El inglés práctico superior

El inglés práctico superior

Tomo II

Josep Capdevila Batllés

libros en red

www.librosenred.com

Dirección General: Marcelo Perazolo
Diseño de cubierta: Patricio Olivera

Primera edición en español - Impresión bajo demanda

ISBN: 978-1-62915-494-7

Para encargar más copias de este libro o conocer otros libros de esta colección visite www.librosenred.com

Introducción

Presentémonos ante todo como **ideólogos, críticos progresistas y defensores de las letras, ciencias y artes**, de allí la riqueza de este texto; y en segundo lugar, para evitar conjeturas falsas de apoyos inmerecidos, frecuentes, manifestarles también la neutralidad ideológica del mismo. Así vengo laborando desde hace cuarenta años (observen por ejemplo los títulos de mis publicaciones), ahora le toca el turno al inglés superior de todos los días y de todas las arenas. Antes de dar más explicaciones me resumiré con una frase: dejen de estudiar a lo bruto todo lo que les echen, desde los métodos miopes a los excesivamente soberbios, y vayen al inglés cotidiano que un servidor ha escogido en las revistas de prestigio: día tras día, año tras año y decenio tras decenio.

Me animé por este útil proyecto después de escuchar copiosas quejas tales como: "He estudiado con tal o tal método pero llego a los Estados unidos y me pierdo", "Llevo x años estudiando inglés y debo recurrir excesivamente al diccionario", "Aunque saqué un excelente en la escuela, si sabes de un buen método, me lo indicas, buena falta me hace", etc. ¡Es pues hora de buscar algo estratégico!

Comprendo perfectamente las quejas mencionadas arriba, pues yo mismo aún tengo problemas, a pesar de mis insistencias: soy la persona indicada para sostener que los resultados académicos (excepto, náturalmente, el caso de los profesionales del sector) son bien insuficientes. Con un sobresaliente en 5º de bachiller y haberme acercado a notables en la lengua extranjera de La Sorbona, sin este último prolongado esfuerzo hubiese andado siempre muy cojo, por no decir impotente. Pues los periodistas y escritores anglófonos también se lucen con expresiones y vocabulario complicados. Y mi caso puede extenderse a muchos colectivos.

¿Por qué he contado esto? Pues para subrayar mejor que se trata de un universo realmente complejo y difícil. Veamos los pilares de apoyo:

- Pretendo que se pueda aprender cómodamente este ya mencionado inglés práctico elegante de cada día.

- Los estudiosos a quienes me dirijo se supone que ya conocen la gramática, así como los verbos y el vocabulario elementales, tal como me ocurría a mí. Así queda más espacio para este proyecto que les ofrezco. Quedando claro que cada uno de nosotros podremos completarlo a medida que diagnostiquemos preciosas novedades cuando nuestras lecturas. Incluirlo todo aquí es un imposible, por definición; quien quiera conocer integralmente esta lengua deberá acudir a los magnos diccionarios Larrousse, Collins y demás, de más de 3.000 páginas si los traladamos a letras de carácter 10.

- El objetivo principal es que se pueda leer cualquier texto con mínimas consultas del diccionario. La escritura elegante y poética irá emergiendo automáticamente y sin esfuerzo. Aquí está la novedad práctica.

- En buena medida mi proposición también puede servir para que los angloparlantes perfeccionen el español.

- Para mejor flexibilidad y eficacia, cada lector puede escoger las frases y términos que crea más convenientes y hacerlos grabar por un nativo. Perfecto ¿Para qué escuchar horas y horas las grabaciones de los cursos que el mercado nos ofrece cuando ya conocemos parcialmente esos contenidos, o si cantidad de esas expresiones no nos interesan?

- Sabiendo que esta lengua resulta cada vez más imprescindible (preferentemente mientras dure la globalización) para cualquier profesión, ahora que yo he masticado un poco el terreno, les invito a digerirlo, insisto. Ante todo les recomiendo unas dosis de ilusión, aunque no caprichosas sino útiles.

- No olvidemos que jugando y disfrutando, poco a poco dominarán las dos principales lenguas de Occidente. Si en los Estados unidos estudian cada vez más el español como segunda lengua (con frecuencia al preguntar a los americanos algo en inglés ellos replican "Hábleme en español, mi abuela era de Sevilla, Galicia...), ¿Por qué no nosotros estudiar más motivadamente el inglés, pues es más importante?

- Será un placer más tarde complementar este libro, con una temática aún más compleja. Pero de momento, ahí está la novedad del método y un nivel bastante elevado.

- Además, matemos dos pájaros de un tiro. Me refiero a la metodología que presento abajo, cuya estructura obedece a nuestras ansias de facilitar la memorización y de estimular la creatividad. Justo, de la misma manera que hacer *footing* cada mañana por la misma ruta atrofia nuestros cerebros, también los métodos monótonos. En cuanto a la memorización, sin duda: quien ostente una buena memoria visual gravará bien y con facilidad los conceptos, pues a través de las próximas secciones descubriremos un esquema bien **variado**.

- Finalmente, desde el flanco formativo e informativo, con tanta pena como razón, expresaré mi desconsuelo de cuando comparo posiciones en la UE (Unión europea): España lidera algunos deportes, primerísimamente el fútbol, también sobresalen los playeros y los esquiadores, aún más el deambular por las calles..., pero nuestras bibliotecas están excesivamente vacías. Esto repercute en nuestros resultados: en patentes, en atracción de materia gris (en España es más bien al revés), en exportación de tecnolgías… Cuento todo esto porque el conocimiento de lenguas extranjeras, con el inglés en primerísima fila, es más común en el norte de la Europa integrante que en el sur de la misma. Aunque en España estamos avanzando agradablemente.

Metodología

Muchos son los trucos que nos hemos inventado para un objetivo común: aprender al máximo esta bonita lengua sintetizando estratégicamente para más **escuetos espacios** y **mínimo esfuerzo**. La siguiente lista parece complicada, pero su pura lógica la convierte en sencilla.

- Tanto en el vocabulario como en las pequeñas frases y en los giros sobresaldrá la dirección inglés → español. Digo sobresaldrá porque por razones prácticas y para mejor facilidad de aprendizaje, a veces será conveniente la dirección contraria: por ejemplo la expresión "A trancas y barrancas", por tener dos equivalentes en inglés: *with great difficulties/ overcoming many obstacles*.

- A veces la dirección pedagógica inglés → español quedaba corta, por lo que un determinado vocablo así rubricado en español se complementará más con otros términos que también sean útiles, sirviéndonos del signo (+), simplificando de paso el aprendizaje. Así por ejemplo el término *crest* significa cresta, cima, etc. Entonces conviene reseñar que cima significa también y sobre todo *top* (para edificio), *summit* (para montaña) y *peak* y *heigh* (de su carrera). En nuestro texto leeremos: *Crest*: cresta, cima + *top, summit, peak, heigh*). Tan decisivas son estas añadiduras que me atrevo a decir "Las traducciones unilaterales y tradicionales provocan impotencias y graves errores".

Debemos pues reaccionar, no soslayando más los términos imprescindibles. Esta idea revolucionaria y de muy exigida labor de consulta constituye uno de los puntos fuertes del libro. En todos esos casos, de no consultar en dirección contraria nos quedaríamos con conceptos parcialmente equívocos y limitados. Insisto en este útil detalle porque en la vida cotidiana solemos conformarnos con sólo la consulta unilateral, y eso es grave. Esta y otras innovaciones convierten nuestra oferta en muy recomendable.

- Dada la fabulosa cantidad de verbos utilizados (algunos de ellos docenas y docenas de veces, caso de los auxiliares), optamos por prescindir del *To*. Así participaremos al ahorro de un excesivamente voluminoso texto. Pero cuidado: sólo en las traducciones de verbos infinitivos considerados aisladamente (ejemplo: llevar: *carry, wear, bring*); no los *to* de las frases (quedaría realmente confuso y feo). Así por ejemplo lo respetaremos en "The right *to* testify".

- Con vías a facilitar el aprendizaje de los diferentes términos, en muchos casos agruparemos estratégicamente los diversos significados de cada palabra. Insisto en ello porque de manera incomprensible incluso los más prestigiosos diccionarios lo han olvidado excesivamente. Cojamos las diferentes traducciones de la dicción *clash*: en los diccionarios se agrupan sin criterio alguno, repito, pero hay que facilitar enormemente la memorización. Así, para *clash* tendremos: conflicto; enfrentamiento, oposición; choque, estruendo, ruido metálico. Para memorizar con menos pena clasificaremos los diferentes significados según parecido, con la ayuda del signo";". Por ejemplo aquí lo hemos utilizado sólo dos veces.

- El signo "/" se utilizará en varias acepciones: ante todo para separar sinónimos, por ejemplo "*The lower/ bottom bunk*" (litera) y para dos adjetivos del mismo substantivo, por ejemplo "*Downriver/ stream*" (aquí ahorramos un "Down" y subrayamos los dos sustantivos a los cuales califica), etc.

- Dada la infinidad de veces que se utilizaría el término "And", lo reemplazaremos por el simple signo "&". Ahorraremos espacio.

- También para mejor aprovechar el espacio, nos serviremos de dos estrategias esenciales: a) En los diccionarios, para tal o tal término se suelen presentar primero los significados sustantivos, adjetivos y adverbios, y luego los verbos. Aquí presentaremos el primer grupo y cuando proceda añadiremos la V (que significa verbo de los mismos). Por ejemplo *plug* (tapón, enchufe,V). O sea que significa también tapar y enchufar. Aunque para no sobrecargar con tantas V, sólo se asentarán las más esenciales, el lector puede imaginar el resto; b) ¿Para qué cargar el espacio con términos ya comprensibles? Nos referimos a los que se parecen mucho en las dos lenguas. Por ejemplo *nanometre* = nanómetro, *tumult* = tumulto,... y todos los acabados en um, así *vacuum* = vacío. En todos estos casos pondremos un (=) al lado del término inglés.

- No hemos eludido el ajuste de términos opuestos o diferentes: con el signo ↔ si tienen significado opuesto. Así: *It was favourably received* ↔ -- -- *bad/poorly received*; con el signo =/= si lo tienen simplemente diferente pero que gráficamente se parezcan. Por ejemplo el término *belie* (defraudar, desdecir, ocultar) =/= *belief* (creencia). Encontrarán infinidad de aplicaciones. La flecha (→) se utilizará para enriquecer con pequeñas frases prácticas.

- A cada palabra traducida de un idioma al otro le suelen corresponder muchas en el segundo, sobre todo en los verbos. Al escoger cual palabra es la adecuada, frecuentemente dejamos al lector (o estudiante) el placer de ejercitarse, según la lógica y el contexto de la frase. Así por ejemplo en "*Hinge on*" (depender de, moverse sobre) *the weather,* es de lógica aplastante el escoger "Depender de". Esta postura nos acerca un poco al revolucionario método berlitziano y será útil.

- Descubrirán Uds. muchas pequeñas frases sin traducir, por fáciles, ante todo en la primera parte. Aunque alojarán algo estratégico, o al menos interesante. Por ejemplo: *he was good at his job, I work on them, I'm scared of you,...* y cualquier otra palabra. Aquí se debe retener *at, on* y *of* en su lugar.

- Encontrarán hartas veces palabras divididas con un paréntesis, por ejemplo: *(black) smith.* Se interpretarán como de igual valor con o sin el contenido del paréntesis: aquí tanto *smith* como *blacksmith* significan herrero. También paréntesis para ahorrar espacio, por ejemplo en *pick up*: (re)coger se traduce por coger + recoger.

- En las primeras páginas he sido muy generoso, recapitulando muchas pequeñas frases y un rico vocabulario, para mejor comprender la riqueza y la personalidad de la lengua inglesa. Luego, poco a poco he sido más parco en frases y vocablos fáciles, basculando hacia los más difíciles, aunque exquisitos.

- Sobre toco: respecto al gran surtido de pequeñas frases del día a día, me he esmerado en seleccionarlas en las revistas y no en el diccionario. Esa **familiaridad**, con protagonistas y espacios conocidos, y a veces famosos, facilitará mejor la memorización que los fríos ejemplos de aquel.

- Nos inmunizaremos frente a una más que segura crítica: el no haber organizado el texto temáticamente o por orden alfabético. Pues porque los innovadores instrumentes (=/=, →, ↔) no lo permiten. Aquí prima la facilidad de memorización que con ello aseguramos.

- Las abreviaciones son las corrientes: el signo =/= significa distinto; Com.: comercio; Comp.: computer; Mús.: música; o.s.: uno mismo; sb.: alguien; sth.: algo; Sp.: deporte; Aut.: autoridad, Atm.: atmósfera; p.: personas, m.: metros y mercancías (según contexto); Med.: medicina; T.: temperature; Ec.: economía; Pol.: política; Jur.: jurídico; Agr.: agricultura; pb.: problema; Mil.: militar; Rel.: religión; Biol. (biología); Líq. (líquido); Hist.: historia; Geog.: geografía; Náut.: náutica; Téc.:

técnica; Mec.: mecánica; Tf.: teléfono; Electr. (electricidad), (m.) mercancías, etc.

- En este segundo tomo del libro se han introducido dos novedades prácticas para (como siempre) facilitar la memorización:

(1) Observemos la palabra Scrawny (esquelético + =, skimmy): el (=) se refiere a skeletal, o sea que esquelético tiene dos significados. Este (=), como siempre, significa que o coinciden o se parecen mucho. Pero muy frecuentemente optamos por (" = "). Es porque sólo hay un significado. Por ejemplo: ringingly/steadfastly (categóricamente + "="). También utilizamos este método para las traducciones directas de un solo sentido, ej.: become incontinent ("="). Si consultamos categóricamente en el diccionario, sólo encontramos categorically. Aunque esto son sólo aproximaciones selectivas, no matemáticas: a veces escogemos el "=" únicamente porque se trata del significado más importante y en general también depende de las fuentes consultadas.

(2) Jugamos con la coma y el punto y coma, para agrupar los significados parecidos. Veamos la frase siguiente: launch a major (fuerte, enorme; clave) publicity campaign. El sentido de enorme y fuerte es cercano, por eso se separan con coma. Pero con punto y coma el vocablo "clave", con significado muy distinto al de los dos anteriores.

El libro estará compuesto de tres partes: (primera) diez cortos apartados de temas muy cotidianos, muchos de ellos científicos, que conciene conocer; (segunda) el gran bloque de términos y frases más o menos largas; (tercera) sectores compuestos de varias frases en los que además del vocabulario se aprende a construir aquellas, sin olvidar el aprendizaje de temas complejos. Aunque estas explicaciones complejas también las encontramos en algún otro apartado, por ejemplo en el del coronavirus.

PRIMERA PARTE:
Diez cortos apartados de temas muy cotidianos, muchos de ellos científicos, que conviene conocer

Esta breve parte comportará once apartados que a mi parecer son partcularmente interesantes: el primero por la complejidad de muchos conceptos (A- expresiones complejas), el segundo obedece a la importancia conocida para nuestras vidas, tanto del mundo animal como vegetal, más los secretos que se irán investigando (B- la naturaleza vegetal y animal y nociones complementarias), en el tercero nos ahondaremos agrupando conceptos que de lo contario serían casi imposible memorizar (C- pequeñas expresiones que se prestan a confusión), en el cuarto hemos selecciondo esquemas que resultan atractrivos y novedosos para los aprenedices (D- algunas expresiones más selectas para más elegante redacción del inglés), el quinto se ocupará del tema más acuciante y actualmente de moda (E- medio ambiente y energía), luego el de los quebraderos de cabezas de que todos y cada día somos objeto (F- finanzas), tampoco olvidaremos algo de medicina (humana o animal indistintamente) en el G, imposible descuidar el Coronavirus o C-19 (apartado H), la inteligencia artificial (AI) en el I, la recopilación especial de algunos verbos (J) y sinopsis plural obligada para conceptos diferentes aunque gráficamente parecidos (K). Evidentemente, este libro no es un diccionario para consulta, se trata de preparar el gran púbico para que pueda leer y entender toda clase de textos divulgativos en los medios de comunicación. Queda pues al mercado como un **libro abierto** que conviene conocer, sean cuales sean sus profesiones, y cada uno puede ir añadiendo los términos técnicos que poco a poco irán surgiendo.

A- Expresiones complejas

Las separamos del resto por su más dificultosa memorización, además de su importancia. Tanto en esta parte como en la segunda, observarán como para muchos detalles de las explicaciones ya utilizamos más el inglés que en el tomo I.

Español → inglés

- Arrancar: (página, papel) tear out, pull the plant up by the roots; pull out some hair; (coche) start; snatch the letter out of my hand, he snatched her bag; here was a struggle (forcejeo) & he wrenched the pistol away from her, he burst into tears (a llorar). Arrancar: (diente, pelo) pull out, (piel) pull off; dig the stuff up =/= disinter & unearth (desenterrar).

- Arrastrar: (suelo) drag, (vehículo) tow, (barco) tug, swept along by the river, (pers. arrastrarse) crawl, dragging on the cough (tos) since ..., the current carried him out of the sea, when the stock exchange/market collapsed it dragged down the whole sector.

- Inverso: in reverse order, the -- side/order, the -- gear (marcha atrás), engage -- (meter marcha atrás), endorse (endosar) the check on the --, quite the --, the results are the -- of ..., the roles are --ed, -- the charges (llamar a cobro revertido); contrary to what happen, conversely (a la inversa), arrange it other way round.

- Manía: have it in for sb (tener -- a alguien), stop saying such silly things or being silly (déjate de manías), he's old, he has some odd habits, he has an obsession or mania about cleaning, the peculiar habit of looking under the bed before he gets into it, the fad/craze (moda, manía) of always dressing in black, the obsession that people are laughing at him.

- Quejarse, lamentarse: complain, grumble, grouse =/= gemir: (animal) whine, (viento) moan, (pers.) moan, groan =/= aullar: (perro, lobo, viento) howl =/= (quejido, lloriqueo) whimper =/= bramar (elephant & bull): bellow =/= (mugido o quejido lastimero, llanto) moaning.

- Saltar: (brincar, lanzarse, en atletismo, tren, valla, obstáculo, semáforo) jump; (más alto, lejos) leap, (pelota) bounce, the spark flew out of the fire, (plomos) blow, (botón) come off, (línea, página) skip.

- Tenue: (olor) pale, (línea) faint, fine, (luz, voz, sonido) weak, (llovizna, neblina) light, (tela) flimsy, fine, (razón, relaciones) tenuous, insubstantial, (estilo) simple, plain, (hilo) fine, slender =/= fine: (opportunity, worker) magníficos, (crystal) fino, (wine) de primera calidad, (mind) brillante, (work) admirable, (health, weather) good, we had a fine time (lo pasamos bien), (fabric, tela) fina, (hair, thread) delgado; sharpen the pencil to a sharp point; (embroidery: bordado; workmanship) delicado; (adequately) bien.

Inglés → español

- Assert (afirmar, hacer valer)ion: aseveración, afirmación; assertive: firme, enérgico, (tono) autoritario, (derechos) hacer valer; --ly (con firmeza), --ness (seguridad en sí mismo) =/= asses: calcular, evaluar.

- Awkward: I feel awkward (not at ease) when I'm with you, (violent) to discuss it with him; movimiento torpe, frase poco elegante, an -- (incómodo, difícil) question, -- place to get to by rail; Twesday's -- for me (no me viene bien), call at -- (inoportuno) moment, an -- (embarazosa) position.

- Beat: golpear, sacudir, latido,V → -- of the heart, -- about the bush (irse por las ramas), (carpet) sacudir, -- his children, he was --ed to death, this model can't be --en (es el mejor), buy now & --en (anticípate a) the new tax, the sea was --ing against the cliff.

- Bend,t,t: torcer, (rodila, vara) doblar; curva, ángulo → it seems --t (dirigido, empeñado, inclinado) on eradicating … =/= bind, ou, ou: atar, rodear, (libro) encuadernar, (cimiento) cuajar, obligar, aprieto, apuro.

- Blast: atacar, derribar; malograr, marchitar + ráfaga, chorro; sacudida, explosion, an ice -- (ráfaga de frío), -- out: emitir a todo volume =/= bust: (máquina) romper → we --ed the window open; degradar; go -- (quebrar, dejar sin blanca), combate: inflation, crime, …

- Br<u>e</u>ach (brecha, violación, infracción) of rule/contract, heal the -- (hacer las paces), -- (abuso) of confidence, -- the peace (orden público), -- a promise, -- of security, fill the -- (vacío + fill the gap) between demand & supply =/= br<u>o</u>ach (mencionar, abordar) it implies …

- Build- up: acumulación, (tensión, presión) incrementar, (tropas) concentrarse, give sth a big -- (hacer mucha propaganda de) =/= build up: make bigger, stronger, (muscle, one's strength) fortalecerse, (supplies, experience) acumular, (reserves, for instance: Mil.) acrecentar, (reputation) forjarse, (confidence) desarrollar, they -- you -- (te ponen por las nubes) & then they knock you down (te echan por tierra), (dirt, debts, malice, grudge, hard, feeling, resentment) acumular, (presión, ruido) aumentar.

- C<u>h</u>unky (pers.: fornida; furniture: achaparrado) =/= chunk (trozo,V, hacer un ruido metálico) =/= clunk (golpetear, golpetazo mecánico) =/= c<u>l</u>unky (anticuado, tosco y pesado) =/= Clumsy (torpe, patoso, tosco: basto, rudo).

- Clear; =, claro, despejado día, a -- advantage, (floor/room) despejada, (debt, account) saldar; (check) compensation; clear up: (crime) resolver, esclarecer, (doubts) aclarar, (drawer) vaciar, ordenar.

- Craft (arte, oficio) --s & arts (artesania), spacecraft (nave especial), -- fair (feria artesanal), a well --ed (bien construida) novel, he showed his -- as an actor, new -- breveries popped up (aparecieron).

- Crawl: avanzar lentamente, gatear, arrastrarse → --ing (muchos) tourists =/= garabatear: scrawl, scribble; garabato: (dibujo) doodle, (escritura) scribble.

- Creep (arrastrarse, trepar; asqueroso, adulador)y: (film, story) espeluznante, (pers.) asquerosa → creep into/out (entrar/salir sigilosamente) of a room, creep under the fences; the water -- higher (va subiendo poco a poco).

- Desagüe: draining, plugholes, wastepipe; sewer (cloaca, alcantarillas); drain: sumidero, drenaje, desagüe, vaciar, drenar; drainage: desagüe de las aguas residuales, canalización de las aguas de lluvia; desechos: waste, leftovers, scraps. Unblock (desatascar, desatrancar) the wastepipe, etcetera.

- Discuss: conversar sobre un problema, hablar, tartar =/= argue: discutir, pelearse, reñir → they are always arguing about the bycicle, a well exposed (expuesto) point.

- Disposal (inhumación) of the body, waste disposal (deshacerse de) unit: triturador de basuras; be at sb's disposal; disposable pen (de usar y tirar), -- (disponible) finance; he is irrelevant (sin importancia) to be disposed of (es supérfluo, se puede prescindir de él); dispose (deshacerse) of them; he disposed of (se deshizo de) his mentor.

- Ease (facilidad) of access; be at -- (relajado...) with her; put sb's mind at -- (tranquilizar), (pain) aliviar; -- sb's mind; -- (mejorar) the traffic flow, -- (allanar) the way for sb; (interest rates, prices, monetary policy, rules) relajar.

- Edge: filo, afilar; orilla, borde, (be on --) estar nervioso, menacing -- (tono), -- (ventaja) over competition, -- (acercar) the chair, cutting -- (de vanguardia) artificial intelligence (AI) projects, a movement toward the cutting --.

- Embattled y parecidos gráficamente → (city, garrison) asedio, (troops) en combate, (citizen, politicians) acuciados de problemas =/= embush (tender una emboscada) at him =/= enable (permitir) =/= enact (promulgar, decretar) =/= encroach (invadir, cortar, suprimir), endear (ganarse la voluntad) → this endeared her (le granjeó el encanto, la hizo muy querida) to everyone; endearing (atractivo, simpático); endearment (expresión de cariño) =/= endeavo(u)r: intento, esfuerzo, empeño (+ striving) =/= endorse: aprobar, refrendar, (check) endosar =/= endowment: dotes, atributos; legados, donaciones =/= endure: (pain) soportar, (system) sostener → enduring (duradero) =/= enhance: (beauty) realzar, (values) incrementar, (performance) mejorar =/= enjoy (disfrutar) =/= enraptured/captivated (cautivado) =/= ensnared (atrapado) in a legal fight/in a trap =/= the ensuing (siguientes) days, policies ensued by the US (United states) =/= Entail (conllevar, suponer, implicar) =/= entanglement (enredo, ej. con una mujer, ...; alambrada, ej. with barbed wire fence (valla) =/= entice (atraer) people into the shops; nothing can -- him (convencerlo) away from his studies =/= entitle (dar derecho a) =/= entrench (enraizar, consolidar, afianzar) =/= enthuse (entusiasmar) over/about technical challenges =/= entrust (confiar) the economy/your savings to ...

- Even y parecidos → even: he didn't -- (ni siquiera) said hellow to us; incluso; plano, llano, liso; desinflado; soso, apagado; equitable; igualar, allanar, uniforme, (T., velocidad, progreso) constante; <u>un</u>even (desiguales) borders =/= <u>flat</u>: (honorarios, precios) uniformes, sales were -- (pocas), flatten/level (allanar), a -- (rotundo) no/rechazo, flattened (allanadas, lisas) faces; (batería) descargada, television (TV): pantalla plana, it flattened (arrasó) crops, (peaks: picos) allanar, estar sin un céntimo =/= level: high level of literacy, water --, above the -- of the window, at ministerial --, a top -- meeting, the picture's not -- (derecho), both are on the same level, draw -- (empatar), -- in hability, average earnings have kept --lled with inflation, (terreno) nivelar, aplanar, igualar =/= llano: (sin desniveles) flat, (no inclinado) level, (lenguaje) simple.

- Feature: rasgo, característica, facción → delicate --; (radio, TV) documental, full/lengh --; article of a journal; -- in a list; the home has many original (de época) --; his legs are his best --; the film --ed her as (aparece con el papel de), (ofrecer, mostrar): it --es the closest thing (lo más parecido) the US has to a president.

- Feeling: (sensibilidad) for art/in my fingers; with -- (con sentimiento) of tiredness or náuseas + play the piece with real -- (sentimiento), a -- (sensación) of joy/isolation; what are your --s (opiniones) on the matter? =/= sense: of sight, of hearing, of smell, of taste, of touch, of time; in his (right) sense: sano juicio, bring her to her --s (hacerle entrar en razón), when I came to my --s (recobré el conocimiento), a -- of space, of betrayal, of business, of decency; humor/rhythm/direction (orientación); (equilibrio): the incident --ed him, a well --ed pers., the scales are --ed, the -- between supply & demand, he lost his --, -- the budget.

- Flock: (sheep) rebaño, (birds) bandada, (pers.) tropel/multitud =/= drove (manada de animles), they came in --s (acudieron en tropel) =/= fold (redil, establo; pliegue,V) → return to the -- =/= herd: (cattle) manada, vacada, goats) rebaño, (pigs) piara/manada + ir en manada los animals, apiarse las personas.

- Flush: cisterna, (in cheeks) colores; resplandecer de salud, de belleza, a -- (arrebato) of excitement (emoción), -- (tirar) the toilet, hot -- (bochornos), in the first -- (euforia) of the success, the first -- of youth (la flor de la juventud).

- Flutter: (aves) revoloteo,V), (pers.) revuelo, (bandera) hondear; agitarse, ponerse nervioso =/= flatter (adular) =/= flatten (allanar, echar abajo, arrasar una ciudad).

- Foster: incentivo, estímulo, impulso,Vs, (talento) fomenter, (reconciliación) promover =/= fester: inflamar, irritar → a --ing (purulenta) sore (llaga), anger --ed (degeneró) into a deep resentment =/= bolster: reforzar, (argumento) reafirmar, (moral) levanter =/= bluster: fanfarronear, bravuconear, bravatas, (wind) bramar =/= booster (estímulo): (TV) repetidor, (Med.) vacuna + "vaccine".

- Foul: hablar grosero, asqueroso; fétido; he fell -- of the law (tubo problemas con la justcia) =/= haul (transportar, trayecto) =/= heal/cure (curar) =/= howl (alullar) =/= hail (granizo,V; llamar, aclamar) =/= fowl (ave de corral).

- Further (más, además; promover, fomenter) → -- away (más lejos), how much -- is it (nos queda)?, we went a little -- (avanzamos un poco), -- west/east, get -- into a matter, without -- delay, not -- need of your service, nothing -- to say, a bit -- aheat/forward (un poco más para adelante) =/= farther → at the --/far (lejano) end of the room, on the -- bank (al otro lado) of the river, on the -- right (extrema derecha) of the party.

- Get along: I must be --ing along (irme) now, we -- -- (estamos de acuerdo) with you, we -- -- (nos las arreglamos) without money, we -- -- fine, he's --ing -- fine (le va bien) at the school, how are you -- -- (le va) without the preparations?

- Get around: We can't -- -- (caber en) this table, I'll get the boxes -- to you (te las hare llegar), I must -- -- (ponerme a) writing the letter, you certainly got -- (has viajado) in your job.

- Get at: (object) alcanzar, (place) llegar a/hasta, it's hard to -- -- (llegar al) wire (cable), -- -- (disponer) of money, you are always --ing -- (metiéndote) with him.

- Get away (salir, apartarse) with (llevarse), (privilege) suprimir.

- Glimpse (vislumbrar, visión momentánea, alcanzar a ver) =/= glitzy (deslumbrante) =/= glare (luz deslumbrante, mirada feroz) =/= dazzle (deslumbrar, brillo). Brillante: (luz, color, estrella) bright, (pelo, papel, metal, zapatos, ...) shiny, (pintura) gloss, (brillo, resplandor,V) glow =/= gown (toga, bata de estar por casa).

- Gloom: penumbra, oscuridad; melancolía, pesimismo → gloomy (sombrio, lúgubre, fúnebre, pesimismo) → I'm feling -- (bajo de moral); he takes a -- view of everything (todo lo ve negro) =/= glum: (pers.) apesadumbrada, apagada, triste, cabizbaja =/= dull: apagado, sin brillo, aburrido, desanimado, torpe, flojo =/= dim: débil, tenue, borroso, idea vaga, nada alagüeño; atenuar, debilitar, irse borrando.

- Go on with sb (ir/llevarse bien con alguien) ↔ don't -- -- -- --. We will go by (nos las arreglaremos), we can't go on like this.

- Grim: duro, penoso, deprimente, lúgrube, triste, espantoso → --ly: (speak) con gravedad, (smile) forzadamente, (struggle) denodadamente =/= grin: sonrisa, burlón, reir abiertamente → -- & bear it (mal tiempo buena cara) =/= grind (café ...) moler, afilar; trabajo pesado, trabajar con dificultad, estudiar mucho; rechinar =/= grip: asir, apretar más, adherer; tight -- (agarrar con fuerza), --ed by pain.

- Harbo(u)r: puerto, refugio; (pers., animal) esconder, (hopes, desire, fugitive, suspicion) albergar =/= hoarding: acumulación, valla de pub., cartelera (+ billboard) =/= boarding: -- house (pension), -- pass (tarjeta de embarque) =/= boarder (alumno interno, huesped).

- Harm: do most harm than good,warning can't do any --, it won't -- you get up early, harmless (inofensivo) =/= hurt: you are --ing me, you've -- my ankle (tobillo), I'm not badly --, I've -- (lastimado) yours feelings, did you -- yourself?, watch don't get --!, were's the --? Kick where --ts, it --s to admid it/by his attitude.

- Have: the UK (United kingdom) would -- to try; they would -- killed each other; we would have failed, should I've to obey?, had it not been ..., he would have won; they could have said they were coming. You shouln't have taken it like that. We should have (deberísamos) to economize; blak as he had been beaten; he might have to pass through! If …, I'd have been drowned. I reflect on/think about what we could have had to pay.

- Heave: he heaved himself off the floor (haciendo un gran esfuerzo); we --ed the box onto the shelf; -- a sight (suspirar) of relief (alivio); -- (tirar) on a rope (cuerda)/line (cable); -- up & down in the swell (marejada, oleaje, hincharse, crecer la corriente); give it another -- (empujón, tirón); -- (cargar) briks.

- Hew, ed, ed/ewn: (carbón, piedra) extraer, (moda) tallar, labrar → -- a path (abrir un sendero) through the undergrouth (maleza), -- (ceñirse) to sth: the unions are --ing to (mantienen) its demands/requirements.

- Hold out: (hand) tender, (possibilities) ofrecer → I don't -- -- much hope of …, (pers.) aguantar, (shoes) durar, the holdouts (los que se resisten) to negotiate =/= the beleagered (asediado) president hold off (rechazó) the attempt (intento) =/= hands-off (no intervención) =/= hand out: (advise) dar, (foot, benefits) distribuir =/= hands-on (práctica) experience =/= wait a moment/hold on =/= hold up: (trophy/hand/banner) sostener, levanter, (roof, wall) sostener, (arrival) retarder, (progress) impedir =/= hold on tight (agárrate bien) =/= move on (hacer circular, seguir adelante).

- Inch (moverse lentamente) in/out + -- forward (avanzar lentamente).

- Jostle: empujar (--ed by the protesters, -- people one another) =/= jot down (apuntar/anotar rápidamente) =/= jotter (bloc de notas: note pad) =/= jitter (ponerse nervioso) =/= jolt (sacudir, conmover) → give a -- (susto).

- Lie, lay, lain: echarse, acostarse; yacer → the papers lay (estaban) …, he lay down (se tumbó) =/= lay, laid, laid: (mesa) poner/colocar, (plan) hacer, (trampa) prender, (queja) presenter → -- a complaint against sb, lay o.s. down (tumbarse, echarse).

- Log: tronco, leño; registrar, tomar nota → the backlog (atraso, pedido pendiente) of aircraft worth $ 3 trn.; logjam (atolladero), waterlogged or flooded or swamped (inundado + =); illegal --ging (explotación forestall ilegal), the --gers (leñadores) were nailed (agarrados).

- Look over: (trabajo, contrato) revisar, chequear, (casa) inspeccionar). Look on us (considéranos) cheap labor (mano de obra barata) =/= oversee (supervisar)r: supervisor =/= outlook (punto de vista) on sth, my -- (actitud) on life, perspectivas → the -- for tomorrow/for the industry are bleak (sombrías, deprimentes, …) =/= overlook: (mistake, detail) pasar por alto → --ed for promotion; misdemeanour (delito menor, fechoría) disculpar; a room --ing the sea; vista, panorama =/= overview (vista de conjunto).

- Mind: creative mind, it came to my -- that (se me ocurrió que), do you -- if I smoke? It --s to admid it, I don't -- cold/waiting, to my -- (juicio), nothing further from my --, lose one's -- (juicio), --! (¡cuida!), --s by his attitude, the --est (más privilegiado) of the period (época), -- you don't fall! -- what you are doing, do you -- telling me? --less (sin sentido), if you are so --ed (si quisieras hacerlo), fair --ed (justo, imparcial), an industrial --ed nation, scientifically --ed; minder (gorila, guardaespaldas + bodyguard), lose one's --/get mad.

- Pin (afilar, sujetar con alfileres; clavija, pinza) → I --ned the papers together (sujeté con alfiler), wear the hair --ned up (recojido), a flower --ed on/to her dress, she --ned her hopes (depositar sus esperanzas) on him, -- the blame to him (cargarle con las culpas).

- Pinch (pellizco,V, apretar → feel the -- (estar apretados), (idea) robar, at a -- (si fuse necesario) → -- (necesaria) new technology to kit out (equipar) their factories; atrapar, agarrar, robar → I had my pen --ed.

- Pitch: punto, extreme, grado → reach such -- that …, the tension has risen to an unbearable -- (hasta hacerse intolerable);

(Sp.) campo; lugar, sitio, puesto, ... He had a very effective sales -- (sabía convencer); an insurance agent's -- (discurso); (tienda) armar, montar.

- Rate: velocidad/ritmo → I'm reading at a rhythm of 100 pages a day; -- of climb (velocidad de ascensión, death -- (tasa), literacy -- (nivel), -- of interest/exchange, the drop-out -- in schools, peak (altos) standards -- (tarifas; impuestos), birth -- (índice).

- Reward (recompensa) to the finder, the well- behaved (niño/perro obedientes); rewarding (gratificación) =/= award a prize, money, condecoration =/= allow: (pets) admitir, (smoke, ...) permitir + allow o.s. sth (permitirse algo) =/= allot (repartición, distribución, adjudicación).

- Roll: inscribir, registro,V, enrollar; rollo, fajo, panecillo, (ball, barrel) rodar; be on a -- (estar de racha); I --ed her onto her back (le dí la vuelta poniéndolo boca arriba), -- back: (enemigo) hacer retroceder, (precios, sueldos, autonomía) disminuir; the electoral -- (registro).

- Rooster (gallo) =/= roost (palo) → rule the -- (batuta) =/= be rostered for (estar de turno) =/= roster (lista de turnos) =/= rustle: (llaves) susurro), (papel) crujido.

- Rough: áspero, rugoso, (mar) picada, vida dura, tosco, aproximado → a -- estimate.

→ " & tumble: avatares (of politics), vaivenes (of life) + ups & downs =/= harsh: aspero, riguroso, severo, violento, duro → don't be too -- with him.

- Routine: the daily --, routine inspection, monotonous (rutinario), routinely (rutinariammente) =/= humdrum (rutinario, aburrido, monótono).

- Ruffle: alborotado, despeinado, (hoja) espinosa, erizada; arrugado,Vs) → ruffle sb's feathers (enojar a alguien) ↔ unruffled (sereno + =, calm) =/= ripple: rizo, onda,Vs, (of excitments) oleada, (pers., water, wind) murmullo → ripple effect: reacción en cadena, onda expansiva =/= rustle (susurro, murmullo).

- Scrap: trocito, pizca; pelearse, (plan) abandonar, (idea) descartar → --s (sobras) --e: lío, apuro → get into a --, help him out of a --; raspar, rascar, desguace, --y: irregular, desilvanado.
- Shake before use, the dog --ed himself energetically, -- the fruit from the branches, -- dust off/from my coat, -- the sand out of the towel, -- hands with sb, -- one's head, -- off (deshacerse de, quitarse de encima).
- Sell y su familia → sell-out (éxito de taquilla) =/= sell out: (existencias/stocks/ tickets) agotar =/= sell- off (venta generalizada de activos) =/= pay off (liquidar, pagar; valer la pena =/= pay-off (ajuste de cuentas: settle of scores; soborno + brivery =/= bail out (rescatar con dinero) =/= writeoff: cancelar una deuda, declarar siniestro.
- Smitte, o, tten: her conscience --ote her (le atormenta), golpear → -- (azotado) with he plague, -- (entusiasmado) with the idea, -- (afligido) with remorse, -- (aquejado) with the flu (gripe); in a hit - and - run (quienes produjeron el accidente se fugan) road he was smitten (tocado).
- Sneak, (p, pp) --uck/--eaket: soplón,V, chivato, acusón; -- in/out (entrar/salir a hurtadillas (escondido) → -- a bottle into a room/under a coat/through a custom + sneaky: astuto, hipócrita, disimulado, que oculta el pensamiento =/= --er (zapatos de deporte).
- Snug: (room, house, sanctuary) acogedor, (bed) confortable, agradable, (tight) ceñido/ajustado, (too tight) apretado =/= snub: (pers.) desairar, volverle la cara, (proposal, offer, plan) desdeñar, rechazar.
- Spring: (saltar) out of the bed, over the wall (muro, pared)/ fence (valla)/gate (verja); nacer, surgir, (shoot) brote, retoño; brotar; go against the --, blood -- from the wound; manantial, muelle, primavera.
- Spurt: he works in --s (rachas), --s (llamaradas: blazes) of fire, with a final -- (esfuerzo, sprint) won him the race, (líquido) salir a choros + the blood poured/gushed out =/= spite

(maldad, resentimiento, rencor + grudge)ful (malicioso, malo, rencoroso + resentful) =/= scornful (desdeñoso) =/= spate (avalanche, serie, racha).

- Stake/bet/bid: stake: estaca, apuesta, marcar con estacas; the --s are high (es mucho lo que se apuesta), (dinero, reputación, vida) jugarse, he has too much at -- (se juega demasiado en ello), have a -- (participación) in the company, he --s his reputation on the result; --holder (depositario) =/= skate (patín,V)board (monopatín) =/= bet: apuesta (ej. en caballos) → win/lose a --, I wouldn't to bet on it (no estaría tan seguro de ello), I hat a bet (aposté) that..., place your bet, please (hagan sus apuestas), he bet him (le apuesta) $ 50 that ... I bet you that =/= bid: a -- (intento) for power, freedom, bid (pujar) for the picture, make a bid, raise one's bid, bid up (hacer subir el precio), a takeover bid (una oferta pública de adquisición (OPA).

- Stand: lugar, sitio → I took my -- at the entrance, stand/platform (tribuna), -- at fair, what is your -- (postura) on the issue? Newspaper/fruit --, quiosco, he was tired of --ing (de estar de pié), he had to -- for the whole of the journey, he tried to -- (ponerse de pié), -- over there (ponte, párate allí), they stood & stared (miraban fíjamente) open-mouthy, don't just -- there! (¡No te quedes ahí parado!), -- still (quedarse quieto) two minutes, no --ing (establecimiento prohibido), -- firm/fast (mantenerse firme), as things --, -- (presentarse) for treasurer (tesorero), I can't -- him (tragarlo), I can't -- it any longer (no aguanto más), -- (resistir) another disapointment (desengaño, decepción), the invitation/ofer still --s.

- Steady: (gaze: mirada) fijo, (ladder, table ...) firme, breeze (brisa) constante, (pace, rhythm, rain, speed) constante, regular, (job, income) fijo → --ies, --ying, --ied (tranquilizar, calmar; sujetar, estabilizar); --ly (regularmente, a ridmo constante).

- Straight: (stick, nose, road) recto, (picture) derecho; franco, directo, claro, categórico; straighten: ordenar, arreglar, (picture) enderezar, (hair/bedclothes) estirar =/= straightforward (franco, honrado, sencillo) =/= forthright (franco, directo) =/= outright (rotundo, absoluto, indiscutible) =/= upright (vertical, derecho, erguido).

- Strand: ramal, filamento, tendencia, a -- of hair (un pelo); a ship --ed (encallado) on a sandbank, --ed (en apuros) tourists, --ed (varado) in the desert, (barco en la playa) encallar, (ballena) hacer embarrancar; pebble (con guijarros)/sandy -- (playa de arena).

- Stretch: tramo, trecho, (leg) estirar, extender, (sea, estate, forest) extenderse, (wings) extenderse, desplegarse, extend out the hand to turn off the alarm clock, (have a --) estirarse, desperezarse, (resources) empleadas al máximo, (meaning) forzar, (wire, rope) estirarse, (money, resources, supply: suministro) ser suficientes.

- Strip: vaciar, deshacer, (ropa, pintura): -- off (quitar) =/= chip away: pintura, ...: desconchar); strip of sth: despojar (bienes, ...) + tira, cinta, franja; pista de aterrizaje (landing strip).

- Sweep: (alcance + reach, scope of law), (extension + "=", stretch of land); barrido, barrer, azotar una región); --ed: arrastrado (by the avalanche), (fire: extenderse).

- Take on: (pers.) recoger, (m.) cargar, (staff) contratar; asumir, aceptar, encargarse de; enfrentarse a, aceptar el reto) =/= take up: recoger/agarrar, continuar con, ocupar un tiempo/espacio → it --s up three days.

- Tetchy/testy (irritable) =/= tacky (hortero, chabacano) =/= touchy (delicado, susceptible) =/= thicket (matorral + busch, scrub (+ fregar) =/= twitch (moverse, tick) → a nervous --, (twitchy) agitado, nervioso.

- Tight: --/taut: tirante, (belt/strap/dress) ceñidos, (control) estricto, (screw) apretado, escaso, difícil → be in the -- rope (en la cuerda floja, en dificultades); tight- lipped (hermético, silencoso) =/= tough: (fabric/rubber/clothing) resistente, (meat) dura, (boss) severo/exigente, (policy/legislation) dura, (examen) dificil.

-- Wager (apuesta,V) + punter (apostador) =/= waive (exonerar) =/= wayer (vacilar, flaquear, tambalear, titubear → in a --ing (temblorosa) voice.

-- Worth: be -- (valer), it's worth a lot more than I paid for it, it isn't -- this money, goods of -- € 600 were stolen, he was -- (tenía) € 1 bn. when he died, it's -- nothing for me (para mí no vale nada), for what it's --? It's worth a try (vale la pena intentarlo)/the risk, the museum is -- a visit, that's worth knowing (vale la pena saberlo), $ 1 bn. -- of furniture, prove one's -- (demostrar su valía), it worth it (vale la pena) ↔ it isn't worth it; a position (puesto) of worthiness (mérito, valía), -- heeding (vale la pena hacer caso), praiseworthy (elogiable), it's a worthy subject for so much attention, be -- of sth/sb (ser digno de --/--), this work is -- of you, worth of attention/his name, a pers. of great --, he proves his -- (valor), --thy (importante, ilustre), newsworthy (de interés periodístico), trustworthy (formal, fiable).

- Would: if you asked him, he -- do it; I said I -- do it; what -- you want me do? The car --n't start, -- you close the door? Cain -- overcome (vencería) the sin; I --n't do it; if I had known, I --n't have come; I --n't worry too much if I were you; I wish you --n't worry, -- you like a cup of tea?

- Wrest (arrancar) gold from a rock, wrestle (luchar) =/= wrench (torcedura, desgarro, arrancar, llave inglesa + spanner) → throw a spanner into the works (fastidiarlo todo) =/= wreck: naufragio + shipwreck; hacer naufragar, derribar → --ing: demolición, derribo, --age (ruinas, escombros), wrecked (destruido, estropeado, hundido =/= Wretched (desdichado, desgraciado; horrible, tiempo espantoso).

B- Naturaleza vegetal y animal y nociones complementarias

Hemos pensado que la inclusión de muchos nombres de vegetales y de animals puede ser acertada por dos motivos: **a**) porque con la ayuda de la tecnología, del tiempo y de la honradez, los comestibles se irán investigando con vistas a la mejora de nuestra salud, **b**) en muchas actividades humanas, industriales, soioambientales y otras, sobre todo los animales nos reservan un potencial ahora inexplicable e inimaginable. Tres secciones animarán esta exposición: vegetales (1), animales (2) y nociones complementarias varias (3). Se ha escogido la lista a partir de los que han aparecido en los textos de nuestras lecturas.

1- Vegetales

Antes que nada les comunico que el conjunto de plantas medicinales, con propiedades, diagnóstico y fotos lo presento en el libro totulado "Vall d'Assua", 2014. Me transmitió los conocimientos el amigo y experto Qued de Llessui cuando se retiró. En el que titulé como "Ética, dignidad y trauma" (2007) al final hay una larga exposición inédita de algunas maravillas que nos ofrece el reino animal, hasta en política. Resumamos:

Abedul (birch), abeto (fir) tree, acelga (Swisschard), ajo (garlic), álamo (poplar), albaricoque (apricot), albóndiga (meatball), alce (maple), alfalfa (lucerne), almond (almendra), apio (celery), arándano (bilberry, blueberry), arroz (rice)al: ricefield, paddy, avellano (hazelnut), avena (oat), azafrán (crocus, saffran), baya (berry) → coffee --, berenjena (aubergine), boniatos (sweet potatoes), cacahuete (peanut), café descafeinado (decaffeinate coffee), calabaza (pumpkin), canela (cinnamon), casis (blackcurrant), castaña (chestnut), cebada (barley), cebolla (onion), centeno (rye), cereza (cherry), champiñón (mushroom), chopo (blak poplar), choucraute (=), ciruela (plum), cítricos: (citrus + lemon), clavo (clove), col (cabbage), col de Bruselas (Brussels sprout), colza (=, rape), compota (compote), chirimoya (custard apple), daisy (margarita), ébano (ebony), ensalada (salad), escarola (endive, escarole), espárrago (asparragus), flour (harina), frambuesa (raspberry), fresa (strauberry), frutos secos (dried fruits), garbanzo (chickpea), genciana (gentian), grano (grain), grano de café (bean), guisante (pea), haba (legumbre: broad been, de café: coffee bean), heno (hay), hoja (leaf), hoja de laurel (bay leaf), judía (bean), lechuga (lettuce), legumbre (pulse, legume), lenteja (lentil), lino: (planta, fibra) flax, (tela) linen, lirio (lily), (lúpulo (hop), macedonia (=, of fruits: fruit salat, of vegetables: vegetables salat), maiz (maize, corn), malta (malt): cebada para la cerveza, mandarina (tangerine), mandioca/cassava (starchy roots), mangle (manglobe), manzanilla (chamomile tea), melocotón (peach), menta (mint), mermelada (marmalade), mora (blackberry, mulberry); morera (mulberry tree), mosto (grape juice, must), nenúfar (water lily), nuez (walnut), olivar (olive grove), ortiga (netle), pera (pear), perejil (parsley), pimienta (white/black pepper), pimienta picante (hot papikra), pimiento: green/red pepper, rábano (raddish), remolacha (beet, beetroot), roble (oak), ricino (castor-oil plant), tallarines (noodles), tomillo (thym), trigo (wheat) → whole (integral) wheat, tulipán (tulip), vainilla (vanille) → -- ice- cream, vegan (vegetariano estricto), (vid, parra, enredadera) vine, viñedo (vineyard), yedra (ivy), zarza (bramble).

2 - Animales

Águila (eagle), alce (elk), almeja (clam), anguila (eel), arenque (herring), ave de corral (fowl), ave de rapiña (bird of pray), babuino (baboon), babosa (slug), bacalao (cod), ballena (whale), caballa (mackerel), cabrito (kit), calamar (squid), camarón (shrimp), camello (camel), cangrejo: (de río) crayfish, (de mar) crab, canguro (kangaroo), caracol (snail), ciervo (deer), cigüeña (stork), cisne (swam), cobaya (guinea pig), codorniz (quail), comadreja (weasel), crustáceos (crustacean), cuervo (raven, crow), cordero (lamb), cuervo (raven, crow), chacal (jackal), chimpanzee (=), delfín (dolphin), erizo (hedgehog), escarabajo (beetle), esturión (sturgeon), flamenco (flemish), foca (seal), gallina: (Zoo) hen, chiken + pollo, gamba (prawn), garza (heron), gato montés (wildcat), gorrión (sparrow), guepardo (cheehtah), halcón (falcon), lagartija (small glizard), lagarto (glizard), lamb (young sheep), langosta: (crustáceo) lobster, (insecto) locust, langostino (prawn), lechal (suckling lamb/ pig), lobo (wolf, Pl.: wolves), lombriz de tierra (threadworms), marisco (sellfish, seafood), medusa (jellyfish), merluza (hake), moluscos (molluscks), oca (goose), oso polar (polar bear), ostra (oyster), oveja: (genérico) sheep, oveja hembra (ewe), pájaros cantores (song birds), pájaros carpinteros (woodpeckers), paloma (pigeon), paloma mensajera (homing pigeon), pangolín/ anteater (oso hormiguero), pato (duck), pavo (turkey), pavo real (peacock), perdiz (partridge), pez (flesh), piojo (louse, Pl.: lice), pollito/pajarito (chick), pollo adulto (chiken), potro (foal), rana (frog), rata (rat), ratón (mouse, Pl.: mice), reno (reindeer), ruiseñor (nightingale), saltamontes (grasshoppers), sanguijuela (leech), sapo (toad), sardina (sardine), sepia (cottlefish), serpiente (snake/serpent), s. cascabel (rattle snake), serpiente pitón (pithon), simio (ape), tábano (horsefly, gadfly), tejón (badger), ternero/a (calf), tórtola (turtledove), tortuga de tierra (turtoise), t. de mar (turtle), trucha (trout), urraca (magpie), urugallo (grouse), verraco macho (boar), visón (mink), zarigueya (possum).

3- NOCIONES COMPLEMENTARIAS VARIAS

Aceite de pescado (fish oil); aguardiente (brandy), alimento adelgazante: slimming & weight-reducing food ↔ alimento que engorda: it get fat, it put on weigh; ahumado: smoked fish, meats, ...; alimentario (food stuff/industry, ...) =/= alimenticio (nourishing, nutritive) → (valor) alimenticio (nutritive value), alimento (food), alimento casero (homemade food/ kooking), alimentos curativos (curative, therapeutical foods), alimento de deshecho (waste food product), alimento de primera necesidad (stapple food), alimentos embotellados (bottled foods), alimentos enlatados (canned/tinned foods), alimentos genéricos (generic foods), alimentos integrales (whole foods), alimentos naturales (health foods), alimentos poco nutritivos (of little nutritional value), alimentos precocinados (ready, precooked meals), alimentos secos (nuts & dried fruits), alimentos tropicales (tropical foods, tropical fruits), alimentos venenosos (poisonous foods), anaemia, ancas de rana (frogs'legs), anis (anisette), aperitivo: (bebida) aperitif, drink, (comida) snack, appetizer; apetitoso: (gustoso) appeticing, (sabroso) tasty; aprovisionamiento: (acción) provisioning, (sujeto) supplies; arroz integral (brown rice); asado: horno (roast), parrilla (barbecued, grilled); bebida (drink, beverage), --/comida helada (ice- cold) ..., -- no alcohólica o refrescante (soft drink), dado a la -- (hart- drinking), (darse a la -- (take to drink); bizcocho (sponge cake), buñuelo (fritter), café descafeinado (caffeine-free), caldo (clar soup), canalones (cannelloni), capullo: Bot. (bud), (Zoo) cocoon); caramelizar (coat with caramel), carne: de ave & de mamíferos (meat), de cañón (cannon fodder), de cerdo (pork), -- congelada (frozen meat), de gallina (goose-flesh, goose pimples), magra (lean meat), mechada (con tocino: larded meat), de ovino de más de un año (mutton), de reses de edad (beef), de ternera (veal), de venado (venison); celulósico (cellulosic) ethanol would not impinge (afectar) upon food production; cerveza sin alchhol (alcohol-free beer), colmillo (tusk), comida para bebés (baby foods), comestible (edible), coñac (=, brandy), cook (cocinar), cordero asado (roast lamb), crema (cream) → nourishing cream, -- batida (whipped), -- inglesa (custard); crudo: (food) raw =/= poco hecho (underdone), cultivo comercial (cash crop), chuleta de cordero (chop), churros (hot cakes), descremado (skimmed, low-fat), desnutrido (undernourished) ↔ well-nourished, dieta (go, be on a diet: regimen), digestión: digest one's food, empanadillas (patties), entremeses (hors d'oeuvre), escalope (=), escoger (choose) → there isn't a great deal to -- =/= chosen/selected from among 90 applicants, esterilización (sterlization), estofado (stewed), (las) existencias cayeron en picado (the stocks plummeted/plunged), extreñir (constipate), fácil de digerir (easily digestible), foie gras, fresco: (agua) cold, (bebida) cold/cool, fresh fish =/= (viento) cool/fresh, wet paint; frutos del pais (agricultural produce), frutos secos (nuts & dried fruit), galleta (biscuit, cookie), galleta dulce (digestive biscuit), galleta salada (pretzel), (otro) gallo cantaría (things would be different), garra (claw); gastrónomo (gourmet), gastronomía (gourmet cooking), gelatinas: gelatina de postre (jelly), gelatina de carne, etc. (aspic), como ingrediente (gelatin(e); grasa (fat), grasa de ballena o foca (blubber), de panceta (bacon), graso (fatty); guarnición (garnish) =/= (Mil) garrison, grosella (redcurrant), hambre (hungry), harina/pan integrales (wholemeal), harto de algo (stuffed with sth), (cayó una) helada (there was a frost), helado (ice- cream); hervido (boiled), hervir (boil), hielo: en cubitos (ice cubes), crashed (picado) ice; huevos duros (hard-boiled eggs), jamón (ham), jarabe (syrup), jugo gástrico (digestive juice), laxante: laxative, it looses the bowls; libro de cocina (cookery book), liquefaction of foods, madalena (fairy cake), mantequilla de crema de cacahute (peanut butter), manufactured product, melocotón en almíbar (peach in syrup), menu del día (set menu), mermelada: (de albaricoque) apricot jam, (de naranja) marmalade; nata: cream, (de leche hervida) skin + descremar, desnatar, natilla/crema (custard); nutriente (nutrient), nutritivo (nutritious, nourishing, of nutritional value); pastel de bodas (weeding cake), pastel de cumpleaños (birthday cake), pastel de nata (cream cake), pastel de natilla (custard pie), pastel de queso (cheese- cake), pastelería (cake shop, patisserie); pasteurization, picado: (carne) grinding, cebolla (chopping); postre (dessert, pudding (=) → rice --; pote de mermelada (jam jar), producto derivado (spin- off); producto principal (staple) =/= producto secundario (by-product); provisiones (provisiones, supplies), queso (cheese), raza (breed) → a pedigree (de raza) dog; salsa (sauce); salazón (salting) → salted meat/fish; salvado (bran), sed (thirst), seta venenosa (toadstool), soda (soda water), sopa de cangrejos (crab bisque), sopa de mariscos (bisque), sopa vegetal (vegetable soup); tarta (pie, cake) → birthday cake, cheesecake, fruitcake, wedding cake, tarta de manzana (apple tart); torrefacto (café, ...): darkroasted, tortilla a la francesa (french/plain omelet), turrón: a candy (golosina) for Christmas, unsaturated fatty (graso) acid, (al) vapor (steamed) vegetables, ...; vasija (vessel), vegetales de temporada (seasonal vegetables).

C- PEQUEÑAS EXPRESIONES QUE SE PRESTAN A CONFUSIÓN

Se trata de un complemento a cuanto ya avanzamos al final del primer tomo. Como entonces, han ido surgiendo en los temas consultados:

a) At (the) last (al final), at least (por lo menos, como mínimo), at the latest (a lo más tardar), at best (en el major de los casos), at length (por fin, extensamente, con detenimiento), at the larger (a más tardía) date, at most (a lo sumo), of atmost (de mayor) importance, lest (no sea que, por si acaso), unless (a menos que, a no ser que), the atmost/greatest care, dificultéis; of the atmost (suma) importance, all the more (aún más), in no time at all (en un santiamén).

b) So it is in labour at large (en general), an allout (total, global) blanket (manta, total)/(suprema) war, after all (después de todo), overall (globales, generales) impressions, overall is a good work, look the problem as a whole, form a whole, disclose (revelar) it altogether (total, totalmente), in broad (general) terms, public at large (público en general), usually (por lo general), the estate (propidad) is to be sold as a whole (como una unidad), in general, an allout (total, general) strike, a global disaster/vision/study, the total output/number, an amount (cantidad) of the overall result, all- in (total, con todo incluido), utterly (completamente, absolutamente, totalmente), all-encompassing (lo engloba, rodea todo), all-embrassing (lo abarca todo).

c) It flew round & down (volcó dando vueltas), by & large (en general), ebb (reflujo, retroceder) & flow: ir y venir, keep ebbing up & down (no poder estar quieto), booms (alzas, auges) & busts (puñetazo, golpe; romper, quebrar): grandes altibajos = ups - & - downs; by & by (de pasada), at once/right away (enseguida), be down & out (vagabundo, indigente + destitute): no saber donde caer muerto, little by little/gradually (poco a poco), stop & go (alternante) growth, up & down (arriba y abajo), to & fro (de acá para allá).

d) Caring (generoso, afectuoso, humanitario, bondadoso), careless (descuidado, negligente, despreocupado), old people home (asilo), he took care of them, care home (residencia de ancianos), health care (asistencia sanitaria), carer or care giver (cuidador/a), care act, medical care (asistecia médica), careless: (pers.) descuidada, (conducta) negligente, careless of a danger (despreocupado). Patient care (cuidado de pacientes), daily (diario) child care.

e) Hand over: (armas) entregar, (poder) transferir, (Tf.) pasar, hand Colombia over (entregarla) to ..., the handing over (entrega) of weapons; mull over (meditar, reflexionar sobre), takeover (adquisición, toma de posesión, entrada en funciones, Mil.: golpe de estado. America took over Brazil as the World's mightiest Ec., take over: asumir, relevar, hacerse cargo, (territorio) tomar, (empresa) absorber, (líquido) absorber + soak up; Indians took over (se sustituyeron) from the Spanish, students won over (conquistados) by the speech.

f) All at once (de una vez), it happens at once, come here at once (inmediatamente), don't all shout at once (al mismo tiempo)!, for -- (por una vez), pay at once (de un golpe), not once (ni una vez) since ..., take it at once (enseguida), it was once a success, the once idyllic communities, once terpid (aletargada) city, once in a while (de vez en cuando), once for all/forever (de una vez para siempre), once the dust settles (cuando haya pasado la tormenta), for once (por una vez), come here at once (inmediatamente)! It happens at once (al mismo tiempo), such a symbol once could not have existed, meet a lodestar (estrella polar, norte, guía) once in a lifetime =/= tourist guide, Tf. directory.

g) Captivate (encantar, captivar), embattled: (city, garrison) asediados, (troops) en combate, (citizens, politicians) asediados de pbs.; embed (enterrar, incrustar, insertar) → -- an idea in the public mind, -- sounds & videos inside e- books; embush (tender una emboscada) at him; enable (permitir), enact (promulgar, decretar), encroach (invadir; quitar, usurpar) → encroach on/upon sth (invadir algo), (rights) limitar, restringir); endear o.s. to sb (ganarse el cariño de alguien) → this --ed her to everyone, endearing (atractivo, simpático); endeavour (esfuerzo, intento, determinación), endorse (aprobar, respaldar, refrendar, check: endosar); endowment (dote, atributo; legado, donación) → a school for --ed children; endurance (fondo, aguante, resistencia), endure: (dolor) soportar, (system) sostener, enduring (imperecedero); enhance: (beauty) realzar, (value) incrementar, (performance) mejorar; enjoy (disfrutar); enraptured (embelesado); ensnared (atrapado) in a legal fight/ in a trap/cheating; the ensuing (siguientes) days, policies ensued by the European union (EU); entail: conllevar, suponer, implicar; entanglement (enrredo con mujeres, ...; barbed wire (alambrada), enthuse (entusiasmar) over/about tech. challenges; entice (atraer) people into the shops → --ing (atractivo, apetecible, tentador); entitle (dar derecho a), entrenched (enraizado, afianzado, consolidado); entrust (confiar) the Ec. to ...; envision (prevenir).

D- Algunas esquemas más selectas para más elegante redacción del inglés

Para empezar les recuerdo el interés de los anejos del tomo I (the first volume), sin menospreciar el apartado C arriba presentado y el K, abajo. Añadamos muchas más expresiones:

Whereby (por lo que, según lo cual, por donde) → the rule -- it is not allowed to … (la regla según la cual no se permite …), Wherefore (por qué). Thereby (así, de este modo). Thereafter (a parir de entonces), all the more so because/as/since (tanto más en cuanto que). Whatever I say (diga lo que diga), -- the consequences, we must act; -- it may be, … So long as (con tal de que, siempre y cuando) → -- -- -- he was alive, I won't interfere in his life -- -- -- he doesn't in mine =/= as far as/insofar as (en tanto y cuando) → -- -- -- I know/I'm concerned, -- -- -- I'm aware (según me consta) =/= the state stretches -- -- -- the river, you can see -- -- -- the bay. It suits me in so far as I'd be nearer the work. As long as (con tal de que) you get back by 5 h. As things stand (tal como están las cosas). Wether … or (tanto si … como si). Know what's going on (por donde van los tiros). In depth (a fondo). Work flat out (a tope) for three months, I'm to my eyes (a tope) in work, take the bull by the horns. Clear the logjam (atolladero, atascadero): desbloquer la situación. Sorry for repeating myself (valga la redundancia). Under full sail (a toda vela). At the death door (entre la vida y la muerte). Live from the incomes of the investments (de renta), live beyond her means (posibilidades), live in a dream world (de ilusiones), roast (asado, V) =/= be the boss/rule the roost (percha): llevar la batuta → white men ruled the roost. He caught on immediately (lo cogió al vuelo). Bit (trozo, parte, un poco) → do one's bit (aportar su grano de arena). Richer countries are pushing forward (siguen adelante). He prefers easy does it (espacio y buena letra). In compliance with (conforme a). Orientate o.s./get one's bearing ↔ lose one's -- (desorientarse). Smell a rat (sospechar algo). Digression (divagación) → stop -- & go to the point (y ve al grano). It's a snap (eso está tirado). The proposal runs counter to/is at odds with (se opone a) … Turn out to be (resultar ser). Hat I but know it (de haberlo sabido) I should had hidden. Screw up (arrugar, apretar, atornillar; poner neura, fastidiar) one's courage: armarse de valor. We can get away with (nos bastaría con) painting. He is matter - of - fact (prosaico, práctico, realista). The hard power China can bring to bear (ejercer). Know the European fate/bad luck/misfortune (fatalidad) to one's fingers (al dedillo). Spain is the laughing stock (hazmerreir) of Europe. North America free trade agreement (NAFTA) got off to a flying start (empezó a flotar) ... Curse (maldición)d = maldito =/= damn (condenar) → the project was --ed (condenado al fracaso) from the start + damn it! (¡maldito sea! + it's not worth a -- (no vale la pena). Keep inflation at way (acorralada). Onrush: avalancha, crecida de río → an onrushing (creciente) wave of immigrants. Be/get into a fizz (burbuja, efervescencia, silvido,Vs): meterse en pbs. Weather (capear) the storm. Be quick on the uptakes (consumo, aceptación): coger las cosas al vuelo ↔ be slow -- -- -- (ser corto de entendederas). In compliance with (conformemente a). Be mindful (tener en cuenta) of the risk. Brave (afrontar, desafiar) the storm (campear el temporal). America & Europe alike worry about losing out (salir perdiendo) to Asian rivals. Catalonian firms are casting about/around (buscan) Asia & elsewhere for customers. Not to mince (fruit: picar; meat: moler) one's words: no tener pelos en la lengua, no andar con rodeos. E-tail (venta por Internet). Defeat (vencer) the revels; -- one's own purpose (ir contra su interés). Beware!/watch out!/be careful! (¡ten cuidado, etc.!). Wound (herida,V) the pride: tocar el amor propio. There are nothing left but rubble (sólo queda escombros). I had to owe him (tuve que quedarle a deber). Turned out to be (result ser). Do at their own risk (por su cuenta y riesgo), -- -- -- -- pace (ridmo). Get one's way (salirse con la suya). I don't care three hoots (bocinazos, toque de sirena): me importa un bledo. Provided that/whenever/as long as (siempre que). Take a liking (simpatía) to sb, a liking (afición) for sth. Get on (well together) with: llevarse bien con + I was getting on (me iba bien) till he cames along (llegó). Jumped on/fell upon (se avalancha sobre) him. Don't let off the rope, …! (¡no sueltes la cuerda, …!). Sky-high (por las nubes) unemployment. Pump up (reactivar, hinchar) the Ec. Turning point (momento decisivo, punto de inflexion). It is in the making (fabricación, preparación). Flog sth to death (repetir hasta la saciedad). Leash (correa) → easy money unleashed (soltado, desencadenado) by Fed's bond-bying is over. Regulators did away with (suprimieron) that in 2000. At nightfall (anochecer). The civil guard was on the take (dispuesto a ser sobornado). Be at loggerheads with sb (estar a matar con). Middle of the rock (mediocre, moderado + =) voters. The eyes twinkling (centelleo,V, brillar) → in the -- of an eye (en un abrir y cerrar de ojos). Be fighting for one's life (estar entre la espada y la pared). Pending tray (bandeja): cajón de asuntos pendientes. The likes of him (gente como él). Face up to (hacer frente a) the overseers (supervisores). Be on a hiding (estar escondido) to nothing: llevar las de perder. Slog it out (luchar hasta el final). My opinión/view → I've had my say (he dado mi opinión). Leaps & bounds (límites, delimitar; salto, brinco,V): pasos ajigantados. Lie about/around it (estar sin hacer nada, por ahí tirado). Wake (despertar, estela) → in the wake of (tras, a raiz de). The shot was right on the target; be on the target (seguir la trayectoria prevista). Do away with (suprimir). Sit through (aguantar hasta el final) → I sat -- two boring lectures (conferencias). Be on the downgrades (en plena decadencia) → he has been --ed to assistant manager (ayudante de dirección). The agreement is fatally flawed (con defectos que lo conducen al fracaso). The opportunity is slipping away (se va). He swept into office (arrasó y cogió el poder) =/= he snatched (arrebató) the power. Antics (payasadas, travesuras) → he is to her old -- (está hacienda de las suyas). Dog (perseguir) sb's footsteps/heels (pisar los talones a alguien). Bereft (desprovisto) of hope. Catch-all: (regulation, clause, etc.) general, (phrase) para todo) → a -- piece of legislation (que abarca muchos casos). Whatsoever (whatever): sea lo que sea, fuera lo que fuera → none/nothing -- (ningumo, nada en absoluto). Scale-back (disminuir, recortar) their loss- making (negocios no rentables). Top- of- the- line/range: de primerísima calidad + model (el mejor modelo de la gama). Raise salaries & backdate (dar efecto retroactivo a) the increases. He doesn't trust a soul (no se fía ni de su sombra). Come to terms with sth (asumir, asimilar) algo; -- -- -- -- sb (llegar a un acuerdo). Not back out now (no te eches atrás ahora). Dwindle (disminuir) away to nothing (disminuir hasta quedar a cero). The more, the merrier (cuantos más, major). Rank (rango) & file: soldado raso, tropa; the -- - -- (de las bases del) party/union. They are torn apart (hechos trizas) by pointless (sin sentido) disputes. They are all the more (aún más) unwillingly to inhibit/restrain action. Be out of kilter: (mechanism (descentrado), business are -- - -- (desorganizados). Goalpost (poste) → move the -- (cambiar las reglas de juego). Size him up (evaluar como es) → he --ed -- -- straight away (lo caló enseguida). He drew a straight line, in a -- -- (en línea recta), dotted line (línea de puntos). He will lose out (saldrá perdiendo). Be always on the move (de uno a otro lado). Flab/fat(ness): gordura → fight the flab (cuidar la línea). Save for a rainy-day (dias de vacas flacas). Butt: extremo, culata, colilla, blanco; trasero → sit on one's -- (rascarse la barriga), work one's butt off (romperse la cabeza). His gambit (táctica) flopped (fracasó). Federal law trumps (supera) state law. Be/live comfortably - off (vivir holgadamente). Put sb through the hoop (aro): hacerle pasarlas negras. Our worst ever results, as -- (como siempre), -- since (desde que) we first saw her, for --. The nub (quit, meollo, parte esencial) of the hard pb. (de la cuestión). It's all up for grabs (estar a disposición de cualquiera). Truco: trick/gimmick → advertisement -- + get the snack (coger el truco). For the time being (por ahora). Strike out on their own (volar por sus propias alas, trabajar por su cuenta), strike wildly (dar golpes sin mirar a quien). Go with the flow (fluir): dejarse llevar por la corriente. Make a headline news (salir en primera página). Wax (luna: crecer) & wane (menguar, decaer): crecer y decrecer, sufrir altibajos (ej. de popularidad). Falcon Heavy: by far the beefiest (más fornido/robusto) rocket, second only to Saturn. We can but try (por intentarlo que no quede). Let things slide (se vengan abajo). Whatsoever none (absolutamente no) + whatsoever duties (sean cuales sean las tareas) you may be called to perform (obligación: cumplir) =/= whoever he/she is (sea quien sea). Even if belatedly (con retraso) they got tough (de mano dura) policies. Pall (paño mortuorio), pall of smoke (cortina de humo), it --s after a time (después de un cierto tiempo deja de gustar). Kick up a fuss (armar una bronca, montar un nº). He hardly (apenas) know him, -- anyone (casi nadie) respect the democratic norms. This equates (corresponde) to one for every 50 Germans. Chapuza: bungle, botched job, shoddy piece of work, odd job; meter la apta: gaffe; blunder, put one's foot in it; metepatas (blunderer), a slapdash/botched (chapucero) work; shoddy: (trabajo) chapuza, (infrastructura) mala calidad. Decepcionar, defraudar: disappoint, let down. Inasmush as (dado que). Insofar as (en la medida en que). At the very least (como mínimo) ↔ -- -- -- most. Put it mildly (por decirlo de alguna manera), I was only mildly criticized. Aside from (aparte de). He demur (objeta, pone reparos) ↔ without --. At any rate (en cualquier caso). For the being (por ahora). By any means (de cualquier manera, del modo que sea) ↔ not -- -- -- (de ningún modo). Not even (ni tan siquiera). At the latest (a más tardar). It make it all the more (aún más) important. The ranks (=, º, fila) of informal workers grew along those of unemployment. Keep up with sth (seguir o continuar con algo). Let's split up into groups (dividámonos en grupos). The Ec. in the full blush (rubor) of recovery. Line up (ponerse en la cola) to vie (disputar) … Go off (desviarse del) path (curso, trayectoria). To put it in a nutshell (para decirlo con pocas palabras). Veiled (encubiertos) attacks → thinly -- dislike (antipatía apenas disimulada). Unskilled migrants depress (deprimen) pay for locals. Seize him up (valorarlo como es), they seized him straight away (lo calaron enseguida). Satellites sent out (lanzados). Out of the way (remotas, poco conocidas) provinces. Catch sb snapping (desprevenidos). Divy up (repartir) money, government jobs, … He is not up (no reune las condiciones) to the job. I bumped (topé) with … Oxigen round (por todo) the body. Turn out (dar media vuelta) & go off (irse, salir). I shouldn't wonder (no me sorprendería) …, be lost in -- (quedar maravillado). Make it clear that (dejar sentado que) … Blot one's copybook (manchar su reputación), a blot in his --. Bluster: fanfarronada, intimidación + (viento) soplar con fuerza. Vow (voto, promesa, V) → -- never to rest (descansar) until ... Return request (solicitud) for comment → the stuff was declared void (malo). The onlookers (espectadores) were gripped (emocionados). Wiped out (aniquilado, limpiado) within five years. Ease (aliviar, calmar) through handouts (donativos). Volkwagen derives (proporciona) over half its turnover (facturación) from after-sale services. The Union is fraying (lucha, se irrita, se desgasta, pierde la paciencia). The state driving investment is tapering off (disminuye poco a poco). The paltriest (el más ínfimo, mísero) return. Laugh off (tomarse a risa). Expulsar: drive out, expel, send off. Flounce: movimiento mostrando excesivo espanto o admiración, -- in/out (entrar, salir indignado). He blew (desperdició) his opportunity & flopped (fracasó). The sea of the northernmost tip (extremo) of the island is stirring (agitado). Forbearance (tolerancia, paciencia) toward fiscal winners. Put up with (soporta, aguantar) Mr's Abe provocation. Nuts & bolds of a sheme (los aspecos prácticos de un proyecto). A very confident/self-assured (seguro de sí mismo) person. Dying cities are doomed to fade away (apagarse, consumirse). My distrust (descofianza) of my own habilities (capacidades). Skulk (esconderse) → I saw him --ing in the background (en el fondo). She bore the pain (aguantó el dolor) without flinching (estremecerse, sobresaltarse (+ shudder, shaken, tremble) ↔ without -- (sin inmutarse). My sister had to hurry me/chivy me (apurarme, meterme prisa) into applying for a grant. The poor have fared badly (lo han pasado mal) under this government. A closesd bank is in next street, a close relative, they're very close (unidos) friends, stay close or you'll get lost, the tragedy brought them closer. Smooth: -- sb's path/way (allanarle el camino), alisar, pulir, suavizar, (transición) facilitar. Go with the flow (dejarse llevar por la corriente). Keep up with sb (seguir en contacto con alguien). He chunned (impidió) to give them a try (probarlos, darles una oportunidad). Fraugh (tenso, difícil) with (cargado de) folly (locura). The remnants (lo que queda) of her self-respect (amor propio). Exhalaration (euforia, júbilo) → --ing (estimulante, excitante, vigorizante) turnaround (cambiar de ridmo, giro radical). It lifts people out (saca la gente) from deep povery. The ground gave way (cedió) beneath his feed; those beneath him. Land area, beneath of which lie vast reserves of oil. The fulfilment (cumplimiento, realización) of her ambitions. Released (puesto en libertad) under bail, animal -- (devueltos) to the wild, -- from ailment (enfermedad, dolencia), -- (dispensado) from his normal duties (tareas habituales). Tenso: (administración, relaciones) fraught, (cable) taut, tight, (músculo) tense, tight, (nervioso) tense, nervous, uptight before the exam. Bring America back in to the pact. Appointed/designated (designado). He unwinds (desarrolla, revela) what he did. His nearest challenger in the party. Saudis work mostly in cushy (fácil, cómodos) government jobs. Foreboding (premunición, presentimiento) of troubles ahead. Shengen embodies (encarna, expresa, incorpora) the dream of frictionless movement across the EU's single market. The vacant (=, vacío) building is emblematic of the city's descend into despair. Trump's ill-fated (infortunada) policy. His opponents are flummoxed (desconcertados, asombrados) by his popularity. I told you so (ya te lo dije yo). He fired off (disparó, lanzó) a barrage (aluvión) of tweets. Banks are guilty of at least minor (=, secundario) jiggery-pokery (chanchullo, tejemaneje). America's allies should stand up (resistir, soportar; ponerse de pie) to its reckless (irresponsible, insensato + foolish, stupid) trade policy; stand up for (defender) Canadian interests. Peer-to-peer (de igual a igual) summit for years. The international system is ossified (=, anquilosado). Turn about/around: (car) dar la vuelta completa, (wind) cambiar de dirección, (business/Ec.) recuperarse. Insofar as (en la medida en que) such an extend (extensión)... The EU has been on a roll (de buena racha). Broadly speaking (a grandes rasgos). The AI will not make human experts redundant (superfluos, innecesarios). Few stick around (se quedan). An anti- corruption campaign frightened investors. Arrange it however you like. Entrapment: incitación por agentes de la ley a cometer un delito para arrestarlo. Irrespective (a pesar de, sin tener en cuenta) of races. Their enthusiasm is paying off (da fruto). Notwithstanding (a pesar de, no obstante, sin embargo) recent events. France was fecund to none (como ningún otro pais) saving national honor. Somehow or other (de una manera o de otra). As much as anyone (tanto como el que más). How long is it since he wrote to you? A flash of lightening lit up the sky. As long as (con tal de que) you get back by six hour. We'll finish it somehow (sea como sea). It won't be easy, whoever does it (no impota quien lo haga). I can't interfere in his life so long as (mientras) he doesn't in mine. Cry (llora) as muchas as you like. We did as much as we could. As soon as he saw me … The most he has, the most he wants. The most I think about it, the less I understand. It was as much mine as yours. The due (fecha de vencimiento) date was only one day away. Why/how on earth … (¿qué demonios ..?). You could have as much as coffee as you wanted. In accordance with (con arreglo a). From here up (para arriba). However much you shout … (por más que grites) …

E- Medio ambiente y energía

Este sector, juntamente con el del C-19, tal como están las cosas, invitan más que el resto a retener la conceptología real, además del vocabulario y la sintaxis:

Environment pollution. Care for the environment is inseparable from the fight against global inequality. Amazonia'crucial role as a buffer against climate change. In Amazonia it's basin contains 40% of Earth rainforest & serves as a carbon sink (hundirse; tragar, enterrar), mitigating warming. Raising deforestation, on the pretext of development, threatens the sustainability of the ecosystem. The insouciance (despreocupación) of regional governments, specially Brazil's, put them on a collision course (camino de enfrentamiento) with the church. The government has shrugged off (no ha hecho caso de) deforestation, bowed (comprometido, inclinado) to legalise mining on indigenous lands. The subsequent exodus left the tribes feeling (sintiéndose) more vulnerable. The church's chequered history (altibajos): credited with educating children but blamed for its complicity with colonialism & Ec. explotation. It helps indigenous tribes secure (seguro; sujetar, proteger; conseguir, garantizar) land rights & put pressure on governments to uphold (mantener, apoyar) them. The Catholic church wants to save souls as well as tries. Inculturisation: adaptation of a religion to alien (extraños, extraterrestres, extranjeras) cultures. A social-media firestorm (tormenta ignea) of indignation. Ordenar (arrange, order), (priests) ordain → ordaining married priests was quarantined within the region. The industrialised nations in 2019 aded 43 bn. of carbon dioxide to the atmosphere. They will to go beyond today's insufficients efforts to stop. Artic weather has gone haywire (se ha averiado, ha perdido la chaveta). Headwaves (holas de calor) once considered freakish (variables, caprichosas) are becoming common place (común y corriente). Meeting the 1.5 goal will mean capturing & storing hundreds of bn. of tonnes of carbon dioxide by 2100. Methods of providing negative emissions need to be developed right now. Sequestring (=, aislar) underground, plantig trees on ascale even remotely (remotamente) adequate to the task requires … The mere idea that will one day be possible eats away (corroe, desgasta) at (=, devora) the perceived (=, considerada) urgency of cutting emissions today. Greeenhouse effect (efecto invernadero). Electricity generated from sunlight going directly to a railway line: unused land next to railway lines to place solar panels =/= the plan/gold was panned (cribado) in his own party. India is keen on using sun power. Limited space available for solar panels on train roofs. A part of the world is blessed with plenty of sunshine; hours of --. Shutdown (cierre) of the reactor. Microbes that inhabit the stomachs of ruminants: this bugs transform those fibrous fare (comida) into energy-rich molecules. Animals belch metane into the atmosphere. It's a problem because methane is a greenhouse gas that has a warning effect 28 times as powerful as carbon dioxide. A cow has about the same greenhouse effect as a car. The antimethagenic power of a seaweed (alga), the *Asparagopsis*. Cultivate it or gather it from the wild (silvestre). Alternative energy sources. Take CO2 out of chimneys of coal-fired power plants & pump it deep underground. The great bulk of Beld & road initiative (BRI) energy spending is in carbon intensive areas, especially coal-fired poor stations. Fuel (combustible, carburante) → fossil-fuel (hidrocarburos + hydrocarbons). They thought modern coal-fired plants are cleaner. The grey energy bits (partes) are wilting (marchitas) under the impact of oil prices =/= thwart (desbaratar, frustar). Nitrous oxide: gas con potente efecto invernadero. Tree huggers (fánáticos del medio ambiente), greening (concienciación ecológica). The issue (asunto) of global warming. Good farming practices (técnicas agrícolas recomendadas). Whole food (alimentos integrales), health food (alimentaión natural). Ecology-related worries/concerns. The ice melted (se fundió, fu derretido) & worried the environmentalists. Ozone layer (capa) is not for ever. Stringent (riguroso + strict, severe) emission regulations. Endanger (poner en peligro) → the critiqually endangered (in danger of extinction) birds suggests the logging (de madereros) wars are not over. A campaign to raise public awareness (concienciación ciudadana) on environmental topics. Deplete (disminuir; stock, ...: agotar) the ozone that protects Earth. Tidal power (energia maremotriz). The 10 % solid waste discharged (vertido) each day is plastic. The figure of plastics for farming in 2019 is $ 3 trn. Utilities prefer cheaper & cleaner natural gas. As the energy industry braces (apuntala) for (se preparar para) future disruption. Geothermal is cheaper & as dependable (formal, digno de confianza, fiable). Norway yearns (ansia) to be green but depends on fossil fuels. Kapital spending in renewable energy. Borrow (solicitar prestado, toma, sacar) the carbon in the air in the form of CO2. Conventional wisdom (opinión convencional) holds that battery powered cars are the future of motoring. A campaign extolling the virtues of an alterative source of electricity power: fuel cells. Instead of storing & then releasing electricity gathered from the mains in the way that battery does, fuel cells generates current from a chemical reaction between hydrogen & oxygen. The oxygen comes from the air & water for electrolysis is everywhere. The hydrogen, suitably compressed, is stored in a tank on board (a bordo) the vehicles, & is replenished at a filling station like petrol. Unlike a battery, a fuel cell does create exhaust (gases de escape). Hydrogen is enjoying a purple patch (estado de garcia). It may also propell buses & lorries, & ship & aircraft. There is talks of it replacing natural gas as a source of heat, of it being employed as a chemical feedstock & even of it replacing coke (coque) to extract metallic iron from its ore. In the 1970s & 1990s has been talks to replacing hydrocarbons with hydrogen. It didn't happen: for a start, ripping up (haciendo pedazos) & replacing the world's fossil- fuel infrastructure is a high job. And even if were that an easy thing to accomplish, hydrogen himself has drawbacks (inconvenientes). Until 2019, for instance, Britain has planed to cut carbon emissions by 80 % from their levels in 1990 by 2050. Full decarbonisation is as much bigger task, & one for which hydrogen may prove necessary. Engineers have toyed with (jugueteado con) everything from nuclear propulsion to high- tech sails. A switch to renewably powered electrical heating would therefore (por tanto) require a dramatic & expensive beefing up (refuerzo) of the electricity network. Keep hydrogen in underground caverns (as currently happens with natural gas) could increase capacity enough to manage not just day-to-day (cotidianas) fluctuations but interseasonal ones as well. On top of this ideas, heavy industry may provide other niches (nichos, huecos) for hydrogen to fill. Climate change may turn much of the northern China into an arid semi-desert. The south is lashed by frequent super-thyphoons & flash floods (riadas). Lack of water has thwarted (frustrado, interrumpido) plans to bring over (ir a buscar, convencer) more mainland settlers. Environmental activists staged (organizaron) a string of lightning (relámpago) protests. Powered by the sun, the machines suck carbon dioxide from the atmosphere & pump it into the sedimentary rocks formation below. Renewable energy in

Japan: promises reinventions of the power is not making much headway (no avanza o progresa mucho). Dozens of fims sprang up (surgieron, brotaron). The hoped-for (esperada) transformation has been slow & invisible. After the disaster of Fukushima most of nuclear plant have been shut down. Fot the most part, they habe been replaced not by wind turbines & solar panels but power stations that burn coal & natural gas. In 2021, the current government wants nuclear plants to provide at least 20 % electricity by 2030; the target for renewables is well below the current global average. Problems for signifiquant energy transition: geography & geology, government policies also help stifle (ahogar, suprimir) growth of renewable energy. The sea floor drops away (disminuye) more steeply off-Japan's coast than it does in places where off-shore wind has boomed. A petrol head (fanático del automobilismo) is thwarting the development of renewable energy. Lopez Obrador administration said would suspend the inspections that solar & wind farms must undergo to begin operating. There is little sign that this bets will pay off (liquidar, amortizar, pagar y despedir; merecer la pena). The Arab world's most abundant clean-energy source is the sun. Convention on climate change took on (asumió, aceptó) a commitment to global adaptation framework. A punch- up (pelea, refriega) serious enough to leave many in hospital. A standoffish (distante, reservado) regime of self-reliance (independencia, autosuficiencia). Tipping: dar propina, vertido de ruinas. Chemical engineering: there is the possibilty of helping the chemical weathering process by grinding up silicate rocks into fine dusts, thus speeding up the reactions that store carbon dioxide away in stable minerals. Paris agreement: under existing schemes the median tonne of carbon emissions is priced at only $ 15. A serious attempt would require a price in the range of $ 40- $ 80 to be levied on all the world's industrial greenhouse-gas emissions (as well as some other interventions). The bad reputation of carbon offsetting (compensación) may one day change. Paris agreement commit its signatories to keep the raise in global temperature, compared to that of the preindustrial climate, well below 2° C by 2050. Renewable energy agency estimates that $ 800 bn of investments in renewables is need each year until 2050 for the world to be on course for less than 2° C of warning. Some states commitments (obligaciones, compromisos) to move to net zero emissions by 2050 means to take out as much greenhouse gas as they loose (sueltan). If the world is to achieve net cero emissions, the only permissible offsets need to be genuine (auténticas, naturales) negative emissions. Scrub (fregar, cancelar) sulphur dioxide from the smokestacks (chimeneas). If the price underperforms (rinde poco, se comporta mal) ... Insanely (terriblemente, locamente) cheap solar enrgy. If techniques for pulling carbon dioxide back out of the air improve, such hydrogene (obtained splitting the water), could be combined with that scavenged (recogido de la basura) carbon to make fossil-free oils. Lithium-ion batteries are too bulky to power big planes on long fights. Some industrial processes give out carbon dioxide. New tehniques may intercept the carbon dioxide before it gets into the atmosphere & squirrel it away (almacenarlo) underground. Potable nuclear reactions could substitute for unreliable (poco de fiar) power grids. In China they would rather not hasten the cloture of carbon-spewing power stations that are working for a good three decades. Emissions slashed (reducidas rádicalmente) today will be felt only in the middle of the century: international efforts are focused on cutting emissions of greenhouse gases, chief (la principal) among them is carbon dioxide. Global average temperatures are rougly 1.1° C warmer today than pre-industrial temperatures & CO2 is the main culprit. Greenhouse gases are produced when fossil fuels are burned to generate energy or power engines, by farming & deforestation. Statistically reliable results suggest that cutting

CO_2 emissions could slow the rate of warming as early as 2033. But only if they are ended worldwide in 2020. Reducing C02 by 5 % per year, starting in 2020, would produe a statistically significant deviation from what temeperatures would have otherwise been only in 2044. The 4-7 % drop estimated this year as a result of C-19, without concerted efforts from governments, it is likely to rise again as economics reopen. The 90 % of energy trapped (=, retenida) by the greenhouse gas emissions produced in the half past century has ben stored in the oceans & released to the atmosphere as head only slowly. Carbon dioxide emited today will remain in the atmosphere for decades to centuries before it is reabsorbed by vegetations & the oceans. That is not true for other industrial emissions. Each molecule of methane warms the planet 84-87 times more than CO_2, but it stays aloft (arriba) for merely years instead of decades or centuries. This has resulted in calls for immediate action to slash metane emissions, for instance by plugging leaks in natural-gas infrastructure, & reducing emisions from farming. But even then, eliminating all sources of methane pollution in 2020 would not affect warming trends before 2039.

The polluant that could have the most immediate impact is one that currently keeps the world cooler: sulphur oxides are a by-product of burning some fossil fuels, including coal & dirty bunker (carbonera) fuel, & there are a target of policies to clean up maritime emissions & urban air pollution. In the atmosphere, they bounce a portion of solar radiation back (recuperan) into the space, producing a cooling effect. Because they are dragged back to Earth by rain within days of being emited, cutting them out of the industrial activities could boost waming by the end of the decade.

The quest (búsqueda) for renewable hydrogen: the bottom line (lo esencial, lo mínimo aceptable) is that hydrogen must be "truly green" or "renewable". The true challenge is to reduce production costs through economies of scale & tech. evolution. It will be very competitive in around five years. Within the EU strategy for energy systemm integration, hydrogen is one of the solutions for decarbonisation hard- to- abate (amainar, aplacar) sectors. The hydrogen strategy focuses on "renewable hydrogene", described as the most compatible option with the EU's climate neutrality & zero pollution goal in the long term. In the third phase (2030- 2050), renewable hydrogen tech should reach maturity & be deployed at large scale. In the US there would be a more thorough (riguroso, profundo, a fondo) attempt (intento, atentado) to undo loosened environmental protections. But this could be complicated by Mr Trump's judicial legacy: the courts he leaves behind will probably take a cagier (más reservado, cauteloso) attitude to constraints (coacciones, restricciones) on business.

F- Finanzas

Se trata de un complemento a los esquemas presentados en el primer tomo:

The complexity of the financial super-structure build upon the € makes break-up (hace disolver) a terrifying prospect. Unencumbered (sin trabas, libre de gravámenes) free trade. Stakeholder & shareholder (accionistas) → majority (mayoritario) shareholder. Revenue streams (fuentes de ganancias). Stockmarkets shuddered (se estremecieron) on March 2020. Ropy (chunga, floja) economía. Share issue/issuance (emission en bolsa). Subsidise feckless (débiles, irresponsables) southerners. It lets indebted southern countries off the hook (los saca del atolladero). Plough (invertir mucho dinero) → in 2006 Germany investors ploughed $ 63 bn. into Spain; only 3 in 2018. The aggregate (total) net debt of the top 20 gold companies tracked by an specialised exchange-traded fund fell by 40%. He earned investor's trust (confianza, fondo fiduciario) as head (cabeza, director, …) of … He has trimmed (adornado; cortado, reducido) Barricks head office (oficina central) & settled (resolvió + acomodó, colocó; saldó; colonizó) a long running tax dispute. Glue (pegamento, V, estar pegado a) → they were glued to TV screens as the finance minister recited the previsions. The viewers felt deflated (desanimados). News duties were imposed on & lifted of thoroughbred (pura sangre) horses. Share prices sagged (cayeron). Investor increasingly attentive to firms'environmental, social & governance metrics (métrica) eye with suspicion businesses energy-intensive. Investors see grubby (sucio, mugriento) reputational risk of crude. She loaned (prestó) her money. At bottom (en el fondo) a bank is a balance-sheet, a factory that turns capital into financial produts (ej. loans & mortgages). Asian saving glut (superabundancia; Com.: inundar, saciar) as an underlying (subyacente) cause of the housing boom of 2008. There are echoes with 15 years ago: high savings rate in Asia continue to translate into (traducirse en) current account surplusses. The Holy See's image as a refuge for hot money & shady (sombreados; dudosos, turbios) dealings =/= shadowy (oscuro, misterioso) government debt in Germany: public- sector Landesbanks are big creditors of local governments. Partners who manage to invest in the funds liable for the debt & pension costs of companies they adquire. Overheads (gastos generales): expenses incurred (contraidas) in running a business. A way of getting a toehold (agarradero, presa) in financial market. Levy (imponer, recaudar) on banks is tiny compared with the cost of the bail-outs. He hurled (lanzó)10 $ bn. loan. Corporate (de sociedad) tax. Risky credit-arbitrage. Export tariff rebates (descuentos) on 3000 items. Lump-sum (pago único, suma total) → a -- settlement: una idemnización global. China scarcity of domestic funds is crippling (agobiante, gravísimo) because China hold foreing institutions back from investing capital. Franquicia: franchise/exemption → (aduanera): -- from customs, (equipaje): free baggage allowance, (postal): freepost. His financial wizardry (su genio financiero). Mexico's cash outflow (flujo) from its usines was $3 bn. Current account (money loged can be withdrawn on demand by means of cheque) =/= deposit account (notice has to be given in advance of the withdrawal). Dishonoured cheque: a cheque/check rejected by a drawer's bank; drawer: bank in which it has his accounts; drawer man (who writes the cheque); the cheque is worthless (sin valor); endorsement: the person whom the cheque is made out/made payable sign in its back. He refund (reembolsa, restituye) a lot of money. Wait for interest rates in America to drop, then business revive & ease (alivia) unemployment. It is done on a cash basis (al contado). Payee (beneficario) ↔ drawee (pagador). Bank draft/order: document in which a bank undertakes to pay a sum of money. Clearing house (cámara de compensación para equilibrar los mercados a término). Raise a loan (emitir un préstamo). They were willing to pay for the service out of their own pockets: $ 16 bn. out of $ 18. Allocation of funds (recursos) for building. Bounce (estar sin provisiones) → I hope this cheque doesn't -- (no será devuelto) =/= (ball, child) saltar. Road-tax (impuesto de circulación, vigente). The cashier (cajero) totals up the value of … No lose entitlement (derechos) to social benefits. Circulation capital/floating assets (capital circulante), circulation figures (facturación, volumen de negocios). Neither refund (reembolsado) nor exchanged. Go over (rebasar, sobrepasar) the $ 10 million. Outraged (ultrajadas, escandalosas) reductions. A $ 700 millions standby (reemplazante, reservas por si acaso) loan. Adjuster: an independent firm who asses (evalua) the damage. S. Hussein used brives to siphon off (desviar) $ X bn. Sobrante: surplus. Balance in hand (saldo activo). Par of exchange (tipo de cambio), at par with the $ (con paridad de cambio con el $), the share is at 20 % above/below par (sobre la par), par value (valor a la par) =/= be on a par with sth/sb: estar a pie de igualdad con algo/alguien.The budget is referred (sometido) back & forth (de acá para allá) between the Parliament & the Council. Subsidies (subvenciones) & countervailing (compensatorios) duties (obligación, deber, tasas en Ec.: derechos). The budget is waiting for aproval, give your consent. It is repayable (plazo de amortización) over ten years. Duty free (libre de derechos aduaneros). A project deferred (en suspense) through lack of funds. Pay the money biannually to the company account. Deducir: give a discount, deduct 25 % of my salary. He was paid out (desembolsado) € 10 millions. Starting a business involved a large financial outlay. Tax- deductible (desgravable). Cash (pagar) a cheque. A seizure (embargo) order of their property (bienes). With/from public funds (con cargo al erario público). Exempt from tax (libre de impuestos). Optional manufacturing costs (costes de fabricación obtativos), --er (fabricante). A totally reliable (de fiar) investor. The new signing (fichaje)- on fee: dinero del nuevo fichaje. Everyday expenses (gastos ordinarios). Plump (relleno, dejarse caer pesadamente) → bank shares plumped (hincharon) their core (meollo, esencia) equities. Public indebtedness; financial -- inquiry (investigación de la situación fnanciera), financial report (informe). Creditworthiness/solvency (solvencia Ec.). Suspension (=, exclusión) the disbelief (incredulidad), -- of payments. Bad debts are written down (amortizdas por depreciación) & bankrupt state owned enterprises (SOES) shot. Listing (cotización) on the stock (bolsa). Investors have soured (agriado, deteriorado) relations on equity investment. The embargo brought about o resulted in the Ec. ruin. Keel (quilla) → solidity of a bank: amount of money that can afford to (disponer, permitirse) without keeling over (volcar, derrumbarse). Tax avoid (evitar, evadir, esquivar)ance (evasión + lugar: escape, capital: flight). Favourable tax tantamount (equivalente a) government subsidies. By shoving (empujando) rates upward. Rely on (depender de, contar con) foreign capital. The bond market has priced/quoted (cotizado) in a slower pace (paso, ridmo). Its wobbly (cojo, flojo, poco firme) credit rating (credibilidad, clasificación crediticia). Diluted (=, atenuado) to make the taxes more palatable (=, acceptables). Insolvency. Fallback (se usa para lo que es o no possible transigir) → I got my skills as a -- (sin necesidad) ↔ this fund is a -- (sirve de colchón) if profits fall down. A repeal (revocación) of the state tax; state duty (impuesto de sucesión), income tax (impuesto sobre la renta). Raise interest rates further & faster than expected. Russia's access to international capital market, severed (cortado) as a result of sanctions. Windfall tax (impuestos sobre beneficios extras), windfall profits; Indian demonetarisation: no windfall from stashed (ahorrado, acumulado) cash. National income (rentas). Guaranteed securities enterprises (GSES): they buy American mortgages from Banks & other organisations, bundled them into securities & resell them to investors with a guarantee. Limited or liability company (sociedad anónima). Trust company (trust, empresa fiduciaria, de fideicomiso). Net/brut profits. Turnover (movimiento de mercancias, volumen de negocios). Sales figures (cifras de ventas). Tax free area (zona franca). Tax inspector. Tax exemption (desgravación). A mobile-only nobank that offers its own current account/act as a broker for products offered by other financial institutions. Neobank advantages: absence of branches, up- to- date (al día) cloud-based softwear. Entice (atraer, seducir, tentar) funds for ... Term (término, periodo, condición) of a loan. Reduction/discount (rebaja). Inverstors piled in (se lanzaron al ataque) blindly. Property (propiedad inmobiliaria) → -- insurance (seguro inmobiliario). Holding (parcela, pequeña propiedad) → --s (terrenos, valores en carteras) → majority & minority --s. Estate (finca, propiedad) → housing -- (urbanización), -- agent (agente inmobiliario), industrial -- (polígono industrial). Capital goods (bienes de equipo). Property developer (promotor inmobiliario). Mutual funds (fondos de inversión inmobiliaria). Private equity funds (fondos invertidos en empresas que no cotizan en bolsa). Hedge funds (fondos especultivos). Secondary market: where previously were issued securities & financial instruments such as stocks, bonds; options & futures. Repo market (repurchase market: mercado de recompra): contratcs to purchase & future repurchage of financial assets, above all treasure securities (valores y títulos) & treasure stocks (bonos del Tesoro). Bankroll (fondos; mantener, financiar)er (financiero) of terrorism. Holes in public coffers in Africa: taxes squandered (derrochadas), stolen & never collected. Only 13% were filing tax returns (hacian declaraciones de renta); 2 % of the GDP through corporate tax avoidance, 2% through individual wealth stashed offshore; the forgone (renuncia, privación de) revenue through tax expenditures (gastos, desembolsos): 5 %. It can use bespoke (hecho a medida) arrangements with western banks. Whack (golpe/porrazo, parte/porción), out of -- (fastidiado) → financial markets have got out of whack (se han fastidiado). The companies that get the most help cannot pay dividends or bonuses until they repay most of the state aid. Concerns that China & America are pampering (mimar, consenter) their own fims with subsidies are widespread. In 2020, governments kitties (bote; fondo común) have gained cloud during the past two decades. Now they face lean years & potential cash grabs (que tratan de agarar) at home. Meanwhile other sovereign fonds (=) have taken advantage of bargains in stockmarkets. The downturns (Ec.: deterioro; ventas: producción, disminución) present them an opportunity. Credit cloud (tortazo, influencia). International springboards (trampolines) for its investment banks. The last prong (punta, diente) of America's finantial domination. The fed allowed most central banks & international institutions to exchange their American debt securities against greenbacks (US: billetes de banco), thus stalling (parando) the stampede (desbandada). Both awed (asombrados) by its formidable rise. China is concentrating on the emerging world; whose leser sense of loyalty to western structures could make it easier to peel off (quitar, despegar, separar). Domestic savers are still caged in (enjaulados). Less tangible goal have taken on (aceptar, asumir) greater importance. The tumbling (caída) value of assets. Quantitative easig (QE): using newly created money to built risquier assets like long term government bonds, mortgage-backed securities & in some cases equities. (1) 2007: many banks cut their main policy rates to cero in order to revive (reanimar) collapsing economies, (2) to inject further stimulus, most then turned to QE. QE by the ECB is, in effect, mutualisation: a shared liability has been swapped for the sovereign bonds of individual Euro-zone countries. The ECB is a collective endeavour (intento). Financial union could be helpful. Asset purchase in response to C-19 means that balance sheets have ballooned further. Both central banks action & broader apetite for relatively safe assets have inflated government-bond prices across the rich world. If bond prices fall as Ecs. heal (se sanean), for instance, the central banks might make a loss. New forms of emergency lending increase the outright (total) credit risk to which central banks are exposed as well. The ECB is hoovering up/absorbing (absorbe) large quantities of public- & private- sector bonds. The Fed is gobbling up (está engulliendo) corporate bonds, municipal paper & banks loans to firms of all sizes. Impediments to setting monetary policy. A central bank is ultimately part of the government, & in some aspects its liabilities resemble government debt. Monetary policies bleed (sangran, exudan; -- into: se diluyen) into fiscal ones when the government's bills are determined by how much bond-buying takes place. Central banks face a dilemma: make policy independently & avoid governments interference or preempt (adelantar, anticipar) political meddling by minimising loses. Underwriters (aseguradores, inscribidores) for Alibaba's flotation (shares, loans …: emisión; company: salida a bolsa). Fully weaponising (utilizar como arma) the financial system would be a huge escalation (escalada). Promote the Yuan as a global payments currency by pushing digital-payments where Chinese tech. system is world-leading. Households are stoking up (se abastecen) on essentials. Economic melddown (cataclismo, "="). The financial crisis caught banks in its wake (estela, despertar). Sell-off: (stocks & shares) vender, (goods) liquidar → the index compound by the 500 values most representative & liquid of the 500 most important northamerian enterprises (S&P 500) has sold off hard & fast before yields rallied (se recuperen). When their need for cash became dire (funesto, alarmante), they dumped (soltaron, se deshicieron de) even treasuries. Asset sales help reallocate (redistribuir) the stocks of existing cash. Be greedy (codicioso) only when others are fearful (temerosos; espantosos, horribles). Before booking (anotar) losses. They can ill afford (mal pueden) at present ... Share buybacks (recompras). Backstop: (Sp) red alrededor de una cancha para impeder que escapen pelotas → their -- is the Fed, American lender at the last resort. It has gone out of his way to ease (aliviar, relajar, ...) the blockage in the Fed system. Banks could dip into (echar mano de) their buffers (parachoques, amortiguadores) & liquidity --s to lend to firms & households. Corporate bad debt markets are virtually shut. Corporate culture (cultura empresarial), -- headquarters (sede social), -- car, -- crime (delito de empresa). Boeing drew down (bajó) its entire $ 14 bn. in order to stockpile cash. Banks have pbs. of their own (sus propios pbs.). Unavailable (no disponibles) bonds =/= (busy: ocupado, no disponible) exacerb the funding (de financiamiento) crunch (crisis, crujido). The ECB latest salvo (salvedad, reserva) may not be big enough. The ECB generally tries to buy governmet bonds in proportion to the capital each member state puts into it (its capital key). The ECB says its emergency purchases will not be bound by its self-imposed "issuer limit". The ECB is breaking more of its own rules. It will start to buy assets with maturities (vencimiento) of less than a year. Russia has teamed up (asociado) with OPEC. America is stepping in (entra, interviene). The world is entering a new era of souvereign debt management. Management skill (dotes de gestión), -- consultant (consultor de dirección de empresa), -- direction, -- administration, -- gestion, -- studies, -- team (equipo de dirección), -- comité (comoté directivo). Remarking on the bitter experience, Keynes noted assuredly (sin duda, sin titubeo) it does not pay to be good. Borrowing costs have fallen steadily (constantemente). The trials (padecimientos, dificultades) of this crisis could inspire a new wave of investments in tech. & infrastructure. Guaranteed-income schemes gain momentum (cobra vigor, gana fuerzas). He gave away (regaló) cash vía share buy-backs (recompras). Persuade markets that GE (General electric) was no hoary (canosa, my vieja) industrialist but a digital innovator. A distorted $ 10 bn. acquisition of the power (energía) & grid (red) businesses of Alstom. GE capital came to drag the company down (la hizo fracasar). The current boss has so far been unable to turn back the tide (dar la vuelta a la corriente). Further pressure comes from the ruse in carbon taxes, as governments, cash- strapped after C-19 bail-outs, sought new streams of revenue.

Recopilación de algunas terminologías financieras que se prestan a confusión

Drug dealers are released on bail (liberados bajo fianza). The boom turned to burst & bail-outs; buy sb out (pagar la fianza de alguien, echar un cable a alguien); bail-out the enterprise: compra de la empresa por ejecutivos o trabajadores; the bail-out plan foresees Greece debt falling to 120 % of the GDP =/= Bayout (comprar todas las acciones) → management (los gerentes)/workers --. Share-out (repartir) the payout (el pago). Lay off (despedir en masa). Sell-off: (m.) liquidar, (stocks, shares) vender; privatización. Payout by the insurance: pago, reparto (+ share-out), indemnización. Write off (desechar algo) as a total loss (considerar algo comio totalmente perdido), cancelar una deuda impagable o siniestro total. Pay off: merecer la pena, dar resultado, (hipoteca) amortizar; liquidar (pagar y despedir a todos), -- -- old scares (ajuste de cuentas). Clear off: (deuda) liquidar, saldar.

G- Algo de medicina (humana o animal indistintamente)

A título preliminar le diré que, si mal no recuerdo de cuando mis experiencias en el CNRS (París), la mayor parte de la terminología médica española se parece mucho a la francesa, catalana, portuguesa e italiana; bastante a la inglesa y muy poco a la alemana. Mostraremos dos apartados: en el (1) los conceptos aislados ordenados por orden alfabétio y en el (2) un conjunto de frases largas inclasificables por orden alfábetico. Cuando hay mucho parecido o coincidecia no señalamos el equivalente en español.

1- Conceptos aislados ordenados por orden alfabético

Age: you must take it into account. Alimentary canal (tubo digestivo). Alopecia. Allergy → be allergic, nut (a los frutos secos) allergy, allergy to pollen, hay fever (alergia primaveral). Aneurisma. Angina pectoris (angina de pecho). Anguish, distress, anxiety (angustia). Arteriosclerosis, Asthma. Attention → medical attention, personalized attention, primary health (atención primaria), counselling care (atención psicológica), psyquiatric treatment, medical (sanitaria) attention. Autism). Avoidance (el evitar) fatty goods, … Awareness (conciencia, conocimiento) → bring him back to --. Baneful: (poisonous) nocivo, (destructive) funesto, fatal. Beat (latido, pulsación). Bereaved (afligido). Biochemical sensors: subatomic structure can selfasemble (armarse ellos mismos), replicate & repair themselves. Blood drenched (empapado), blood poured/gushed out (salía a chorros). Bout (racha) of flu (gripe)/of illness (enfermedad). Brain tumor. Bugged (infectado) mall (alameda, paseo). Cancer (cáncer). Carrier (portador). Cassava (mandioca) → face up to (enfrentarse a) -- mosaic disease. Cerebral crust (corteza cerebral) inflammation. Cirrhosis of the liver (hígado). Cognitive impairment (discapacidad cognitiva o cognoscitiva); cognitive behavioural therapy (terapia cognitivo-conductual). Cold (catarro). Colic. Collective mental damage. Conjunctivitis. He knew tennis put a strain on his heart (le sometía el corazón a un esfuerzo). Coronary arteries: elasticity of coronary arteries decreases along with oestrogen levels. Cyst (quiste): an ovarial cyst was removed (extirpado). Cystitis. Dandruff (caspa). Deadly (enormemente) pale. Dejected (desanimado) with eyes dubbed (apagados) & shoulders bent. Degeneration. Degenerative disease. Degeneration. Destructive (=) weapon, drug. Diabetes. Diarrhoea. Disabled (minusválido). Dispirited (desanimado). Distress: dolor, anguatia, miseria, aflicción,Vs). Disturbed & unhinged (trastornados mentales). Drip (goteo, salir) feed: suero gota a gota; A drip- feed (alimentación intravenosa, suero gota a gota). Drug epidemic in the Rust Beld (cinturón industrial) → the drug epidemic is ravaging (asolando) the once-idyllic communities. Duct (Med.) tear duct, bile duct, gland duct. (he) Fainted (se desmayó) & was badly hurt. Fatal accident + I feel auful/terrible (fatal). Feverish (con fiebre + have temperature). Fight off: (enfermedad) combatir + deshacerse de. Flu: you've given me the flu (me has pegado la gripe + influnza). Folly (locura). Functional diversity (diversidad functional): what so far was known as functional disability, either physical or mental, i.e. Down's syndrome & paraplegia. Gallstone (cálculo biliar). Genome. Geriatrics (geriatría). Gerontology (=). Grief: pena, dolor, tristeza. Grin (sonrisa, mueca) & bear it: aguantarse, poner al mal tiempo buena cara. Hafefovia. Hay fever (rinitis alérgica). Heart attack (infarto). Hemiplegia. Iptus. Isquemia. Long-sightness (presbicia). Madness/insanity (demencia): disminuido intelectualmente. Maiming (mutilar) will continue. Malignant growth (tumor maligno). Marsh fever (paludismo). Mastitis. Medical assistance. Meningitis. Meningoencephalitis. Metachondria (mitocondrias) are descendants of once-free-living bacteria. Midwife (comadrona). Moxibustion: the burning of dried materials near the skin. Mucus (mucosidad). Multiple sclerosis. Mutations have warped (combado) genetic information. Myalgia. Nephritis. Nervous breakdown (crisis nerviosa). Neurosis. Nurse (enfermera). Obsesive compulsive disorder (trastorno). Oncology. Ophtalmology. Osteoporosis. Otitis. Paediatrics. Paraplegia. Patch (remedio, parche, mancha). Patient → trawl (red de arrastre, buscar) through patient's data collection; patient care, patient confidentiality. Pharyngitis. Pill (píldora, pastilla) → no longer have to take the pills, the pain will soon go. Placebo. Pneumonia: general name for the response of the lungs to a variety of viral, bacterial & fungal infections. Poisoning (síndrome tóxico). Psoriasis. Quack (curandero) medicine. Recover/get back your health; I recovered & the drugs turned me to any normal appearance (apecto, apariencia). Rehearsal (ensayo). Rheumatism (reuma). Scaremongering (alarmismo) & misinformation provoks that menopausical women are missing out (se pierden, se saltan, dejan pasar) on the benefits of hormone-replacement terapy. Schizophrenia. Serum: (suero) saline solution, (de sangre) blood serum; (leche) whey. Sinus (de seno) infections =/= breast (seno). Sleeping (del sueño) sickness. Smallfox (viruela). Smitten (golpeado) with a flu, a plague. Soothing, sedative, tranquiliser (calmante). Spasm

(=, acceso, ataque). Spawn: fresar, prole, generar, producer. Spleen (bazo). Stimulating (excitante). Strabismus/squint (estrabismo). Stroke (apoplejía o derrame cerebral). Struck → the pain -- (alcanzó) her. Symptoms include hot flushes (rubores). Syndrome. Tumour. Ulcer/sore (úlcera) → duodenal --, gastric --. Ulcerous colitis (colitis ulcerosa). Ultrasound (ecografía) → the operator lays the wireless device on patient's arm and views an ultrasound (ecografía) image on a nearly (cercana) screen. Vasoconstrictor, Vasodilatador. (the) Wound was dripping blood.

2- Frases largas no clasificables por orden alfábetico

Ail (aquejar): what ails you? (¿que le sucede?), don't get upset (no se aflijas). Acquired immune deficiency syndrome (AIDS) carries off (mata, se lleva por delante) fit (sanos) young & adults. The connection between mind & body was the cornerstone (piedra angular) of Hippocratic medicine. Already with Homo Sapiens the diet was fat-free of wild game & plants with a lot of fiber & vitamins. Pay for sick leave (baja de enfermedad); give (pegar, contagiar: pass on, transmit) sb a contagious disease, Ancien Chinese physicians palpate the pulse revealing facts about Physical & mental functioning. The singular outstanding (importancia). Asthma is frequently a mental condition, as is irritable bowel syndrome, colitis & anxiety. Make whole organs for transplant remains elusive (difícil, esquivo). Bioprinting: cells cultured & sow into biodegradable mould whose shape resemble ... A small electrocardiogram worn on a belt with a lead (Plomo, delantera, ..., cuerda, cable + wire) that attach (ata, sujeta) to a patient's chest. Ultrasound scanner: it employs high-frequency sound waves to create images of parts of the inside of the body. There are quick skims (desnatados, tratados superficialmente) & painstakingly (meticulosos, esmerados) philosophical studies. An enticing (tentadora, seductora) opportunity for improvements. Know sth about propensities to disease well before any symptoms show up. Previously recognised genetic diseases have been traced to specific genes & can be connected to defects in the proteins they create (almost all genes describe proteins, & proteins do almost all the body's chemical work). Most of these diseases are rare, in that they typically affect no more than one person in 2000. Studies for genetic disease are not just a worthwhile (que vale la pena) end in themselves. They may be helpful for treating other ailments. The growing understanding of how large sets of genes may contribute to disease is making it possible to pick out (elegir, distinguir, ...) the patients most at risk. The pharmaceutical companies used to dominating medicine are working hart to keep up (no quedar atrás, mantener el ridmo). Concerns about medial privacy (intimidad). There are more genes involed in diabetes than we thought. A completion of a rather scrappy (desilvanado, incompleto) draft (redactada, trazada) sequence was announced. The genes string out along (hacen la fila a lo largo de) the genome's chromosomes, of life's key ingredients: proteins. Some genetic changes which are simple misprints (erratas) in the ingredient's specifications are bad. They contracted the virus & spread (propagan) it. Viruses undergo (experimenta) much more rapid evolution than other type of patogens. Hence their hability to adapt to novel hosts. If the microbial ecosystem gets out of balance, illness can, indeed (de hecho), result. Otorrino: ear, nose & throat specialist. Some microbes/germs cause ensuing/sunsequent (subsiguientes) global calamities. It was a warning about aspects of modern life that encourage the spread of previously unknown pathogens. The risk will remain of further zoonosis outbreks, in which a patogen pass from animals to the human beings. But viroses are cause of more than two-thirds of the human diseases. Simian immunodeficiency virus (SIV) got into people & became Human immunodeficiency virus (HIV)-1. Influenza viruses that break out into human beings has cycled through pigs or chikens first. Few wild animals spend as much time cooped up (encerrados) with other animals as do herd (rebaño, manada) animals & their herders. Many common diseases date back to (remontan a) the early days of domestication. Of more than 330 diseases which emerged between 1940 & 2004, over 60 % were zoonosis. Of those over 70 % had their origin in wildlife. War displace civilians, shifting disease from one place to another. The doctor has full confidence with me. Pangolins are very hard to breed in captivity. The convoluted (enrevesada) ruling that made abortion legal.

Refrán alemán: "Ein Unglück kommt selten allein" (un infortunio llega raramente sólo)

H- Coronavirus o COVID-19). Aquí: C-19

Este apartado es el que sin duda merece más atención, mucha más: porque esta epidemia repercute en todos los flancos de nuestra existencia (o sea que el vocabulario será muy completo) y porque frente a un futuro muy incierto todos debemos conocer cuanto más posible acerca de este mortífero virus y de su comportamiento. No alarmamos con el término plural "comportamientos", pero ahí queda la idea de posibles futuros inesperados peligros, por ejemplo mutaciones. Es muy importante para todo viviente humano que se familiarice con el C-19: por cuanto leerán Uds. aquí estarán al corriente de lo que van hallando los mejores investigadores del planeta al respecto; los datos y las anécdotas nos fortalecerán los espíritus a todos para cuanto pueda ocurrir más tarde; y máxime, si todos los habitantes del globo terrestre estamos al corriente de los pormenores de esta tan letal enfermedad; también cooperaremos todos más motivadamente y determinadamente a la salvación de nuestras vidas. Así pues, este capítulo es más que ningún otro un **libro abierto**, en el cual cada persona medianamente aplicada y responsable irá ampliando conceptos, simplemente con la complementaria lectura o escucha de los progresivos resultados de las cotidianas investigaciones. Como que nadie conoce el origen de tal invisible y hasta ahora indetectable y enigmático microbio, todos podemos aplicarnos la frase de Séneca: "sólo sé que no sé nada" y "a luchar se ha dicho" añado yo. Esta presentación evolutiva incluye verdades inequívocas, aproximaciones y también algún estudio o proposición que luego se ha desmentido, por ejemplo cuando se creía que el transmisor era el murciélago. Pero todo es bueno para la Ciencia.

Con todo, la idea no es un estudio exhaustivo del fatídico caso, ello requeriría escribir un libro al respecto. Pero sí la presentación de un florilegio completo de conceptos (epidemiológicos, económicos, sociales, políticos y sobre todo pedagógicos) que tal como están las cosas nos son y nos serán bien razonablemente y empáticamente imprescindibles.

Dividiremos la sección en cuatro partes: cuato ocurrió hasta finales de Junio 2020, o sea primera ola (1), hasta la generalización de la segunda ola a finales de verano e inicios de otoño (2), avatares de la segunda ola en otoño del 2020 con resticciones generalizadas casi universales y finalmente las primeras vacunas (Pfizer & BioNTech el 9-11-2020 y Moderna el 16 del mismo mes) (3) y finalmente la cuarta (4): aspectos socioeconómicos y políticos de cuando la tercera ola y enfoques de vacunación.

Una introdución sobre el universo viral

La genética está a la base de cuanto iremos mostrando:

Viral universe → viruses are deeply alien (extraños, extranjeros) & profoundly powerful: in viruses the link between metabolism & genes that binds together all life you are related, from bacteria to blue whales, is broken. Viral genes have no cells, no metabolism of their own. The tiny particles "virions" (vivriones), in which genes come packaged, are enterely inanimated. The virus is not a virion, it is a process, not a thing. It is truly alive only in the cells of others, a virtual organism running on borrowed hardware to produce more copies of its genome. Some bide their time (esperan el momento preciso), letting the cell they share the life live on (seguir viva). The virus has no plan or desire. The simplest purposes of the simplest life are entirely beyond it. When you ask whether viruses are alive, he answers a yes-&-no. Viruses alternate between non living & living phases. No other biological entities are as ubiquitous, & few as consequential (=, resultantes, importantes). They may have been responsible for more of the most important events in the history of the life. The legacy they have left in the human genome helps produce placentas & may shape the development of the brain. The last universal common ancestor (LUCA) was not the first living thing, it was the one which set the template (plantilla) for the life that exists today. Some viral lineages (linajes) seem to have began quite recently. Others have roots that comfortably predate LUCA itself.

When a particular protein is to be made, the "Desoxyribonucleic acid (DNA) sequence (=) of the relevant (pertinente) gene acts as a template" for the creation of a complementary molecule made from another nucleic acid, the "ribonucleic acid" (RNA). The messenger (mensajero) ribonucleic acid (mRNA) is what the cellular machinery tasked with (encargada de) translating genetic information into proteins uses in order to do so. Because they, too, need to have proteins made to their specifications, viruses also need to produce mRNAs. But they are not restricted to using double-strand (espiral) DNA as a template. Because uninfected cells only ever make RNA on the basis of a DNA template, RNA-based viruses "need distinctive" molecular mechanisms those cells lack. Those mechanisms provide medicine with targets of antiviral attacks. It is widely believed that much of the evolutionary period between the origin of life & the advent (advenimiento) of LUCA was spent in a RNA world-one in which that versatile substance "both" stored information, as DNA now does, & catalysed chemical reactions, as proteins now does. Metagenomics, a part of biology that looks at (mira, considera, examina) all the nucleic acid in a given sample, to get a sense of the range of life forms within it, reveals that this tiny throngs (multitudes) are highly diverse. On the land, most of the photosynthesis which provides the biomass & energy needed for life take place in the plants. In oceans, it is overwhelmingly (arrolladoramente, aplastantemente) the business of various sorts of bacteria & algae collectively known as phytoplankton. Bacterial phytoplankton tipically last less than a week before being killed by viruses.Viruses do not just shape (traza, conforma) the human genome through natural selection. They also insert themselves into it. At least a twelve % of the DNA in the human genome is derived from viruses.

Retroviruses like HIV are called retro because they do things backwards. Where cellular organisms make their RNA from DNA template, retroviruses can do the reverse, making DNA copies of their RNA genomes. The "host" cell" obligingly makes these copies into double- stranded DNA which can be stitched (suturado) into its own genome. If this happens in a cell destined to give rise to eggs or sperm, the vital genes are passed from patients to offspring (descendencia) & on down the generations. Such integrated viral sequences, known as endogenous retroviruses account for 80 % of the human genome. The viruses most prevalent (dominante, extendida) in the human body are not those which infect human cells, they are those which infect the bacteria that live on the body's surface (internal & external). Viruses engineered to engender immunity against pathogens, to kill cancer cells or to encourage the immunity system to attack them, or to deliver needed genes to faulty (defectuosas) cells, all seem likely to find their way into health care (asistencia sanitaria).

I- CUANTO OCURRIÓ HASTA FINALES DE JUNIO 2020 (O SEA LA PRIMERA OLA)

Queramos o no, el fenómno en curso no se comprenderá sin analizar y coordinar adecuadamente el máximo de información posible:

China's initial response to the virus was a bungled (chapuza) cover- up (encubrmiento), but since its harsh lockdown brought C-19 under control. It has touted its success around the world & supplied protective kit to thankful countries. Instead of leaping into action over C-19, the Council of the United nations (UN) mustered (reunió) its first discussion of the crisis only in April. The C-19 crisis is providing a telling (certero, convincente) case study (studio de casos). Whereas (mientras, Jur.: considerando que) America has suspended funding the World health organisation (WHO), in 2020 China has promised $ 2 bn. to fight the pandemic. The Spanish flu of 1918, a world-shaped pandemic, killed more people than the First world war. C-19 has thus far taken its most serious toll (peaje, mortalidad) on rich, peaceful countries. The disease is now rippling (ondeando, murmullando) through less stable places. American firms supply vital parts to C-19 projects. Coffers (=, fondos) → C-19 will strangle the government/nation --s (arcas). A hasty (rápida, precipitada) construction lodging (alojamiento) against Coronavirus. Desoxyribonucleic acid (DNA): double stranded/helix (hélice) of DNA; snatched (agarrado, arrebatado) breath (soplo) samples from sprouting (retoños, brotes) of whales for DNA analyses. Test (probar) a vaccine against C-19. Checkpoint (punto de control) of suspicious of C-19. The general food system is showing surprising resilience to the pandemic. Oxford Uiversity has taken the deal into the race to produce a C-19 vaccine. The Jenner Institute has become the likeliest candidate to produce the world's first vaccine against the C-19.

According to a tally (cuenta, total) maintained by American Milken Institute, 180 vaccines are in development. Some of this vaccines are doing well, but have yet to progress to late-stage testing. They may be immune for future infections. Other Oxford researchers have since identified the first drug proven (de eficacia probada) to reduce mortality from C-19. They have engineered a chimpanzee virus to deliver a portion of C-19 genetic material into the body. There was limited capability to scale (trepar, escalar) to significant volumens of vaccine. It will scale up (ampliar) production. The vaccine is grown inside cells that are cultured in vats (tinas, tinajas). It has suggested that hydroxychloroquine & its analogue, cloroquine, actually increased the death rate in hospitals when taken by those with C-19. This substance is embroided (enredada) in yet more controversy. Leak: (pipe, tank) rotura, (information, document) filtración → a -- draft of the EU post-Covit stimulus plan contains an ambition to install 40 Giga watts (GW) of green Hydrogen capacity by 2030. Messiness (desorden, complicación) of Mexico's response to C-19. President Bolsonaro (Brazil) dismissed (destituyó, rechazó) C-19 as sniffles (resfriado) & breached (violó, cometió infracción contra, …) his own health minister's social distance advise. Most governments in Central & South America acted early & sternly (severamente, con dureza); yet with few exceptions, the spread of the virus has been swift (rápida). Beneficiaries of emergency aid flocked (se apiñaron, fueron en tropel) to cash-points (cajeros automáticos) =/= cash- strapped (escaso de dinero). It causes deadly pneumonies. The disese would again grow rapidly. Almost 4-5 % of people infected by C-19 globaly are likely to become so ill they require hospitalisation. As coutries loosen restrictions & open borders, cases are starting to rise again. Such discoveries are helping officials come up (aparecer, comparecer, surgir) with more targeted rules. Prevent punters (jugadores, apostadores; clients; the --s: el público) jamming together. Everyday social distancing. What you do actually matters. Frequently politicians have lost their trust by contradicting ... There are countries with more fast growing epidemics. In the poor countries such messages may fail to sink in (penetrar, asimilar) if people see disease spread. Some people think there is no point (no viene al caso, no tine sentido) in wearing a mask. We know painful (dolorosas, penosas) memories of the severe acute respiratory syndrome (SARS) epidemic. We can't lower the guard. In Spain outside terraces of bar throng with mainly mask-less young people. In many European countries new C-19 cases have crept up as restrictions have eased. In United kigdom, Germany, France, Spain & Italy migrant workers from Afrika & Eastern Europe live in cramped (estrechas, apretadas) accommodations. A lot of them live in food-packaging (embalaje) factories. Workers stand close to one another, often yelling (gritando, chillando) to make themselves heard over the clatter (estruendo) of machiney. Many are not fluent in the local language & so struggle to understand messages. The risk will remain of further zoonosis outbreaks in which a pathogen passes from animals to human beings. The pandemia has accelerated the growth of competitive video-gaming. Meanwhile (mientras tanto) Germany has agreed with France that the EU should issue € 500 bn. in common debt to fund investments in member states hard hit by C-19. The professional commitment (obligación, compromiso) to fight the C-19 increased. The break-even point (punto de equilibrio, umbral de rentabilidad) is lower where the C-19 attacks. For a long period there was a rise but not fall of the C-19 crisis. When the deaths started the masks came out (se mostraron, se difundieron), said he from behind a sheet of plastic at the hole-in-the-wall (cajero automático) of his convenience store (tienda de conveniencia, chino). This reassures (tranquiliza)customers, he said. Among 25 countries with most cases, none tests fewer people than

Mexico as share of population. Cases rises after streets fill up (se llenan, echar gasoline) during the lax phases. Chile has the highest confirmed infection rate of any non-tidy (diminuto) country. A plan to phase out (retirar progresivamente) their lockdowns this month. Governments hope thereby (así, por tanto) to support their Ec. COV (coronavirus) → C-19 struck the most exciting, global cities hardest. Even as lockdown lift, fear of infection will linger (se rezaga, tarda en marharse). The emergency of the C-19, for exemple, has created demand for laboratory animals that have human versions of a protein called Angiotension- converting- enzyme (ACE2) receptor. This molecule is the hook (gancho,V) that SARS-COV2 (the virus that caused C-19) uses to attach itself to a cell entering & turning the cell into a virus factory. SARS-COV1, which came close (faltó poco) to cause a pandemic in 2003, also uses ACE2 as point of entry. The C-19 also replicates in the brain of a nice. This suggests it may be making use of human nervous tissue. C-19 pandemic has thrust (empujado) such medical applications firmly into the spotlight. Despite a plethora of ideas, C-19 is mostly being fought with old weapons that are already to hand. The British state provides a case study in how not to respond to a pandemic. A cheap steroid cuts deaths from severe C-19. British cientists are still top-notch (de primerísima categoría). The anti-inflammatory dexametasona reduces death by a third among the most severelly ill patients (with eczema, cancers, ...). Some experiencies about C-19 pandemic demonstrate the benefits of always keeping humans in the loop. In early March, as the disease spread, tech. firms sent their content (=, contenido) moderators home, where such security is tough (fuerte, duro) to enforce (imponer). Britain has been slow to increase testing & identify a contact: training (adiestramiento) apps, stop visits to care homes, ban big public events, provide the health working with personal protective equipment (PPE) & require people to wear face covering on public transport. Britain has a high proportion of ethnic minority people, who are specially vulnerable to the disease. British are somewhat (algo, un tanto) overweight. On 16th June 2020 a trial by Oxford University, the first to identify a lifesaving (salvamento) medicine, showed … While the world waits for a vaccine, this lack of trust will make managing (dirigir, manejar) the disease a lot harder. Beating the coronavirus calls for attention to detail, consistency & implementation (poner en práctica), but they are not his forte (fuerte). Bay (bahía), very large bay (golfo + gulf) → bring to bay (acorralar), be at bay (estar acorralado), hold o keep sth/sb at -- (mantaner --/-- a raya). All compassing (cercar, rodear, abarcar) national lockdowns would wreck (arruinar, naufragar, fracasar) Ecs. Some countries are looking for middle ground (terreno neutral) measures that will prevent the disease from overwhelming hospitals while loosening some of the heaviest restrictions. The priority is to shield from infection those who are most likely to become gravelly ill. That becomes difficult if large numbers of people are becoming infected. To prevent the virus from spreading uncontrollably, goverments are relying on a combination of three key measures: testing & quarantine; changes in behaviour that reduce transmissions (which include social distancing, the wearing of masks & handwashing); targeted lockdowns of outbreak hotspots - a practice known as "circuit-breaker" that has been popular in East Asia countries. If autorities can quickly identify new outbreaks, they will be better able to prevent them from spreading. We shouldn't underestimate even a small outbreak. Be off one's guard (estar desprevenido) → countries facing waves of C-19 where caught -- --. People with certain health conditions - including obesity, diabetes & heart diseases - are particularly vulnerable. In America 38 % of adults fall into this category. Ensuring people understand how asses their own risks is crucial, especially in the event of an outbreak in their area. Doctors & patients organisations will be more closely involved, advising vulnerable people & their families on how to balance reducing their risk of contracting C-19 with their need from some degree of social life. It's necessary never stop contact-tracing (rastreo, averiguar el origen, seguir la pista, localizar). Public health professionals say the system needs more staff if it is to function effectively. They had come into close contact with someone infected. In countries as large as India, the success of different places in keeping C-19 at bay will vary. Measures to curb (dominar; frenar, restringir) transmissions are even more vital. Encourage people to wear face-masks & keep their distance. The official advise on masks changes over time. People were initially discouraged. Run down (atropellar, agotar, localizar) the scare supplies for health workers. It is becoming clearer where social distancing matter most. C-19 thrives (prospera) on close contact. Three things are known to exacerbate its spread: being at close (cerrados) quarters (barrios) for a prolongued period of time, in a large crowd, & taking part in activities that lead people to breathe out forcefully (enérgicamente; convincentemente, violentamente). In combination these create "super- spreading" conditions. Such discoveries are helping officials come up (subir; aparecer, surgir) with (sugerir, ofrecer) more targeted rules. You need to win over (convencer, ganarse) the influencers in certain groups to convey (conducir) themselves in a credible way. The exhortations of online celebrities (famous, well known) will carry more weight with young people. Politicians have to convey the message to the people that it's really up to them to decide what's happening. Politicians have lost the trust of their people by contradicting their experts on basic facts about pandemic, publishing implausible numbers on C-19 deaths or propagating conspiracy theories. He chairs (sillas, cátedras, presidencias,V) advisory committee on C-19: we need to change the mindsed (actitud, disposición) of people compliances (conformidades, sumisiones) with guidelines. Fear, backed up (respaldado) by fines & strict policing may contribute to the colletive discipline. Contemplate (=, considerar, plantearse) longed-for (ansiadas) summer holidays. New C-19 cases have crept up (subido, aparecido sigilosamente) as restrictions have eased. Clusters (gupos) frequently linked to parties or other celebrations. The future precautions add up to (suman en total) three- layered (de tres capas) defence: (1) worldwide effort to find & track the hundreds of thousands of as-yet-unseen pathogens that might threaten human health, (2) the monitoring (siguimiento, control) of blood samples & other indications from people living in places where new diseases are most likely to emerge, (3) a concerted programm that emplois all the data thus collected to get a head- stand (posición en cabeza) in the development of droups & vaccines to meet an emerging disease halfway. C-19 is a new challenge. Make fool on sb (poner o dejar a alguien en ridículo). A vacuum exists where the world would normaly look for American leadership. Instead it sees president Trump making fool of himself, suggesting wacky (pers.: chiflado; idea: disparatada) cures. Under C-19 casual sex (relaciones promiscuas) are out. Demand for petroleum has collapsed as a result of C-19 lockdown. Producers are cutting investment & shutting down wells. There is good reason for caution/foresight (precaución). A fine-tuning (puesta a punto, último retoque) of measures to stop the illness spreading. The post lockdown phase will involve a return to classic epidemiology: it will be calibrated (=) to the places & people involved. People in their 60s are twise as likely to die of C-19. Focusing effords on care homes would cut the death toll considerably. C-19 deaths have been disproportionately concentrated among blacks & Hispanics. Some of the biggest outbreaks have been in slaughterhouses, where crowded (abarrotados, hacinados) working conditions & the cold ... Vulnerability of multigenerational households. Shield the close (detallados) regular controls with the most vulnerable. The pangolin (oso hormiguero) could have spread the C-19 virus to humans. America has passed grim (crudo, lúgubre) milestone (mojón, hito): 150,000 deaths from a novel (novela; novedoso, orginal) virus. Contrary to demands for national rules, this is a strength, not a weakness & will become more so as the pandemic runs into course. Mr Trump could have acted sooner. Flare up: (fire) llamear, (pers., riots) estallar, (epidemic) declararse → -- ups can be spotted quickly & rules adjusted accordingly. In Brazil the president has distaste for masks, so is wreaking (causando) havoc (estragos). Fare alike (correr la misma suerte) + America & Europe have fare (lo pasan) similarly in the pandemic. Mr Trump's inhability to cleave (partir, surcar) to (adherer a, no seprarse de) a consistent message; cleave together (ser inseparables). The lifting (levantamiento, disipación, desaparición) of the lockdowns is likely to hasten its spread again. Swabs (trapo, algodón; frotis) from the nose. The lockdown begets (engendra) thoughts of settling down (acomodar, tranquilizar). In India the treatment of endemic diseases has also been impeded (dificultado, obstaculizado). The pandemic is an unmitigated (verdadera) calamity, & in some quarters is stirring innovations. Say the China's Ec. has been hurt by C-19 is putting it mildly (es quedarse corto). C-19 is keeping vegetable-pickers (recolectores) at home. How the virus make his way from bats to humans ... jeopardising (arriesgando, comprometiendo) sensible scientific discoveries. What is needed is rationality, cooperation & full transparency from the countries. America's dry run (ensayo) to defend Europe is derailed by C-19. True for a majority of patients, but it is not so far a sizeable (importante, considerable) minority. They present the new virus as having many faces. The same way influenza behaves. Why this virus's symptoms are so protean (proteicos)? The tendency of influenza to mutate every year & yet still cause the same symptoms of rapid onset (principio, aparición): fever, malaise (malestar), headaches & coughing. SARS-COV2: it causes C-19, literature on it suggest that C-19 is a master of disguise (disfraz, cambio, disimulo). Possible normal temperature & good breathing & it is not suspected; they examine samples & stools (heces: deposiciones) & they found none. They saw no beneficial effects from antbiotics. Only the fourth day of her stay at the hospital she developed a cough. Influenza rarely gets deep into the lungs. Sometimes makes its initial appearance in the digestive system. The only way to be sur is to take samples from places other than the respiratory tract. Purpose (propósito, objetivo, utilidad) → existing drugs might be purposed (=, utilizadas) for the job: Remdisivir (antiviral) is a nucleoid, its structure mimics one of the chemical letters of the virus's genetic code. The ill-fitting shoes (que le quedan mal) → -- - -- chemical letter grums up (paraliza, estropea) its replication. Those particles gain entry to the lungs, where they start reproducing themselves. It robs sense of smell, in other patients the toes or fingers darkens as bruised (magullados, amoratados), heart swells, blood clots (coagula), immune system cripple (inutiliza, lisia) organs they are meant to be saving. How much these various symptoms are attribuable to direct effects of the virus, to secondary effects, to the treatments, ...? For the virus to attack a cell, the cell's surface need to be adorned with a protein which plays a role in the regulation of blood presure & inflammation: the ACE2. In some cases the virus may get into those intestinal cells directly. Before the body's defences take care of it so well that presence is never even noticed. The 70 % of those who tested positive were asymptomatic. Most of those who fall ill suffer flulike symptoms, typically with a fever & cough, sometimes with diarrhoea. After a time they start to feel a shortness of breath (falta de aliento) as blood's ability to oxygenate the blood weakens ... The immune response to the virus starts with intellect cells producing a suite of signalling molecules called cytoxines. Nurses must reposition (=) them every few hours to prevent be sores. In some people the antibody-making process can go away, & then newly developed antibodies may confuse a healthy cell for an infected on, making it for destruction by the immune system. In some cases, it is the generalised immune response inflamation that goes into overdrive (empieza a funcionar a toda marcha). The biggest risk factors have been hypertension, diabetes & obesity. People with these factors & heart disease have more ACE2 on their cells as a response of higher level of inflammation. Many of those who survive a severe bout (ataque) of C-19 are likely to have long-term health problems. There is no evidence so far that SARS-COV2 directly harms the brain. The mere fact of being an Intensive care unit (ICU) can lead to a cognitive impairment (discapacidad, deterioro). Delirium is a particular problem of C-19. The pandemic put a dampener (que agua, entristece) on the scene's growth. Middle eastern respiratory syndrome (MERS) heralded the arrival of MERS-COV. Then SARS-COV & MERS-COV are closely related to coronavirus found in wild bats. If, like MERS- COV, the virus is still circulating in an animal reservoir, it could break out again in the future. If not, some other virus will surely try sth similar. Its proponents (defensores) … They can nonetheless (aun así) be found on menus. Leak out: (líquido) salirse, información) filtrarse. Ominously (inquietante, amenazante, con mal augurio), the mechanim of reform is also broke. Virus-laden droplets of spit. But to break the chain, it behaves (incumbe) even the symptomless to assume they may be infected. There is not watertight (hermética, perfecta) evidence of the efficacity of the masks. A stretched-out (extendida, estirada, alargada) face mask. Correlation between mask-wearing & rapid suppression of C-19. Widespread (generalizada, extendida) mask-wearing to be worn in crowding public spaces. As a result of C-19 some projects have come to a halt (se han parado). Lack of readiness (buena disposición). The pandemic has hit demand for commodites. They lacked protective gear (marcha, equipo, engranaje, ...). The government recruit 50,000 retired or former health workers. Steadfast (firme, resuelto) nes: firmeza, resolución, consistencia, tenacidad. Nightly (nocturn) applauses. Immediacy (inmediatez, urgencia). The government erred in its tardy reaction to the virus. The ministers were fixated (obsesionados) on healing (sanear, reconciliar, salvar sus distanciamientos) their divisions. The government has oscillated between loyalty & snipping (brusquedad). In a recent poll Catalonia was the only region where respondents gave higher marks (marco, mancha; señal, nota) to the central government than their local one. The Th. Roosvelt, an American aircraft-carrier, is stuck (atascado) thanks to C-19 outbreak among its screw. States are clamping down (ponen frenos, toman fuertes medidas). Will they loosen up (relajar, desentumecer) when the crisis is over? The restrictions keep out border-crosers. Mexico president encouraged families to visit restaurants, as this strengthen the Ec. A would be (aspirante a) strongman (forzudo; Pol.: hombre fuerte) to fight the C-19. A coronavirus law in Hungary giving the prime minister almost unlimited powers'mechanism; he may relinquish (ceder, renunciar) some of his new powers; he nobble (soborna) the courts, tilt (inclina) the electoral sytem & urge his cronies to gobble up (engullir) independent TV/radio stations; this may involve intrusive (molesta, indiscreta) sourveillance. Moscou is mulling over (reflexiona sobre) a scheme ... Some governments have criminlised any disparagement (menosprecio) of their response to the pandemic. The Chinese government muzzled (puso bozal, amordazó) the doctors who sounded (que hicieron sonar) the warning. Election campaign (campaña electoral) for/against. Statesmanlike (digno de estadista) =/=

statesmanship (habilidad política, capacidad para gobernar). The epidemic has subsided (ha descendido, se ha hundido) in China. The stringency (rigor, severidad) of official lockdowns & changes to the people behaviour. Lockdowns stringency is strongly correlated with the hit to Ec. activity. The pandemic is a nasty (desagradable, grave, .., blast (oleada, ráfaga) from this ugly past. Health is a purview (ámbito, esfera) of northern governments. Remove the manacles (esposas, grillos) that fetter (encadenan, ponen gillos a) Leviathan (=, barco grande). States that take the blame from the bereaved (afligidos). Top dogs (mandamases). The system, especially the UN is impotent & old fashioned, without excepting the US'health administration. America's health industry complex will be recast (refundido). America, which led global campaigns to defeat HIV, AIDS & Ebola, has been absorbed in its internal arguments & the UN Security council has confirmed its disfunctionality in many cases. The UN wants to use it 75th anniversary for a grand consultation on the future of multilateralism. For instance & above all, each of the 193 countries in the General assembly has one vote: India with 1.4 bn. people & Tuvalu with 12,000. C-19 has hijacked the global agenda, but it also created an opportunity: rather than destroying the system, the upheaval (trastorno) could spur countries strengthening it.

2- Hasta la generalización de la segunda ola a finales de verano e inicios de otoño

La estructuración por sectores (a) y por paises (b) facilitará mejor el estudio de tan complejo panorama. Estas complementarias informaciones con respecto al partado 1 nos ayudarán a comprender aún mejor cuanto ocurre, y como.

(A) Estructuración por sectores

La microbiología es extremadamente delicada. De allí que conviene archivar las individualidades de cada sector:

- Airlines: to see the danger of C-19 to aviation, look up. The industry can rebound (rebotar) leaner (más racionalizada) & greener, so long as governments stop favouring incumbents when ideas rebound, the twin (hermanas) priorities should be to put the industry on a sounder financial footing, & to make flying less polluting. For both objectives the way forward is the same: loosen icumbents'grip on the skies. For many years aviation mostly had a free pass (paso gratuito) when it came to regulations of the type that forces carmakers to clean themselves up (sanearse). The pandemic impact: plan next generation of cleaner planes. The effords to keep incumbent airlines flying threaten to prevent bolder (más atrevidos, más audaces + =) carriers from spending. Waivers (exenciones, descargos, right/fee: renuncias) on airport-slot (hueco) rules will further hamper new entrants. Regulators around the world suspended use-it-or-lose-it rules for the summer to help stricken (dañados, afligidos) carriers. If the idustries are in the deep- freeze (congelada), it will show the development of clean airports. Airbus has a goal of developing such an aircraft by 2035. So dynamic airline industry searching for new ways of growth would require new aircraft, encouraging Airbus & Boeing to make air travel greener. As well as setting back (retrasando, apartando) the industry, cosseting (mimando, consintiendo) the old guard (vieja guardia) will do more damage to the planet.

- Care homes: the pandemic has shown the urgency of reforming care for the elderly. She was sent to help out (ayudar, echar una mano) at the 236-bed facility in April as C-19 ripped through (iba a todo gas en) its narrow corridors & crowded wards (en hospitals: salas). Across the world nearly half of all death from C-19 have happened in care & nursing homes. Countries with fewer care homes have had fewer C-19 deaths, all else being equal (sin que cambien los otros factores). In the future, many experts argue, the vast majority of old people should be looked after at home as long as possible. In all but the most severe cases this is cheaper & it is also what most old people want. What they value most is autonmy & independency. And for those who still need it, residential care should be transformed. In countries such as Brazil & America, tax-payer financed care is intended as a last resort (como último recurso) for the poorest & sickest. The sector is understaffed. In several countries it is underhelpfully (con pocos ánimos de ayudar) detached from the health system. In countries such as Hong kong & Taiwan that experienced the SARS outbreak in 2002- 2003, care homes has stockpiles of personal protective equipment (PPE). In other places they were very poorly supplied (aprovisionados). People working in British care homes say the pandemic has confirmed their "Cinderella" (hermano pobre) status. All around the world staff at care home run over (cambia de trabajo) quickly. That is not surprising given that carers are paid in average 35 % less than people that do similar jobs in the hospitals. At the height (cima, momentos más críticos) of the outbreak in London more than one quarter of staff in care homes for elderly could not work, or would not. Officials sent in temporary workers to replace them. That probably spread the virus even further. As well as (tanto como) exposing fragile business models, the pandemic has highlighted (destacado, puesto de relieve) tensions between keeping old people safe & keeping them happy & well. Technology can help a better system to make it easier for most people to age at home. Care givers begin to spot unexplained bumps (choques, abolladuras, hinchazones, ...) & bruises (cardenales, moratones). Some of the most compelling (convincente, apasionante) recent scientific

& technological develpments aim to help people with dementia. A product produced by Elovee allows them to have simple conversations with a digital avatar (in video games) styled to look & sound like one of their relatives. The idea is to produce reassurance (consuelo, confianza) during moments of anxiety or boredom that occur when their loved ones are not around. They will never replace the loving attention of a carer, but date-crunching (devorar datos) would make it easier to work out (calcular, resolver) how to deploy carers more efficiently. Technology could improve residential care, even as it reduces the number of people who needs it. Sensors placed in Norway & Netherlands have reduced hospitalisations. Telemedicine is having the same effect in Estonia & Israel. The number of care workers in the rich countries will need to increase by 60 % by 2040, just to maintain the present ratio of carers to elderly people. The pandemic is persuading more people that "the mass institutionalisation" of older people isn't such a good idea". Congress & C-19: an extended (extendido, prolongado) partisan (partidista) showdown (enfrentamiento) over another stimulus package will hurt millions of Amricans. The same dynamic will shape the latest gargantuan (gigantesco, colosal) stimulus package needed to cushion the fallout (lluvia radiactiva, repercusiones) of C-19.

- International monetary fund (IMF) & World bank: in Febuary more than 500 millions people in China where experiencing some form of lockdown & C-19 has spread to Italy. By April the IMF had cut its forecasts of global GDP growth by 6.2 percentage points. By June it has sawn off (cortado) another 1.9 points. About 40 IMF staff expected another downward revision in October. This rosy (rosáceo, halagüeño) forecast can have serious consequences, especially in poor countries today,where C-19 is ravaging Ecs. & governmets, international organisations & investors are using forecasts to guide their decisions. IMF & World bank projections can be very influential in some countries: investments, borrowing, sustainability (sostenibilidad) of debts & so bail-outs, ... The fund uses to be optimistic & even once a recession has began, forecasters are still slow to accept the news. Lockdowns & social distancing are at least as severe in poor countries as in rich ones, but fiscal policy in poor countries is weaker & capital outflows & currency pressure are bigger threats.

- Locked out (dejados fuera con la puerta cerrada): when & how to let migrants move again (marcharse, apartarse, alejarse)? Globally, tens of millions of migrants have been stranded (hilo, ramal; aspecto, faceta; encallar; quedar sin dinero o medios de transporte), burning through the savings they had hoped would lift their families out of poverty. Migration policy is far from the top of any country's agenda for now. But governmnts sooner or later have to grapple with (enfrentarse a) an important question; as they gradually & fitfully (de manera irregular) open up again for tourists & business travellers, will they also welcome migrants? There are emotive responses why C-19 might make countries less willing (dispuestos) to accept foreigners even after a vaccine is discovered. Suspicions of foreigners is why people who look (parece) Chinese have been harassed (acosados, hostigados) in many countries. It is why D. Tump has boasted (alardeado, presumido) about banning Chinese travellers, even as he downplayed (quitó importancia a) masks. In addition, C-19 has caused mass unemployment. Many voters believe that migrants take jobs from the native-born. The executive order in June suspending most kinds of works visa was well aimed for many. Both these fears are electorally potent, but neither (ninguno) is well-founded (fundamentado). Tourists & business travellers outnumber migrants. D. Trump has locked out skilled workers, internal company transfers & even foreign students. This is a recipe for a poorer, most insular America, where domestic firms cannot hire the best, foreign investors cannot send it technicians to unblock bottlenecks & brainy youngsters opt to study & settle in Canada. South Africa temporarily closed migrant-owner shops in townships (asentamientos para gente de raza negra in Africa creados cuando el apartheid), forcing customers to walk miles to distant grocery stores, thereby spreading the virus. When people bang pots for health-care workers, they applaud a lot of foreigners. Britain will be less open to migrants from the EU, because the Brexit, but just offers residence up to three millions of Hong kongers without backlash (reacción violenta) at home. When the coronavirus is vanquished migrations will be what it was before: a powerful tool that can lift up (levantar) poor, rejuvenate rich countries & spread new ideas around the world.

- SARS-COV-2: where the SARS-COV-2, the virus that causes C-19, came from? It is thought the answer involves bats, because they harbour a variety of SARS-like viruses. Yunnan, one of the China's southernmost (más meridional) provinces, has drawn the attention of virus hunters, as the closest-known relations of SARS-CUV-2 are found there. Since the outbreak, in 2003, of the original SARS (now known as SARS-COV), scientists have paid close attention into coronavirus. Around 16,000 bats have been sampled & around 100 new SARS-COV like viruses discovered. In particular, some bats found in China are now known to harbour coronavirus that seem pre-adapted to infect people. The chiropteran (quirópteros) host of viruses have versions of a protein called ACE2 that closely resemble the equivalent in people. Some people in Myanmar, Laos & Vietnam carry similar SARS-related coronavirus, maybe a huge diversity of them, & that some of them could be close to SARS-COV-2. A former professor of tropical medicine says his guess (suposición, estimación) is that either SARS-COV-2 or sth similar to it have been circulating in people in parts of South east Asia & southern China, probably for many years, & that intermediate hosts have not yet been identified. Bats are able to carry a huge diversity of viruses without getting sick, & are most mobile that people realise. As he puts it, bats congregate in huge colonies & poo/defecate everywhere. Other mammals live off (viven de) that poo & then act as a mixing vessel (barco, vasija, Bot./Med.: vaso) of those sorts of viruses. Sth ressembling SARS-COV-2 have been circulating in South east Asia, particularly in Vietnam. Above all in Vietam, the circulation of other SARS-like viruses could have conferred a generalised immunity to such pathogenes. If a new one emerged in the region, it was able to take hold (coger, agarrar) in the human population only when it travelled all the way to the central China, where the people did not have this natural resistence. That would tie in with/agree with (concordar con) the idea that infections with one coronavirus can provide protection against others, & that even in countries away from South Est Asia part of the population may have some protection against the current pandemic. There are suggestions that protection maight be conferred mainly via part of the immune system called T-cells, that work by killing virus-infected cells, not via antibodies. If that is the case, then serological studies which look at antibodies may be underestimating natural immunity. It is widely assured that 50 % of people need to be vaccinated to prevent a resurgence of SARS-COV-2. This figure could be much lower if a significant part of the population is already resistant to infection. The virus may have jumped directly from bats to people or come via intermediate species.

- (the beginning of the) Second wave: on August first it is worring Australia, Japan & Hong kong. Young Australian returnees in quarantine hotels made whoopee (se divirtieron mucho) with the security guards who were supposedly supervising their isolation. Not since the Spanish flu has the great untrammelled (ilimitado + unlimited, limitless) continent thrown up (construido) internal barriers in that way.

Australia is recording more daily cases (744 on July 30th) than at the peak of the firt wave in March & April. In recent days Japan has recorded sharply (fuertemente, bruscamente) higher number of infections than during the first peak (200 in Tokio). Abe Shinzo has ruled out (descartado) another state of emergency in the lead-up (periodo previo) to a four-day national holiday. Hong kong was exemplary early this year (closed borders, schools & restaurants) & urged office workers to work from home, & instituted a strict system of returnees. Though there was never full lockdown, just seven people died of C-19 in the first wave. Quarantine rules were laxer for pilots & seafarers (marineros). Even with this latest spikes (púas), the performances of these three countries show the US, Latin America & parts of Europa & struggling India in a dismal (triste, sombría) light. Nor can other Asian standouts (destacados, que se mantienen firmes), notably New Zealand, South korea & Taiwan, afford to feel smug (creídos, engreídos) about their abilities to detect, contain & treat.

- Slaughterhouse (matadero, pero la idea puede ilustrar para toda la industria alimentaria): vow (promesa,V, compromiso + commitment) → a big European abattoir vow to reform. He made comments belittling (menospreciando) Africans. The plant (fábica) triggered (provocó) Germany's biggest single outbreak of C-19. Workers are supplied by 24 subcontractors who recruit them mainly in Poland, Bulgaria & Rumania. They live in cramped (estrechez de condiciones) infection-prone quarters. There is not a digital time sheet, making it hard to work. Instead shifts of 12 hours of blood-soaked-labour. Subcontractors charge them for knives, boots & other equipments. They also make them pay for boards in squalid (miserables) rooms shared with half a dozen others. Locals do not mingle with the migrants. He did not resign. Instead he vowed to right the ship. He promises to scrap (descartar, desechar) subcontractors & employs all workers directly. The outbreak was caused by poor ventilation. That meant it was not the firm's problem, but of the entire industry.

- Testing C-19 on August 8th.: dive into the water (tirarse en picado), dive into the crowd (meterse entre la muchedumbre) → Testing laboratories are overwhelmed (agobiados, abrumados, atosigados). Pool (piscina, charca; fondo común) sampling (muestreo) may be the solution. Now, as countries emerge from lockdown, & case numbers begin to raise, the strain is being felt once more. Overwhelmed laboratories mean that results are taking weeks, sometimes two, to come through, instead of a couple of days. It is obvious: pool together samples taken from several individuals & test the pool. Only if the pool comes up positive his individual testing required. Pool-sampling has been used in America, Germany & Israel & has been introduced in China, India, Pakistan & Singapore. More than 16 samples would be difficult to manage & could have a higher risk of a false vegetative result. Only on July 18th America's Food & drug administration issued its first emergency authorisation for the whole country follow suit (seguir el ejemplo) of Nebraska. It is best used on the asymptomatic, since those with symptoms are most likely to test positive. But at the beginnings & ends of outbreaks, when most candidates for testing are people without symptoms, it looks like a valuable time- & money- saving tool that might become a standard procedure.

- Universities: high education was in trouble before the pandemic; C-19 could puff (soplo,V; pipa: chupar;...) some institutions over the brink (precipitar al borde). If big investments in Universities made sense in a world where students were crosing borders in droves, today they seem barmy (chiflados). Now they are considering cuts. C-19 has put immense pressure on all Universitis. But problems are about to get particularly severe in America, Australia, Canada & Britain, as they have come to rely on international students to fill their coffers.

Academis, used to tricky questions, now face an existential on: how will Universities survive with many fewer students in them? The problem is that campuses make an excellent breeding ground (caldo de cultivo) for the virus, & students travelling across the world are a good way to spread it. Some 6.600 cases can be linked to American colleges. The risk is that, beyond the lecture hall youngsters will ignore many restrictions. A lot of teaching will be online. Lots gravitate to big cities: in America, New York University is home to the most international students, with 19,605. In Britain, University College of London, with 19,535. The collapse of air travel means there may not be enough flights. Currently Canada will not let in students who did not get a visa before March. Some Indian students are allowed into America, but Chinese ones are not. Both would be welcome in Britain, so long as they quarantined for a fortnight. The British University most at risk of insolvency are those that entered the pandemic with weak finances. Of Australia's top-ranking Universities, only Monash is among the seven at "high risk". Lobby groups everywhere have sought bail-outs. University Australia estimated that its members'revenue would drop by A$ 3bn. In America, Congress gave American colleges around $ 14bn in March. In Britain some funding has been brought forward (propuesto; presentado, adelantado) & loans will be on offer to cover 80 % of lost income from international students. President Trump has complained that colleges are focused on "radical left indoctrination", not education, & has asked the Treasure to re-examine their tax-exempt status. Mr Johnson has said he may follow Australia, where the government plans to more than double the cost ho humanities "courses" while lowering fees for subjects it reckons are in areas of future employment or are otherwise importat. All three governments have taken more hawkish (de línea dura) stances towards China. Britain's opposition to a new national-security law in Hong Kong has infuriating Beijing. The first two decades of the 21th century where ones of extraordinary growth for the University in many countries. That golden age is over.

(B) Estructuración por países

Cuanto avanzamos para los diversos sectores es aplicable para los diferentes paises:

- Africa: on early August Africa bears one million reported cases of C-19. The true number is much higher. He has to bury some corpses away. South Africa has the world's fifth highest number of reported cases. The full extend of the undercount is unknown. The share of tests that come up positive is below 5 % in only a few countries, suggesting underreporting elsewhere. Another hint of underresponsibility is found in the number of cases among Africa's elites, who are more likely to get tests. Patchy (incompleto, no uniforme) data make it hart to asses many African countries'responses. Cases seems to be growing quickly in most countries as they loosen lockdown to try to revive their Ecs. States that appeared to have the virus under control, such as Ethiopia, Kenya & Zambia, are all experiencing daily growth rates above the regional average. Hold back: (guardar; flood/river: retener; progress: refrenar; infotmation: no revelar, emotion: reprimir) → in Nigeria, home of nearly one-sixth of Africans, testing is hold back by shortages of reagents (reactivos) & kits. The relative isolation of rural areas was meant slow transmissions. The continent's youthfulness is more of an obvious boon (gran ayuda). Most Africans were born in the 21th century. Africa has a lower share of population over the age of 65 than any other continent. South Africa has an older population than other African states. About 2 % of Africans diagnosed with C-19 have died. That is only half the global average. Such numbers should be treated with great caution. Only a few African countries keep good cause-of-deaths records. Politicians may not see it as in their interest to reveal how many people have died on their watch. In Ugandaa member of the opposition in the Parliament bought some rice & sugar & had it delivered to his neediest constituents (electors). Then, the soldiers dragged him into a van & threw him in a cell. He says they beat, kicked & cut him, crushed his testicles, sprayed a blinding chemicalito his eyes, called him a dog & told him to quit politics.

- Australia: Melbourne, country's second city, battens down the hatches (atranca las escotillas) again. On July 8th, its premier of Victoria was forced to impose a second lockdown to five millions residents of Melbourne, the state capital, were a second wave of C-19 has been ralling on (llegó). Contact-tracers (indicadores de contacto) are overwhelmed. Local acquired cases were virtually stamped out, largely because of stay- at- home rules & the quarantining. They had not been using protective gear (equipo) properly & have been accused of breaching social distancing rules by sharing cigarettes & car-pooling (uso compartido de transportes) to go to work. Several of the guards contracted the virus & passed it on (contagiaron) friends & family, just as Victorian's first lockdown was being lifted. The new restrictions will do "untold" (nunca reveladas, incalculables) damage to the Ec. & employment. A testing blith (campaña, guerra relámpago) is under way. Ill health (mala salud) makes them especially vulnerable to C-19. They will use drones to hunt for (buscar) scofflaws (scoff: mofarse) trying to sneak across (escabullirse) via bush (arbustos) tracks (rastros, senderos) o along rivers. There are too many roads for police control them all, for exemple waist-high plastic barricades, & prevent people entering Queensland (the north & central East) from avoiding police checkpoints. But also walls of less visible variety of obstacles erected all over Australia. Nevertheless, imported cases continue to pop up (aparecer inesperadamente), spurring (espoleando, incitando) constant tightening (reforzamiento) of restrictions on interstate travel. C. Palmer, a mining magnate, has sued (demandado en justicia) the government arguing that the constitution declares that trade, commerce & intercourse among the states shall be absolutely free. But the pandemic qualifies (=, condiciona) & constitutional niceties (sutilezas) ... The federal government initially argued (discutía, sostenía) for looser restrictions. Western Australia's approach was indiscriminate & uncompromising (intransigente, inflexible; loyalty: absoluta). The federal government has since (desde entonces) withdrawn (retirado, sacado) support for Mr Palmer. The Commonwealth has taken into account the changed state of the pandemic & the high level concerns about C-19 in the west of the country.

- Brazil: the alarm of pandemic was heightened (fue aumentada, realzada, destacada) because C-19 could hurt indigenous people more than those with access to modern health care. It seems that, given governments'inhability to protect indigenous lands, isolated groups are not viable in the long term. The idea of controlled contact ignores native people'right to self determination. Many groups retourned to isolation after traumatic encounters (=), such as enslavement by rubber tappers (cazadores, tramperos). The prevalence (predominance) of C-19 among indigenous people in cities is five times that among white Brazilians. Evangelists see the disease as a reason to initiate contact. Congres evangelical lobby tacked on (añadió) to a law that allocate money to protect indigenous people from C-19 an amendement that allows missionaries to remain on indigenous land.

- Central Asia: on July 25th of 2020 the isolationist Turkmenistan is one of the last countries still claiming to be coronavirus free, along with North korea & some remote Pacific islands. Out are the patriotic festivals, football matches & horse races that stood out (que sobresalóan, destacaban) as the rest of the world shutdown earlier this year. Elsewhere in

Central Asia, the disease is well into a second wave & restrictions are being reimposed. Many in the region are anxious to resort (recurso, recurrir) to spurious (=, falsos) folk remedies, from ginger (jengibre) & horseradish (rábano picante) to horse milk & dog fat. In Kazakhstan officially diagnose cases have rocketed by around 1,400 % since the easing of a stringent lockdown. Rules requiring people to keep their distance & wear maskes have been flouted (ignoradas, burladas). Groups of most than three people are banned, Kazakhstan, like other countries in Central Asia has struggled to discourage this, but gatherings of the extended family (familia extendida), an ingrained custom, have helped spread the pandemic. Kyrgyzstan recently adjusted its statistics to include probable C-19 cases previously classified as pneumonia, causing the number of infections to double overnight & fatalities (muertes) to jump almost fivefold. Uzbekistan has reimposed a lockdown. It began easing (aliviando, relajando) in May, althought its government is still attempting to lure tourists with a promise to pay $ 3,000 should they catch the coronavirus during their visit.

- China: Slack/few diligent public servants in China: Chinese officials-followed by the logic of their unaccountable, secretive one-party system failed to report an unknown virus in the central city of Wuhan for several critical weks, giving C-19 time to take hold. As one government after another botched its own response, China's rulers refused to take any blame for the pandemic, instead slapping Ec. sanctions on such countries as Australia that called for inquiries into the outbreak's origins.

- East Asia: as far as pandemic is concerned, E. A. Budist lands seem blessed. One of the biggest riddles (acertijos, enigmas) of the global pandemic lies in S-E Asia: despite being close to the source of C-19, in China, & to one of the current hotspots of the outbreak, India, the partly or largely Buddhist countries of Cambodia, Laos, Myanmar, Thailand & Vietnam have scarcely sneezed (estornudado). Vietnam is the standout (el que destaca): with 97 millions people, it claims no deaths from C-19. Compare that with the nearby archipelagic nations of Indonesia (3,400 deaths) & Philipines (1,400), where on July 11th the pandemic still rages (se propaga con furia). Set aside Karmic (religion Karma) as an explanation, especially given that Vietnam's communist dictatorship is atheist. Few governments have both the overweening (altivo, arrogante) power & effective health system needed to emulate China & Vietnam. But Thailand, a sham (falsa) democracy overseen by the geneals, perhaps come closer. The quality of its health care makes Thailand a popular destination for medical system. Moreover, the government was quick to set up a vigorous Covit-fighting task force (destacamento especial, grupo de trabajo). Why did visitors from China not sow more S-E Asia outbreaks? One widespread suspicion is that they did, but these were not reported. We have to consider other factors: a religious element, as the *wai*, a Buddhist greeting (acogida, bienvenida) of palm pressed together; people living in the countryside rather than in crowded cities; the relative youth of the region; people more likely to live with fans & windows open; preexisting proclivity for masks. The question is whether S-E Asia's Buddhist successes can weather (aguantar, superar) second or third waves. Low transmission from China was not a miracle.

- <u>Europe</u>: that may change, even if on August first a surge (oleada) of C-19 is mostly (en su mayor parte) under control. The waves of an epidemic tend to raise like a tsunami-slowly, almost (casi) surreptitiously/furtivelly (furtivamente) before a precipitous (escarpada, precipitada) surge. There are now fears that C-19 cases may again be nearing a menacing infection point. Less dramatic than in Spain but worrying increases in cases are starting to bubble up (burbujear) in other European countries. Infection rates are particularly high in the Balkans & Spain, which has notched up (apuntado) 27 cases per 100,000 people in the past week. The raise in cases across Europe is not surprising: as lockdown were lifted & people resumed (reanudó) travel & mingling (se mezcló), both imported cases & the local spread of the virus have pushed tallies (el total) up (hacia arriba). Covit clusters (grupos) have emerged across Germany, in care homes, workplace & private parties, forcing officials to impose localised lockdowns. As cases in Spain notched up, Britain and Norway swiftly brought back (restauró) quarantine for people coming from Spain. Vacationers in Greece from some Balkan countries must now show proof of a negative C-19 test to enter the country. That has dealt a blow to whatever remained of the foreign tourist season in much of southern Europe. But there has been a collective sigh (suspiro) of relief among health officials watching with trepidation (inquietud, agitación) clubs & beaches crowded with drunk foreigners. German politicians have warned that citizens are growing complacent about the danger; surveys confirm suspicions that fewer people are avoiding crowded public spaces or private gathering. Priotity to Europe now is to ensure that young people comply more with such precautions. If that fails, it won't be long before infections spread to older vulnerable people. A huge worry in all countries is the Autum, when people start to spend more time indoors & flu & other respirations infections rise. Across Europe, they are better prepared for a second wave than they were for the first, with new measures to curb the spread of C-19 in hospitals & extra beds & field (de campaña) hospitals that are mothballed (aparcados, en reserva) now.

- (the) Gulf: in normal times jetting off (salir de viaje) to Dubai in July is an act of masochism. Now fived-star hotel rooms that cost $ 272 a night in high season go for a third of that. Dubai allowed tourists back on July 7th, one of the first destination to open its doors after C-19 slammed them shut (les cerró de golpe). From August first arrivals from hard-hit countries will need two tests. Masks are mandatory in public, with a $ 716 fine for scofflaws (burlas de la la ley). Some hotels have done away with valet parking (servicios de aparcamiento a cargo del hotel). United arab emirates (UAE) has lodged (anotado) about 60,000 cases of C-19. At 6,000 per one million people it ranks in the top level of all countries. But the death toll, at 35 per one million is well below most Arab & European countries. Other emirates are less hung-go (optimistas, entusiastas) about reopening. The airport of Abu Dhabi, the UAE's capital, is shut to non-residents.

- India: Flattening (aplanar, nivelar) the wrong courve. Unlike Brazil or America, India responded quickly & forcefully (de manera convincente). Perhaps too quickly: two months of nationwide lockdown shattered the Ec., but only sowly the disease. One deadly error was to freeze all travel with no warning, trapping millions of migrant workers where they were no longer wanted, in the big cities with the highest rates of infection, & then later, to let them go, carrying the infection with them. At south of Chennai, fishermen complain that when lockdown was lifted after eight weeks, a seasonal ban on fishing kept the fleet grounded (encallada). This was followed by a closure of the market, so that when thay could at least cash fish they had no place to sell it. Nearby farmers voice similar despair. A transport ban at harvest time kept many out from selling their crops. Nationwide sales remained a dismal (sombría, deprimente) 67 % lower than in the same period last year. In India big cities, hospitals can now send Covit patients home as soon as they feel better, rather than having to wait for test results to prove they are free of virus. India's people fear that India would run out of ventilators. So Indian manufactrers boosted production from 30 millions a day to 30,000. Indian industry has proved so responsive (sensible, que reacciona) to the crisis that it is now lobbying the government to drop restrictions on exports of medical equipment &

protective gear. So the fears are misplaced (inoportunos + "=", que no vienen a cuenta).

- Iran: on end August 2020 the clerics argue over how to hold a month-long shia festival. So vast crowds will file (desfilar) through the streets. Beating their chests, banging huge drums & re-enacting (volviendo a promulgar/decretar) the passion with mock (imitadas, simuladas; burladas) words. They will wail (gemir) their laments in back-draped (cubiertos) basements (sótanos) & share food close together. Masks won't stop transmissions by sweat & tears. Nothing could spread the virus faster. But Hassan Rouhani, the president, says the pageant (desfile, espectáculo) cannot be cancelled. So doom (desastre, destino funesto)-mongers (difundidores) are being muzzled (amordazados). Not all clerics are so rash (temerarios).

- Israel: One day Netanyahu said "so far we've hold it better than nearly any other country in the world, other countries are adopting the steps (pasos, medidas) we took". Although Israel pushed new cases of C-19 down to a handful a day in the late May & early June, on July 25th they are close to 2,000. The disease is spreading faster in Israel than in most other developed countries (thought not America). Unemployment sits (se coloca) at 21 %, compared with 3-4 % before the outbreak. Mr Netanyahu has hinted (insinuado) that another full lockdown could be in the offing (en perspectiva) if things do not improve. And the fact is that on September 13th, its authorities signed it. Israel is a leader in testing per person, but its contact-tracing system has been overwhelmed. The health ministry has too few nurses to track (rastrear) people, so there are ideas to transfer the responsibility to the defence ministry, which has more manpower (mano de obra, Mil.: soldados). One silver lining (resquicio de esperanzas, oportunidad) of Israel's C-19 crisis is that relatively few people have died. The trial on corruption charges is postponed because the lockdown. The court will convene (convocar, reunirse) three times a week.

- North Korea → self- strangulation of the Ec.: N. Korean dictators are not given to self-deprecation (auto desaprobación). To ward off (rechazar; infección: potegerse de, peligro: protegerse contra) the pandemic, the regions has imposed one of the world's strictest quarantines. North korea shut its borders soon after the initial outbreak in the Chinese city of Wuhan in January. Efforts of humanitarian organisation have never been straightfoward (sencillas) given the regime's obsesion wth self- reliance (auto- suficiencia). Mr. Kim, although keen to showcase (exhibir, mostrar) his concern (preocupación, interés) for "the people's well-being"during the visit to a flood-hit areas, has reject offers of foreign help, ostensibly (aparentemente) for fear that it might bring the virus into the country. The vast majority of foreign aid workers have been forced to leave in recent month, along with most diplomats.

- Philippines: on July 11th a ferocious lockdown lingers on (persiste), despite of uncertain benefits. Its lockdown is among the fiercest (más feroz/terrible) & longest-lasting in the world. It has been repeatedly extended, but the rules have been applied unevenly. The University of Philippines reckons there may have been 3.6 millions people without the lockdown, a figure the government linked to trumpet (aunciar a son de trompeta). The number of deaths each day dropped sharply since March. Irregularities & anomalies that have attracted attention of the government ombudsman (defensor del publo). The lockdowns have been lifted in some cities, only to be reimposed when cases began rising widly (violentamente). They argued for more targeted (dirigidos específicamente) quarantines. Relaxed restrictions should soothe (pers.: calmar; mind: relajar; anger: aplacar) the country's pummelled (aporreada) Ec. The C-19 has brought to an end

84 quarters (trimestres) of an uninterrumped growth. The lifeline (cordon umbilical, cuerda de salvamento) that help Philippines to stay afloat (mantenerse a flote) during the financial crisis are frying (se desgastan, se deshilachan), too the remitences from the Filipìnos working abroad. In July 2020, 83 % of working-age Filipinos say their quality of life has declined versus (frente al del de) a year ago. Delays have beset (acosado: -- by fears; plagado: -- with obstacles) other schemes (planes, proyectos). Mr Duterte (the president)'s priority appears to be boosting his own authority. On July 3rd the Congress signed into law a sweeping (movimiento rápido, cambio radical, victoria arrolladora) antiterrorism bill, which allows suspects to be detained without judge approval.

- Scotland: how C-19 strengthened (reforzaron, consolidaron) Scotish independence. On August 8th more than 4,200 Scotish deaths are due to coronavirus. Even so the pandemic has left national's first minister in rude health (buena salud). In contrast, B. Johnson has been stricken by the virus personally & professionally. Unlike the rumpled (despeinado) Mr Johnson, she has given poised (serenos) daily TV press conferences packed with useful information. The government thus fulfilled the unionists'promise in the 2014 referendum that Britain's would be Scotland's protector in hart time. The thread of hard order between Englan & Scotland after divorce has been the unionists's trump card (mejor carta). 37 % of scots polled in early July said border controls to stop Covit-19 " should already be happening".

- Sweden: Sweden is held up (se ha mostrado) as a champion of liberty. Liberty-loving Swedes are supposedly pursuing a mask-free, loodown light strategy that will create herd immunity wothout bankrupting the Ec. Its strategy entails (implica) large-scale testing & contact-tracing (seguimiento) so as to identify & suppress outbreaks early. A clear, consistent message is sustainable because it gives people autonomy. The government weighs up (considera) the trade-off of each restriction. Sweden is a high- trust (de alta confianza) sociey, where people follow the rules. After all, its policy is based on evidence (prueba, testimonio) & pragmatism (not blind principle). Case numbers are creeping up, but more slowly than in much of Europe. Sweden is starting to ramp up contact-tracing & quarantining, but in ways that, once again, set it apart (destaca). Beyond (más allá de, aparte de) care homes, C-19 has hit ethnic minorities particularly hard. Official guidance reached immigrants groups too late. The elderly in these tight-knit (muy unidas e integradas) communities have busy social lives. On protet the elderly Sweden failed. Sweden is changing course to prevent a second wave, it is putting new meaures into the mix: resume contact-tracing & quarantiny & expand (ampliar) testing. Sweden's quarantine is for seven days & only for those who lives with an infected person. The goal is to stop as much transmissions as possible, without unduly disrupting personal's life… But Swedish king recognised that in the end the first wave has been a disaster.

3- Avatares de la segunda ola en otoño del 2020 con resticciones generalizadas casi universales y finalmente las primeras vacunas (Pfizer & BioNTech el 9-11-2020 y Moderna el 16 del mismo mes)

Compilemos el fenómeno en tres flancos: fundamentos evolutivos, con decisivo apoyo de la Ciencia, en la segunda ola (a) y optimismo mundial gracias a las vacunas descubiertas y riesgos ineludible de nuevas olas (b)

(a) Fundamentos evolutivos, con decisivo apoyo de la Ciencia, en la segunda ola

Esta ola ha sido menos cruenta gracias a la experiencia cobrada de la primera y a las instalaciones ya previstas para esta. También el nivel de las investigaciones ha escalado considerablemente, siendo cada vez más profundas. Los acontecimientos han ayudado, desde la técnica a la rectificación de los múltiples errores políticos y populares. Pero no podemos soslayar los egoistas e irresponsables comportamientos de casi todos los pueblos, con sobresaliente para España. Y dentro de ella, Andalucía y en general todas las regiones beneficiarias de la solidaridad protagonizada por Cataluña, Madrid, Baleares y Navarra; cuando parte de esa solidaridad la destinaron a organizar peligrosísimas fiestas, para que dichas cuatro regiones y muchos españoles paguen las consecuencias (muchas docenas de miles de ellos con sus vidas). Encima, los infractores de las normas se burlan de nosotres, por ejemplo una joven que participó a una fiesta ilegal en Navidad del 2020 explicó por TV "que ella tenía derecho a no renunciar a su juventud".

En este sentido, sabiendo que el dinero centrifugado desde dichas cuatro comunidades constituye el principal factor de lógico descontento en ellas, la corrección del comportamiento de las receptoras, en todos los sentidos, conllevaría un hermoso amainamiento de las reivindicaciones independentistas. Una vez más, tal como vengo insistiendo para muchas esferas, la principal bandera de todos debe ser el honor y para los egoístas, también la vergüenza. De lo contrario, los independentismos agudizarán y las consecuencias pueden ser graves.

Dos párrafos compondrán estos aspectos: (1) Elementos evolutivos coadyuvantes y (2) la primera recidiva.

(1) Elementos evoluticos coadyuvantes

- China has effectively controlled C-19 & its Ec. is returning to life. Meanwhile, goverments in America, Europe & beyond face second waves of infections & business bankruptcies & exploding public deficits. Several elected incumbents will lose office. China's leaders call their coputry's recovered proof that Communist party rule offers a uniquely effective blend f organisational prowes, respect for science, & traditional Chinese morality. Foreign anger will in turn promp (provocar) resentment within Chna.

- Cronic illness & C-19: Doctors have learned a lot. They have stopped rushing patients onto ventilators (which can cause lung disease). Oxigen supplied through small prongs (dientes, puntas) in the nostrils (orificio nasals) is much less invasive & often does the job. In most people, C-19 is a brief, mild illness. But between a third & a half of those infected do not notice any symptom. The share of C-19 patients with lingering (persistentes) problems is far higher than is seen with other vital illness such as influenza. Some long-term C-19 patients may be suffering from undiagnosed conditions (such as diabetes or tyroid dysfunctions) which are unmasked (descubiertas) by the infection. The hallmark (sello) of many C-19 cases is damage to the lungs. The scarring, in turn, impedes the flow of oxygen from the lungs into the blood. Breathing problems can also arise from its tendency to cause blood clots (coágulos). When the clots can choke off (cortar) blood flow, C-19 can also damage the heard, it can inflame the tissues that surround the organ, as well as the blood vessels that ferry nutrients to it. Patients with lingering post-covet symptoms complain of headaches, tingling (hormigueo) & numbness (entumecimiento) in the feet, &another neurological problems. Britain, Belgium & other countries are setting up specialised C-19 rehabilitation programs for those recovering from the disease.

- Trials & tribulations (aflicciones, penas, desgracias) and C-19: on August 11th 2020, V. Putin said his government was the world's first to approve a coronavirus vaccine "despite a lack of proper (adecuados) tests". That regulators move fast in emergencies is to be applauded. Unfortunately, on August 29th his Sputnik vaccine has not yet been through the trials. America's behaviour is not better. The approach (enfoque, propuesta) behind the product approved is reasonable insufficient tested. Convalescent plasma therapy transfuses blood plasma (rich in antibodies) from those who have recovered from an infection. Trials of it as a treatment of C-19 are therefore under way around planed. On early September, the results are "no conclusive", & the trials themselves have been small. Meanwhile, in Hong kong neaws have emerged of someone who, having had C-19 once & recovered has now been infected by a slightly (ligeramente) different strain of the virus. The pandemic will leave Ecs. less globalised, more digitalised & less equal. Every country will be called to adapt, but America faces a daunting (desalentador, amedrentador) task. To lead a post- pandemic world, it will have to reset (reajustar, reiniciar) its politics.

- Deaths & C-19: on september 26th 2020, recorded deaths from C-19 will surpass 1 million. Perhaps another million have gone unrecorded (no registrado). Roughly1 % of survivors have long-time viral damages such as crippling (grave, abrumadora, que conduce a parálisis) fatigue & scarred (marcados, cicatrizados) lungs. In developing countries, especially bereavement (pérdida, pesar, aflicción) is compounded (agravados) by poverty & hunger. The northern winter will force pople indoors, where disease spread much more easily than in open air. Countries like India, with an average age of 28 years, suffer fewer deaths because the virus is easier (más pausado, más relajado) on the young than on the elderly. More progress is in store (reserva, almacén). Nonclonal antibodies (anticuerpos), which disable (deja inválido) the virus, could be available by the end of the year. Even if vaccine emerges, nobody expects it to be 99 % effective. Protection may be temporary or weak in the ederly, whose immune systems are less responsive (sensible). Early vaccie may well need two shots (dosis, inyecciones). Muly-country polls suggest that a quarter of adults (including half of Russians) would refuse vaccination, another reason why the disease may persist). Hence for the foreseeable (previsible) future the first line of defence will remain testing & tracing (seguimiento), social distancing & clear government communication. There is not mistery of what this involves. And yet countries like America, Britain, Israel & Spain persist in getting it disastrously wrong. The right lauds (elogia) Sweden for supposedly letting the virus rip (desenfrenarse), while it makes a priority of Ec. & liberty. The left lauds New Zeland, which shut down to save lives. It had suffered only 0.5 deaths per 100.000, but in the second quarter its Ec. shrank by 12.2 %. By contrast Taiwan remained more open but hat seen 0.03 deaths & 1.4 % fall in GDP. Countries like Germany, S. Korea & Taiwan have used fine-grained testing & tracing to spot (observar, reconocer) individual superspreading venues (lugares de reunion), & slow the spread using quarantines. If testing is slow, as in France, it will fall (fracasará). If contact-tracing is not trusted (de confianza) as in Israel, where the job fell to the intelligence serices, people will evade detection. Opening schools, as in Denmark & Germany, should be a priority; opening noisy, uninhabited places should not. Governments, like the British one, that bark out (grita, escupe) a series of ever-changing orders which are broken with impunity by their own officials will find that compliance (conformidad, sumisión) is low. Spain let down its guard, Britains's testing is not working. America's centres for disease control & prevention has been plagued by errors, poor leadership & presidential denigration (infamias, ofensas).

Israel's leaders fell victim of hubris (orgullo desmesurado) & infighting (peleas internas, as is the case for Spain & other countries). The C-19 will abate (se calmará) but government must get a grip (tomar las riendas).

- Mental health & C-19: how to grapple with (confrontarse con) the psychological scars of the pandemic. The mental scars will linger (persistir, tardar en marcharse). For many the pandemia is a merely annoyance (irritación, enfado, molestia). But some groups face a particular risk of post-traumatic stress disorder (PTSD), the symptoms of which include nightmares, flashbacks (escenas retrospectivas) & feelings of guilt, ansiety or isolation. The most vulnerable are those who have been very ill, or lost relatives, as well as victims of previous traumas (such as refugees), & those front-line (de primera líea) jobs, such as doctors & nurses. In Spain, nearly a sixth of those infected are health-care workers. In Bangldesh, where the incomes of poor people briefly (brevemente) fell by 80 % when lockdowns were tight, 86 % people in one poll reported (cominicó, informó, denunció, resultó) C-19 related stress. Even the mass-bombing of cities in the Second world war did not break civilian morale. Nonetheles, the World should take the collective mental damage of C-19 seriously. Governments have to chip in (participar). The Ec. shock of C-19 has undermined (minado, socavado) mental-health services everywhere, but specially in poor countries. Mutual-aid networks, which tend to peter out (irse agotando) once the initial disaster subsides (amaina), should instead (sin embargo, en vez de eso) be formalised & focused to the most vulnerables. Mental health professionals should connect patients to such services, & train (formar, capacitar) more lay folk as counsellors.

- Migration after the first wage of C-19: this virus has immobilised the world. Planes are grounded (obligados a permanecer en en tierra), people are hunkered down (tratan de pasar desapercibidos) at home. Play close attention to what I am going to say. Families that used to rely on cash from a migrand son or aunt find that this flows of cash from abroud has dried up. Fear could make people more hostile, letting in migrants is a health risk. Bigots (intolerantes) in China have evicted back migrants from their homes & barred them from hotels, after hearing a rumour that Africans were likely to be infected. It may become virtually (prácticamente) impossible to live without papers. On the other hand, the pandemic could make people friendlier towards migrants: risked their lives & Health services of rich countries could not function without them: some 40 % of medical & life scientists in America are foreign-born; Oxford vaccine group includes scientists from practically everywhere. One of the first thing South Africa's government did to fight C-19 was to construct fence on the border with Zimbabwe.

- The relapse (recidiva): on the early days of C-19 pandemic doctors were befuddled (aturdidos) by a peculiar phenomenon: some patients responded well to treatment, recovering almost enough to be discharged, before suddenly deteriorating again. Then, in October 2020, the pandemic exploded again. Today the cases are doubling across the continentevery two weeks. On November 5th, 20 countries had shut gyms, restaurants, museums, & other public venues, introduced curfews, banned people from going out for non-essential business or all of the above. The most striking difference is that now ost schools & universities are staying open. The second most striking is that this tie it is winter, not summer, that is coming, with all that means for the inhospitality of outdoors activity & the stir-crazines (locura, insensatez) of being cooped up (encerrados).

- The structure of Remdisivir mimics one of the chemical letters of the virus genetic code. Then the ill-fitting chemical letters grums up (paraliza) its replication.

(2) La primera recidiva

On the early days of C-19 pandemic doctors were befuddled (aturdidos) by a peculiar phenomenon: some patients ill enough to be admitted to hospital seemed at first to respond well to treatment, recovering almost enough to be discharged, before suddenly deteriorating again. Then, in October 2020, the pandemic exploded again. Today the cases are doubling across the continentevery two weeks. On November 5th, 20 coutries had shut. Asian nations, some democratic, some not, have proved it possible to force infection rates slow as to more or les eradicate the disease. But when they came out of their first lockdown European countries were unwilling to impose the strictures they thought would be necessary for true eradication. A large part of the reason for the resurgence is that the policies Europe put I place to keep the disease manageable did not take full accout of its peculiarities. The number of others to whom an infeted person will pass the covid virus varies a lot. Most will not pass it on to anyone; a few will pass it on to many. It is estimated that just 10-20 % of infected people account for about 80 % of subsequent infections. These ones often occurring in clusters.

In Japan, this aspect of the disease was appreciated from the outset, in part through studies of the outbreak on *Diamond Princess*, a cruise liner. As early as March the Japanese government began warning its citizens to avoid the "3Cs" (closed spaces, crowded places & close-contact settings). The 3 Cs message was far less clear in Europe. Public-health autorities stressed continued mask-wearing, which increased almost everywhere, reaching Asian levels quite early on in Italy & Spain. Yet many countries also allowed bars & nightclubs to re-open with no strings (condiciones) attached. In parts of eastern Europe, where the current outbreak is particularly bad, football fans were filling up stadiums even as cases were on the rise. Holidays abroad did a lot of damage, so as they had in the initial outbreak. Even Germany, which has had one of the Eurpe's best test - & - trace systems, is now struggling. The cheap & fast testing kits (útiles, herramientas, equipos) will redice the burden of contact traces.

Con las recidivas llegan también los más rápidos y resoltivos tests: the current thinking is that higher viral loads make people more contagious, but contagiousness is not fully understood. Doctors are used to make decisions when testing things like cancer, sexuality transmitted infections & so on. But for C-19 things are new & changing rapidly. To deal with that, some test developers are pairing (emparejan) their products with "digital wrap-arounds" (bucles, reciclados) suah as apps in which such decision-meking algorithms are fed up-to-date (al día, actualizados) data on things like trends in local C-19 prevalence & the weight of various personal risk factor derived from various analyses. A rapid over -the-counter (Med.: sin receta) test could be available in America as early as next summer.

(b) Optimismo mundial gracias a las primeras vacunas y riesgo ineludible de nuevas olas

Puesto que nunca estaremos seguros de que todo acabó, principalmente si abundan los testarrudos y tramposos, cuanto más sepamos acerca de este coronavirus, mejor: mutaciones (el 20-12-2020 en el Reino unido anuncian una nueva variante del virus que ya existía hacía una semana, es 70 % más contagiosa que la variedad original; el día siguiente anuncia otra varieda en África el sur; el día 23 del mismo mes se sabe que la variante de Sudáfrica ya ha llegado al Reino unido, luego llega a Madrid,…, se conoce que es más contagiosa que la primera variante y que a su vez la primera variante ya ha llegado a Italia), microbios excesivamente parientes con él, falsas inmunidades, reinfecciones, grupos humanos menos protegibles por las vacunas, efectos secundarios y terciarios de estas, … e incluso algunas sorpresas para la medicina moderna. y ante todo (condición *sine qua non*) su identidad y origen y los portadores (los organismos animales, vegetales y otros, así como el medio ambiente, guardan muchos secretos). Como siempre, el dinero y la técnica, sin olvidar las religiones y la política, tienen la palabra. Adelantamos unas líneas generales sobre los semblantes económicos de las vacunasn(1) y luego nos adentraremos en los aspectos técnicos de las mismas (2).

(1) Líneas generales sobre los semblantes económicos de las vacunas

Even South korea, which has managed the virus better than almost any other country, has not scaped a deep recession. On August 8th goverments so far have invested more than $ 10 bn. in C-19 vaccine purchases of about 4 bn. doses. A large share of purchases could turn out (aparecer, resultar) to be duds (cheque: sin fondos; marchandises: invencibles; machine: estropeada). A typical vaccine in final trials has 20 % chance of failure. Some of the candidate C-19 vaccines involve new tech., so the risk of failure could be higher. Despite the scramble in America & Europe to get to the front of the queue, countries elsewhere are likely to be undersupplied. On average, emerging markets have secured enough to cover less than a third of their citizens. A company normally sets up production once a vaccine wins regulatory approval. But these are not normal times. To speed things up, some firms have started mass-production vaccines that in early August 2020 are still in clinical trials. Companies may have promised 4 bn. doses, but some of their vaccines may not past trials & will have to be poured away (tiradas). Many experts think supply will also be constrained by global shortages of thinks: vials (frasquitos), syringues, … They put a more realistic estimate of global supply of vaccines by the end of next year at near 2 bn. During the Swine flu (H1N1) pandemic in 2009-2010 rich countries cornered (acapararon, pers.: acorralar) supplies of the vaccine to fight the disease. Only when they had more than they needed did they offer some of it to poor countries. Early in the C-19 pandemic, too, global co-operation quickly broke down. By late April, eight jurisdictions had restrict exports, with governments specially keen to hoard supplies of disinfectants, personal protective equipment & thermometers. The World health organisation (WHO) is also trying to avert (possibility: evitar; danger: prevenir; blow: desviar) vaccine politics. The first doses would go to health & socialcare workers & the next batch (lote, remesa, pers.: grupo) to the 20 % of people who are most likeny to day from C-19 if infected. The rest would go to places with the highest risk of outbreaks. There are slim hopes that America, China, Russia, among others, will allow exports of vaccine made on their territory before enough is available for all of their citicens. A global free-for-all (pelea), then, seems inevitable. One way to mitigate it would be to spend more. Separate groups of researchers reckon that the world needs to invest round $ 100 bn. in order to make vaccines early & in sufficient quantity. On August 8th of 2020 that would be tenfold increase in what has been spent. But set against the output lost & the $ 7 bn. in stimulus injected to the Ec. so far, it is peanuts (una miseria).

Como siempre conviene advertir acerca de los defectos humanos que yacen en el centro de tanto distubio: si bien es cierto que no se pueden ahogar las Ecs. y que por tanto hay que ser humanos con las restricciones, también lo es el hecho de que en gran parte las nuevas olas responden a los comportamientos irresponsables de miles de ciudadanos que tanto aman las juergas y las actividads justamente prohibidas.

How C-19 is disrupting the fight against Malaria, for instance in Thiba (Kenya): many city-dwellers believe it is safer to send their children to rural relatives. Others hope to save money: the pandemic has destroyed jobs & closed schools, where poor children are often given a free lunch. So, dispatching kids to the countryside, where it easier to live off (vivir de, a costa de) the land, means fewer mouths to feed. Yet there are hidden dangers: the irrigation ditches in the paddy fields breed mosquitoes, which transmit mlariualprasites from human bloodstream to human bloodstream.

(2) Aspectos técnicos de las vacunas

Conviene saber que el futuro dará más sorpresas, aunque los pasos imprescindibles ya se han dado. A partir de esta premisa, como siempre, cada lector puede añadir los nuevos adelantos a estas bases esenciales que exponemos aquí:

- A study made by Ramanan Laxminarayan of Princeton university & eight co-authors finds that C-19 transmission is highly concentrated: fully 71 % of infected people did not transmit the virus on. Most new trasmssions were from a few "super-spreaders": about 10 % of the people caused 60 % of new infections, giving Covit-19 to three other people, on average.

- Anothr important actor is the T-cell: rather than attacking viruses directly, T-cells attak infected cells, to stop the virus reproducing. The balance of importance of the antibody & T-cells arms of the immune system varies with the illness in question. And, as far as this particular infection is concerned, although almost all patients who catch SARS-COV-2 are thought to create T-cells in response, an understanding of their significance has been elusive (esquivo, difícil de conseguir). The implicatiopns of this is that those searching for vaccines against C-19 should give priority to the production of the T-cells. As for the vanishing antibodies, there may be grounds for optimism here, too. The fact that levels of these proteins wane rapidly after infection, when they are no longer needed, should not be so surprising. It might not matter (importar), either. The immune system could well be primed (preparado) to make them in large numbers again, if & when it encounters SARS-COV-2. It is also worth remembering that, even if researchers cannot defect antibodies, that does not mean they are not there at all. On early November 2020, while it is true that Science has not yet jammed (aglomerado, abarrotado) the pandemic exit doors open, there are now at least a few shafts of light (rayos de luz) emerging around the doorway (puerta, sendero).

-The T-cell response to C-19 last at least six months: antibodies are parts of the immune system that attack the virus directly. They are expected to be involved in any long-term protection protection against reinfection. Worriers (preocupaciones) also highlight the facts that immunity types of coronavirus which cause the symptoms described as "a cold" is short-lived, & that there are already a number of provencases of infection with SARS-COV-2, the virus that causes C-19.

- On November 14th 2020 vaccine development is based on viral genomes: researchers look for a gene which describes a protein the immune system seems likely to recognise. Then they put that gene into a new context. The idea for the three first vaccines is the same: to introduce into the human body RNA that carries the recipe (receta) for spike (proteina S), a protein abundant on the outsides of particles of SARS-COV-2. The body then uses this **recipe to manufacture spikes**, & the immune system, recognising the protein as an allien, mounts a response to it. Thus, stimulated, the immune system can react rapidly if it subsequently encouters the spike proteins of actual viruses. The vaccines from Pfitzer & Moderna introduce the RNA directly, as molecules known as messenger (mRNA) held inside small, fatty particles called liposomes. The mRNA approach is regarded as particularly interesting, because this is the first successful example of what researches hope will be a new class of drugs that work by feeding cells instrutions to make therapeutic protein *in situ*. Understanding the structure of the SARS-COV-2 on the basis of their experience with other coronavirus, would-be (aspirantes) vaccine-makers immediately homed in on (se dirigen hacia) the gene for the distinctive spike protein with which the viruses membrane is studded (clavada): just the sort of thing to provoke a response from the immune system.

At BioNTech (a German company specialised in the use of mRNAS)-sequences of genetic material that provide cells with recipes for making proteins, its researchers made an mRNA version of it that could be injected into the body in tiny capsules made of lipids. There it would lead cells to produce the spike protein, & the immune system would then take note. In Oxford a version of the spike gene was instead put into the genome of a harmless adenovirus originally found in monkeys; when the resultant virus infects cells, too, makes them produce spike proteins that attract the immune system's attention. Moderna also shows that targeting the spike protein pays off. Moderna is pursuing mRNA as the basis for other vaccines, against such patogenes as cytomegalovirus, influenza, paediatric-respiratory-syncytial virus & Zika. BioNTech, meanwhile (entretanto), is exploring the use of mRNA to stimulate the immune system to fight cancer. Its pipeline (proyecto) includes treatments for malignant melanoma & for prostate, head-&-neck & breast cancer. As for C-19, the success of this rapidly created mRNA vaccines bodes well (es de buen augurio) for dealing with any future mutations of SARS-COV-2. As the pandemic continues to spread, & such mutations accrue, it is possible that the excellent responses these vaccines now produce could wane (menguar). That, though, should not be a problem. Just as natural selection can tinker (toquetear, juguetercon) with the virus's genetic code, so too can scientists tinker with the code in the vaccines. And, once they have proved themselves, those vaccines could be adjusted every year, as happens already with the influza vaccine. Over 320 vaccines are in development.

If the Pfitzer vaccine does not provide sterilising immunity, there will be a need for one that does. And there are other ways that subsequent vaccines might probe preferable. Different vaccines can work better or worse with different populations, & for C-19 it is important to find a vaccine which works well in old people. Their immune system can often be unresponsible to vaccination, & they may do better with vaccines which, in general population, do not look as effective. There is no guarantee that the best vaccine overall will be the best for the elderly.

- Social distancing & mask wearing will stay important for some times to come even after vaccination becomes widespread. But a more normal form of life looks unlikely to be too long delayed.

A survey of 20,000 adults in 27 countries undertaken for the World economic forum this August found that 74 % would get a vaccine if it were available. In China the figure was 97 %, in India 87 %, in America 67 %. Countries with low rates of acceptance were Russia (54 %), Poland & Hungary (both 56 %) & France 59 %.

4- Aspectos socioeconómicos y políticos de cuando la tercera ola y enfoques de vacunación

Escogeremos algunos aspetos indicadores de las diversas reacciones frente al C-19:

- **Assian governments** are hampering (dificultando, impidiendo) vaccination drives (empujes, impulsos, campañas, ...) with extraneous agendas: no country perfectly insulates public health from extraneous considerations, & none has a spotless (sin mancha, impecable) record fighting C-19. The president of **Indonesia** took the first shot (tiro, inyeción). On Januay 13th a doctor trembling hands jabbed (pinchó, clavó, inyectó) him on live TV. Unlike many other countries, Indonesia is not putting the elderly - who account for 5 % of covit deaths - at the front of the queue for vaccines. Instead, recipients must be between 18 & 59. Indonesia never instituted a nationwide lockdown for fear of pushing workers into penury. However the data on whether Sinovac's jab stops people passing on the virus (as opposed to falling ill from it) are just as scanty (escasos, insuficientes) as those on whether it works on old people. **India** followed soon after. India is a good example. It has done a lot right. Its health ministry devised special software to target & track vaccine recipients. Its pharmaceutical firms, already the world's largest makers of vaccines, licensed foreign shots & developed their own, & its drugs regulator was quick to act, approving AstraZeneca for immediate emergency use on January 3th. The company that makes Covaxin, the India's vaccine, denies any misconduct & insists the vaccine is safe. Officials simply noted that those who do not want to take Covaxin could refuse to be vaccinats. That is what people appear to be doing, even though trust in doctors & medicines is typically strong in India. The president of **Philippines** was reluctant to pay upfront (por adelantado) for Western vaccines. He was confident that China would ride to the rescue. His spokesman sugested that those who prefer Western vaccines suffered from a "colonial mentality". Yet his government secured enough vaccine from China to inoculate barely a tenth of the population & hat to run belately (con retraso) to the western firm again. The government of **South corea**, which has been more succesful than most at slowing the disease's spread, initially schewed (evitó, renunció a) foreign vaccines, assuming that local firms could develop an indigenous one. Its confidence, unfortunately, was misplaced.

All over the world, politics & health make poor bedfellows (extrañas parejas).

- **Automotive industry**: the creation of the world's fifth-largest carmaker (Stellantis) by vehicles produced is well set to deal with the effects of Covit-19, & to navigate the other dificulties facing the automotive business. Annual worldwide sales fell from 94 millions units in 2017 to 90 m in 2019. C-19 depressed sales by 15 % in 2020, to 76.5 m. Despite the rebound, the industry is not likely to get back to its size in 2019 before 2023.

- **Brexit & C-19**: England's third national lockdown began on January 5th, shutting much of the hospitality industry (ind. hotelera) & retail sectors. The chancelor of the exhequer announced a further $ 6.2 bn package of grands for firms as the lockdown began & signalled that more support may be forthcoming at this year budget, due in early March. But although the resurgence of C-19 has overshadowed (eclipsado) Brexit, the latter is causing problems. Rules-of-origin checks (controles, inspecciones) have emerged as a particular bugbear (pesadilla).

- **China:** in Beijin, on January 2021, growing fears of a second wave have led to ever-tigher rules. This range from the irritating - some pharmacies stopopping over-the-counter painkiller sales, to prevent people hidding fevers - to the heartbreaking (desgarrador). Chinese New Year, which this year falls on February 12th, has been, in effect, cancelled for government workers: they may not travel home to see families around China. Almost every movement in the city must be registered. Such restrictions are burdersome (onerosas, molestas, pesadas), indeed a bit sinister, but effective. At the time of writting (January 16th, 2021) Beijing has detected 44 cases of covit in the past month, after millions of tests. For comparison, London is finding more than 8,500 new cases a day. China's strict virus controls are rarely criticised, even in private. Indeed, a common grumble (queja) is that rules are not being enforced harshly enough. A lazy (poco meditada) explanation for this virus exceptionalism is that people in China do not care about personal freedoms or privacy. In particular, the idea of catching it inspires a real fear, even dread (terror). The reasons include politics & propaganda, economics, culture & history, ... In part, propaganda chiefs want to demonstrate the superiority of modern Communist party rule. In part, they are drawing on (se inspiran en, recurren a) older traditions: an outbreak of bubonic plague during the civil war in 1947 saw party workers in the north-east recruit villagers with a "patriotic higiene" campaign involving compulsory vaccinations & fines for failing to report deaths. Further back, in the last days of the Quing dinasty, reformist officials fighting plague in Manchuria in 1919-11 linked modern medicine with national rejuvenation (=), stressing the need to quarantine "irresponsible" migrant workers & make them wear masks. In China, the urge (impulso, deseo) to control has deep roots.

- **India**: India's education system was failing its children long before C-19 forced them out of their classroom. Only 55 % of the country's ten-year-olds an read & understand a simple story. In October 2020 the World bank estimated that mising out on (perder, dejar pasar) school for six month would reduce pupils' lifetime earnings by 5 %, at a cost to the country of around $ 450 bn.

- **Spain**: Spain's Gross domestic product (GDP) shrank by about 11 % in 2020, the worst in the Euro-zone; in January 2021, some 750,000 workers are still furloughed; public debt is heading for 120 % of the GDP. The government's hopes are now pinned (cifrados, depositados) on aid from the Eurpean recovery fund: it expects to get € 27 bn in 2021.

- (the) **United states of America**: On January 23rd 2021, 68 % of white parents want they children to return to school this academic year; only 36 % of black parents & 50 % of Hispanic parents feel the same way. Black & Hispanic Americans have many reasons to be even more afraid of C-19 than white families: they are four times more likely to be hospitalised as a result of the virus & three times more likely to die than white Americans are.

- **Vaccinating the world**: who gets the jab? Who survives & what is the sort of the world they inherit? How countries approach the problem, ...:

. A big worry is that the presence of a fairly (bastante) large population of only-partially immune patients might encourage the development of viral strains that can get around (superar) the sort of protection that the different vaccines offer.

. Another way to stretch (estirar, hacer que llegue) supplies is to administer more first doses by delaying the booster (refuerzo), as Britain & Denmark will & Germany may. Critics argue that the vaccine may be less effective, undermining confidence in vaccination, & that exposure to partially protected people may help the virus acquire resistence. Supporters say they have some evidence that delayed boosters will work & that immunology suggests people will retain plenty of protection against the virus.

. In a world where the supply of a cheap Western vaccines was already plentiful (abundante) there would be little interest in the less-attested (bien legalizadas) vaccines from China, India & Russia. As it is, they provide a welcome option for some countries, as well as a fillip (estímulo: =) for their originators (creadores, inventores).

. It is possible that in time Western governments will increase the amount of vaccine available to others.

. Some comparisons: although Israel hat inoculated 16 % of the people by January 5th, France managed just 0.01 % & the Netherlands has just started. In Spain Madrid uses 6 % of the vials it had received; the region of Asturias administered over 80 %. In America, by January 7th, the federal government has shipped 17.3 m doses, well short of its target. Only 5.3 m people had received shots.

Sputnik V is similar in its design to the AstraZeneca- Oxford vaccine.

. Africans are not humans? We have not enough data about its vaccination process.

. America & Britain have coverage of 290 % & 200 %, respectively. The regulators of both countries have been quicker. If America comes to see value in competing with Russia & China for the soft power bestowed (conferido) by providing vaccines beyond its borders, that will be all to the good. This is the first global-health emergency in which new treatments are being rolled out (lanzados al mercado) to poor countries at about the same time as in richer ones. That process will undoubtedly be fraught (tenso, cargado) with inequity (injusticia). The fiscal stimulus signed by D. Trump may help speed up reopenings of the schools. It includes $ 54 bn to help public ones cover costs including masks & extra cleaning. J. Biden promised yet more cash. He will have little direct authority over shool districts' reopening plans.

- Brazil seems the sort of place where vacinations against C-19 should have taken off (despegado, empezado a tener éxito) quickly, & not just because it is suffering heavily from the disease. Impressive vaccine-making institutes - Butantan in Sao Pablo % Fiocruz in Rio de Janeiro - provide excellent support for its existing immunisation programmes. Brazil has been intimately involved in the validation of C-19 vaccines developed elsewhere. But at the frst week of January, Brazil, with 212 m inhabitants, had just 6 m doses of a C-19 vaccine within its borders. On January 9th, because that vaccine has yet to be aproved by the country's regulators, not one dose has ben used.

. Canada has dibs on enough doses to immunise 505 % of its population.

. China has a long history of vaccine scandals. But the 1.5 m vaccine doses that were distributed during 2020 did not all go to people obliged by the government to take them, such as soldiers, party officials & labourers being sent abroad; some of the rich & well connected happily snagged doses for themselves.

. The EU, acting as bulk (al por mayor) purchaser of its member tates, plumped much heavely for AstraZeneka's product than for Pfizer's.

- The United arab emirates, of which Dubai is a part, rank second in the world in vaccination per head. By January 13th it has administrated almost 13 doses for every two residents. Bahrain & the the Emirates rely on a vaccine made by Sinopharm, a state-backed Chinese firm. Some residents prefer Sinopharm jab because it is based on an inactivated strain of the SARS-COV-2 virus, a long-established way of making vaccines, rather than the new mRNA technology used by Pfizer & other Western manufacturers. The Emirate embrace of Sinopharm will bring them closer still: in this relationship there is not social distancing.

- **Welfare programmes**: in the annual meeting of the American economic association (AEA), the pandemic upended the rite this year, & instead enabled conference attendees to peer (mirar) into the living rooms & offices of scholars as they presented their work, much of it focused on the consequences of C-19 on Zoom. Scholars presented work showing that higher levels of trust & social responsibility were associated with less scepticism of media reporting on C-19 & greater willingnss to accept stringent lockdown measures.

"Whoever doesn't fight Covit-19 commit a crime against humanity" (quien no lucha contra el Covit-19 comete un crimen contra la humanidad)

"As things stand each minute is a year" (tal como están las cosas, cada minuto es un año)

"We are afraid of the unknown" (tenemos miedo de lo desconocido)
"Some questions remain unanswered" (algunas preguntas siguen sin respuesta)
"Keep trying!, don't give up! (¡paciencia y barajar!)
"Let Science take its course" (que la Ciencia siga su camino)
"Where there's the will, thre's the way" (querer es poder)
"Aim at other people" (pensar en los demás)
"Close to each other or together, but not in each other's pockets" (juntos pero no revueltos)
"Each peron may succeed if he want" (el hombre llega allá donde quiere)
"So far many millions of irresponsables on a worldwide scale have defeated their authorities" (hasta ahora muchos millones de irresponsables a escala mundial
se han burlado de sus autoridades)
"Offenders of rules must be more severely punished than till now" (los infractores de las normas deben ser más severamente castigados que hasta ahora)
"Don't let difficulties get the better of you" (no te dejes vencer por las dificultades)
"It has less expert knowledge than us" (el tiene menos pericia que nosotros)
"We beat it!" (¡le ganamos!)

Apreciación personal del año 2020 y perspectivas y voluntades para el 2021 y después

As saying goes, "where not reach the Science reach the Philosophy", & if we take into acount the complexity of the subject, we can't dismiss anything. Above all if the behaviour of authorites & citizens don't acts correctly. In most countries thousands of people have violated the rules: celebrating thousands of forbidden parties, gathering & demonstrations around the world, go unmasked, not respect of social distancing, producers and dealers of vaccines fobbed (engatusaron) consumers off, some deadlines have not ben met, and so on. And what is more, from the early stages of the vaccination appeared the law of money: some producers of vaccines breached the agreements carried out with the buyers in favour of some unscrupulous entities: black markets, distribution of unlawful medial certificates dor prostitutes, widespread (generalizado) fraud, etcetera. It will be new strains of C-19 much more virulent of it later on? Maybe, and it could be catastrophic for humanity. Where? What is sure is that if they come they will hit more the poorer countries. With great dificulty (a trancas y a barrancas) Science will gain the battle, but to the frights (susto) coming from the different strains of this virus we may add those derivated from vested interests. We must think about a new instruments of domination, above all those in the direction North-south in the broad sense? The everlasting & obiquitous logic of vital space incite us to answer positivelly. Let's hope I'm wrong (ojalá me equicoque).

So far, world authorities don't take care of all the details: imposing social distancing is excessively arbitrary, as the contagion also depends of the wind direction, for instance; on the other hand, the fines are arbitraries: they never bother rich people. It would be better to fine according to the purchasing power of every person; we also have to be more flexibles (so that not to overshadow the personality of the people) when they say hellow to each other; it would be beter to gesture at the pleasure of everyone, though correctly, ... It also would have been interesting to give a course of virology on the TV from the early stage of its appearance, with obligatory attendance & trying to wound the pride (tocar el amor propio) of any irresponsible citizens; and so on. Looking after those &

other details would loose the need of too tough restrictions. These are wrecking our economies. Above all, the behaviour of politicians & public servants as a whole must serve as an example; and whatever may befall all of us must cooperate with as much empathy as we can. In this sense the fraternity called by the Pope Francis on Christmas day of 2020 is worth mentioning. In spite of the vaccinations, the only way to reduce more conveniently the wreckage of our Ecs. is the universal love & the discipline of all human beings. Hope this won't happen again!

It will be new waves after the third one, even if being different? I answer in the affirmative. Even the third wave (above all in January & February 2021) shows us the inexcusable irresponsibilities of many people and the negligence of many authorities. Unfortunately people like too much make whoopee (divertirse). The new waves will catch us unaware (desprevenidos) again? If so, what a pity! Propbaly we will need some years to get adapted to them. We must beg God (rogemos a Dios) for no more virulent strains than first C-19.

The danger of this virus is bigger than what we may appreciate, even for the vaccinated people: the vaccines are asymptomatic but they can transmit the virus, the people having been vaccinated may be like the asymptomatic, and so on. Little by little (poco a poco) we will discover the secrets of the C-19 & those of its strains.

Actually, so far it's a calamity that no one can be blamed for.

I- Inteligencia artificial (Artificial intelligence) (AI)

A smartphone cheks the battery/instruct the behicle to park itself. They avoid one another at road crossings. Space words evenly (uniformemente) settled. Connectivity will bring customers & carmakers closer together & safely spaced. V2x: a wireless tech in cars. Share of the pie (pastel) for AI companies. Supervising learning (it belongs to AI) requires feeding software stacks of pre-tagged examples. The system of machine-learning software is trained (entrenado, educado, adiestrado) to recognise objects. Gesture recognition: a user might swap (intercambiar, trueque,V) tracks (huellas, pistas) by swipping (golpeo) over the surface the lider is scanning. Face recognition relies (confía, se basa) on machine learning (a subfield of AI) in which computers teach themselves, to do tasks that their programmers are unable to explain to them explicitely. AI is poised (suspendida, colocada; preparada) to changes, it change warfare (guerra) by seeping (filtrarse) into military decision-making. AI finds tumours that radiologists miss. China's national- security establishment is also sobered (se vuelve más serio, formal, duro, crudo) by AI's potential. Officials gung-ho (fanáticos, exaltados; optimistas) about AI as a path to prosperity. AI may win a war ahead of global stability, ej. game- playing (interactividad en videojuegos) "doomsday" machine. AI parses (analiza sintácticamente) résumés (=, CV) for key works without which an applicant's odds (possibilidades) of an interview lengthen. Social-media firms use AI to flag (flaquear, decaer; señalar, marcar) posts for human's attention. The rise of AI & cloud computing is making it possible to analyse this torrent of data. Provide (proveer, suministrar) =/= Chinese plan 2025 envisions (prevé) that foreign firms are excluded from areas such AI. AI startups rent their processing power from cloud-computing firms like Amazon & Microsoft. AI heralds (heraldos, precursores) say further transformation are still to come. Grand: (building) imponente, (clothes) elegantes, (pers.) distinguida, (scheme, plan) ambicioso → the fact remains that many of the grandest claims (demandas, solicitudes, reivindicaciones) about AI have once again failed to become reality. Self-driving cars have become more capable, but remain perpetually on the cusp of being safe enough to ... The state of AI hype has far exceeded the state of AI science, especially when it pertains (concierne, pertenece) to validatons & readiness for implementation in patient care. Even when data do exist, they can contain hidden assumptions that can trip (hace tropezar) the unawary/imprudents. Machine learning use thousands of millions of examples to train (entrenar, formar) a software model (the structure of which is loosely-ligeramente-based on the neural architecture of the brain). In theory, the world is awash with data, the lifeblood (sustento, sangre vital) of modern AI. Data issues are one of the most common sticking points (puntos de fricción) in any AI project. Amazon used graphs software to create virtual shoppers (clientes, compradores). Those ersatz (sucedaneos) of humans were used to train the machines on many hard or unusual situations that had not arisen in the real training data. Many AI models are subject to a drift. The world changeability means more training, which means providing the machines with more data. Huge piles of user (usuario)-generated data. AI experts are scarce. AI systems learn from examples rather than following explicit rules. AI will remain a backroom (entre bastidores, desconocido) tool, no a drop-in replacement for human medics (médicos, estudiantes de medicina); drop-in center (centro de acogida). Swarms of this robots zip (se mueven zumbando) around a grid of rails (carriles). Train machinelearning model to predit when a damaged or worn robot was likely to fail. Predictive (de predicción) maintenance (machine: mantenimiento; house: manutención). What holds (guarda, refrena, oculta) a lot of IA projects back. Keeping up (manteniendo el ridmo) with falling costs of scans (escáners). Provide big speed-ups for some sorts of computation. Take inspiration from biology: Cerebral's chips consume 15 Kw =/= human brain consumes 20 W & is many ways cleverer than it silicon counterpart. Intel & International business machines (IBM) are therefore (por lo tanto) investigating "neuromorphic" chips, which contain components designed to minimice more closely to the electrical behaviour of the neurons that make up biological brains. Quantum computers are relatively well-understood in theory, but actually building them remains an engineering challenge. Their designers are hamstrung (paralizados) by the fact that the neuroscientists still do not understand what exactly brains do, & how they do it. Driveless cars … along with (junto con) getting computers to conduct plausible (=, verosímil, convincente) conversations. Aerial combat: America's defence advanced research project agency (DARPA), an adventurous arm of the Pentagon, considered the future of the air - to - air combat & the role of AI within that future. Computers never tire, & their attention never wander (erra, divaga, deambula). Accidents caused by fallible (falible) human drivers ↔ advocates of driveless hoped to cut those numbers drastically. Embody (encarnar, incorporar; expresar, plasmar) → embodied cognition in AI: if they minds to understand the world properly, they need to be fully embodied in it, not confined to an abstract existence as pulses (pulsaciones) of electricity in a data-centre. Incumbend car makers prefer to talk about driver-assistance, as automatic lane-keeping or parking system, rather than full-blown (hecho y derecho, a gran escala) autonomous car. Vehicles which trundle (empujan, tiran, ruedan) slowly along pavements (aceras, andenes). Tracing: (of phone calls) seguimiento; (rastreo) → -- device (instrumento de localización). Researches hoping to apply AI to C-19 might reflect on (reflexionar en) a poll which suggested that around half of Americans would refuse to install a contact-tracing/location tracing app (aplicación para móviles o tabletas) on their phones. A new language-generating AI can be eerily (sorprendemente) human-like. A computer can crunch through the laborious task of mapping out (strategy: planificar; plan: trazar) those statistical relationships. What sets the algorithm apart is its unprecedented scale. The model that underpins (sustenta, respalda) general pre-trained (GPT)-3 boasts (ostenta) 175 bn. parameters. The model could be used to translate rude messages into politer ones. It has noted that words like "woman" are frequently associated with misogynistic writing, & will mindlessly (estupidamente, sin pensar) reproduce that correlation when asked. Open AI itself was founded to examine ways to mitigate the risk posed by AI systems, which makes GPT-3 lapses (lapsus, fallos) all the more (aún más) noteworthy (digno de atención). GPT-3 may well be detroned by an even more monstruously complex & data-hungry model before long. … Even AI systems of great virtuosity (virtuosismo) have shortcomings (defectos). They tend not to be able to convey (transmitir) how they came to a decision, which makes it harder to understand why they made a mistake. AI is only as smart as the training you give it. … In China the country's digital giants, from Alibaba to Tencent, have already become AI & cloud-computing powers in their own right. The units of analysis for today's nascent technopolitics are platfoms: the technologies on which other technologies are built-& alongside them, increasingly, businesses, governments & ways of life. The platform of all platforms is Internet. The rise of the cloud computing & AI - the first a truly global infrastructure, the second its most important application - has heightened the tensions between these plarforms. More & more value is created using oodles (cantidad, montones) of computing power to extract AI models from digital information generated by people, machines & sensors. Many rich countries have drawn up (redactado, dispuesto) ambitious industrial-policy plans for AI. This summer took place the launch of the Global partnership in AI, which is meant to come up with rules for the responsible use of AI, & for the Inter-parliamentary alliance on China ... In the long run, the World needs more than bilateral deals & a loose form of co-operation, but something more robust & specialised. It may even have to be something like a **World date organisation**.

Some exemples of usefulness (utilidad) of AI in the warlike (bélicos) exercises: the exponential progress in computing was on the verge (borde) of delivering explosive advances in machines capabilities. Headline-grabbing (que salta a los titulares) breakthroughs in AI seemed to support the idea that the robots would soon upend (volcar) every workplace. Given that, on the eve of th pandemic jobs were as plentiful as ever, you may conclude that the warnings were overdone. Economists have, on the whole, been fairly sangine about the impact of robos & AI on workers. History is strewn (esparcida) with incorrect predictions of the looming (amenazante, inminente) irrelevance (irrelevancia, intrascendencia) of human labour. Some researches of the AEA identify tasks & jobs in the dataset that could be done by AI today (& are therefore vulnerable to displacemet). Unsurprisingly, the researches find that businessess that are well-suited to the adption of AI are indeed hiring people with AI expertise.

AI is an important ingredient for the future of armed conflicts. Among other things AI can work out the combination of hardwere best suited to take on (asumir, aceptar, enfrentarse) threats popping up (que aparecen inesperadamente) in th battlespace. The more decentralised the AI processing is, the better. Applying AI to more C2 (in the military jargon it's known as common & control) processes

will also increase the celerity with which strikes can be ordered. Existing procedures often require raw sensor data to be sent to operations centre, where they are stitched together & studied by staff before commanders order strikes. This can take tens of minuts, during which a target may slip away (escabullirse) or fight back. California AI should cut that delay. A JADC2 rich in AI promises not just faster decisions, but better ones. It could, for exemple, assign planes to bombing missions that require serial refuelling to complete. By taking into account things like wind speeds, air defencs, flight altitudes & the weights & stealth (sigilo) of the planes concerned, AI can find efficiencies (=) that might exlude rushed human dispatchers (tranportistas). AI can, for exemple, keep track of a government's myriad cyber capabilities & propose actions that might be relevant for an operation. It might inform a commander that a building to be destroyed could be first been emptied thanks to an ability to activate its fire alarm or sprinklers (aparatos de rociadura automática). Or it might determine that temporarily disabling an area's electricity or telecommunications network would render a strike unnecesary. It can also sort through (revisar) probable knock-on effects (repercusiones) of an action, to warn, say, that a certain type of blast might contaminate a local water supply. AI could flag (señalar, marcar) a troubling (inquietante) change in activity in a port. Postings (destinos) on social media could alert AI to unusual troop movements abroad. There are, however, numerous obstaclesto the success of all this. For a start, developing unjackable software for the purpose will be hard. China's AI developers are able to train algorithms using unparalleled (sin precedentes) pools (reservas) of data, garnered (conseguidas) thanks to the country's weak privacy protections & huge population. China & Russia are also investing heavily in disrupting C2. The help of AI allow us to turn our physiognomy into de one of anybody.

J- RECOPILACIÓN ESPECIAL DE ALGUNOS VERBOS

Abide, ed, ed (tolerar, soportar) by: acatar); abide, ode, ided (permanecer, morar); bear, bore, borne (resistir, soportar, aguantar, sostener, cargar con la responsabilidad, news: traer, fruit: dar, interest: devengar); befall, e, allen (acontecer); beget, o/a, begotten (engendrar, provocar); behold, e, e (contemplar → be --ing to sb (estar en deuda con) + behold! (¡mira!); bellow (rugir, bramar); bend, t, t (torcer, doblar), bent, ou, ou (atar, rodear, encudernar); bespeak. o, en/e (indicar, m.: encargar, reservar); beset, =, beseting (acuciar, acosar); betroth (pometer en matrimonio, be --ed: desposarse); bid, bid, bid (ofrecer, pujar); bid, bad(e), bidden (mandar) =/= bit (apuesta); bite, i, itten (morder, picar); bless, st, st (bendecir); bling, i, i (adornarse ostentando riqueza); chide, ded/did, ed/id/idden (censurar, reprender); fall, e, llen (caer); fling, ung, ung (arrojar, lanzar); forgo, went, gone (preceder; renunciar a, pasarse de); gild (dorar) → --ed (dorada) youth, ...; hamstring, u, u (paralizar, atar de pies y manos); hew, ed, de/ewn (cortar, shape: labrar/tallar, tree: talar); lead, ed, ed (ocupar un primer puesto, guiar, conducir, encabezar, ...); lean, --ed, --eant (inclinar → the tower --s, -- forward, the party --s to the left), apoyarse (against the wall, ...); seek, ought, ought (buscar, ambicionar, pedir); overrun, a, u (invadir, exceder, rebasar); overshood, o, o (destination: ir más allá de, -- the runway: salirse de la pista de aterrizaje, budget/target: exceder), -- the mark: pasarse de la raya, excederse); overtake (rebasar, exceder, ir más allá de, adelantar); saw, ed, ed/awn (serrar); slay, ew, ain (asesinar), también murder, pero assassinate si es político); slide, id, id (deslizar); slit, i, i (cortar, rajar); smit, o, itten (golpear, castigar); sneak, p y pp: uck/eaked → he --ed it throught the customs (pasó de contrabando), -- the bottle under the coat, -- in/out: entrar/salir a hurtadillas; -- about/away (escabullirse); strew, wn, wn/ed (seeds: esparcir, objects: desparramar); stricke, uck, uck (atacar, golpear, dar con; idea: ocurrirse) → --en (aflijido, dañado, ej.: drought --); stride, o, iden (ir a zancadas); wake, o, o (despertar, despertarse → -- from a dream, deep sleep, koma).

K- Sinopsis plural obligada para conceptos diferentes aunque gráficamente o fonéticamente parecidos

- Blast: ráfaga, chorro; explosión, sacudida; tempestad; -- off: (spacecraft) despegar, (mine) volar, (Bot.) marchitar, (hopes) malograr, (ball) estallar.

- Bust: busto; caída; estropear, romper, degradar; go -- (quebrar); busting (combate) → inflation/crime --.

- Clash: (de intereses) conflicto, (culturas) choque, (colores) sin armonía; (ejércitos, facciones, líderes) chocar; their heads --ed (se dieron un cabezazo); enfrentamiento → our views -- on every subject =/= point of view.

- Harsh: áspero; clima: duro; violento, grosero, severo + a stern (severa) mirada/economic test; popa).

Harshly: (judge, treat, speak, criticize) duramente → -- put down (dejar, anotar; reprimido).

Harshness: dolor, dureza, (punishment) severidad, rigor (of a prison regime, of a law, of the climate).

- Rigor: severity, harshness, toughness of prison regime, rigour of the climate, of a law.

- Robusto: =, sturdy, tough (+ fuerte, duro), strong.

- Rough: accidentado, escabroso, desigual; rugoso, áspero (to the touch) → roughness: violencia, tosquedad, (fabric) aspereza, (road) desigualdad, (mar) agitación =/= rugged (accidentado, escarpado, escabroso; duro, rudo, áspero) =/= coarseness (aspereza, tosquedad) =/= hardy: fuerte, robusto; potente, resistente + strong, tough (+ fuerte) =/= sturdy: fuerte, robusto; enérgico, tenaz.

- Smash: choque, golpe, estruendo; aplastar, rotura, quiebra; exitazo (+ great success, big hit) =/= - Quash: (protest) acallar, (rebellion) sofocar, (proposition) rechazar, (veredict) anular.

- Quell (uprising) sofocar, (opposition) dominar; (fear) desechar =/= Squelsh (chapotear) through the mud.

- Stark: (warning, reality) dura, cruda, -- (clear, patent) poverty, in -- (marked, accentuated) contrast, (landscape) agreste, inóspito; sin adornos, desnudo, escueto (libre, descubierto; sin ambagues).

- Starkly: (austeramente) austeramente, (describe) sucintamente, (outline: contorno, esbozo) claramente, (different, apparent, evident) completamente, (illustrate) crudamente.

- Starkness: (landscape) lo agreste, inóspito, (conditions) severidad, (description) lo escueto/sucinto.

- Stiff: duro, rígido, tieso, (test, climb) difícil, (resistence) feroz, tenaz; almidonado; frozen -- (helado hasta los huesos), I've a -- neck (tortícolis).

- Stiffening (muscles) contracción, (joints: articulaciones) agarrotamiento.

- Stiffness (paper, chair, fabric, corpse) rigidez, dureza, (paste) compacta, (muscles) entumezamiento, agarrotamiento.

- Strain: (rope, wire, cable) tension → break under strain (tension), (bridge, structure) presión; -- (efford) of the heart, stant (reistente) to the --; carga, esfuerzo, forzar al límite, crear tensión. The demand of welfare state is straining public finances to a limit.

- Strength (solidez) of a building, relationship & material; fuerza, fortaleza, entereza → get one's-- back; overestimate one's--, value/force of a currency; strengthen/reinfoirce: fortalecer, consolidar, afianzar (+ secure).

- Strenuous: pyhisically demanding (exigente, agotador), (effort) intenso, arduo, (work, exercise) agotador, (objection, protest, opposition) enérgicos, (denial) rotundo.

- Strong: (physically, mentally, team; material, structure, currency; wine, wind, voice; colour, smell) fuerte, (teeth, bones) sanos, (heart) fuerte, sano, (argument, evidence) sólido, (magnet, lens) potente, (opinion, belief) firme.

- Taut: (rope, skin) tirante, (pers., face, voice) tenso, (body) firme.

- Tense: fraugh with (cargados de) tensión, things got a bit tense (la situación se puso difícil), tense (=, difícil) friendship; the tensions (presiones) of the Ec./of modern life.

- Tenso: (tirante) tense, taut, (pers., situation) tense; be uptight before an examen; (relations) strained.

- Thickness: denseness of a wall, door, layer; (line, fabric, lens) grosor, (hair) abundancia, (fur: piel, sarro; carpet: alfombra) tupido, (smoke) densidad, (cream, sauce) lo espeso; it's 4 mm in -- (espesor).

- Tight; tensar, (shoe, belt) apretar, (discipline) reforzar; tight (justo, ceñido) credit; the rope is -- (tirante), tight-waisted jacket, tighten the strings of a racket, hold tight to the rail (barandilla), grip her arms tightly (con fuerza); tighness: tirantez, (relations, environment) tensos.

- Tirante: (skin; rope, string, cord) tight, taut, (step) firm, (relation) tense, strained with her boss.

- Tough: (robust) fuerte, (pers., meat, skin; polices, situation, stance: postura) duros, (choice, question) difíicil; get --er on its unruly (rebeldes) clients; --en (endurecer, fortalecer) democracy, …

(b)- Atizar: (fire) spoke, stir, (oven, stove, furnace, kiln) stoke, (discord, disagreement) stir up, (passion, flames) fan.

- Back: espalda/dorso/parte de atrás/(hall) fondo/(chair) respaldo; -- (up); (plan. pers.) apoyar, respaldar =/= pump up (reactivar) the Ec.

- Poke: --/stir (atizar) the fire, -- sb's eyes out (arrancar los ojos a alguien + gouge out the eyes; pull out a tooth/a plant, a floor), -- sb in the ribs with an umbrella, -- a fork into the meat, -- (dar un puñetazo a) sb in the nose, -- (darle) at a mouse with …; codazo (nudge: -- disinulado, elbow: -- fuerte); mamporro (golpe con la mano: clout, bash; al caer: bump.

- Prop: (puntal,V, apoyo); (Ec., región) respaldar, (estructura, arquitectura) apuntalar + share up (apuntalar, reforzar; apoyar, sostener) its allies confidence, …; shore (empujar) shares upward.

- Stir: (liquid, fluid) remover, (fire) atizar, hurgar, mover; a breeze (brisa) --red the leaves; (interest) despertar; (liquid) revilver; (emotions) provocar; -- (incite) sb to sth, -- up (remover) the past, (discord) sow: meter o sembrar cizaña, Earth northernmost sea is --ing (agitado).

- Stoke: (up): (fire) atizar, (hopes, fears) cebar. Stoke up: cebar el hogar, echar carbón a la lumbre, (eat) atiborrarse.

(c)- Ruffle: agitar, alborotar; rizo,V, despeinar, (feathers) erizar.

- Strife (conflict) → -- prone (propenso a) =/= stiffening (agarrotamiento) of the muscles.

- Strive: try (intento,V)/endeavour (intentar, procurar), make an effort (esforzarse) to …, -- ater/for sth (fight to get/obtain sth), -- (fight) against sth =/= --/struggle to achieve (conseguir) sth.

- Stifle (por humo: suffocate, por fuego: smother), (pers.) overwhelm: agobiar; (expression) reprimir; stifling (overwhelming, suffocating, asphyxiating).

- Scoff: burlarse at sth/sb, at the idea; --ing (mofas, burlas) + --s & cheers (mofas y abucheos); zamparse → she --ed the lot (todo), all the sandwiches.

(d)- Baffed (desconcertado, frustrado), chafe (rozar, irritar), chaff (cascarilla, pienso, paja), chuffed (contento), scuffle (enfrentamiento, escaramuza) with the protesters, stuffy/shameful (bochornoso), miff (disgusto,V, ofender), miffed (ofendido), scoff at (burlarse de) → --ing (mofa, burla), shuffle along (arrastrar los pies) + drag one's feet, (paperwork: papel administrativo) revolver, waffle: (meras) words, hablar y no decir nada.

(e)- Affable: (=, sociable, cortés), agile (ágil), delightful (encantador, delicioso), nice & pleasant & likeable & congenial (simpático), correct (correcto), corteous & polite (cortés) → courtesy.

- Lightly: (touch, knock, kiss) suavemente, (walk) con paso ligero; (ligeramente, levemente) → -- clad, season -- with pepper.

- Lightness: (weight, Culin.) ligereza, suavidad (+ voice), feeling of -- (ligereza), -- of step, (sentence) leveda.

- Slightly: (un poco, ligeramente, levemente), -- better (algo mejor), -- injured, -- less/more, he looks -- J. Dean.

- Slightness: (difference, change, increase) insignificancia, (injury, pb.) levedad, poco importante, (accent) poco marcado, (movement) leve.

(f) - Creak: crujido, chirrido → --y: poco sólido (ej. la revolución cubana).

- Crack: (de primera) tropas, golpe, grieta (+ fissure); golpear, rajar.

- Crash: estruendo, choque, (1929…) crack, estrellarse contra, (Ec.) quebrar.

- It crushed/squashed (aplastó) her, an insect, ….

(g)- Varios:

- Abashed (avergonzado); awashed (inundado) with applicants, with cash …; oomph (brío); shoo the bird off/away (ahuyentarlo); sooth (verdad, realidad) → --e (calmar, tranquilizar); swath (venda, banda, franja)e: (wrap: envolver, bandage: vendar) in a furry (vello, pelusa afelpada)/in a gauze (gasa); swish: silvido de cañas o agua, susurro; whoop (grito,V, chillar; chillido); whoosh: ruido de tráfico o del viento fuerte o del agua a presión, zumbido (zoom) de coche, ruido de puerta corrediza; woozy (mareado).

- Mug: bobo, ingenuo; taza, barra =/= guy (tipo, tío) =/= bloke (novio, compañero; tío, tipo) =/= chap (tío, tipo) → a good -- =/= groom (mozo, novio; cepillo, acicalar, preparar).

- Stump up (apoquinar) = shell out = catch up = kick in = chip in = fork out = defray (sufragar) costs.

-Timber (madero/a, viga) =/= plank (tabla, tablón, puntal) → be as thick as two short -- (ser más buto que un arado) =/= lumber: maderos, trastos viejos; endilgar (-- sb with); moverse pesadamente =/= junk: chatarra, baratija, trastos viejos, porquería; tirar a la basura, (theory, play: obra) desechar.

SEGUNDA PARTE:
diez cortos apartados de temas muy cotidianos, muchos de ellos científicos, que conviene conocer

La organizaremos en dos secciones. Sección primera: vocabulario y sobre todo frases cortas. Segunda sección: frases más largas, muchas veces ya compuestas

Sección primera: vocabulario y sobre todo frases cortas

Procuraremos que este vocabulario sea también complementario de cuanto expusimos en el primer tomo. Si en algunas contadas ocasiones se repite, es para utilizarlo en otro sentido, o también porque es muy necesario y difícil de conceptualizar. Vayamos al grano:

Keep tabs on (vigilar) ships. Startup upstarts (arribistas). Perfect posterboys (iconos) for the new Korea. All the trappings (adornos; horse: arreos) of the genre. A bubbly (burbujeante, pers. llena de vida) 22-year old. Lent (cuaresma). No obstante: nonetheless, however, all the same, in spite of, still. A windswept (agotado) pier (muelle). Ferry: barca de pasaje, (cars, ...) transbordador. Floppy (flexible)-haired, a dog with floppy (caídas) ears. Wreck: naufragio, (hope, plan) fracaso. A presidential aide (asesor + adviser, advisory, consultant). Responsive: sensible, interesado; que reacciona con entusiasmo. That would spell (significar) the end of the Kim dynasty. Halo (halo, aureola)- like glow (brillo, resplandor). Mis-selling (vender de forma abusiva) adictive narcotics. The villain (maleante, delincuente, malo) of the novel. Unrest against Hong kong's Beijing-backed governments. Hallowed (sagrado, santificado) political status. Verbose (=, hablador) speech. The midpoint of the street. Manuscript (=). Forgeries (falsificaciones). Kung-Fu like exercises. Palm-fringed (bordeados) places.

Oversee (supervisar) an empire; overseer (capataz, supervisor). Of high end (de gama alta, de qualidad superior) malls. A senseless (sin sentido) dividing line. Earthquake warnings. Bravo: (animal) fierce/ferocious, (pers.) boastful, swaggering; bravo!, (mar) rough, stormy. Blitz: guerra relámpago, bombardeo aéreo. Ape (mono, imitar) the success of ... A bogstandard (común y corriente, normalita) nation state. Parenthood (paternidad) → the responsibilities of --; acknowledge of paternity (reconocer la paternidad); fatherhood, motherhood; marriage is ailing (enfermo, con problemas). His boorish (grosero) former ambassador. Áspero: (piel, tacto) rough, (terreno) uneven, (sabor) sharp. Rue: lamenter + regret, be sorry, mourn); lamentarse: complain, grumble, moan. Arrepentirse: be sorry, change one's mind. Skit (sátira, "="). Events involving gargantuan (gigantescos, descomunales, titánicos) bodies (cuerpos, organismos, cadáveres + personas: corpses; animals: carcasses). Pristine: =, puro, limpio, impoluto (sin mácula, sin mancha). Stronghold (fortaleza, bastión, baluarte) → the last -- of ...). The man in the street (el ciudadano de a pie), citizen of the world, rights of citizenship. Relacionarse con un grupo (mix with a group). Ecstasy (éxtasis). Bowels (intestino; entrañas + entrails) → the -- of the earth, -- movement (evacuación). Recant: retractarse + back down, take back what o.s. said. Abjure: (belief) abjurar, (claims, activity) renounce. Herejía (Rel.: heresy) → his heretical view. Get up to the stage (subirse al escenario) & rap (golpe, acusación/ crítica,Vs) against each other. Drive a wedge ("sow discord): abrir brecha, sembrar discordia entre ... The plane nose- dived, the bird plunged/dived into the water, his reputation has taken a dive (ha caído en picado). Slippery (resbaladizo, de no fiar) ↔ he confided me a secret, he let me have the food on credit. Unearth (sacar a la luz) specs (especulaciones), unearthly (sobrenatural, del otro mundo). Spectacle (espectáculo)s: anteojos, lentes, make a scene (dar un espectáculo). Appliance (aparato) → electrical -- (electrodomésticos). Contraption (aparato, artilugio) fuelled (alimentado) by …; anti-theft device. Slum-dueller (barriobajero + common). He seems minded (inclinado, que desea) to interfere, reform/liberal minded. Price (tener en gran estima) better among them. (Fine)-tune: (automóvil) ajustar, poner a punto, (melodía, plan; hablidad, destreza) afinar, (TV) sintonizar la longitud de honda; be in tune with (sintonizar con). Non-binding (no vinculante) plebiscite ↔ make one's fate (suerte) dependent (vinculante) on sb else's, they are closely bound together (tienen estrecha relación). Lost- out (salir perdiendo) to the (frente al) world/on this deal. Wit (inteligencia, genio, agudeza) → wittingly (a sabiendas), unwittingly (sin ser conscientes, sin darse cuenta, (Med.) unconscious. Make landfall (divisar tierra) =/= landfill (enterrar resíduos) site: vertedero. Charade: farsa + farce, sham (+ parodia, fingido,Vs). The crowing (cacareo, gorjeo; jatarse) of the cockerel (gallo joven, gallito). Arise, o, osen → difficulties have arosen; the question arose later last year. The bedrock (lo fundamental) of German prosperity. Fill the gaps in its pockmarked (picado de viruelas, marcada de hoyos) Constitutions. Corroer: (tech.) corrode, (Geol.) erode → he is eaten up with jealously. Mess up: desorden, desarreglar, ensuciar; destrozar la vida, estropear los planes. Rot: podredumbre, pudrir → pudrirse: (food) rot, decay, (valores) deteriorate, (pers.) rot, languish. Primary (principal → our -- concern is …, primordial, fundamental → of -- importance). Cagey: cauteloso + cautious; reservado + = → he was very --ed about his plans. Footprint: huella, impacto → social -- (impacto social). Steamroller (de apisonadora) tactics: tácticas avasalladoras, opresiones + (sensation, feeling) oppression, (place, situation) oppressiveness. Mad (demente, furioso) → car/marriage -- (loco por --/--). Dutiful (consciente de sus deberes) + conscious/aware of sth. Tiara (diadema) sellers. Feelings of emptiness (vacío) =/= unfurnished flat. Lean/fat years. Cohort (seguidor, cohorte) =/=

follower (discípulo, seguidor), (Sp.) supporter, fan. Tropa: rank & file/ordinary soldiers; -- de choque: storm troops; las tropas (the troops). Shape: forma,V, configurar, moldear, (proyecto) desarrollar. A sky high (por las nubes) household rates; praise sb to the skies, have one's head in the clouds. Squirrel away (guardar) 50% of disposable income, -- -- (almacenar) nuts. Contact lens (lentillas), space telescope. Pegar: glue (+ pegamento)/paste (+ pasta)/stick. Longevity of people's intimate (íntimo, estrecho) bonds (vínculos). Upper-middle-class children. The progeny (=, familia, linaje, descendencia + descendants). Picks & shovels (pala para nieve y carbón) =/= spade (pala para cavar). Cherisch: (persona) valorar, apreciar, respetar, (memoria, esperanzas) conservar y mantener. Reckless (imprudente, temerario + rash, bold). Dope (=, droga) smuggled in speedboats (lanchas motoras), dopey (drogado, colocado). Ding-dong (disputa, agarrada, reñidismo + row, ruckus). The astronauts won- over (ganados, conquistados) by the speech. The mooted (planteada, discutida) demotion (disminución de categoría). Stomp in/out (entrar, salir, pisando fuerte) to/off the (World Trade Organisation) WTO. Hard won (get with efford) wisdom. Rigmarole (lío, follón; trámites, papeleo). Gibberish (galimatias, lenguaje incoherente). Gobbledygook (jerga: jargon; lenguaje enfático y de muy mal gusto, acción ridícula). Enloquecer (drive mad) =/= enfurecer: enrage, madden, drive crazy. Deny (negar, desmentir) → -- having done sth, she denied eveything). Disclaim (negar, descargar toda la responsabilidad → he --ed all knowledge of it. Taberna (bar, inn, pub, tavern) =/= saloon (=, bar, taberna) =/= drinks cabinet (mueble-bar). The progressive (progresistas) embraced rigurous exemptions (exenciones, exoneraciones). He rubbished (puso por los suelos a) the foolish/stupid peope (insensatos), he talk a lot of rubbish (tonterías). Be bereft (estar privado) of a common purpose, have a purpose in life; purposely (expresamente). Courteous/polite (cortés, correcto) =/=

courtly (fino, distinguido + =, celebrated, outstanding) =/= celebrated writer, outstanding former pupil (antiguo alumno). Finicky (melindroso, con pulidez extremada) supplier (proveedor)/eater (con la comida). The users (usuarios) of the public transports; road user (usuario de la vía pública). Please everybody/everyone's wishes (contentar a todos) =/= keep the customer happy. Fulfill (cumplir con, llevar a cabo, realizar) + satisfacer (he has a fulfillig job) =/= satisfy (=) + -- o.s. with sth (contentarse con algo). Offpeak (fuera de horas punta, de menos consumo, de tarifa reducida) ↔ rush hour, peak times. Coitus/intercourse (coito). Tussle (discusión, pelea,V) with the police, ... Dongle (=: dispositivo de protección de software). Deplete (disminuir) the ozone that protects Earth, the holiday rather --ed our savings. Child abuse (abuso, insulto, maltrato,V). Highly (sumamente) acclaimed (elogiado), --charged (tensa) amosphere. Ágil: agile, dynamic, lively (animado, alegre). The bow (lazo)tied (con pajarita) waiters with supercilious (desdén, altaneras) smirks (sonrisas superficiales, de complicidad). Obstrusive (presencia: demasiado prominente, ruido: molesto, olor: penetrante) ↔ un--: discreto + (colour, dress) sober, (warning) discreet. Uglify (afear), idiocy (idiotez) + that's nonsense! Well-liked (muy querido) by … + dear friends, we are assembled here to … Slur: difamación,V; reputación: manchar, dificultad en hablar). Tontorrón/bobo: stupid, silly, fool, idiot, dummy; tarado/imbecile: dimwit, (Med.) imbecile. The pings (metalic sounds, sounds (silvidos) of bullets); sounds the bells emit. Bush (arbusto, mata, matorral), Bush scandals aside (apartar, no hacer caso de) ... Resemblance to sb, similar experience/custom; remembrane Day/Sunday: día de recuerdo a los caídos en guerras. Fellowmen (pers., tipos, compañeros). Happiness is fleeting/ephemeral (efímero). Take head (tener cuidado) & pay homage/court/tribute (render homenaje). Bond (juntura, enlace, vínculo; bono; obligación)age: cautiverio (+ captivity), esclavitud (slavery); bond of friendship. Arraigado: (custom, tradition) deep-rooted, (belief) deep-seated, (pers.) property-owning. Mofa (mockery, ridicule), make fun of sb/sth, scoff at sb/sth. Abucheo: booing, jeering. Burden (cargar) with the responsibility, fiscal burden =/= load the sacs onto a lorry, carry the heavy cross; he swung a huge rucksack (mochla) up onto his back. Low cost regime lighten (aligera) the indusry's otherwise wafer-thin (muy finos) margins; fine-tipped ball-point pen (bolígrafo). Be in the eye of the beholder (espectador, observador): depender del cristal con que se mira. Observar algo a alguien: draw sb's attention to sth. It did not met (satisfizo) our expectations. Draw inferences (sacar conclusions, deducir) from sth. Markup (margen de beneficios) firms can charge over the production costs =/= safety margin (margen de seguridad), margin of error. Tease: tomar el pelo → he is --ing; hacer rabiar, (sex) provocar. Swell: hinchare, (stream) crecer, (population) aumentar. It adds (amplía, añade, agrega) volatility (=, inestabilidad). Chusma/gentuza (riffraff, rabble) must be out of the politics; what a rabble! Fragmento: ej. of jug/pitcher (jarro) shard; of bone (fragment). Staid (serio, formal; clothes: sobrio, serio) culture/ tech.; why you are so serious? He looked at me very seriously, take a matter seriously. Bloated: (face) abotargada, (budged, estimates) inflados, -- of civil servants. Surfeit (saciar: -- o.s., exceso: there is a -- of) =/= forfeit: fine, (chunks of equity to the banks) confiscation, (honour, rights) lose. America has earmarked/ allocated (destinado) funding (finanzas) to help people adjust to trade-related shocks. The downtrodden (oprimidas) masses; the oppressed (oprimidos). Seleccionar: select, pick, choose), shortlisted (preselecconados) candidates. Support (apoyo) of the people to an initiative, use the stool as a -- for your feet, steel -- (soportes de acero), his knees wouln't -- him any more, (financially) mantener. Gush (chorro, salir a borbotones, efusión) → politicians -- over (elogian mucho) him, -- out (chorrear). China is no longer beholden (en deuda, con obligaciones) to Hong kong for its Ec. welfare. Bankrolls (financiar, recursos económicos); the kingdom fund (financia, costea) … Torpe: clumsy → how --/stupid of me!, (necio) dim, slow, heavyhanded (torpe) blockade (bloqueo). Emit wearisome (pesado, aburrido) stream (corriente, chorro, …) of announcements. Biased (tendencioso, parcial, partidista) → -- toward sth/sb (predisposed in favour of --/--), tendency to ged colds) =/= lopsided (torcido, chueco; table: coja, view: desequilibrado). Sap: savia; debilitar, minar, socavar + undermine). Unreadable/illegible. An undercover (secreto) journalist, … In secret, secretely, because the matter is sub judice (debido al secreto sumarial, en manos del tribunal). Paltry/miserable (mísero, mezquino) → for a -- (míseros) $ 60; miserable: (tacaño) mean, stingy, (sueldo) miserable, paltry, vil (+ vile, despicable). Lump: trozo, terrón, pedazo; bulto, inchazón, zoquete → -- together: (things) amontonar, (pers.) agrupar; if you don't like it, you -- it (te aguantas). Callar: silence, be o keep quiet → he got the children be o keep quiet; shut your mouth (cállate)! Forthcoming: (event, election) próximos, (week, month) venideros, -- books (edición en preparación), -- exercise. Scrub: matorral, campo lleno de maleza; fregar, restregar → it was --bed clean, -- a stain off. China's sizeable (importante) share in American imports. Long range: (missile) largo alcance, (flights) larga distancia. Sober (sobrio, serio, formal) → afer -- reflection, (realidad) cruda; sobering: aleccionador → it had a -- effect on me. Ferret: hurón, hurgar (remover, incitar), husmear (olfatear, indagar), -- out: (pers.) dar con, (secret, truth) desentrañar. Disputa: =, quarrel, argument, altercation, fight, row → the matters in dispute/at issue. Winning: (team, pers.) ganador, (smile) encantadora, -- over (conquistar, ganarse) several colleagues. Deflect (desviar) criticism/bullet/pers., deflection (desvío). Cleaning/cleanness (limpieza) → -- cream/ lotion; ethnic --. Techies (estudiantes de tecnología, de informática) got plum (importantes, chollos) jobs in the administration; what a cushy job (que chollo)!, the appartment is a snop/bargain at this price. Scooter (patinete, vespa). Ardiente: (que quema) burning, (que brilla) blazing, (partidario, defensor, amor) ardent, (aficioado, amante) passionate. Santuario: sanctuary, shrine. Know-it-all/know -all (sabelotodo). Play off: oponer, (Sp.) desempatar → he liked to play his wives'off against each other. Ravenous (voraz, hambrinto). Bruise: (pers.) cardenal, moretón, (fruit) magulladura, maca,Vs → --ing (doloroso, penoso). By coercion or compulsion (coacción,V) → con coacción (under dures). Caught (cogido) in the crossfire (entre dos fuegos). Timelier (más oportuno, =) loan provisions. With accurate (precisos, exactos) models =/= a precise description, enough time to eat, the necessary qualities, it is essential to have a car. A lovers'tiff (riña) → trade --s & nuclear braggadocio (jactancia + bragging, boasting) =/= (discusión) quarrel, (lucha) fight/brawl, cockfight, dogfight. Dragnet: red barredera, de arrastre; operación judicial de captura, emboscada. Shake up (agitar, conmocionar; reformar) the *status quo*. Cushion (cojín, almohadilla) → cushioned (amortiguado) by 25 % increase of sales. Largely (en gran medida) cut Iran off from the global market. Bemused (perplejo, aturdido) at Mrs May refusal =/= the film leaves you rather puzzled, disconcerted. Fretting (preocupado) about (estar neura por) an intra European spat (rencilla) + worried about his wife'unfaithful. Escalate: (fight, violence) intensify, pollution --ed to disastrous levels, (costs, claims) increase. Redress (reparación, compensación) for aggrieved (ofendidos) investors + as compensation for … I don't expect any reward for my effort. Rajoy did his damnedest (lo máximo posible) to gain the local (municipales) elections… Trivial: (details, matter) trivial/banal, (pers.) frívolo, (sum) insignificante. Regardless (pese a quien pese, cueste lo que cueste) … =/= relentless (implacable, incesante, despiadado, sin tregua). Trump appears to dwell (vivir, morar) little on/upon (pensar/detenerse poco en) Taiwan. Roof of glazed (con vidrio) green tiles. Cotton/silk (seda) spinning (hilado). Lift (impulso, avión: propulsión; ascensor, levanter(se), -- off (despegar), -- (levantar) the blockade (bloqueo) =/= heft (levantar con esfuerzo, sopesar), hefty: robusto, fuerte, (salary, price) high. Upstanding: íntegro, (texto) unabridged, de pie → the court (sala) will be (se pondrá) --ing! Be -- the whole play (obra). Hotspot (club nocturno, punto conflictivo) in a puzzled/disconcerted world. Because of the C-19 European banks drag (arrastran, rezagan) down (se debilitan). Lush (exuberante, suntuoso, lozano) forests =/= louche (turbio, dudoso). Vigilar: watch, keep an eye on the suspect, the children, … Leisure (ocio)lly (pausado, lento + slow) approach to life. The main gripe (queja + "complaint") about the high cost of living. He holds great allure (atractivo, encanto). Raven (cuervo), be ravenously hungry (tener mucha hambre) =/= rave: delirar, despotricar; alavar, poner por las nubes, gustarles. China's loot (botín, saquear)ing: saqueo) bothers/annoys the US. Mischief (daño, diablura)-making, boisterous, troublemaker: alborotador; (Pol.) seditious. Freight: carga, flete, mercancía, transporte, coste del transporte → -- paid/charges/free, -- car (vagón de mercanías + coach, carriage). Bring out (sacar, hacer salir) the worst of India's politicians. Plodding (paso lento y pesado) of a student but with determination/effort (empeño); we go at a steady plod (caminar a ridmo lento pero constante). Act with caution (cautela) in awkward/embarrasing (comprometidos) scenarios. Feud (enemistad + enmity; contienda + disputa,Vs) → a family --. Brime/pickle (salmuera). Infringe/contravene (incumplir) upon/on sth: violar algo. Tab: etiqueta, (Mil.) insignia, (bill) cuenta → keep tabs on sb (vigilar a alguien), pick up the -- (pagar la cuenta, asumir la responsabilidad). Excise (eliminar, suprimir, Med.: extirpar) zombies (=) from the screens; (-- duty) impuestos indirectos. The government devolved (descentralizó) powers of some public service; delegate (delegar). Bring down: (price, T.) disminuir, (tree, wall) tirar, (pers., animals) abatir + (chiken, birds; planes) shoot down, (gobernment) derrocar. Get Huawai off the hook (sacarla de apuros); let sb -- -- -- (dejar escapar a alguien). Amid/amidst (entre, en medio de) … Pigybacking (ir a caballo) → give sb a -- (llevar alguien a cuestas). Matter-of-fact (práctico, realista)ly (con toda naturalidad) … Get up, stand up (levantarse). Impropriety (incorrección + discourtesy) + it was bad manners/impolite not to inform them. Beneficiary: =, (de un cheque) payee + his children are the main beneficiaries. Hamstring/--ung/ung: atado de pies a cabeza, fracasado (+ failed, unsuccessful) + the reform is doomed to falure/destined to fail. Vouch (responder) for sth, I cannot -- for its authenticity, -- for sb (salir como fiador de alguien); voucher (vale, justificante, Com.: bono) → luncheon/travel --. With wanton (terca, sin sentido, libertina) falsehood (falsedad + falseness, insincerity). The Republican standard-bearer (abanderado, portaestandarte). Seat: asiento → save me a --, take one's --, banco; (Pol.) escaño, (gobierno) sede; -- belt (cinturón de seguridad). A slow-burning (que quema lentamente) C- 19 struggle which may last long after lockdowns are lifted. The wishful (deseoso) thinking. Paralización: Med.: paralysation, Com.: stagnation, -- total: complete *stand still*. World trade: trucks queues & blues (tisteza, melancholia). Stiffen: almidonar, entumecer, agarrotar → I'm all stiff (tengo los músculos agarrotados), (moral) reforzada =/= (fortalecer en general) reinforce, strenghten. Record: document (+ "="), registro (=), archivo, Ec. --, antecedentes (political/criminal --), anotar, hacer constar, grabar =/= he engraved his initials on the medal, it's etched in my memory. Flash point (punto álgido, de inflamación), crucial/decisive (álgido) moment. Made-or-break (intento desesperado, situación decisiva), made-to-measure, British-made (fabricado), made-to-order (de encargo). Find out: (averiguar) → -- -- everything you can;

descubrir → they never found out how he escaped). Localizar: (encontrar) where can I find/get/hold him?; (llamada Tf.) trace; (Med.) localize; where the industry will be sited. Storm (tormenta) → it unleashed (desencadenó) a -- of passions; vociferar; tomar por asalto) into (irrumpir en) her son's swanky (pijo, fanfarra) apartment/flat. Vet (revisar, axaminar) → vet potential. He reverts (vuelve) to the ancient model, he reverted to type (a ser el de siempre), --ing to the matter under discussion. Secularise the state by fiat (orden, decreto) =/= by royal decree. Tepid: (liquid) tibio + likewarm), (welcome) poco entusiasta. Meal (comida, harina) → --&- mouthed (excesivamente comedido, complaciente, con miramientos) response. Supremacist (who defends the supremacy) of th race. Reach out (alarga la mano) for the knife, -- -- to the poor & oppressed (oprimidos). A battered (aporreado, golpeado, estropeado) enclave; to get a battering from the critics. Gloss: glosar, comentar; lustre, brillo (+ shine), -- paint (pintura esmalte), lustrar, pulir. Disimular: (dolor, alegría) hide, conceal; a cleverly hided scar (cicatriz); she saw me but he pretended she hand't; be more discreet, please! Reverberate (resonance, repercussion) far beyond the tribunal courtroom; far-reaching, with profoud effects. Take the stand (postura, actitud) on/against sb, how can you stand (estar) in such an unconfortable position? =/= he adopted an unreasonable stance/position. Pull out: (page, tooth, plug/socket) arrancar, (supplement, section) separar (+ separate, divide). Urge sb to incite sb against another person. With no heed (sin considerar), he paid no heed to my advise =/= think about/consider the advantages, I must give this matter some thought, he is guilty of the robbery. Worried, preoccupied, uneasy (inquieto, intranquilo) → uneasiness (inquietud, desasosiego). Tread: (pisar) softly, (paso) of marching feet; can I walk on the kitchen floor?, sorry, I trod o stepped on your foot, step on the accelerator. Fist (puño de la mano), cuffs (de la camisa) → fistcuffs (puñetazo + punch,V =/=

handcuffs (esposas) → -- sb/put sb in --. Breastfeeding (amamantamiento). Shy (vergonzoso, tímido) away (asustarse) from sth (rehuir de algo, (-- -- from doing sth (tener miedo a hacer algo) → Buthan has shied away (rehuido) from world diplomacy. Hartarse: get fed up (harto) with telling him …, they're getting tired of/fet up with/sick of your fooling around (sus bobadas). Harto: (tired, bored) fed up; (food) full, full up. Sleaze: sórdido/sucio, turbio → --zy: (place) sórdido, asqueroso, (pers.) desaseado, (deal) poco limpio. Alijo: contraband, smuggled goods, an arms cache/haul, a drugs shipment + an official stash (alijo, esconder, ir acumulando) wad (fajo, montón; tapón,V, rellenar) → millions --ded in a Suiss bank. Risk one's neck (jugarse el pellejo), it's not worth the --, there's too much -- involved, the benefits outweigh the --s, a health/security --. They mixed up the index cards (fichas de datos) =/= card index (en cajón: fichero). Retroceder: move back/backwards, he went/move bak a few steps, the police made the crowd move back, he is backtracking (retrocediendo). Tímido (shy, coy, timid); timidez: shyness/timidity =/= vergonzoso: shameful, disgraceful, shameful, shy) → it's disgraceful that … Private parts: (Anat.) partes vergonzosas. Desgracia: misfortune, sth terrible =/= disgrace (vergüenza, deshonor). Online matchmaking (servicios “de emparejamiento”). A rise in inquiries (preguntas, cuestionamientos). Incorrigible prone (propenso) to wickedness (maldad, crueldad). He would have been among the rebels. Laser weapons. America come close to develop a chemical --. American laser weapon: a hangover (resaca; traza, vestigio (=) from Star war. Snuff (apagar + put out) out: extinguir (=). Therein (en eso) lies the trap. Mars is dull (soso, aburrido, apagado). Incomparable, matchless (sin parangón), in comparison with … In previous days, without prior warning, preliminary examen, prior authoristion, permission, by appointment only (cita previa obligada). Front legs/forelegs. Drizzle (llovizna,V) → a drizzly (lluviznoso). A cautionary (de escarmiento, aleccionador) tale. The car vired off (se salió de) the road. Dummy: muñeco + doll; maniquí + puppet (títere), maqueta de libro. Imitación: (copia) imitation → beware of --s, an -- leather bag, a fake gun. Imitator. The sights (lugares de interés). Be racked/tormented (atormentado) with pain/guild (culpa)/remorse (remordimiento). Cleanse (limpiar, purificar) state institutions. Sostener: (structure, ceiling) hold up/support, (responsibility, weight) bear, (familia) support/maintain, (packet) hold. I can't find my coat (anywhere) (en ningún lugar), have you seen it --? He didn't consider to be important (no le dio importancia). Neither of them came; she didn't bring either of them. They called an early election. Auditor (=, --ía) → financial, ... audit + audit a course (asistir a un curso como oyente). Garland (engalanar + decorate, trim, embellish, adorn, festoon). Asesor: advisory, consultant, think-tank (comité asesor, gabinete estratégico). Trammel (ataduras), feel trammelled (atrapado) by sth ↔ un-- (ilimitado) =/= atadura (acción): tying, fastening. Depression enable/allow/permit (posibilita, permite) radical changes. Weave (tejer) one's way (abrirse camino) through the crowd. Paddle (pala, pequeño remo, rueda hidráulica de paletas, mojarse los pies) steamer: barco a vapour. Thrall (esclavo, esclavitud) → enthralling (embelosador, cautivador). Brusco: sharp, sudden, abrupt → the sudden turn (giro) of the events; avoid braking sharply/suddenly; (character, manners: modales) rough, brusque; abrupt gest/tone/reply. A cheetah (gepardo) running at a top speed. The drones ingress (acceden) & regress (salen) to/from the police station. Wrap (up) envolver, -- up well: abrigase bien; wrap up (cerrar) a deal; dar fin a: that --es it up for today; --ed up in his own world/himself. Lockup: calabozo + hell; garaje + garage; local commercial. I was got fed up (hasta las narices) of my youth employment, I've run out my patience. Healthy: (pers., animal, vegetal, clima) sanos, saludables, (Ec.) próspera. Plead for/defend (abogar por) =/= defend your country, yours interests, to protect o.s. from (defenderse de). Take advantage (aprovecharse) of sth/sb → everybody -- -- of me =/= have an -- over sb, she had the -- of knowing the language. Abuse of authority, abuse of sb (sexo) → let's do away with (abolir, eliminar, acabar con, liquidar) ... Council (ayuntamiento) posts (empleos =/= instructions for use. Uneventful (sin accidente, poco interesante) life ↔ try to attract attention. Aferrarse: harden o.s., stick to a principle, cling to a hope, remain firm in one's opinion. Industrial wasteland (terreno industrial baldío). A source of concern (asunto, negocio, preocupación, interés). Live-&-death (a vida y muerte) decisions. Speed has become paramount (sumo, primordial) → of -- importance. Reaping (siega) what one has sown. Condena: capital punishment/death penalty; a reprehensible (condenable) act =/= condenar: desaprobar, (pena capital) condemn, (Jur.) convict, find guilty, sentence, (Rel.) damn. It's time to take action. Toughten (endurecer, fortalecer) the democracy =/= (Mat.) harden → varnish that -- your nails, exercises to strenghten the muscles, (pena, castigo) make more severe. Hit the target (acertar los disparos), the car -- a road sign; you got right (acertaste), you got it right (adivinaste), make/have a guess (adivinar), guess (adivinanza). Answer the question correctly. After a lot of thought we managed to find the solution. Honorary/honorific citizen =/= adopted son (hijo adoptivo). A caughing fit (un ataque de tos) when I got off the lake. Aprieto/apuro: predicament, fix, tight spot. They are being harassed by the journalists. They held up (atracaron) a branch of the bank. Bone marrow (médula ósea). Make sb aware (concienzar) of the disaster =/= totally useless as a painter, I'm terrible/hopeless at drawing. His threats don't frighten me =/= don't be alarmed! Whereas (mientras que) =/= meanwhile/in the meantime (mientras tanto). His clothes attract looks from the indiscret/tactless people. Whichever way/however you look it (lo mires como lo mires). Whenever I want (cuando me parezca).

Those who are in my side (de mi parte). He doesn't miss a thing (no le escapa nada). Special characteristic, peculiarity; distinctive feature. Our sorrow (pena) at his premature death. Heat is oppressive (=, sofocante), it make it difficult to breathe. Shorts (calzones de deporte) =/= underpins (calzoncillos). Dustcart (camión de la basura). Refrigerated lorry for perishable goods. The countryside looks lovely (precioso), we hat a -- time (lo pasamos muy bien), it was -- (me ha encantado) to see you again. Hood: capote (en general + de coche), capucha. This wound is itching (pica) a lot but he'll put up with/endure. He said it mischievously (con picardía, malicia). A fur coat (un abrigo de pieles) for an atrocious, cruel, dreatful, awful winter. The booing (pitada) of the dissatisfied/discontend people was deafening. Completion data (plazo de ejecución). Be in the peak of his creative powers. Rottennes (podredumbre) of the desmoralized young people. A postal order (un giro postal) for the ruined nephew & grandson. Labour costs. Caramba!: (sorpresa) good heavens!, (enfado) for heaven's sake! Take charge of (hacerse cargo de) watch/keep an eye on the malicious (malintencionados) people. Hardly (apenas) anybody/let us say a word. Unavoidable circumstances (causas de fuerza mayor). The play (obra de teatro) has been praised (alabada) by the critics but not by the stuntmen (especialistas en escenas peligrosas en cine y teatro). In proximity to (cerca, en las proximidades de). Take a bend too tighly & too late. The allegued (presunto) murder. The so called (pretendido) inspector. The Monday prior (previo) to the elections. Even some murderers profess the Catholic faith. Aproximately shortly (dentro de poco). Cautiously (con prudencia) & patience, resolve to be patient (cargarse de paciencia). Boiling/melting (fundición) point ↔ freezing point. To what extend is that true? He said it to look good (para quedar bien) in front of the desperate/hopeless familiar (conocido) people. He dit it on purpose (queriendo) & he sorried himself (se arrepintió) A highly topical subject (un tema de mucha actualidad). It tastes rancid. A material highly prized (apreciado) because of his rarity. Rascar: (uñas) scratch, (utensilio) scrape. Clotting (coagulante) agent. Fitted kitchen (cocina amueblada). Civil law (código civil), mercantile law, tax/private/public law. Collect: coleccionar, reunir, juntar → the teacher --ed the exercise books (cuadernos), I'll collect you at eight, go to -- the mail (correo). Hang on a coat- hanger. Smother (asfixiar, sofocar) sb with kisses (comerlo a besos). "Brainwash" sb. Win at all costs (ganar como sea). As much as anyone (tanto como el que más). A little while later the Tf. rang. But I was daydreaming (ausente mentalmente, en sueños). How long is it since he wrote to you? Soften (ablandar, suavizar) → -- the blow (amortiguar el golpe). Best wishes (recibe un caluroso saludo) on behalf of your great-great-grandfather. Retrain (reciclarse) from time to time. Present a reclamation/make a complaint. Recruitment (reclutamiento). Come to nothing (quedar reducido a nada). Cooling system/air conditioning. Launch a major (fuerte, enorme; clave) publicity campaign. The whole family attended the ceremony. Politically commited (comprometido). A condemned to death man asked for the judje's pardon. Kindness/goodness (bondad, condescendencia). Ready made ↔ made to measure. They entrusted (confiaron) their children to my care. Traditional (casero) remedy. The waistcoat (chaleco) is too tight. They blackmailed (chantajearon) the substitute. Clarity: (statement, sound, image) claridad/nitidez, (water, glass) claridad, transparencia. In remembrance (recuerdo, conmemoración) of… Move up three places in the qualification (clasificación). The new machine products twise as much. Renounce (renegar) your religion. A hard-fight (reñido) match. Repraisals (represalias), retaliate (meter en marcha represalias). Rescue (rescatar) the hostages (rehenes). Eyes shining (resplandecientes) with happiness =/= the brightness (resplandor) of the light. Review: (survey, stock) examen, (troops) revista,

(Jur.) revisión, (crítica) reseña. How dare you to make fun of me? Blood flow (riego sanguineo). In accordance with the law. Give your consent (conformidad). A top tennis/music player. Atender: deal with the people =/= look after the patient. Vital functions (constantes vitales) of our spokesman (portavoz). Rigor: severity, harshness, toughness → the harshness of the prison regime, the full rigour of the law/climate. Hear the children's laughter (risas). My wrist is sore (irritada) where my bracelet has been rubbing (ha frotado). The biro (bolígrafo) rolled (rodó) across the floor. S<u>m</u>ashed to pieces (roto a pedazos). Leave you on your own (dejarlo solo). Corkscrew (sacacorchos). Saludar: greet + saludo; say hello =/= warm regards (cariñosos saludos) =/= a kind (amable, cordial) offer of help. Life here is terrific (se vive bien aquí). Half-naked (semidesnudo). Sensitive: (sensible) to the sun, (susceptible) to the critics. Be kind-hearted (tener buenos sentimientos: feelings) → feel sorry (pena, lamentación) for him. In compensation of the disturbance (perturbación, disturbio). Stand (ponte) agaist the wall. An attempt on the president life. Cordialidad (cordiality/friendliness + simpatía). Cordón: (umbilical, cuerda + string) cord, (zapatos) lace. A correspondance (por correspondencia) course in Russian. Proportion between aims & achievements. You are entitled (tiene derecho a) a third of the shares. Too astute/clever/crafty/sly (astuto) to be ousted (echado). The slightest spark could set it off (hacerlo explotar). Full of landslide (desprendidos) rubble (escombros). Le Pen outdid (superó) the socialist candidate. Greece & Turkey have growled (regañado) each other over Cyprus. Taint (imperfección, contaminación, mancha, corrupción,Vs) ↔ untainted brand. Cautela: wariness, (pre)caution, prudentness. Irrelevant (sin relación, que no viene al caso) accusation, charge, indictment. Mutilation main young girls: from a nick (sección) to the complete excision → surgeons pull the tip (punta) out & stitch (coser, Med.: suturar) it to the skin. Using the Olympics to flaunt (hacer gala, alardear, pavonearse de) its control over Tibet. At 82 & unwell he has endorsed (apoyado, aprobado) his colleage of over 30 years. Despite sluggish (lento, flojo, perezoso) growth, he is in the mood (de humor). Disavowal (negación, desmentido) guilt/culpability. Make minority rights a plank (tabla, elemento fundamental) of his campaign. Alex III: the last Tsar but one. Sobornar: buy off, bribe, nobble, suborn. Get away! (¡apartaos! Self: --absorbed & centric (egocéntrico), --appointed (autoproclamado), --assesment (autoevaluación). Unaware: (of danger) inconsciente, I --ed (ignoraba) that ..., catch/take sb --ed (desprevenido). The key doesn't fit the lock. Don't come whining (quejándote) at me. Half of all seaborn (transporte naval) oil shipments. A recurrence (reaparición, repetición) of illness. Toga: (dressing, evening, wedding) gown. The shadowness (poca profundidad) of the valley/dale. The cost is at our expense (corre a nuestro cargo). On board of ship, plane or other conveyance (medio o vehículo de transporte). Greece needs X millions to stay at float (mantenerse a flote), regardless (pase lo que pase en) ... With a view to (con vistas a). Franquicia: franchise/exemption → (aduanera): -- from customs, (equipaje): free baggage allowance, (postal) freepost. Ocuparse de: issuing (concesión) of licences, deal with, take interest in, take care of. Have fun! (¡que te diviertas!). What's up? (¿qué pasa?). Hardly ever (casi nunca). Be away (ausente) for a quarter. Agotar: (fuerzas, desgastar la ropa/un motor) wear out =/= this mine is worked out =/= we used up our coal. A primera vista (at the first sight). Cuban peasants are emaciated (demacrados). A peasant revolt. We are throught (se acabó entre nosotros). A rewarding (gratificante) experience. Universally knowledged (reconocido). Date of birth, today's date. I found him keen (con ganas) to try out (probar) new ideas. He's always envied (envidiado) me, no reasons to envy. Order intake (llegada de los pedidos), gas intake (toma), food intake (consumo). Insalubre: (insano) unhealthy, (condiciones) insanity. Postcode (código postal). Not really (no necesariamente) exhausting. She will be refunded in full (se le reembolsará todo el dinero). Safari parks (reservas zoológicas). She is due back (llegará) at midday/noon. Abreviar: shorten an speech, abridge a text, abbreviate a word. The broad outlines (los grandes rasgos), in broad terms (en términus generales), in the whole (en conjunto). Bind (atar, sujetar; vendar, encuadernar) → closely bound up (muy atado). A hard-fought/close game (un partido muy reñido). Since the onset (principio). Thre US has eased (aliviado, relajado) on its military build up (incremento). Road-worthiness (validez): the fitness (aptitud) of a car to run in a public road. Set out/forth: exponer un pb./una condicón =/= expose to cold/sun =/= present (proyecto, teoría). Offtake (despacho, salida) of warlike (bélicos) productos. My name is missed out (ha pasado por alto). Impending demise (imminente desaparición). An overhawl (revisión, examen) of accounts (cuentas) shows what ails (aflije) the industry. Bake (cocer) =/= back his candidacy for the post of … Forward: Rush -- (precipitarse), from this time -- (en adelante), -- buying (compra a término), -- (a largo plazo) planning. Miss your footing (dar un traspié). Don't miss our bargain (ganga) offers. Score one hit & one miss. In my stead (en mi lugar). Trolly (carrito) → luggage --, super market --. The state of the track slow down the train. Hereafter (en el futuro) I will work more. After all (al fin y al cabo). Be about (a punto) to do sth. Appraising (valorar, apreciar) applicants → in evaluating more accurately the academic credentials (credenciales). City life becons (atrae) many country dwellers (habitantes). He hold the state (finca) much to his family's dismay (consternación). He's eating up (se corroe) with jealously. I'll take a chance on it (voy a correr el riesgo). It's good to be ready somehow (de algún modo) to assemble (montar) the stand. Control desck (escritorio, mostrador) for infected people of coronavirus. Behold (contemplar) → it was a wonder to behold (era digno de verse). Current events (actualidades). Manufacture sth under licen<u>ce</u> =/= licen<u>se</u>: autorizar, expedir una patente/ un permiso. Give me particulars (detalles), please. The sea is smoothness (calma). Longstanding (permanente) policy, on -- stand-by (alerta, preparado). Recrutar/contratar (recruit). Withhold: (dinero) retener, (información) ocultar. Tigthen (apretar) the grip (empuñadura, agarradero). We can afford a few luxuries (lujos). Sunbeam (rayo de sol) =/= lightening (relámpago) & thunderbolt (rayo de meteo) =/= thunderclap (trueno). Thoughtlesly (sin pensar, inconscientemente + unconsciously) =/= negligence (=). Offender: (infractor) → a traffic --, (delincuente) → a persistent --/recidivist (un reincidente). Beware! (¡atención!) → -- of falling (caer), of dogs, of pickpokets. Matters of public policy (de interés public). His work is remote (alejado) from our concerns, in the remote future, it isn't remotely possible (no hay la posibildad más remota). He was beckoning (hacía señas) that police was behind. Friendship bonds (vínculos), chemical bonds (enlaces). Award (otorgar) a penalty/an island to Chile. Argue about silly (tontas, ridículas) little things. Ditches (zanjas, trincheras, fosas) made by digging. A child outgrow his clothes. Hear the key turn in the lock. On your own account (por su cuenta y riesgo). Take sth into account. Unoficial source/strike. Steward (administrador), the shop steward (enlace sindical) is behind us. Your own union would disown (desconocería, desaprobaría, desautorizaría, negaría) you. Uphill (cuesta arriba), difícil → an -- struggle. Be in deep water (con el agua al cuello). Holy water (agua bendita). Fiefdom (feudos) of top politicians. Misgiving: feeling of doubt, distrust, suspicion, apprehension. Tread (pisar) grapes, -- carefully (andar con pies de plomo). Merry/cheery (alegre, acogedor). Move away (apartarse) from the window. It went ashore (desembarcó). Mishandling (mal tratamiento) of agricultural equipment, there are lack of drying facilities (instalaciones, servicios). Irak is off the list of nations abetting (induciendo, instigando, favoreciendo) terrorism. Run across (atravesar corriendo) =/= -- away (irse) → -- -- with (dinero: llevarse, pers.: fugarse con) =/= -- out (salir corriendo). Rank (clasificar, poner en fila) the book on the shelf. Les has caido en gracia: they have taken a liking to you =/= take a -- for sth (tener afición a algo). Be funny (tener gracia) → I don't find that joke at all funny. There'll be room if we all squeeze up a bit. A celebration/party to her honour. Trudeau rule out (descarta) rumours. Reach: her hair --ed down to the waist, be within arm's -- (al alcance de), keep out of -- of children. Malabarista (juggler). There's no hurry, unplug it ↔ what's the hurry? (¿por que tantas prisas?), make a hasty decision (tomar ua decisión acelerada), make haste (darse prisa). Our figures were too low (nos quedamos cortos en los cálculos). As impressive as the sea. The raising of the river level threatened to flood the area. As usual (como siempre). The innocent always pay in the end (pagan justos por pecadores). Trade unionism (sindicalismo). Regard the text as hallmarcks (contraste, distintivo, sello) of professional thoroughness (esmero, meticulosidad). Many sneer (desprecian, se mofan) without a shred (trozo) of evidence to support their conviction (condena, convicción). A source of our distress & an arena (ruedo) for relieving it. *Yin*: shadow part of the hill ↔ *Yang*: the sunny part. Release the steeling- lock (liberar el anti- vol). Neutral point (punto muerto). Bodywork (carrocería). Counterfoil: tocón de ábol, matriz, talón de cheque, resguardo. A clever little gadged (un aparato ingenioso). Exempt from (dispensado de). Palm Sunday (Domingo de ramos). Be at the pit (foso, hoyo)- brink: al borde del precipcio. He despise (desprecia) a nice girl. Flow/fall into (desembocar en) the Mediterranean. In the mind (spirit) of the public. Intermediate products (bienes de equipo), intermediate level (nivel intermedio). Be trapped underground (bajo tierra). The document bears his signature + just sing here, the singning of a treaty. They bore (llevaron) his body to the tumb. Bumbling (inepto, habla a tropezones) during a debate. It's a nonsense (es un sin sentido). Be in tune (sintonizar). I think they are onto us (nos siguen la pista). Punk: inútil, sin valor, podrido, (in the US) gamberro, Music --/Rock -- (con protesta). It pains me (me da lástima) to have to say you … Umpteen: montón de veces, innumerable; umteenth (enésimo) Key passages (textos fundamentales) of he treaty. Properly (adecuadamente) dressed for the reception (acogida, recibimiento), use the tool --, -- speaking (a decir verdad). Have a nice stay (estancia). Overload (sobrecarga). Overdose (sobredosis). The family was taken aback (quedaron sorprendidos) by the news; be overcome (superado, dominado, vencido) with emotion/fear. Throught flight/non stop -- (vuelo directo). Be concussed (sufrir una conmoción cerebral). For my liking (a mi gusto) … Glowing (entusiasta) approval. Examined here in turn (sucesivamente). Lose entitlements (derechos) to social benefits. In the early stages (escenarios, tarimas, etapas). Unatended (abandonada) suitcase. Meet (respetar) delivery dates (plazos de entrega). Exaggerate. Further to (con relación a) your letter … The relevant/appropriate (pertinente) document, experience. Training scheme (etapa de formación). The public at large (el gran público). On my way home (al volver). The older the boss gets, the less aware (consciente) he is. The trial (juicio) was adjourned for a week; a trial (de prueba) period. Acelerar: (coche) accelerate, (motor) rev (up), (trámite, proceso) speed up. The banners of efficience are being unfurled (desplegadas). Overshooting (sobrepasando) the deadline (fecha tope), the plane overshoot (se pasó de) the runway (pista de aterrizaje); meet a deadline (respetar el plazo). Mass medium (medios de comunicación de masas). The faulty art (parte defectuosa). Showroom (sala de exposiciones). A fancy-dress party (fiesta de disfraces). A smashing party (una fiesta muy lograda). A stall-holder (un comerciante que tiene un puesto en el mercado) =/= a storekeeper (tendero, almacenero + whorehousemen). Shopping precints (zona). Can't make neither head nor tail of it (no comprende nada). Don't let us be outpaced (distanciados) by the competitors. Fitness (adecuación, aptitud) to do sth. I'm the host ↔ he is the guest (invitado) + guest house (casa de huespedes, pensión). Don't panic! (¡no exaltarse!). Horse-racing (carrera). It would suit me (me iria) best. Primary school, comprehensive (secundaria) school. Schooling (escolarización) is compulsory. Vow (promesa solemne, Rel.: voto) + 40 votes for & 40 against; give one's votes to. The election is four years off. The eagle spread (despliega) its wings. I account myself lucky (me siento feliz). Achievement (logro, éxito) → female underachievement (menor rendimiento del normal). Seaside resort (lugar de veraneo en la costa). He despised (despreciaba) him for being weak. Be on the skid (patinar): estar al borde del precipicio. Take the one underneath (el de abajo). Front-runner (corredor en cabeza). See our situation in a broader perspective. He relinquished/renounced his claim to the presidency. Soltar: the thief dropped (dejó caer) the bag; let the cable out a bit. He was in a odd estate of mind (de mal humor). Turn the system upside down. Leeway (margen) → it leaves us plenty of -- (flexibilidad), make up -- (recuperar el tiempo perdido). It behaves (corresponde, incumbe a) the Spanish government … Borderland (pais limítrofe, region fronteriza). To & fro (de un lado a otro). Metampsychose (metampsicosis): un alma va de un cuerpo a otro, con más o menos perfección según los merecimientos de la vida anterior. Arrancar: pull out a nail/tooth, pull up a tree, (feather) pluck, (arrebatar) snatch. Selfishness (egoismo) ↔ unselfish (generoso, =). Kindness (amabilidad, bondad + goodness) is always rewarded (recompensada). Chirac has steadfastly (resueltamente, firmemente) supported Turkey. Three years hence (de aquí a tres años). Season-tickets holders (abonados). Familiarize o.s. with (familiarizarse con). Date back to (remontar a). Obliging/helpful (servicial).

Connive (confabularse, hacer la vista gorda, consentir + allow, tolerate, agree, consent) in the spread of Islamic extremism. Mat (estera, enmarañar) → hair matted (enmarañado) into dreadlocks (rulos del estilo rastafari). Be serious about sb (ir en serio con alguien). Spin sth round (hacer girar algo), send sth to -- (echar algo a rodar), my head is --ing (me estoy mareando). They queue up (hacen la cola) to remove Chavez, we --ed up for tickets. Netles (ortigas) → grasp the -- (coger el toro por los cuernos). An outstanding (sobresaliente) performance (actuación). Charitable organisation (sociedad benefactora, bienechora). A rude (soez) gesture (gesto, ademán). Sufocating: (smoke) asfixiante, (heat) sofocante. Excess weight (sobrepeso). They died of radiation exposure shortly after the accident. Noncommital (evasivo). Add-ones (accesorios, complementos). Detestable: (acto) atrocious, (persona) hateful. Braconnage (caza/pesca furtiva). Selfless (desinteresado) leadership. It depends on whom you write. The elephant fell into passion (se enfureció) & trampled (down) (pisoteaba) everything before it. He kept off (apartó, evitó, espantó) the vermins (vichos) in the drains (desagües), keep your dog off my lawn (evita que tu perro me pise el cesped). Particular: in this -- (concreto) case, pay -- (especial) attention, he's very -- (exigente) about food, for no -- (especial) reason. For further --s (información, detalle) apply to (escriba a) … The pattern (patron, pauta, norma) shows a roughly (más o menos) equal divide (partición) between intra-community trade & world trade. I was beaten up/ thrashed (apaleado). Lay down (establecer, formular) a thoroughgoing (veritable) strategy. It stays (permanece) in the background (2º plano) ↔ in the foreground; at top ↔ at the bottom, the bottom right-hand (derecho) corner. The novelty (novedoso) of an approach. Came into existence officially (fue oficialmente creado). Applications (demandas) for assistant/ deputy manager (subdirector de empresa), deputy director (subdirector de organización). I'd watch out (yo tendría cuidado). Often falls far short (mucho menos lejos) of the wishes of our products. The windspeed exceeded 170 km. an hour. A meeting to request (solicitar) permission. They went on strike on solidarity with the students & they support the miners. The strength (solidez) of a building, of a relationship. Lonely (solitarias) streets, people, ... Be (left) on your own (quedarse solo). An abrupt end of the road, she was -- with me, abruptness (brusquedad). An incidental, accesory (accesorio) detail. He had to hasten (acelerar, precipitar, darse prisa) sb to do sth ←→ delay (retardar) our departure. The stadium holds one million people. I'm going to lay down (acostarme + dejar, poner a un lado) for a while. A judge with proben impartiality. Go to the court (tribunales), through the court (por lo judicial). Show signs (+ Med.: symptoms) of tiredness. Indisciplined countries will overtake us (adelantarnos). Be ahead of your time, we are an hour -- in Spain, she is 10 minutes -- of the other runners. Magnets stick to metals. Read sb's mind (adivinar + guess). Disrespectful (irrespetuoso). Certificate of attendance (asistencia). A youthful (juvenil) outlook (actitud, punto de vista, perspeciva) =/= look/aspect. Teamwork (labor de equipo). The occupation (profesión) housewife (sus labores). Industrious (trabajador, aplicado, diligente) =/= hardworking (trabajador). Stand aside (echarse a un lado). The decoration (adornos) spoils (afean) the overall effect. Afianzar: reinforce a wall, secure the ladder, consolidate a business. His refusal distressed (apenó, afligió) her. Be pleasant (agradable) to the eyes/ears. I'm very grateful (agradecido) to you. Lecture theatre/hall (salón de actos). Sharpen (agudeza) of mind (inteligencia). The hotel has laundry (lavandería) services. Be in a houl mood (de mal humor). They started arging & in the end came to blows. Be single & unattached. Get her up at seven, get out of bed on the wrong side. Be too clever (pasarse de listo). Attract (llamar) attention. Feature (característica) → the most striking (llamativa) new feature (novedad). I habe stiff (agujetas) in my abdominals. They were full of praise (alabanzas) for you/they praised you. The alarm went off (disparó). Troublemakers/roudy (alborotadores) students. A victory within his reach ↔ out of his reach. I shouted to scare the delinquent away/off (espantar, auyentar). I'm leaving to get away (escapar, apartame) from this atmosphere. I cried (lloré) as the coastline (litoral) disappeared from view. Go astray (extraviarse), lead sb -- (alejarlo del buen camino). Lack of stimulus dulls (embota, apaga) the mind. Dress (aliñar) a salad. Relieve the pain, the boredom (aburrimiento). Hire (alquilar para periodos cortos, ej. a car) ↔ rent, ej. a wo-bedroomed flat. The aircraft was losing heigh. The baby woke me up with its crying. The water comes up to my shoulder ↔ her hair comes down to the waist. Full attendance in the Chamber of Deputies. The ball hit me full in the face. I slipped & went straight (dí de lleno) into the door. You lead (llevas) a too hectic/busy (ajetreada) life. She is in charge of the programme. Weep for joy/anger. He moans (gime)/complains (se queja) about .../mourn (llora) his death. Arbitro: (fútbol, boxeo) referee, (Jus.) arbiter, arbitrator, (tenis) umpire. Luxurious → --ly (lujosamente). Brightness (luminosidad, claridad; alegría) in a shiny (brillante, lustroso) floor. Be bitter (amargado), --ness about sth =/= that left me with a nasty taste (amargo sabor). In a friendly way (tono amigable). A longstanding (vieja, antigua) friendship (amistad). Wide range (abanico) of possibilities. Aerials (antenas) =/= animal antenna =/= communal aerial =/= satellite dish (antena parabólica). Anulación: (contract, agreement) cancellation, (marriage) annulment, (sanctions) be lifted, (licence) withdrawal. Every other year (año sí, año no). We stayed (nos alojamos) in a youth hostel (abergue juvenil, residencia), in a shelter/refuge. Yearning: añoranza, ansia, anhelo. Pacify/calm (apaciguar). The fall in prices calmed people down (calma los ánimos). Implement (aplicar) a 5% increase of salary. What are their grounds for blaming us? Classical antiquity =/= antiquies fair on Sunday. Be short (apurado) of money/time. I'm embarrassed (me da apuro, estoy incómodo, violento, con vergüenza) to congratulate sb a happy Christmas. He is careful (cuidadoso) with his scientific instruments. A load (cúmulo) of suggestions (propuestas). Dañino: (salud) harmful, (el desarrollo de algo) damaging. He couldn't have known (no podía haberlo sabido) because he looked (parecía) no surprised. At the proper (debido) tiempo, with -- precautions, hold your saxophone properly. A weakness for women, a soft spot (debilidad) for my daughter, depressed (deprimido). So to speak (como quien dice). Anyone would say (cualquiera diría que). A dedo: without going through formal procedure. His eyes were swollen from so much blows/punchs. Don't drive so fast (no corras tanto). The macaroni were slightly defective (defectuosos). Type (teclear) in your personal identification number. The spider (araña) was spinning (tejiendo) her web (red, telaraña). Hard-wearing fabric (tejido resistente). He was startled, frightened, schocked (asustada) & with a rambling (inconexo) speech. I was afraid of that (me lo temía) =/= I fear (temo) the worst, the witch's curse (maldición de la bruja). Point the finger (señalar) at ... Not to lift a finger (no mover un dedo). Knock down a partition (tabique). A faultless (sin mancha) married/conjugal life. Seasonal (de temporada) vegetables/workers, an early (temprana) crop. The race (carrera) shattered me (me dejó molido). Stop larking about! (¡déjate de bromas!), it's no joke, it's serious! Leave it! (¡deja eso!). You dropped (dejado caer) your keys, let himself drop (dejarse caer). Gentleness (delicadeza), treat the books gently, you have the curtesy of ..., to be kind enough to do sth. She is very sensitive (quisquillosa + touchy, irritable + =) & easily offended. Cross two breeds of dogs, get your wires (telegramas) crossed. Over the slightest thing (por cualquier cosa). The more I think about it, the less I understand. What gear are you in? Fourth. For no reason (sin venir a cuentas) ↔ be relevant (pertinente). Make sur that (cuidado de que) ... He gave me all the change (suelto) he hat. The seat belt holds you firmly; hold tight, there is a bend coming up; two policemen were holding him down (lo tenian sujeto). Imploring/pleading (suplicante + =). Suprimir: (freedom) suppress, (firearms control) abolition, (inequalities) elimination, removal, deletion of a paragraph. I failed (suspendí) two subjects. Willingness (disposición, buena cara) ↔ relunctantly. Weigh up (tantear, sopesar) the pros & cons. Don't give me so much (tantos) troubles (disgustos). Someter: (dominar) subdue, (proyecto) submit, (a censura) censor, (sometimiento) subjection. Sleeping pill/ sleep-inducing (somnífero). This wall sounds hollow (hueco). Sorteo: (lotería) draw, (rifa) raffle, (Sp.) toss. Disimulado: (cosa) disguised, (pers.) you are discreet. Accrue: (acumular) some legitimazy, (originarse): the great damages --ed from the war. Steadily (a ridmo constante) → his health is going -- worse, he is working -- (sin parar) since 8 o clock =/= steadiness: solidez, firmeza, (lluvia, T.) constante, (flujo) continuo, (precios) estabilidad. Unwell (indispuesto, que sufre). Heal thyself (curate tú mismo), know thyself. Crisis in China is a pretext for hardening regulatory impediments to all but State controlled local firms. Rumble: ruido sordo, rumor, estruendo; pillar, calar → I soon rumbled him/his game. Walk out: salir, marcharse → you can't -- -- now!, (on strike) abandonar el trabajo. He dumped (tiró, abandonó) her on the bed ↔ He tugged (estiraba con fuerza) of her. Sportmanship (deportividad). Discredit (desacreditar) the beneficient (benefactores). Treat his subordinates coldly (con desafecto). Some unfortunate (desacertado) statement → the discrepancy between the two statements. Desagradecido: (trabajo) thankless, (pers.) ungrateful (to his family, ...). He spoke with displeasure (desagrado), do sth unwillingly. Soaking (remojo) to remove the salt =/= desalination (el aguade mar). Discouraging (desalentador) → he was -- about it (habló de ello en tono pesimista).

Tenderness (ternura) → speak/treat sb tenderly. This history is a joke (tomadura de pelo, chiste, broma,Vs). Invigorating: (shower: ducha, chubasco; walk) vigorizante, tonificante, (conversation, talk) estimulante. The embasy is processing (tramitando) his work permit. I tripped/stumbled (tropecé) & fell. Cervantes would turn in his grave if … Untar: (smear), con aceite o grasa (grease). Unblock (desatascar) the pipe (tubería). Descapotable: uncovered/open-top car. The descent was difficult, the plane come down very fast. Disenchantment (desencanto, desilusión). Disillusioned: =, desengañado. Spend the summer (veranear). The fact that he's mean (tacaño) is self-evident (una verdad como un temple). Highway (vía pública) code: código de circulación. She was widow(ed) (viuda) at an early age. She turned to me with tears in her eyes. Turn sth over (dar una vuelta a algo). Unroll (desenrollar). Infuriating/maddening (desesperante). Reject (desestimar) the offer. I feel faint (desfallezco) with exhaustion (de cansancio). The fog blurred (desfiguraba) the outlines (contornos). Drop of popularity. Careless (falta de atención, de cuidado) → -- ness (desidia). The ceremony was spoiled by the naked invaders =/= I have painted three nude, the child is half nude. Malnourrished (desnutrido). Desocupado: (asiento, habitación) vacant, empty, (mesa) free, (casa) unocupped, (pers.) unemployed. He is paying for the excess of his youth. Barechested (despechugado). Desdeñoso o despectivo → speak in a scornful voice, a disparaging remark. An industrial, residential disaster (catastrófica + "=") area. From sunup to nightfall. A sunlight streaming (mana) into the room. Clung (abrazarse estrechamente; agarrarse, pegarse) each other. A cyclist left the bunch (grupo) behind. He was stripped (despojado) of her wealth. Catch sb anawared (desprevenido). Destinatario: (giro) payee, (carta) addressee. The hair/nails done. She blew out the candels on her cake. A shiver (escalofrío) ran down her spine (columna vertebral). The return of defective goods. I'll return your visit as soon as I can. Be up to date (estar al día). A gang (pandilla) of unruly (desmadrados, revoltosos) youths. An open-minded (dialogante) person. Blur: (contorno) borroso; borrar, enturbiar, desdibujar. God forbid! (¡no quiera Dios!), for God's sake! (¡por Dios!). Disimular: hide (+ esconder), pretend (+ fingir, simular), conceal (+ esconder) → it's not good pretending with me, he pretended not hear. Solvent (disolvente), stir to make it dissolve. Disparar: the soldiers fired on the civilian population, (alarma) shoot off, inflation has shot up. The police dispersed the demonstrators. Alarm/safety device (dispositivo). Housing state (urbanización). Treat everybody alike. He enjoys being with his grandchildren. My favourite pastime (diversión), I paint for fun (diversión), the places of entertainment (diversión) =/= divertido: (gracioso) funny/amusing comments, (agradable) an enjoyable holiday. The river separates two countries. Divide & conquer. So likeable (agradable) & appealing (atractivo). A day off to enjoy (disfrutar); enjoyment: placer, (health, etc.) posesión, disfrute. His name on the underside (parte de abajo). She spend the time with him. The sex bond (vínculo) went downhill (de capa caida). Sure of herself without being overbearing (dominante). They doubled the offer, he is twise the heigh, it cost twise as much, twise as much flour as butter, there was twise as many people, books, … twise as wide, long. Cries (gritos) of pain → aspirins relieve pain. Be common knowledge (de dominio público). Interfere (meterse donde no le llaman). Ration (dosificar, racionar) your efforts. A good deal/dose of patience. Droguería: shop selling household items & cleaning material. The plastic surgeon. Wear sexy high heels. Grinning (decir de oreja a oreja, sonriendo) =/= whisper (cuchichear, decir en voz baja). Apprenticeship, apprentice to become a chief. The music drowned (ahogaba) the noise. Homemade bun (panecillo, madalena, pasta + moño). Intoxicated or drunk (ebrio) =/= poisoned. He jumped into the water. He fainted (se desmayó) in the middle of the lecture (conferencia). I noticed the effect straight away. Delayed (retardada) action. Front/rear axle. The focal point (centro de atención) of the talks. They are not hers, they are his (de él). A qualifying (eliminatorio) examen. The plans are being implemented. Register (empadronar) a child. Her determination (empeño, resolución) to learn. Fit (encajar) the pieces of the jigsaw together. Earnest (serio, formal, trabajar con afán)ly: encarecidamente. Metal sheet (chapa). They entrusted (encomendaron) the business to him. Quick-tempered (enfadadizo). Picture/coat hook (garfio). Fatten (engordar) → get fat. The shoes have stretched (alargado, extendido). Bloodstained (ensangrentado). Imply that (dar a entender que) you are wrong. Entry into the EU =/= entrance in the theatre. Entrañas: entrails, in the bowels of he Earth. Between ourselves (entre nosotros). Entrenamiento: (ejercicios) training, (por el entrenador) coaching. The pirouettes thrilled (entusiasmaron) the audience. Make sb's feel seek (dar ganas de vomitar). The hanging over (entrega) of the money, weapons, documents. Home delivery (entrega a domicilio). Fairness: justicia, imparcialidad. Management board (equipo directivo). Let off (disparar, hacer explotar, dejar salir, perdonar) =/= let out: acompañar a la puerta, dejar escaper, poner en libertad → I ---- a sigh (suspiro); sigh of relief (suspiro de alivio). Enslave (esclavizar). A new broom sweeps clean (escoba nueva barre bien). Attend: (school) asistir, church (ir a), (waiter) servir, (Méd.) atender, prestar atención. A pers. without scruple (escrúpulos). They got lost in the depths (espesura) of the wood, at the -- (profundidad) of three m., study a subject in --. Rib (costilla), breastbone (externón), kneecap (rótula). During my stay (estancia) in London. They pay me travel & living expenses (gastos de mantenimiento). Narrow the gab between north & south. The news shook (estremeció) the whole family, the servant (criado) & the servant/maid (criada). Studious (estudioso) =/= expert =/= scholar (estudioso, experto) =/=

hard-working (trabajador). I'll be forever (eternamente + --lly) grateful to you. He spends ages (se eterniza) in the bathroom. Much too fond (aficionado) to drinking. A gymnastics display (exhibición). The swindler/(en Ec.) racketeer (estafador) spent many years in exile. Mass production (fabricación en serie). Nasty: a -- (desagradable) business (asunto), a -- feeling (horrible sensación), a -- shock (terrible susto), the situation turned -- (se puso fea), a -- - looking (mal encarado) individual, be -- to sb (ser cruel con alguien). Notice (notar) sth is missing. They lack affection (les falta cariño). Doesn't it bother (molesta) having to get up so early? What a nuisance! (¡que lata!), what a -- (fastidio) having to shave (tener que afeitarse)! What a -- you are! (¡eres un pesado!). Luxurious (lujoso). They behaved really badly (se portaron fatal). I can't stand the new shop assistand (dependiente). He was his mother's favourite. Date of purchase (adquisición), fecha de caducidad: expiry date, (alim.) sell-by date; fecha límite: (solicitud) closing date, (plazo de realización de un proyecto) deadline. The outside of the house, outside influences. Three appliances (aparatos) were involved in extinguishing the fire. Praise (elogios) for you. Smear (embadurnar, manchar) her blouse (blusa) with your greasy hands. Yacimiento: (Geol.) bed, deposit, (Arqueol.) site, (petrolífero) oilfield. Draw/move with ease (desenvoltura).The directive obliged telecom companies to unbundle the local loop (bucle, lazo, circuito cerrado). A personal vendetta, revenge, vengeance. Have pre-emption (preferentes) rights; preferential treatment. Deafening (ensordecedor) noise. A marble base supports the column. She's too weak to stand (sostenerse). Suavidad: (color, facciones, piel, tela) softness, (maniobra) smoothness → change gear smoothly, (clima, temperatura) mildness. Time (cronometrar). Crudo: (alimento) raw, (poco hecho) underdown, (clima) harsh → the harshness of the Winter, (realidad) stark. Cruz: cross → "--", "I win", tails → heads or tails (cara o cruz). I beg (suplico) you to express your regrets; do anything you may regret (arrepentirse + repent, be repentant/sorry). Announcement (comunicación, declaración) → I've an -- to make (algo que comunicarles). Lounging (descansar comodamente) in the sun. Pakage deal: large variety of goods at a special "all - in price". Write in every other line, every other Iranian of 25- 29 years. All 27 states operate under binding (obligatorio) common rules. It cost (me) more than it was worth. It is terribly good (buenísimo). Actual scope (alcance real). The body/corpse (cadáver) was floating on the water =/= the flags fluttering in the wind. The R. Madrid was likely to win, the goal put Barça ahead → be ahead by two points. Ganglio: nervous ganglion, lymph node/gland. Be chilly (hacer fresco). I appreciate (agradezco) your kidness/courtesy. Look a real mess (ir hecho un gitano). She hit me (me dió un golpe) with her baton (Mús.: batuta; policeman: porra). He is absolutely charming (de una gracia inigualable). In broad terms (rasgos) it seems unbearable, intolerable. The general public (el publico en general), an overall, general view of the pb., general comments (declaraciones de carácter gneral). Have a great time (pasarlo en grande). Grano: grain of sand, (en piel) spot, fine/coarse (grueso) grained. The pleasant (grata) surprise of the captain (comandante de vuelo). Pensioners (pensionistas, jubilados) travel free. Shout (gritar) with joy (alegría). Guapo: (hombre) handsome, good-loking; (mujer) pretty, attractive, good-looking. Two soldiers guard the front/back entrance. Have your eyes tested. He left me speechless (sin habla). Talk for the sake of talking (hablar por hablar), for the sake of (en interés de), for my sake. Vested (creados) intereses. It was a private ceremony (se celebró en la intimidad). An intimate gathering (fiesta, conversación). Tranquilo: calm, with peace of mind. Flood (inundar) the market with garment/articles of clothing, underwear (prendas interiores), sportwear, work clothes. Market research → investigative methods → private detective → judicial enquiry (investigación)

→ trial → indicted/accused → verdict, judgment → convicted, found guilty. Involve (involucrar) you in the dispute. Down the corridor (bajando el pasillo) on te right; the corridors of power (los altos estamentos del poder). Got bless you! (¡que Dios te bendiga!), Got bless the Pope! They fed us (nos hartaban) on nothing but lentils. Hermetically sealed (cerrada). Hang by a thread (pender de un hilo), pick the thread (coger el hilo). Come today whithot fail. The wall of the military prison (calabozo) is damp (húmeda). Comings & doings (idas y venidas). The fight was even (igualada). On equal terms (en igualdad de condiciones). I'm worried/anxious/agitated (intranquilo) =/= I'm excited (=, ilusionado, alborotado) & hopeful (esperanzado) about the cruise (crucero). Make sb angry ↔ put sb in a good mood. A stricking (impactante, espectacular) building complex (complejo urbanístico), striking/impressive (impresionante) ugliness/beauty. The good weather has given tourism a boost (impulso). Be unnoticed (pasar inadvertido). Inagotable: (recursos) inexhaustible, (pers., paciencia) tireless. Which cannot be put off/postponed (inaplazable). Unatainable goal. Undeniable (incontestable) guilt/culpability. Indemne: (pers.) unharmed, (cosa) undamaged. Indagar: make inquiries, (investigar) investigate, inquire into, (averiguar) find out, ascertain. Unavoidable (ineludible). Unaccurate (inexacto). Be at disadvantage (en inferioridad de condiciones). The petrol tank caught fire (se inflamó). Subhuman (infrahumano). Infravalorar: (pers.) underestimate, (price) undervalue. Unfounded fears/rumours. Entlistement (reclutamiento) → join (ingresar) the army. On your own (propia) initiative. In the vicinity (=, inmediaciones, cercanías). Indeniable (innegable). Insensatez (foolishness) → don't talk such nonsense. An unusual (insólito) event, unbearable (insoportable). Two works for supplies (suministros). Intriga: amorous/political intrigue, (teatro) plot, (cine) suspense. Audience ratings (índice). Outrageous (escandaloso, exorbitante) &

infuriating (indignante). Indisponer: make sb feel (sentirse) unwell. Encourage him to apply for this job. Implicación: (project) involvement, (crime/ofence (delito) implication; (complicidad) involvement, complicity. Pinza: clothes peg/ pin, tent peg. Ravings (delirio + --um). Pot of paint, teapot, flowerpot, coffee pot. Beer glass (copa larga) =/= beer mug (taza alta) =/= wineglass (copa alta con tope grande). Componentes de la rueda: tyre, valve, sprocket (piñón). Some crumbles (migajas) left over (que quedan) for you. Getting the house into shape (acondicionar la casa). As boring as hell (a morir de aburrimiento). A while back (hace algún tiempo). The dish (guiso) of the day. A slice/the crust of loaf (pan de molde). Collar: cuello (de camisa, ...). As/when dawn broke (cuando despuntaba la aurora), the dawning of a new era, of a civilisation. We need to project a forward-looking (prospectiva, con miras al future) image. Exhibition site (lugar, escenario). Cubierto: covered, a bad/unbaked cheque, the place has already been filled, take shelter/cover (ponerse a --). Esquemas para estadística: bar chart (gráfico con columnas) =/= pie chart (gráfico con compartimentos radiales en una circunferencia) =/= graph for extrapolation. Within the framework (marco, armazón) of the existing rules. Frame: (ship, building, door) armazón, estructura, (picture) marco, enmarcar, (plan) elaborar. Beg for forgiveness (implorar perdón). Atend lectures (asistir a clase). Health is what matters most. Powerless (impotente) ↔ powerness of a conqueror or ladykiller. Inexcusable or imperdonable. Luxuriant (exuberante, lozano, frondoso) =/= lustful/lecherous (lascivo, lujurioso). On the way out (a la salida). Of no fixed abode (morada, domicilio). Run them at arms length (guardar a distancia). Shuttle (lanzadera) =/= Ariane rocket (cohete) is notching up (se apunta) a record for parking (estacionamiento) satellites. Easygoing (calmado, relajado) chancellor. The star-gazing (mirando a las estrellas) observatory. Breathe in (aspirar) ↔ the soil soaks up (absorbe) the rain & the trees breathe it back into the atmosphere. Gory (sangrientas) & erotic images. Sick benefit (subsidio de enfermedad). Left-handed (zurdo). Iran's sluggish (lento, perezoso, aletargado) privatisation program. Escape unscathed or unharmed (ileso). Sierra Leona: vagines were sewn up with fishing lines. Yonder (allí, a lo lejos) → up -- (allá arriba) ↔ down --. Unlovable (adorable, simple): unpleasant, antipatic. Liking (agrado) → have -- (afición) for sth. Be willing/prepared to (estar dispuesto a). Pensioned-off (jubilado, retirado). A topsy-turvey (en desorden, revuelto) world. Unfurnished (no amuebldo). Pip pills (euforizantes). Well-being (bien estar). Triunfantly (por la puerta grande), hit the nail on the head (dar en el clavo). Bring into operation (puesta en funcionamiento). They showed him no mercy (misericordia). He isn't the same anymore. Surpass → be ahead. Already 25% of the students are on grants. It takes up (ocupa) half a page. Mind your own business! (¡ocúpate de lo tuyo!). Did you enjoy yourselves? (¿os divertisteis?), clap his hands with joy (alegría). The balcony faces (está orientado hacia) west. I dented (abollé) the car. Have sb in your pocket (al bote). How often? Whenever (cada vez que). Padlock & chain (cadena antirrobo). Tempers (ánimos) were beginning to fray (caldearse, combate, deshilachar). Culture medium (caldo de cultivo). Somewhat worried (algo inquieto) I left my keys somewhere else (en otro sitio). Have good contacts (tener padrinos). In any emergency, pull the lever (palanca). Be as thin as a rake (palillo + toothpiece). Get off (bájate) at the stop outside (frente a) my home. The corridor will accommodate (hospedar) the exhibition. Certificate of baptism. Bill (carta) of indictment (acusación). Defiant posture (postura, pose) =/= attitude/approach (actitud). Current affairs, events, situation (actualidad). For children of three & upwards. A step forward (adelante) of the law. Out at see (mar adentro). Fortune-teller (adivino). A little while ago (hace poco tiempo) =/= a long -- -- (hace mucho tiempo). Compressed air. Stale: rancio, marchito, (aire) viciado, (idea) vieja. Wire-netting (alambrada). Outdoors: in the open (libre) air. In their own air (a su aire) ↔ be in a rush/hurry (prisa) to get married. Bend down oneself (agacharse) = stoop (+ encorvarse). Hold it by his end (extremo). Shook him to bring him round (para que vuelva en sí). Hold your handbag (cartera, bolso) firmly. Be grateful (agradecido) for … Chort-range (alcance). Alegar: plead, Jur.: allege, claim that (alegar que). Move/run away (alejarse). There is bound to be (tiene que haber) ... Watch out (alerta)! Get one's breath back. It strengthened, fuelled (alimentó, estimuló) my desire to ↔ ease/relieve (aliviar). A charitable/kind soul. Substitute/surrogate (suplente) → surrogate (de alquiler) mother. Don't be upset (no te alteres)! Three terms in office (en el poder). Apply the ointment (pomada, ungüento), -- the brakes gently (suavemente), -- in writing, -- for a job. Overcome the obstacles. Encouraging (alentador, alagüeño). I live in lodging (pensión)/rented accommodation, a friend gave us accommodation. Anticipar: pay in advance, (fecha, acontecimiento) bring forward. Tranquilizar: calm down, (muchas pers.) pacify, (Pol.) appease. Aspirante: applicant, contender for the title, aspirant to power. The phase (etapa) he's going through (pasando). More ingenuos in the third world than in Europe. Abuchear: boo(ing) = give sb the bird. At a rough guess (a bulto) politics. Bulge: bulto, a --ing stomach, a population -- (aumento); sobresalir → her eyes --ed at the thought, -- with sth (estar repleto de algo). Cansancio: tiredness, exhaustion, weariness, be worn out. Hastío/aburrimiento (boredom) in the meetings of the EU. Fanciful/whimsical (caprichoso). Delicacy: =, fragilidad, (food) exquisitez. Turn off the tap (grifo)/faucet before leave home. Make up (resolver) one's differences. Idle (ocio, holgazán, sin trabajo) gossip: habladurías. Color chillón: (colour) garish, loud, (clothes, paintwork) gaudy. The quoted (citadas) sources. Sow discord (cizaña) &

harvest enemies. Cry out (clamar) → the system is crying out for reform, the car is -- -- to be resprayed (darle una capa de pintura). Stew (guisado, estofado) in the families of nuveau riches. Inhibited (cohibido) in face of the Constitutional court (tribunal). Feel sorry for (compadecer) D. Trump. Specify (concretar) =/= arrange/set up (concertar) an interview. Free admission, closing data for application is extended. He querries (duda, pregunta, cuestiona) the methodology. Hunch: corazonada, presentimiento (premonition), joroba, encorvarse =/= hump (joroba, encorvar) =/= jorobado: humpbacked, hunchbacked. Warm: cordial (=), afectuoso, templado. Worship (devoción, veneración, culto), -- sth/sb, --per (devoto). Llorar: cry, (loss, tragedy) mourn =/= snivelling (lloriqueo). I never come across (encuentro) the word + tropezar, dar con. The books are samey (parecidos) but not the spirits & the encouragements (estímulos + stimulus, incentive). Well liked (querido) by his followers (seguidores) but hateful (detestable) by the opposition. Tiresome: (pers.) unpleasant (pesada), (task) tedious (aburrido); boredom (aburrimiento). Factious: (debate, argumento) contencioso, (grupo) faccioso, revolucionario → the factious groups are all round the world. Account: explicación, informe (report), cuenta, dar cuentas → -- to your superiors. Toss (lanzar, lanzamiento; sacudir, agitar) out/ throw the remains (restos) & the waste/refuse (basura) to the bin. Squeaky (chirriante, chillón; muy) clean. A binding (vinculante) vote, even for the differing (disconformes) or being in disagreement. Longstanding (que vienen de lejos) disastrous policies. Shoo! (¡fuera!) → -- the children into the house; -- off/ away: ahuyentar, (ladrón, animal) frighten off/away, (mantener a distancia) keep away, (mosquitos) repel/ward off. Drone: zángano, esclavo; zumbido; avión teledirigido. Bear, bore, borne (soportado, resistido, llevado) by the poor. Flagrante: (mentira) blatant, (en justicia) glaring/flagrant; catch sb in the act or catch sb redhanded (en flagrante delito). Gross: obeso, ordinario, grosero, (injusticia) flagrante, (negligencia) grave, (gross income) ingresos brutos. Hook up: abrochar + chaqueta/cinturón (fasten); enganchar + (fish/chain) hook, (trailer) attach, (horse) harness. Preclude: excluir (+ exclude), descartar (+ rule out, reject) ↔ pervasive: (influence of occidental cult) omnipresente, (idea) dominante, (smell) penetrante → spread --ly: (ideas) extenderse de manera dominante. Clamber: (over the wall) trepar, subir gateando, difícilmente =/= climb: subir a un árbol, escalar una montaña, subir las esaleras. Political Islam come into terms with (acepta) liberal democraties, but with certain reservations (reservas). It accords undue (indebida, excesiva (=) deference (=, respeto) to promoters. In the wreakage (ruinas, escombros) of the Arab world. Affable (=), (pleasant, nice) agradable, friendly (sociable, =). Scoff at (burlarse de), baffled (desconcertado, frustrado) by the words =/= waffle (palabrería, hablar mucho y no decir nada). Charlatán: talkative, chatty, hawker + vendedor ambulante). In the aftermath (periodo subsiguiente) of terrorism. Store: provisión, reserva; almacén, tienda,V. Subvert: (government, system) socavar las bases, (belief, morality) subvertir (trastornar, derribar, revolver). Genuino: sincere, authentic, true (verdadero), real, own (propio), legitimate. Goon (imbécil, matón), thug (gorila, bruto, matón). Blithe (risueño, despreocupado, alegre). Norma (rule, regulation). Decoro: have a decent standard of living. Corrección: correctness; a well-mannered/correct man. Liver, bile → bile duct (conducto). Bile (de hígado) attack =/= it made me furious (me dio un ataque de rabia). Singleminded (decidido/resuelto) → his -- devotion (=, lealtad) to duty (deber). Backslapping (campechano + straightforward). Grouse: gruñir, protestar; refunfuñar, murmurar =/= Catalan whine (aullido, queja,V). Strike down: abatir, derribar, (Mil.) bombardear, (vida) segar. North atlantic treaty organization (NATO) jets pound (machacan, aporrean; Mil.: bombardean) Belgrado to halt atrocities. Regular (habitual) client/customer. Commit:

(muerte, robo) cometer, (dinero) asignar; obligar, comprometer → commitment: compromiso, obligación, responsabilidad. Give succo(u)r to the weak, helpless/defenceless (indefensos). Let me introduce you to the speaker → how do you do? Pleasant to meet you. Jam-packed (repleto) with sensors. Squirm: retorcerse → he --ed with embarrassment (bochorno, situación embarazosa): le dió mucha vergüenza. Watch/shoes trap (correa), straps onto (sujetar con correa) a baby when you are away. Delayed (retardados) talks, trains, … Loose: sueltos, holgados (espaciosos), flexibles, flojos. Disclosure: revelación (=) of a secret. Print (imprimir, estampar, publicar)er: impresora. Rancour/resentment for the way I was treated. Get one's strength back (reponer fuerzas) after a hard-working/industrious day. Repugnancia: revulsion, aversion, loathing. Rescue/save (rescatar) the unfortunate sailors. Rebelde: rebellious, (Jur.) defaulting. Retirar: (dinero, permiso, ayuda) withdrawal + (alejar, apartar) move away. Retractarse: retract, withdraw. Mushrom (seta, hongo) in the meadow/prairie, moss (musgo de árbol); rust (musgo de hierro, herrumbre) in an abandoned agricultural tractor, mould (moho de los alimentos) to intoxicate enemies. Bally (bombo, bombo y platino)ed: tan cacareado. Blistering: (calor) abrasador, (crítica) feroz, (velocidad) frenética (con rabia, frenesí, delirio). Blowout/flat-tire (reventón). Broiling: achicharramiento. Defray: sufragar (costear, satisfacer), sufragio (of the holiday/vacation). Daub: embadurnar, pintarrajear; mamarracho. Grosero (vulgar, rude, crude, coarse, loutish)ias: loutishness. Flights have shifted to bigger hubs (centros) → hub-airport (aeropuerto principal). Tailor (sastre; confeccionar, adaptar)-made (hecho a media) wedding-dress. Reluciente: glitering, sparkling, shining =/= glow/brilliance: brillo, resplandor. Sluggish: (growth) lento, (mercado) inactivo, (economía) deprimida. Revelious/troublemaker (revoltoso). Wizardry: brujería, hechicería; maravilla, destreza prodigiosa. Beefing (fortalecer, reforzar) =/= backup (respaldo, apoyo) copy: copia de seguridad. Peering (mirar detenidamente) back to the enemy. Truce: tregua ↔ relentlessly. Put political investors off (aplazar, posponer). Rotundo: categorical, emphatical answer; resounding success. Slosh (echar) tides (mareas) of money =/= make a -- (causar sensación) in the travelling (ambulante) circus. Ready to the dustbin. Saciar: (desire, hunger) satisfy, (thirst) quench, (ambition) fulfill. Lay the foundations. Good sense (sensatez). Conscious/aware) from sth. Despicable (despreciable). Sedative (calmante, tranquilizante). Handsaw (serrucho). Simpa: pleasant, nice, likeable. A sham (por dinero, falso, fingido) love. Nonsense (tontería). Strength (solidez) of the material =/= soundness (buen estado, sensatez, solvencia). Break the chain (cadena) before the attac of a castle. Back (atrasado) pay. It's quite (bastante) warm today. Underlying: (cause, rock) subyacente. Subsidized (subvencionado). Banish (desterrar, prohibir)ment. Hurl o.s. to the ground, hurl abuse or insults at sb, hurl o.s. over a cliff (por un precipicio). He can't bear/stand his boss. My duties as political man bind me here. Hypermarket/superstore (hipermercado). Aplazar: postpone, put off, adjourn, (pago) defer. Get one's own way (salirse con la suya). Cheque payable to the bearer. Get one's share/take one's cut (sacar tajada) of the crisis. A glaring truth (una verdad como un templo) in the Vatican. Foreground (primer plano, término) ↔ at the end. In the background (en el segundo plano), green against (sobre) a white background. In good terms (relaciones) with sb. Testing ground (terreno de pruebas). A defeat or draw (empate) away. Rich pickings (ganancias, recolecciones, elecciones) of foreign investments. Attachment (cariño, acoplamiento) to one's native soil. Attest (testificar). Cool, unenthusiastic welcome (recepción). Ring the bell (timbre). Shyness/timidity. Leave me alone. Keep/recover one's composture (serenidad, calma). Get by (arreglárselas) with less money. I'm fair to middling (voy tirando). Arching (tirar con arco) in the outskirts of a city. Be within one's reach (alcance). Feel (tócale) his forehead. Due to be done next week. Reprimand (reprender) him when he acts badly. Don't pick (tocar, ...) yours spots with your dirty thumb. Sandwich of streaky (veteado) bacon. Realisation (toma de conciencia) of future bad times. He signed a false statement (declaración). They have been fond of him (le han tomado mucho cariño) but he is ungrateful (desagradecido). Don't take it that way/so badly, the basic/underlying problem is another. Topar con: run/bump into, come across. Work flat out (a tope) from dawn to dusk. Fondle/caress her. Grew fond (ncariñarse) of sb. Fiddly (difíciles, complicados)/shady (sombreados, turbios) deals: negocios sucios. What a relief (tranquilidad) in times of peace. Shred: triturar; brizna, tira, trozo,Vs. Transigir: give in/away, bow, tolerate. Solidarity with sth/sb. Bleak: (panorama, view, outlook) imhóspito, desolador, (prospects, day) gris, deprimente, (winter) crudo), (painting) sombrío, (pers.) adormilada, con desaliento, (news) sombrias. Queep quiet (no decir nada, no hacer ruido). Misfortune (desgracia) → have constant bad luck. He is an offender/infractor (delincuente) wherever he goes. Defeat/beat (derrotar) =/= derrocar: overthrow/topple + caerse). Hopeless/desperate (=), exasperating (desesperante, que saca de quicio). Despair (desesperación,V), the plaintif (demandante) losed his patience. Uproot (desarraigado) from his beloved counry. A helpless invalid (totalmente imposibilitado). Unscrupulous (=, poco honesto, desaprensivo, sin conciencia). Figure out: descifrar, entender, resolver un problema → I just can't -- it out (no me lo explico). Desconsolado: discondolated, grief-striken. Distressing (angustioso, penoso) → three hours of anxious waiting. Acuciante: urgent, pressing, (deseo) burning. Embezzlement (desfalco, malversación de fondos públicos) to win o earn popularity. Supersede (una técnica, etc.): desbancar, reemplazar → the pack (pelotón) overtook the leader five km. from the finish (meta). Combed ↔ ruffled, messed up.

Desigual: (terreno, calidad) uneven, (Pol., Ec.) unequal. Despedir: sack/dismiss; say goodbye → they said -- to each other at odd times (a deshora). Fiar: sell on credit =/= I confided my secret to him. A tasteful touch (un detalle de buen gusto) for his best mistress. Despojar: (bienes) strip, (honores, derechos) divest; despojarse: (ropa) remove/undress/take off, (poderes) relinquish (renunciar a). Wander (paseo,V)ing (errante), wander off (alejarse) of the course (rumbo). Treacherous (traicionero), traición: (deslealtad) betrayal → betray sb; (alevosía) treachery. Divagar: digress, ramble → ¡no divagues! (get on with it!, come to the point!). Namely (a saber) → another possibility, -- that it was not working. Frail: frágil; débil, delicado + a seemingly (aparentemente) fragile woman. Mischief (travesura). Assert one's authority (imponerse) during an eternity in the power. Compel: -- (obligar) sb to, (obedience, respect) imponer; compelling: conveniente, (necesidad) imperiosa. Have the eyes tested (graduar la vista) when drug abuse becomes an addiction. She can't bear him (le cae gordo) when he's cheating her. Game (juego, caza)keeper (guardabosque privado) ↔ warner (en parque nacional). Forest ranger (guarda forestall). Cloak (capa, manta; (en)cubrir) → --room: guardarropa en teatro y restaurantes; the affair was cloaked in secrecy. Hito: (hecho transcendental): landmark (+ monumento, punto de referencia, mojón), milestone + señal, mojón) → a --/-- (hito) in our history, …, bound (salto, límite,Vs, atado, obligado); boundary post/line; traffic cone, kilometre stone. Humildad: (de carácter) humility/humbleness, (de origen) humbleness, lowliness. The lack of integrity/honesty (honestidad) if you are scare of money. Ilusionar: (entusiasmar) excite, thrill → I'm really excited about the jurney, (alentar falsamente) get sb's hopes up. Indelible/lasting (imborrable, duradero, perdurable). Flaw (defecto) → fallible/imperfect/flawed. Discapacitado: disabled, handicaped + physically/mentally --. Impressive/striking (alarmante + alarming, impresionante + moving, shocking). Inaccesible: (price) prohibitive, (pers.) unapproachable, (objectivo) unattainable. Maladjusted/misfit (inadaptado) ↔ be able to adapt to the circumstances. Unnoticed, unobserved, unseen (inadvertido) =/= inattentive/absentminded (despistado), I'm terribly muddled (confuso) about all this. Uncautious (incauto), unsuspecting (confiado), unwary (imprudente). Unfit: -- (inepta, incapaz) mother, -- (incapacitado) for a job, -- for human habitation, for consumption, for military service, you are -- (no en forma), -- (no en condiciones) to drive. Inmobilizar: tie (up), immobilize. Urge: deseo → -- to write, (animar, alentar) → -- that sth should be done, (recomendar, abogar por) → -- a policy on the government. Add/incorporate/include sth to sth; a camera with an incorporated/build flash. Fulfill: llevar a cabo, realizar, (contrato, promesa) cumplir → fall to fulfill (incumplir): (law, promise) break, (contract) breach + infraction). Infringement (infracción, incumplimiento) of a law by a wity (ingenioso) & indesirable cheater (tramposo). Horror (=), terrific (tremendo, terrible, espantoso; estupendo, genial) =/= terror (=). Fame/reputation. Intruder/trespasser/outsider (intruso), (en Mil., Pol.) infiltrator. Jubilar: (objeto) discard, (trabajador) pension off, retire; prejubilación: early retirement. Bark: corteza/(pan) crosta; ladrar, también yell (grito, chillido) para las personas. Lay/secular (laico) → secular education. Offence/se: (crime) delito, (moral) pecado, falta; agravio/ofensa → no -- was intended. Lápida: heat/gravestone, memorial tablet. Loable: laudable, commendable, praiseworthy. Lesionado (hurt, injured), (Jur.) the -- party: la parte perjudicada. Serious (=, formal, grave)ly: seriamente, gravemente, fatalmente). Reasonable (=), reasoning (razonamiento). Come what may come/against or at all costs (contra vieto y marea). I keep going (sigo adelante). Promising (prometedor) + encouraging (alentador, esperanzador). Catch: their enthusiasm was --ing, (Med.:) it isn't contagious/catching; I give in/up (me rindo + surrender). She lied out of revenge/vengeance; swear vengeance on sb. (Hard) cash (dinero cantante y sonante) is recommended. Executioner (verdugo) for the guilty people. Unfortunate/unhappy (desgraciado) → you'd better not do that! (¡desgraciado de tí si lo haces!). The smart (elegante, listo) way he dresses. Verter: (water, wine, wheat) pour, (liquid) spill, (blood, tears) shed, (basura, residuos) bin, dump, tip =/= volcar: (vaso, botella) knock over, (carga) dump, tip, (barco) capsize, (camión) overthrow. Grain: (cereal, salt, sugar, sand) grano. Supply (suministro, provisión) for healthy & for ill, sick, unwell. Access route, free -- to the library, a port with easy --, accession to the throne ↔ no entry, no admitance. They moved forwards/advanced few steps, move/push a pawn forward. Make sb's life miserly (mezquina, ruin, mísera) =/= amargado: bitter, embittered. Upsetting: triste, terrible; ofensivo, perturbador → the incident was -- for me, it's-- for him to talk about … ↔ imperturbable even in times of war. Come into effect on White Sunday (Pentecostés) → regulation currently in force (vigor) → go out of use on St. Valentine's day. Be close bound together (estar muy vinvulados) when money is abundant/plentiful. I didn't feel like (no tuve ganas de) go, even if they insisted. Willingly/glad (de buena gana) → I'd -- help you ↔ poco dispuesto: reluctantly, grudgingly, unwillingly. Reluctant (reticente). Viscous/thick/slimy & not transparent. It's her own possession/ownership. The child came all on his own. Housing (de vivienda) problems. Live on/by one's wits (de su ingenio, del cuento) in a disastrous/calamitous society. Go ballooning (en globo) & not set fire to it/light it. Derrochador: spendthrift, wasteful. An extinct (extinto, apagado) volcano threaten spew again. The ordinary (de la calle) people, out of ordinary (común): excepcional =/= you rarely get any snow here (aquí las nevadas son excepcionales). The picture is upside down ↔ the right way up/straight, go straight home (derecho para casa). If you don't want to fall, lace up your shoes. It's yours, theirs is in the garden. Wakeful (desvelado) =/= watchful/vigilant (alerta). Wan (pálido, lánguido, débil)e: disminuir, menguar, decaer, languidecer. Diluir: (líquido) dilute, (sólido) dissolve, (aguar vino) water down, (politics, criticism) suavizar. Woodcraft (silvicultura), woodman (leñador). That's quite enough (ya está bien)! Dive/plunge (zambullida) into a frozen lake. He is a sly (astuto, atrevido) crafty old fox. Portrayal: (Lit.) descripción, (teatr.) interpretación, (arte) representación. Walled (amurallado) =/= wallet (monedero), folder (carpeta), Minister without portfolio (cartera). He go abroad in a dinghy (lancha) → leap (saltar) ashore (a tierra). Suave: (surface) smooth/even, (colour, movement) gentle, (pers.) affable, (climate, taste, tobacco) mild, (voice, drugs) soft, (smell) slight. Temblor: (hand) tremble, (frío) chiver, (casa) shake. Rather: I rather (más bien) like a fancy (caprichoso, lujoso, idea extravagante, ...) subject, I'd rather (preferiría) you don't smoke, it's rather (más bien) a long way/walk =/= hardly (casi) ever/anybody. Do without/dispense (prescindir). I'm in a hurry (prisa), --up! Stop --ing me! I --ed in/out, I was --ed into a decision. Be on trial (proceso) for murder, flight trial (pruebas), trial of strength, on -- (de prueba) =/= give sb a try (probarlo), a try/attempt (intento). Blood pressure increase with age. Not so many (tantos). I expect so (supongo que sí), so he says. Don't spend so much. I love you so (tanto). So I do (yo también). Ten or so people. Foulmouthed (malhablado). The (b)rim (borde) of the sum; -- (rebosar) with energy if you are well nourrished. Insult/offend. Remote spot (lugar apartado). Think out (madurar) a delicate decision. Mastery/skill (maestría). Malcriado: (mimado) spoiled; (travieso) naughty, mischievous, bad-mannered =/= mischief (travesura). Bear malice (guardar rencor, resentimiento) to sb. Ocupado: (pers.) busy, (taxi) taken, (Tf.) engaged. Nasty minded (mal pensado), you always think the worst of people (eres un malpensado), think ill/badly (malpensar) of sb. Maltratar: maltread, mistread, (pegar un niño o mujer, aporrear, apalear) batter =/= abuse (=,V, physical abuse: malos tratos; sexual abuse). Flimsiness: ligereza, inconsciencia, poca solidez. Overcrowding: (bus) abarrotamiento, (city) superpoblación, -- in the University. What a bump (golpe) I had. A reproachable look ... ↔ above/beyond reproach (irreproachable). Cute (monada, precioso; listo). Compassion/mercy (misericordia), be on sb's mercy (merced), be at the -- of the elements (=). Nanny (niñera). Nivelar: (terreno) level, (budged) balance, (diferencias) even. Ondulado: (carretera) uneven, rough, (terreno/superficie) undulating, (pelo) wavy. Borrador: (redacción) rough copy, first draft, (dibujo) rough sketch, (contrato, proyecto) draft. Beget (engendrar) more hope than distress. Turn pale (palidecer). Beating (paliza + hiding, thrashing). Drop (tirar) food by parachute. Palpitar: palpitate, (corazón) throb, beat; throb with emotion. Catchy (pegadizo, fácil de recorder) =/= sticky: (autoadhesivo, (superficie) pegajosa, (día) bochornoso, (problema) peliagudo, (situación) difícil. Pending/inresolved (pendiente) litigation (pleito, litigio), dispute. Perishable (perecedero) ↔ (memory) immortal, undying, (legacy) eternal, (fame) eternal, overlasting. Piercing: (look, cry, pain) penetrante, (cold, wind) cortante, (scream) desgarrador, (wit) ingenioso, (sarcasm: burla sarcástica) hiriente, agudo. Quit: dejar de hacer, abandonar, irse, dimitir. Cope (hacer frente, arreglárselas) → he is coping with (sobrelleva) the stress, -- with responsibility ↔ he can't cope with his work/woman. Prey: (animal, víctima) presa, (seize) hacer presa → fall a -- to a disease, be -- to (de)... He presumes he is innocent but nobody believes him. He loved showing off (fanfarronear, lucirse) when a woman was there. Supposed/alleged (presunto). Gather: (crowd) congregarse, juntarse, (flowers, mushrooms) juntar, recoger, (strength, energy) juntar, hacer acopio. Irk (irritar, molestar) some: fastidioso, pesado =/= itch: picor → I was --ing all over (me picaba todo),V; deseo → he's --ing for a fight (pelea), ansia,V). Lean back (reclinarse) on the shoulders of the defending counsel (abogado defensor). Reinstate: rehabilitar, =). A recidivist/reoffender (reincidente) ruthless (sin escrúpulos) murderer. Rebosar: be radiant with health, brim/bubble with health/joy (alegría)/gladness (satisfacción), (embalse) overflow, be fried in batter (rebozado). Batter: aporrear, (mujer, niño) maltratar; (con huevos) rebozar. Hobnob with (codearse con) well-off people (gente bien). Stay up late/all night. Have a blazing (ardiente, abrasador) row: tirar los trastos por la cabeza. A good way (un buen trecho) up to the next valley. The suburban (de cercanías) train is always packed (abarrotado). Sadness/sorrow (pesar) in his troubled/eventful (accidentada) life. Live in style (a todo tren) but not forever. Profits (ganancias) for the conscientious/diligent (aplicado) people. Saddly notorious (de mala fama) well know place: lugar tristemente famoso. Triturador: grinder/crushing machine, (culinario) mincer. Tutela: guardianship → in ward (bajo tutela). The duty chemist (farmacia de turnos) on Sunday is often closed. Deep-freezer (ultracongelador) for the meat industry. Poverty line (umbral de pobreza) is lower in the most wretched (miserables) countries. Unite therapy, join effords, (mecánica) junction, united we stand (la unión hace la fuerza). Adhesive tape (cinta). Usefulness (utilidad) ↔ inútil: (intento) unsuccessful, fruitless, (inepto) useless, hopeless. So it seems (se ve que sí). Vagar: wander, roam =/= waste your time (perder el tiempo de Ud.) =/= prowl, loiter (merodear) =/= lazy devil (muy vago). Bank note (billete de banco), a $ bill. The two properties (fincas) are adjoining (vecinas) but the landowners are bad friends. The sleep (sueño) overcome him, but he refuse go to bed. Manage (conseguir) complete all the tests. Graceful (lleno de gracia, elegante (= + stylish, smart). Exaggerate/magnigy (+ aumentar) the truth. Gregorious (=, sociable). Being tripsy (achispado: ligeramente pipa) he went to see them off (a despedirles). Silent/taciturn (silencioso, melancólico). Habilidad (skill, cleverness). I despair (pierdo la esperanza) ↔ don't -- (no abandones). Uproar (alboroto), disturbance (disturbio). Gape (mirar boquiabierto). Grub (larva)by: sucio, asqueroso =/= grumpy (gruñón: malhumorado, que murmura). Groundless (infundado). Gruesome (cruel, atroz, horrible) =/= gruelling (agotador, duro, penoso). Cautious/prudent (precavido). Gunrunner (traficante de armas). Half-caste (mestizo, =). Racha: run/spell of bad luck, serie/string of scandals, illnesses, misfortunes, I'm in a winnung streak (--, veta, vena) in tennis, gust of wind. Guzzle (zampar, engullir)r: comilón. Hamper: cesta; entorpecer, obstruir un proceso + (carretera, vena) obstruct, (tubería) block, clog (+ zueco). Haphazard (caótico, desordenado) airport. Ronco: (pers.) hoarse, (voz) husky, (sonido) harsh, irritated throat. Join: -- (juntar) things together, ingress in, (stream) confluir, unirse. The lorry was dumping (vertiendo) sand. Interrumpir: (progreso, meeting) =, stop the speaking, (supplies) cut off, (services) suspend, (traffic) hold up, (arrival) retrasar. Lax: poco estricto, relajado. Improvise a tune (melodía). Live off sth (alimentarse/vivir a costa de algo). Lockout (cierre del lugar del trabajo, de la patronal). Inquilino: tenant → tenant farmer, pero current occupant of the White House. Compulsory/mandatory (obligatorio). Manned/with the crew (tripulado). Makeshift (provisional, improvisado) Angustioso: (grito) anguished, (situación) distressing + penosa). Slipknot (lazo corredizo) to strangle crook/villain people (maleantes). Noticeworthy (digno de mención). Overconfident (exceso de seguridad en sí mismo). Misfire: (tiro, máquina, plan) fallar. Sullen (sombrío, triste, pers. huraña) =/= moody (deprimido, mal humorado, de mal genio bad-tempered). Override: hacer caso omiso, anular, ignorar, our protests were --en ↔ of overriding (primordial) importance. Surrounded (rodeado) by the police. Obliging (servicial + helpful). Outburst (arrebato) → an angry -- (arrebato de ira). Outcast/ alienated (marginado) & not dear (querido, majo, bonito) by his former loved ones (seres queridos). Outlast (durar más que). Forgiveness/pardon (=). Exemption (exención) → tax --. Pauper (indigente + destitute). Remove the Political party's power to veto the budget in the Senate. Dismiss ↔ resign, surrender (rendición), relinquish (renunciar a), deterrence (dissuasion). Soso: (insípedo) tasteless, (pers., film) boring, dull, (estilo) flat, drab =/= undefinited/vague form =/= insipid (sin valor). Slot (ranura, puesto) → conjure up (evocar; spirits: invocar) a structure slotted into (encajada en, introducida en)… I resent that (me ofende que) …, he --ted her success. Assemble (montar, ensamblar; reunir, congregarse) → tearful & backing off/away (retrocediendo) from an --ed staff. Loom (avecinarse) → in the face of --ing tax increases + the mist (niebla) cleared (desapareció). Keep up: (store, shop) mantenerse, (rain, noise, studies) continuar. There's some money missing in the till (caja). Ines is missing (no está). Search/check your bag (bolso). There's no handle (asa) on this cup (taza). Faint: ligero, sencillo, leve, apenas visible; desmayarse, ej. with hunger; --ed (tímido) → ritual chants were --ed in Iran. Extricate (sacar) the pilot from the wreckage (restos del avión secuestrado). Atrocity/madness (barbaridad). At grass (de la base) level. Warden: traffic warden (guardián, encargado), Rector de Univ., celador de prisión) =/= (de edificio público) guard, (parques y museos) keeper, (vigilar, custodiar, guardia) guard. A squat (agachado, rechoncho; ocupas) drumlike cylinder. Animal droppings (excrementos). The leaders face down (hacen frente a) all comers (público en general, todos los interesados a participar). It had been mooted (planteado, sometido a discusión) in the hope he might … Lurking: (acechando) the enemy, he was -- (merodeaba) around the buildong. Be down - at- heel (venido a menos). Regulators & courts are chipping away (descascando, fruta: peel off; desconchando; socavando, minando) at the legal immunity of international firms. Policemen bearing riot shields (escudos antidisturbios),

-- arms, a letter --ing good news; bear signs (características) of ... Be a burden (carga) on/to sb, tax/financial --. Admonishment (advertencia, amonestación, reprimanda). The elections are shrill (estridentes, chillonas, frenéticas) with accusations. Harrying (hostigando, acusando) the rest. Deprecation: menosprecio, reprobación, desprecio. Beg/implore/plead (suplicar). Pas over: pasar por encima en una promoción, pasar por alto, omitir. Please (complacer). Patrocinar: sponsor, back, support. Penance: castigo, penitencia. I'm plain (franco, claro) with you =/= plain/prairie (pradera) llanura, he dresses plainly (sobriamente). Pop in (entrar un momento). Pounce on/upon: abalancharse sobre el torero (bull fighter). Joke (broma). Jokster: bromista. Practical joke (broma pesada). Play a prank/ joke on sb. Gracioso: joker, facetious, funny, cute. Push aside (dejar de lado). Fasten (abrochar) the seat belts =/= tighten one's belt, the rope, ... Quarry: cantera, explotación de una cantera. Farola: (luz) streetlight/--lamp, (poste) lam - post/-- - light. Blow out the candel in ine's blow. Puff: ráfaga, calada de tabaco, de aliento, soplo de aire → the run has puffed me out (dejado sin aliento), -- up (inflar) the trade deficit. The ship tied up (atracó + atar) at the wharf. Hideous (horrible, espantoso) → a -- mistake. Silencioso (quiet, silent). Vagabundo: (pers.) wandering, (animal) stray + extraviarse. Sostener: (estructura, techo) hold up, support, (peso) bear, support the weight of the roof, hold the parcels (paquetes) for me while ... Height: (objeto) altura, (pers.) talla, (avión) gain/lose --, (cima) of one's power, fame, recession, (colmo, no va más) of luxury =/= heighten: acrecentar, realzar, intensificar (=). Quarrelsome (peleador, buscapleitos). Heardbroken (desconsolado). Hearty (cordial, campechano). Covered/heated swimming pool. Patrimonio: =, wealth/cultural heritage, world heritage site, national wealth. Gently/smoothly/mildly (dulcemente, suavemente). Rotundamente: categorically, flatly, rotundly. Frivolity (ligereza), --ous (poco formal).

Delightful: delicioso, (pers.) encantadora, (time, event) delicioso, agradable, (dress) precioso. First rate (de primera calidad). Fit out (acondicionar) the premises (locales) for fashion shows. Inflate the figures (cifras). Atractive (=)/engaging (interesante, encantador). On the eve (víspera) of fair/New Year, … As a rule (por lo regular) people is scrounger, freeloader, sponger (gorrero). Aventajar: be ahead, (superar) excel/surpass. Excruciating (atroz, espantoso, terrible, insoportable). Hazaña: exploit, passing the examination was quite a feat. Set aside (reservar, apartar) your savings to pay … Enclosure: cercamiento, recinto. Things enclosed/attached (anexadas en la carta/en el informe); anexo: (edificio) joined, (en carta) annexed, attached, (cláusula) added. The jealously is beating up (consumiendo) him. Ordeal: dura prueba, terrible experiencia, suplicio. Enmity (enemistad). Edgy (crispado)/nervous. Lodge: alojarse, portería =/= (Sp.) "goal"; porter's lodge (conserjería); caretaker: conserje, recepcionista de hotel =/= goalkeeper. Do sums (cuentas) in one's head. Summarize the text, sum up a speech/argument. Weep/suppurate/ooze. The reservoir (pantano) supplies the surrounding (vecinos) villages. Liable (susceptible) to be privatized. Moratorium (demora) of payments. Whisper (susurrar) sth in my ears. Subtle: delicado, sutil, ingenioso → --etly (sutileza) =/= delicacy. Board (tabla, tablón; junta, consejo; atracar, hospedar) → diving -- (trampolín fijo), springboard (el flexible + tablero, tabla de anuncios). Plank (tabla, tablón). Fautless (sin tacha) employee. Recognize by touch. Seasonal vegetables (v. de temporada) =/= off season (fuera de temporada), fruits in --/out of --. Spend as much as you can. Carving/sculpture → carve a statue. The candidate is up (apto) to the job, know one's job (conocer el oficio). A prominent (de talla) lawyear. Tight-waisted jacket. Shoot: brote, retoño; coto de caza (+ game/fish preserve), tirar, disparar. The officials sifted (tamizaron) the data/the applications. Not even (ni tan siquiera). Cover (tapadera) of shady (turbio) deals =/=

lid of a saucepan (cazuela), cap (gorra, tapón)/top (cumbre, parte superior, tapón) of a bottle. Plaster (yeso,V) a wall. Block sb's view (vista, opinión). Tapiar: (jardin, terreno) wall in, build a wall round, (puerta, ventana con ladrillos) brick up, (con tablas) board up. Plug: enchufe macho, tapón the lavabo + cork, screw top (tapón en rosca). Box- office hit (éxito de taquilla), -- - -- receipts (ingresos de taquilla). Warm sth up ↔ cool (fresco, frío, tranquilo) → --sth down, it's cool outside. The oil stained the sea black. Weather the storm (capear el temporal) when a new disease turns up o appears. Capricious (=), delicate (=). They defeated or beat the visiting team 3-2. Time is pressing. Tread sb tenderly/with tenderness. I don't like vagueness (medias tintas). Sit with your back straight + stand up s (ponte tieso)! Cleaner's (tintorería) for linen goods (géneros). What a ugly (feo, peligroso) guy (tipo)! In your innermost (más íntimos, recónditos) thoughts. A draught (corriente de aire, bocanada) from the window + --/draft (de barril) beer =/= drought (sequía) + dry season. The weasel (comadreja) is within range (a tiro). Tug (tirón,V; remolcar, arrastrar) → I felt a -- in my sleeve. Shoot out (salir disparado) =/= Shoot-out/shooting (tiroteo) → we heared shooting (tiroteos) in the pitched battle (batalla campal). Shakily (temblorosa) voice =/= striking (chocante, llamativo) spending. Academic qualifications (títulos), degree certificate (diploma de licenciado), universitary degree (título universitario). The finished touch (toque) before to consume it. I can't bear (tolerar) demanding o exacting (exigentes) people. Quietly (silenciosamente + discretely). He indulges (permite, complace) his whim =/= he induces (=, provoca) … Conspicuous: llamativo, notorio, evidente, que destaca) ↔ discreet ("="), invisible ("="). Thorough (cuidadoso, minucioso) rinse (enjuague) of the glasses, a -- (total) waste of time, --breed (pura sangre, animal de raza). In depth (a fondo), at a -- of 20 meters, in --s of the ocean/forest. A crumb (miga) wend down on he throat (se me atragantó). Stir (remover, agitación, V) → the rigging (tongo) caused quite a stir (fue muy sonado). Stop messing about/ around (de hacer travesuras) when the employees are idling (ganduleando). Tono: (voz) pitch, tone, (color) shades of brawn, ... → an outlook (vista, perspectiva; punto de vista) in tune with young people. Tune: melodía, canción, change one's-- (cambir de parecer), (instrumento) afinar, ... Serious wound → you'll soon be allright. I bumped with (topé con) my granddaughter & my grandchildren, they bumped into each other (chocaron) in the street. An age limit (tope) for the competitors. Fill the glass to the brim (a tope). I banged (golpéé) into (me dí contra) a door; the car crashed into a tree. Crash (alboroto,V, crac financiero, chocar, estrellarse); (enemy, car) aplastar. Tactless (poco discreto/diplomático) mentioning ... The smoke & the vapo(u)r makes me cough. Shift the scenary (decorado), work the early/late shift (primero, ultimo turno), work in --s. Junk (trastos, tirar a la basura) =/= lumber (madera, trastos viejos) room: trastero + boxroom). They reassured/ calmed down (tranquilizaron) the police when they cought the thieving (ladrón, robo). Laid- ack (despreocupado, relajado, tranquilo) in the Upper house (cámara alta). The actor appears/turns up on the stage. The passers-by (transeuntes) obstructed the traffic. See through the blouse. Be accommodating (complaciente)/compromising (comprometido). Oxigen round (por todo) the body. The bottom/buttocks (nalgas) hurts me + get up (levanta) your backside (trasero). Inauguration/opening date of the Olympis games. Opaque ↔ translucid. Transfer the money to her partner (socio); -- me (ponerme) with sales (ventas), (pers.) -- to Boston, teams --ed (transbordados) at Chicago. A mislead (traspapelado) document. The bullet went through his liver but it didn't killed him. Can I turn the sound down? Compensate for all inconveniences (trastornos) issued from the discussion (debate)/argument (riña). The management (direción) ruined the business/her hopes. She drived him crazy (lo sacó de quicio, lo enamoró). Bocina: (car) horn → sound the --, (factory) hooter, (ship) siren/mermaid. Evadir: (pb., difficulty, danger) avoid/ evade + eludir; (responsibility) avoid, (question) avoid, sidestep. A man squints (estrabismo, entrecerrar los ojos, torcer la vista) up at (mira a) telecoms mast (mástil). Apasionante: (wok) exciting, enthralling + cautivador, (subject) fascinating, thrilling. Engrossing (fascinante, apasionante) book. Call in: hacer entrar, (Com.) retirar los malos, -- -- on sb (pasar a verle), -- -- any time (cuando quieras). Secuestrar: (pers.) kidnap, (plane) hijack, (newspaper) seize, (goods) sequestrate/confiscate. Prone (propenso) to muffle (amortiguar; oars/hooves: envolver)d (sordo, apagado) shouting (vocerío). Admirers called J. Serra a Champion of the underdogs (los más déiles, desvalidos) in South America. In aggregate (conjunto, total) consumption looked smooth (liso, en calma, fluido, sin problemas)er than income. The truck broke through (abrió camino)/ down (averió). Rock-bottom (parte más profunda, bajísimos) approval ratings. Practicality (utilidad, sentido práctico + practical; instrumento: handy) of a wedding. Fend for themselves (arreglárselas solos) + -- o.s. (valerse por sí mismos) =/= fend off (desviar, rechazar, esquivar). Tender: tierno, delicado; (oferta, propuesta por un contrato) -- for a contract, put out sth to a -- (sacar algo a concurso). The linguistic prowess (valor, destreza, capacidad, habilidad) as a proxy (poder) for intellectual agility. Auspicious (=, prometedor) → un--: (inoportuna/poco propicia) place to meander (deambular). Imprint: (marca, huella) → leave an -- on/in sth; imprimir, (in mind) grabar =/= impression: (sensación) impression, (acción) printing. Godliness (devoción + "=", piedad (+ piety). Piety: pena, misericordia (+ mercy, compassion). Snatch (agarrar rápido) → --ed the case (maleta) & ran out (salir corriendo); -- the children to safety, -- sth from sb; arrebatar/robar. Trounce: (defeat: derrota) de forma aplastante; zurrar → give sb a -- (paliza).

A sound (acertado) treatment of the subject, as if it were its own. He is too familiar (se toma demasiadas libertades) with the recruits (reclutas); be in familiar terms ←→ they call each other Ud.; treat sb as an equal; how do you address the new manager. In my job I deal with … Get there in time. The trajectory of a rocket. Plait (trenza). Stunner: mujer despampanante, persona estupenda, cosa maravillosa. Climbing (trepadoras) plants for the sad buildings. The court (tribunal) found/ruled (falló) in my favour. When I was running away (me fugaba) I stumbled/tripped & fell. Trophy ("="). Come up against (topar con, enfrentarse a) serious difficulties + confront, have a confrontation. Extract: (juice, tooth, gold) extraer, (of a novel) fragmento, trozo, extracto, (beef/yeast: levadura) extracto. This cheese stings (hace tufo) & it is toxic & poisonous (venenoso) + -- snake. Throes (agonía), he is dying ←→ -- of childbirth (en trance de), -- of (sumido a) a civil war. Quite a few (más de uno) ←→ no one survived. On the top of the other, on top of each other. Cream ("="), ointment ("pomada"), unguent (ungüento). Grease (embadurnar) sth =/= Smear: mancha,V + mark, stain), difamar/calumniar + slander/libel. Brive (soborno, cohecho) him to turn a blue eye. Asbestos (=, amianto, uralita). Planning (urbanismo, planificación), town planner (urbanista) =/= urban development (desarrollo). Fomentar: (industria, turismo) promote, (inversions, ahorros) boost, (odio, disturbio, alboroto) incite. We need emergently …, emergency department (sala de urgencias) in the stadium. Ever since I can remember, he has been always an academic failure. Drain: sumidero/alcantarilla (cloaca); vaciar, drenar, agotar, escurrir, --a glass in one gulp (trago). The police cleared (despejó, aclaró) the premises (locales) & disinfected them. Walk unsteadily (firme, constante) = vacilante. Wander (vagar, deambular) → -- around (vagabundear sin rumbo fijo). Brawn (fuerza muscular)y: musculoso → -- but not attractive. Better later than never. Brave/valiant/

courageous. Diplomatic bag (maleta). Defeat the rival. I don't give up (no abandono, no me doy por vencido) easily. Put a blindfold (vendar los hojos) to sb. Have happy memories of… It amounts to the same thing (viene a ser lo mismo). Mail order. The truth hurts, the true (cierto, verdadero, verídico) is …, trust me (confía en mí)/-- in sth/sb; truly: realmente, verdaderamente. It's embarrassing (envarazoso) to speak in public. Veteran =/= vet (revisar, examinar). Housing (vivienda) shortage, second home, house to let or rent. Apenado: sorry, ashamed, grieved, saddened. Iron railing (reja, cerca, verja, barandilla) =/= railroad/railway (ferrocarril). Loose (suelto) living (mala vida) of the politicians. Dear (querido) → darling (vida mía)! Despicable/nefarious (malvado, despreciable) =/= obnoxious (repugnante, detestable, asqueroso). Bond (vínculo) of friendship =/= blood tie (vinculo sanguíneo). Violador (rapist), violación: (ley) infringement, (acuerdo, principio) violation, breach, (pers.) rape. Sudden (repentino) swerve (viraje). He plays amazing (alucinante, asombroso)/fantastic (una virguería) job. The view from the room has a good sight. Shortsightedness (miopía, falta de perspectiva, de clarevidencia) ↔ a farsighted politician, long-sighted (presvicia, vista cansada). Hatchery (vivero de peces); oyster bed; nursery (guardería, vívero, semillero). Angustiado: worried, anxious, distressed (+ aflijido). Live from hand to mouth (al día). She volunteered (se ofreció voluntario), garment industry (industria de la confección). Loud/quiet voice, in low voice. Shout to be heard. Turn: vuelta, dar vueltas a, girar → the engine --s (hace girar) the wheel, -- round (volverse, dar la espalda); go off (irse, salir). Be quiet (calla)! The swallow flew away (emprendió el vuelo). A high-flying: (executive) de alto vuelo, (career, student) prometedor. Sheduled (regulado) flight. Low-fat (desnatado) youghourt. Stop in our way back. Three laps at the track, the lap of honour, the outcome is in the -- of the gods now (la suerte está echada, ya veremos que pasa). Token (vale, ficha; muestra de apreciación/recuerdo) → as a -- of respect. Social network (red, cadena) ablaze (en llamas, resplandece, prender fuego) → he -- with passion. Pond: (man-made) estanque, (natural) laguna =/= pool (charco natural o artificial, piscina) =/= puddle (charco natural). Mao-suited (apropiado, adaptado) interior. Pin down (identificar, concreter; inmobilizar) a brand loyalty (=, fidelidad). Outbound (dirigir hacia el exterior) tourists. The Earth was cracked (agrietada) & the streams (corrientes) stopped. Dig wells. The wind blew dust down the valley. Shallow (pers., profundidad) superficial. He swung (se balanceó) at him & both fell over the ground. Rapid footsteps (pisadas). Sinless (inocente) boy + innocent, not guilty. Misgivings (dudas, recelos) about a scheme (plan, proyecto, esquema). Main lines (grandes lineas). Cake shop (pastelería). Air strike (ataque), launch an attack, surprise attack, heart attack, nervous breakdown. Connection: (Tf., Electr., trenes) conexión. It sounds great (de maravilla). Rise/ascend ↔ descend, the place came down. Full (lleno, completo), take -- advantage of (aprovecharse al máximo the) the situation. Pull the alarm, release the brake. Make inquiries (buscar, investigación,V). Stand waiting (parado, de pié), we were standing. Christian day (onomástica). Chapeau (brave, well down)! He tried to kiss me but I moved away/stood aside. Fold your arms (crúzate de brazos)!, folding a chair/table/bed for better convenience or suitability (acomodamiento). He supplied (suministró) goods of questionable quality. An eventful (lleno de incidentes, memorable + "=") period. They rised (crearon) nine children. Eventually/finally =/= actually/in reality. A street off (que sale de) the square. A timeless/eternal question. I pretended to be s.o. else, but I didn't achieve it. Tourists from wherever (de donde sea) are welcomed. My mind was disturbed/upside down (trastornada) + turned the house upside down (revolverla). They are similar in character (=, reputation) → he bears good --; personaje + star/main character (protagonista), he starred (protagonizó) 6 films. The settlers (colonos) moved west. Growing awareness (conciencia, =) of ..., be aware (consciente) of ..., Awareness campaign (de concienciación), Pol. --, make aware (concienciar). Accuracy (exactitud), accurate (exacto, preciso) → he is usually -- in his forecasts. Holistic (--o): algo considerado como un todo. Demise: fallecimiento, desaparición + (pers., object) disappearance, (de especies) extinction. The rented/leased premises (locales, inmuebles). Scruffy (dejado, desaliñado) backpacker (mochillero). Rubber (caucho, goma) → rubbery (correoso, gomoso), uncork (descorchar) the bottle; cork (corcho). Jag: (edge, cut) irregular, (rock, cliff: acantilado) cortado, con picos → glaciers jagged peaks. Tube (tubo, TV, metro). Spread: (feet, arms) extensión, (infection, disease) propagación, (idea, information) difusión, (education) extensión, generalización, (wings, maps) despliegue, (disinfectant) esparcir; Vs. Blandly: (say, reply) débilmente, (smile) de manera insulsa (sosa, insípeda: tasteless). Confound: (pers.) confuse, (plan) desbaratar + spoil, ruin, mess up, (sistema) disrupt, (attempt) frustrate. Their annual leave of the stork (cigüeñas) in April. I wore a skirt & matching tie. Outsized (de talla enorme, gigantescas) ambitions. Alarm friends & foes (enemies) alike. Wheezes (respirar con dificultad, con silvidos) =/= wheedle sth out of sb (sonsacar); he --ed me (me engatusó) into going with her. He has stepped up (incrementado) American defense. He remains wedded (casado; empeñado, entusiasmado) to a zero-sum game/view. With defiance (desafío) to anybody (al mass pintado). Hot-heated (exaltado). Weight down (sujetar con un peso). Strong nations look out (tienen cuidado) only for themselves. He is rattling the sabre (lanza amenazas) at Iran. Papelería: (shop/store: tienda) stationer's, (writing'items) stationary. Sheaf (fajo) of papers. Shock (=, impacto, susto; horrorizar, impresionar). Freewheeling (irresponsable, despreocupado). Noose: slipknot (nudo corredizo), rope for hanging (colgarse). Trammel (poner trabas a)led (atado, atrapado) → un-- (libre, ilimitado). Sign: señal, firmar, hacer señas; alistarse, inscribirse, matriularse; reclutar, Sp.: firmar un contrato, Med.: síntoma; -- language (lenguaje por señas). Some areas it vacated (desalojó). Quagmire: atolladero, atascarse, congestión + =, jam-packed (abarrotado de gente), repleto de cosas. Princely: espléndidas, hermosas) sums. Well-heeled (tienen nucho dinero) figures (=,V, cifras, tipos → a nice (buen) --. Louvre A. Dahbi: the new beacon (faro, modelo) to the World. Resplandor: (sol) glare, brightness, (glass, moon) gleam, (rayo, explosión) flash. Vindictiveness: revenge, vengeance, eagerness (afán) of vengeance. Astronomy is stuck (atascada) in a rut (rutina + =, surco; Biol.: celo). The whole set-up (sistema, organización, montaje) weighs … Statutory (establecido por la ley). Get away (escapar) from sth/sb. Plague (=, asediar, acosar) ed by the strikes. Blaze: (fuego) arder; brillar, resplandecer, (ojos) centellear, Putin's brand (marca)/style (estilo) of authoritarianism blazed the trail (marcó el sendero). Recycle bin (papelera de --), empty the bin. It floats faced down. Do you want go anywhere else?, s.o. else got the job. He was caught (atrapado) in the trap (trampa). Think alike (igual). Leave them alone (solos), be alone, in my own, a lonely (solitario) man/childhood. Hernia (=, rupture). He swam back to the shores. They came down & run up to the mountains. He arranged (ordenó, planeó, …) the murder, -- as planed (como previsto). Ghost (escribir) sb's book, speech. Speak from memory (=). Learn by heart. I just (sólo) came up (he subido) to prevent you from te peril/risk. You beg (me pides) to get in (entrar), I beg you! (¡te lo suplico!), beg forgiveness. Say aload (en voz alta). Be faithful (fiel) to one's promises. Fond (tiernas) memories, a-- (tierno) embrace, he is -- of her (le tiene mucho cariño). Wait a little while. The way your body stands (tal como se te ve) you'll win the love (enamorarás) of whoever you try. The water was nice/pleasant (agradable). He wanted to think of sb else except you.

Put away (aparte) the defective, faulty goods/marchandises. Get lost (desorientarse). Tighten (up): (rope) tensar, estirar, (nut, belt, shoes) apretar, (regulations) hacer más severas, (discipline, security) reforzar. Avoid discomford (incomodidad). Desperdiciar una oportunidad: miss/waste/throw away an opportunity. Swimming trunks (de hombre) ↔ s. costume. Run/get away from sb/sth (huir de --/ --); keep away from him! Enjoy (disfrutar) of this magnificient, wonderful day; enjoyable (agradable, divertido). He managed it somehow (de una u otra manera). The love we felt to each other. I shouldn't wonder (no me sorprenderían) the bad news from the Open (a distancia) Unversity, Polytechnic (Universidad laboral). He has a worry/concern (preocupación) that his wife is unfaithful to him. Bother/annoy (molestar) → is this man annoying you?, don't be --ed if I cant come. All the walls (muros, paredes, murallas) were broken down. They took a long time (tardaron mucho) to reply. Resort (centro vacacional, recurso + options, resources) to violence. Thirsty for revenge. Split up: (marriage, matrimony) separarse, (crowd) dispersarse, (re)partir. He laught at me/about … Climb over a wall/to power. The crowd run onto the pitch (campo de Sp.). It's my duty to … Drop the mail into a postbox/mailbox. Two hits (aciertos) & two misses, miss the target, I near -- the train/truck, he narrowly (por poco) --ed the tour (viaje, visita, gira)/being killed. He was frozen of fear as he had been beaten (batido, derrotado). There was not one around (por allí). Where the prisoner have come from? As time went by (transcurría) we became ever & ever poor. They wrestled & she beat him to death. She's zipped into the town (se fue deprisa a la ciudad), zip the bag shut (cerrar la bolsa, la malet) + saco: sandbag, sleeping bag. Be at the forefront (frente, vanguardia) of sth. He was unpleasand (desagradable) with his subordinates. I don't dislike it (no me disgustan) but in the fair are cheapest; his dislike/anthipathy of him. Restless: (mar, viento) agitado, (pers.) inquieta. Throw off (quitarse rápido) the clothes, the illness, … Shake off: (snow) sacudir, (habit) quitarse de encima, (illness) librarse de. Ride off (partir, alejarse de) home ↔ he rode back home. Her eyes grew watchful (vigilantes), under the -- (atenta) eyes (mirada) of him. Dropper (contagotas), ophthalmologic eyedrops (colirio). The pain struck (alcanzó, golpeó) her. Beer, let alone (y aún menos) champagne. A faraway (perdida, remota) look (mirada; aspecto, aire, estilo). Dulled (apagados) eyes & bent shoulders. Bank (orilla) of sand → she climbed up to the level (llano) land & after that he was shot to death. Disrespectful (irrespetuoso). Beauty/prettiness. Get him sent away/dismissed (despedido, Min.: destituido)/fired. Long haired, curly (rizado) --, red -- (pelirrojo). Her repply puzzled me/disconcerted me (me desconcertó). Arose: (suspicion) despertó, (pb.) surgió. He parted/separated the thin branches that hang down to the ground. He sat up/got up (se levantó, subió) & joined (se incorporó) to the work. Turn up: (sleeve) subir, (heat, sound …) poner más fuerte), (the brim of his hat) levantar; aparecer + appear, come out → he --ed two hours late. Live the way they used to … A faintly (debilmente, levemente) remembered friendly relationship (relación amistosa). Unwrap the bandage with gentleness (delicadeza). He made her feel fear & hatred. She slid (deslizó, metió) the capsule into the tube. Very pleased (satisfecho) to meet you, we'll be -- to answer any question (todas sus preguntas), he wasn't too -- that I had sold it, what are you looking so -- about? He looked straight ahead (derecho hacia adelante) multiple/road accidents. Wait your turn, even if you are tired & you need a rest. Lively (alegre, animado) =/= lovely (belleza, encanto/encantador, bonito, alegre; amoroso). We are powerless (no podemos hacer nada) to help you. I & my pet are both defenceless, the wall (muralla) undefended (indefensa). Further up/under the river. We are getting further away (nos alejamos) from … I was sure nobody was aground (encallado). I remained quite still. What was going on (pasaba) there when he got away or escaped? He felt the touch of a hand. I'll be in touch with you as soon as I can. She glanced around (dió un vistazo alrededor) & got (se llevó) a surprise. Did you see anybody? All else (todos los demás) ↔ no one --, what --? (¿qué más?), how --? (¿de qué otra manera?). Behold! (¡mira!) =/= see o detect (observar) an improvement. Appointment (cita, nombramiento) bureau/office + appointed (designado) to be read in the church =/= enlistment (alistamiento), recruitment (reclutamiento). Write plainly (claramente), speak -- to sb. Strongminded (decidido, resuelto) to change the office up a floor. A stage further (una etapa más). Blown bull (bombilla). He swung (osciló) his head toward the desperate people. The offenders (infractores)'s account (cuenta; explicar, considerar) was seized (embargada). Because we are towing (vamos a remolque) we'll arrive or get there late. Roncar: (dormir) snore, (mar) roar. Rule of three, three squared (3 elevado al cuadrado). Provide: suministrar, proporcionar; (against sth) tomar precaución, (for sth) prevenir; provided that (siempre que) … An current (en curso) search. Hermético: =, airtight, watertight, water resistent. Secretive: reservado + reserved/discreed, (subject, document) confidential (secreto). Climb out (salir trepando), climb (up) a tree. He rode away (partió). Race back (volver a toda prisa) if you'll get dinner. Counter desk (contador de facturación, registro). He looked severe (serio, grave), a -- (difícil, riguroso) matter. A fine for speeding (exceso de velocidad). Cabin: cabaña; camarote, cabina =/= booth (cabina de disyokey, de intérprete). He dropped all charges against him. The rope mark (huella) disappear without trace. Your devoted/humble/fervent servant, your obedient (afectísimo). You took me out of the darkness. He stretched out (se extendió) on the grass. Assailant (agresor, atacante). We saw each other every week. Turn over a page. Reach out (extender) his arm. Be/fall asleep, I feel asleep, get to -- (conciliar el sueño). Reparar: undo: desatar, deshacer (the harm), repair/mend/restore forces, correct errors, compensate damages. Tirante: (skin: piel, rope: cuerda) tight/taut, (situation, relations) tense, strained (with her boss). The door became wider & deeper. He made the theory his own. He has money for his own. Cheer (ovación, consuelo; aclamar)ing: ovaciones; alentador, esperanzador. Cheerful: alegre, jovial; alentador, animado. It was beginning to be light. They haven't spoken to each other since… You should have listened to me. Meadow/pasture (dehesa) =/= prairies/grasslands (praderas). Duck (esconderse, agacharse) out of: escabullirse de =/= Buck: pas the -- (escurrir el bulto: eludir el riesgo), -- up (animarse), deer/rabit male, $ =/= bulck: bulto, masa, the -- (mayoría) of th work; buy in --s (al por mayor). Unforeseen, unexpected, sudden (imprevista) bank failure, fraudulent bankruptcy. He went to look for him. Cólera: anger, rage; colérico: angry, furious, irritable, bad-tempered; coléricamente: angrily. He was holding (sostenía) the letter. Peaceful (pacifico, =). He got off her horse & went in. You are unkind (duro, desagradable) to him. Unfurl/unfold (desplegar) the flag. D-Lama: Internet freedom is naked (desnuda; manifiesta, visible, ostensible) scheming (intrigante, maquinador (que trama). Obviously/evidently (ostensiblemente). Cog: diente, piñón; rueda dentada) → just a -- in the wheel (una pieza del mecanismo, nada nás). Compound: (nº/química/palabra) compuestos, (pb.) agravar), (riesgo) incrementar, (interés) compuesto, be --ed (acompañado) with sb, be -- (compuesto) of sth (algo). Without demur (objection): recatado, we have --ed/doubt (dudado). In sheer amazement (absolutamente asombrado, estupefacto). Off stage: fuera de escena, entre bastidores, preparar en secreto. Soviet sump (sumidero, foso séptico, letrina). Vendetta (persecución) → pursue/carry on a -- against sb (… campaña contra alguien). Be operative/applicable (en vigor). Sprinkle (rociar, salpicadura, V, esparcir)r: esparsor, regadera → -- out (esparcir). Cook- up (tramar) an excuse. Raising prosperity.

Rub (frotar, restregar) → don't -- your eye, -- the glass clean, -- the shoes against/on my heels, -- off (quitar frotando, restregando). Unseemly (decente, decoroso): impropio, indecente, indecoroso =/= seamless: perfecto, (knitting: tejido) sin costuras, de una pieza. Pessimistic ↔ upbeat (optimista + (=, hopeful) =/= downbeat: (gloomy) deprimente, (mood, atmosphere) relajados. Bankers would to grip with (enfrentarse a) weakness. Store: reserva/almacén, tienda; guardar, acumular, almacenar, amasar dinero. Munch/chew: masticar. A middle of the road (mediocre) man. The crisis bring success in the junk (pulgas) market. Tap into: (Comp.) acceder ilegalmente, (sb's market/ideas, one's potential) aprovechar. Humble (humilde) → --bly (humildemente). Meek (dócil) → (docilidad) meekness/docility. Stocky: fornido (bajo y robusto) =/= sturdy (robusto, macizo, resistente; tenaz. Boggling (que deja pasmado/patidifuso, alucinante). Crowding-out (desplazamiento) → the exotic plants crowd the native out; crowed (abarrotados). Head off: interceptar, atajar, cortar el paso; prevenir (a resurgence in Catalonia, ...). Remain in detention (=, arresto). Keen/admirer (entusiasta) ↔ half heartedly (poco entusiasta), she is delighted (encantado) with the dress; deleite: placer, deleite, regocijo. Foundation (de base, preparatorio) course, -- stone (primera piedra). Purchase the whole set (juego) or individual items (artículos, piezas de una colección). Organisations or individual/particular citizens. Suit (traje; satisfacer, convenirle) =/= it should be remembered (convendría recordar) that this is a serious matter). The cusp (cúspide) of development. Segregated: (races, sexes) segregar, (rival groups) mantener aparte. Ugly: feo, (crime) horrible, (news) inquietantes. It will freeze tonight + quedarse inmóvil: -- of fear; -- to death. Outflow: desagüe, flujo de capital. Junk bonds (bonos basura) & a lot of traps (trampas). Prime (principal, de primera) property. He doesn't look his age, but he is too old for you. Flotation: issue new shares/loans, (barco) flotar. Frantic/

frencied: desesperado, frenético (con frenesí: delirio, locura) → -- lending, at a -- pace (a ridmo vertiginous). Grey market: mercado negro para cuando hay escasez de algo. Sanctimony: moralización, mojigatería (de hipócrita/beato), humildad y beatería para conseguir algo. Topple (volcar, derrocar) the long-running Tokugawa on 1867 + long-running (que viene de largo, con mucho tiempo en cartelera). Stones missing in the wall. Of humble/noble parentage (ascendencia familiar), of unknown --. Be in the pink: estar en plena forma, rebosante de salud. Tidy o.s. (asearse). Taxi stand/rank (parada) + cardial arrest, a direct (sin paradas) train, bus stop. Store up (almacenar) hatred. Samples for testing new virus, test new vaccines =/= hacer testamento (make a will). A stampede (desbandada) for the door. Go along (hacer algo sobre la marcha) with (acompañar, secundar) his plans + I make corrections/I chek as I -- -- (sobre la marcha). He took the book away (se lo llevó). The room directly below this one, 50 m. below the surface, below average (de la media). My dream became true. A woman screamed/shrieked (chillaba). Insipid/tasteless ↔ tasty/delicious (sabroso). The sheet of instructions. He lost consciousness of his main duties. Ramp renewable electrical generation up (aumentar) to half the total. He pushed the lever (palanca) & the Electr. shot through his body. The lecturer (conferenciante) speaks aload (en voz alta). The robe (traje, bata, túnica) rub (frota) his skin when time is hot/warm. Pray (orar), say the rosary. They must be millions left (quedaron) … There was little left of the body, of his previous wealth. Badly (gravemente) hurt. Burns (quemaduras), sunburns, third-degree --. Whose prisoner am I? Burn the body to hide evidence. Gain weight steadily (constantemente). Overbilling/overcharge (cobrar de más). He wrote plays (obras, juegos) for TV. Basement/cellar (sótano). Acertijo (riddle, puzzle, jigsaw, conundrum) → puzzling (desconcertante) → it is -- (curioso, raro) que …; he was puzzled (perplejo, desconcertado). Farewell (de despedida) party, dinner, gift & words. He had to make him take the pills before he becomes ill. Outer (exterior) wall/island/garment. He waved his arms at the taxi, but the cab driver was deaf to his entreatises (súplicas). Lobby (=; antesala, vestibulo, pasillo). Serious: serio, formal, grave. Anthipaty/dislike. They didn't like each other/one another. A yawning (enorme) wealth gap. In its guise (apariencia, forma) as Islamic front; under the guise of ... Stability is not a turning point (punto decisivo). The ivy (yedra) is not edible. He strode up & down (iba y venía a zancadas en) the platform (plataforma, tarima, tablado, estrado). He came striding (a zancadas) down the street. The brewing (elaboración, tramado) of troubles. A defeat attributed to fraud. Dole out (repartir) building contracts, money, food =/= (repartir ganancias) distribute/share out, (propaganda) hand out. Renano did not junks (chatarra, tirar a la basura, desechar una teotía) the peace deal. The government badly (malamente, miserablemente) was misguided (equivocado, desencaminado). Public mood (clima, aire, humor) =/= moot (plantear, establecer una discussion)ed: discutible. The forces arrayed (expuestas, desplegadas, en formación) against it. The stablishment twise saw off (despidió) subsequent (=, posterior) loyals to ... Incensed (furiosos, encolerizados) that the judge let off (perdonó, dejó salir) ... Rable (chusma, gentío)- rousing (enardecedor, entusiasta) → -- - -- (demagogo, agitador) speech. Deliberatelly/on purpose. A remote-controled aircraft prowling (rondando, merodeando) the skies. Petrifying/terrifying (aterrador, espantoso). Outflank: aventajar, (Mil.) flanquear, batir por los lados. Bride (novia) =/= he bridles (se pica, se molesta + get annoyed/upset). Spew: (water) salir a borbotones, (volcano) vomitar, (flames) arrojar. Retrenchment (racionalización, disminución the gastos) of the government. Staunch: incondicional, firme, fiel, vigoroso, acérrimo, (sangre) contener. He went broke (se arruinó) & his woman went with another man. The court pronounced/passed (dictó) sentence. Dragooned (presionado, obligado a hacer algo). Snubbed (despreciado, desairado, rechazado) Abe. Bordering on (limitando con) C. Asia. The Amazon is by far the longest. Plummeting (cayendo en picado) on a 16 km. stretch (tramo) of tunnels. Joined (unido) by the bridge. The car ploughed/plowed; chocked, crasched, collided against the pedestrians. Turnabout/around: giro radical. Progressive ↔ regressive countries shudder (vibran, se estremecen) at all this; estermecer: (de orror) shudder, (casa) shake, (miedo) tremble. Grievances/complaints (quejas). They attribute/ascribe (atribuyen) outbreaks of violence, disease, hostilities to … Potholes (baches, grutas). Property (=, inmueble) bust (quiebra, bancarrota). Nestled (acurrucados, enclavados) in the hillside. It ranks (rango) fourth + rank among (figura entre) … Undergoing (sufrir, experimentar) a harsh (riguroso) enconunter (choque) with reality. A painfully (dolorosa) recession. Levy (imponer, cobrar) on … + (multa, pena) impose; a duty (obligación, impuesto + tax). Punishment ↔ such an act cannnot go unpunished. ebt- ridden (agobiados). A one-off (único, excepcional) forgiveness (perdón). The World bank comments sparked a rout (causaron una derrota aplastante, hicieron salir en desvandada). Past (más allá de) its vettings (exámenes, investigaciones). The edge (borde) of the cliffs (precipicios). Fight back/counterattack. Munificiently (generosamente) funded (financiados). Swoop (redada) =/= snoop: (atisbar/acechar; fisgar: husmear, olfatear, indagar; si es por costunbre: fisgonear). Catalonia was championed (defendida) by Natonal aeroautics and space administration (NASA). Get in (entrar) on: tomar parte en =/= get on in (entrar en el sistema). Tracked down (localizado + localised) in Westminster. Display (expo, muestra; presentación, manifestación). Google has brought forward (adelantado, presentado) … Bajar: (mano, cabeza) put down, (persiana, precio) lower; (fiebre) bring down. Unaware that anything was amiss (había ningún problema). Words & deeds. Next of kin (familiares más cercanos). Bare (desnudo)-bone (hueso): muy limitado → a -- - -- living (vivir con lo mínimo). Astutamente: shrewdly, cleverly, astutely, craftily, cunningly. He schmoozes (cotillea, chismorrea, habla para establecer contactos) with his opponents. Business mogul (magnates) + shipment magnat/tycoon + oilmen --. Tackle (abordar, emprender) it piecemeal (poco a poco) rather than in comprehensive (total, integral) bill (programa completo). Over-reach (ir más allá de lo possible) abroad & a string (cinta, cuerda; serie, hilera) of pbs. at home. Halting (entrecortado, titubeante, vacilante) speech. Slim (esbelto, escaso, delgado; adelgazar), I'm --ming. Grid (rejilla, red) → national -- (red de suministro de electricidad nacional), gridlock: colapso, paralización de la circulacón, punto muerto de las negociaciones. Dilatory (lentos, tardíos) regulators. Tardiness (lentitud, retraso), slowness (lentitud, torpeza), life moves at a slow pace. The bank saddled (cargado) with defaults (impagos). Glitzer (más ostentoso/glamoroso) grow of premises (establecimientos, locales, oficinas). Financial trauma is as row (crudo; serie, fila; riña; remar) as if it had just happened. Outdoor (al aire libre). A 3% drawdown (bajada) implied an expansioning (expansionista) impulse of the Ec. Cull: (flores) escoger, (información) seleccionar, matanza selectiva. Traipse (recorrerse, patearse, andar penosamente) from administration to finances → it's a bit of a -- (buen trecho, caminata) to the shop. Yard (patio, jardín, corral; almacén) → slippery (resbaladizo) junkyard (chatarrería). Rutted (llenas de roderas) roads. Group of every stripe (lista, raya, tendencia). Climbdown/reverse (marcha atrás) ↔ showdown (enfrentamiento + confrontation, Sp.: encounter) =/= the Ec. has taken a downturn (bajón, deterioro). Shrine (santuario) → en- (consagra) equal voting rights regardless of race. Go unnoticed (pasar desapercibido) + slip away (escabullirse) unnoticed. Disgruntled: (tone, boy, look: mirada) contrariados, (employee, clerck/office worker) disatisfecho. Spawn (engendrar, producir) vile (=, repugnante) harmless (inofensivos, =) extremists. Corruption is patchy (desigual). They passed around (de uno a otro, entre todos) photografies. Breakneck (vertiginosa) speed. The strength (fuerza, solidez, entereza, energía) to carry on (seguir adelante, continuar con). Snippets (fragmentos, extractos) of Mozard. The oil riches (abundancias) anchor (ancla, anclar; aseguran, afianzan) the federation. The core (centro, núcleo) of interest in America is terrorism. The world's tallest building is a symbol of what looks like heedless (despreocupado, irresponsable) excess. High-rises blocks (edificios de muchas plantas, muy altos). Dull (triste, aburrido; insípedo, apagado) =/= dud (falso, estropeado, invendible, pila descargada, cheque sin fondos) =/= dim: oscuro, borroso, nada prometedor, lerdo/tarugo; debilitar, atenuar). The opposite direction/side/opinion. Unaware (ignorar) =/= unprepared/unready (desprevenido) → catch -- =/= unwary (imprudente). They outnumbered us. Dubious/suspect/suspicious acquaintances → maque the -- of sb =/= acquiescence (consentimiento) =/= assumption (suposición). High ranking (categoría, grado) =/= (piso) luxury =/= (mujer) high standing. I must get a move on (cambiar de trabajo) to a biggest company. Suspicion/mistrust (suspicacia/sospecha). Cub: (animal) cachorro → wolf/lion --; (youngster) jovenzuelo. This detergent vanish (elimina) dirt. The archaeology findings (hallazgos) suggest a previous settlement. The wheels are secured by 3 nuts (tuercas). It doesn't make sense (no tiene sentido). They aren't sold singly/separately. A lucky man & a wrech(ed) (desgraciada) woman. Left (abandonado) to his fate. Band (banda, tira) to hold the hair up =/= ribbon: cinta de adorno o para envolver =/= tape recorder (grabadora) with magnetic tape. Peg (clavija; asegurar, ropa: fijar) → properly pegged (sujetadas) clothes, so the wind doesn't blow them away. The bill adds up/comes up to …, lump sum (suma total), the total expense, add this two accounts. Add (together), divide/split, substract/take away, multiply, deduct. The fare (pasaje, billete; precio, tarifa) exceed ours expectations. The film turned out (resultó) ... Various pbs. came up. He was a carpenter by trade (de oficio), learn a trade. Assortment (colección, surtido). Trend/tendency → a word which is tending to become archaic; dominant trend or prevailing tendency (tendencia imperante). Fundamental (=), basis (=, fundamentos) + groundless or unfounded belief. Asistencia: (school) attendance, (help) assistance =/= assistand (ayudante). Hold back (retener; información: ocultar) + keep out of sight (ocultar de la vista). Delay our departure, delayed action bomb. On time/punctual (puntual). Impresive (impresionante) career. Revival: (custom, usage) recuperación/vuelta, (old ideas) resurgimiento, (Med.) reanimación. Charge to sb's account. You're a special case (situación aparte), he took her aside to confide in her (se la llevó aparte para contarle sus confidencias). Statement (estado) of accounts (cuentas). A well/badly brought up child. Affectionate/warm (cariñoso). Impolite (mal educado, descortés). Set: (keys) juego, -- of dishes/crockery (vajilla), the jelly (gelatina) is -- (cuajada), at a -- (señalado) time. Atrasado: the train left late, (pago) overdue, arrears; reloj (slow ↔ fast), (pb.) be a bit behind. Don't contradict (contradecir) me! (¡no me repliques!). The oven has a timing mechanism (reloj automático). Appraise (tasar, valorar, apreciar) + the damages has been estimated or assessed at thousands of millions). Get off: (del tren) apearse, what time you -- -- (sales)?, lid, top, ring, stain, shoes (quitar + remove). Extraer: remove + =, pull out. Rescatar: (minero, prisionero) rescue, free, (dinero, bracelete) recover, get back. Get better (mejorar) + business is picking up (los negocios mejoran). He does it to impress (impresionar). Enjoy yourself/your meal, did you enjoy the game? Meanwhile/meantime (mientras tanto) → I'll be right there, --/-- you get it all ready (llegaré enseguida, mientras tanto, prepáralo todo). Enfadarse: get annoyed/

angry. I have to speak in public. Rentabilidad: profitability/ return of an investment. Achieve a return (ganancia, rendimiento) of $ 1 bn, quick --s, --s of investment. It's worthwhile (vale la pena) getting there early. Hostess (anfitrion/a) ↔ guess. Tank: depósito, cisterna, tanque. He entrusted the task to an assistant (=). Make waves (causar sensación) + I've a feeling (sensación) that... Ondas: (hair) waves, (land) ondulating, shortwave, medium wave, sound wave. I'm extremely worriet about the matters pending (pendientes). Get/have a secure (firme) foothold (punto the apoyo) in the market/in politis. Charming/delight (placer, deleite) → delightful: encantador, delicioso, muy agradable. Decline: descenso, disminuir; decadencia, deterioro,V. Puesto/tenderete: news stand/kiosk, (market) stall. Demanding/exacting (exigente) → she is very particular about cleanliness (limpieza). Blend: (pers.) grupo, (ingrediente, colores) mezcla + mix children of different abilities (niveles) in the same clase. Tranquilo: ¡--! (relax!) → I feel better now that I --ed; (lugar) quiet, peaceful, tranquil; lead a quiet life, (medio ambiente, mar, pers.) calm. His mother is in the hospital & he is not worried, bothered or perturbed. Swan (cisne) about/around (andar pavoneándose) =/= swank (fanfarronada), --ky (fanfarrón + loudmouth, show-off, bragger; (brag) jactarse. Sign up for (apuntarse para). Work out: idear, calcular; resolver, resultar. Thick-headed (tozudo). Final demand/call: last notice (último aviso). Utilizar: which means of transport do you use?, he let me use this computer, (recursos) harness. Tranquilizante: reassuring, (Med.) tranquilizing + she stopped worrying (se tranquilizó) when she found out (al saber) that they had arrived safely. A brandy will calm you down. Deploy: (riquezas) utilizer, (Mil.) desplegar. Thoughtful (amable, pensativo, considerado)ness: amabilidad, consideración. Bear (soportar) misfortunes (desgracias). Affable: =, atento, agradable, cordial, afectuoso. It will have taken heart (ánimos) from Catalonia. We do our best to please, do as you please, he's eager to please, -- the customers ←→ reluctantly (de mala gana) → he accepted their advise --. Rizar: (pelo) curl, (mar) ripple + onda. The phrase is underlined to make it stand out (que resalte); he --s out thanks to his modesty. Crush/put down (sofocar) a rebellion. What length is it? Twise the -- of the golf course & the football field/pitch. Elude (=, burlar, escapar, esquivar) =/= escurridizo: (nudo) slipknot, (pers.) slippery, (idea, actitud, respuesta) elusive. What height are you?, of average --, gain/lose --, at a -- of 200 m. above he sea level. --ten (acentuar, realzar, destacar). Extend the room, expand the period, enlarge the photo, amplify the son/voltios, broaden studies. Emit shutter (de obturador, pestigo, persiana) sound. Promotor: (constructión) developer, (show) promoter, (strike) instigator. The web thronged (atestada) with furtive/ surreptitious photos. Debris: escombros, desechos, detritus. A low-lying (bajo) cost to eke out (estirar, hacer alcanzar) a living (ganarse la vida) by fishing. Pork-barrel: destinar dinero a proyectos que pueden no ser rentables con fines electoralistas (electioneering). Ludicrous, absurd, ridiculous buzz (de moda) words. He has collided (chocado, colisionado, enfrentado) with ... The lens covers providers seclusion (aislamiento), live in seclusion. Chairman (president)ship: presidencia. A run-of-the-mill (ordinario, común y corriente) camera, they're very common (ordinario) people. Impaired/damaged (dañadas) memories, people with impaired vision. Hyped: exagerado, promocionado con bombo y platillo. Loss of frankness (franqueza), I'll be quite frank with you. Take photos simply by a blinking (pestañeo, parpadeo). Build up area (zona urbanizable) ←→ green belt. A good recall, don't remind me ... Hair with a blond highlight (reflejo; destacar, realzar). Ass (asno, imbécil; culo) → lick sb's ass. Edge: it --s (bordea) ..., leaves --ed with read, his performance lacks -- (mordacidad), sharp -- (cortante), --gy (de vanguardia). Empty the glass, empty/ turn out the pokets, hollow out (ahuecar). Todavía: still in bed, haven't you finished yet, they are even/still richer, you still defend him. Rubber ring/life preservar (flotador para la cintura). Alluring (de manera seductora) → seduce, attract, captivate. Aniquilar: annihilate/destroy/destruct: (relations, hopes, ...) destrozar, (vermin) exterminar. Outing/excursion (=); excursionista: tourist, hiker (+ senderista) + treck (caminar, caminata) → treker. Front: (edificio) fachada, (camisa) pechera, (automóvil) parte delantera, be in -- (llevar la delantera), portada de libro (title cover, front cover) ↔ back cover. Conjunto: (clothes) outfit, combined operations/effords; (works) collection, (pers.) group. Cravenly/cowardly. Proceed: proceder; avanzar, proseguir. Collection (tax: recaudación), tax collector, (post, rubbish) recogida. Shut out (excluir) from ... Applications for vacancies (vacantes). Aplicado: (ciencia, técnica) applied; diligent, hardworking. Ongoing: (en curso) → the -- (no resuelto) pb.; en desarrollo. Back away/off/down: retroceder + move back, go backwards. Envolver: (paquete) wrap, (con capa, con membrana) surround; shrouded in fog/gloom (niebla/tristeza), --ed in a mistery. Blub/snivelling (lloriqueo). Take heart (coger ánimo) + he is in better spirits (tiene mejor ánimo), be in low spirits, cheer sb up (dar ánimos a alguien), rise one's spirits. Rouse: despertar, (león...) provocar, the speech --ed (enardeció) the crowd. Slumber: sueño, dormitar → the village lay --ing (la ciudad dormía apaciblemente). X-ray (radiografía). Renta: (beneficio) income, (alquiler) rent, (del trabajo) earned incomes; customs duties, taxable income/source of income =/= revenue: ingresos, rentas, (of country) rentas públicas, (of investments) rédito, oil/... --. Break off: (ej.: chocolate) partir, (engagements, relations, diplomacy) romper, (piece of ice) desprenderse. Blare (estruendo, trompetazo). Priceless (inestimable, invalorable). Social status. Marker (marcador, jalón, poste indicador) → put down a -- (dejar una señal); status markers (indicadores) =/= buoy: boya, aboyar, señalar con --. Mother tonge for the indigenous/native.

Sponsor: patrocinar, --dor + patron, mecenas (+ maecenas). Heavy-handed (severo, torpe) control. Turncoat (chaquetero), become a turncoat (cambiar de chaqueta + change sides). Lacquer, hair spray (laca), nail polish. Describe it poignantly, moving, touching (conmovedor) =/= knock (golpe) → fight bare-knocked (sin guantes, a puño limpio), bare to the waist, barefooted. Onslaught: arremeter, ataque + attack → make a furious -- on a critic (=). Peter- out (irse agotando + run out). Profits/crowd funnelled (encauzados) into ... Masquerade (baile de mascaras, farsa) =/= fencing (para esgrima) mask, unmask sb. Madriguera: (conejos) warren, (zorros) earth, (tejones) set, (maleantes) den, lair. Highly praised (elogiados) by the critics. Lata: tin, can; bore, nuisance. Mushy (blando, pulposo; sensiblero, sentimentaloide). Penny pinches (coger, pellizco, V, robar): tacaño, pesetero. The waiting seemed to go on forever. Put in hold (espera) while judges ..., it was an endless wait (la espera fue interminable). Property (=, inmueble) development (promoción, "="). Skillful/clever/ingenious (mañoso). Screwdriver (destornillador). Seco: (piel, pelo) dry, (higos, ...) dried =/= skinny/thin (flaco) → get --, his weak point/his weaknes (su punto flaco). Stupid, idiot, dump (+ mudo), silly, dummy. Selfcentered (egocéntrico). Beforehand (de antemano, con anticipación) + do sth in good time, arrive early o in good time, book (reservar) early or in advance. Sholar (erudito, sabio, estudioso) → a famous Dickens -- (un conocido especialista de --). Fair play (juego limpio), a neat play (una bonita jugada), be out of -- (estar fuera de fuego). Try on (probarse) → can I try this shirt on?, try a larger size. Self-conscious (tímido, cohibido, afectado). Press clipping (recortes) for my superior. Self-reliant (independiente + independent) → independientemente que: irrespective or regardless of whether ... Turn down: (vol., T) bajar, (obra, trabajo) rechazar ←→ -- up: (aparecer) → we waited but she didn't -- --; he --ed up two hors late). He revealed the names of her accomplices (cómplices), complicity/involvement (complicidad). Apply for (solicitar), apply in writing. Aclarar: (tiempo) clear up, (pb.) clarify. Open up yauning (enormes) gaps (vacíos, brechas, desfiladeros, (vegetación) claros, espacios, huellas, huecos, intervalos, abismos (+ chasms). Silliness (tonterías) ↔ let's be serious (=, formal). The dog scratched (arañó) at the door, it's just a -- (solo es un rasguño), start from-- (empezar de cero), be or come up to -- (cumplir con los requisitos). Rush headlong at (lanzarse de cabeza). The bus stalled (paró) suddenly, unexpectedly. Dwarf: enano, (building, person) empequeñecer, hacer que parezca pequeño, (achievement) eclipsar → I felt --ed by him (me sentia pequeño ...), his achievements --ed those of his rivals. Google grapples (forcejea, se confronta) to the ruling (fallo + decision, ruling) on the boundary (límite) between privacy & free speech. It is on the rampage (pasa arrasando) across the pond (charco, estanque). The storm/tempest devastated the crops or swept the crops away. Bulging (muy llenos, a reventar) order books. Inwardlooking (intrometida, centrada en sí mima) person. An enduring (duradero) friendship, affection (cariño, afecto); (en cartas) your affectionately. Ravine/gully (barranco) =/= gulp: bocanada de aire, trago de líquido → "yes", he said with a -- (tragando saliva). Stubbornly/obstinately (obstinadamente). They devoted themselves (se dedicaron a) ... Set bounds (límites) to one's ambitions + (Pol./Geogr.) boundaries, borders. Status (rango, situación) maker (=, jalón, indicador) in high-tech. hubs → ideas are as much as a -- -- as cars are in the oil belt (zona, cinturón). Debit balance (saldo deudor), debit card (tarjeta de cobro automático) =/= cart (carro, carretilla) → I had to -- his books about all day. Push ahead (seguir adelante) & pounce on (lanzarse sobre) the prey. Devise/device (concebir) new devices (artefactos, aparatos, mecanismos, estratagemas). He is but a child (sólo un crío) & without experience. Disenfranchisment (privar de derecho de representación y de voto). Be moved to tears (llorar de emoción). Longuish (bastante largos) texts. Lounge/parlor (salón), en el hotel: reception room. Feudo: (Hist.) fief, (Sp.) they won on their own ground. Burnishing (mejorando) its image, (en Ec.) improve, pick up. Patch up (hacer las paces, remendar) with the South. On the back (a consecuencia) of growing trade. Brand-new (flamante) underwater, submarine. Towed back (remolcado hacia atrás). Go with/against stream + come on stream (en funcionamiento). Overstate/exaggerate. Treasured/prized (preciada + amigo: valued, steemed) autonomy. Be skint/on the rocks (no tener un céntimo). Rescue (de salvamento) operations. A ragtag/mishmash (mescolanza + hotchpotch, hodgepodge) of smaller political parties surrounded the main two. Restrictive measures, measurements of the table =/= restrain (refrenar, contener, disuadir) sb from doing sth, -- o.s. (contenerse). Disclos<u>e</u> (revelar) it altogether (total); disclos<u>ur</u>e (revelación) of its dockyards/shipyards (astilleros). A good smooth start of Hong kong; its ideas may catch on (imponerse + impose; cuajar, tener éxito) elsewhere. House (alojar) troves (tesoros + treasures) + be worth a fortune (valer un tesoro), yes, my darling! (¡sí, tesoro!). The disgruntled (descontentos + dissatisfied) of affluence (opulencia, bienestar económico). The new tech. stars can get away (salir) with (llevarse, permitirse) diversification. Depressed (deprimidos). Amnisty, tax break (amnistía fiscal) ↔ taxpayer (contribuyente) =/= each person contributed with € 20. International push (empuje, esfuerzo, (Mil.) ofensiva). Rosy (optimista + "=", hopeful) dusk (atardecer + get dark). Flagship (buque insignia, punta de lanza) → odd newspaper is the -- of his media empire (medios de comunicación de masas). Peru tackled (abordó, se enfrentó a) tax evasion. Stock depleted (agotados) by overfishing. Screen: mosquitera, pantalla; the big --, ocultar (the hose by the trees), protect from the enemy, (TV) emitir, (cine) proyectar. Lousy: (Ec.) pésima, (comida, tiempo) asqueroso. Uphold (sostener, mantener, Jur.:confirmar) religion rights. Give/lend sb a hand. Run out of (quedarse sin) time =/= runt: (animal) el pequeño, (pers.) mequetrofe, (Grecia) pequeño en la € zona. The submarine ran aground (encalló). The machine is gummed up (paralizada + "="). The chomage stands (resiste, aguanta) at 15%. Turmoil: (confusión, agitación + upheaval), (upheaval en Geo.) levantamiento. Save one's carcass (pellejo). I can't abide (soportar) cowards + --ing (duraderas, permanents) fixations (obsesiones) Bombastic (pomposo, grandilocuente + "="). Procrastinaton (indecisión) → he procrastinated (aplazó) a decision; his procrastination cost him the deal (contrato). Muhammad rubbed (frotó) shoulders (se codeó) with Jews. Cherish (querer, apreciar, acariciar); get ma/be furious (ponerse furioso). Hard to fathom (Náut,: sondear; misterio: entender, desenterrar). Despise (despreciar). Grievances procedures (trámites de quejas). Barter (trueque) deal. Red crosses hoisted (izadas) off the building. Heap (montón) of praises (elogios). Foremost (principal, en primer lugar) credit. It puts paid (puso fin) to all that. He is beholden (tiene obligaciones) to them; behold the result! (¡he aquí los resultados!). Ruddy (rojizo, coloradote)-cheeked. He has conjoined (unido) Taiwanese Ec. closer to China. Solace (consuelo, comfort,V), console o.s. (consolarse) → it's one consolation for not having gone. A change in the offing (perspectiva); good prospects (perspectivas) of/for improvement (mejoras). He talked up (exageró; valor/Ec.: inflar) the Constitution. Spell out (deletrear, explicar con detalle), talk out/speak out (hablar abiertamente, expresar su opinión); speak up (hablar más alto, decir lo que piensas). Mouthpiece/spokesman (portavoz). The poroduct line-up (Sp.: alinenación + alignment; teatr.: reparto); the sharing out of the inheritance gave rise to (originó) disputes, wealth is not evenly (equilibradamente) distributed. Courtier/polite: cortesano/cortés (atento, comedido, amable). The pledge (garantía, señal, promesa) of sincerity; a company's -- of satisfaction to its cunsomers, pledge of support (promesa de apoyo) from 150 MPs. Make inroads (avanzadas) into the japanese market, -- -- into (comerse) the savings, make -- -- (avanzan) into enemy territories. The desired effect of an fast-acting (efecto inmediato) painkiller; it begins to work/take effect immediately/at once. Harried (acosado, agobiado, hostigado) by 22 legionaries & by 20 conscientious objectors. Indeed (en efecto), side effect (-- secundario) of delayed (de efecto retardado) action. The public carping (las quejas continuas sin motivo). A confused explanation; his brain's confused, let's not confuse things, please. Racy: picante; brioso, animado. Wrongheaded (pers.) obstinada, ofuscada, (attempt) desatinado, desacertado) → --ness: desatino + foolishness, tactlessness (sin tacto). Zealots (fanáticos, "=") to critizise =/= censure, censorship. Ridículo: =, absurd, ludicrous. Broken down before being dumped (tirado, abandonado). Suscitar: arouse interests, raise doubts. Kindle: despertar (enthusiasm, hope) in sth; fire/light/wood/desire (encender) → rekindle (reanimar). Rant: vocerío, sermón, despotriqueo,Vs; vituperio (reprobación). A splurge (derroche) of coal will make it harder for African states to uphold (mantener) growth. Rape (violación, destrucción, expoliación). Buckle (hebilla, torcer) → Madrid --s (se dobla) under the weigh of cleaner's strike. Repeal/abrogation (abrogación, revocación) =/= repel/repulse (repeler). Plucky (valeroso, bravo; valiente) ↔ feckless (débil, irresponsable, incapaz). Items in the in-tray (bandeja de entrada, asunto principal) → it's at the top of my -- (es lo primero que haré). Young men lounge (salón, gandulear; (estar arrellanado) in his chair. Upmarket: (hotel, vehicle, store) para gente pudiente) ↔ the grottier (más cutre, asquerosa) industry. Cobrar (charge) ↔ client/customer: pagar (pay). Gambit (táctica, estrategia) of the schrewd/astute. Caja de caudales: safe, strongbox. A downgrading (decadente, que pierde categoría) management. Blandishments (alagos, lisonjas) to the ruling/leader (gobernante). Tantalising (oferta, perfume, …: tentador, que atrae) → six World powers & Irán came --ly (tentadoramente) close (a punto de entenderse). In exchange for relief (alivio) on debt-sanctions. Trump flew into (llegó en avión) to clinch (abrazar, cerrar) a deal. Israel's existing stockpile (acumular, reservas) being turned into the weapons-grade (de uso military) stuff. It falls short of (no alcanza) Iran giving away (obsequiando, revelando) in ful their demands. Foreigners in S. Arabia are packed off (mandados, despachados) joining an exodus, so they will free jobs for locals. Those of menial (servil, de poca confianza, de baja calidad) kind. Most Saudis endorse (endosan, respaldan) the crackdown. When the electricity flickers (parpadea) on the TV screen. Lock him up (con llave) for ever. They live in shelters (refugios, alojamientos) & go to school on armoured buses. Closing data (fecha límite) → -- -- sale (liquidación por cierre). Harshness (rigor, dureza) towards dissent (disidencia, disconformidad). Private health in Africa: insurers have spotted (descubierto, manchado) an opening for no-frills (sencillo, sin lujo) but life-saving (que salva la vida, socorrismo) health care. Unlicensed outpatients departments (dispensarios para los de fuera). Spare (de más, de sobras, de reserva) =/= scare (susto, V, bomb --: amenaza de bomba, be --ed: tener miedo, estar asustados) =/= scarce (escasos) health inspectors → they are getting shirty (se cabrean) about it. Mauled (atacado; vapuleado, destrozado, aplastado) by a fighting bull; Obama was flayed (despellejado, recibió una paliza) from the critics. Trespassing (entrar sin permiso, entrometerse) against (violando) … The sentences, judjements & rulings are mandatory/compulsory (obligatorios). Ruling: (clase) dirigente, (partido pol.) en el poder, (monarquía) reinante; factor dominante, precio vigente, Jur.: resolución, fallo. Blaks are 29 times more likely to receive such sentences: in some states the number is yet more skiwed li(torcido, desviado). Make drugs harder to buy or Americans less likely to get high ("colocarse").

Probation: libertad provisional, periodo de prueba. Public benefits: food stamp, housing assistance. Garbled: (information/ account) confused, (text) undescifrable, (image) blured. Poach (birlan) foreign brainpowers. Foreign students rised by 40% over the past decade to a high of one million. The numbers are levelling off (se están nivelando). The Saudis make up the fourth largest group. Abashed (tímido) → the un-- (descarado) pursuit (búsqueda) of profits. Hang about/around → there is no point (no vale la pena) hanging --/-- (esperar), I hung --/-- (me quedé por allí) to see .../waiting for her call. Flaky: raro (=), strange. Bumper (parachoques) sticker (pegatina). Leverage: influencia, apalancamiento. Colombia spin out (prolomgó) the process as cover for ... The bogey (duende, pesadilla), bogeyman (coco, fantasma) of choice: the armed robbery (robo a mano armada). Israel-America entanglements (enredos, líos amorosos), (Mil.) alambradas. The plot gave ammonition (munición, argumentos) to conservatives. He is barred (impedido, bloqueado) from running away (fugarse, perderse) for president. Shops besieged (asediadas) by bargaining hunters (cazadores), we are -- by calls (nos llaman constantemente). Gold diggers (cazafortunas). The plane inimical (hosti, adverso) to peace is not brought down (derribado, abatido). Impact on the figures (cifras), -- of a book/speech, good -- (buena impresión) in the country. Fireworks (fuegos artificiales), man-made (artificial (=), synthetic (=)/artificial climate changes. Slowness of the rescue (=, salvar) effort. Children hold up (sostienen) crudely (groseramente, de manera rudimentaria) cardboards (cartones) signs (señales, letreros, símbolos) saying: please help. Cardboard box (caja de cartón). They have been trooping (ido en tropel, multitud) to get out (marcharse). A port so prone (propenso) to storms. Notice to appear (citación en justicia). Indoor swimming pool/tennis court; shoes -- (para estar por casa). Six meters surge (oleada) of the water. Foundations: cimientos; bases/fundamentos de un trabajo; story without --. Well-meaning (bien intenionados) plans drawn-up (redactados) to …; a badly written (redactado) essai. Be, get on the defensive. Investors look giddy (atolondrados, mareados). Put the squeeze (apretón,V, extraer …) on sb (apretar los tornillos a alguien). Bad sampling (muestreo) means respondents (demandados, que llenan el cuestionario) are not picked at random. Showcased (exhibidas) in the special zones before being extended … + showcase (escaparate) for capitalism, … Government has held down (mantenido baja) the help devoted (dedicada, destinada) to rice. The explosion blew its roof off. Pluck (desplumar, arrancar; valor, coraje) → -- out (arrancar) radioactive rods (barras); rule with rods of iron. Swithch the nuclear power back on. The government has stepped in (tomado parte, intervenido). He is staying on (se queda) as a consultant. A tap (micrófono de escucha) on sb's phone. The shrill (chillón, estridente, agudo) peeps (ojeadas,V, vistazos). It looks as unbridgeable (infranqueable) as ever; it could drag on (durar mucho) like that. Scotch: (rumor) acallar, (plan) frustar + =, thwart, foil) → the guards foiled their escape attempt. Pick up (reanimar, continuar) the pace (=, ridmo) of reforms =/= outstrip (adelantarse a, sobrepasar, dejar atrás) sales of … Pave (enlosar, pavimentar, …) the way (preparar el terreno) for … The choicest (los más selectos) spots (sitios) for research. The lasting (duradero) unspoiled (no pierde la belleza natural) wilderness (desierto, jungle, tierra virgen). Bare (sin hojas) branches of the fir (abeto). All around (en todo el alrededor) are blasts (ráfaga, explosions…). The pross & cons. If we find out a specific flu vaccine, the decline of jobs will merely (simplemente) botton out (tocará fondo). Grading (calificar, clasificar) ruthlessly (despiadadamente) the incompetents. Clear off! (¡lárgate!). It ranks (se clasifica) near the bottom. Forklift (truck) (carretilla elevadora) for the likes (gustos) of the more demanding (pers.: exigentes, works: agotadores & exacting (duros, exigentes, severos, rigurosos). They whisked him off (se lo llevaron volando). Recite by rote (de memoria), rote learning: memorización con mucha repetición. In the fullness (con el correr) of time a solution will be found. He fixed up or arranged everything for the interview ... Be mindful of (tener presente, estar consciente de). Weber credited (reconoció, dió crédito a) the protestant ethic, I've -- you (le creía) with more common sense. Mindfulness/awareness (conciencia). Lavishly (generosamente, suntuosamente) shared (out) o divided (out) his whole wealth. Inmiscuirse en algo (interfere, meddle in) without have been invited to it. American military spending far outstrips (sobresale, aventaja) anyone else. Belated (atrasados) attempts are rare in times of war =/= extraño: he's a very strange or odd man. It costs a bundle (mucho dinero). Mitigate (aliviar)d (atenuadas) circumstances ↔ un-- (rotundo, claro, decisivo) disaster. The glitches (pbs. técnicos) bring about o lead to mediocre outcomes (resultados). The affordable (asequible) Care act was less fair/just as Obama pretended. Explanatory (explicativas) regulations have to be more widespread. The average length/stretch (extension) of the laws. This perks (beneficios adicionales) lured in (cautivaron) textiles. The bond market sopped up (absorbió) paper exempt for taxation. Walk away (alejarse, irse) from the stern (severas, duras) measures. China scours (friega, busca, registra) the World for raw materials. Worldbeaten (liderazgo mundial) → worldbeater. Unpopular moment, unrivalled power. China's challenge (competición, desafío + a muerte/a un peligro: defiance) to America is not over global primacy (=, superioridad). American capitalism is as spirited (enérgico, fogoso) as ever. Recovery (recuperación). These advantages are wearing out (se desgastan, agotan) =/= the weary (pesados, cansados) theatrics of Congress's furloughs (licencias, permisos + on leave: de permiso) sequestered (=, aislaron, confiscaron (=, seized) ... He observed wrily (irónicamente) that America chastised (reprobó, regañó; castigó) for meddlimg (intromisión) in the region. The removal of S. Hussein was meant to eradicate … Obama has made a stab (intento, navajazo) at setting a new balance (=, equilibrio). Smart: elegante, listo, vivo, fuerte + eyes/wound (escocer) → they are --ing (se resienten) from the defeat in the elections. China is sneering (desprecia, es desdeñosa de) the main advisers because they have stretched (estirado, extendido) too thin (exigido al máximo. Many years can elapse/pass (transcurrir). With nerves twitching (tirantes, contraidos,V) after a spike (punta, …) in kidnapping (rapto)/extorsion. Not be charged (acusado), let alone (aún menos) convicted or jailed → acquittal (absolución). Dismiss (descartar, despedir, Jur.: anular) a flurry (racha) of arcane (secretas, misteriosas) appeals (llamadas, apelaciones). Din (barullo, estruendo) of slot (ranuras) machiunes =/= rowdy (alborotadoras) protests. Livelihood (sustento) asistencia for the poor is not permanent, constant. He is under fire (ataque) for seeming (aparente) … Its temerity (=, osadía) in standing up to (hacer frente a) China. Niggardly (tacaño, miserable). Full funded (financiado) by the tenants (inquilinos). Predictably (previsible + foreseeable). The cookies (galletas) crumble (se desmigajan). Press ahead (seguir adelante) with … The falcon (halcón)/heron (garza) took flight. Marshy (pantanoso) wasteland (inculto, erial, yermo). Be blamed for foreign banks blowing up (bomba: estallar; globo: hincharse) in their market. The sea water houses algae & seafood. The handheld (portátil) camera appalled (consternó, horrorizó) the 19th. Merrily (alegremente) celebrated. He armtwisted (presionó) the deal. Let sb escape. He got me out of a tight spot (de apuros). Three blocks (=, manzanas, secciones) that he leave out (deja fuera, omite). New found (recientemente descubierta) determination to strike. Crucero: cruise → -- de lujo (luxury cruise ship, (hacer un -- (go on a cruise). Gap (espacio, laguna, vacío) → stop-- (medida provisional), plug --s (llenar huecos). Fleeced (esquilado, desplumado); desplumar: (ave) pluck, (estafar) fleece. A stunning (deslumbrante, sensacional) debt. Running (gestión, funcionamiento) the foul (asqueroso, fétido, grosero) of the law: enfrentarse a la justicia. Scary (de terror) film → North Korea is even scarier (da más miedo). Appearance (aparición, aspecto, Jur.: comparecencia) can bet the most deceptive (engañoso + pers.: deceitful) of disguises (disfraces). His downfall (caída) was the origin of his decline (decadencia, declive); fall into --. Western policy boils down (se reduce) to hope. Political hues (colores). Before his visit expires (=, vence, finalice). A tame (dócil, fiable, sumiso) people, report. Glow (que irradia, rebosante; brillo, resplandor,V) with health. She slipped out (salió un momento, escapó de) the regulatory control. Undercover (actividad: clandestina ("="), agente: secreto. Sighted (vidente). Forthcoming (próximos) legal wrangles (pleitos, disputas) =/= fight/brawl/row (camorra) + go looking for trouble (buscar camorra). Jolly (alegre, gracioso; muy) glad (contento), you did jolly well, jolly mood (muy contento). Arriesgada (risky, hazardous) acción; brave/daring, bold, cheeky, risqué (atrevida) person. Suicida: suicidal, a pers. about to commit a suicide. redit-rating (de tasación) agency. Forephaders/bears (antepasados). He struts (se pavonea) of having a treasure in La Habana. We have bitten the bull (nos hemos enfrentado al toro), even at the risk of being hurt. Yank (tirar) each other's hairs. The supply cannot keep up (sostenerse) with booming demand. Of luxurious collections. Wastaged (perdidos, mermados) rates. Verbiage (verborrea) in the parliament. It spearheaded (fue punta de lanza, encabezaba) an effort. Wring (escorrer, retorcer) → -- out: ídem, (dinero, verdad) sacar. They fume (echan humos, están furiosos) about the €. An endorsement (respaldo, aprobación) of the battered (magullada, estropeada) single currency. Mint (menta, acuñar), (dinero, sellos) sin usar; in -- conditions (como nuevo). Less than a fifth that what he could have hat to pay … Pore over: escudriñar/examinar, estudiar muchas horas, inquirir/investigar) his books ... Barking (ladrando) up the wrong tree (ir muy desencaminado) about the political diarrheas; corteza: (árbol) bark, (limón) peel/rind, (pan) crust. The simple-minded (resuelto, delicado) focus on mastering risks is commended (elogiado, recomentado). Overplaying (exagerando) his hand: pasarse, ir demasiado lejos. Al-Quaeda holed up (escondido, refugiado) in Pakistan's tribal badlands (terrenos yermos, desérticos). Ec.'s teetering (balanceo), -- toward me. Dollops (cucharadas, porciones) of debts to encourage/stimulate returns. Fizzy (gaseoso, efervescente) =/= fizzle (silvar, fracasar) out: apagar, quedar en agua de borrajas. Shot off (salir disparado). Single-handed (sin ayuda, a ella sola). He delights (se deleita) drawing (trazando) contrasts between flashiness (exhibicionismo) & nondescript (anodinas, insípidas, sosas, indiferentes) offices. Break-up (desintegración, fracaso, disolución, Vs) =/= -- away (desprenderse, escindirse). Shake off (deshacerse de, dust: sacudir, habit: eliminar, depresión: salir de) the Soviet legacy. Underwear (ropa interior) for any age. King makers (personas muy influyentes). The human excrements dot (punto, salpican) the back wall where the destitute (indigentes) huddle (pers.: tropel, apiñarse, acurrucarse; cosas: montón,Vs) at night. Distante: far off, remote). Self-restrain (auto-control). Corroer: (metal) corrode, (mármol) erode, wear away, erode with envy, eate up with jealously. Shear: (sheep) esquilar, (hair) cortar; shorn heads (cabezas rapadas)'soldiers; shearer (esquilador) → fleece (lana, vellón). Round them up (acorralar) → shepherd (pastor, guiar/hacer entrar) them into the lorries. Rarely inconvenienced (=, incomodado). Thunderous (estruendoso). Poshness (elegancia, pijería) =/= lavish (suntuoso/lujoso; espléndido/gneroso). Plumb (right, exactly) in the middle; a plomo, plomo =/= --p (relleno, regordete, dejarse caer) → voters -- for (optan por) upper class. Its powpow (asamblea, reunión, consejo) rose (se levantó) to applaud/clap. Straightfaced: serio (=), sin reir). Franqueza (frankess, familiarity) → (frankly) con franqueza; I am on close enough terms (con suficiente --) with him to disagree. A stern (severo) faced pers. It worth his while (vale la pena) to criticize bad actions. One clenched (apretado) fist at his said. Whip (látigo, azote, V) → he --s up: agita, incita, bate; exaltar, provocar, fomentar, (dust) levanter, (wind) agitar. Moun<u>d</u>: montón,V, montículo → a -- of earth/rubble (escombros) =/= moun<u>t</u>: monte, (donkey/motorcycle) montar, (throne/stairs) subir, (campaign, offensive, event ...) preparer. Parecidos: they are alike, similar features (parecidos de cara), a similar skirt, resemblance/likeness to him. Plunder: saqueo,V, botín. Crackles (crepitaciones, crujidos, chisporroteos,Vs) & shrieks (chillidos). Better hold their tongue (morderse la lengua) than be included in the blacklist. Stout (resistente, robusto, enérgico) → he denies this stoutly (sólidamente, rotundamente). Ec. doldrum (abatimiento, estancamiento). Derison: escarnio, desdén, burla → this was greeted (recibido) with hoots of -- (con gran mofa). Range: gama, variedad; alcance, ámbito; mountain -- (cordillera), (skill, cleverness: habilidad) niveles, be within -- (a tiro). Ec. drift (cambio, deriva, current/wind: dejarse llevar) gains a new following/audience (=)/hearing (seguidores) =/= admirers. Have food (tener intereses) in both camps. List: lista,V, enumerar, incluir; cotizar, catalogar (=) → --less: apático ("="), indiferente ("="), lánguido, débil. Conviction shared by the members. Britain pressure gradually (=) cracks (raja, agrieta, se desmorona) open services market. The mainstream (corriente principal) of American life: el Americano medio. Downsize: recorte de personal; design: disminuir la talla. Fully (completamente, por lo menos) 55% would not be ruled out (descartados). Criss-crosse (entrelazar, entrecruzar, surcar) with battle lines. Split the flimsy (muy ligero, poco sólidas) nations into a clash (conflicto, choque, enfrentamiento) among sects & tribes. Unremitting (incansable, devoción: total, absoluta) gloom (melancolía, oscuridad, pesimismo) ↔ bolshie: pers.: rebellious, government: rebel, child: unruly. Rebelde: (troops) rebel, (boy, character) unruly, rebelious. Less red tape (papeleo) & more results. Overstated/ exagerated (exagerado); I thing that it would be going a bit far (que eso sería exagerar las cosas). Stitch (punzada del lado, Med.: sutura). Be in the saddle (silla,V): en el poder + -- (cargar) sb with sth. Partisan (partidario, partidista) of more strict policies in Spain. Pin (afilar, sujetar con agujas, clavija, pinza) → I --ned the papers together (sujeté con alfiler), wear the hair --ned up (recojido), a flower --ed on/to her dress, she --ed her hopes (depositar sus esperanzas) on him. Padlock (candado,V) =/= break the deadlock (salir del punto muerto/del impasse). Tenure: tenencia, ocupación; titularidad → teacher with -- (titularidad). Leer: mirada lasciva (lujuriosa), con recelos. Apalizar (fastidiar): bug + situar un micrófono, un chinche; hassle + lío, rollo =/= clobber: dar una paloza =/= beat: golpear, batir. Vested interests: derechos adquiridos, interés personal. Undercurrent: corriente submarina, tendencia oculta. Taxpayers fund (finanzan) education to be rolled out (introducida, presentada, lanzada ...). Influential contacts in governmets circles. Wave off (decir adiós), -- on (animar). Censure/ condemn/criticize. Rest (descanso) from ciry life, may day of --, the -- of the money/World, (pers.) not disturb him, he's resting, everything --s (depende) on their goodwill, -- my feet, eyes, ... Shudder: (pers.) estremecimiento, (máquina) vibrar/ sacudir, (casa) temblar. Strike back (contraataque,V + counterattack). Pity: pena, lástima, compasión, piedad. Cold-hearted (frío, insensible) code. Deprecation (desprecio, desaprobación). Mantener: (pers., familia) support, maintain, (promesa) keep, (contactos) maintain. The maintenance/upkeep of the sport facilities (instalaciones). Burlarse: make fun of sth. Mexican potholes (con baches) roads & blaring (estruendosos) horns (cuernos, bocinas) ... Reproach (reproche) → he looked us reproachfully. Pungent (mordaz, acre: áspero) oil smells.

Soul stirring (conmovedor) hammering (martilleo, duras críticas). Chopper (hacha pequeña, helicóptero). Culprit: culpable de un delito, guilty. The gulf (=, abyss (=) between China & India. Founder ("=", barco: hundirse, plan: fracasar). Hearsay (rumores) + there's a rumour going round that .... The second to last. Roadblock (control, barricada). Swap (estropajo, algodón) down: limpiar herida con -- =/= swat: (aplastar, matar), give a -- (zurriagazo). Handcuffing (esposas,V). Fan out: avanzar en abanico, cortar el paso. Dissent: =, disconformidad, (Pol., Rel.) disidencia. Its support fell away (se desmoronó). They trot (trote,V) into an stunning (sensacional) room. Hung upside-down. Ten pitches (campos) long & 15 km. of conveyor belt. The centrepiece (eje/atracción principal). Tight knit (tejer): muy unido/integrado. He summed up (resumió) his vision as sth of strenuous (intensa, agotadora, ardua) life. Chase (perseguir) a hardy (resistente, fuerte) ... Rake: rastrillo, V, remover, barrer. The bedrock (lo fundamental, la base, lecho/cama de roca) of the junction (cruce, empalme), go to the -- of a theory. Uncharted (inexplorado, desconocido) fourth amendements. Officials (--les, funcionarios) =/= officer (agente de policía, dirigente de club/de partido político). Quarrel (pelea)some (pendenciero, peleón, camorrista). Toss (agitar, sacudir; echar) peanuts to each other; one of the nuts hit the driver. Ended up charged with felony (delito grave) assault. Repository (depósito) of scholarship (beca, erudición). Sleepovers (que pasan la noche). Escalator (escalera mecánica) on the outside of the building. Non- for- profit municipal art gallery. Sweet-smelling/fragrant (fragante) mist (neblina) =/= flagrant (evidente)/blatant/glaring. Script (escritura, argumento, guión,Vs). Hook (percha, gancho,V, pescar) up: (TV, radio) transmitir en cadena, conectar; abrocharse. Argue (discutir, alegar, sugerir)ably: posiblemente, se puede decir =/= allegedly (presuntamente). Duly (como previsto, debilmente) trounced (derrotó, apalizó) their opponents. Starving (famélico, muerto de hambre) business. Doctors turn (vuelta, volver(se), giro,V …) them away (los rechazan, desvian) because the government rates (índice, ritmo, tasa, precio, cotización) are too low. The elderly (ancianos) America switch to a medicare plan: managed by private insurers, the government pays the premium (prima de seguros). Ec.'humming (canturreo, ir viento en popa). Populist anger (ira, enojo) at banks. Drive down interest rates. Pine: consumirse, languidecer (+ languish) for sth/sb (suspirar por --/--). Albeit/even though/(al)tough (aunque) wanly (ténuamente, ligeramente, pálidamente). Growth pick up (se reanima) & budget deficit decline =/= the British drove the French out of Egypt & picket out (elgieron, destacaron, reconocieron) their anticuarian (coleccionista) loot (botín) =/= antique shop, antiques. Lacklustre (deslucido, candidato mediocre, pelos/ojos apagados) & underpinned (sostenida, respaldada) by banks'loose policy. Get over (superar) the failed promise of the May 68 students uprising (sublevación). The upshot (resultado) is that … Jet-set (alta sociedad) → an inveterated (arraigado, empedernido) -- - -- member. Rock-bottom (tirados) prices + hit/reach -- (tocar fondo, ej.: of our moral). Bafflement (desconcierto, desorden, confusión, incertidumbre + uncertainty), baffling (desconcertante …). A civilisation has been brought down (derribada). Hiss (silvar, abuchear) the losing/defeated team. Filling to bursting point (a reventar). Severed (cortadas) relations, rope, chain, communications; one shoulder & the top right side of his head is sheared (cortado). The cockup (lío, fastidio) tend to be bad judjed; I made a -- of it (la fastidié), what a --! (¡que lío, que fastidio!). The lone (solitarios) egomaniacs (ególatras: que dan culto a ellos mismos) are excluded. Crossbreed (cruce, híbrido) of starry-eyed (idealista) dreamer & hard-nosed (duro) businessman. Guiddy (vertiginoso, que marea) heigh of 100 km. above the Earth. Outer: exterior, de fuera, outer space (espacio sidereal: de astros). Biff (bofetada), (punch) puñetazo,Vs =/= bang (estallido, explosión, golpear). It pained at him (le dolía) to imagin … Cros-bar: listón, (vicicleta) barrera, (goalpost) larguero). Float along (circulando) with a skiff (barquito). Oily droplets (gotitas). He reverted (volvió) to its passivity, to its subject ↔ he receded (se alejó/retiró from …). Pull/squeeze the trigger (gatillo). Footloose (libre y sin compromiso) & fancy free: libre como el viento. Dodder/totter: tambaleante (+ stagger), con paso inseguro + sway (tambaleo), lurch: bandazo, sacudida; (vehículo) dar sacudidas, (pers.) tambalearse. Income (renta) tax. Substantial/sizeable (considerable). At his behest (instancia, petición). We should have to reapply (solicitar de nuevo). Virtual realm (reino, campo). Independent judiciary. The government hobbles (hace cojear) its private sector =/= hump (joroba, encorvar, get the --: enfurruñarse), humback (jorobado). Sinfulness (pecaminosidad) that entitles it (da derecho a) …. Lump: bulto, trozo, pedazo, terrón, hinchazón → he had a nasty -- (chichón) on his head. The conspicuous (=, insigne, ilustre) dazzle (deslumbrar) of the games masks (=, oculta) deepening (cada vez más) trouble. The sturdy (fuertes, robustos) supporters are drifting away (se dispersan, se dejan llevar por la corriente). Vest (chaleco,V) sb with sth (investir a alguien de algo, ej.: with special powers). The competition head-on (de frente), cars collided --. Team up (asociarse) with reliable people. It stood out (destacó) as … + stress, emphasize, underline. Apresurar: hurry, speed up, hasten =/= the events that precipitated his downfall (caida, ruina) + it will be his --. The best-looking (de mejor aspecto) people of the planet. The supreme court has been tampered with (manipulada, forzada, falsificada + forget, faked, counterfeited, resultado/decision: rigged, fiddled). Create twice as much pbs/as many jobs as the next biggest polluter. An awakening (naciente, que despierta) giant. Manufacturing's share of GDP in Sub-Saharian Africa has held steady at 10-14% in recent years. We were cramped (íbamos muy apretados). Overrun:

(invasión,V) → -- sth (prolongar algo) → the meeting oberran by one hour, (exceso) → (exceder/rebasar) the budget. Bench (banco, asiento, mesa de trabajo, judicatura/tribunal, mandar al banquillo) =/= --marks (cotas, precios de referencia) such Libor: it traks (sigue la pista de) the price of loans between banks in London. Submit assignments (misiones, tareas) by e-mail. Snap up (agarrar) rich world assets. Stand-alone (autónomas, independientes) instructions on line. Overlie/overlay (recubrir) =/= overly (demasiado). Squarrely (directamente, como es debido). Transistors tininess (que son muy minúsculos). Cram (empollar, meter) them into slices of silicon. Chips: fabricated in batches (grupos, lotes, tandas …) on silicon wafes (hostias; Comp.: oblea de silicio). Spintronics: use the spin of subatomic particles to make a chip from transistors. Do away with (suprimir) the battle dress swathed (envuelto) with cables & batteries. Reverenciar/vnerar (revere, venerate, worship). Debt burden (carga). Mug (bobo, ingenuo; taza, tarra). Pluck a goose (ganso) with smallest hissing (silvido, abucheo) =/= Haze (bruma, neblina) → be in -- (estar atontado). A madcap (alocado, tarambana, descabellado) idle (holgazán, sin trabajo). Sidling in/out (entrar/salir furtivamente) → -- up to sb (acercarse sigilosamete). Comment (comentario, observación) → no --, make a --, cause --s =/= recommend (recomendar) → I -- this novel to you. Lagos disgorges (vomita, arroja) 10,000 metric tonnes of waste a day. Salvage: (operation) rescatar, (from the wreckage) salvar, (of ship) salvamento; salvaged: reutilizado, (theory) rescatada. Charges (tarifas) for state primary schools. Crave: reclamar (+ claim) → may I -- your attention, (food for pregnant woman): -- for (tener anto de). Cyber-security: law-abiding (cumplidores) hackers help business … Crook (doblar, cayado; ladrón, sinvergüenza) & spook (fantasma, policía secreta) fight off (repelen, rechazan) the bad guys (tipos). Chinks (grietas, tintineos) in digital armour (blindaje). Rig (manipular + elecciones: amañar) the market.

Turn around (darse la vuelta; sanear, recuperar) to timing (ridmo, hora fijada). Slush (aguanieve)y: cubierto de nieve medio derretida. Scalp (cuero cabeludo) sb: arrancar la cabellera a alguien. Mock/scoff (mofarse). Mitigate (aliviar, atenuar)ed circumstances ↔ un-- (puro, auténtico). Seat-stuffed (relleno) with ... Trundle: (carro, ...) tirar de, empujar, (barril) hacer rodar, -- in/out (entrar, salir pesadamente); the car --ed along the lane (camino). Padded-shoulders (hombreras). Freeing up (liberando) airplace. Terrify (aterrorizar) → it terrifies me to think that I might lose her. Stateless (apátrida). Cumplir: (promesa) keep, (amenaza) carry out, (objetivo, sueño) achieve, (ambición) fulfill. Sever (cortar, romper) the doom (fatalidad). In no mood (de mal humor) to listen to the excuses. He looks set (fijo, forzado) to ... Chirrido: (puerta) squeaking, creaking, (frenos, neumáticos) squeaking, (de pena, dolor) screech, (pers., animal: chillar, gritar) squeal. Quiescent: inactivo, quieto; (pers., volcán) inactivo so far (hasta ahora). So as to + inf. (para). It's too dear (caro) for us/it's beyond our means. Peel (=) off: (painting) desconchar, (stamp: sello; sticker: etiqueta, pegatina, adhesivo) quitar, despegar. Unfriendly (unpleasant, antipatic) towards sb. Banking is spluttering (ranqueando, chisporroteando, pers./engine: resoplando). Underline (subrayar, destacar + highlight, stress, emphasize) =/= underwrite: asegurar contra el riesgo, soportar, respaldar, (finanza) apoyar. Be arrears (atrasado) with the rent. Puncture (pinchazo,V) his popularity. Short-stemed (de tallo corto) crops. Leggy (de pierna larga). Blow torch (antorcha): soplete. Eyecatching (vistosos, llamativos). Grudgingly (de mala gana). Grandstanding (demagogía, pavoneo). Tepid (tibio, poco entusiasta). Trail (estela) → lay a --; (huella, rastro, seguir la pista de) the separated groups, ... General dismay (consternación, espanto, desolación). Clean-up (limpieza) of the banking. Pelts (pellejos, cueros) of fluffy (plumosos + feathery; materil: mullido, toy: de peluche) creatures. Pelt sb (acrivillar a alguien) with questions, stones, insults. Busker (músico callejero) on a clapped out (desvencijado) bus. Mincing (menuditos) rascals (granujas). Protracted (prolongada) Ec. war. Mincer: máquina de moler y picar. Quit: parar, abandonar, irse → -- while you are ahead; don't -- now. Between cradle & coffin. Inquebrantable: (fe) unshakeable, (fidelildad, lealtad) unswerving, (entusiasmo) undying. He has an iron constitution. Trendsetter (indicador de una moda), trendsetting (que impone la moda). Satelites launchpads (plataformas de lanzamiento) =/= (ideas, carrera) trampolines (+ springboard). Scale back (recortar) its power. Critter (bicho + small animal, bug). Get by/manage to (ir tirando, arreglárselas). Onslaughts (el arremeter, ataques) of summer visitors. Uplift: (spirit) elevación, exaltación, (physical support) sostén. Miss/waste an opportunity/chance. Tide: marea, corrientre → tidal power (energía maremotriz), tide of violence. Filled with gravel (grava). Miss out: (línea, …: saltarse), (-- -- on) dejar pasar, (life, good deals ...) desperdiciar. Mash: moler, pure de patatas,V. Power supply + oil, coal, water, goods, m.) reservas, existencias. Tax levied in a product. So (that): para que, de manera que → I brought it -- (--) ... Makeover (sesión de maquillaje y peluqiería) =/=he had (le habrá) made over (traspasado)the farm to his son. Doblar: (shirt, paper, napkin) fold, (arm, knee, rod/bar: vara) bend. He held the cup aloft (hacia arriba). Wildcat (perforación petrolífera) =/= catwalk (pasarela). Sequel (secuelas, consecuencias, continuación). Golpe: hit, knock. He comes out (sale, se muestra, florece) fighting. Anger & folly (locura). He is hated & scorned (despreciado) + scornful/contemptuous (despreciativo). Laden (cargado) with gold; he was carrying the heavy cross. A country torn (destrozado) by civil war. The sources of income are very scarce, be short of food, of money. Eye (mirar, observar) a bubbly (burbujeante, lleno de vida) housing market. Pernikety (perfeccionista + "="). Bait (cebo de pesca), decoy (ceñuelo, reclamo). Torpor/letargy (letargo, sopor + Med.: drowsiness). Xenophobic innuendo (indirecta + =, insinuación). Indirectly affected (perjudicado). Put the screws on (apretar las tuercas). Abetted (insistió, secundó, instigó, fue cómplice) =/= abate: amainar → wind/storm --, manufacturing decline has no signs o --; the fighting has --ed, (pain) mitigar, (pollution) acabar con. Critically injured people. Suspend: colgar, (flights) suspender + -- sb. from office. An offensive/defensive tactic/strategy/radars to register incoming objects. A blast (ráfaga) demolished (=, echó abajo) a disused (abandonado) ship/deserted city. Cartritge belt (cartuchera). Barely (apenas) notices (avisa, nota) the slow down/speed up. Wedged in (encajado) between two lorries; I've managed to fit the two parts together. Encubrir: (ocultar) hide, (delincuente) harbour + dar refugio; (delito) cover up. Be accomplished (realizado, llevado a cabo) with the utmost (mayor) urgency. Trackers (rastreadores) to reduce theft considerably. Monitor: (elections) observar, (process) controlar, supervisor → --ed by air-traffic controlers. Data leakage (gotera, escape) → they use football as an -- from or as a way of escaping from their pbs. Light them up (iluminarlos). Ofimate (oficina de automación). Cared (preocupado) for … The quirkier: los más peculiares, raros, singulares. By-elections (elecciones parciales) to solve local problems. The demeanour/behaviour (conducta, =) is reprehensible (criticable), you can't blame him for standing against you (por oponérsete). He has drawn up (redactado) eventual/contingency plans (medidas de emergencia). The gang bunch (banda) of delinquents has been publicly chastised (castigados, reprendidos). Galvanize (animar) sb into reprehensible action. Tax hike (incrementa) strangle business. Overstretch (forzar/exigir demasiado) with harsh treatment (mano dura). He eschewed (evitó + avoided; derecho: renunció) state action. Venue: (lugar) for the recital …; lugar de celebración, (Jur.) change of venue: cambio de jurisdicción ("="). Sickly (enfermizo, débil; empalagoso). Syria rose up (se precipitó, se levantó) against IS with Russian help. Circunscripción/distrito electoral (circunscription, constituency, electoral district); jurisdicción: (autoridad) jurisdiction, (distrito) district, administration area. Cortejo fúnebre: funeral cortege, procession. Cajoled/fob-off (camelado, engatusado + coaxed into doing sth). Claw back (recuperar, volver a tomar) the lost spirits (ánimos). Ringed/surrounded (rodeado) by astute/clever helpers, assistants. Twise the usual audience turned in (sintonizó) the TV to watch the film about the Age of Enlightenment (Siglo de las Luces). Alleged (supuesta) friendship with the highest sphere of influence. Wanton: (attack, destruction) sin sentido, (neglect: negligencia; waste) que disgusta, de mal humor; lifestyle (licencioso, disipado). Despilfarrar: waste, (dinero) squander =/= desperdiciar: (food …) waste, (oportunidad) throw away, miss, waste. Pilfering (robos, raterias), pilfer (ratero; hurtar, robar). Jumpy (nervioso, asustadizo + easily frightened). Shiften out (desviado) into vessels. Come to fruition (cumplimiento) as planned or according to the plan. Startle (sobresaltar, asustar + frighten)ing: alarmante, sorprendente, asombroso; --ed tourist. Bond: bono, vínculo (of friendship, …), juntura, (química) enlace + Tf. linkup. Interspersed (intercalado, incluido); todo incluido: (Com.) inclusive, all-in, an inclusive price of $ 40 (un precio de $ 40, todo incluido). Vie <u>for sth</u> (dispuesto a algo), <u>with sb</u> (competir, rivalizar). Enthuse (entusiasmarse) over o about sth/sb; the news arosed (despertaron) little enthusiasm in the White House. Hardly (apenas) tactful (discreto + discreet), diplomatic (+ "=") & too rude. Fritter away: malgastar, derrochar + (dinero) squander, (electricidad, agua, gas) waste. Tonificante: toner, invigorating, stimulating. Fabricar: manufacture, produce → the plant --s three harvests (cosechas) a year, friction --s heat, he is optimistic that his visit coult -- results. Dribble: baba, chorrito,V; (Sp) driblar → he -d his milk all down his chin (le chorreaba la leche por la barbilla). Saliva/

spit + escupir → be the dead spit (vivo retrato) of sb. The idle (vacías, ociosas, flojas) batteries need to be charged. Eyebrow (ceja), eyelash (pestaña), eyelid (párpado). Drudgery (trabajo pesado) → skul-- (tejemaneje, trapicheo, embuste). Parpadeo: (eyes) blinking, (light) flickering, (star) twinkling → in the blink of an eye (en un abrir y cerrar de ojos); -- at sb (guiñarle el ojo). The Spring uprising (levantamiento, sublevación) began in Tunisia & it will never end. Cesspit/--pool/septic tank =/= oil well. Roaming: vagabundo, excursión, animal: vagar). Rust (herrumbre) → --belt (industrial belt). It looks like he know/it rains/a caramel + he looks ill/older/unhappy. There appears/seems to be a solution. Kingship/royalty (realeza). Tarugo: (of wood) lump, chunk, (of cheese, bread, cake) hunk, (pers.) dimwit/block/stupid. Get one's share (sacar tajada). Drill (taladrar) a hole. Tenderness (ternura). So much/many (tantos) as it will be possible. Delete (eliminar, tachar) key: tecla de borrado. Keep still (estate quieto), why don't you try to sleep again? There is nothing left for him. Through ages (a través de los tiempos) we've discovered a sad experience. They searched (registraron) the whole forest. By sheer (pura) chance, by -- desperation (en último término), by -- (total) impossibility of. You must work faster; she got dressed quickly. With all speed/in all haste, do sth in haste (deprisa), make haste (apúrate), haste to do sth. Everyone (todos) who wants it, anyone (quien) who knows it. Cadáver (body, corpse) → ¡sobre mi cadáver! (over my dead body!), he was dead on arrival. It smells disgusting (un asco) & in addition it's expensive. Awful: (tiempo) terrible, (clothe, crime) horroroso. (smell) terrible, you are awful! (¡que malo eres!), don't be naughty! (¡no seas malo!), Behave yourself! (¡se bueno!). That's a bad sign (es un mala señal), the trouble is that (lo malo es que) … It's around here somewhere, but only God knoes exactly. Do it to make himself look good (para quedar bien) ↔ you made us look bad. The sun is scarching (quema), they were burned at the stake (en la hoguera), the home was ablaze, (fogata) bonfire. Pine forest, pinewood (pinar). He did it on purpose, deliberately. It happens that (da la casualidad de que) …; what a coincidence! Who did you gives it to? Who were you with last night? Whyever did you do it? (¿por qué demonios lo hiciste?) It won't be easy, whoever does it (no importa quien lo haga). Whoever finds it can keep it (puede quedarse con él). He do the football polls (juega a las quinielas). As a result of (a raiz de)... A bookworm (ratón de biblioteca) to solve the identity crisis. He vanished (desapareció) without traces (rastro, señal), but finally we'll find him. The last but three, the third to last. Stay a bit longer; a short while later/shortly afterwards. A spare (que no te hace falta) paper, in one's -- (perdidos) momentos, lend me a -- umbrella. He knows quite a bit (bastante) of …, overstep the mark (go too far). Dash in/out/rush past (entrar, salir, pasar como un rayo), dash away/back: salir/entrar corriendo. Wall/fortify (amurallar) → walled (amurallado) enclosure (recinto). Grow a crop (cultivo) → reap/harvest it, reap (recoger) the benefits of sth; what time is the mail or post collected? Pick up flowers, legumes, vegetables (hortalizas), get your things together, gather up your things. Award of his effords. Data collection/capture. Recrudecer: worsen, intensify, recrudesce. Wire mesh (mallas, engranar): red de alambre. Defeat/vanquish the enemy. Bring down (reducir) to a minimum. For more safety we'll register the mail. The University statute, by -- (por ley), through legal channels. Unlawful (ilícito, ilegal), lawful wife, legitimate heir, son, governement. Move off (ponerse en marcha); (automóvil) arrancar + start, (Comp.) boot (up), start up. A fair (justa) reappraisal (revaluación) of politicians, of currency. Three month of the sentence were remited (perdonados, remitidos), remitted to a lower court. Remitance (envio, remesa), costs of postage & packing (de envío). Remolcador: (Náut.) tug, (automóvil) breakdown lorry/van, tow truck; remolcar: tug, tow; (remolque) trailer;

llevar un coche a --: tow a car. A close/hard fight (reñido) game. Be in bad terms (relaciones) with ... Sanctioned (aprobado) project. A layer of insulating material. Briefing: (press) reunión informativa; órdenes, instrucciones. Go on pilgrinage (romería). The house doesn't match up (reune) the requirements (requisitos). The souldiers surrounded (rodearon) the home with barbed wire. Revender: (entradas) tout/scalp, (artículos) resell, (acciones) sell off. Split: división, descosido; grieta, ruptura, abertura, rajadura,Vs, (Pol) escisión, (religión) cisma. Adhesive, sticky ↔ non- stick (antiadherente). Revestimiento: coating, covering; lining the ceiling with fibreglass; -- antiadhrente (non-stick coating). Namely (a saber, concretamente) → another possibility, --, that it was not working. A steel frame (armazón) clad (vesido) in concrete (hormigón) → reinforced concrete (hormigón armaso). Gnawing/ rodent (roedor), knaw/nibble at (roer). The occupation hazard (riesgo profesional) becomes the more & more considered. De rigor: the hottest part of the summer (el -- del verano), the scientific precision, after the usual or customary greetings. Tosquedad: roughness, rudeness, coarseness. Poco refinado, rudo, basto: vulgar, common. Saber hacer: be in the habit of doing. Jackpot (premio gordo), as a reward for her services. Correct one's course (rumbo), (río) curso, (planet) órbita. Repeat at nauseum (a saciedad) but nobody listen to, pay attention to, heed it. Tasteless & without salt ↔ tasty & delicious (comida, bebida), delightful (momento, sonido). An opportunity comes up/arises; at an opportune or at the right moment, his call could not have come at a better moment. How did the performance go? It worked out right (salió bien), the plan has come out very well ↔ the plan didn't work, all was spoiled by rain. Life jacket (chaleco salvavidas) to confront or face up to the danger + deal with o tackle the problem. It's nice here (se está bien aquí) but I've three hours work left, where are my work clothes? Get annoyed/angry:

enfadarse, hacer mala cara =/= angrily/furiously (con enfado). Brake sharply/stop dead (en seco) to save our life. Nothing can come between us (nada podrá separarnos) ↔ they tried not to meet each other. Cross: we have our -- to bear, cruce de calle, híbrido ("hybrid"), crossed cheque, cross o.s. (santiguarse). A sharp (seco) bang (golpe). Dry up a well/a stream. A deposit (=),V) of $ 50 + sediment. Go ahead (ponerse delante, en abeza) from now on. Look after yourself (siga Ud. bien) & not bother me more. His path (trayectoria) as a film maker. Is excellent, unbeatable. He highlights/stands out (destaca) … The way things are (tal como estan las cosas) I prefer forget the participating countries. The best ones are split up from the rest. Fix (atar) the load, -- (grabar) it in one's memory, -- the eyes/gaze on her, --ed at 3 h. PM, be in a -- (apuro). Sure of himself/confident on the stage (escenario) but unlucky at carts/in love. Postage (franqueo) stamp … It appears twice monthly but people want it only once a week. The simplicity (=, sencillez), she dresses very simply, she didn't understand a thing despite the simplicity or straightforwardness of the matter. The ageing (senescencia, envejecimieno) process, (vino) envejecimiento, crianza). Lay (sentar) the fundations for the electricity pylon (torre de conducción eléctria). Be liable (responsible) for sth, not -- (exento) for military service, -- for tax, -- (probable) to forget, -- (propenso) to suffer damages. Make it clear (dejar sentado that) the husband will not command her. Black disagree with me (no me sienta bien) & white disagree with military staff. Pronounce (en Jus.: dictar) sentence; what common sense suggests or dictates =/= dictate to one's secretary. Moving forward (avanzando) in the opposite direction. It arouses (suscita, despìerta) the nationalistic feelings; it whet (estimula) my apetite, the awakening (despertar) of the spring. I suddenly felt cold/some effects. Exclamation mark. Cry (grito) for help; at the top of one's voice (a gritos), shouts of protests. He gestured me to move aside (me apartase). Leave a sum as a deposit, leave message after a bip/tone. At birth (al nacer) we have already different fate. I sorted (clasifiqué, arreglé) them out (los separé) in several piles. Burial (entierro), tomb/grave, bury (V). We'd have to get rid of them, we rid the home of mouse (Pl. mice). Sequedad: (terreno) dryness, (respuesta, tono) curtness → he greeted us curtly. If it hadn't have been for him I'd have drowned. He will be shot. Give a lecture (clase, conferencia) for disadvantaged northerns (norteños). Moved/touched (conmovidos) by the scandalous/shocking news. Calmly/serenely. Serenar: calm down, (pb.) settle. Mass (en serie) production cripple (ahoga) little producers. Reliable/ trustworthy (fiable) but elusive (difícil de encontrar) & evasive. It's too late to back out (echarse atrás + back down) & withdraw what he said (retractarse). Black is serious/severe for a girl, seriousness of a repport, an information & an account (explicación, informe, cuenta). I've saved (guardado) you a place. Subsidio (subsidy, grant), subsidize a project. A hectic (agitada) life + (mar) rough/choppy, (perss.) agitated. The sesion time (sesión the control al gobierno) will be awkward/ uncomfortable (violenta). Firme: (silla, mesa, escalera) steady, paso f. (firm step), he remained --, firm belief/conviction, be firmer with him. I don't bet in it (no estés tan seguro), it'll betray you. You were paying not high enough, so he found it hard (le costó mucho) to agree. He has given his all (lo major de sí), but she is looking onto all circumstances. Status (=, de prestigio) symbol. Charmed (cautivado) by his friendliness/ warmth (simpatía) to sb. In nine cases out of ten money is law. Ingratiating himself (congraciarse, hacerse el simpático) with … At sunrise/rising sun we are rested/freshed (descansados) ↔ at set we are tired. A minimum income (renta, ingresos, pensión) will be provided for the humanity as a whole. Surplus: exceso, sobrante, (Ec.) superavit. Imposing impressive (imponente, sobrecogedora) unfairness (falta de equidad). Soberly (con moderación) dressed, I recommend you eat in moderation. The receptionist was solicitous: (pers.) diligente/complaciente + (inquiry: indagación) llena de interés. Let me go! At a/one blow (de un golpe) the plane was blown off course (fue desviado por el viento). Shade (sombra, tono en arte) =/= he's not a shadow (sombra proyección) of his former self (mismo). Complain (quejarse) =/= (de dolor) moan, groan. Deaf to her entreatises/pleas (ruegos, súplicas) =/= request (solicitud + Jur.: petición). Travel enables to plot (parcela, argumento; conjura, fraguar) our future more clearly. A question lurks (merodea, está en acecho) about his patience... Long-winded: (pers.) prolijo, largo, (speech, explanation) prolijo, interminable. A meatier (más sustancioso) range of power. Prime mover (promotor + promoter) to develop a steppe. The stalling (paro) of Europe integration worries me. Lame-duck: (pers.) caso perdido, (proyecto) fracasar. The crowning (más supremo) point of the process. Flood (inundar) the market, the kitchen was flooded (inundada), the -- damages (los daños causados por inundación), the -- victims. Leave not loose ends (cabos sueltos), leave everything properly (bien) tied up. He paid lip service to (defendió de boquilla) an ideal. All are bludgeoned (aporreado, coaccionado) by austerity but the affair will be a happy ending. Boredom (aburrimiento) in the arena; these meetings bored me. Labour in vain (sembrar en arena), State's fuel subsidies to affluent (prósperos, acomodados) farmers beget (engendran, provocan) more hate to little ones. Wellbeing (bienestar social) worldwide will be never attained. China rise unsettles (descontenta, intranquiliza) some in the West. China could lash (látigo, azotar) out (atacar, arremeter) abroad. From the subtle (flavour: suave, pers.: súbtil, perspicaz) to the blatant (evidente, flagrante, descarado), he is blatant about it (no lo disimula), he was blatant about cheating (copió con todo descaro). The Ec. default (omisión, falta, rebeldía, no pagar). Incompetent mindset (actitud, manera de pensar) =/= mindful (tener en cuenta, ser consciente). Concevable (possible, imaginable) rebound (=, Ec.: recuperarse, repuntar). Impromptu (improvisadas, espontáneas) neighbourhoods visits. The likelier scenario: India's fresh (reciente) start. The flood-prone (propenso) riverbank (orilla, ribera), the flood grow along the banks of the river Ebro. The EU sluggishness (flojedad, pereza + haziness) has damped (humedecido, sound: amortiguado, vibration: mitigado) demand for commodities. Come to naught (malograrse). Compile (recopilar) the ten forms (impresos) needed to open a business. So outcomes (resultados, consecuencias) will disappoint hopeful citicens. The club has billed (pasado factura, anunciado) 2025 as … An union is in the offing (se avecina, está en perspectivas). Unasailable (inatacable, irrefutable + =) theory. Bask (disfrutar) with the acclaimed (aclamado, elogiado, proclamado) winner; bask in the sun/in the head, bask in sb's favour (disfrutar del favour de alguien). Light-footed: rápido, veloz. Progresista (progressive). Vivid: (color) vivo, intenso, (personalidad) con mucha vitalidad, (imaginación) rica, fertil (=). Israel bucks (se opone) to regional trend. Holy (sagrados) temples & lively (alegres) local celebrations. We need foresee (adivinar, estimar; plan: proyectar) an afterthought (idea adicional) for the dissatisfayed, disgruntled, discontented/dissatisfied. I owe you $ 5 but you owe 10 to me. Sure-foodness (seguro, conocedor de lo que pisa) of foreign police. No dumping garbage or sewage (aguas fecales) in the groundwater (aguas subterráneas). Dredge: (canal, río) dragado, (culinario) espolvorear + dust, sprinkle. Stamping out: (resistencia) aplastar, (rebellion) sofocar, (crimen) erradicar. Scale down (disminuir) its effords to take out (sacar, eliminar, excluir) his job. Drop (soltar) two bombs. Outbounded (hacia fuera) investments from China. At the daylight (luz del día): al amanecer → I'm beginning to see -- (a ver las cosas claras). The success of Islamic state (IS) ows as much to the awfulness (lo terrible) of rulers in Damasc as to the prowess of the fighters. Spin (hacer rodar) out:

alargar, (dinero, bebida) estirar; if you stretch it any more, it'll break, make his money stretch to the end of the month. Spouse/husband/partner (cónyugue), married couple (cónyugues), the couple husband & wife. Adoptar: she adopted him as her son, take a critical stance (postura) against the government, she sleeps in a bad position (... adopta una mala postura). Baathist ideology. The pledge has not been met. Under blockade (bloqueo), mental block (bloqueo), they bloked or barricaded the door with an armchair, the police barred our way. A build-up (acumulación) of borrowing. The offer is oversubscribed four times (es 4 veces superior). A record-breaking sale. Carry on: (conversación) mantener, (tradición) continuar, (negocio) tirar adelante + the train continued its journey (marcha), we will go on with or continue the lesson tomorrow. Lifeblood (alma, sustento) of Africa's rise. Flagging (que flaquea/enfría/decae) rise of social unrest. Flog (azotar, vender) their prized assets; Israel tough stance (postura) toward Arab world. Map (plano) → he --s (planifica) both gains/earnings; profit & losses (ganancias y pérdidas), gross output (producción bruta), net output), gross profit, net profit. The bottom line (lo mínimo aceptable + acceptable, passable). From trency (de moda) attire (atavío, adorno, acicalamiento) & mats (esteras) to ... Live up (animar) as much as you can & walk out (salir). The signatories are grumpy (gruñones, malhumorados + bat-tempered). Flashpoint (punto álgido/crítico) for a war/of the disease. Resources extraction underpins (sostiene) grouth. The debt overhangs (sobresale) from the 2008 housing burst; grab an overhanging (saliente, que sobresale) branch. Too broad (ancho, extenso, amplio) to plot (conspirar, determinar; fraguar, trazar). Crunch (mascar) → the -- (la hora de la verdad + when it comes to a --), hammered by credit -- (crisis, crujido), -- sth up (triturar + crush, grind). Faint (débil) sign of life. Occasional splurge (derroche; news: spread acros the front page, ...) to mollify (aplacar) a weary (cansado) public. Proponents (defensores) of discipline are to the fore (van delante, en proa) after the president. Held back (retener, refrenar) by an electoral willing. It may edge (abrir) its way into power. Battered (estropeado, reputación: maltrecha; rebozado; (bombardeo/paliza) from the critics. The Ec. in the full blush (sonrojo, rubor) of recovery. Tread (pisar) warily: andar con cautela. Prime: principal, excelente, de primera calidad; preparar → prime the fuel subsidies. A hand-picked: (cuidadosamente) selectioned picture. Toe with Xi's line (conformarse, aplacar la disciplina of Xi). Extend paid parental leave (permiso) get welfare (de asistencia social) recipients back to work. Be on the alert (en alerta), Keep sb in line (a raya). A penchant (predilección, inclinación, tendencia) for ... A potent brew (variedad de cerveza, hacer una infusion de té; scheme/mischief/plot: tramarse) to quench (saciar la sed, satisfacer una pasión) the thirst of loans. Be in the doldrums: estar abatido, (business) estar estanco. The last full year of his term. The target is hit (alcanzado, afectado ...). The catch-up (puesta al día) growth is no longer on the cards (programa). The contest (contienda, concurso, impugner) for succession takes centre-stage (va en primer plano). Ireland is charting (traza) conciliatory course. A shared stake (participación) in running the Ec. Irk (irritada, fastidiada) & is coming/falling apart (se deshace) at the seams (costura, juntura, sutura) → irksome/annoying (irritado, fastidodo). A full-blown (hecho y derecho; a gran esala) insurgency alongside (junto a) local malcontents (=, revoltosos). The Ec. is rallying (se recupera). Ec. dispiriting (desalentandor) shape (forma, configuración). The bigger hazard/ risk (riesgos) will lurk (acechar) in debt-ridden (cargada) Europa. On their own behalf (por su cuenta y riesgo). Polish (pulir, refinar, perfeccionar) the program. EU is phasing (escalonando, organizando) in trend-setting (que implica la moda) fleet (flota)-average (promedio). Faltering (voice: titubea; movimiento/Ec.: tambalea) president. Chart (trazar) an altogether (total, completo) surer course (rumbo, curso). The nuclear plants could empower (autorizar + =) safety checks (controles). Roadkill (matar animales en la carretera). Bumper/ shock absorber (parachoques). A remorse (remordimiento)less: (despiadadas) advances: =, sugerencia, dinero: anticipación. Swell: (knee, …) hincharse, (river, stream) crecer, --ollen (hinchados) with pride, oleaje, the -- (protuberancias, ondulaciones) of the hills. Compact: sólido, compacto (apretado y poco poroso), conciso (breve, preciso, lacónico). Self-restrain (autocontrol, self-aware (concienzarse bien). From shoddy (chapucero, baja calidad) to fancier (más caprichosos + fanciful, whimsical) flats. Shot up (disparó, creció) → sales -- -- by 30%. Trophy (trofeo, que gusta exhibir) apartment. Incur: (anger) provocar, (risk) correr, (debt) contraer, (gasto) incurrir, incur a 20% capital-gain tax. Oversupply of unsold homes. He was indebted & reportedly (según se dice) outbid (oferta/puja más que alguien,V). Town house (residencia urbana). Return the bail out (pagar la fianza). Bolster (reforzar) the banks balance-sheet. Heavy-handed (torpe) control; control traffic (c. de la circulación), take c. or charge of sth (hacerse con el control de algo), loss c. (of o.s., …). Recruitment (reclutamiento). A more restful (sitio tranquilo, color relajante) capitalism. Banks assuage (calman) the misgivings (dudas, recelos) of the brightest (más brillantes, fuertes, inteligentes) institutions. Neglected: (casa) abandonada, (poeta) olvidado, (oportunidad) desaprovechada. Applications for 10 slots (vacantes; ranuras, huecos); there is a vacancy in the office, fill a post (proveer una v.). Art (=, destreza); the arts (las Bellas artes), Faculty of Arts (Facultad de Filosofía y Letras). He walked/ran up to the house, he hat up to 16% more offspring (cría) =/= offshoots: retoño, niño pequeño, (árbol) vástago, (empresa) filial, (familia) rama. American colonists cross Bering before sea level rose to flood it at the end of the last ice age. He punctured (pinchó) its share price, I had -- in the motorway, -- the pride (bajó los humos). Space X & Orbital: outfits that ferry (transportan, transbordan, transbordador) supplies (suministros). Acquire their lift (ascensor; ánimo, levanter, propulsión) from ...; jet propulsion, jet propelled (con -- a chorro). Cruise (navegar) at X km. above H_2O level. A host (anfitrión, receptor de un transplante, gran cantidad, hostia, huesped de parásitos). Out of balance, supply/demand imbalanced, what is my -- (saldo)? Filibuster (obstaculizar, obstruir, por ejemplo en la votación de las leyes). High-handedness (despotismo, arbitrariedad). Clamp (abrazadera) down (medidas drásticas, restricciones) on foreign-own media. Moonlight/having more than one job (pluriempleo). Squalls (borrasca, tempestad; chillidos,V) in some places, there are --s ahead (el futuro se anuncia no muy tranquilo). Playground: paraiso/lugar preferido de los millonarios, patio de recreo. Crafting/crafty (artesanía, astucia) of the rules in contention (discusión, argumento). The lopsided (desequilibrada) inversion has been stuck (atascada) + I got -- with him (lo tuve que aguantar, soportar). Shore up (apoyar, reforzar) the system; we must reinforce or strengthen our sales. The weird thing (lo raro) is that in despite of his revolutionary program he never gain elections. The country was agog (convulso, con mucha emoción); I was agog (curioso) to hear the news. Half-backed (mal concebido) & worst fit (adecuado, en forma) experiment. Breach: (law) infracción, (contract) incumplimiento, (danger) causar, (public order) alterar. Hem (dobladillo); hem in (cercar, arrinconar + put in a corner) → our forces were hemmed in to both east & west. Touchdown/ land (aterrizar). Lofts (desvanes, pajares) of the pigeon; dove of peace. Fanciful (caprichoso) & ramshackled (destartalado) empire; rickety (destartalado, inseguro, tambaleante) car. Mostly (en la mayoría, la mayor parte) unappealing (poco atractivos); mostly (sobre todo) in the evening. Hit the target/ bull's seye (diana): dar al blanco. Erran<u>t</u> (descarriado, errante) =/= erran<u>d</u> (recado, misión, mandato,V) → -- boy/messenger (recadero), run errands (hacer recados. They are fed up (hartos) with bickering (riñas, discusiones) between the two main political parties. Until further notice (aviso). Bulging (que sobresale, repleto, abombado, ojos saltones) waistlines (cintura, talla) → I'm watching my -- (estoy guardando la línea). Soportar: withstand/endure 500° C, not tolerate this treartment, stand/bear this person. Shokingly (terriblemente, pésimamente) difficile. Bliss (gozo, éxtasis)ful (maravillosa, dichosa, de mucha felicidad) impunity as displayed in the protracted (prolongado + prolonged, lengthy) theft; in blissful ignorance (feliz en la ignorancia). Right minded (honrado). Evitar: avoid a pb., prevent a tragedy, save troubles (molestias). Backroom team: equipo que trabaja en la sombra, (negocio) entre bastidores. Overturn: derrocar, derribar; anular, invalidar, (mesa, automóvil) volcar. Get carried away (entusiasmado) in a ruinous, disastrous; splendid, magnificent project. Newly minted (acuñado, que se gradúa en la Universidad); mentolado. Redraw (volver a trazar, revisar) borders … Carve up (repartirse) the old empire. Step up (incrementar) effords/production. He usually lays out (se echa) late at night. Tunnelling (socavando) seemingly (aparentemente + "=") insuperable, unsurmontable, unbearable barriers. Grazing (de pastoreo) land. Spear (lanza,V, arpón + arpoon,V) a fish. Emulate (copiar y mejorar) a move (movimiento, jugada, mudanza) from … Harmful/injurious (nocivo) populism. Rights he upholds (mantiene, defiende) at home. War-torn (destrozada) easter Ukraine. Bird's eye view. Forcibles (forzosas, =) mass conversions =/= forzudo (tough, brawny). Ghastly (horrible) law, how -- (que horror)! + aghast/horrify/appall (horrorizar). Skating (patinaje), figure (artístico) --, ice-skating, roller-skating =/= scathing (áspero, que corroe, cáustico, feroz). A more enlighted (progresista, inteligente) stance (postura, actitud). He junked (se deshizo de, tiró a la basura) his social policies. The plan backfired on him; his trick misfired (falló).

Impair/damage/harm (dañar, afectar) ↔ un--ed (intacto + =; untouched). Borg (cyborg): =, organism cibernético. Inquest: (Jur.) investigación, pesquisia judicial + they have an -- (análisis en profundidad) into or in their election defeat. Husbandry: agricultura, animal -- (cría); good -- (buena administración + thrifty management). Clemencia: (misericordia) clemency, mercy → beg for mercy (clemencia), have mercy on sb, (Jur.) leniency (indulgencia). Avalancha: --e of letters, a flood or torrent of people. Net (por Internet) phone. Obsessed in becoming an actress. The enmity (=) of the likes of Baltics. He bemoans (lamenta) his inability (incapacidad) to express himself. The grovel (grava) pit (hoyo, foso, cantera + quarry); Scotland produced many (es una cantera de) talented (grandes) footballers. Friendliness/sympaty (simpatía) with Germany; it's a show (muestra) of sympathy towards the victim; win everybody's (de todos) affection. Tough-guy (tipo duro); a tough stance (postura) or hard line (postura) against drugs, you have to be firm or strict with the students. Loathed (detestado) as wildly (locamente desenfrenado) popular. Demonstrators' falseness/falsehood. The likes (gustos) for bricks & mortars (morteros): inmuebles, construcción; under construction: en (vía) de construcción. The death knell (toque de difuntos, sentencia de muerte) fot the party; the TV was the -- -- for the movie; the death knell (caída) of the empire). Boundary (límite) line (línea divisoria) → make -- changes (hacer cambios en las circunscripciones), -- dispute,-- fence (cerca). Over & above (además de) its Ec. power; -- & -- normal requirements. First-past-the post system (elegir por mayoría relativa, quien tenga más votos). Bounce back/get back (recuperar + recover) to power. Its splinter (astilla)ing (fragmentado) vote & likelihood (probabilidad, =) of coalition government in Spain. Conscious (consciente) mind (mente), be conscious or aware of sth. The lingering (persistentes) effects against the downturn (deteriorización, bajón económico).

Endless (interminables) stimuly; encourage sb to do sth, stimulate the Ec., savings, efforts, appetite; promote a debate. Undermined (minados, debilitados, socavados) drains (desagües, sumideros, alcantarillas). Free will (voluntad, antojo): libre albedrio, antojo, capricho. Bearth (escasez) of money, of sincerity. Lovable (adorable, amoroso) boneshaker (cacharro, carraca). Effete: (instituciones, civilización) decadentes, (persona) agotada + exhausted) =/= books, ...: sold out, out of stock. Winding (hacer girar, serpentear). Other upgrades (mejoras). Humans & delfine are very close. Know by sight, disappear from --, lose one's --. Pinpoint (precisar, diagnosticar, localizar, identificar) where the dog comes from. Smug (engreídos, petulantes) talks → --ness. Habitable zone, only the Earth is habitable. Maven will blast off (despegar) in an attempt to work out (calcular, resolver) the most intriguing aspects of the Univers. The wraith (fantasma, + ghost, phatom). Outlying (remoto, alejado, periférico + outlying district. Recelo: (mirar con recelo) look with suspicion at sb, (temor) misgiving, apprehension, (desconfianza) mistrust, distrust. Glad to make your acquaintance + we're old acquaintants but not for many years. Backward: hacia atrás, nación atrasada, niño retrasado + (estar retrasado en una actividad) be behind, ej.: in or with one's paymentes, we are lagging behind in the production. Stool (taburete; heces: deposición) in the middle or centre of the square. Look up: buscar en diccionario, (pers.) visitor + the physician is holding his surgery (cirugía, consultorio): está visitando. Wherefore (por qué, por tanto, por lo cual). Deposition: quitar una dignidad, (ley) deposición, (Geog.) sedimentación, (King) destronar, (president, director) destituir + overthrow. In the midst (pleno, medio) of a battle. Covenant: pacto, (Biblia) alianza. Ye (vosotros), thou (tú, tus). Rectitud: righteousness, rectitude =/= honestidad: honesty, honour, decency. Stumbling block (escollo + pitfall) to sth → the many pitfalls of English. Whosoever (quien, todo aquel que) unite (une, confluye)/join together) carefully. Her father betrothed (prometió en matrimonio) her but she didn'accept ... Scourge (azotar) → a region --ed by famine. Agradecimiento (gratitude, appreciation) → with our more sincere thanks, in appreciation of what you ... Avoid the enticing (atractivo; tentador + tempting) sinning. Glad (feliz)ness: gozo, alegría → -- of heart/spirit, happiness (felicidad), be glad about sth ↔ sadden → make sad (entristecer). Perversity (contrariedad, terquedad) =/= --sely (sin lógica, obstinadamente, tercamente). Transgressor/offender (infractor). Applicants are rigorously screened (tamizados). Long-standing: (duradero) agreement, dispute, friendship). Feeling of drowsiness/sleepiness (modorra, somnolencia). Tracker (rastreador) dog. Feld (fieltro) =/= filter (fitro), filter-tipped cigarette. Add-on/accessory: accesorio, componento adicional. Let's sit further (más, más lejos, fomentar) forward (más para adelante) =/= farther (lejano + far off, distant) → further --/far away: más lejos, en otras partes. Disposable (desechables) batteries, not-returnable containers (envases), the offer is not to be turned down lightly. Showcased (exhibido, mostrado) in the front-page. Residential mortgage inflame (=, enciende) America's housing bubble. Self- demeaning (autodegradante) =/= biodegradable. Byword (synonym) for nastiness (gravedad, lo repugnante) into a rainbow (arcoiris) nation. For your own good (bien). An utter (total, completo + =) disaster. Harshly (duramente, ásperamente) judged. Misguidedness (desacierto, torpeza); that was really tactless or clumsy of you! (¡menuda torpeza la tuya!). Good/bad reputation. Congress was walloped (apalizado, golpeado) + they hit her on the head, the teacher banged on the desk with his hand, the rain was beating against the window. Sot (borrachín) →--ted (locas, enamoradas) for him. Fire up (enardecer, entusiasmar) the Ec., be fired up (estar enardecido) about sth. Skullcaps (gorros, casquetes), bathing cap. Connived (confabulado, cómplice, con vista gorda), complicity, involvement. A rapturous (enthusiastic, =) reception; I trayed to seem (parecer) enthusiastic. Outweigh (ser más que) → this step --s all other considerations. Ostentar: hold a position, show off; they flaunt/parade their wealth. Chunks (pedazos) of fast-growing bits (partes) of the market. Felons (delincuentes) of a hackable (piratizable) base; juvenile delinquent, abitual offender. Adman (profesional de la pub, publicista). Succour (Socorro,V) → relief (alivio) or aid, she went to his aid; he gave a sigh (suspiro) of relief (alivio). Bookish (estudioso), an expert in or a scholar of medieval literature. The chief (=, principal) mover (promotor). Longhaul (de larga distancia) market. Inoxidable (rustproof), stainless (inoxidable)- steel. Louds (altas, fuertes) complaints; he has a loud voice. Disobey. Bump (chocar) into the fences. Spur (estimular, espuela,V) them to greater effords. Indoor (interior, cubierto) ski slopes (pendientes). Attract sb's attention, --ed by sb's idea. Its revenues dragged down (decayeron) by price competition. Hair-rising/horrifying. Bring a prosecution (juicio, proceso) against sb + case for prosecution; indictment (acusación, procesamiento) ↔ defence. Acelerar: (motor) accelerate, (proceso, cambio) speed up, (paso) kicken, walk a bit faster. Face the consequences. Reacquaint: (reconocimiento), (error) admid, (pers., sonido) recognize. This squeeze (restricción) will intensify. Western Ec. climb out (sale trepando) of the slump (bajón). Swivel round (girar sobre los talones), -- chair. Our mind can be warped (pervertida, deformada, combada). Fewer pointless (inútil, inmotivada) initiative; on his initiative, on one's own --. Insane: loco, descabellado, insensato → the -- (enfermos mentales). Anticuado: (pers., ideas, ropa) old-fashioned, (sitema, aparato) antiquated. Parting (de despedida) words, -- (de gracia) shot, -- of ways (encrucijada, despedida definitiva). Fun (alegría, diversión) ended when …, a fun pers., have a -- (divertirse); fun run (marathon popular con fines benéficos), funny (gracioso, raro). Embrace (abrazo,V, adoptar, adherirse a; aprovechar, emprender, lanzarse en). Grilling (cuestionario + questioning). Board (tabla; junta, consejo)rooms: sala de juntas; advisorial board (consejo consultivo). Namedropping (dárselas de conocer personas importantes). Heartily (a carcajadas, enardeciente, efusivamente) embraces … Puff: (air) soplo, (wind) racha, -- of smoke (calada), out of -- (aliento) =/= off-putting (desalentador, desagradable), be unpleasant to sb. Mass-market (mercado popular). Petrol-powered saloon, pub, bar, tavern (=, bar, taberna, cantina). Nowhere will match (igualar, emparejar) the lefty (robustos, fornidos) subsidies. Reveal personal secrets (sacar trapos sucios a relucir). Adaptor (adaptador, enchufe multiple). Paperback (libro de bolsillo, rústico, para gran público). A stream (corriente, arroyo) alongside (junto a, al lado de) the garden + stream blood from the wound/nose. My primary (principal, primario) purpose. The congestion (vehicles, Med.) is tamed (amansada, dominada). Prever: foresee, anticipate. Avoid rear-impact crashes; rear- engined. Put spin (efecto) on a ball; go for a -- (dar una vuelta). Enloquecer (drive mad, madden, go out of one's mind). Libya's hoped-for (esperada) transition. Fast (rápido; firme, sólido, inalterable) ness of Syria. Hand in: (homework) entregar, (one's resignation) presentar. Reproach (=, recriminar) sth to sb =/= approach: acercarse, (pers.) abordar. Sack: saco, bolsa de papel; give sb the -- (botar), saquear. Meddling (intromisión), meddlesome (intrometido). Raid: incursión, ataque aéreo, asalto,V. Stamp: sello, timbre, -- album; cupón, vale; the -- (impronta) of a genious in his work, -- collecting (filatelia). Sideshow (atracción secundaria). Outspend sb (gastar más que alguien). Relentless (imparable + unstoppable) courtship (cortejo, noviazgo) of centrist voters. Sibbling (de hermanos) rivalry. It unleashed (desncadenó) a storm of passions. They sullied (mancharon) their cause. The capitalist drubbling (paliza, derrota) to the third world. Whimper (lloriquear, quejido/gemido,Vs + groan, moan, whine, wailing; howling (aullar).

Infrastructure upgrades (mejoras). Bask (disfrutar) of his benighted (ignorante) people; -- in the sun (tomar el sol); tan: (piel) curtir, (sun) ponerse moreno. The thornier (más espinoso) problem of streamlining (racionalización de) a tangled (enredado) tax regime. Gall (descaro; bilis, irritar, hiel + bile) → galling (mortificante, que domina las pasiones). Curtailment: disminución, restricción; without restrictions, power cuts (restricciones eléctricas), budgetary constrain (coacción, restricción). Rag (trapo viejo, periodicucho; broma pesada, tomar el pelo) → I was only --ing. Picker (recolector). Toss (sacudida, tirada) rings around the cup, the boat was --ed by the waves, the horse --ed his head. The lion circled (rodeó) its prey, old people are easy prey for unscrupulous salesman (dependiente, vendedor, representante, viajante). China's secretive (reservado) space program. A deadly (mortal, funesta, terrible) crisis. Cynicism is warranted (garantizado). Onlookers (espectadores, =) lingered (persistieron, tardaron en desaparecer). High speed rail (carril) has clawed (arañado) a market shared from airlines. Cover up (ocultar/cubrir totalmente; disimular (+ hide, conceal). Villain (maleante + crook)'s sidekick (compañero, secuaz + follower, henchman). His tenets (principios, =) are outlandish: (idea, conducta) extraña, descabellada, (vestido) estrafalario. Stand-lone (autónomo, independiente) → -- - -- firm, selfemployer worker; (periodista, fotógrafo) freelancer. Onslaught/attack → he left himself open (expuesto) to attack, go on the offensive (pasar al ataque), surprise --, suicide -- (atentado), pre-emptive strike. The offline (desconectado, autónomo) world. Destello (rayo de luz, resplandor): sparkle, twinckle, glitter → centelleo: sparkling, twinkling, glittering; glint (centelleo, destello,Vs). Pare: (nail) cortar, (fruta) pelar → -- financial crisis; -- down (costes: reducir) to a minimum. Taper off (disminuir poco a poco) → his populary is --ing off. Their everyday/daily (cotidianos) rallies, lifes, etc. Run down (descender, atropellar, hundir, agotarse) a steep (escarpado) hill. The protesters struck up (entablaron, empezaron a tocar) the chorus (coro). A perception took hold/root (se reafirmó), favour cliques (camarillas). Bonus (prima, recompensa, bonificación; ventaja) → -- scheme (plan de incentivos), tax incentive. Apresurar: hurry, hasten, speed up. Fasten: (caso) cerrar, (coat, belt) abrochar, atar, sujetar, (stick/glue) pegar. Rearguard (retaguardia). The crowd greeted (saludaba, recibía) his arrival. Break down (derribar, descomponer) chemical agents into sludge (resíduos, fango). Salary/wage earners (asalariados). Saver (ahorrador) of words. Officials toiled (se esforzaron) ... Leafletting (reparto) leaflets (folletos, panfletos). Tintin (tintineo), tingling (hormigueo). A basement (sótano habitable)/ cellar (s. almacén) without ventilation + an extractor fan. Attempt to slip (resbalar, pasar desapercibido) the spyware (programa de espía). Barrow (carretilla) to rescue (rescatar) ..., rescue operations, land reclamations (rescate de terrenos). Meneo: (tail) wag, (head) shake, (liquid) stir, (hips: caderas) swing. By a roundabout (rotonda, indirecto/alternative way). The desirable American stood for (significaba, representaba) ... What did it stand for (significaba)? An empty feeling inside, empty his pockets. Contingency (=, de urgencia) plan (=, esquema, medida, disposición). Draw up: (testament/will, contract) redactar, (plan) elaborar, (trups) ordenar. Animar: encourage (+ Ec...: estimular), (espíritu) cheer up, (reunión, fiesta) liven up; (señas para que sigan adelante) wave up. Mess around (pasar el rato, hacer tonterias) + that's nonsense or rubbish, let's be serious (dejémonos de tonterias). Reach (alcanzar/ llegar a, ponerse en contacto con) out: tender la mano. Strip down/away: (monopolio) desmantelar, (máquina) desmontar + take to pieces. Ejercer: (ejercicio) practise/ce, (right) exercise. Inveigh: vituperio (reprobación), arremeter, lanzar invectivas → -- against ... Trespass (entrar ilegalmente) upon: abusar de + contract (infringer, violar) + not -- (prohibida la entrada). Entry to common market/a military zone, -- requirements, refuse the entry. Bring down: (government) derrocar, (opponent) derribar, (price) disminuir. A flurry (oleada) of emotion, of wind (ráfaga), a flurry (aluvión) of proposals =/= the flags fluttered (se agitaban) alongside each other (juntas codo a codo) =/= flatter (halagar, favorecer) ↔ unflattering (poco alagüeño) =/= flatten (allanar) =/= glaring: (luz) deslumbrante, (injusticia) grande, (flaw: defecto) flagrante, evidente. Curl: bucle, curva…, (hair) rizo, (smoke) espiral, (chard/paper) arrollar, (snake) enrollarse sobre, (leaf) abarquillarse, (waves) encresparse, -- up (acurrucarse). He got nothing out/derived no benefits (provechos) from the course; for his own benefit (bien, provecho) =/= make profits (ganancias); sell sth at a profit. Chill out: relajarse + relax; calmarse + calm. Lock up/away: (valuables, home) cerrar con llave, (criminal) encarcelar. Come up: (pers.) ascender, (sol) salir. A pool (reserva) of untapped (sin explotar) labour-vengeful (vengativo) status. To a lesser extend (º). Just a sliver (tajada, rodaja fina, astilla + chip, splinter) away from junk (baratija/trastos, basura, V) status. The miss-selling (mala venta). Fire-proofing (a prueba de fuego) =/= cortafuegos: firebreak, fire wall. Funda: case, cover, (pillow) pillowcase, (raket) cover, (pistol) holster, spectacles/glasses case. Excesivamente ("=") troubled (molesto, preocupado, con problemas/dificultades). American banks got out (salieron) of perish (que perecian) business. Britain falls inbetween (en medio). The challenges (desafios, retos, intentos) are nibbling (ágiles, diestros); challenger: desafiador, aspirante, contrincante. Sinvergüenza: (canalla) swine/scoundrel, (pícaro) rascal, little devil. Miscreant (malas, ruines, sagaces) firms have instilled (inspirado, infundido) fear. Ec. growth is measly (mezquino, miserable). Asset managers hunted (=, buscaban, perseguian desperately) … =/= hounded (perseguidos, acosados) by the press. Weigh down: sujetar con pesos + agobiar, abrumar → -- -- with debt/ -- -- on sb (a alguien). Index (=) to inflation; cost of living --. The paltriest (más ínfimo, mísero) of the returns, for a few -- pennies, for som -- reason. Inflation proof (resistente a la inflación) income. You stay right here! (¡no te muevas de aquí!). Top up (llenar, recargar + recharge) batteries. Eking out (estirar, hacer que alcance) the power. Hound (acosar) → bloodhound: (perro, detectivo: sleuth) sabueso (indagador). Swallow the bait (morder el cebo/anzuelo) + 50 pellets (gránulos) of poisonous bait. Updraft/draught/current (corriente ascendente). Fur (piel/pelo de animal, sarro) → -- coat. Wiped out (limpiado, aniquilado) within 50 years. New Horizon blasted off (despegó) in 2006. A mottled (moteado, manchado, jaspeado) world =/= demoted (degradado, de menor categoría). Striking (llamativos, sorprendentes) geisers. Sedatelly (sobriamente, reposadamente, con calma). A covering of frost (escarcha). Beyond (más allá de) the seas. Superbug (bactería asesina, transgenésica). A sandbar (barrera de arena). A saying summed up/summarized (resumido in …). Eficazmente: tellingly, effectively, efficaciously, efficiently. They won't relish (no les gustará) having to walk; I don't relish the prospect, relish with a film, relishing (saboreando) his triumph, astronomers will relish (entusiasmarse, disfrutar con) this close-up (primer plano) glimpse (vislumbre: ver débilmente) of Plato; glimpse her feelings (entrever sus sentimientos). The bleached (blanqueada, decolorada) atmosphere of the desert. Laugh off (tomarse a risa). A taster (catador, muestra) exhibition. A slight (un poco de) temperature (fiebre), --est (mínimas) ideas, chances. Build it anew. Put cartoonists (humoristas, dibujantes de chistes) on the payroll (nómina). Wilderness (desierto, monte, tierra virgen). Bombshell: obus, (chocking news) bomba; a real bombsell (un bombón). Fool: tontear, engañar) about/around (hacer payasadas). The onlookers (espectadores) are gripped/moved/excited (emocionados); I get all emotional when I watch romantic films. Exposure: (light, heat, risk) exposition, (impostor: =; who feigns: que finge; who deceive: que engaña) desenmascarar, a home with southern --. Spare (escatimar) no effords. Drove him out: expulsó + expelled, sent off. Plentiful/abundant (abundante). Be on leave (permiso), take one's -- of sb (despedirse de), say goodby; I'll -- you at the station, the car -- the road. Good riddance! (¡adios y buen viaje!) for them (que se pudran). Caravana: (=), (retención del tráfico) backup/tailback, (fila hacia el mismo punto) convoy + =. Roaming (vagabundear, vagar, deambular) =/= lounge (gandulear, salón); departure (salida) lounge/gate (puerto de embarque). Alien: extraño, extranjero, extraterrestre. Leave tail (rastro, sendero, estela) behind us. Customer/shopper (cliente). The tracking (rastreo) is inexorable. Ten or thereabouts (más o menos, allí cerca). Mesh (malla) → get enmeshed (enredarse, ser cogido) into a net. Slimness (delgadez) =/= slimy (viscoso, =, (pers.) falsa → sliminess (+ "viscosity"). To a great/certain/lesser (menor) extend. Acosado: hounded, harassed, beset, pestered + molestado) → -- by doubts, with questions about political troubles. Put one's foot in it (meter la pata). Hold (retener) sb in thrall (esclavitud). The new generations are eating away (desgastan, corroen) the ancient model. Sightly (agradable a la vista) ↔ un--: feo + ugly, nasty (+ asqueroso, ...), unpleasant. Maim: lisiar, mutilar (+ =). His biggest achievement/success is the conquest of the market. Assets (activos) =/= pass on (pasa, da, contagia) to their children an asset (atractivo, baza, ventaja) that can't be frittered away (malgastado, desperdiciado). They are 60% of high-school dropouts (abandonan la Uni., marginados). Pull strings (mover palancas) into a top-noch (de categoría) colleges. Repressed (reprimido) people. Back: (animal) lomo, (silla) respaldo; trasero → back's troubles (molestias). At the top of the pile (montón). The tilt (inclinación) of Earth's axis, --ed back in his chair, -- sth back/forward. Bloodlust (sed, codicia). Flippantly (ligeramente, con poca seriedad). Senior officials skim off (separan, quitan) money for the kit (equipo, útiles, cosas personales, ropa), belongings (bártulos). Give sb a piggyback (llevar alguien a cuestas). Pageant (festividad, espectáculo al aire libre), pageantry (pompa, esplendor). Over tough (duras, fuertes) rules. Preventive, preventative & precautionary measure. Slight (ligeros) accent, improvement, temperatura, idea. Slights (ligeros, escasos; desaires, desprecios + disdains, disregards) against Islam. Tier (grada, hilera superpusta, piso, nivel) → two -- health/education system. The safeguard (salvaguardia, protección,Vs) afforded (ofrecido, permitido) to ethnic groups. Advocacy/defence & caveat (advertencia)/warning & advise. Plunder (saquear) the reserves, water supplies, stocks of coal, food supplies, currency reserves. Surmising (suponiendo + supposing, assuming; conjecturing) that people at the top are a rotten crowd. Dirigir: (película) direct, (debate) lead, chair, (hotel) run, (orquesta) conduct/drive. It ran (estuvo en cartelera) for three years. Cantankerous/grouch (cascarrabias, gruñón). This is the last straw (el colmo), the straw (paja) that breaks the camel's back (la gota que colma el vaso). Shore (costa, orilla; puntal) → date (fecha) to shore up (sostener, apoyar) or shoot down (derribar, echar por tierra). Skewer (pincho, broqueta; ensartar). Slit (corte, abertura,V) a sac open: abrir un saco con una cuchillada. Pretend, feign, fake (fingir). Some are gazing (miran fijamente) fondly (con cariño, ingenuamente), kindly (amablemente) & friendly (amistosamente). Skyline (horizonte, =) =/= horizontal (=). Bland: sociable, acogedor, (pers.) afable, (food) insípida, fácil de digerir, soso, anodino. Apartments block, block of flats. Square (cuadrado) → the town -- (la plaza del pueblo), try to -- the circle, -- sth with sth: conciliar (=). Tourists guide, to your guidance (para que le sirva de guía). Backtrack: retroceder, (explicaciones) ir más atrás, (decisiones) echarse atrás =/= backward: fall/walk -- + --looking (retrógrado). Be in cahoots with (conspirar con, confabular, asociar). Munificiency: esplendidez, generosidad. Without pandering (consentimiento) → pander sb's whim. He spurned (rechazó, desdeñó) the risk sharing ... Fellow: pers., tipo, compañero → he's an old --, -- inmate (asylum: interno; prison: preso; (hospital: paciente), -- student. Country man/compatriot. Overblown: estilo pomposo, pretencioso, (flor) demasiado abierta. Onrush (oleada, avalancha) of immigrants. The refugees were drown or dying of exposition (at heat/cold). Mr's Cameron promise in/out referendum. Warmth/affection (cariño). He was principled (basado en fuertes principios). Mop (fregona, estropajo, fregar); wash the dishes, do the washing up. Gamble (riesgo; apuesta,Vs, jugar) → -- my reputation. The trusty (leal, fiel) defence minister =/= trust me, trust in sth/sb. Germany earns accolades (elogios, entusiasmos, honores, galardones). Bring to bear (ejercer) → abroad France bring ... to bear. Cherrypick: (Universidad, empresa ...) seleccionar cuidadosamente los mejores; -- the benefits of integration. Apoyar: lean/rest the ladder; back/support me if I complain; support/bear hypothesis; support of people. Warm-up (preparación, Sp.: precalentamiento) act. Hyllary: the hostile Congressist is shaping (forma, determina) her ... He unseated: (government) derribó, (rider) hizo caer. Ethos (espíritu de grupo, escala de valores) → the middle class --; the -- of free enterprise. Approximate/rough (aproximativo) =/= the train is approaching Abu-Dhabi =/= gesstimate (cálculo aroximado). A has-been (vieja gloria). The swagger (arrogante) man strut about/around (se pavonea) along with a blonde. The typical marcher (manifestante) is a middle-aged. The impending (inminente, =) announcement; I'd like to make an announcement to you. Tabloid (periódico popular), the --s (la prensa amarilla). They likened (compararon + "=") him to ... Manhunt (persecución, búsqueda de delincuente o desaparecido). Preserve (=, consevar, proteger + protect, defend) → heaven -- us! (¡Dios nos proteja!). Ec. upturn (mejora, incremento). Mishandle (maltratar, manejar mal) his response. Bombastic: (estilo) enfático, ampuloso (hinchado, presuntuoso), (pers.) pomposa, regordeta. Dot, --, -- (puntos suspensivos) + deep craters -- (puntean, se esparcen en) the runway, a family --ted about (esparcida) all over Europe. Dislocated (=, trastornados) plans. Shot up: (T., valor) dispararse, crecer muy rápido) → it -- -- by 30%. Pound: Libra, perrera, depósito de coches; (especias) machacar, (mesa) golpear; aporrear. IS incomes (ingresos) are taking a pounding (paliza). Morge (depósito de cadaveres) =/= dirge (canto fúnebre). Take off: (avión) despegar, (mancha) eliminar, (ropas) quitarse, (miembro) amputar, (precio) descontar + discount. House (domiciliario) arrest. Hardship (miseria, apuro, penuria) clause: cláusula de salvaguardia + live in poverty, the misfortune of the war. Suffer hardship (pasar apuros). Test the staying power (resistencia, aguante) of the new upstart (arrivista, presuntuoso) left-wing political party. Mas'plan has been dropped at the instance (=, petición) of his rival. The campaigners (defensores) have turned the national day to a mass (de masa) event =/= say/celebrate/offer mass (misa). Be distracted (trastornado) with anxiety (estar loco de ansiedad, angustiado). Road-map (hoja de ruta). Surveyor: topógrafo, (industria) périto (tasador). He tutted (chasqueó la lengua con signo de desaprobación). A sketchy (incompleto, sin detalles) grasp (agarrar, entender ...) of the religion. Grease (suciedad en mecánica). Train militias deemed (consideradas) helpful (eficientes, serviciales, útiles + useful). Snort: (animal) resoplido, (pers.) ronquido, (cerdo) gruñido. Their largesse (generosidad) to Hizbollah. Stockpile (acumular, almacenar; reservas). Firecracker/banger (petardo). Mr Rato released (liberado) from police retention. Overrun: (cockroaches) invadir, (presupuesto) exceder. Striking (llamativo, sorprendente) peace; it is hardly (difícilmente) surpising that. In their stead (lugar); meeting place (lugar de encuentro), the concert will take place indoors or at an indoor venue (en un lugar cerrdo). Raven (cuervo) =/= rave (delirar) about sth/sb (poner por las nubes) →

rave reviews (críticas muy positivas). Presentar: (show) present, launch; submit a repport/application (solicitud). Their dependants (pers. a cargo) =/= he has held the office or post of European commissionner forth three years, he left his post as ambassador, a top/senior official (un alto cargo) has resigned, person in public office (cargo público). Fed up (harto) → get -- --. Rage: furia, rabia, cólera; (storm, sea) mujir, bramar; protests against sth/sb. Gamberrismo (hooliganism, loutish behaviour). Revamped (renovado, modernizado; image/strategy: poner al día) on an inmate reoffending (reincidencia). Did not return request (solicitud) for comment. Blizzard (ventisca), (letters, bills, etc.) avalancha (=) → the -- sent it off course (fuera de rumbo). The House (session de la cámara) sat (duró) all night. Fondness: (thing) afición, (pers.) cariño. Humdrum (rutinario, monótono + =) =/= tedious (aburrido + bored) → his speech was --. Mislead (engañar, inducir a error, corromper + corrupt). His sight (vista, mira) is set on general elections. Seal (cerrar) a pact. Testarrudo: mule, pigheaded, stubborn. Nakedly (manifestamente) self-interested (con interés personal). Scenery: (paisaje + landscape, coutryside), (teatro) escenografía, decorado + decoration. Akin (semejante) to those that thronged (atestaban) the streets; stuff (atestar) sb with fruits. Digging (excavación + =). Squarely (directamente, justamente) → the blow hit him -- on the nose + it happened just when the energy crisis broke out. It snakes (serpentea) around the dusty rubbish. Morras (cenegal, lugar pantanoso). Loose one's footing (equilibrio), the Ec. is on a shaky -- (sin bases sólidas), on an equal -- (en pie de igualdad), on an emergency -- (situación), on a war -- (al pie de guerra). Heaven knows. Namesake (homónimo, =). <u>A</u>front (ofensa, insulto) to sovereignty =/= <u>up</u>front (abierto, franco; pago inicial, por adelantado). Men languishing (languideciendo, consumiéndose) on the "death row" has been executed. Crucial (primordial) role; it is of fundamental (=, primordial) concern, it is essential (primordial) to now. Underlie (subyacer) → their underlying (subyacentes) hardly (apenas) have time to … The cities engulfed (tragaron, sumergieron) the villages (aldeas). Crank (excéntrico, maniático, raro, cascarrabias). Desencadenar: (prisoner) unchain, (dog) unleash, (crise, reaction) trigger. Sexual relationship/intercourse (relaciones), our relationship (relación amorosa) lasted until 2020; trade relations, business relations. Yummy (riquísimas) mumies. Stuffed (lleno, disecado) with steering (de dirección) commitees. Obsessed with the idea → become -- to make up (confeccionar un vestido, etc). Sweltering (abrasador, sofocante) heat. Mooted (discutido) point. The treasurer (tesorero) has been feasting (se dió un banquete). Actuator (impulsor, accionador). Stanching (restañar: parar el curso) of bleeding. With no say (voz) in drawing them up (redactar, preparar) ↔ have one's say (voz y voto). The crisis get them restive (inquietos). Who owns the pen? (¿de quien es el bolígrafo?). Screenplay (guión + script =/= (--) hyphen → depart (salir) from the script. He made the theory his own, but he convinced nobody. Untimely (prematura, inoportuna) demise (desaparición, fallecimiento). Milk (ordeñar, exprimir; sacar partida de) the historic importance of … Bonhomie (afabilidad, =). Firm (=, sólido, estricto). The collective nemesis (=, castigo) of the Gods. As customers flutter/flit (revolotean) in/out (entran/salen precipitadamente: headingly, very suddenly, precipitately, rashly). Hablador: chatty, talkative. Stodgy: (pers., style) pesado, aburrido, (science fiction novel) aburrida, densa, (cacke, pie: de carne) pesado. Scintillating: (star, jewel) centelleante, (wit, conversation) chispeante, brillante. Fingertips search (investigación exhaustiva). He used to go by the position of the sun. Their jaws dropped (quedaron boquiabiertas). The proceeding (proceso, proceder) was kept secret. The state had turned on (en contra de) its own citizens. Hitler staff carted off (se llevaron) the artworks from Rumania & hired an art stuntman to evaluate the find (hallazgo).

Outlaw sexual intercourse (coito) between Jews & non Jews. Soft (blando) pronouncement (declaración, dictamen) against influential people. He will go ahead (seguir adelante) with Chinese deal. Turkey picked (eligió) Chinese missile, even if he is in the NATO. This stood for (significaba) blue jeans, chewing gum & few strains (esfuerzos). Unlawful (ilegales) practices. The outer (externo, alejado) London boroughs (municipios) are more polluted. Plenty of spare (no utilizado) land in the rocky Spain put society at risk; new kind of business have to be invented to lift productivity. Cope with (arreglárselas) paying workers up to $10 (hasta 10 $ nada más) an hour. Strange hum (murmullo, cantorreo, zumbido) are head in Mars's surface. With gallantry (=, valentía + bravery, courage), he was playing along (siguiendo el juego) gamely (valientemente). They dropped down before graduating & he became just a seasonal worker. Remembrance (memoria, recuerdo) day → in -- of sth. Refrán (saying, proverb + "=") → as the saying goes: "be completely open about thing" (ir con la verdad por delante). Simple/modest (sencillo) → it's a simply but tasty dish (es un plato fácil de preparer pero es apetitoso). Fulsome (exagerado, empalagoso, demasiado efusivo) praise (elogio). Be here albeit/even iff/although (aunque) briefly. Soaring rents wreck/destroy business & indirectly ruin workers. The lopsided (torcido/desequilibrado) 70% result. He exudes (=, irradia) emphaty. The contrast to middle class's pain (dolor) is telling/revealing (revelador). Manners (modales, educación) =/= manner (manera, actitud, estilo) → French --. Bow: reverencia, inclinación; prometer solemnemente: solemnly → he --ed pay for universal pre-school (jardín de infancia). Curb the tax by half a percentage point. Crime has fallen twise as far as in the rest of America. It crunches (cruje, chirria; n^{os}: devora) data but its calculations are not very accurate. Deter (desalentar, disuadir) them from carrying guns =/= deteriorar: (estropear) damage, (Mec.) wear & tear. No one city public shool was in

NY state's leading 25. Proficient (competentes) in Maths but incompetent in Humanities. Tracked (seguía la pista) of complaints (denuncias) & linked (relacionó, hizo connexion de) them to tax irregularities. Pinpoint (precisar, identificar) illegal building conversions against fire hazards (riesgos) American politics can be distilled ("=", reducido a lo esencial) in one word: the strong America =/= haphazard (al azar o sistemático). Where is Republican party heading. Archetypical (=, modelo) of backroom (trastienda, anónimos, =) politicians. A polling (votación) deficit to see off (despedir, deshacerse de, derrotar) a proposal for compulsory labelling (etiquetado). Take away (apartar, llevarse) the perks (beneficios, ventajas) of the defenceless people. Drudgery (trabajo pesado) → machines take -- out of the housework in compliance with (conforme a) ... Seal (foca, sello/precinto) off: (house/room: cerrar, área/street: acordonar) + surroud the place when the Pope visits Paris. Insularity ("=", estrechez de mente). Coterie (grupo, peña + group/circle) → cultural -- of investors. Steadier (más firme, continuo, constante) hand (pulso) in conducting foreign affairs. Kite (cometa, cheque sin fondos + bad check). Unnoticed (inadvertido, desapercibido) → go (pasar) unnoticed, slip away (marcharse) unnoticed. Ungir: (Rel.) anoint → --ed (ungido) with oil, (Med.) put ointment on, rub with ointment. Deemed (considerado) wayward (indisciplinado + unruled; rebelde + =ious). (1) Mangrove (mangle) + (2) swamp (pantano, marisma, inundar) → (1) (2) (manglar). Streets thronged/crammed (atestados) with people & craps (porquería, estupideces, mierda + shit,V) in the roads respectively. Be dredged (dragado) through (por un) pristine (=, original/antiguo, inmaculado/impoluto) lake; rain forests (selvas tropicales) are uprooted (desarraigadas) ... The shady (sombreado, frondoso; negocio turbio) palm trees buttress (apoyo, sostén; apoyar, apuntalar) K. Lumpur's outermost (más extremo) sprawl (expansión). In the shade: a la sombra, put sb on the

-- (hacer sombra a alguien, tono =/= shadow: sombra de un objeto; oscuridad, tinieblas, ensombrecer, oscurecer. Great (excelente) man/artist, wine =/= large/big home, family. Segregación: racial segregation, (Anat.) secretion ("="). Sought-after (codiciados, solicitados) exotic foods. Ganga (trato, negocio: bargain) → it's a --! (¡trato hecho!), make a -- (cerrar trato). Premature receding hairline (entradas). Play up: dar guerra/coba, exagerar/entretener con engaños/halagos. Greeting: recuerdos, saludos → she sends -- for you; -- card (carta de felicitaciones). The tear (rotura) of the duct (conducto) ruined our village. Arrebato: de ira (rage) → flew into a rage; outburst of anger (cólera), a sudden fit of enthusiasm, anger, passion. Outbound (dirigido hacia fuera) from Plato. Discount: (=, V) + you have to deduct $ 10, they give you 19 % deduction if you pay cash, excluding or not including accomodation expenses. Whet: (instrumento) afinar + sharpen/hone, (interés, curiosidad) estimular → whetting of scientific appetites. Parish (parroquia), priest (párroco), curate (ayudante de). Unpleasant experience, learn by --, work (laboral) --, pilot scheme (experiencia piloto), the new drug is being tested. The coffee-berry (baya) borer (taladrador) is an annoying (molesto) beetle (escarabajo). Strut about/around sth or boast about or of sth (jactarse de algo). Sketching (incompleto, sin detalles) bill of rights (declaración de derechos). Hauled up in Court (llevado a los tribunals) → be released (liberado). Timing (fijar el tiempo) → the -- of the meeting was inconvenient (tiempo, appointment: inoportuno; location, design: poco práctico, incómodo), the timing of this is important. Revile: injuriar, vilipendiar (despreciar, maltratar), Assembly line (cadena de montaje), assembly production (producción en cadena) =/= the chain came off my bike, distribution chain. Unforeseen (unexpected) → they turn up (aparecen) in the most -- places, it was all very --. Upon: encima, (tiempo) después → -- his arrival. A rival paper brought out a spoiler (publica una exclusiva para desfavorecer al rival). Overstretch (forzar demasiado) → --ed: (system, service) desbordado, que funciona al límite de su capacidad, ej.: the police force, my budget. My throad/vocal cords hurts me = I've a sore throad. You have few friends in common with. Crime history collection (rubish/post: recogida, (taxes: recaudación), Crime Squad (Brigada de Invesigación Crimina). A kiss before dying. The results have exceeded our expectations; life expectancy is rising & becomes problematic. Date of receipt (recibo) → I received an important sum, "message received". Perplejidad: perplexity, puzzlement + desconcierto. Disfrutar: enjoy o.s.; disfrute (enjoyment). Taxing potency (lo fuerte, lo poderoso); potencia sexual ↔ sexual impotene). Acobardado (intimidated) + be chicken/ daunted =/= asustado: frightened, startled. Submarinismo: scuba diving, (para pescar) underwater fishing; (submarinista) scuba diver; (su tubo para respirar snorkel. Alluring (atrayentes, seductores) packages; I'm not taken with the idea (la idea no me seduce), she captivated everyone with her charm. The showiest (los más ostentosos + ostentatious). Demand for tobacco seems to go up along with demand for cannabis. Get tougher on its unruly (indisciplinado, rebelde + rebel, rebellious) client. Mildness: palidez, bondad, suavidad, lo templado). He looks (mira, parece) inefficient ("="), ineffectual (inútil + useless), ineffective (ineficaz). Business<u>wise</u> (en cuanto a). Policymakers (politólogos) sneer (comentan con desprecio, desdeñan) =/= despreciativo: disparaging, sneering, disdainful, scornful. Intricated (=, complejo) pink (rosados, felices) structures. Bleached (decolorados, descoloridos) looking (pinta, aspecto) skeletons (=, en vehículo: estructura, armazón). The cream (crema, nata) soaks in (penetra) in … Thorns (espinas) of starfish. Coran- chompers (masticadores). Sediments cloud (nube, enturbian) waters. Its upkeep (mantenimiento) will require … Repopulate ravaged (devastados, saqueados, hechos estragos) reef. Long propeller (hélice) shafts (ejes, astiles). Chew up: masticar bien

→ the dog --ed up (destrozó) the carpet (alfombra). The murk (oscuridad, tinieblas) became clear (=, despejado, ...; aclarar, despejar ...). The climate parching (que reseca + make dry, dry up). Harvester: segador, recolector de fruta, cosechadora. The chummy (de muy amigo) relations. Women are chatty (habladoras). Double-edged (dos sentidos) words, sword (de doble filo). A case in point (un ej. al respecto) for the circumspect. Pot (olla, testo, ...), belly (barriga) → Pot-bellied (panzudo). A new-fangled (de moda) language, it's just a passing fad (moda pasajera), tight jeans are really in fashion, this area is getting very trendy ↔ out of fashion. Ammo (ammunitions: municions). Revolts have been harshly (duramente) put down. Blasphemy laws carried (llevaban, transmitian + "=", passed on) death penalty before 1789. Wavering (indeciso, vacilante, que flaquea) ideal; ideally the parking would be free. The debate heats up (se calienta). Soils razed to the ground (se asolaron). A lecherous (lujurioso, lascivo) thug (matón), lasciviousness (lujuria, liscivia). Scruffy: (pers.) desaliñada, dejada, (clothes) desaliñadas, (building) destartalado) → he looks -- (tiene aspeco descuidado). An unrest (que molesta/inquieta,V) rumbling (rumor,V, ruido sordo, ...). Oil & gas rig (torre de perforación, equipo, aparejo; amañar elecciones). A leaner (más magro) approach for the ungrateful. Investors are trickling in (entrar poco a poco, goteo); trickle irrigation, our money is --ing away (se consume poco a poco). Assuage (calmar) American grievances. Dodgy: the brakes are a bit -- (no andan muy bien); (tricky) peliagudo, (risky) arriesgado. Pop: (pequeño estallido, taponazo), (balón) reventar, his eyes nearly popped out of his head, gaseosa. Outwit (burlar, ser más listo que) → they have been -- by the enemy; I'm serious (yo no me burlo). Crouch (agacharse) → the cat --ed, ready to pounce (saltar, lanzarse) at your head & pull out your eyes. Wake (despertar, estela) → in the -- of riots (disturbios, motines, sublevaciones): tras la tormenta. Cook up (inventar, tramar) new stances (actitudes). Sizzle: (al freir) crepitar, chisporrotear; chispa → the idea doesn't have any --. Mindful (tener presente) of tight (ajustado, ceñido, estrecho) credit. Municipio: municipality, (US) township. Dais (tarima). Boom (estruendo; empresa...: auge) market. Vastness (inmensidad + "="). Stab: puñalada,V; a -- (punzada) of pain; --bing (apuñalamiento), -- sb to death, -- sb in the back. Scan: (inspect closely) escudriñar, (Med.) explorar con escáner, (tec.) explorer, registrar, (Comp.) examiner, explorer, echar un vistazo. Verificar: verify, check, crosscheck → you'd better (sería major) --. Regardless/whatever conditions. Serpenteante: zigzagging, (way) winding, twisting, (ravine: barranco) winding, meandering (vagar, deambular). Purport (pretender) to be ... → --tedly (supuestamente) =/= pretend (fingir, aparentar; pretender). Nature's bounty (generosidad, beneficiencia). Blob (gota, mancha, borron)by: borroso. Borroso: (photo, image) blurred, indistinct, (escrito: writing) smudgy, lo veo todo -- (everything is blurred). Exterior: (surface) outer, (wall) external, (extranjero) foreign, (world) exterior, outside, (habitación exterior) a room facing onto the street. Outermost (más exterior) layer (capa, estela). Mastermind: genio, cerebro; (robo, crimen) planear, organizar → he --ed the robbery (asalto). Loosen: aflojar, soltar, desentumecer. Convenience (comodidad, conveniencia) → -- foods (fáciles de preparer); do it at your --. Second half (segunda parte). Forecast: (tiempo) pronosticar, (ventas) provisión =/= foresee (prever). Struck: he -- a blow (dio un golpe), you seem very -- with her (que te ha caido muy bien), -- on him (loca por él). Run up to the house, be up (a la altura) to the task, be up (en condiciones) to doing sth, are you up going for a walk? The tide (marea, corriente) of the events; go against the tide ↔ swim the tide. The quake (temblor) that struck Haiti. Transigir: (give in/way) on sth ↔ I refuse to -- -- -- --. Make/kick a fuss (alboroto) about sth. Realm (reino, campo) → beyond the --s of possibility (totalmente imposible), it belongs to the -- of metaphysic. Spurning (rechazo, desdén). Misstrust (desconfianza) of oficialism (=, burocracia + red tape). Schmoothing (hablar mucho, estar de cháchara + chatter). Belated (tardía) attention, --ly (con retraso). Virilidad (=, manliness). La edad feliz (the prime of life), edad adulta (aduldhood, tercera edad (older people. Full stop (punto final), -- -- new paragraph, (;) semicolon, in inverted commas, brakets (paréntesis). I'm babysitting (canguro) tonight. Nice salute (saludo) for the second lieutenant (alférez). A breathtaking (imponente) landscape. Boggle (quedar atónito, patidifuo) → mind - --ing (increibles, alucinantes) protests. Multy-storey building. Harebrained (descabellado + crazy, wild, preposterous). Be lovelorn (sufrir mal de amor). Pigmy ("=", enano + dwarf). Britain is superseding (desbancada, suplantada, cambia de sentido) in Eurpe; the superseded technique. Unfaced (no inmutado, tan pancho) by contest (lucha/competición, contradicción, refutación). The budget is punny (endeble, enclenque + weak, sickly). Most fast growing European nations. The drugs were dumped (descargadas, ... desechadas) overboard (por el bordo). Suciedad: dirt, dirty, dirtiness. Glare: brillo,V, deslumbrar; mirada de enojo (of anger) ..., --ing (deslumbrante) of disaprobal. We draw on (nos inspiramos de) ...; I prefer to inspire respect rather than instill fear. Estercolero: (dunghill, heap, manure) → I made a -- of my examen (lo cagué). Warring (en guerra, enfrentados) politicians; the inheritance set the brothers against each other or at loggerheads. Exchequer/Treasury (Ministerio de Hacienda) → the -- (el fisco), -- bonds. She greets (saluda, recibe) her impeachers. Foreign/Home (Interior) office. Show off (presumir, destacar, hacer resaltar). It is churlish (grosero, maleducado) not to thank him. He ponders (reflexiona, considera) =/= he panders (consiente) sb's desire for sth. Whisk (batir, agitar, quitar) → -- India away/off the decade- long doldrums (abatimiento, estancamiento) of rule by a jaded (harto) Congress Party; he wisked away the plates/the cloth of the table. His mingle/ragtag (mezcla) with the crowd =/= mingy: mísero, tacaño + misery, mean, stingy). Find (encontrar, hallazgo) → finding (descubrimiento, resultado), findings (conclusions, resultados). Asaltante: (de caminos) highwayman (pers.) assailand, (bancos, tiendas) raider. Valuable (valioso)s: objetos de valor; a valuable contribution (aportación). U-turn (cambiar de sentido en U. Contender: competidor, que aspira → competitor (rival). At his behest (petición + request, petition), petition for divorce, request for extradition. Uncool: anticuado + oldfashioned; conservador + conservative. Help keep afloat (a flote). Discern (distinguir, percibir)ing (exigente, con criterio) experts; discernible: perceptible, apreciable, ostensible. He resent (le molesta) being duped (engañado). Snack (truco) → get the -- (don) of doing sth. Get carried away/enthusiastic (entusiasmarse). Brownnosing/crawler (lameculo). Pet (mascota, preferido) → the teacher's--. The market slide (desliza,V, bajón; diapo). In broad daylight (en pleno día). Appeal (solicitud, petición, Jur.: =) against the judgement/ruling (fallo). Funnel: (ship) chimenea =/= (of home: chimney), embudo; (traffic) canalizar, (help, finance) encauzar. Academe (mundo académico), academy (academia). Surf (ola,V; navegar por Internet: surf the net). Argentina severed (cortó) its decade-long link with the $ in 2002. Grove (arboleda, bosquecillo, pinar: pine grove) of poplars (chopos): alameda. A bird's flapping (aleteo). Airborne (transporte por el aire) → become -- (elevarse en el aire); the skyscrapers soars or rises above the park. Be onto sth (seguir la pista, encontrar algo). Give sb a lift (propulsion, ánimo): levantarle el ánimo. Undergrads (estudiantes no licenciados). Hackles (pelo herizado del lomo del perro) → have one's -- up (estar furioso), his -- rose (se enfureció). Administered partway, partly, partially (parcialmente, a mitad) through, … Column/pillar (pilar). Post: empleo, poste, correo, send by --. Overstep (sobrepasar, rebosar) =/= the coffee cup is running over, the group filled the room to overflowing, be radiant with health. Hazard (peligro) → -- warning lights (luces de emergencia) → a fire -- --, --ous (peligroso, arriesgado). The state's role in the Ec.: less heavy-handed (torpe, inepto). Freed & arrived safely (sin pb.) at home. France has grown painfully (=, penosamente, dolorosamente, terriblemente) accustomed to seeing its countrymen taken hostages (reenes) abroad. Minuciosamente: meticulously, thoroughly, conscientiously. In your sense (sano juicio) → out of --. Syllabus (plan de estudios, programa de algo) for a course. The upshot (resultado final) is a sense of less security; the -- was that he resigned. The nazis derided (ridiculizaron) avant-garde arts as degenerated. Shore up (reforzar, sostener) the single currency. Juerga: go out on the town/partying, go out for a good time. Chic/stylish (elegante). Land área beneath of which it lies vast reserves of oil. It has some challenges ahead. It backs (apoya) India. Oil rich nations gets a quarter of its government revenue from well-managed state controle. If Ec. slide (desliza, cae, baja) he will spoil the chances of reelection. Outcomes (resultados, consecuencias) which …; a decission of unforeseeables consequences, as a result of. Agree upon (sobre) joint common action. Teamwork (trabajo en equipo), team spirit. It has a hart time (lo pasa mal). Backbone (columna vertebral) of online efforts is security. Librarians (bibliotecarios). He fails to back tough measures. Meaningful (significativo) usage of domestic violence. Some human needs are not covered within the framework (marco) of the Constitution. Purpose (intención, propósito) → accomplishment (logro, realización). Notify interested parties on available (disponible) objects (=, objetivos). Deteriorar: (material) damage, (relación, imagen) affect. Used for orders (pedidos) fulfilment (satisfacción, cumplimiento, llevar a cabo). Your standing (=, prestigio) as a professional with whom the Institute is proud to associate. Legislation drafted (redactada) to … leaves public at risk. Hindrance (obstáculo, =). Inequity/unfairness (injusticia) → we have to overcome it. Eyecatching (llamativo, vistoso). This exposure triggers microorganisms to release ... Nanoparticles found in ten top brand cosmetics. Failing to disclose (divulgar, revelar) its use for fear of consumer backlash (reacción adversa). Delayed (retrasado) by the traffic. Nanomateria delay rice flowering & reduce seed set (cuajar, replantar ...). The UK inquiry (investigación) hears expert evidence (pruebas) but nanofood risks remain largely unknown. The odd one out (desaparejado) in Europe + which is the odd one out (el que no pega)? Reflection/think about (reflexion, consideración) of gradual spread (propagación). He's forever (sin cese) complaining. Foolishness/stupid think (sandez). Rechazar: reject, repel, refuse, repulse, spurn, push away, drive away, turn down =/= despreciar: disdain, disregard, snub, scorn, sneer, look down. Charlatán: talkative, gossipy, chatty, quack + curandero. Fellowship (compañerismo) for lifelong training (entrenamiento, capacitación). They all rallied (se reunieron). Purchase of moisturers (hidratantes + moisturizings) rely on (dependen de) online. Pemex tussled (luchó) with Repsol. Clouds of black smoke mottled (motearon) the snowcovered ground. He cold-shouldered (volvió la espalda) at ... Despite these hiccups (hipos, dificultades, tropiezos), S. America was a shock absorver during Spanish slump. Hardly a day goes away/pass ... The clashes (conflictos, estruendos, enfrentamientos) show vividly (vivamente) the refusal. Dismantle monopoles commanding Ec. Turkey is turning away (se separa) from ... Energy sources die down (decrecen). Brutishness (brutalidad). Praisworthy/commendable (digno, elogiable). A war fought out (competida, resuelta) by China & Japon. The Ec. is held back (contenida, frenada) by private debts. Designer (diseñador), +computer-aided (asistido) design. Britain is going all out (con maxima fuerza, haciendo lo imposible) for shale gas. Plazo: period, instalment (de pago) → pay in --s. An spot (lugar) off (algo apartado de) … The costline/shore. People entitled (con derecho a) free schools. The isle endured (soportó) a muddled (confusa, hecha un lío) transition. Dollops (dosis, =) of government cash =/= a walloping (paliza, colossal; enorme) 98 % yes. Offload/unloading (descarga de un peso) =/= discharge/shot (tiro); electrical discharge. Get a real fright (llevarse un buen susto, tener miedo). Kick (coz): the police --ed the door open. Infringement (violación, no cumplimiento) the contract + breach of contract; traffic offence, traffic violation. Habitar: inhabit, live in, occupy (habitar, vivir, ocupar). Impedir: prevent, block, hinder, inhibit (=). Role reversal (invertido) in the supramodern family. Intimacy (=), intimately (íntimamente), intimate friends/details, be intimated familiarized, acquainted with sth (estar familiarizado con). Laborious (laborioso, escrito: poco claro) task/process. Owner: propietario + landlord/landlady. Gangling/lanky (larguirucho). Lash out: tirar coces, arremeter contra, emprender a golpes. The sweat of one's brow, his shirt was soaked with ... Lay (poner, colocar): (aside) ahorrar, (down) deponer, (off) despedir, (on) proporcionar, (out) disponer/presentar. Be soft in the heat (estar tocado). We assumed we would have tolt it to you. Nag (fastidiar, dar la lata; gruñón) sb to + inf.: dar la lata para … Nagging: (doubts, worries) persistentes, acuciantes; (husband/wife) rezongón(a)/gruñón(a). Egypt's press as a cheerleading (animación) ... Turkish- ruled Nord of Cyprus. The magic of truffles (trufas) is their scent (perfume, fragancia), a savoury & drowsy (perezoso, somnoliento) smell. Civil war is scaring away/off (auyentarndo) big oil companies. Unblock/clear (desatascar). Diet pill (píldora de adelgazamiento). Consultation: Med., lawyer, dictionary, notes, unions … (consulta). Imprudente: imprudent, rash, careless, reckless =/= bold/rash (temerario). P2P: a network (cadena, red) where each workstation has an equivalent capability & responsibility. Aerosol offset (compensa) part of the overall warning trend (tendencia). Unplug it during the storm. By hook (gancho) & by crook (cayado): por las buenas o por las malas. Press & hold the power button 5 sg., then release it. The start up (puesta en marcha) process. Status: member -- (categoría de), legal -- (situación), marital -- (estado). Select objects in the display (expo, aquí: pantalla). Remove dust & grease trapped under the keys (teclas). Abet (inducir, instigar, secundar). The effort is unsuccessful/fruitless. Work for a pittance & not time-off. It heralds (es =, es precursor, anuncia) distant prospect (perspectiva, panorama, posibilidad). Complex traits (rasgos) in humanity. Throwback (vuelta atrás, tiene sus raices) to ancient styles. Hold to (atenerse a) the account (cuenta, factura; información). Elicit: (interés) suscitar, (reacción) provocar; obtener algo de alguien. Intake: (aire, gas, ...) entrada, (water) toma, (food) consumo, student -- (matriculación, -- valve (válvula de entrada). Cram: meter (things into a case, foods into one's mouth), llenar a reventar → the hall is --med, empollar, empollón (--er). This trove (treasury) of data is fiddly (delicado, complicado) to download. Ask for an early wake-up call. Comb (peine,V, rastrear, rebuscar) for celebrities. Clear up: (dificultad) aclarar, (crimen, misterio) resolver, (habitación) ordenar, (duda) disipar/eliminar. Clear out: vaciar, quitar, hacer salir, ej.: rebels. This political party clears (salva) the 5% hurdle (valla, obstáculo) to get into Parliament. Bugbear/nightmare (pesadilla). Literate (saber leer y escribir). Taiwan is thought to be crawling, crammed, cluttered (lleno de) Chinese spies. Badly (gravemente) damaged. Vengarse: avenge, take revenge; revengeful (vengativo). Cain was furious/angry/cross (enfadado). Swear: jurar, decir palabrotas, tacos + swearword. Girdle (cinturón, faja; ceñir, rodear). Make an atonement (expiación) for ... Dizziness/giddiness (mareo, vértigo). It is all swings (oscilaciones) & roundabouts (glorietas, indirectas): lo que se gana por un lado se pierde por otro. Bog (ciénaga)ged down: estancarse, quedar empantanado. Striking (llamativo, sorprendente) =/= stri<u>c</u>ken:

afectado, afligido, enfermo) → -- with guilt (culpabilidad), -- with remorse, drought -- (asolado por la sequía). I withdraw the accusation. The beefiest (más fornido) party survive its founder demise (fallecimiento, desaparición). Think alout ↔ think in low voice. Foist sth on/onto sb (endosar, endilgar algo a alguien) → the job was --ed to me. They find an annoyance (fastidio, molestia) + get annoyed. A very supportive (que apoya) family. Land (del suelo) speculation. Nicaragua's canal, with twice the draught (corriente de agua, calado) of Panama's draught. Fulfill/carry out his obligations, carry out the task ↔ unfulfilled (no cumplida) pledge (promesa). Candelabro: candlestick, limelight + centro de atención* =/= spotlight (atención, poner de relieve, (teatro) foco, be in the -- (centro de atención*). Cannily/cunningly (astutamente) ↔ uncannily (asombrosamente, increiblemente). Trace (huella, rastro; dar con alguien) → --ing a messy (desordenada, sucia, descuidada) pers. is a grim (lúgubre, deprimente; nefasta, macabra) task. Hype (exageración, bombo publicitario) → -- its products, a media --. Funds that pay out (se gastan) when catastrophe strikes. Tease (bromista/tomar el pelo, fastidiar) → he is a dreadful (espantoso) --: es muy bromista; tease out: desenredar, (información) sonsacar. Merciful (clementes, compasivos) directors. Obamacare from its inception (inicio) to implementation (ejecución). Uplifting (inspiradora, edificante) story. Partisanship (partidismo). Maze/labyrinth. He did such (tal) thing. Inútil: (esfuerzo) fruitless, (inepto) useless. It is no point/it is of no avail in keeping on trying, avail o.s. of sth (valerse de, aprovecharse de algo). Central bankers are running down (staff: reducer, bateria: agotar, fábrica/negocio: hundir) their arsenal (muchos datos, mucho material bélico). Licensing (autorización de bebidas alcohólicas) laws/hours. Golpe: knock (choque, impacto), blow (pegar a una pers.; contratiempo, soplar). These ideas fuse (fusible; funden, fusionan) fiscal & monetary policy. Shoving (empujando,V) it back into the campaigner (partidario, defensor)'s hand; shovel (palada) of earth, he --ed a path through the snow. Conventional/traditional ↔ contingent/incidental (eventual). Clad (vestido,V) → scantily -- girls; -- with trademark (marca de fábrica). He ambled (andó sin prisa) to the marquee (entoldado, marquesina) to listen to the tribute (=, homenaje). A spokeswoman (portavoz) denied (=, desmintió) it. He has made a filing (archivó los documentos) on his finance. His wealth may have been overstated (exagerada). He has outperformed (superó) the S&P 500 index of big firms. Tantrum (rabieta, berrinche). Syria bleeds (sangra). A hornlike protrusion (protuberancia). Media companies can gather (agrupar) firms with higher resolution (=, Comp.: definición). Upgrade (ascender de categoría, Comp.: actualizar) their 5G network to comply (=, acatar, acceder) to a global standard. The radio spectrum used by 4G is running out (acabado). He pinned (sujetó) his treatise (tratado) to a church door. Self-harm, self-mutilation. Pump up (inflar), -- -- (reactivar) the Ec. The taxman did not repay (reembolsa, devuelve) the kindness (favor, detalle, amabilidad). Pas the time (pasar el rato) with the friends, stick around (quédate, no te vayas). Fall out of fashion. That was a ruin/mess, dire strait (situación desesperada); dire prediction (funesto pronóstico). A courtly (cortés, elegante) song. A chilling (frío, escalofriante) encounter. The deal will lapse/expire (caducar). Hold out (ofrecer, tender) sth to sb as an inducement (aliciente, incentivo). An oldie (cosa anticuada), go out of date (queda anticuado). Needle (aguja)ing (pinchándose, fastidiándose) each other. Win the first prize, the lottery. Custom (costumbre, cliente)s: aduana → as --s expenses dwindle. Naturalness (--lidad) in painting. Heavenly (celestial) body. His work is rooted (enraizado) in the everybody life (vida cotidiana). On the brink (borde) of the war, in the -- (a punto) of doing sth/resigning. Earthly delights (placeres, deleites, encantos) → -- in sth (disfrute de algo). The Christ who is bowed (reverenciado) &

lacerated (magullado, dañado) with whippings (palizas) & dripping (chorreando) with blood. Overbearing (dominante, autoritaria) American mother ↔ bearish (tendencia bajista, pesimismo); downwards/upwards trend. Cowered (encojido de miedo) & naked on a moor (páramo, amarrar un barco) pretending (fingiendo, pretendiendo, aparentando) ... Barely (apenas) veiled (encubiertos) attacks. A carterpiller (oruga)'s grunt (gruñido) as it noses on (olfatea). The police wonks (tambaleos) favoured ... Wonky: cojo, tambaleante, torcido; estropeado → go -- (estropearse). Torn (desgarrado). Bles, st, st (bendecir). Handy (a mano, práctico, hábil). An spoused (adoptado, defendido, apoyado) plan. His overarching (general, global) aim. Lopped (off): podado. Willifully (terco, obstinado + =, stubborn, dodged, tenacious). Trump (triunfo), her father always come up trumps (nunca le fallaba). She has a strangehold (poder, dominio) on him (lo domina totalmente). Cast-iron (hecho de hierro fundido; sólido, ferreo) → a -- - -- constitution (una salud de hierro). Wishy-washy: endeble, insípedo, sin gracia ni personalidad =/= mish-mash: revoltijo, lío, desorden + mess, jumble. Sullying (que mancha la reputación). Notch (corte/muesca, desfiladero + defile, gorge) up: apuntarse, conseguir (its own record, victory ...). Top-notch (de primera calidad). Disrepute: desprestigio, discredit + descrédito =/= disparagement/"contempt" (menosprecio). Reputation (=). Secretive (reservada, callada) army; everything was very quiet (callado), keep quiet about sth (tener algo callado), pay for sb's silence. Strive after/for (esfuerzo/V para conseguir algo). America is bent (empeñada) on China's destruction. Their relations built on (agregan) stronger foundations (fundaciones, fundamentos, cementos). At its apex (cúspide + Geog.: summit, peak). Garrison: (troops) acuartelar, guarnición + (decoración) adornment, (verdura) guarnish. They hail (aclaman, granizo,V) he as leader. Trolls (duendes + a magical/ enchanting village). Seesaw: oscilante,V, vacilante, vaivén,

-- in Earth climate. Perp (perpetrator: autor, responsable). Proxenetismo: priming, procuring =/= soliciting (abordar clients). A secular creed (credo). The back seat driver. Feisty (batallador, animado). Understanding (entendimiento) → measures to foster (fomentar) a better understanding of the laws. Lurid: escabroso, (image, picture) inmoral, (garment, colour) chillón: loud). An elongated (alargado) rant (vocerio, injuria,V) on behalf of (de parte de, en favor de) the desilusioned. Spend oodle (cantidad, montones) of … Wooliness (lanosidad, imprecisión). Disjointed (inconexo, desilvanado) speech & writing. He should be streets ahead (adelante por mucho). Flicker: parpadear, vacilar, vibrar, (llama) destello; (de diversión) explosión → --ing (vacilante, parpadeante). Gutter (cuneta, canal; barrio bajo) → he rose from the -- (nada). Gag: silencio, mordaza,Vs) → the Gulf statelets are --gged (silenciados, prisioneros). Unabridged (resumido): íntegro. Blended (mezclado) into a light dough (pasta, masa) that is fried. Tied-up & flogged (azotado). Ruling: (Jur.) fallo; in power, -- class (clase dominante), (precio) vigente. Steelworks/ iron & steel industry (fundición). Commandeer: apropiarse (appropriate sth), (tierra, casa) expropiar, (pers.) reclutar (recruit) por la fuerza. It surfaced (emergió, salió a la luz/a relucir) unexpectedly (sin aviso). Shore/prop up (apuntalar, reforzar) his support; I've had a lot of -- from my family, our -- comes from the workers. Convince/persuade many disillusioned. Temper (suavizar, atenuar, templar) the system =/= he has trampled (pisoteado, atropellado) all over (por todas partes). Resort: without resort (recurso) to violence, as a last --; you -- (acudes) to me for help, holiday (turismo) -- (lugar). Eatery (restaurante). The electoral system he bequeathed (legó). The winning (ganador) candidate; presentar su candidatura: put o.s. forward for a post, stand for a post. They were given more weight than they warranted (merecían + deserved), autorizaban, garantizaban). He helped fire-up (infundir) enthusiasm. Offender (delincuente, infractor) + previous reoffender (reincidente). At full/top speed (a toda marcha). Bloom (flor, florecer, prosperar) → in the -- of life, the censure motion was unsuccessful or was defeated (no prosperó). Bouquets (ramos) to sell briskly (enérgicamente, con brío). He blew (desperdició) his opportunity & flopped (fracasó). Line up (alinear) too many candidates. High handed (despótico, arbitrario) & aloof (distante). The wild-eyed (con ojos desorbitados, de loco) radicals. Graze: (injure) rasparse; the bullet --ed his arm; rasguño + scratch; pastar → --ing (pastoreo). Pista: (atletismo) track, (rastreo) trail, track; (circo) ring; (hipódromo) race course, track avenue, (tennis) court, ski slope, ice rink/skating rink. Back paw: pata/garra trasera. It stopped dead (se paró en seco). Down: abajo, write down (apuntar), the tyres are -- (desinflados), it's -- to him (le toca a él), the computer is --, derribar, abatir. The terrified pup/puppy (cachorro) eyes stared (miraban fijmente) from a metal cage. Hanger (perchero) + (de pared) clothes rack. He flexes his musles (alardea de poder, hace ejercicios de precalentamiento). Commissioned: encargado, (Mil.) --ed (nombrado) officer. Add up: (cuentas) cuadrar, (n^{os}) sumar. Timely/well timed (oportuno + =, appropriate). Cutting down (suprimir) middlemen. Sidestep (eludir) them. Soar: (birds) levantar el vuelo, (hopes) incrementar, (prices) dispararse, (popularity) aumentar. Get onto/get on to: (moto, caballo) montar, (tren) subirse → we -- -- the motorway at the junction (cruce, empalme) 15. More businesslike (serio, formal, eficiente) than ever. Books that fly (salen volando) from the shelves. Salesmanship (arte de vender). I've nothing to reproach him for … Compile/gather together (recopilar). Survival of the fittest (ley del más fuerte), that's not fitting (digno) for an officer. Delve (escarbar) into (ahondar, buscar en, ej.: into the past). The surface is pittet (picada) & ridged (estriada, acanalada) + the ice thaws (deshiela) forming ponds (charcos) between ridges (caballones, cadenas de montañas). Mold → mould: molde, moho. The raising of primary (fundamental, principal, de base) products which sustains biological awakening may be capped (limitado …). Wed (casarse)ding (boda). Lucha: fight (pelea), wrestling (lucha libre), struggle (lucha, pb.), contest (disputa, contienda). Desmentir: (news, accusation) deny, (theory) refute. Girlie (chiquilla). Entrant: (competición) participante + =; (examen) competidor/candidato (=), (Universidad) los que entran. Correa: safety bel, tighten one's --, dog's leach, (tira) stray, watchband. Grating: rejilla. Chirriante (squeaky), crispante (infuriating). Winning (premiado) film. Full of praise for her; speak in -- of her staff; songs of -- (alabanza). He pushed back the chair. He replaced/took over his uncle & her aunt as leaders, replace the soap with (por) a detergent. Restless/agitated men. She was nothing but the clothes she was bearing up. Feel a bit low (ser bajo de moral) → raise sb's spirits/morale. My heart sanks (se me cayó por los suelos). Conmovedor: soulful, moving, touching. Expelled (expulsado) migrants in the delusion (delirio, falsa ilusion; error, engaño). Offence/se (infracción, ataque, atentado, delito) → commit an --, cause an -- to sb, I was offended by an offender (infractor). Be full of go (energía). Cumbersome: voluminoso, incómodo, engorroso + (subject) bothersome, trying, (situation) awkward. Fade: apagar, desvanecer, debilitar, desteñir → dying cities: some are doomed to fade away (apagarse, consumirse). Robbers/railers (asaltantes). Behind that aggressive exterior there are a heap of gold. Consoling (que consola, reconfortante) profit (beneficio, ganancias). Seriousness (seriedad), lack of responsibility (=, seriedad). Electoral outing (excursión, paseo) + outing, ride on horseback, boat trip, bike ride, (en coche) drive, ride; space walk, natural trail. Tatters (andrajos + rags) =/= titter (risa ahogada, reirse disimuladamente). Estafar: rip off, defraud, diddle, swindle. Mistrust (desconfianza)ful: desconfiado + mistrust sth, sb, beware of imitations. An unruly (rebelde) ruffled (rizada, erizada, agitada) Germany. Three-cornered (triangular, "="). Heartland (interior, zona central). Freak: fenómeno, hecho insólito; ejemplar anormal, monstruo; fanático → peace/tennis --; freaky (muy raro, extraño). My nerves are shattered (hechos trizas), tear sth to shreds (halcer algo trizas). Astucia: astuteness/shrewdness; craftiness, cunning; the slyness of a fox; ruse/trick/ploy. Dazed/stun (aturdido). It was once backwater: (water) remanso, (place) atrasado. Team up (asociarse). Ramp (rampa) =/= desnivel: (land) uneven, (table) not levelled. Flinty (de silex), (soil) silíceo, duro. Fault: defecto + default, flaw; culpa, avería + breakdown) → with all their faults. Foremost: principal, destacado, en 1ª linea. Fetter (trabar, encadenar) ↔ un--ed (sin trabas). Scale down: disminuir a escala, make proportionally smaller, (investment, operation) drop, decrease ↔ -- up. Flurry (ráfaga/racha, locura, frenesí) of activity. Backtrack (marcha atrás) reform. Sulky (a los malhumorados) voters resent (les molesta) stumping (apoquinar) any more for Greece. Tear: lágrima; rotura, rasgar; (ropa, papel) romperse → -- up: (papel, carta) romper, (terreno) abrir, (poster, árbol) arrancar + -- off/out. Forbearance (tolerancia + =, paciencia + =) toward fiscal winners. Derrocar: (edificio) knock down, demolish, (Minister) oust, (Gob.) overthrow. Opresión: (sensation, feeling) oppression, (of regime/system) oppressiveness; (opresor) oppressive. A rat he hat cornered (acorralado) hat nowere to go & jumped out at him. Black-leather-clad (vestidos de) bikers (motociclistas). Being greeted (recibido) with howls (aullidos, clamores, gritos) & rotten tomatoes. Their friendship/relation is fraught (tensa, difícil), --with (lleno/cargado de) dangers/pbs. Give fodder (pienso, forraje) to critics, to anti-Semitism. We are remotely related (parientes lejanos); in the not too distant future, in those distant o far-off times. Unnerving (que pone nervioso, desconcierta + disconcerting). Asking/trying is futile (=, vano).

Refugees endure (resisten, soportan) appalling (horroroso) joblessness. Oddly (raramente) upbeat (optimista, =; própero) ←→ down--. Upsides (ventajas, lados positivos) of the war ←→ downsides. The grass was frosted over (cubierta de escarcha). Drill (taladradora, V) → --ing (perforar) a well is noisy & disruptive (perturbador, prejudicial). Bleeding (hemorragia, =). It has no equal (semejante). Power would have to be handed to next generations, but what prince would be worthy (digno, respetable)? The smooth (suave, tranquilo) of power contradicts the view that S. Arabia must collapse. Ooth/swear (juramento) of allegiance (lealtad) to Crown. Goddam (puñetera, maldita) stone; goddam! (¡maldición!). Put up: (persiana) subir, (mano) levanter, (cuadro) colgar, (casa) construir, (satellite) lanzar, (resistencia) oponer, alojar, presenter un plan. Sliver: (slice) tajada, (wood) astilla + wood chip, splinter; (rodaja) sliced onions … Kinship: parentesco, similitud =/= relationship: parentesco, relación (blood --). He relate sth with sth, related by blood, be related (sintonizado) to sb, distantly --, the incidents are related, drug -- crimes. Be vilified (vilipendiado, despreciado). Moscow's moles (espías, tipos). Some swear by (son entusistas, creen ciegamente en) debunked (desacreditada) Escuela nacional administración (ENA) =/= he panned (dejó por los suelos the film) =/= pillory (ridiculizar, burlarse de) + laugh at sth/ sb, make fun of sth/sb. An on-screen (en pantalla) character (=, personaje). Outwardly (por fuera, aparentemente + "="). A round-up (rodeo, redada) of undercover (secretos, clandestinos, =) illegals. A sort (especie) of amicable relations. Vacuous: (pleasure, pastime) vacío, (remarck, statement) insustancial. Starlet (joven aspirante a estrella). Read out/aloud (en voz alta), reading (lectura); ++++mind- reading (lectura del pensamiento). Wind down (disminuir poco a poco). Play down/gloss over (minimizar, disminuir la importancia, disculpar) of the threat. Stand up: levantarse, estar de pie =/= sit up: ponerse derecho, incorporarse + join. Gruesome/

horrifying (truculento, cruel, atroz). Largerly (en gran medida) due to... Descaradamente (shamelessly, brazenly). Coupled (unido, asociado) with ... Cleavage (división, escisión) between leaders, the split in the party. Briefly/quik as a lighting (rayo): fugazmente. The fingerprints match with those of the murder. Set off: (journey) salir, (bomb) explotar, (strike ...) desencadenar → -- -- a rash (erupción, avalancha; imprudente) of killings. Mishandle (maltratar) =/= misguided (insensato, herróneo) enough to believe in him; a -- (torpe) attempt (intento). Ploufh/ plow (arado, V). Transigir: relent, give in/away, tolerate → mercilessly, relentlessly: implacablemente, sin tregua (truce). Frail: (débil, delicado) fragile/breakable, (salud) delicate. Headgear (casco, gorra, sombrero). Sprout (brotar) new shoots (retoños). Bathroom (cuarto de baño + toilet), (servicios) lavatorios; lavatory paper (papel higiénico). Cause furor (=, sensación, escándalo); it's outrageous or shocking! (¡es un escándalo!); make a scene, cause a row or an uproar (armar un escándalo). Matchmaker (Celestina) + Sp. (promotor). Maker (creador), maker (fabricante + "manufacturer"). Scientists slim (delgados, escasos) enough to crave (ansiar + permission: rogar, pardon: suplicar) crawl into (entrar gateando). Fraterniry (hermandad, círculo estudiantil) & sororities. Novatada: beginner's mistake, practical joke. Cad: canalla/sinvergüenza + shameless/dishonest. Burbuja (bubble) → a fizzy/bubbly of wine. Germany was more at ease (más tranquila) with itself/ her ... Rail: rail de tren, barandilla, valla → -- against sb (recriminar a alguien, -- against sth (clamar contra algo). Anodyne (insignificante, insípedo, indoloro) statements. The screen went blank. Slash - land - burn (talar y quemar); he was burned alive, he had a sunburned face, the guerrillas burned several villages. Such measures are long overdue (ya tendrian que ser establecidas).The Worl's poorest: not far to catch up/reach/ get to the population of India. He binned (tiró a la basura) it. Hooded (encapuchados) eyes: de párpados caidos, de matón.

Boomed (hizo estruendo, resonó) her dissent (discrepancia, disconformidad): No, No. Europe since transfixed (atravesada, traspasada, paralizada) with fear, terror & has sundered (roto, dividido) the Conservative Paty. Tedious (pesadas, aburridas) intricacies (lo intrincado, complejidades + complexities). Arrimarse a: come nearer/closer to. Snuggle (down) (acurrucarse) under the settee (sofa) + it snuggled up (se arrimó) & released the sperm. Tattered: (fence) destrozada, (pers.) andrajosa, (reputation) hecha trizas. The catalyst for foreigner-bashing (ataque, paliza). Burla: fun, mock, joke → everyone makes fun of/mockes her + this makes a mockery of regulations (reglamentos, normas, ...). It sparked (provocó, suscitó, desencadenó) elation (entusiasmo/euphoria + =). The market was jubilant (jubiloso). Weakness (flaqueza), weakens (flaquear); slaken: (rope) aflojar, (speed) reducer. Be in abeyance (atividad: haber caido en desuso (disuse). A three tier educational system/hierarchy. The paragon (dechado: modelo) of cold-blooded (desalmado, peces de sangre fría) rationality. Take us unflattering (poco favorecedor) a self-portrait as possible. A fib (mentirijilla, bola) blows up (vuela; hincha, explota) into an international incident. Collateral (garantía/finanza subsidiaria) → -- loan (préstamo colateral). Vilipendiar: (insultar) vilify, insult; (humillar) revile, humiliate. The only hint (insinuación, indirecta; pista, consejo) of the untoward (adverso) ... Protect from logging (explotación forestal) =/= I googled (busqué en) four Universities. How bust-ups (riñas, roturas) ... Agitado: (mar) rough/choppy, (vida, día) hectic/busy; period of unrest, (pers.) agitated, clouded muddy (enturbiadas) waters. Tertiary (superior) education. Rearguard (retaguardia). In the grand (=, magnífico, imponente, fabuloso) manner: a lo grande → they live in a -- style. He is jobless & broke/penniless (sin un duro). Leery (receloso, cauteloso) of globalisation. Overreach (ir más allá de, sobrepasar, ser demasiado ambicioso) followed by remorse. Unaccountable (incomprensible, inexplicable, irresponsible). He sleeps in bunk (camastro, lecho pobre) & uses a buckle to wash in. Attainment (logro, consecución, realización) in Science & Maths. Unskilled migrants depress (disminuyen deprimen) pay for locals. Backbreaking (deslomador) toil (esfuerzo, trabajo duro). Stepmother (madrastra). A clear-headed (lúcida) choice. The troops treate diamonds as a spoil (botín) + estropear, malcriar. Hail: (leader) acclaim, (pers.) llamar, (taxi) hacer señas → the discovery was hailed (acogida) as a major (importante) breakthrow (avance). Clow (garra, arañar) back (recuperar: goods/losses: recover; (freedom/controle: regain) lost tax. Responsive: sensible, receptivo → the orchestra was -- to the conductor (director). A rock that cannot sustain human life. Encourage border blockage (bloqueo). Glaciers retreated/receded by 20%. Contrite (arrepentido + Relig.: repentant + reformed terrorist). A reminder (recuerdo) of his party's tolerance to help pad out (inflar) the budget & defray (sufragar) costs of... Interlocking (entrelazado, engranado) system. In cramped (estrecho, apretado in the car) mouldy (mohoso) quarters (barrios, una cuarta parte). He run up to the house. Ring: anillo, (of Saturn) aro, (re)sonar, repicar, llamar por Tf., sonar el Tf., (bell) tocar. Ringing: grandilocuente, sonoro, rotundo; repique, toque, (ears) zumbido, --ing (de llamada) tone. A blond boy went up to her (se le acercó). Decommissioning: (desguace, desmantelamiento) of monopolies, of weapons, of nuclear reactor. Dung (estiercol) → -- - fuelled (combustible) fires, drug - -- crimes. Waste (de desperdicio) products. Horno: (culin.) oven, stove, (tech.) furnace, (para cerámica) kiln. They agreed to show up (poner en evidencia; revelarse, aparecer). Fluke (chiripa) → by a --. Belittling (menosprecio, minimización). The late (tardía) Renaissance. The issue rankles (molesta, duele + hurt) in South Korea. Circumventing (burlar, salvar) the control. Dad (papa) ↔ mum (mama). Plug: tapón,V → -- this clothes into the hole; enchufe, toma de corriente.

Tosh (paparucha: noticias falsas, tontería, obra literaria insustanial). Twixt: → be-- (between). Underwent (sufrió, experimentó) knotty (espinosos) pbs. Chimera/illusion: quimera (animal fabuloso, fábula). Ironing (de planchar) board (table, trampolín, tablero). Weeping (lloroso) over ... Plunder (saquear, robar; botín). Mercurial (=, inestable, veleidoso, voluble, versatil). Paleness/pallor (palidez), pale/pallid (pálido). Unsettling (desestabilizante). Forgiveness (perdón + =). Go to a killing spree (matar todo lo que se encuentra), public spending spree (derroche de dinero public). Face/nominal value (valor nominal). Vent: (respiradero) chimenea; descarga, desahogo; give -- (dar rienda suelta) to his leftist urges (impulsos, ánimos,V, exhortar/instar). Repercutir: have repercussions on, (sonido) echo. The onset (principio) of the crisis. False alarm. Gold-braided (con galones, trenzas + plait) gown (toga). Not welcomed. An ineffable (=, inexplicable) taste. Undemanding (poco exigente, que pide pocos esfuerzos). Power befitting (apropiado) to ... Say one's farewell (despedirse); his parting (de despedida) words/thoughs. Forced them into the corner (los arrinconó). He looks grubby (sucio, repugnante + disgusting, revolting). Becon sb in (hacer señal para que entre), he --ed me over this table, I'm sorry, work --s me. Heartwarming (reconfortante, emocionante, grato + pleasant; agradecido: grateful). Unveiling (descubrir, inaugurar) a monument; (teatro, expo) opening. Seaweed/alga (alga). Assistant: dependiente, empleado, ayudante. Realize sth (caer en la cuenta). Pull one's punch (puñetazo, perforadora,Vs): andarse con miramientos ↔ without considerations. The paymaster (mecenas + "sponsor", "patron") balk (impiden, evitan; no aprovechan) at: se plantan ante: -- at the first fence (valla, cerco). Sabroso: flavoursome, delicious, tasty stuff. A branding (imagen de marca) exercise rather than a scientific one. Weighings (pesajes) machines (básculas + scales). Ceres has a core & a mantle (manta, capa). It was quietly (discretamente, silenciosamente) demoted (degradado, disminuido de categoría). Wail (lamento, gemido, lloro, queja, protesta, Vs) & gnashing (rechinar) the tooth. Loosely (sin apretar, sin demasiado rigor, poco rígido). Probes approach (se dirige a, se acerca a) a pair of former planets) & five truly (realmente, de veras) Worlds turn up (aparecen). Sizzling: chisporrear (produce chispas), crepitar (la leña al arder) =/= stifling (agobiante, sofocante). The exhilaration (júbilo/alegría, excitación/euforia) of scruffy (dejado, desaliñado) people. Voice (expresar) concerns (asuntos, incumbencias, interés) about ... Hit back (devolver el golpe) at tycoons who bullied (intimidaban) around him into doing sth. Lambast (azotar, fustigar, arremeter contra). Mammoth (mamut, descomunal). Downfall (caída, perdición, ruina) of his investments. Wipe out: (deficit) cancelar, (container) limpiar; erradicar, (pers.) aniquilar, exterminar. Trumped-up (falsificado, inventado) fraud charges (acusaciones). Ably (habilmente ghost (fantasma) written (por otros). Holy ghost (Espíritu Santo). Unanimously (por unanimidad). Befriend (hacerse amigo de) → they were -- by a stary (callejero, perdido) dog (se les pegó). Screenwritter (guionista). Amazingly/astonishingly (asombrosamente) good. A more quietier life bewitching (cautivador, encantador, seductor). Fun loving (amigo de diversión). Sidestep (eludir, esquivar) =/= sideway (lateral, de lado) → look/walk -- (de reojo). Follow-up: continuación (of his novel); -- - -- (de seguimiento, postoperatorio) care (atención). Witless (tonto, estúpido + =, silly). Playfully (de broma, alegremente + happily, cheerfully). Disquieting (inquietante + disturbing, worrying). Roam (vagar, errar, deambular) around: andar sin rumbo fijo. Vividness (intensidad, viveza), vividly (vivamente). Unbridled (desenfrenada) sensuality. Sinuous/winding. Primal: primero, original, principal → primarily (ante todo, principalmente). Alegría: joy, happiness, delight + deleite. Raw: crudo, puro, sin refinar; (sewage, rubbish, ...) sin tartar. Belavour: ataque, fustigar;

azotar; asediar con cuestiones → bereave (afligir, desconsolar → the --ed (los familiars del difunto); counselling (apoyo psicológico). Brasero: brazier, (Electr.) heater. A puny (enclenque) sword; -- (insignificante) impact. Fling (arrojar, lanzar → -- sb into jail, go on a -- (lanzar una cañita al aire), -- one's arms around sb. Tone down: disminuir, suavizar, atenuar. By striking (alcanzando) an agreement. He slinks (se escabulle, va sigiloso) into the rubbish dumps (vertederos). A warm glow (brillo, sensación,Vs) of their country. Expansionist mindsets (actitudes, disposiciones). Satisfied/pleased, he is never, be -- with that. Lain fallow (dejado en barbecho). Restaurants are popping up (establecidos inesperadamente). Tingle: (ears) zumbar, (piel) hormiguear, (emoción) estremecimiento. The hilltop (cumbre, cima). Assuage (calmar, aliviar, …): he was not easily --ed. Sewers (cloacas) hardly been upgraded (reformadas, mejoradas, Comp.: actualizadas). Brought-down (bajado, derribado). Massage parlour (sala). Befall (suceder) → whatever may-- (pase lo que pase). Face-saving (salvar las apariencias) → take the easier -- - -- (las más fáciles soluciones). Avowed (declarado) nationalist. The oponents outmanoeuvred (se mostraron más hábiles (skilful, clever) than …; (coche) más maniobrable (easier to maneuver) than. The scourge (plaga, azote,V) of poaching (caza y pesca furtiva) by foreign fishermen/hunters. Set up: erigir un monumento, montar una tienda, fundar una escuela, crear un comité o una comision. Jettisoning: -- (deshacerse de) its GDP projects, (aviación) vaciar, (Náut.) echar por el borde. He steamed into (entró echando vapor). Ballyhoo (bombo, propaganda estrepitosa)ed: tan cacareado. A maker of air-coolers. Workforce: población activa (+ working population), plantilla, mano de obra. He spotted (observó). Fiduciary (fiduciario: valores ficticios dependiendo del crédito y de la confianza). Stock: surtido, provisiones, (teatro) repertorio, acciones. Brush: cepillo, roce,V → -- with failure, death, authorities. Wind: (enrollar) → the rope wound itself round the branch, (ovillar) → -- wool into a ball, -- one's arms round sb. Observer/expectator =/= events/accidents (onlookers. Become rather bothersome (molesto, pesado, fastidioso). The rationale (base, fundamento, motivo) for the emergency. Practise foreign law. State owned enterprises. Pickup: -- (de reparto) truck (camión)/van (furgoneta), -- point (lugar de recogida), (Ec.) repunte, -- arm (brazo del tocadiscos). Onset (aparición, inicio) of the slowdown (Ec.: relentización). Swiftness (velocidad, rapidez); she got dressed quickly. The simplicity (sencillez) of style =/= a simple (=, sencillo) manner of speaking. Draw the line: (at sth) no aceptar, (somewhere) fijar límites, (under) poner punto final. Saviour (salvador), salvation (=). Stuffy: mal ventilado, (pers.) de miras estrechas, retrogrado. He sought for/after (buscaba) animal spirits. Contemplate one's navel/belly button =/= lifeline (cuerda de salvamento). Pool: fondo común (to buy sth), charca (of water, blood, talent), reserva (of resources). Gasp: (grito ahogado) with amazement (de asombro), for breath (respiración entrecortada, -- for a beer & liquidity, --ing for sth (morirse por algo). Cloister (claustro) → lead a --ed (de hermitaño) life. A century-old stamp-duty (impuesto al timbre). Dust down/off (desempolvar). Gain a mastery of (llegar a dominar) violin/trumpet. Militar rule, the -- (imperio) of the law, -- the roost/hanger/hook (percha): llevar la batuta + be the boss. Rule a dificult/troubled (de conflictiva) zona. The simplicity (sencillez) of style. Speak simply & unaffected (con naturalidad), he dress simply/modestly. Put on one's make up (maquillaje), put on weigh/3 kg., put the heating on, put a clok <u>on</u> one hour ↔ -- - -- <u>back</u> one hour. Spoil: dañar, estropear, (voting paper) invalidar (nullify), the coast spoiled by development (=, urbanización). Herror is human. Play dead (hacerse el muerto). sccept/take (asumir) the blame (culpa), lay/put the blame on sb, be to blame for (tener culpa de), I'm not to --, who is to --? Claim (demanda, reivindicación): wage --, he lost his -- for damage (daños & perjuicios), make a -- (reclamar), renounce his --/throne. Drown (ahogado) → -- o.s., -- out by demands (demandas comerciales), (earth) inundar, his cries were --ed by the noise of the waves. Bump (choque, golpe; sacudida, abolladura, hinchazón). Shred: (papel) tira + strip; a shred (mínimo) of decency (honradez)/evidence (prueba); tear sth to shreds (hacer trizas). Locate (situar, ubicar) → the switch (interruptor) is --ed under the seat. Renounce to a right/to a violent plan. Pick up the tap/bill (pagar la cuenta, asumir la responsabilidad) =/= fit the bill (cumplir con los requisites) =/= foot the bill (apoquinar). Estropear: break (down), damage a car, ruin/spoil the crop, (pers.) he has aged realy badly. Badly (mal) explained, the play (obra) was -- (mal) received, -- (gravemente) injured, be -- (muy) mistaken. Baby creche (orfanato, belén). Electorate. Denims (vaqueros) → jacket --. Polish: betún, cera, esmalte; brillo, lustre,Vs; pulir, perfeccionar. He mentioned it by & by (de pasada). Woe (angustia, desgracia, aflicción) → Nigeria has --fully (lamentablemente + regrettably) failed to defeat an insurgency of B. Haram. Airfreighted (enviar por avión), airborne (transportado por el aire) → exposure to -- pollution during the pregnancy. Fightback (contraataque + "="). Meal (comida)- skip(saltarse)ing during the pregnancy. The decreasing, dropping, falling rating (popularidad,=) of the desperated party. Overdraft (cuenta al descubierto); he went out bare-chested, an open área of the wood. Enjambre (swarm)/colmena (hive) → a hive of industry (donde se trabaja mucho), a hive (hervidero) of activity. Wire (alambre, mandar un telegrama) → wiring: cableado eléctrico, conectar, comunicar (the World, …). Sequence (orden) → in --, in historical (chronological) --, the -- of events (como se sucedieron los hechos). Give sb's short shrift (despachar a alguien sin rodeos), he gave that idea -- -- (mostró dificultad con esta idea), he got -- -- from the boss. He will sit atop (encima). Brass: latón, oficial, mandamás + bigwig. Fare well/badly: pasarlo bien, mal; how did he fare in the examens? Scale: escala, balanza (trade --), (Zool.) escama → -- drawing (dibujo a escala). Apocryphal: finjido, supuesto, falsamente atribuido. Muster (reunir, lograr formar equipo) up courage: armarse de valor. Drag (arrastrar), dragnet: red de arrastre, operación de captura, policía (emboscada). He was within a whisker (le faltó un pelo) for being millionaire. Revs (revoluciones). Wedding/birthday anniversary. He answered me dryly/drily (secamente, con sequedad). Coarse (basta, áspera, ordinaria) wool. Groove (surco, ranura; estriar, acanalar). (1) Spark (chispa,V); (2) plug (tapón, enchufe, rellenar, ...) → (1) (2) spark plug (bujía =/= candle). Wallop (golpe fuerte,V)ing: paliza → give sb a --. Wanderer: viajero, vagabundo, nómada (nomad). Globetrotter (trotamundos). Novel (novela; original, novedoso) after hurtling (alejarse violentamente) 6 km.; hurtle: precipitarse, arrojar (violentamente) → hurtle along/by (pasar volando); hurtle past (pasar a toda velocidad). The political party is not pulling away (arrancando) ... Wizardry (brujería, hechicería). Overall/overarching (global, total, general) goals (=, portería; objetivo) & tarjets (objetivos, dianas) → development --. Lick (lametazo,V) → -- one's wounds, -- sb's boots. Bone: hueso, espina de pescado,V =/= bane (ruina, pesadilla)ful: funesto, triste, desgraciado, terrible, nefasto. He scoffed (se mofó) at sth/sb; it makes a mockery of our beliefs (es una mofa a nuestras creencias). Elation: euforia + =, entusiasmo, júbilo (jubilation). Underground: soldiers of the Jewish underground (subteraneo) movement; (periódico, organización) clandestinos + =, secret, (Ec.) informal. Imprudent/carelss pedestrian. A gouty (gotoso: afectado de gota) gait (modo de andar) → a curious --. I looked out (tenia cuidado, busqué, encontré) my boot& I shook out a stone. Rouse (suscitar, provocar) sb's ire, anger, rage. Tax avoidance (evitar); avoidance of physical contacts. Alluring (seductor, atractivo) country in tax terms. Harry (ostigar, acosar, azotar =/= the hardy (potentes, resistents + strong, tough + fuerte) faithful (fieles). Tear (lágrima,V, romper/rasgar, hacer pedazos) a stained act of contrition (arrepentimiento) → tear up (romper, anular) wasteful (derrochadores) subsidies. Satellites sent out (lanzados). Exhibirse: (mostrarse en público) show o.s. off, (pavonearse) flaunt/boast o.s. Quaint: (personal clothes) peculiares, poco corrientes, (cottage, village) pintoresco (vivo, animado, digno de ser pintado). Delay (demora), delaying (dilatoria) tactic to allow … The slope (inclinación) of the land, plate, bottle, head + at full tilt (inclinación,V): a toda velocidad. You wan't overhoot (rebasar, ir más allá de) the deadline (plazo establecido). It's scary (da miedo) here in the dark.You ought to be grateful. You shouln't be so strict/ashamed, you ought to have seen her face. State of emergency (excepción). Vine: vid/parra, enredadera (climbing plant); wine grower (viticultor). Gush: (ej.: oil) salir a borbotones/chorros → he --ed (se deshizo) with gratitude, --ed over (deshacerse en elogios para) the child; water --ing (a grandes chorros) down street. I'm counting on your assistance, help, collaboration. Charter: estatutos, fuero, escritura de una empresa; fletamiento (precio de alquiler del barco, contrato, carga del barco). Snowden infuriated digital-privacy advocates (defensores). Beset: (acosado) by doubts, (acuciado) by fear, his --ing sin (su principal defecto). He eyes (observaba + =) the holy land. Carried away (entusiasmado). A brisk (enérgico) business in safeguarding (protegiendo, resguardando) guns; as a safeguard (como medida preventiva ("=""). Easily available (fácil de conseguir), the -- (disponibles) funds. A ship that loiters (se entretiene, se rezaga) in international waters. Breadbasket (granero, panera) → Ukraine was the -- of the Europe. The mastermind (genio, cerebro; planear, dirigir) finds solace/comfort (=, consuelo) + live in --, words of --. They raced down (entraron corriendo en) the hillside (ladera). Asesino: murderer, murderous, homicidal, (animales) killer. Get a move on (darse prisa; -- - -- -! (¡daos prisa!). Barely budged (movido, cambiado de opinión). Gunpowder (pólvora) for the hired (contratados) gunman & Islamic terrorist. They are coining (acuñando, inventando) ... A flabby (fofo, soso, músculo flojo; argumento endeble) state sector is a let-down (decepción + disappointment). Hug (abrazo, arrimarse) → figure-hugging (ceñido, ajustado al cuerpo). Bog (ciénaga) → boggy/swampy (pantanoso). The Ec. is sliding (cayendo) into recession. Enfadarse: get annoyed, angry, mad + loco). Don't be offended (te ofendas) but... Do one's utmost to do sth. (hacer lo imposible por hacer algo). Glimmer (luz tremola, débil, espejo del agua). Hurl (tirar, arrojar) insults to the police. Hawk (falcon, línea dura) → from hawkishness (dureza) to dovishness (blandura + softness, tenderness). Grind: moler, (negocio) llegar al punto muerto, funcionar con dcultad → a --ing movement + come to a --ing halt (detenerse en seco). Clutching (embragando; cogiendo/agarrando) battered (abolladas, maltrechas, maltratadas) engines. Communities at the fore (proa + prow, bow ↔ stern). Paint brush (pincel). Stifle (sofocar) yawns: contener los bostezos. Nap (dormitar, sueñecito) → catch sb -- (desprevenido). The fairy (hada) land (pais), fairy tale. Stray (extraviarse, vagar sin rumbo fijo) & badly directed (orientados). Undernourrished children with swollen bellies/ stomachs in Africa. The rape (rapto, violar) of the Sabine + fell short (no llegó a) rape. Tar (alquitrán) → tarred with the same brush: cortados con el mismo patrón). A lopsided (inclinado, desequilibrado) migrant sex ratios. Avow (reconocer, confesar, declarar) → an avowedly (declaradamente) confrontational (=, polémico) government. The household chores (tareas). The sleazy (de mala pinta, desaseado) suitor (pretendiente) has little prospects of success. Seat's heatcount (plantilla) has grown. Do it for her own benefit (=, bien). Inquieto: worried, anxious, restless, enterprising. It's hemmed (hecho el bordillo) in: (terreno) enclosed (cercado, arrinconado), (ciudad) surrounded. Chinese firms that rushed to expand are now gasping (respiran difícil). Snowstorms, avalanches & crevasses (grietas de glaciar) =/= crack (de pared y techo). Homing: (device: dispositivo, mecanismo) buscador, (instinto) de volver al hogar → homing pigeon: paloma mensajera. Scodland severance (ruptura, despido), severance pay. Abhor (aborrecer, detestar, abominar) → abhorrence (repugnancia, aborrecimiento, el detester). Hard-headed (realista, prático, testarrudo, cabeza dura). Desenlace: (film, book) ending, (aventura) outcome + resultado. Watchfulness (vigilancia) of security services; vigilance of children, security of the hotel. Deficitario: with deficit or negative balance; loss-making. Slake (aplacar, apagar) slaves's thirst =/= alienated by stale (duras, ideas trasnochadas; marchitadas, añejo, rancio, aire viciado) politics. Endanger (poner en peligro) → the critiqually endangered (en peligro de extinción) birds suggests the logging (de madereros) wars are not over. Retain some high fliers (ambiciosos de prestigio) ... China frequently lobbed (volaba por lo alto; shells: obuses: lanzaba). Raise the school-leaving age (edad de escolaridad obligatoria) compulsory. You run on (continua adelante), Catch: agarrar, alcanzar, coger, tomar; contagiar + transmit/ pass on. Clearheaded (lúcido). Global downturn (deterioro) ←→ upturn (repunte, mejora). Fill up (recargar, llenar) the batteries. Fire (fuego, disparar, incendiar, despedir) volley (descarga, lluvia) of applauses. Weighty (pesado, responsabilidad: grande; argumento: importante) ordnance (artillería, material de guerra). Aimless (sin pronóstico ni rumbo); the purpose of your visit, I didn't do it on purpose or deliberately. Shore up (sostener, apuntalar) its allies confidence. Smallish (más bien pequeño) butget in crissis times. Cock up (fastidiar, joderla) all over (en todas partes, completamente, integralmente) + we coked it up! (¡la jodimos!). Sisi frequently misguidedly (equivocadamente + mistakenly, wrongly) conflates (combina, refunde) it with terrorism. Unchallenged (incontestable + indeniable, irrefutable, indisputable) master of suspense. His record (documento, archivo; "break/set" a --; historial) shows how Tatcher nudged (codeaba, refrescaba la memoria a) the African parties. Courtship (cortejo, comitiva) → wedding party (cortejo nupcial); escort (escolta, séquito, acompañamiento); entourage (séquito), retenue (en el Rey y gobierno); funeral cortege (en religión), Main: cañería principal) =/= the --s (red de suministro), gas --s tap (grifo; en bañera: faucet), gas mains supply. Prenda usada: (clothing) worn-out, (dictionary) well-thumbed. Landline (Tf. fijo). Fast track (por la vía rápida). A surface covered in craters scorched (quemados, abrasados) by the nearly sun. Tumble down (desplomarse, venirse abajo). Gravitational kneading (masaje,V) from the sun. Abstenerse: (votación) abstain, (alcohol) avoid, refrain from doing sth. Glow (brillo, resplandor) → aglow (radiante, brillante) with happiness. Sawtooth (diente de sierra). Light bulb (bombilla). The vista (=, panorama) at either end opens up few vistas (perspectivas). Struggling (lucha, forcejeo, pasar apuros, luchar para abtirse camino en los negocios, en el equipo). The Samurai were rather bulky (corpulentos). String-pulling (amiguismo, enchufismo). Estufa: (calefacción) stove, (Electr./gas) heater; (cocina) cooker. Islam is incorrigibly flawed (mercancía: defectuosa; teoría: erronea). <u>Go</u> on the blink (estropearse + break down), (plan) go wrong, (shoes) ruin; <u>be</u> on the -- (no marchar, no andar bien). Ejecución: (pers.) execution, (plan) implementation, execution; (orden, promesa, trabajo) carry out; the execution or enforcement (hacer cumplir) of the eviction (deshaucio) order. I was disconcerted by the unexpected (inesperada) question. The war is a morass (cenegal, pantano) of pbs./regulations. The spear, the lance & the dagger (=, puñal). He sang before a spellbound (embelosada, cautivada, hechizada) audience. The 250 ethnic groups in Nigeria can divvy up (repartir) oil & jobs. Extortionate (excesivos, exorbitantes) house prices. Why are you avoiding me (me evitas)? Prevent (impedir) her from leaving before dinner.

Mezquino (mean, stingy, miserable, paltry). Disgruntled: descontento, malhumorado (+ peevish, bad tempered). Less racially segregated, thanks to suburban (zonas residenciales, aburguesadas) sprawl ↔ poor neighbourhood. Light shining off (que brilla/deslumbra desde) a puddle (charco) is harmless. A tech. luminary/leading light (lumbrera). Profits may seep (filtrarse) towards producers. They spirited (animaron) Tibetans. Ser perjudicial: be detrimental/prejudicial, harm, have adverse effects. It is cleaving (se parte, raja, surca) itself away from the rest; cleave through the throng (muchedumbre, atestado de gente). He nosed (olfateó) out: averiguó, descubrió ... The harmless, inoffensive people can't incur (=, debt: contraer; provocar) the wrath. Morale-boasting (estímulo, inyección). Expunging (eliminar, suprimir) the memory of the fight. Berate (regañar, reñir + scold, tell off) women for bearing too flirty (coquetas) skirts. Cloak (capa, encubrir)ed: silueta envuelta en una capa; the layers or strata of the atmosphere, broad strata of a society, aquifer o phreatic stratum, a sheet of ice, a blancket of snow. With the hair on a mess ↔ her hair looks nice. Play (gastar) a prank (una broma) on sb. Fight (pelea) → a closely (estrechamente, rigurosamente, de cerca) fought (reñida) battle. Mantle: (of fog) capa, (of office: poder) responsibility. Be short of sth (quedar sin algo) → Ukraine was -- of its elites. Largese (generosidad, esplendidez) of small municipalities. Crisol: crucible, melting point → the city is a -- -- of cultures. He shot at point blank (boca jarro). Dolphins throw fish up onto the jetty (muelle). Nudge (codazo, empujón suave) sb's memory (refrescar la memoria de alguien). Manipulate implements (implementar, poner en práctica; herramienta, instrumento), ej. the clubs (porras: sticks, truncheons) to beat with. Apisonadora: road roller, steamroller (rodillo, rulo). Legalizar: (party, situation) legalize, (documents) authentication → legalizing pot (olla, marihuana) in Cuba. Squeeze (restricción, apretón,Vs) in (buscar un hueco) →

you can't squeeze anything else in (aquí ya no cabe ni un alfiler). Bleach (lejía; decolorar, blanquear). Canadians got creaker (más crujientes, chirriantes). Light up (p. y p.p.: lit): iluminar, encender un cigarro + (match) strike, (light, radio) turn on, switch on, put on, (gas) light, turn on, (enthusiasm) arouse. With suicide vests (chalecos, camisetas) the crowd rampaged (pasó arrasando). Be rude, disrespectful. Encantador: winsome, charming, delightful; snake charmer. Cause ruckus/rucktions (follones, tensiones) → They was a hell of a row (se armó un follón tremendo), what a mess of papers! (¡que follón de papeles!). Bossness (autoritarismo), the overbearing (autoritario) Kim & the scraggy (flacucha) vegetation. The show is bound to be a crowd-puller (no cabe duda de que este espectáculo atraerá mucha gente). Flake (copo, escama) → the pillars of social controle are flaking (desmenuzados, desconchados, pierden revestimiento) at the edge. Pit (hoyo, foso) → he rubs (frota) his armpit (axila) while patting (dar palmadas, acariciar) his head; rub sth off (quitar algo frotando). Frolic (juguetear; travesura, fiesta), juguetear con (play with). A spasm (=, acceso, ataque) of coughing. Equipment to grown-ups (adultos). Theoretical, hypothetical offsetting (compensación, pago). A hop (brinco con un pie) across the rue. Estelar (stellar), sideral: (Astron.) sidéreo/astral, (coste, precio) astronomic. It seems barmy (chalado) until you realize … A one-off item (caso único) held up (alzó, sostuvo, mostró) it best. Bat (murciélago) → blind as a --; love is -- (el amor es ciego). Frantic (desesperado, frenético; fuera de quicio), these things make me see red o drive me mad (me sacan de quicio). Fraudsters (defraudadores). The soldiers kitted-up (equipados with). The nipples (pezones, tetinas) lightly (suavemente) puckered (arrugados, fruncidos). Uptight (tenso, nervioso) → she is very -- today, don't get so --! (¡no te pongas tan nervioso!). Reckoning (cálculo,V) the total; in my -- (a mi juicio), what is your -- (opinión)?; theory of probability (-- de probabiliudades), mental arithmetic (cálculo mental). His look is wry (irónico) & humorous (divertido), ironically =/= sarcastically (con burla). Festoon (festón, guirnalda), garlanded (adornado, engalanado). Heretics (herejes). Run down (agotar, atropellar) before recharging; we have to pay 22 % surcharge (nos han recargdo un 22 %). They boarded/accommodated 40 people; they showed us to our seats (nos acomodaron en nuestros asientos), make yourself confortable! (¡accommodating!). Rencor: hard feeling + I bear you no malice, I don't bear you any grudge (rencilla). The goodies (golosinas, regalos); goodness (bondad, amabilidad) & baddies + do gooding (hacer buenas cosas). Denial (denegación, rechazo + refusal) → selfdenial (abnegación, generosidad) ↔ wrapped in a cloack (manto, capa) of selflessness (desinterás + unselfishness). Faned (excitado, avivado, abanicado, llamas: atizadas). Dazzled (deslumbrado) by the glitz (ostentación) of China ersatz (imitaciones, sucedáneos). The bank lending is subdued (suave, apagado); estar apagado: (fuego) be out, (luz, radio) be off, (voz) quiet, (sonido) dull, (botón de apagado) off switch/off button. Awe (terror, intimidación, sobrecogimiento) → in -- of her superior. The news caused a sensation; a sensation o feeling of pleasure, I've the feeling that ... Quizzical: socarrón (astuto), burlesco, no formal. Raro: strange, odd, funny + with rare exceptions. Astounding (asombrado, admirable) claim. The end is nigh (próximo), it is -- on (casi) finished. Deny a charge flatly/roundly (rotundamente), he gave me an emphatic yes (¡me dio un sí rotundo!). Round: -- tower, (golf) partida, (drink, business) ronda. Pick (elegir) one new. Lightness: (tejido) ligereza, (tráfico) fluidez, (tarea) sencillez. A mooted, controversial (discutible) question; when the question was first mooted (discutida). Ec. blemish: mancha → -- on his reputation; imperfección → the table is imperfect. Slowly & calmly; I tried calm her down but she kept crying (llorando), this measure will reduce tension in the country. Pie (pastel, empanada) → it's easy as

-- (pan comido). Cortar el bacalao: be the boss, have the final say, run the show. Cut the apple in half, cut or chop (+ chuleta) the celery into pieces, they've closed (cortado) the traffic, the gas had been cut off, stop the bleeding (hemorragia). Contradict (llevar la contraria), don't -- me! (¡no me repliques!). Put off (aplazar) pesky (molestos, latosos)/awkward (torpes, poco elegantes; difíciles, incómodos) pbs. Stagnation: (agua, Ec.) estancamiento. Breezy: tiempo de viento/con brisa; animado, simpático, despreocupado. Years elapsed (transcurridos). Dismay (consternación,V, =) =/= dismal: (día, pensamiento) sombrío, (rendimiento, performance) pésimos. Demeaning (degradantes) terms. Muddy: (=, confusos, turbios) outposts (avanzadas) → the shelling/bombing (bombardeo) of its --. Wist: pensativo (+ thoughtful), nostálgico, =). Indulgence (=, tolerance); this cannot be tolerated, he won't allow them to say that, eggs don't agree with him. Roof/floor/wall tiles. Statues dotted (esparcidas en) the wide street. It ails (aflige + afflict) five municipalities (comarca de cinco municipios). A grassroots (de base) campaign has been wide (de gran) ranging; grassroots politics (donde se tartan los pbs. corrientes). Overflow (desbordar), flood (desbordar, inundación); open the floodgate (compuerta) to sth. They totalled up (sumaban + accumulated, amassed, added up) income from salary & alimony (pensión alimentaria) payments =/= ailment (enfermedad, achaque, pb.). Be bereft (estar desprovisto, privado) of …; deprive sb of sth, forbid sb to do sth, render sb unconscious (privar a alguien del conocimiento), they lack nothing (no se privan de nada). One in ten Americans are striken (dañados) by … Stay (permanencia) over (pasar la noche, quedarse a dormir) at a fixed point. High-flying (de altos vuelos) curator (comisario o conservador de museo). The work is on exhibition in this gallery. Droll (gracioso, curioso, con chispa) paintings. Pattern: dibujo, patron → the Constitution was --ed on the American one; diseño, modelo → -- of consumption. Africa potentates (potentados). Pluck (desplumar, arrancar) from the bosom (seno, pecho) of his family. Tug: tirón,V, (barco) remolcar =/= tow: (autos) remolque, remolcar; coraje → it takes tow to do sth; be plenty of -- (tener agallas). Number crushing (cálculo numérico). Bridge the gap (salvar la distancia). Well equipped office, a ship -- with radar, -- for such a task. Harp (arpa) on (estar siempre con la misma historia) about. He has performed dismally (pésimamente), the play was bad performed. The dog snarled (gruñó) at us. Cash (dinero en efectivo, cobrar + charge) hoard (acumular, acaparar; reserva); cash crops (cultivos comerciales). Hinge (bisagra, girar sobre, depender de) in this direction. The grocer's (tienda de comestibles) team up (se asocian). Drawing board (mesa de dibujo). The quarrelsome (peleones) states; have a quarrel with sb. The contenders (competidores) are ailing (flojean, decaen; están enfermos). Bear the brunt of sth (aguantar lo más duro, ser el más afectado) of recession & casualities. In tandem/jointly (conjuntamente), jointly liable (responsable). Slug (babosa; puñetazo, pegar) → two heaviweights are. Beneath of bonhomie (afabilidad, atención, cordialidad) lies the undisclosed (no reveladas) donations (=, donativo). The warping (distorsión, deformación) of the Ec. sail (vela,V, velero, navegar, zarpar; gobernar, manejar) → set --/weigh anchor (zarpar). Shrink (encogerse, área: disminuir; recular) back (retroceder) from the danger. There's a generation gap. Braket (soporte, entre paréntesis; categoría, gama) → the best car in his -- (gama + range). Bout (racha) of flu (gripe)/of illness (enfermedad), -- of activity, -- (ronda) of negotiations. A token (obsequio) of our gratitude (agradecimiento), remove the hats as a -- (señal) of respect, as a -- of my love. Be furious, get mad. Lackadaisical: apático + "apathetic"), desagradable, perezoso. Estar distraído: be miles away, be absendminded, I wasn't paying attention. Most fish spooked (se asustó) & jellyfish avoids bubles (burbujas). Come along (vamos)! +

presentarse: you -- -- at the right (preciso) time. Wholeheartedly (con entusiasmo, incondicionalmente). Renew: (enthousiasm) renovar, (friendship, business) reanudar. Fly over (salir volando; alejarse + move away, get away from). Restoration: (poder, Monarquía) restauración, restablecimiento =/= refurbish (renovar, reformar, restaurar + restore). Desgastar: (rope) wear out, (roca) -- away/erode. Annoy (fastidiar, molestar); cabrearse: infuriate, get angry/mad, get fed up with sth/sb; it infuriates me having to ... Hardly anyone (casi nadie), hardly ever (casi siempre); always ready (dispuesto) to help, the day had began (había empezado) as usual (como siempre), they've always done it this way (así). Everlasting (eterna, =) life, (hoja) evergreen ↔ decidious tree. Networking: (Comp.) interconexión, (radio, TV) transmisión en cadena, establecimiento de una red de contactos. Marauder (merodeador, intruso + intruder). The Ec. recovery continues apace (a ridmo acelerado). He bankrolled (financió) & seconded (=, apoyó) 50 men in its ranks (rangos, Mil.: filas). Engaged in crass (gordo, graso, grosero) anti-Semitism. Pakistan is amassing (acumulando) nuclear weapons to make up its inferiority to India in conventional forces. Banks are in no mood (clima, humor) to quibble (ser quisquillosos,V, hacer pequeñas objeciones, crear pbs. con nimiedades). He is losing out (sale perdiendo). Smugness (petulancia, engreimiento, vanidad, suficiencia) =/= petty (insignificante, mezquino), --fogging (lawyer: pedante, paperwork: latoso). It didn't live up to (no vive a la altura de) my expectations, they --ed up to their name (hacían honor a su nombre). Cover up: cubrir, ocultar, disimular. Whitewash (encubrimiento, tapar + put the lid/top on; fill in the hole), tapadera, blanquear. Eat away (corroer) the inside of the tree. Uplift: (inspiración + =), animación, elevación del espíritu. Sober (sobrio, serio, formal) up: (drunk pers.) despejarse, volverse más serio. Scale back (recorte, disminución en número). Rickshaw: carrito oriental tirado por pers. Hairspring (muelle muy fino en espiral). Shirk: hacer el gandul, esquivar un deber, una responsabilidad. Whiff: tufillo, olorcillo → go out for a -- of air (salir a tomar el fresco), not a -- of wind (ni un soplo de viento), (corrupción) indicio =/= stuffy (mal ventilado, aire viciado) → it's -- in here (aquí huele a cerrado). Critter (bicho) → I've been bitten; poor --. Irrigar: (jardín) water, (con manguera) hose out, (campo) irrigate. Fuss: escándalo, alboroto bulla =/= rowdy (pers.: escandaloso, peleona; meeting: alborotado). Take in: (harvest) recoger + pick up), (starry dog) acoger, (pers.) hacer entrar. Flunk: (examen) suspender + fail; reprobar. They caught up (agarraron) close to $ 50m. Abduction: plagio; secuestro, rapto + kidnapping. Knick-knacks/trinkets (baratijas). Rizado: (pelo) curly; (superficie) ridged (con caballones, pretuberancias), (terreno) ondulating, (mar) choppy. Wall (muralla, pared), fence (valla, cerco). Cercar: (terreno) enclose, surround; (pers., Mil.) besiege, surround, (con vallas) fence in, (con pared) wall in. Lane: camino, callejuela, carril; Sp. --, bus --, sea --, single --, cycle --, boat --. Prop: (puntal, sostén) → -- a ladder against the wall, the door --ed open with a bucket (cubo). Shy away from (rehuir de) emotional hell (infierno), we musn't -- -- (no debemos tener miedo) from taking a decision; get frightened/scared. Japan's companies are concealing (ocultando)/retaining $ 2 trn. in cash. Torpeza: (acción) clumsiness; (andar) awkwardness. School year (curso escolar), a course in business administration, I'm doing a degree in Ec., (profesión) career; course of a river/life/ship. Ticket: billete/pasaje, round -- (de ida y vuelta), get a parking (de estacionamiento) --, -- counter (mostrador), desk, machine; ticket collector. The shortages of Electr. are holding back (retienen) growth. Concoct: (food, drink) confeccionar, (lie, story) inventar, (plot) tramar, fraguar. The party makeover (maquillaje; modernización, reorganización, cambio de imagen). Correr riesgos (take risks). Men in suits (trajes) swarmed (pululaban, estaban en enjambre). Take the lid off (exponer a la luz pública). Haven (refugio) of misfits (inadaptados). Fortune seekers, he has been sought in many countries, it is much sought after (está muy cotizado), seek death, seek to do sth (tratar de o buscar hacer algo). Maim (mutilar, cortar miembros) → be --ed for life (quedar lisiado de por vida). This glitch (fallo técnico) leaves people with goggle (mirar sin comprender). Curmudgeonly (arisco, cascarrabias + "grouch"). Arrest: (pers.) detención (=), (goods) secuestro; make an --, be under --, you're under -- (queda Ud. detenido). Meld the brash (demasiado presuntuoso, desenvuelto, gran desparpajo) & brainy (inteligente). Gift: regalo, (Jur.) donación), it's a --! (¡es una ganga! ¡está tirado!), talento, don, ej.: artistic --s. Smartness for self-promotion. Demerge (dividir, fragmentar). Quirk (rareza + rarity, oddity, peculiarity). Coal less deadly (mortal, mortífero) to extract. Informal: (pers.) unreliable, (cena, reunión, charla, ropa) informal, unofficial sector of the Ec. Play down (disminución) of Iran's antagonism. Forgive any debt outright (indiscutible, absoluto, rotundo; en el acto). Be satisfied (=, conformarse). Part (=, separar(se), abrirse). Pun: play of words. Iran devoted (dedicó) resources to Syria. Afterthought (idea adicional, ocurrírsele más tarde)→ as an --, just in case (por si acaso). Orderliness (orden, método, disciplina) =/= orderly (ordenado, metódico). Make sure it's steady (constante, firme, seguro, formal, serio) ↔ loosen (aflojar) up: entrar en calor, relajar, desentumecer los músculos. Winning (ganadores, encantadores) manners (modales, maneras). Step down: bajar (from the), renunciar, dimitir. Disgruntled: (employee) dissatisfied, (look, tone) contrariado, malhumorado. The City is a mainstay (pilar, puntal) of British Ec. Its grandees (grandezas) → the nobility or greatness of hide or hidden humanitarian action, the Spanish nobility. Malware (softwere malicioso), a mischievous (pícaro, travieso) look. $ 50 millions to have de attacks called off, cancel, annul. I need somewhere to stay (alojarme). Get a seat on the board (estar en la junta directiva). Heist: atraco, robo a mano armada + armed robbery, hold-up. Asphalted =/= paved (con adoquines, enlosado). It defies (=) descripion (supera toda descripción), inefability (=, indescriptibilidad). Anuncio: (noticia) announcement, (periódico) advertisement, (TV) advertisement, commercial. Bank (orilla, terraplén, ...) → beneath the outer (exterior) bank of the superhighway (autopista de muchos carriles). Earthwork: (terraplén+ embankment), trabajos de preparación del terreno). Jaw-dropping (alucinante) + it's mind-blowing. The floor remains/leftovers (vestigios) suggest she came to host (fue anfitrión, Biol.: fue huesped de) a dense village. Cave: (cueva, caverna) + cave painting (pintura rupestre), cave dweller (cavernícola). Derrumbar: knock, domolish; derrumbarse: (home) collapse, fall down, (pers.) go to pieces, (expectation, illusion) be shattered, collapsed. Footnote (nota de pie de página). The specimens (muestras, ejemplares) of thigh (muslo) bone (fémur) have ridges (perturbaciones, crestas). It is rare to catch (coger, comprender, entender) this transition. Lawless/ anarchy. Mainland: tierra firme, continente → islanders want to move to the --; -- kin (parientes). F. the Great of Prusia is buried in a tomb next to his dogs. Circumnavegate (dar la vuelta al mundo por mar) his kingdom (reino). Goblin (duende, espíritu travieso) in magical, enchanting villages. Parade (desfile) ground: plaza de armas. Eventful (azaroso, lleno de incidentes). Shanty (chabola) towns that cling (se pegan) to the slopes (cuestas) above. The car go stuck (se atasca) on a slope, there is a slope down to the town, the road begins to slope downward. Despreocupado: unworried, unconcerned, he has a careless existence (vive -- de todo), (al hablar, jugar) nonchalantly, (libremente) freely. It like taking a candy (golosina) from a baby (es coser y cantar). Convey: (m.) transportar, (corriente) transmitir, (olor) llevar, (gracias) comunicar, (significado) expresar, (Jur.) traspasar, transferir. It reveals its hidden depths (profundidades). The laughing-stock (hazmerreir) of he country. Deport immigrants. Boorishness (groserias) → be coarse/crude (decir groserias). He creamed off (separó, se llevó) the best. Trip: viaje, visita,V, excursión; zancadilla, tropezón. Proclaim it from the rooftop (a los cuatro vientos). A motorway that cuts through (atraviesa) the town. Look-alike: (pers.) doble, (producto, máquina) imitación (=). Toothless (ineficaz + ineffectual, ineficient). Favoured insiders (que tienen acceso a la información privilegiada). Mobster (gangster, =). Chumminess (amiguismo). The underworld: infierno, hampa, los bajos fondos. Hearse (carro fúnebre). Officials mutter (murmullo), a -- of voices. Avert: (view, thoughts) apartar, (suspicion, danger) evitar, (accident, strike) impedir. Assembly: asamblea, reunión; ensamblaje. Pull off: quitar, arrancar, (plan, Ec.) llevar a cabo. Traveling/itinerant theatre. Palatable/appetizing (apetitoso). Agitar: (líquido) shake, (brazo, bandera) wave. Advert(isement): (radio, Tv) anuncio, spot publicitario =/= allude (aludir), refer (referirse a) =/= notice (darse cuenta, preaviso, letrero; crítica, reseña). A wide/large readership (nº de lectores). I was only 16, thus unable to vote. He profess (manifiesta, faith/Rel.: profesa …). Miff (molestar, offender + offend) → they feel miffed about free decision. Sardonicism (=, burla). Nestle (acurrucarse, arrinconarse) in their showcases (vitrinas) =/= display (exposición, demostración) of sincerity. Propulsar: (development) promote, stimulate; (action, automobile, rocket) propel. In the upper income braket (nivel de ingresos). Brave (aguantar) the storm (asalto, tormenta) → take a town by storm. Vociferar (yell, shout). Bemused (desconcertado + =; aturdido). Fears of sustained depression (= en Ec. + recession). He ate it all in one bite (bocado + morsel). That pile (montón, dineral) has cushioned (amortiguado) against serious fallouts (lluvia radioactiva; consecuencias, secuelas) of the C-19. Exhaust o.s. (agotarse). Exhausting (agotamiento) of Islamic opponents. Relapse (recaída) into bad habits =/= a public rebucke/reprimand (reprimenda) =/=

rapapolvo: telling-off, ticking-off, dressing-down. Retrieve: (dato) recuperar, (jewels) rescatar, (situación) salvar, (damage) reparar =/= reprieve (aplazamiento, indulto, conmutación). Munch (masticar + masticate) merrily (felizmente). A bombastic (elocuente, grandilocuente) ideology. On the sly (pícaro, travieso, astuto): a escondidas + secretely, by stealth. Abridged (resumido, compendiado) ↔ un-- (íntegros). Unintended (no buscado, planeado, deliberado) =/= involuntary. Mild (moderado, suave, dulce, affable) mannered: de modales suaves ... Impenitente (=, unrepentant). A bounty (generosidad, presente; recompensa: reward) of millions $ 2 on his head. He tosses (tira, lanza; agita, sacude) Congress a challenge. Apagar: turn/switch off, (ira: anger; rage) appease, (fire) put out/stinguish, (thirst) quench. Beset: (atormentado, acosado) by dismal (pésimos, deprimentes) Ec. data; a path beset (plagado) with obstacles. Single (< de 10)-figure approval ratings. Play hardball (mostrarse implacable (+ =, relentless). Brownouts (apagones parciales) =/= blackouts, power cuts, power outages. Revisar: (texto) revise, look over, (cuenta) check, (Ec.) audit, (teoría, Jud.) review. He was shaking (sacudiendo para que hagan algo) legislators into making hard decision, rather than simply blocking. Reinstate a tax that would have brought $ 5 bn. Canadian indigenous faiths (fes, creencias) use sage (sabio, savia) in their rites. Conviction (condena, sentencia; convicción). Political posture (postura, pose) =/= pretense/ce (fingimiento) → make a -- of doing sth. Joystick: (aviación) palanca de mando; (Electr., Comp.) mando. Getting the craft (destreza) to climb up (subirse) onto the hydrofoil (hidrodeslizador). Scroll (rollo, pergamino + parchment) → --ing (desplazamiento) + --ing up & down: hacer avanzar & retroceder el texto en la pantalla. The overcast (cielo nublado) of Britain has limited the amound of solar Electr. which can be fed into th grid (red). Propeller (hélice) with a flapping (que aletea, se agita; lío, crisis) fin (ala). Gusty (borrascosos) winds.

Render useless (inútil) the device. The operation was codenamed (dado nombre clave a) Alberta. Covert (encubierto, secreto, furtivo) weapon. Fiend (diablo, desalmado), fiendishly (terriblemente, diabólicamente) difficult; drugs fiend (maníaco), sex -- + "sex maniac". A spun out (alargada) company by a furniture market. It should be 25 % lighter & should last five times longer. Contest: disputa, contienda; concurso (→ beauty --), rebatir → I -- your right to …; impugnar (combatir), contradecir. Put forward: proponer, presenter, (reloj) adelantar ↔ -- back + (proyecto) retrasar, volver a poner. Be secretive (reservado) about … + these documents are confidential. Lavish (suntuoso, generoso) gift. Venture: operación, empresa; aventura, arriesgar + (poner en riesgo) risk, hazart, (oportunidad) endanger, put at risk; arriesgarse: take a risk, expose o.s. to danger. Widespread (generalizada) adoption. Cebar/engordar: (animal) fatten (up), (pers.) get or grow fat. Feeder: (Mec.) alimentador, (Geogr.) afluente (tributary). Jet propulsion (a reacción). Dairy farming industry outside (fuera de) the birth barn (centro de partos). Cows step onto a slow-motion merry-go-round (caballitos). It runs through sieves (cribas, tamices) to capture long fibres. R<u>ea</u>ssure/calm down (tranquilizar) =/= resumption (reanudación, continuación) of the sitting (turno, sesión). Dish out: (food) servir, money (repartir), (consejo) dar. It's not up to me whether you … China gets along (se las arregla) with the US. They worry about losing out (salir perdiendo). Urging (rogar, insistir) Russian companies not to be depend on western ones. Shot down a hostile Muslim. A man whom she married while in office. A budget commensurated (que se corresponde con) his ambitions. File/bring a suit (pleito) against sb. Judjing & ruling in his favour. It turned out that (resultó que) … I worked it out in my head (lo calculé mentalmente) + I worked out (ideé) a plan. Firms with huge (inmensa, enorme) valuation & hardly any staff. The tones of the painting. He prepares to stand down/resign (dimitir). A plea (súplica) for mercy (clemencia, misericordia, (Jur.) leniency (indulgencia, benevolencia) → show leniency to/towards sb. Emphasis on teamwork (trabajo en equipo). Burst (reventar) out the room (salir rápido). I've so much (tanto) to do … So many/such a lot of tourists. We must get on with (seguir adelante con) your work, please. Be inappropriate (=, inoportuno (+ =, ill-timed) complain. Weeny (chiquito, minúsculo) → his chun (amigo) gave him the devotion (=, lealtad) his overweening (arrogancia + =/soberbia: haughtiness) vanity demand. He has conjointed (unido) Thaiwan Ec. ever closer to China in 2015. Up there (allí arriba), higher up (más arriba). China: innovative private entrepreneurs are suffocated (asfixiados) losing out to (perdiendo frente a) state entreprises. While you are up (puesto que estás de pie) … The inner history (=, secreto, historial) of an affair. You can depend on me (cuente conmigo), your success depends on how … Meet for lunch in down town (centro), outside off (a la puerta de) a cinema. We are up at seven. In any case/by any means (medios). With the means to do it. Come in handy (a manos, manitas, práctico, hábil): ser muy útil, (dinero) venir muy bien. How are you? Middling (regular). Impact on events, I only play for my own entertainment. She will command at all cost (a toda costa), even when her ideas dosen't make any sense (no tienen sentido). I guess so (supongo que sí). Leave out (omitir, =). I haven't so/as much time as you. Take sb down a peg ot two (bajar los humos a alguien). Throw themselves to the ground =/= American soil. No te dejes engañar: don't be mislead, fooled, deceived, taken in. Get used (acostumbrado) to the new regime. Think/dress alike (parecido), they all look alike to me, you're all alike. Pay off old scares (ajuste de cuentas); structural/wage adjustment, redeployment of labour (ajuste de plantilla). There's sth fishing going on (hay gato escondido); do sth behind sb's back. Either of them (cualquiera de ellos) can do it. You can ask whowever you want. In real terms the income has fallen, terms of trade (condiciones de transacción), be in good terms with sb, come to terms with sb (llegar a un acuerdo con)/ -- -- -- with sth (asumir, aceptar algo). He does anything any old how/anyway (de todas formas). Put it mildly (por decirlo de alguna manera) the world has become incomprehensible. Rock solid (sólido como una roca); his business went on the rocks (se fue al carajo) last year. He blew his top/lid (se le fundieron los plomos). Break under the strain (romperse debido a la tension), the --s (presiones) on the Ec./of modern life, the demands of the welfare state are --ing public finances to the limit, she gets strain to the point (no se anda con rodeos). Down from 70 % a year earlier ↔ down to 40. Putting taxes up by half a percentage point. Crime has fallen as far in NY as in the rest of America. The line (=, cuerda, hilera) will exend (=, alargar) by one fifth compared with its current length. Spain ranked 125th out of 148. The president popularity was down by 20 % in a decade. The Spain's milk production quota. He revealed how would like to conduct elections. Its ranks (=, º, fila) of informal workers grew along (junto a) those of unemployment. She lay down (se tumbó)/ spread out (estaba tendida) on the floor. Put the squeeze (apretar los tornillos) to sb. Wormhole (agujero de gusano), moth (polilla), woodworm (polilla de la madera). Formal ball/dress (de etiqueta). No scrupule about saying it. Let off: (anyone accused) perdonar; hacer explotar; (steam) soltar; let the children off (salir). Plonk: dejar caer → -- o.s. down, she --ed down on the sofa, it fell -- ("plaf") onto the floor. Destrozar: (glass) smash, (edificio) destroy, (pers., vida, zapatos) ruin, (pers., nervios) shatter. He objects (objeta/pone reparos), do you -- to me smoking? He objects that ..., without demur (sin objetar). Confiding (confiado), confidence (confianza), --tly (con confianza) & titillated (estimulado, excitado) by ... Euristica (=, arte de inventar). Purse (monedera, bolso), purse one's lips (fruncir los labios). Sinvergüenza: brazenly, cheeky, shameless.

Indian unflattering (poco alagüeño, poco favorecedor) relief (=, alivio, auxilio, liberación). Death penalty. Defraud (=, estafar) the state =/= the low-key (discreta, sencilla) home belies (defrauda, desdice) with a home placed there; a low-key police presence; desdecirse: but later he went back on sth, on his word, on what he said. Bot (robot) → botnets (utilizados en cibernética): vast network of compromised (comprometidos) computers. He went up (se acercó) & said hellow to him. Codear: nudge, (con fuerza) elbow → they --ed us out of the way (nos apartaron a empujones)/toward sth; --ed their way through (se abrieron paso a codazos). Widget/gadget: artilugio, chisme, aparato. Landgrab (apoderarse/compra de terrenos). Itinerant (=, ambulante). Buck up (animarse, espavilarse), -- --! (¡date prisa: rush, hurry)!), hurry up or you'll … At the risk of one's life, at one's risk (por su cuenta y riesgo). Whistlestop (visita relámpago, apeadero). (Foreign direct investment) FDI is wilting (débil, marchito, mustio). Make sb blush (hacer sonrojar a alguien). Spread/difuse (difundir). Circumvent: (sorteo, evite) of the obstacles, (burla) of the law. Swank (fanfarronear, chulear)y: fanfarrón =/= posh/classy (chic, pijo). Enraptured (embelesado, cautivado + =). Prescindible, dispensable ↔ indispensable, essential. Disconcerted ("="). Astucia: astuteness, shrewdness, craftiness; ruse/trick. Destrozado: (zapato) ruined, (físico) exhausted, (moral abatida) devastated & shattered. Headship (dirección) of a club/college. Intranquilo (worried, anxious, restless). Mareado: (nauseas/ganas de vomitar) sick, queasy; (pérdida del equilibrio) dizzy, guiddy. Snazzy (vistoso, llamativo) =/= snappy: rápido, enérgico; elegante, alegre =/= zippy: brioso, veloz. Difamatory, slanderous (calumnioso). Insidious (insidioso: engañoso, que prepara cautelosamnte los medios para), treacherous (traidor, peligroso), deceitful (falso, mentiroso, engañoso). Inclinación: (roof, land) slope, lean/inclination of a tower, greeting (saludo) with a slight bow. Slant: (ground) inclinación, (floor/roof) pendiente, ...; punto de vista: what is your -- on this? get a -- (pareceres) on a topic (asunto). Descend/ going down ←→ ascend, rise, climb. Toss: lanzamiento; tirar, aventar, lanzar, sacudir(se) → -- up (echar a cara cruz. Profiteers (especuladores, "="). Diluted ("=",) to make it more palatable (aceptable, agradable). Sync. (sincronización). Sanitice: desinfectar, hacer potable. China's seniors echelons (capas) → the top -- (altos mandos). Terrifying/fearsome (aterrador, que espanta). Grosero: vulgar, coarse, rude. Coarse: (texture, skin) áspera, (sand) gruesa, (character, remark) ordinarios. Prime (principal) time: horas de maxima audiencia. Centinela: sentry, (Mil.) guard. The mob (muchedumbre) got roudier (más alborotada). Undisclosed (no revelados) loans. The government will step in (intervener). A neatly manicured (muy cuidado) garden. Squeak (gruñido, chillido,V) → have a narrow (limitado, estrecho) -- (salvar las apariencias: no dejar parecer nada criticable. Prey (presa) on/upon (alimentarse de) → the dealers who --/-- (explotan) youngers immigrants in detriment of the locals. Trendy (modernos) buildings. Be a showstopper (que causa sensación + feeling). I've gone over (examindo, revisado) the pb. Drag (arrastrar) down: (moralmente a su nivel) arrastrar, (físico) debilitar. Marital bliss (felicidad). Superficial/ shallow: (pers.) superficial, (river) poco profundo. Dissecting (=, análisis minucioso). Traffic snarling (gruñiente + maraña) cavalcadas (= + parada, procesión). Copy & paste (pegar). Racha: a rash of strikes, winning (de éxito) streak, run/spell of bad luck, gust of wind, serie/string of illness. Debatable (discutible, dudoso). A moot (discutible) point + it has been --ed that (se ha sugerido que). Hard won (ganada con esfuerzo) wisdom. Cold-hearted (frío, insensible), half-hearted (poco entusiasta). Paper tiger/tigress: (pers., institución) que parecen poderosos y que no lo son. Trusted (de confianza) record (=, documento, registro; anotar, grabar). Extricate (sacar) sth from sth/sb, ej.: Britain from the EU, a pilot from a wreckage (avión siniestrado). Be bereft (privado) of a purpose, intention. They leafed through (hojeaban) piles of magazines & catalogues. Convenient/advisable =/= apropiado (fitting, suitable) =/= apt (acertado, apropiado). The low-hanging fruit has been plucked (arrancado, desplumado). Ordenador: (sobremesa) lunchbox, desktop; (portable) laptop, portable computer. Picking (harvesting + recolección). The rain flooded (inundó) the countryside & the market with products + swamped with offers, work, applications. Contractor (contratista). Poster (=, afiche, cartel). Holey (con muchos agujeros) veil. Underhand ("turbio") way to risk capital; turbio: shady, murky, (agua) clowdy, muddy. China is amenable (dócil, flexible, responsible). A ham (actor de teatro extravagante, exagerado; melodramático, cómico + =, funny). Go back into autocrazy. Brass fanfare (fanfarria): jactancia de jefazos. Upgrade: cuesta arriba, actualización, mejora. Lifeboats (botes salvavidas). Move containers around (de un lado a otro). Glowing: brillante, (pers.) rebosante, (descripción) entusiasta. The World trade is becalmed (estancado + (agua) stagnant, (pb.) stuck. Inmóvil: still, motionless, immible. Intemperate (inmoderado). Be on display (expuestos). He is balls (testículos) & guts (intestinos, panza, tripa): es un tío con cojones. Attempts to weed out (arrancar, suprimir) wilfully (adrede + on purpose) distorted (distorsionados) risks weightings (ponderaciones, primas, pluses, ej. por vivir en Londres). Foolproof: (plan) infalible, (máquina, control) sencillo, manejable. Incentive (=, estímulo). The lot (mucho, montón, todo; terreno, solar) → they ate the --; their lot: destino, suerte + fate); draw/cast lots (echar a suerte). Piecemeal: poco sistemático; poco a poco + gradually, little by little, (desarrollo) irregular. In-flight emissions, meal, movie. Cruising (navegando) at an altitude of … Crafty (astuto, hábil) foxy (astute, sexy). Faster-acting material can seal (tapar, precintar) holes in any emergency. Copycats (imitadores + =); plagiar: plagiarize, copy illegally, pirate. Come into being (nacer) + bring into being (realizar, llevar a cabo + carry out). Daylight-savings time (horario de verano). Indemnity ↔ uncompensated. At first sight/glance. Laugh like crazy/mad. Fun: the -- (diversión) ended, have -- (divertirse), poke -- (reirse) at Churchill. Stalin chain-smoked (uno tras otro) & doodled (garabateaba) volves heads & improvised … Powerhouse: central eléctrica; (company) centro motriz, (ideas) fuente inagotable. The more ludicrous (ridículo) navel-gazing (mirándose a) traditions. Empedernido: (vicio) hardened, inveterated, (player) compulsive. Clamor/shouting (vocerío). The model has run out of steam (quedó sin fuerza). Oddball (raro, excéntrico + =). Scrabble (escarbar) about/around (revolverlo todo) for sth. Tight spot/corner (situación apurada). Redeemed (redimido). Nay (no) → the naysayers (que dicen lo contrario) will muster (reunir) votes. He saw off (despidió, venció, acabó con) an attempt. Scream (chillido, chirrido, grito,V) → they were --ing with laugher (reian a carcajadas). Mistrust or desconfiance. Four hallmarks (contrastes,V, sellos distintivos) from the era stand out (sobresalen). Sludge (lodo, residuo) that filled the water ways (vías fluviales) =/= muck (estiercol, suciedad)y: sucio =/= dung (estiercol, excremento), manure (estiercol abono) + artificial manures (abonos o fertilizantes). Deeds (actos, hechos) of derring-do (great deeds/exploits: azañas (+ feats). Hardcore (incondicional + =, pura porno). Snare (trampa, atrapar) such a pretty girl. Prospects of shut (down). Demeaning (degradante) by apologizing with him. Imitation (=). Inimical (adverso, hostil) to the idea. Gloat over sth.: regocijarse, deleitarse, recrearse en algo + enjoy o.s. It blends (mezcla, armoniza, combina) ersatz (sintético, sucedáneo, imitadas) arquitectures. Canopy (toldos) → a -- (manto) of leaves. The space will be abuzz (ocupado + engaged, busy) with machines → the whole office was --ed with news (las comentaban). Momentum (=, impulso, ímpetu). Quip (ocurrencia, broma), witty (ingenioso, gracioso + funny). That saps (mina, debilita) the domestic Ec. Utter (total) → Pope's utterance (declaración, = + statement). Drones to scout (explorador, reconocimiento, búsqueda) houses for burglars (ladrones). Inimical (adverso, hostil) to the idea. Hopper (tolva) → grasshoppers (saltamontes). Razor wire: alambre de seguridad, con cuchillas. Sealed (off) (cerrado) behind his iron curtain. Not to mention (y no digamos ya) ... Hydroelectric power stations (centralitas hidroeléctricas) would mar (estropear) unique (=, excepcionales, =) landscapes. Slippage (deslizamiento, patinaje, bajón) → the -- seems inevitable. He tops (cubre) his billowy (hondeante, hinchado) menswear (ropa de caballero), the turban. Pilgrinage, which Koran enjoins every believer who can afford it to perform once in a lifetime. They lack (están desprovistos de) school. The grief striken (afligida) widow. More hoopla (bombo y platillo) for the looming (inminente, que amenaza) ... It brough into focus (enfocó + focused on) the wearsome (pesado, aburrido + boring, tedious) ... Political brawl (camorra, pelea). Revered (venerado) by some. The fight will outlast (sobrevivir) his canonization. He sorrowed (se aflijía, sentía pena) over the excess. Mentally, emotionally disturbed (con pbs.) + I was gravely, seriously --ed (afectado) of this misfortune + I had a --ed (agitada) night. Hunted down (cazados) & beaten or chained. He suggested flogging (flagelación), which he likened (comparó + =) to stern (severa) discipline. Saquear: (ciudad) sack/plunder, (tienda) boot + botín). Pipe ("=", tubería,V). Outvote (vencer en elecciones). War-path (pie de guerra, búsqueda de camorra). After years of abstaining, aborigenes can be swing (basculantes) voters. Premiership: primera división de fútbol, puesto de Primer ministro, tropas: crack. A. Prank (de broma) call. Enliven (animar). Lagging (rezagándose) behind (quedando atrás). Ease (aliviar, calmar, rebajar) China's curbs (frenos, restricciones,V) on internal migrations. Pamper (mimar, consentir). Be under cloud (sospecha) + have one's head on the -- (estar en las nubes). A wide ranking (=, clasificación, graduación) of agreements. Well-heeled (ricacho). He noted approvingly (con aprobación). The EU doused (apagó, mojó con agua) it, though the embers (brasas) still glow (brillan). He no longer practice his profession. Plug (tapar) the current-account gap. Without demur/objection. Receipt (recibo) → tax --s (ingresos) frittered (away) (malgastados) on middle-class giveaways (regalos). The committee crushed (estrujó, aplastó) a proposal. Phoney: (pers.) farsante, (name, address) falsos. Cut a dash: emphasize, highlight: destaca, attract (llama) the attention. Ambicioso: ambitious, self seeking, unterprising, careerist. Vulgarity of elite/crack troops. A baboon (babuino) heart as stopgap (recurso provisional) until a donor comes up. Crap: estupidez (talk --), (film) mierda, cagar + shit), gilipollez. Deepen: profundizar, incrementar, agudizar, intensificar. The likes (los semejantes). Prestidigitation (juego de manos). We are not getting much feedback (reacción, respuesta, retroalimentación): no nos tienen demasiado informados. Tanker: buque cisterna. In England of two million people eligible to give feedback on devolution only a handred replied. Frozen (congelado) soil. Our Democracy is backsliding (recae, reincide). Dra<u>pe</u> (cubrir, poner sobre) → -- the furniture with sheets =/= dra<u>b</u> (color apagado, gris; soso, vida monótona) office block which is home of … Vividly (vivamente). Sixty % of its World's output lies (se encuentra) within de facto 4 % zone. Putin blamed America for unsettling (desestabilizar) the Middle east. The concert was disappointing (decepcionante). He doesn't like be scripted (no acepta guiones, lo preparado de antemano). Holmes's sidekick (secuaz, que sigue un partido político, compañero). Brand (tildar) sb (as) a racist. A run of good/bad luck. The wall (pared, muro, barrera) of martians craters. The latest research bolsters (refuerza, moral: levantar). Clinging (pegado, aferrado) on dwindling (menguantes, cada vez menos) pockets of dampness (humedad). Laughable (irrisorio). Spew (arrojar, vomitar) fire brimstone (azufre + sulphur) =/= salmuera (brine). Foil: papel de aluminio, florete, (pers.) desbaratar los planes, (attempt) frustrar. Glitter (brillo,V)ati: famoso, celebridad del mundo literario. Hit-or-miss (al azar + at random, by chance). Hazardous (peligroso, arriesgado). Everything depends on you. It's my turn to play, it's not up to me (no depende de mi) ↔ if it were up to me … You will come? It depends. Cashpoint/cash machine (cajero automático). Molluscs branched (off) (se ramificaron, se desviaron) to form … A tasty morsel (pedazo, comida: bocado). The city became eponymous (tomó el nombre) of his ideas. Monuments to the unknown soldier =/= war memorial (monumento a los caídos). Hand-picked (muy seleccionado). Mall (alameda, paseo; calle peatonal) → shopping --s: (centros comerciales) are American front (fachada, delantera). Latins decried (criticaban, menospreciaban) German bullheadedness (terquedad). Data collection. Intimidad: (amistad) intimacy, familiarity, (en privado) o.s. privacy. Toddler (niño que empieza a andar o que está en edad de aprender a andar), tiddler (pececillo; nene, renacuajo) =/= minnow (pequeño pez de agua dulce). Comfy: (chair, bed, room) comfortables, cómodas → I'm nice & -- here (estoy súper cómodo aquí). As a feat (hazaña) of brawn (fuerza muscular) is impressive (impresionante) → he is all -- & no brain. Fate (destino, suerte)d: predestinado, condenado → it was --ed (inevitable) that … → fateful (funesto, fatídico, triste, desgraciado) + ominous (mal augurio). Summon: llamar, convocar, (help) pedir, (Jur.) citar. Paliza: drubbling, thrashing, beating → the R. Madrid thrashed Barcelona, give sb a beating; the critics panned or slated the novel; the journey was a real bore (taladro, perforar; pesado, pelmazo; una lata, aburrir. Ordenado: (habitación, escritorio) tidy, (oficina) well organised, ordered → they lead a normal, ordered or orderly life, the children entered the museun in an orderly fashion (manera) ↔ untidy, messy. Lead-up (periodo previo, precampaña). Flash: destello, arrebato de ira (a fit of anger) … in a -- (instante), ráfaga (of inspiration), -- (rayo) of hope, news .. (noticia de última hora). The Arab spring unleashed (soltó, desató, desencadenó) more than hopes for change. In the poor (pobres, marginales) & outlying (periféricas, distantes) areas of the society. Brilliant marksman/shooter (tirador), he is a good marksman (tiene buena punteria). Retrenchment (recorte/racionalización de gastos) of army-backed rule in Egypt. Unabashedly (tímidamente, avergonzadamente): descaradamente, sin inmutarse. Flit (revolotear) in/out (entrar/salir precipitadamente) + flit from one topic to the next (ir continuadamente de uno a otro tema). His piety (=, devoción, beatería). Not learned (=, erudito) or bookish (libresco, pers. estudiosa). He left unseen (oculto, inadvertido). The official data is iffy (dudoso, inierto). He had/threw a tantrum (le dio un berrinche). Scoop: (flour, grain) recoger con pala (shovel), (crema: cream) cucharón, (newspaper) exclusiva (exclusive/sole rights), (Com.) ganar un dineral, logro financiero). Her underlings (subordinados, subalternos + pers.: auxiliary). Flow: (Electr., blood, …) fluir, correr; (traffic) circular con fluidez; flujo, (lava, agua) corriente. Hop (saltar) back to he coop/henhouse (gallinero). Artimaña: (caza) trick, trap, (ingenio) cunny. Campaigner: partidario, defensor + in favour/supporter) → environment --. Trestle (caballete), (de arte) easel). Compliant (sumisas) courts, compliance (sumisión, conformidad). Spy story (novela de espionaje), spy out (hacer un reconocimiento al) land. Short change: no dar % del cambio, defraudar, tartar mal un proyecto → -- -- (defrauder) the governments through artificial (ingenioux) use of loopholes (fisuras, lagunas) in laws. He shumed (evitó, impidió) to give them a try (probarlos, darles la oportunidad). Users (usuarios) of public transport. Turf (cesped, hierba artificial) → -- out: (pers.) echar de patitas a la calle, (ropa) botar. Shorthand (taquigrafia). Fulfill: cumplir con, realizar, llevar a cabo + satisfy

(=). Tenderness (ternura, cariño). Cautivar: captivate, (prisoner) capture. Defiance (desafío a peligro o muerte) + it is a challenger to us all, challenge or dare sb to sth. Samey (similar, parecido, semejante) + she is like her in character, they are very much alike or very similar, it has no equal, there is nothing to equal it. Erasure: borrado, tachadura (+ delete, cross out). A homegrown (del estado, de la nación, local) quackery (curanderismo, charlatanerismo). Chopping (cortando) business into ever smaller shunks. High tech. wizards (brujos, magos). She is well-liked (amada, querida) by ... Drug racket/ traffic (tráfico de drogas). Randomized (aleatorio, fortuito). Cardboard city (para los sin techo). Court (corte, tribunal, cortejar) → --ly: cortés, elegante, fino, distinguido. Barred from standing (posición, prestigio, (e)status, ...). Status: (pers.) estado, (of agreement) situación → marital -- (estado civil), *(e) statu quo*, -- symbol (símbolo de rango). Foreign doctors to fill chronic vacancies (vacantes). Nugget: (gold) pepita, (information) datos de mucho valor. Failure to comply with the law, to keep his promise; breach of a contract. Partisan: (supporter) partidario, (decission, crowd) partidista. Evil (mal, malvado, asqueroso) system. Rastrear: (zona) search/comb, (pers.) track, trail, (rio, lago) trawl, (policía) drag, (limpiar el fondo, dragar) dredge. Perched (posados) above mineshafts (pozos de mina) =/= well. Execrable (=, deplorable, abominable, aborrecible). Thin-skinned (susceptible, sensible) leader. Cocky (chulo, gallito) → he got all -- (se puso en plan chulo), don't get -- with me, what a lovely (chulo) dress! Malinterpretar: misconstrue, misinterpret. Diary (agenda, diario) of an opportunistic. Charco: puddle, pool + estanque, piscina → an untapped pool of ability (una reserva de inteligencia no utilizada). Wicked (perverso, malo, vil, pícaro) → a -- (socarrón) sense of humor; wickedly: malvadamente, cruelmente. A passionate (apasionado) retold (contó de nuevo) ... Domed: (roof) abombado, (building) con cúpula. Plaudits (aplausos, aclamaciones) →

elect sb by acclamation; amid applause from the audience (entre las aclamaciones del público). Jack (gato mecánico, enchufe hembra) ↔ plug: el del macho) → a jack- of- all- traders (manitas, sabe un poco de todo) → he's a -- -- -- -- & master of none. It come about (ocurre) when … =/= come across: (pers.) encontrarse, ser comprendida → he -- -- very well in the interview. Gyrations (giros, rotaciones, virajes); viraje: (Náut.) tack, (coche) turn, (repentino) swerve, (en carretera) bend, curve. Spruce: arreglar, acicalar → -- o.s. up; (room, garden) arreglar. Archways (arcos de entrada). Stress/emphasize (poner énfasis). The trial put on hold (en suspenso + in pause for a moment). Chronicle: (=, registrar, describir + describe); registrar: (birth/death) register, (son) record, (home, zone) search. Under no compulsion (coacción, obligación) to do it. Empeñar: (pertenencias) pawn, hock; empeñarse: get/go into a debt. Mesmerize (fascinar, hipnotizar, cautivar, dejar boquiabierto). Stroke: golpe (of luck), on the -- of 11, apply using light/quick --s (toques), She is most eyebrow- raising (arquea las cejas, se asombrar de algo). Insider trading/dealing (abuso de información privilegiada) + ruinous --/--. The road skirts (out) (bordea) the lake, we had to -- round the mountain, we sailed along the edge of a coast, the street bordering the park. The well-meaning (bien intencionadas) parties (partes). Sudan secede. It's decked (out), decorated/festooned (engalanado) in fairy (de color) (light) bulls =/= lamps (lámparas). Qualify for (clasificarse, titularse, tener derecho a) green cart (permiso de residencia). Remission (=, perdón). Go downriver. I stick out for (defiendo + defend, protect), saco la cara para) Democracy. I advise you for your own good (port tu bien). Crushingly (de manera aplastante) =/= the president's veto is ringingly/steadfastly (categóricamente + "=") overturned (anulado, erradicado) by Congres. (Brainwave, fantastic, brilliant, genial) idea. It's doable (hacedero) in three weeks. His state of the Union address (discurso del estado de la unión). Atic/loft (desván) =/= penthouse (piso ático). Pore (poro) over (hacer un estudio minucioso) → we --ed it over hours (lo estudiamos durante horas y horas). Simmered (hirvió a fuego lento, estuvo a punto de estallar) without pushback (crowd/army: retroceder). Yeast/leaven (levadura) =/= his speech was leavened (aligerado) with lively (divertidas) anecdotes + Marxism was leavened by the Liberation Theology. Feel/suffer the effects of ... Break into (introducirse en) the mainstream, the market ... Retrenchment (disminución, racionalización de gastos). China has lobbied (presionado) the Group of seven (G7). Opportunities galore (en abundancia). Adequately. Evitar: elude, avoid, evade, dodge. Cloistered ("enclaustrados"). Forbid (prohibir) → --ing: (pers., look) severa, intimidante, (landscape/cliff) imponente, (task) difícil. Revelious projeny (--ie: descendencia) ↔ ancestry. He continued, despite the ministrations (cuidados, atenciones). Meet targets by higher-ups (los de arriba) even if other unexpected facts befall (ocurren). Wire (conectar) sth with sth. Incubar: (eggs, diseases) incubate, (crisis) brew, (eggs) hatch, (ideas, plot) tramar. They blew themselves up: estallaron, saltaron por los aires. Simpathetic: compresivo, favorable, receptivo, bien dispuesto; cordial, affable (afectuoso, agradable). Dirigir: (pers.) direct, (comentario, pregunta) address, (programa, producto) aim. The oncoming (viene en sentido contrario) winter. A head-on (de frente) clash with the union, the two cars collided --. So far/up to/hitherto (hasta ahora) obscure ... First of all (antes que nada) the plan came to fruition (se realizó). Slip (error, resbalón,V, caída; patinar) → -- in/out (entrar/salirse rápido sin que lo vieran). Esponjoso: spongy, fluffy). A glittering (brillante) throne overlooking (dominando) red-leather benches (bancos, escaños). Study afresh (otra vez, de nuevo). All it purports to be (pretende ser) ... Squeeze: apretón,V, (venta, crédito) disminuir; estrujar, (fruta) exprimir, extraer, -- inflation out; -- in (buscarse un sitio, meterse). Be brief, concise, succinct in the explanation. Global positioning system (GPS) signals are jammed (atascadas). Heel (tacón, talón) → a down- at- heel (venida a menos, de mala muerte) town. Mr. Li was harder-line (más radical) than even his two immediate predecessors. In plenty (en abundancia). Ligero: (paquete, comida) light, (dolor, sabor, olor, fiebre; acento) slight. Premunition: presenimiento + I've the feeling that … Have a strategic control, authority, domination on sth. Agrieved (ofendido) → in an -- (de queja) tone. Lick sb's boots; suck up to sb (hacer la pelota, lamerle el culo). An American icon covers up (oculta, tapa completamente, disimula). Lash/whip (azotar) out: (pegar golpes, arremeter contra) the democracy. The creaking (crujiente, poco sólido) empire will decay (se desmoronará, irá en decadencia). Angle: ángulo, punto de vista, perspectiva, enfoque. Vexed (enfadado, confuse). The plant's radioactive plume (=, smoke: columna) headed (encabezaba, iba en dirección de) N-W. Terms: (words) términos, condiciones de un contrato; plazos, períodos, trimestres → winter --. Insípedo: (insipid, bland). Terror waged (remunerado) by the regime. Slavishly (servilmente). Local officials hurry (corretean, se apresuran) to adjust their rethoric to fall in line with the land. Post-stress: symptoms of hypevigilance & flashbacks (escenas retrospectivas). Bunny (conejito, tía buena). Scent: perfume,V, aroma; olfatear, (peligro) presentir → be on the -- (sobre la pista) =/= a brief footnote containing scant (escasos) details. Limited/slender (escasas) resources + delgado). The Federal reserve board (Fed) is set (resuelto, decidido) … Aboard (embarcar, …, a bordo). Vessel: vaso, recipiente, (Bot.) vaso. Tepid: tibio, (reacción, público) poco entusiasta. Clamber (trepar, subir gateando) out of it: salir con penas + they --ed over the wall, into a car. Be a show-stopper (que causa sensación)ing: sensacional + =, fantastic, marvellous. Executive committee. Lop (cortar, podar) sided: desequilibrado, torcido, desigual. Voters rebuked (reprendieron, reprocharon) a regressive regime. Will subvert (=, trastornar, perturbar) the new National Assembly. Get off (bajarse de, salirse, mancha: eliminar) my land! Pattern: dibujo → draw a --; patron → a clear -- (pautas definidas) began to emerge, behaviour --, healthy eating -- (hábitos), sleep -- (hábitos). Bristle: they bristled (se resintieron); cerda de animal & pelo de planta: (erizarse), many --ed at what they saw; --ed (repleto) with tourists. The upstanding (honesto, honrado; de pie) future citizens → the court (sala) will be --. The doctors relying on (basarse en, confiando con) leeches & blootletting (sangria, carnicería). Trolley: trolebús, tranvía, (de mercado, estación) carrito. The fertility rate has fallen blistering (calor abrasador,velocidad vertiginosa, crítica devastadora) fast. Doll (muñeca) → paper -- (monigote de cartón) + a cardboard cutout (monigote/figura de carton) of a sleek (impecable) smiling couple. Gather strength: recobrar fuerzas, solidez, resistencia. They flog (azotan, venden) discounted hairspray & nail varnish. Regional elections are just a stepping-stone (pasadera). Ostracised (desterrados, exiled) by mainstream (corriente principal) politicians. Torpe: (pers., acciones, comentario) clumsy, (andar) awkward, (entendimiento) slow, dim. Gasping: decir jadeando, grito ahogado, respirar con dificultad. A roaring (estruendoso) business. Its focus is at ease (cómodo, relajado) with free market. Ballyhoo (bombo, propaganda)ed (de propaganda estrepitosa) breakthrough (gran avance). Thaw: diplomatic -- (deshielo), (food) descongelar, (ice) fundir. Cottage (casita), -- (artisanal) industry + handcrafted furniture. Africa's bows (lazos) in the continent. Muggy (bochornoso) evening, it's -- today. Dapper: atildado, pulcro, aseado (+ tidy, clean, neat) ↔ Seedy (cutre + shabby; sórdido: sucio, tacaño) room. Shepherd (conducir, guiar; pastor) → she has shepherded (llevado, acompañado, …) the legislation through the Senate. Facelift: lifting; reforma superficial de un edificio. Man: (barco) tripular; fortaleza (fortress): guarnecer, ocuparse de. The Chicago gangland (mundo del crimen) boss. It was arson: el incendio fue premditado + deliberated. Arrange the furniture however you like (como quieras). The solution they have devised (ideado, concebido, inventando). His thug (matón)gery (matonismo, brutalidad) with convicts (prisoners/ inmates) evoluted leniently (indulgentemente). Unsparing (moderado: moderate): (incansable, despiadado) poursuit of suspects. Uphold: (Jur.) veredicto: confirmar, (costumbre) conservar, (fe: fith; principio) mantener. Nannying (profesión de niñera, protección excesiva) migrants. It lifts out (saca personas) of deep poverty. Censors'shocability, shoked, scandalized (escandalización por poco) has varied over time. Viewer (telespectador); for home viewing (ver). Unequal (desigual) amounts. Re-edit shots (tiros, tiradas) that include plunging (muy profundo) necklines: escotes muy bajos. Dripping (empapados) corpses (cadáveres), be wet (empapado, chorreante). A film heavely censured. Grind (moler, triturar; chirriar)ing noise (chirrido); come to a --ing halt/stop: (vehículo) detenrse con un chirrido, (negociaciones) estancarse, --ing poverty (miseria absluta + abject poverty); a --ing race/examen (que deja molido). Offer/proposal for successive encounters. On the issue of political prisoners. The tone (=, sonido, señal sonora) was removed (sacado) from the tension surrounding (de alrededor, rodear) meetings (reuniones, encuentros). Fail (fracasar, frustrar, malograrse, suspender un examen); he failed to live up to (no estuvo a la altura de) our expectations. Superar: overcome, Lím.: go beyond; the success surpass our expectations. Unintended (no buscada, planteada) consequence. Pricing (fijación de precios). Spar/train (entrenar). A region racked (sacudida) by earthquakes + be --ed with pain (sufrir atroces dolores). (Wire)tap (escucha telefónica). The quintessential (por excelencia) Sunni. Custombuilds (hechos de encargo) ships. Show up (evidenciar, poner de manifiesto). Rightful: (hijo, partido politico) legítimo + legitimated, lawful, (recompensa) justa. Its earlier offer. The endgame (final) of Chinese rulers is not for tomorrow. Spineless (débil, sin carácter). Soft (suave) landing. A provisional, temporary arrangement. Clearance: autorización, (stock) liquidación, (mercancias) despacho de aduanas, (finanzas) compensación. He travels light (con poco equipaje). A wash (capa) of greenery (vegetación), of painting. Ride (cabalgar) abreast (al lado) of sb + keep sb -- (al corriente). Bring deals to fruition (a buen término). Capa (layer) → the veneer (enchapado,V) is beginning to chip (desconchar + chip away). Flags superimposed (superpuestas) atop (sobre) a pile of ... Debase: (idea, principio) degradar, (lenguaje) viciar, corromper, (pers.) degradar, rebajar. Interference: (=, intromisión, meterse donde no le llaman). Lack of discretion, tacktless (indiscreto + =). Playthings/toys (juguetes) of the imperialists. Staffers (pers. de plantilla). With trays (bandejas) of pastries (pastelitos, cakes) → wedding cake. Loony (chiflada, disparatada) right → she's completely -- (está como una cabra). Towered (descollaba) a head along the pudgy (rechoncho, regordete) Khrushchev. Tossed about/around (lanzado acá y allá, estar agitado) but not sunk (perdido). Drawbridges (puentes levadizos). This attire (atavío) for a startling (alarmante, extraño, llamativo) 99 % of women. Float: flotar (al agua ...), -- a company (introducir una compañía en bolsa), I felt (me sentía) --ing on the air, the waves --ed the seaweed (algas) ashore. Retroceso: backward movement, (army) withdrawal, (ceder) backing down. Retroceder: (pers., automóbil) go back, move back, withdraw, retreat. Mosquearse: get suspicious, smell a rat. Gather/form a group. Aficionado: keen/fond, enthusiastic, amateur. A do-it-yourself (bricolage) enthusiast. Taking no sides (no participar) in the conflict. Live on the day- to- day (cotidiano) basis (al día). Underachiever: pers. que no rinde el nivel exigido por su capacidad. Hive (colmena) off (separar, escindir; vender, enagenar) two millions Palestinians. Portend (augurar + predict, foretell =/= portent (augurio + omen, prediction). Whiteboard (pizarra blanca, electrónica). Very narrow-minded (estrecho de miras). The bottom line (lo mínimo aceptable, lo essential) is that … Unfaithful/unbeliever. Disloyal to the king. The press gloated (se regodeaba, deleitaba + delighted). He spars (discute, se entrena) with crusty (pan…: crujiente, mal humoradas) girls. The trial was put on hold (en suspense). An alternative to the stiffness/rigidity (rigidez) of the college. You are under no compulsion (obligación) to do it. He dons (assume, =) his role. Bodes ill ←→ -- well (buena señal). Breathtaking (impresionante) pace (paso, Mús.) ridmo, at a slow --(lentamente), at my own --. Caress (caricia) =/= charity (organización, obra benéfica). The well-meaning (bienintencionadas) parties. Take it on trial. Burglar (ladrones)proof mechanism, bulletproof glass. Stick up for one's rights (hacer valer) + -- out for (defender, sacar la cara por). Upstream/upriver (río arriba). Moving (emotivo, conmovedor) → I found it -- (me entusiasmó). The driving force (impulsor) behind the policy. Arousing (causar, suscitar, provocar, despertar) perorations (peroratas: razonamientos pesados, inoportunos). Watchword: (motto) lema, órdenes, consigna =/= (password) contraseña. Asombrado: astonished, amazed =/= stunned/dazed (aturdido) =/= boggle: atónito, sorprendido, patidifuso. Taint (mancha, contaminación; deshonor,V). Scout (explorar, patrulla de reconocimiento, explorador) → have a -- around, talent -- (cazatalentos), -- for (buscar) sth. Make fun of (burlarse de). Polvorín: (almacén) magazine/arsenal, (lugar/país peligrosos) powder keg. The book is timely (oportuno + =) → opportunities galore (en abundancia). Atravesar: (river, customs) cross, the road goes through the town/valley. The bullet went through the heart. Broth/clear soup (caldo). The present Prime minister. Proffer: (gift, apology) ofrecer, (advise) dar, (condoleances) presentar. Betcha (a que no) can't climb. Tibetans feel shut out (sienten quedarse fuera) from China's boom. Rematch (revancha + return game, revenge + venganza). Caption:

(cuadro) leyenda, (artículo) título, (cine) subtítol. The headlines (los resúmenes informativos). Fly, flew, flown → he flies (ondea, vuela; enarbola: levanta) the flag. Disinfect (desinfecta,V) Internet. A feeling (sensación) of sadness. The mob (muchedumbre) got rowdier (más alborotado, pendenciero). Dosis (dose) + a good deal of humor in the play (obra). The government will step in (intervenir). The headrest covers (fundas) on the seats. Modern man =/= (dress, hairstyle) fashionable, trendy. Boot-camps (campamentos de entrenamiento). Waste of time (perder el tiempo + there's no time to lose + make up (recuperar) the lost time + to save time (para ganar tiempo) + time is gold/precious. Marital bliss (felicidad). Longer (persistir, entretenerse, quedarse un rato) in the fair. Open-minded: (attitude) abierta; (assessment) imparcial + =, unbiased, without preconceibed ideas, preconceptions. Tremors (seismos, temblores, estremicimientos). Sulk (enfurruñarse, enfadarse, estar de mal humor). Lose their drags (perder los estribos). Labourers (peones industrials) =/= farm labourers. Reps: representantes → Spain's only representative in this event (Sp.: prueba), one of the greatest exponents or representatives of surrealism. While his career fizzed (silvaba, burbujeaba) brightly it also fizzled (silvaba, fracasaba) out (se apagó) early. Pop-ups (emergentes schools). Traffic lights are/go on the blink (están averiados, se averían). Diddle (estafar + swindle, rip-off, defraud) over the change. Chalk (tiza)s up (escribir, anotar) the shortfalls (deficits + no alcanzar la meta de producción) to (a cuenta de) strong $. Some growth had dimmed (atenuado, debilitado, borrado) memories. Weed out: (plantas) arrancar, (errores) eliminar. Automobilismo (motoring). Lakeys (lacayos), servants (servidores) → all them are baaing (balando). Bug-eyed (que mira con ojos saltones). Impinge (incidir, afectar) on sb's rights & privacy (intimidad). Fail (fracasar)lure (fracaso). Wrong-doing (maldad, delincuencia). Eulogy: elogio, encomio. Get into (adquirir) bad/good habits.

Be in the dock (dársena) =/= the dock (banquillo de los acusados). Be wired-up (conectado) to a Internet society. Straw poll (sondeo informal de opinions). Chorradas: bullshits, guffs, drivel, piffle, twaddle/nonsenses =/= twiddle (girar, dar vueltas) with: jugar con. Outsource this function to fickle (inconstantes) outsiders (de fuera) =/= (foreigner) extranjero, (trade & relations): exterior; forfeign-debt (deuda externa), a strange boddy, -- (ajeno) to sb. Frantic/frencied (frenético, exaltado, desesperado) antic (payasada, travesura). Custody (=, detención, be in --). Desvenzijado: (vehicle) dilapidated, rickety, (chair, table) clapped out. A finiky (melindroso, demasiado delicado) trabajo. Repatriate. Movable properties (bienes muebles), movable feasts. Despreocupación: nonchalance, lack of concern, carefree. They clog (atascaron) water-intake pipes. Self-serving (egoista, interesada) political class in full swung (balanceo), apogee & heigh. The argument laid down (expuesta) by the lawyear. His name has cropped up (aflorado, surgido) repeatedly. The longer Ec. downturn (bajón, empeoramiento) since 1930's. Abasement (humillación + =) Sb. squealed/grassed (se chivó) on sb. Yardstick: criterio + =, opinión, medida (measure) =/= para las mediciones (standard). Grinder (afilador, molendero) → kaffee --, knife --. This is the selected criterion that we have followed =/= I'm struck by his lack of judgement or discernment. Smokescreen (cortina de humo: masa donde ocultarse). Solvencia (solvency, creditworthiness). Consentido/mimado: cosseted, pampered, spoiled. His marketing expertise/skill (pericia). Credit bender (borrachera, juerga). Disparate (dispares) currencies. Leafy (frondoso) N. Theran. Lightness: (fabric, cake, attitude) ligereza, (traffic) fluidez, (task) sencillez. Scale back: disminucón del nº de actividades, (producción, gasto) reducir. Cockpit: (aéreo, Náut.) cabina de mando. This solidarity has rankled (defeat: dolido, attitude: resentido) the US. A lossmaking (deficitaria) startup. Labour force (mano de obra, -- leader, -- union).

Obama's words sound cloying (pers. empalagosa). Flabby (fofo, flojo; gordo). A stillborn (nacida muerta) Democracy. Chuk (echar, tirar, desperdiciar, (job) dejar → get the -- (ser despedido), give sb the -- (plantarlo en la calle). Scare (susto,V) → be frightened =/= scared (cicatrizado, marcado) by violence. View (vista, opinión, ver, mirar + look). Nunnery (convento de monjas). In quantum theory everyzing is bitty (deshilachado, sin connexión). Mutter/grumble (hablar entre dientes, refunfuñar, murmurar) =/= murmur: murmullo de pers. que hablan al mismo tiempo, del viento, del agua. Unlike Hong kong's bastion (=, baluarte) of global capitalism. Mr. Obama is unfaced (tan pancho, como sin nada) by critics; he considers them were ingenuous (falsos, insinceros) & naïve (=, ilusos). He resent (le molesta) her success, I -- (no puedo admitir) that, I -- (tengo celos) of my syster. Mr so- and- so (fulano) snubbed (rechazó) the relations with the US in favour of friendship with ... He purged the clique/cronies (camarillas) officers. Dualownership or jointownership (condominio), joint control. Pursuit (persecución, búsqueda; actitud) of wealth was frouned on/upon (desaprobados). Myanmar's swift (rápida) transition is heartening (alentadora). Arab countries have not local country beacon (faro) of democracy to guide. The adequate, suitable, right moment. Offsetting (compensando) the pain of recession. For every yuan of loans he takes out (obtiene) ... Lorry-loads (camionadas) of banknotes relieve (alivia) banks. Dingy (deslustradas, deprimidas, sombrias) back alleys (callejuelas). Ledge: saliente, anaquel, (wall) cornisa, (window) repisa =/= loft (desván)y: (ideals, aims, sentiments) nobles, elevados, (haughty) altivo, altanero, (mountains) altas, majestuosas, (room) high ceilings. Pull the chain, he pulled his boots off, pull out (arrancar; separarse, retirarse). Munch (masticar + chew, masticate). The industry wilts (marchita). Improvisación: improvisation. Be in sth (right) up to one's neck. 10- or- so spontaneous lift-offs (despegues). Balmy (templado y agradable) space coast. Drive sb crazy (sacar alguien de quicio). Senior position (puesto de responsabilidad), -- officer, the -- (más antiguo) of the club, an officer -- to me. Ritz/luxurious (lujurioso). Fob off: engatusar, dar excusas, evasivas & pretextos. Condom/sheath + funda, vaina =/= preservatives (conservantes) are required to avoid/prevent (evitar) termites & decay (descomposición) + (cultura, civilización, imperio) decaer. Wood =/= timber/lumber (madera de construcción). Tensile (elástico, extensible) & strength (resistente a la tensión). Shoot up (crecer mucho), (precios) dispararse. Chirp (piar, chirriar, decir alegremente). Assuage: (hunger, thirst, desire) saciar, (pain, loneliness) aliviar, (anxiety) calmar, (fear) disipar. Namely (concretamente, a saber) stricke back (contraataque, volver el golpe) at his critics (detractors). Poise: colocar → he poised himself (en posición de) to jump; --ed (suspendido) in the air; porte, elegancia, desenvoltura. Cutting edge (filo) of tech. (estar a la vanguardia de la técnica). A lighthearted (alegre, de buen humor) guide. Sort (tipo, clase; clasificar, arreglar) → -- out: (books, room) ordenar, (pb.) solucionar. Clotted (coagulado,V, muy espeso). Opening, inaugural speech. Carry regular patrols (patrullas) or send on a one-off (excepcional) human-controlled missions. His intervention has mellowed (maduraro, suavizado, hacerse añeja, endulzado …). Stricke down (anular, matar) "sodomy" laws. The particles the theory conjecture (supone, augura) ... Media firms are defaulting (omiten, faltan a) to deletion (tachadura, supresión)… Salman went off (salió, se apagó, estalló) with little fuss (escándalo, inquietud, alboroto, preocupación). Grid (rejilla, red) → national -- (red de energia Eléctr.); the lean years of gridlock (negociación: punto muerto; traffic: paralización). Despreocupado: don't be bothered, worried about the darkness; carefree, easigoing (with children, …). He is ill-suited (poco indicado) to the presidency. Bring lapsed ones (que han dejado de practicar) to the fold (doblar, pliegue, redil); he lapsed his customary courteousness (cortesia habitual). Pending (en espera de) a credible effort. This bone-dry (completamente seca) region, plates, dishes, clothes, plant, character. Gnarled: (tree) retorcido, (wood, finger) nudosos (knotty + pb. espinoso). Greenness (verdor, inexperiencia). Stamp out (apagar con los pies, erradicar, rebelión: sofocar + stifle) ancestor worship (veneración, adoración + culto (of success, ...). Prever: foresee, anticipate, (time) forecast; this issue was expected. Charla: (conferencia) talk, (conversación) chat. Parasol, sunshade, beach umbrella. Taper: (astilla + chip, splinter; afilar, estrechar) → the stick (palo) tapers (termina) to the point. Furl: (flag, sail, umbrella) plegar ↔ un-- the flag, -- his limbs (extremidades). It's ischief-maker (alboratador). Adherir: this tires (neumáticos) grip/hold to the road, (pegar) stick, adhere, (organización, partido politico) join. Side with (ponerse de parte de) Russia. Trump bestowed (otorgó) his state-visit on/ upon his French counterpart. Molinero (miller), molino: mill, water mill, wind mill. Grinder: afiladora, molinillo de café, picadora de carne. He advocates (defiende: defend; protect; recommend) to link ancient Franc to a basked of currincies. Disproportionate. Distracted (distraído). Preocupado: fretful, preoccupied, worried. Be a millstone around sb's neck (carga para alguien). Exigente: exacting, demanding, riguroux, exigent. Canada: car-parts industry which caters (dirige) mainly to American carmakers. The abituary (nota cronólogia, difunción) of a deal. Gritty (arenoso, enérgico). Intransigente ("="). Sailing under the Panamian flag (pabellón). The entangling (enredarse, involucrarse) of mainstream (corriente dominante) political party. Grew out of (nacido de) anticolonialist government. Dwell (vivir) on (detenerse en, insistir en) → the documentary (documental) -- -- her life; try not to -- -- (pensar en) the past. Family provider (sostén Ec.). Amontonar: (apilar) pile (up), head (up), (datos) gather, collect =/= amontonarse (accumulate, gather, crowd together, pile up). Reflex action (acto reflejo). Health records (registros, archivos) are increasingly electronics. Trusted (leales, de confianza) providers. T. May: intolerable but unshackable (inquebrantable). Jerk (tirón, sacudida) → the train --ed to a stop, he --ed awake, the impact --ed him forward. A question of principles. Treat sb like dirt (trapos, suciedad, barro, porquería). Hawk (halcón; pregonar, vender)ing his wares in the street. Turning point (momento crucial).Quandary (dilemma, =). Such concerns (asuntos, inquietudes, incumbencias) are overblown (ampulosos, pretenciosos; flores: demasiado abiertas, marchitas); that's not concerns of yours, there is a cause for concern. Yemen proclaims independence from the northern taskmasters (tiranos + =, despotic; exigentes). Scale back (reducir) North Krea's military excess. Bobadas: stop being so stupid/silly, he said a lot of silly things. Varied (variados) trade planes. Stem (contener) Iran's push (empuje, esfuerzo). A great rivalry. Overstate (exagerar) ↔ understate (subestimar). Chinese tech. is blurring (borrosa, poco clara) =/= borrón: smudge, blot, (de tinta) inkblot. Inroads (avances) into Japanese market. A 47 years old greenhorn (inexperto + =, unskilled, inexperienced + novato). The markets are perking up (se reaniman). Swallow (golondrina, tragar) =/= engullir: guzzle, gobble, gulp down. Cheat (tramposo, fraude, trampa) on (engañar a) sb → be unfaithful to sb. Nigh (próximo, cercano, casi) impossible tasks. Placate (apaciguar, aplacar la cólera de) Trump. They want peace at any price (cueste lo que cueste). All rally round (se juntan) to help... Gut (intestino, limpiar, vaciar; destruir el interior) & redo (rehacer) the interior rather than knock them down (derribarlos). Splutter (balbuceo, resoplido, chisporroteo,V) =/= stutter/stammer (tartamudear) before to give an evasive reply. Halting (titubear), hesitate before accept. The speech (discurso) elicited (provocó, suscitó) cheers (ovaciones, alegrías). America further (fomenta)/fuel (estimula, alimenta) Sino-scepticism. Estafador: (timador) swindler, trickster; fraudster, rip-off artists & merchands. Noticeable (perceptible, evidente) pollutant. Irrecuperable: (delinquente) incorrigible, (debt) unrecoverable, (object) irretrievable. Cockiness (engreimiento, smugness). Spanish courts censor (censuran) rap (golpe; charla, crítica, acusación,Vs) lyrics. Bare (desnudo) → -- armed. Slap: (abofetear, golpear, dar palmadas; tirar con fuerza, incrementar el precio) tariffs on imports from Canadá; (de lleno) → he run -- into a tree. Gatecrash: (fiesta, match) colarse + cut the lines, jump the queue. Vest: chaleco, investir (ej.; of special powers). Checkpoint (control) =/= road-block, barricade, control. Unassailable (inexpugnable, irrefutable, incuestionable, (right) unalienable). Insolvency. I totally agree with you. Draw/sketch (dibujar), (tech.) design. Suffering was showed in his face (el sufrimiento se dibujaba en su cara). drawing (dibujo) → charcoal --, technical --, cartoons (dibujos animados). Dent: abolladura, make a -- in your savings, (popularidad) afectar, (orgullo) hacer mella. Bother (fastidiar, molestar, fiesta: spoil) politicians & browbeat (intimidar) customers to kick (hábito: tirar; heroina: desenganchar; recular; patada,V) … Spine: (animal) pua, (flor) espina), columna vertebral, espina dorsal. Siphon (desviar) funds meant to … Mirroed (reflejado) in the lake below. Soil erodes & grows saltier. Drain (vaciar, sumidero) → First minister leaves office drained (agotado: exhausted, sold out). Reach out (extender la mano) to people who left behind (olvidados, dejados atrás). Fringed (bordeado) by yucca & rotting (pudriéndose) cacao trees. Goods that infringe (=, viola) trademarks (marcas distintivas). The plane nose-dived (cayó en picado) = the stock/bird plunged. Huge tracts (extensions, folletos) of ancient vegetation. The decline has been steeped (empinado, abrupto, brusco, que descendió en picado). A gangling (larguirucho, delgado; desgarbado, sin elegancia) appearance. I didn't recognize him at first. Coddle (consentir, mimar) by giving preference in procurement (obtención) contracts. Malignant (malign) tumor =/= once maligned (calumniado, = + defamated, slandered, libelled) for its paucity (penuria, escasez + shortage, dearth, poverty). They've alike, similar faces. Heavy-duty: (material) mucha resistencia, (máquina) de uso industrial, (clothing) de trabajo. Burble: (agua) borbotear al hervir; (hablar) impaciente, con excitación: excitedly). Stocks promptly (rápidamente) ran out (se acabaron). Contrapartida (compensation, in contrast. The most sparsely (escasamente) populated. I recovered my money, I got back my energy & I regained my credibility single-handedly (sin ayuda de nadie). Barring (a menos que exista) accident, delay. He aimed (apuntó) his pistol at her, the missiles --ed to the capital, -- somewhere else. Take on/assume responsibility for looking after (cuidar) the chidren. A full-blown (auténtico) artist. Buzz: (bee/wasp) zumbido, murmullo,Vs, telefonear, (aircraft) acercarse. Concocted (preparado, inventado, tramado) by Russia. It's likely to ensue (seguir). Clog (up): obstruir (the electrical system, ...). Be on the cusp (puerta, borde) of sth. Tether (soga, cadena; atar, amarrar) → I'm at the tether/end of my rope: no aguanto más. Slug: babosa; puñetazo, tortazo,V + I'll hit/wallop you. Intestin/gut =/= vísceras (innards, insides). Make sur there's nothing missing. Alone & unafraid (sin temer). Furrow (surco) → plough lonely, (seguir camino solitario) =/= plough a different furrow. Make the registration of inherited land compulsory. Commit: (tiempo/resources) asign + =, allocate, (error, crimen) cometer; comprometer → pull back (retirarse) from signing a contrac, from commiting an error. Perforar: (pozo, madera) drill, bore, make holes, (bala) pierce/perforate, (papel, tarjeta) perforate/punch holes. Contend (competir, enfrentarse; afimar)ing (contrario, rival, contendien) with ... =/= contempt (desprecio, desdén). The failure to comply with the order. Betray (traicionar) his country, -- (defraudar) sb's trust (onfianza). Her voice revealed (revelaba) ... It was wadded (vadeado) into (se metió, acometió contra) an unwinnable war.

Quieten (calmar, acallar) the dowtroden (oppressed + oprimidos). Side with (ponerse al lado de) the Emirates. A partnership (asociación, sociedad) to supplant/replace (reemplazar, suplantar) the Gulf cooperation council (GCC). Toldo: (terraza) canopy, (tienda) awning. My deceased father, husband. The fiery (ardiente, exaltado, abrasador) rocket reminded (hace recordar) … Artesanía: (actividad) craftsmanship; (objeto) handicraft (ej.: furniture); craftwork. Sweep: barrer, (elecciones) arrasar, (emoción) invadir, (fuego, pánico) extenderse; swipping (amplio, arrollador, radical) energy shift. Shift: (mesa) cambiar de posición → -- resources from public to private; turno. Repercusión: =, echo, effect, reverberation + resonancia), great impact. Dispute the ownership of the land. Brand: marca,V → words --ed in his memory; estilo → his -- (tipo) of socialism, -- image (imagen de marca) =/= firebrand (activista, agitador + "="). City dwellers. Incentive (=, estímulos). Multitud (crowd, horde). Setback (revés, contratiempo). Tailoring (confeccionar, adaptar) + adapt policy (política, programa, normas, póliza de seguros: insurance policy) to your circumstance. A crane (grúa, grulla) stands out (sobresale). Esconder: hide, conceal, stash (ir acumuulando) 90 $ millions. Forestall (prevenir, anticipar); second-guess (anticiparse + cuestionarse a posteriori). At the very least ↔ -- -- -- most (como máximo). Drain: sumidero, drenaje, alcantarilla; vaciar, drenar. Drainage: desagüe, drenaje de aguas residuales, alcantarillado, cloaca, (Med) drenaje. Nuclear warhead (cabeza, ojiva). Walled (tapiados) gardens. Overwhelm: (emotionally) abrumador + --ed with rage, (army) aplastar, (swamp) inundar. Dreamy (soñador). To decide on steep (abrupa, …, excesiva) tariff. The current trends. Heaped (amontonado), friendliness (simpatía). Run-off: (Sp.) eliminatoria; 2ª votación =/= run- up period (-- preelectoral). Raise costs at least fourfold. Spur: espuela,V, aguijón de estímulo. Fortune-teller (adivino). Lure (atraer)d into the trap. Unimpeded (sin obstáculos) access =/= impend (amenazar, ser inminente). Smuggle out (sacar clandestinamente). The caliphate crumbles: (soil, cheese) desmenuzar, (wall, democracy, ...) desmoronar, ... Enfocar: (máquina de fotos) focus on, (pb.) consider, tema (subject) & artículo (item): approach, look at. Not get paid what is owed. Sections of track (huella; pista, sendero) are torn down (derribados). Worldly (material, humano) → other-- (de ensueño, de otro mundo; místico, spiritual)ness: ensueño, espiritualidad. The timbers (maderas) are rotten. It begin in earnest (en serio) + he is in -- (seriamente decidido) to ... Train: entrenar, enseñar, educar. The war reignites (reaviva). Crude (=, ordinarios, groseros, rudimentarios) rails. Acclaims/cheers (aclamaciones). The landscape glints (brilla). Protein-rish fare (billete, precio, comida). Valuable (valioso) cargo (cargamento). A bitter (amargo) aftertaste (regusto). Convenience: = → the date is at your --; comodidad; hotels equipped with every modern --. Convenience store: shop/store, grocery store are opened in fixed hours (horarios no abituales). Visiting hours. They are following suit (siguen el ejemplo). A favourite haunt (rondar, perseguir, aparecerse; frecuentar, lugar preferido) for a bowl of beef/for the artists. Embrujado: (lugar) haunted, (pers.) bewitched. He has done likewise (de la misma manera). Comfy (cómodo) monopoly. Cooling (de refrigeración) system. Last/stay the course: aguantar hasta el final, acabar la carrera. Walkway (puente, pasillo, pasarela). Enrich a nation, a pers., the culture, Uranium. Reprocess (=) nuclear waste. Sweat'shop (fábrica donde se explotan los trabajadores). Elegir: choose/choise =/= (por votación) elect. Befuddled (aturdido, ofuscado) by the drink (el alcohol le embotó el cerebro). Failure, has the Internet failed? Seller's market (mercado favorable al vendedor). Investigators (=, inspectores). Plead: alegar → -- ignorance of (no saber de), -- self-defense; defender → -- the rights of oppressed, -- the cause of powers. Leaky: agujereado, (security) fácil de violar.

Fiscal prosecutor. Oily sludge (barro, sedimento). Affluent (próspero, acomodado, rico) =/= effluents: (líquids, waste) vertidos, (sewage) aguas negras, radioactive effluents (residuos). High-ranking official (funcionario). Wipe out: (escrito) borrar, limpiar, pasar un trapo; (deficit) cancelar, dejar hecho polvo, (ventaja) eliminar, (animal) exterminar, (microbio) erradicar. Se me antojó una cerveza (I felt like (having) a beer; he hat an urge to go swim; he do exactly what he pleases. Clergymen (pastores protestantes) preach in English; preach (dar) a sermon; -- (proclamar) its virtues. Buck ($ …) against sth/sb: revelarse contra --/--; buck against/at --ing (resistirse a --ing). Arruinar: (proyecto, salud, cosecha) ruin, (reputación) ruin, wreck, destroy. Fastidiar: (estómago) upset, (pers.) bother, pester, (mecanismo, plan) mess up, (fiesta, excursión) spoil. American strategy in the Gulf is in flux (cambia, fluctua). The current rate of unemployment. Plug in/into (enchufar) the Internet cables beneath the Red Sea & create a hub (centro) for innovation. Volte-face (giro radical) of politics/opinion … Puritanism. Bounce: rebotar, (-- in) entrar, (check) devolver, ged rid of pb., give sb the -- (botar). Keep each other in check (mutual control). We have strayed (aislado, extraviado) from the path of our righteous (honrados, honestos) forebears. Rider: jinete, motorista, (bus) pasajero. Raid: atraco, redada, (Mil.) asalto, (policia) ataque aéreo. Release: (prisoner) soltar, (unleash) desatar, (information) hacer pública, (gas) despedir, (bomb) arrojar, (book) publication. Stumble: tropezar, (speech) atrancarse, -- in/out (entrar/salir a tropezones), -- across/on/upon (dar con, encontrar) amazing (alucinantes, increibles, asombrosos) new services. The extensions (=, ampliaciones) the Internet has spawned (producido, desovado). This loosely (sin apretar, sin excesivo rigor) coupled (aparejada, asociada, conectada) architecture … It's designed (diseñado) in layers (capas). Bylaws: regulations of a company (normas de empresa), local/municipal ordinances/bylaws (ordenanzas municipals). Rock-climbing (escalada en roca). A defensive wall/rampart (muro). Teamed up (asociados) with the online giants. Keep close tabs (vigilar estrechamente), run a tab on my own (llevar mi propia cuenta). His face curdles (milk/sauce: corta; blood: cuaja, hiela) into a sneer (aire despectivo, desdén) as she traces (trazas, indicios; detalla, localiza) the betrayal (traición). The World-spanning (que abarca) supply chain. Stolen goods (botines) → (de guerra) plunder, booty; (de ladrones) haul, loot. Blank: empty, (page/space) en blanco, (façade/front: fachada de una casa) lisa, (tape) virgen, the screen went --, -- check/cheque. Funcionar: the clock works, how does this thing (cacharro) works? Out of order (no funciona), the relationship wasn't working, the service cannot operate, function; it works on batteries. Breathtaking (impresionante): (success) amazing, incredible ↔ (accident) horrible. Allegiance: lealtad, (criado, amigo) faithfulness, (al gobierno, al Rey) loyalty → oath (jurar) -- to the Constitution; he pledged -- to IS. Data-ravenous (voraz, hambriento). Download: (Comp.) descargar, (ship) descargar (+ unload). Bow (reverencia, agachar; proa, ceder) → the EU is bowing to China. The numbers add up (suman, cuadran). Rejig (readaptar, hacer ajustes). Cought (tos,V) =/= be caught (enganchado) in sth, (enthusiasm) contagiarse. Knowledge (conocimiento). Acknowledgement, recognition (reconocimiento) + express special thanks to … Exceedingly (extremadamente, sumamente) rare =/= excesivelly (=). Be hardpressed (en apuros) + in a tight spot/in a predicament. Made up: confeccionado; story/excuse (inventada) sort (tipo, clase). Fan (abanicar, soplar; avivar) grievances (motivos de quejas). Shroud (sudario)ed (envueltos) in misinformation, a case --ed (envuelto) in mystery. Spring up (surgir, brotar) across Africa. Raise objections (poner reparos). Registered trademark (marca registrada). The ultimate (final, último; máximo, primordial) in sth (el no va más). Salvo (salvedad, reserva). Reliability (responsabilidad, formalidad, fiabilidad). Perseguir: chase, hunt (+ cazar,V, buscar), hounded by the press, China's pursuit (persecución) of European resources =/= persecution (persecución ideológica) =/= (presa, fuguitivo) pursue. Lessen (aliviar, atenuar). Louse, Pl.: lice (piojo); lousy: asqueroso, cargado de piojos. Code: clave, código → descipher a --. Counter: (mostrador), counterattack; counteract (contrarrestar) → go/run counter to sth (ser contrario a algo). Space shuttle: it launchs rockets to space. The key (clave) work/actor, the -- sector of the Ec., …, the -- mystery, pb, success. Foreseen & unforeseen consequences. Widespread (extendido, generalizado). Fence off (separar con una cerca). Drop off: caerse, (sales) disminuir, (pers., goods) dejar/depositar. The deep scattering (esparcir, dispersar) of a layer (capa). Setting the pace (marcando la pauta). Shelf: estante, arrecife (banco de roca, polípero a flor de agua) → continental -- (plataforma). Attached (atado, sujetado) to the shark's fin with a clamp (abrazadera). Tether (soga; atar, amarrar) → replenish (repuesta) fleet of nearly 400 untethered buoys. Sink/a/u → slowly down to about 2000 m. & back up. Track (rastrear, seguir la pista a) fish & pick up pollutants. Take a plate out of an incubator. A research ship to schlep (arrastrar) & deliver them. Profiling (reseñar, hacer una nota, un esbozo) T., salinity & pressure. Resíduo: (química) residue, (desperdicio) waste → toxic, nuclear --, radioactive --, solid --. Interface with sth (funcionar en conjunto con), -- -- sb (relacionarse con alguien) → brain-computer --. Wholeheartedly (con entusiasmo, sin reservas, incondicionalmente). Sweatband (muñequera, cinta de la cabeza). Doff one's hat (quitarse el sombrero) to sb. Whiz (silvido, zumbido) by: pasar zumbando → I --ed down the hill (bajé como una bala). Her switcase was stuffed/full to busting (lleno a reventar). We are cramped (apretados). Narrow hips (caderas). Escalation: (disputa) intensificación, (violencia) escalada. Open cast (a cielo abierto) mining. Adjudicar: (premio, contrato) allow, (vivienda) allot, allocate. Mock: (her accent) burlarse, a -- (fingida) break-out (fuga de cárcel + jailbreak). Lore (saber popular) → in local -- (según la tradición local). Wire: alambre, alambrada; telegrama → -- me when you get there (llegues); be --ed (conectado) to sth. Hit the front page heatliness (salir en la primera página); hit: atacado, golpeado; perjudicado, afectado, Vs =/= hurt (lastimado, dolido, herido), my legs hurts me. Suitor (pretendiente de casamiento, Jur.: demandante) =/= followers (seguidores, ej. en fútbol). Goods stashed (escondidas, que se van acumulando) in freeports (puertos francos). Pliable (flexible, maleable) =/= folding (plegable, ej. a chair). Dismiss (destituir, rechazar, poss.: descartar). Despectivo, despreciativo: contemptious, disparaging, (término) pejorative, (desdeñoso) disdainful, scornful. Political, electoral maneuver (estratagema + =). Skirmish: (demonstrators with the police) refriega, escaramuza. Stroppy (borde, insolente) → pesky (latoso, molesto). Asylum seekers cooped up (encerrados) in a vessel. Work → wrough: changes -- (causados) by …, the devastation -- by the war, the -- forjada) iron tower. Lose his sheen (brillo, lustre). Push through: abrirse paso, (reforms) hacer aprobar. He took the dais (tarima, entablado) at the IMF forum. Debauch: pervertir, corromper, (women) seducir. In sb's stead (lugar). Tingling (hormigueo, cosquilleo) → spine-tingling: emocionante (+ moving, exciting, thrilling), inquietante (+ worrying, disturbing). Resourceful: (pers.) con recursos, (plan, solución) hábil, ingenioso. Enthralling (fascinante, apasionante, cautivador). Redactar: (boceto, borrador) draft, (contrato, tratado) draw up, (texto, periódico) write. Be in tatters (andrajos): hecho trizas, Ec. por los suelos. Rental yields are high. A risible (=, causa risa) canard (bulo). Vituperar (desaprobar): vituperate/inweigh against, censure, codemn =/= revile: insultar, vilipendiar (despreciar, maltratar). Sore (úlcera; dolorido, irritado)ly (mucho) missed: muy echado de menos. It is three times as large as that of nearest relatives. Rep<u>eal</u> (anular, revocar, abrogar) =/= repel (repeler, repugnar), repulse (rechazo, V). Downplay (disminuir la importancia) of peacekeeping (mantenimiento). Bring to heel: sobreponerse, hacer entrar en vereda. Snag (pb., inconveniente) → what is the --? If you run into any snags …; enganchar, enganchón → -- the fishing line on a stone, branch (rama); -- your sweatter on those branches. Syria has fallen ever (más, cada día más) under Israel's spell (encanto, hechizo; período, temporada; significar, augurar). Aloof (distante)ness (actitud distante) toward … Cram: meter, repleto a reventar; aprender, memorizar, preparar intensivamente. Trench (de trinchera) warfare. Prosecutorial: (procesantes) summons, (Jur.: citaciones) & harsh court sentences. Summons: (servant, physicians) llamar, (meeting) convocar, (aid) pedir. Ascribe (atribuir) sth (fault, pb, ….) to sth/sb. Atribuir: attribute, Jur.: impute; atribuirse algo: he claims sth for himself. It mollifies (aplaca, apacigua) the other part. Hoax (engaño,V) call: llamada falsa (a servicios de emergencia). Overturn: dar la vuelta a la mesa, (barco, automóbil) volcar; derrocar el gobierno, anular un juicio/decisión. Plunge: (sumergir, zambullida) a prisoner heat first into a water wessel. Wesel: barco, vasija, vaso). Favo(u)r (favor): be in -- of, do sb a --, -- (honra) us with your presence. Middle-aged couples. Put the country in a war footing (pie de guerra) would enjoy (agradar a) Ukraine + I -- Mús./wine, … =/= is this to your liking? Unrewarding (recompensa, gratificación): (task) poco gratificante, ingrata, (discusión) infructuosa. Bounty (prodigalidad, recompensa); bountiful (pródigo, abundante) source of … Distinctive (=, característico) features (rasgos). Guarro: yucky, dirty, filthy. Despeinado: dishevelled, uncombed, unkempt (+ descuidado, desarreglado). Heat wave (hola de calor). Delgado: fine, thin, slender =/= faint (débil; ligero, borroso, tenue, pálido) → aint-hearted: tímido, pusilánime, con poco ánimo. Contredict (contradecir). Swager: fanfarronería,V, caminar con aire arrogante. Fete (halagar una pers., celebrar un trabajo u obra). Privatised to a certain, large, greater, lesser extend (grado). Reliance (dependencia) on American protection. Used inflated ones as floats (flotadores + rubber rings). Downpours (chaparrones). The offer was turned away (rechazada). Fire staff to get by (arreglárselas), get by with the French learned. Hedge: seto, protección → -- against inflation. Hapless (desafortunado, desventurado) → -- - looking. Get off from the shared currency. He chanced (se arriesgó) on upon (tropezó con, encontró por casualidad) a lover/a wolf-pack (manada + en leones: pride; en ganado: herd). Re-run (TV: reposición, Sp.: repetición). It has galvanised (impulsado) progressive artists. Ogle: comerse con los ojos. The mummies (mamis, mamitas). Bare-knuckle (sin guantes, implacable)d entrepreneurship. Get share tips (consejos, propinas, puntas) from his shoeshiner (limpiabotas): it is time to buy. Trough (bebedero, depresión) of disappointment in a hype (bombo publicitario) cycle. Kid (cabrito, niño, cerebrito; bromear, engañar) → he's kidding you (te bromea, te toma el pelo), who do you are --ing (engañas)? Expire: (permit, passport …) caduca, (contrato) vence, (term of office) finalizar. Assert: afirmar, hacer valer, imponer) → European technological assertiveness (seguridad en sí misma). Bluntly: sin rodeos, claramente, rotundamente. Baker (panadero) =/= backer (partidario + supporter, in favour of; patrocinador + sponsor, arte: patron). Ape (simio) =/= monkey: mono) → his social control apes (imita + copies, imitates) that of the UAE. Inchoate (incipiente, embrionario) trade war. America is increasingly inured/used/accostumed to what the harmless (inofensivo, =) president is doing. Cumbersome (torpe y pesado). Well tailored (confeccionados) suits. Doe (gama, coneja, liebre hembra)-eyed: de dulces y grandes ojos azules. It's true (cierto) that …, truly (ciertamente, verdaderamente),…, I trust you, …, trusty (fiel, leal (+ loyal). Wield: (authority, power) ejercer, (sword) manejar → -- power of veto; I taught him how to -- (usar) the knife & the fork. You run the risk of losing it. Heavily (mucho, en exceso, fuertemente) critizised. Literary/art critic. Convince voters. Complete rest (reposo absoluto). We have never been so busy as we are now; so confident (confiado en sí miso) as he looks; he so hated the job, he left; as to + inf.: I'm not so stupid as to belief ..., I'm not as efficient as he claims to be. He ran as fast as he could; I eat a lot, but he eats as more. Tighten (poner más tenso, apretar) it up as much as you can + (belt, knot) apretar → -- one's belt (cinturón). He has not awareness of the people's feelings + increase public -- of. Avoid/evade (eludir) an obligation. The flow of migration must be smooth, to prevent the sudden surges (subidas, oleadas, ...) that make host societies feel swamped (agobiadas, oprimidas, abrumadas) of supplies. Complain loudest (más alto, fuerte, enérgico) about the huddled (agrupadas, amontonadas, apiñadas) masses. Open-door (de puertas abiertas, no proteccionistas) policies. Mishandle (maltartar, llevar mal) Ec. crisis. Scrap (rascar) dirty saucepans (ollas, cacerolas) & design skyscrapers. Fall through, mess up, fail, be unsuccesful (fracasar) =/= fall away (decaer, desprenderse). Service (hacer el mantenimiento) of its machines. Scientific bias (inclinación); unusually (=, excepcionalmente) biased against talent (con parcialidad): only 15% are granted (subvencionadas) because the applicants skills. Live off begging/charity (limosnas) + the beggars beg (piden) ... Biker rack (soporte para estacionar las bicicleas). Overseas: (trade) exterior, (investment) en el extranjero. The same old gang (banda, pandilla). The footprint (huella del pie, pisada, impacto: ej.: social --) began to grow. Pre-electoral poll (sondeo), go to the polls, decide by ballot (voto), they vote tomorrow. Dodgy: que funciona mal, de poco fiar; peliagudo, arriesgado (+ risky). Aman sidestepped (evadió, eludió, esquivó) his boss. It has been sluggish (lento; Ec.: deprimido). The titles (=, derechos) are not lodged (presentados, depositados, hospedados) with the deeds. Onerous: (task) pesada, (debt) onerosa (costosa). Bogged down (empantanado, inundado). Sturgeon (esturión). Grievance (queja) in the west. A reason for caution: what he gives he can suddenly take away (quitar, llevarse). He is born in Madrid, 3 kg. at birth. Subside: (foundations, road, land) hundirse + sink, collapse, (storm) amainar, (fever, anger) calmarse. The likes (semejantes) of S. America; judges, lawyears & the likes. Qubit (quantum equivalente del transistor) can be connected, so that operation on one has an impact on the others. Qubits are capable of superposition (can be in both states at the same times). House of representatives & senators. Classical computers think in bits (a value of 0 or 1); future computers: in quantum spring. Cultural clash (choque, conflict, enfrentamieno) between native indigenous & Muslim immigrants. Warlords (caudillos) round up (rodean; hacen una redada en) criminal migrants. Toolkit (juego de herramientas). Creativity & censorship. Luminary (luminaria, lumbrera: cuerpo luminoso) of the quantum field. Operate flawlessly (perfectamente) in an unsolved… ↔ a flawed proposal ... Mid-term turnout (nº de votantes, participantes). Investment vetted (investigados) case by case. Reach (alcance) of law. Beloved (queridas) of liberals, land-value taxes have never caught up (alcanzado) … Enjoy the windfalls (unexpected benefits) of a property boom. Duck (agachar(se), esconder(se) behind a pillar. Beheadings (decapitaciones). Cuddle (abrazo,V)y: (niño y oso de peluche: teddy): riquísimos, que dan ganas de comerlos; (pers.) adorable. Canuck (canadiense). Obscene (=, soez; espantoso) costs of … Inútil: useless, hopeless, fruitless, unsuccessful, good-for-nothing. The swain (mozo, festejante) has all the attributes birds (pájaro; chica, pollita) want. Swear, --ore, --orn → he was sworn in (le tomaron juramento). Kindergarten/nursery school: parvulario. Shut down: (business, factory) cerrar, (machinery) apagarse, desconectarse. Overstate (exagerar) their assets. Retirarse: move back/away, retiro, withdraw + yank (retirar) America out of Paris deal. Earth is smouldering (ardiendo, sin llamas) + (hatred/passion) que consume. In smog-schrouded (envuelta) China. Britain prefer pragmatism to ideology, moderation to extremism, continuity to change. Chicanery: embuste/subtlety: sutileza. GDP shrank by 7%, its longer contraction ever. The dye (teñir)/ed, dyeing (tintura) =/= die (morir)/died, dying (moribundo). Defecto: flaw, fault, defect + desertar; defeccionar: (abandoner un partido politico) → keep customers from defecting to rivals. The monopoly has a towering (altísimo, imponente) debt pile (montón,V) of € 50 bn. Take a liking (afición) of that toy. Infatuation (encaprichamiento). Impressive (admirable, impresionante). American Inc. (incorporated) is underweight (pesa menos de lo normal) in the rest of Asia. Nonevent (fiasco, fracaso). Inbound (que llegan) investments. Develop their potential to the fill ←→ the unrealised (=, sin explotar) potential/talent of the women, … War engulfed the country (el pais se sumió en la guerra). Bust-up (ruptura, pelear) at the NATO summit. Backslapping (campechano, palmaditas en la espalda). Vibración: =, vibes. Jurar lealtad: swear, pledge allegiance (to the flag, to the constitution, …). At the behest of (a instancia, solicitud de) pragmatic advisers. Wean (destetar) sb off/away (quitar) from drugs. Gruesome (truculento: cruel, atroz, horrible) ideology. GDP flat (fijo) for a decade =/= garble (terjiversar, enredar) → garbled: (message) incomprensible, (account) confuso. The Gulf broadly (en lineas generals, claramente) avoided the upheaval (agitación, transtorno, perturbacón) of the Arab spring. Turkey is ready to surrender (entregarse, renunciar, rendirse) to the fading (que se agota) dream of EU leaves heartfelt notes of … + my heartfelt (más sentidas) condoleances, sympathy (pésame). Thunderstorm (tormenta Eléctr.). Its power lies in the futility (inutilidad) of ... Hamas (it runs Gaza) threw a defiant wave (oleada) of home-made rockets. Gentrification (aburguesamiento): its benefits go unsung (heroes: olvidados; achievement: no reconocido) success. In the popular telling (relato, narración; elocuente, contundente, revelador) → tellingly: eficazmnte, de forma reveladora =/= telly (cuenta, anotar; coincidencia, cuadrar, concordar). Ousted from the post. A racist, cowardly slur (difamación). United nations right council (UNRC) is remembered for having had Quaddafy as its chairman (presidente). Rant: despotricar, vituperar (censurar, reprochar) against rapists (violadores). Hang around (esperar, merodear, holgazanear). Gamberro: (modales) rowdy, troublemaker, (violento) thug, hooligan. See this as an omen (augurio) of victoty. A long-mooted (discutida) suspicion, it has been mooted (sugerido) that .... Mastermind (planear y organizar) legislation which ... Dable (hacer superficialmente, chapotear) in the river, politics, journalism, warfare. Quaddafy craved (ansió, imploró, anotó) respectability (=, decencia). International atomic energy agency) (IAEA) pinpoint (localiza) where materials may have been diverted (desviados, eludidos, distraidos) =/= divest (despojar, deshacerse de). It'll be a disaster, he predicted; a paragon (modelo) of predictability (=, previsibilidad). Fascinating, captivating. Vacancies: two -- for electrician; -- in the hotel/free rooms ↔ no -- (completo). Chinese slurps (sorbe) goods made in the hinterland. The good time rolls (empieza a rodar, a funcionar). Estates (fincas, propiedades, patrimonio; political/social --) → housing estates: urbanización. Property market (mercado inmobiliario). The State subsidized apartmens & houses, ... (vivienda de protección social). Sunset (en decadencia) industry. Charming, delightful (encantador). Reverberating (que resuena, repercute) in Britain literature. Tried for a third time in the court of appeals. A shimmering (brillante, resplandeciente) glass business park. Artificial radiologists outperforming the ones ... This year styles are a throwback (vuelta) to the twenties + their attitude is a -- to (tiene sus raices en) their experience. Dispatch (despacho,V, envío, expedición) from the melting North. It bullies (acosa, intimida) in referring (remitiendo, aludiendo, enviando) to … It was quickly scotched (frustrado, acallado, puesto fin). Chinese fledgling (novatos) manufacturers undercut (venden más barato, debilitan un argumento) the market. The dissatisfied (descontentos) toast (=, brindan) new arrivals. A platform for booking (reserva) stays (queda) in other country. Chary (cauteloso: cautious, reacio: reluctant). Growth has been dizzying (vertiginoso, que marea) from almost nil. Non performing (productivos) loans. Slam: -- the door (dar un portazo), book --med down the table, he --med (atacó violentamente), -- the safe open (hacer saltar la caja fuerte). Duty: deber, función, responsabilidad, obligación; turno, servicio; impuesto. This figure leave things out (omite cosas): the defensive duties against dumping. A market with bags (bolsas, cantidades) of potential but plenty of perils. A learned/wise (sabio) who excels (destaca) at one particular task. Make a conquest (=). Having campaigned in bile (=, mal genio), he would gobern calmly. Bewildering or disconcerting political polls. Bigot (fanático, intolerante)ry: fanatismo, intolerancia. Feral (=, wild: salvaje) bovine & sheep (ovino). Cunning (astuto, astucia; ingenioso). Picardía: naughty craftiness, cunning, prank + travesura, broma) ↔ incauto: unwary, unsuspecting. Some are getting carried away (maravillado, entusiasmado, extasiado). Stray: extraviarse, (dog) callejero, (lost) perdido, (sheep) extraviada, a -- bullet. Paddy (arrosal)-turned mudbath. Nullified (anulado) by countervailing (compensatorias) consequences. Dump: vertedero de basura, (Mil.) depósito, (waste) deshacerse de, (sand…) descargar, tirar; --goods/products: invadir el mercado con productos baratos, no dumping! Save: ahorrar (money saved), salvar: anable to save him, saved from having to listen to the speech. No truck (tractor, camión) with IS. Far-right parties fed on & fanned (avivaron) such fears. Prayer mats (esteras, alfombras de oración). Impressive (admirable, impresionante). Of noble/Algerian parentage (origen), of unknown parentage (padres). Outbound (que salen) flights, passengers. Puncture (pinchar) their dinghies (botes) to ensure no way back. Bumper (parachoques; record, extra) year/crop. Trade wars have upended (derribado) soyabean market. Glut: superabundancia, saturar. Lopsided (torcido, desigual) trade between ... Skillful avoidance (habilidad con la que evitó) controversial issues (temas polémicos). Entertainment (espectáculo, diversion, =). The trinkets (baratijas) hawked (pregonadas) … Command (dominio, mandar) of Arabia. Roast: asado, tostado,V → the sun which was --ing the city, we --ed there for a whole month. Misfit (inadaptado) to the new circumstances. Jostle each other (empujarse mutuamente). Browsers (navegadores) that use Android operating system. Europe has no giants to rival Amazon or Alphabet & hosts few of the World's dynamic startups. Russian TV viewers shift to online Internet-based-information. Rejecting a coalition from the outset (desde el principio). Pakistan & India bombed one another's territory during an all-out (total) war. The roar (rugir, bramar) of warplanes. Climate change & pollution growth make the water woe (desgracia, aflicción) more urgent; woeful (lamentable, deplorable; afligido, desconsolado). Boats stranded (encallados) aground. Eerie (misterioso, extraño, inquietante)rily (de manera extraña, inquietante). The largest transfert of water between river basins in history. Allowances (complementos, sobresueldos; prestaciones, asignaciones) had to be made for adjustment (ajuste, puesta a punto) in space & back to Earth. Topping (cubierta) → an ice-cream with chocolate-- (por encima). The entire world, clean the entire house, his entire earnings (ingresos) for a year. NS2: Russia-Germany undersea gas-pipe bypassing their territory entirely. A Jihadist spotted in Turkey. The move (medida, movimiento, mudanza, jugada) dismays (consterna, espanta) E. Macron. The dispossessed (desposeídos) Shias. A seminal (fundamental, the mucha influencia) event in 1979. Saudi royals (soberanos) urged their clerics to follow suit (seguir su ejemplo). Hooked (enganchado) for 4 years in opioids; -- on a nail. He gathered up (recogió) her possessions lined up on the floor & left. As a drug gains notoriety, new users flow in. The dune is subtle (sutil, delicada, ingeniosa ...) & secluded (apartada, solitaria, aislada). The daily routine, monotonous life. This books serve as an antidote (contraveneno) to American fears of a Manichean contest (competición, contienda, lucha) with China. Pay tribute (pagar en señal de sumisión) to American intellectual property IP protection. China is a long way from living up to (estar a la altura de) the IP commitments (obligaciones, compromisos) it made on entering the World trade organisation (WTO) in 2001. China still forces firms in joint venture with state-owned enterprises to surrender (rendirse, entregar, cesión) IP; surrender of property (cesión de bienes). China pursues (persigue, continúa con) a communist party. Companies, mostly Chinese ones, sue (demandan, pleitan) each other over patents in China more than in any other country. A higher win rates in patent cases. They were in thrall to (eran esclavas de, estaban sometidas a) American inventiveness. China accepts the rationale (lógica) behind America arm-twisting (presión). Impose IP codes on a humbled (humillada) China. If it were not for American pressure on IP, China would not have come half as far. He belittles (menosprecia) ... It is worth recalling how much of a cultural wrench (tirón, jalón; arrancar, desgarro, torcedura; llave inglesa) the Anglo-Saxon IP system is for China. After its founding (1867) as a confederation, Canada has been sheltered (refugiado, protegido) under the protection of a superpower (Britain & the US). Few small countries succeed when they spurn (rechazan) their neighbours. Canada: skimpy (mezquinas) rations (raciones, víveres) for indigenous peolpe. India, a potential partner, has turned frosty (fríaa, helada). On matters where it already applies, like the single market, member states tend to find fudges (esquivar, amañar; excusas, rodeos) preserving unanimity. Get over (pasar por encima, superar) its past. At a time of mock (burlarse, de prueba) space missions. Prod (dar codazo, pinchar; empujar, estar encima para) → prodded & monitored (seguido, controlado). The third most widely grown (acumulada, desarrollada, crecida) crop in the World. Back-to-back (consecutiva + "=") victory/defeat; the film is run -- -- -- (session continua + continuous performance). A truckers (de camiones)'strike. Wildfire (fuego abrasador). The World top ten beef exporters. Blandishment (alagos, lisonjas: alabanzas). Kit themselves out (equiparse). They indulge (consiente, satisface, mima) them every whim at least once. He gave sworn evidence (declaró bajo juramento). Exaggerate. Low pay rather than toil (trabajo duro) in bleak (oscuras) offices. Five signatories are sticking (se pegan) with (son fieles, no se separan). They perch (se sientan) on stools (taburetes). Undemanding (poco exigentes) for money but exacting (duro, exacto; severo) for work conditions. Montón: a pile/stack of books. An ordinary girl, loads/masses of people. Like-minded (de ideas afines) to work together. Load: carga + charge; peso + weight → lose/gain weight. Articulate core principles of the rules-based orders. Take deep breath (aliento): respirar a fondo; get my -- back, dying (último) breath. Outsized (alta, enorme) influence. Such & such (tal o cual) date. Uncharted (inexplorado ocean). Develop a string (serie) of such berths (literas, camarotes; atracaderos) to extend ship research beyond China's shores (orillas), the eastern -- of the lake. To conclude, I would like to … Wounds that have yet to heal. Conmover (shock, move). Bashing: give sb a bash (paliza); union/media -- (ataque), rather than mindlessly (sin sentido) -- to the WTO, -- (golpear) my knee on/against …, -- the ice with a stone. Curb abuse of temporary contracts. Scrubbly (con maleza) landscape. State: the overall (global) state of Bundeswher is dismal (sombrío, triste, funesto), -- visit, affairs of --, siege (de sitio) --, -- security, -- pension, -- of mind (ánimo), as --ed (como se indica) above. Helicopters circling overhead. Fire-fighters (bomberos), call the fire-brigade (cuerpo de bomberos). Production data were allegedly (supuestamente) faked, the supposed architect proved not to be qualified, they took it for granted (dieron por supuesto) that we were interested. Fire-fighters broke-out across (se fugaron por) the rooftop. Britain: inwardlooking (introvertida, encerrada en sí misma) & anxiety-ridden (con mucha ansiedad). Average citizen, student, an average of 99 people a day, $ 500 a week on --, take the -- on sth (sacar la media), above the --. Takle (abordar) Ch's misdeeds (delitos, fechorias). His peeves (manías) over American trade deficit; it peeves her (le fastidia, le da rabia) that ... I feel rather --ed (estuve molesto, picado) that they didn't invite me. Playing catch-up (para conseguir el empate). Backtraking (retroceso,V) on the Ec. sanctions can be circumvented (burladas) & the nation is a master of subterfuge (=, escapatorias). You are upsetting (terrible, triste, ofensivo) yourself (te molesta) ... That soured (amargó)/spoiled (estropeó) my evening. The sense of the smell, duty & justice. Give sth one's full attention. A censure motion. Roundabout/traffic circle (rotonda). Their true spirit would ultimately (en última instancia, a la larga) ... Crumple: (metal) abollar, (papel) arrugar =/= crumble (cake) desmenuzar, (democracy/wall) desmoronar. Get restive (impacientarse). President runs into (choca con) the obstacles that bedevilled (plagaban) his predecesor. Doer (pers. emprendedora + "enterprising"). What do you reckons (opinas)? Blare: estruendo, trompetazo, vociferar. In due course (a su debido tiempo). The ECB is in charge of ensuring (asegurar, garantizar) monetary & financial stability; in absence of fiscal authority it acts as a safety net (red de seguridad) for the currency block. Nationalistic tinge (matiz: nuance). Even-handed: imparcial (unbiased), ecuánime (equable, even-tempered). A prolongued slump: (Ec.) depresión, (be in a -- (aguda crisis Ec.), the Slump (la gran crisis). Broadily speaking (en lineas generales) → more broadily the sweeping (drástica, draconiana, abrumadora) decentralisation mandated by the Constitution. He showed daring (audacia, coraje + =) & schrewd (ábiles) institutions. Jumble (mezcla, revoltijo) of grievances (quejas + complaints). Tableland (meseta + plateau) of Castilla. Shadowy (impreciso, misterioso, obscuro) committee =/= shallow (poca profundidad). Set the seal on (ratificar + =, confirm). The Supreme court charged (acusó) Puigdemont with offences (infracciones) ranging from rebellion to misuse of funds. Self government, autonomy. My nose itches (me pica). Bushy: (barba) poblada, espesa, (undergrowth: maleza) espesa. Abreviar: (visita, estancia) cut short, (journey) shorten, (texto) abridge. Lookout (perspectiva, atalaya). Sensatez: good sense/wisdom of a project, she acted sensibly. Be on a loosing (suelto, flojo) wicket (terreno): llevar las de perder, be sticky (pegajoso; delicado, en situación comprometida) about lending money, be on a sticky wicket (estar en un aprieto). Reiniciación: (business, studies) resumption, restarting, (Comp.) reboot. Storm: tormenta, taken by the -- (por asalto), weather/ride the -- (campear el temporal), irrumpir en. Kickback (mordida, soborno) + bribery (cohecho, soborno) + perjury (jurar en falso, falso testimonio) + malfeasance (prevaricación, administración desleal). Cluttered (abarrotado + crammed, packed) with advertissements. Candidate, competitor, contestant: concursante. A refuttal (que refuta, rebate, contradice) memos (memorandums: librito de notas). Transcurrir: (tiempo) pass, go by, (acontecer) take place, during the course of the year. False, insincere pers.; false alarm, false testimony; (billete) counterfeit, forged, forged picture; false/forged/fake (copiado). Alarming, surprising; amazing or astonishing (asombroso). Alboroto: (excitación, nerviosismo) excitement, agitation, (ruido, barullo) racket; (jaleo, disturbio) disturbance; commotion;

(motín, disturbio) riot. Uprising (sublevación + rebellion, revolt) =/= sedition, insurrection; rebellion. Void: desprovisto, -- in my life; (accord/check) anular, invalidar, (bladder: vejiga, bowel) evacuar, (accord, votation) nul & void, (pers.) inútil. Gruñir: (pig) grunt, (dog) growl, (pers.) grumble, grouse. Debauchery (depravación), libertinaje + licenciousness, dissolute behaviour). Glut: superabundante, saturar → -- a market with apples. Auxilio: help → ask for --, he helped us; (carreteras) breakdown (grúa) truck/van + breakdown service (servicio de grua) =/= tow truck (grúa de policía). Infatuation (encaprichamiento) with her, take a liking/fancy to that toy. Soft-core (blanda) pornography. Boisterously (escandalosamente, bulliciosamente). Shear (trasquilar) → be shorn off/be stripped of sth (estar despojado de). Sistemas para sujetar algo: (Med.) forceps, (alicates) pliers, clothes pin (alfiler), hairgrip (agarrar). Lack of nous (sentido común) → political, financial --. Smugness, cockiness (petulancia). His estimate (=, aproximación) was wide of the mark (erró por mucho en su cálculo). Trump's bluster (bravatas: fanfarronadas, arrogancia, intimidación) may thwart (frustrar) =/= fail/be unsuccessful (fracasar), failure (fracaso). Acertar: he only got three answers right; see if you can guess who it is; I was right. Ill fate (destino)d: infortunado, desaventurado. Reasume (volver a empezar, reanudar), resumption (reanudación, continuación). Heckle (interrumpir)r: pers. que interrumpe al orador para molestarle. Gladly (con mucho gusto). Embattled (cercado, asediado en combate), (pers.) acuciado de pbs. Peal (repique, V) → the city's clock --s, -- of bells. Tidying (arreglando, afinando) anomalies. Dejadez, negligencia: sloppiness, slovenliness, laziness, slackness. Slack: descuidado, negligente, flojo; slackness: (market) falta de actividad, (wire) falta de tensión, (period) poca actividad, (pers.) poco aplicada. Hands clasped (agarradas) as if in prayer. Other states are catching up (nos alcanzan). Space travel, coastal navigation. Lanzar: throw, launch, bowl + bol, palangana). Bound (atado, envuelto, limitado, obligado; brinco). Slowness (lentitud). Strange bedfellow (pareja) → the crisis bring together -- -- (forja peculiares alianzas) of paramound (primordial) importance. Coin: moneda, acuñar; inventar → the transnationals -- along One bed one road (OBOR): it will span (abarcar) 65 countries. Tab: etiqueta, pagar la cuenta, → I run a -- on my own, -- what we spend =/= tap: llave de gas, grifo, espita; micrófono escucha, palmadita. Shelter (refugio) → air raid --, a -- for battered (maltratadas) women, -- (proteger) sb/sth from ..., a wall provide -- from the wind. Charter: (Universidad) status, (ciudad) fueros + municipal charter (empresa) escritura de propiedad, (Constitución) Carta Magna, (transporte) contrato de fletamiento. I locked up (guardé bajo llave) myself out (me quedé fuera sin llave), lock up money for ... Assets (activos) → current (circulantes) --, fixed -- =/= the city greatest asset (atractivo); know how will be an asset, living so centrally is an --, your degree will be an asset. Breeze (brisa) → be a -- (ser pan comido). During a period of hardship (apuros). Have declined (disminuido) foreign disaster relief (alivio, auxilio). War-torn (devastado por la guerra) country. Freezing (heladas) conditions held up (retrasaron) sowing. He has pledged a shake-up (remodelación) regardless (sin considerar) of whatever deal. Plaudits (aplausos, aclamaciones) + elect sb by acclamation. Some farmers have gone into other lines of business, such as solar energy or bed & breakfast. Servitude, subservience (servidumbre) =/= submission or submissiveness (sumisión). Raise/bring up (educar, criar) =/= America's long-lived (longeva, que perdura) recovery breeds (genera, produce) complacency. He has reasons for complacency (para sentirse contento consigo mismo). Valued between them at almost $ 2 bn., pay $ 50 a month/apiece. Facebook moved into somewhat (una especie de) pusher (más lujoso) dig (escavación, prospección). The longterm outlook (vista, perspectiva) is still cheery (alegre, optimista). Outstrip (adelantar, sobrepasar) its competitors. Autarkic culture goes against the way the Valley used to work: shutting off (Electr.: cortar; máquina: desconectar, persona/sitio: aislar) the flow of talent. We watched the flickering (parpadeantes) shadows (sombras) & flames. Wane (menguar, decaer) → support for the strike has --ed. Beachwear (ropa de playa), urban get-together (reuniones). Make off (salir corriendo) with (llevarse) $ 5 millions =/= take de suspect away (llevarse). Bright-eyed (de ojos vivos) tech. Slow performance (rendimiento). Makeup (maquillaje, composición de grupo, substancia, (pers.) carácter =/= He discarts the strut (pavonearse) of the pundit (experto) & delves into (hurga, ahonda) in areas he knows. The boat skims (pasa casi rozando) along the surface. Replicated (duplicado, reproducido). Petty (insignificantes) hatreds (odios). Fixations (fijaciones, obsesiones) → become or get fixated on/with sth/sb (obsesionarse con algo/alguien). Trump has bullied (acosado, intimidado) his way to what he sees. Shove (empujar) firms into abandoning cross-border supply chains in favour of safe-but-costly. Ec. might (poder). Sleaze: sordidez (sucio, repugnante; indecente, tacaño), corrupción. Back away (evitar, echarse atrás) =/= go/move back (retroceder). Funcionario: government employee, public servant, international organisations staff. The Frente de liberación nacional (FLN) pales (blanco, pálido, pequeño,Vs) in comparison with Fuerzas armadas revolucionadas de Colombia (FARC). His encryption (codificación) system. Call off (suspender, desconvocar) talks. Covered (encubiertas) operations in a Political party. Rid us (libéranos) of irksome (fastidioso, molesto) regime. Irk (fastidiar, molestar). This merely (simplemente, sólo) strengthen, reinforce him. Underpin (sostener) the system. Counter-intelligence (contraespionaje). Worn(out) (gastadas, inservibles) cells + the pages of the book were well-thumbed (manosusadas). An all washed-up (acabado) politician. The Trump officials' liking (gusto, afición), take a liking (simpatía) to sb. Cudgel (porra,V) China into make concessions. Russia has all but dropped (dejarse de) any pretence (pretensión, pretexto, fingimiento,V + pretend, feign). Politeness (cortesía) with EU. Baghdad's resentments have had fancy (lujosas) facelifts (=, renovaciones). Europe's most salient (destacada, notable) political rift (fisura, grieta,V). He typifies (=, es representativo de) this stodgy (denso, aburrido, pesado, ...) machine-political Europe. Full-blown (verdadero auténtico) innovator. Exhort faithful to defent unborn life. Faultliness (líneas de falla). A schrivelling (arrugada) skin, the shrivelling (el marchitar) of Congres, once Indian dominant party ... Incorporate the Muslim-run princely (principescos) states. The shunning (rechazo) of industrialisation in favour of village-based crafts (artesania, arte, oficio) to offset higher labour costs. The crowd dispersed dejectedly (desanimada, desalentada), downhearted (desanimada). Dishevelled (desaliñado, derreglado, despeinado) district capital. Turn his inkling (presentimiento + =, premonition) into a reality. Fascinating, captivating. Admiralty (Ministerio de la marina). The build-in advantages of incumbency (mandato): ventajas que conllevan estar en el poder. Adamant (firme, categórico). Their compassionate (compasivo) behaviour typified (=, era representativo de) the new nation. A less wasteful (derrochador) growth model. He inveighed (arremetió, lanzó invectivas, vituperó: reprochó) against his superiors ... Junker braces for (se prepara para) ... Run up (tropezar) against (con) national reluctances (reticencias). Pay quarterly (por trimestres). Hue (color, tono) =/= trend/tendency (=). The hall was packed (abarrotado) with people, the play packed (arrebató) the theater. Picker (recolector de fruta, de té). Basura: trash, garbage, rubbish, (en sitios públicos) litter → "no --", a -- (montón desordenado) of books, -- the streets (tirar basura por la calle), a pavement (acera) --ed with papers. Chillón: (pers.) loud, shrill, noisy, (tono, sonido) shrill, (color) loud, garish, lurid =/= estridente: (ruido) strident, raucous, (color) loud. Craggy (rocoso, escarpado; features: arrugadas)-faced (facciones bien marcadas) & weather-beaten (curtida) face. Skipper: (Náut.) patrón, (avión) capitán, (Sp.) entrenador. Throwaway (desechable, de usar y tirar) industrial revolution. Resources/means of production. I've the wherewithal (medios, recursos) to seize & hold disputed territories. China breakthroughs (avances importantes) are muted (apagados) by data protection. Plinth: (edificio) zócalo, (estatua) pedestal. Rate (ridmo, índice) → birth --; (considerar) → Italy --s its progress by comparing itself .... At this pace (paso), at an alarming -- (velocidad). Fire started deliberately; deliberate on (sobre) sth, the judge retired to deliberate. (Store) front (frente de almacén, fachada ...). FARC was fond (era aficionada, tenía cariño) of bombing & torching (antorcha, incendiar + set fire, burn down). Tardiness (lentitud, demora). Hope for hours in shirt-drenching (empapada) ... Low profile (=, contorno): poco prominente. Hardball (implacables, despiadadas) tactics. Achieve self-fulfilment (llegar a sentirse realizado). I can do mischief (causar daño) or disappointment (desengaño, decepción). An attentive, thoughtful (atento, pensativo) chap (tipo). Put the coin in the slot (ranura). A second-tier (actor ...: de segunda fila) tournament (torneo). Revamp (reformar, modernizar) education. Brimming (rebosando) with ideas & nothing to eat. Money mostly dressed up (disfrazado) as research funds; criticism -- -- as advise. It dispenses with/do without (prescinde de) the EU's four freedoms. Head (cabeza, dirigir) → the --ing back (regreso) into the government. Saudi Arabia: a TV show which makes fun (se burla) at his kingdom's royal highness (alteza). His longtime (de toda la vida) enemy. London remains the channel (Alzeera)'s backup (respaldo, refuerzo). The microphone cajoles (camela, engatusa) the audience, hearing. Sewing (costura) nail/scisors; nail clippers (cortauñas); secateurs (tijeras de podar) + podar: lop, trim. Concoction (mejunje, invención; food/drink confección) of herbs. Barraca: (puesto) stall, (cabina, caseta) booth, (Mil) barrack/hut. He is heightening (incrementando, recrudeciendo) the debate. The city (es mayor que a town) has held drills (taladros,V; (Mil.) simulacros) from NY missile attack. Streak: a missile carrying nuclear warhead --ed (pasó rápido) over Northern Japan; a -- (reflejo) of light; a --/run/ spell (racha) of luck. Do-gooding (hacer buenas cosas). Demeanours (conductas) → misdemeanours (fechorias, delitos menores). American upmarket (de mayor categoría, que atrae mucha gente) → go/move upmarket; subir de categoría, buscar una clientela más selecta. The market is oversold (sobrevendido + (productos: exagerar sus méritos, promoción exagerada). Step up: (producción, campaña) intensificar, (exportaciones, poder, volumen) incrementar. Politicians want to grab more of the spoil (estropear, echar a perder; mimar demasiado)s (botín) than the transnational companies have gone to control. Istambul has always lent (prestado) itself to rioting. Nozzle (boca, pitorro) =/= nipple (pezón, tetina) =/= muzzle: hocico de perro y de lobo; de cerdo (snout), bozal, amordazar. Loaded up (cargado). Writ: orden o mandato, a royal --, issue a --. Compliance (conformidad). Tear/tore/torn out (arrancar) → tear sb's eyes out; tear one's hair (out): (in exasperation, worry) tirarse de los pelos. A likeminded (de ideas afines) group. Fraught with: (tensión) estar cargado de, (pbs,) estar lleno de), be -- with danger (ser peligrosísimo). Heartland (centro) of American's tech. Leading-edge (de vanguardia, punta de lanza) bodies. Exacting (exigente, riguroso) grooming (acicalamiento, preparación) standard. Magnificient/splendid (magnífico, espléndido). Cyber-attacks are independent of each other (mutuamente). In the guise (disfraz) of monk, in a new guise (con aspecto nuevo). In different guises (formas). Truancy (ausentismo escolar). Shrug off (encojerse de hombros, hacer caso omiso). Recurrir: turn to sb, resort to sth/to hour address (discurso) at the Sorbonne. Trump ought to take note. Acronyms (siglas). Seasoned (sazonado, condimentado). Advancement (fomento, mejora de posición) of backward (atrasada) class. Enthuse (entusiasmar) → -- about/over sth (mostrarse entusiasmado con algo). Pool (hacer un fondo común). Work in relays (relevos), go on relays (ir por turnos), relay station (estación repetidora). Pinnacle: (Archit.) pináculo, (peak of rock) punta, (of mountain) cumbre; the -- (cumbre) of fame/success. Pelearse: quarrel (discutir), fight (pegarse). Tick off: (annoy) fastidiar → what --s me -- ...; (scold) regañar, reprender → he was severely --ed off. He asked for one year's leave of absence (permiso, excedencia). Inquiry (indagación, investigación). Dishono(u)r (deshonor, deshonra). Be in fine/good fettle (forma). The streets glisten (brillan + shine, sparkle) mit ice. Obus: (arma) mortar, howitzer, (proyectil) mortar bomb, missile, shell. Se entrevistó con su homólogo francés (he met with his French counterpart). The mainstream (corriente dominante) centreright family. EU leaders: a rough history of leaps forward & lurches (automóvil: sacudidas, pers.: tambaleos) backward. Quell: (revolt) sofocar, (criticism) acallar =/= quench: (thirst) quitar, (desire, passion) satisfacer, (flames) sofocar. Dissent: discrepancia, disconformidad. Cutting through (abrirse camino a través) a mountain. Soupe kitchen: comedor de beneficiencia. You need a magnifying glass or magnifier (lupa) to read this handwriting (letra). Blazing: (building/torch) encendido, (light) resplandeciente, (eyes) centelleantes → trailblazing, grounbreaking: (pionero + "pioneer") + the cutting-edge (de vanguardia) tech. Inferences (consecuencias, deducciones) → draw -- (sacar conclusions + "="). Damp (húmedo) down: (fire, cyclons) sofocar, (enthusiasm, excitation) apagar, enfriar. They balked (evitaron) a shelling out (apoquinar) ↔ freeloader & scrounger (gorrón). Pull or press or squeeze the trigger (gatillo). Ancillary (auxiliar) → be -- to sth (estar subordinado a algo); administrative assistant, auxiliary nurse; come to sb's aid (auxilio), give help or assistance (prestar auxilio). A discomfited (desconcertada, frustrada) experiency. Prisoners mill (molino, moler) around (dan vueltas, arremolinarse) → mill around inside her head. Atemorizar (frighten, intimidate) him. Imprudentemente: unwisely, imprudently, carelessly, recklessly. They're joking, teasing, pulling her leg: le toman el pelo. Rumbustious (ruidoso) shouting (vocerio). Acrimonious: =, palabras cáusticas, ásperas, (disputa) enconada (inflamada, irritante). Commonality (cosas en común) → there is a -- of interests between them; the commonality (la plebe, el pueblo llano). Recover: recuperar, rescatar, (-- from sth): recuperarse de algo, obtener indemnización, (Ec.) (repunte, reactivación). Haphazard: (elección de aspirantes) al azar, caprichosamente, (trabajo) irregular, (enfoque) incoherente. Lowly/humble soldier. Sumiso: (dócil) submissive, (que no se resiste) unresisting, (que no se queja) uncomplaining. Act with caution (cautela) → --ary words, market. Its underlying (subyacentes) genetics. A climbing (trepadora) plant; this wine goes straight to your head (este vino es bien trepador), (pers.) social climber. Buy off/brive/suborn. Upstaged (eclipsado) by … + (pers.) outshine, eclipse; (star) eclipse. Gallow: horca, colgar; gallous humour (humor negro o macabro). The mainstay (pilar, puntal) of the business, of the society. Agree staunchly (incondicionalmente) about the leadership. Scathing (ironía mordaz, sarcástico, feroz, cáustico) ↔ un--ed (ileso + unhurt, unharmed, uninjured). Earn razor-thin (muy finos, escasos) margins. The war is impending (inminente); his impending (inminente) jubilation, a sign of -- disaster. Skin-deep (superficial) Japanese westernization. Outspoken (franco, directo), outspokenness (franqueza). Understate (subestimar, disminuir la importancia)ed: sobrio, sencillo, directo. Won by a narrow (escaso) margin, write in the margins (márgenes), -- of safety, they live on the -- of society (marginados de la sociedad). Asco: a home in a revolting, disgusting state; it made me feel seek (me dio asco), this corruption is sickening. Seducir: (pers.) seduce, the idea appeals me. Pious (piadoso, beato, santurrón). Hushed (silencioso + quietly) → in -- tones (en voz baja, murmullo), the atmosphere (ambiente) was -- (silencioso). Unholy: (impura, profana) alianza, (mess, row, noise) tremendo. Heel (talón, base) → wellheeled (con dinero, ricacho) tourists. People of this ilk (tipo, clase, índole) =/= tilt (inclinación, V) → -- at/towards/against (arremeter contra + attack), the -- of the earth's axis, the -- of his head when he listened. China brazenly (con toda la frescura, descaradamente + shamelessly) interfered. The wireless (inalámbrica) tech, talk on the -- (por radio). Lucirse: he will be shown off (se lucirá), -- -- one's talents (lucir sus habilidades). Jhon excelled in the examen. Clerk (trabajador administrativo, dependiente). Unskilled, inexpert, inexperienced (desmañado). Coherent (=) → incapable of -- speech. Logical (=) → she's the -- choice for the job, she has a -- mind (es una persona lógica), it is -- that. Consistent (pers., accción: consecuente, uniforme, de calidad constante, coherente, lógico) → he made various statements (declaraciones) which were not --, his actions are not -- (consecuentes) with his beliefs (ideas), the rate of inflation has been --tly low (se ha mantenido bajo. Congenial (simpático, agradable) president, find sb -- (tener simpatía a alguien), he found few people -- to him (con las que congeniaba). He demurred (objetó + =, put forwart), I pointed out to him (le objeté) that there was not enough money. Espinoso: (bramble: zarza) thorny, (fish) bony + huesudo). Drive a drill (taladro, barrena) through two feet lake ice, drill good manners into a child (enseñarle buenos modales), I had it --ed into me (me lo inculcaron) as a boy. A movie for grow-ups (personas mayors). Defendant, indicted, charged (demandado, acusado) outriders (escoltas + escorts). Iron the garment on the inside; the inside of the house, socks (calcetines) on inside out (al revés). They suffered a major (importante) setback/mishap (contratiempo) or a serious reverse in the last elections.

Lynching (linchamiento). Spur (estimular, espuela,V) them to greater effords; --ed by dreams of wealth. Bide your time (esperar el momento preciso); at that precise or very moment, the necessary (precisas) qualities. At grass roots (de las bases) level. The security (vigilancia) will have to be tightened; the building is under surveillance or watch. Security patrol (servicio), be on patrol (estar de patrulla), the frontier is not --ed, he --s up & down (se pasea de un lado a otro). Break loose (soltarse) → all hell broke loose or hell was let loose (se armó la gorda); be armed to the teeth, pluck up courage (armarse de valor), there was a big fuss! (¡Que follón se armó!). Sidestepping (eludiendo) licensing (autorización de) requirements. Back up (respaldar, apoyar). He vaunted (se vantó) of their values of sexual equality, of religious tolerance. Drop (gota), drip (goteo) → drip caffee down your shirt (camisa)/skirt (falda). Never-ending, endless (interminable + =). Captivity (=): presidio donde se cumple la pena. Joy (alegria, júbilo) =/= jolly (alegre, jovial, pasarlo bien) good time. Tertulia: gathering to discuss philosophy or policy. Arraigado: (costumbre) deep-rooted, (persona) property-owning, (creencia) deep- seated → China's deep-seated (profundamente arraigado) bureaucratic traditions. Storyteller (narrador, cuentista, mentiroso). It's outline (contorno, perfil, esbozo, resumen) of social-credit scheme. Bittersweed (agridulce). Spill: derramar, verter, volcar → without --ing a drop, don't -- tea over the tablecloth; the spillover (excedente de población) from the urban centres + there has been a -- of violence into these suburbs, into the neighbourhoods. Hellhole (lugar horrible) ↔ hallow: (religión) consagrar, santificar → --ed: (instituciones, tradiciones; terreno) sagradas. A party is broken & adrift (a la deriva). Oil patch (remiendo, parche,V; parcela, terreno): yacimiento petrolífero + oilfield =/= yacimiento arquitectónico (site). Yore (antaño, de otros tiempos) + antaño: long ago, in years past, in years gone by. Coalesce (fusionar, unirse) + fusionar: fuse (together),

Com.) merge, amalgamate, (información) merge. Amenable (dócil, de acuerdo, convencible) to sth: responsable ante algo. Hedor/apestar (stink, reek), fetidez (smelliness, fetidness), peste (plague, epidemic) → the whole business stink. Noxious, harmful & injurious (nocivas) substances, fumes, ideas, influences. Boon (favor, gran ayuda) → it would be a -- if he went (nos ayudaría muchísimo que él fuera), it would be a -- (gran beneficio) to humanity. Gild (dorar) his biography with an epic lustre (=, brillo). A rocky (tambaleante, con incertidumbre) few years. It did overspend (gastó más de la cuenta) in advance. Resolve the differences by resorting (recurso) to coercion or compulsion (coacción); con coacción (under duress). The senate comitee hearings (sesiones) in NY. Skull: calavera, (Med.) cráneo → I can't get it into his (thick) -- that (no hay quien le meta en la cabeza que …). Farm out items (encargar trabajos) to independent outfits (a terceros). Chill: frío, escalofrío, (food, wine) poner a enfriar =/= freeze: congelar, quedarse inmóvil. He lives abroad =/= outlan<u>dish</u> (extravagante, estrafalario), outland<u>er</u> (desconocido, exranjero + foreigner), outsider (de fuera). Shirk: (task, duty, responsibility) eludir → European's defence shirkers (perezosos, vagos). Battle-hardened (avezado a). Peddler (vendedor) → a drug -- (un traficante de drogas) + drugs & ams dealer, slave trader. Champion: =, World swimming --; defender, abogar por; he defends his opinions with good arguments, the Barça are defending the championchip title, he's defending his doctoral tessis. Iron out: (pb.) resolver, (dificultad) eliminar. Carefully (con cuidado) embraces (=, abarcar, aceptar, religión: adopter) more foreigners. Lucha: fight (pelea, ej. against the cancer; (struggle) para conseguir algo, para superar un problema, para la supervivencia (survival). Blush: rubor,V, bochorno, vergüenza. Mine (extraer, explotar) a deep seam. Seam: (stitching) costura → fall o come apart at the --s (descoserse), (Med.) sutura, (gold, coal) filón, veta. Refugio: (rain, attack) shelter, (mountain) refuge, shelter, (calzada) traffic island. Bumpy: con desniveles, (road) con baches → it was a bumpy ride & he felt sick (se mareó). Let me introduce you Mr Smith → how do you do?, pleased to meet you. I was delighted/very pleased of your work. He is very fond of she (le tiene mucho cariño), gustar mucho (ej. I'm very fond of music), fondness for (afición a la) opera, the fondness for one another was obvious. Did you like/enjoy the book? I enjoy her company, being with her. He likes play the guitar. Would you like some? (¿le gusta?). Flee, fled → flee from (escaper de) sth/sb, flee (huir de) the country, they fled (corrieron) to safety (de seguridad) shelter (refugio), to her mother. I nearly passed out (me desmayé) with fright (del susto), I was nearly fainted. Faint: apenas visible, tenue, débil; (smile, hope, resemblance) ligeros. Downturn (baja, empeoramiento) of the Ec. Culprit (culpable), it's your fault, you are to blame. Manufacturing (de fábrica) fault, defect, flaw =/= physical handicap. Exact (=, exigente)ed hefty budget, -- spot (lugar), -- sciences; exacting/demanding (exigentes). Wage-depressing (deprimentes) levels. European area endures (aguanta, soporta) … It was the first time we habe been apart (separados), the posts (postes) are a meter apart/at one-meter interval/with a gab of one meter. Moot (discutir, planear) bans on … Blend (combinación,V, mezla,V, palabra compuesta + compound word); (sonidos, colores, olores) armonizar. Villages cleared (aclarados, limpios; despejados, vaciados) of B. Haram. Banking clean-up (limpieza). Leaky (agujereada, con goteras, fácil de violar) security. Bequeath (legar) assets. Flag: bandera, (de suelo, piso) losa, señalar, marcar, (pers., animal) desfallecer, (entusiasmo, conversación, interés) decaer. Crimp (onda, rizo; obstáculo, Vs) → regulators abroad have crimped American's ambitions. Look back over his life, in retrospective. Quake (temblor, terremoto), those institutions are quaking (temblando). Decamp (escaparse, Mil.: levanter el campo). Profusión (=, abundance). Credit carts are peddled (ofrecidas puerta a puerta, ambulantes) to acquaintances (conocidos) by freelance (por cuenta propia, independiente) agents. Tuition in sth (clases de algo); he's having (tomando) private (particulares) --; tuition fees (coste de la matrícula) =/= the registration (matrícula) has already began, free (gratuita) registration, foreign registered ships. Competing head-on (frontalmente). Mane (crin de caballo, melena de persona o león) → a --less lion. Uplift: (spirit/mind: mente) elevar, (spiritual) exaltation, (physical support) sostén. Any account-holder (titular de una cuenta). Lent out (prestado) credibility to sth. Keep the Ec. ticking (tick tack). It would be more accurate (exacto, certero) to say that ... People would have said they were satisfied with taxis until Uber came along (llegó) + come along children! (¡Vamos niños!). Dross (escoria, basura) on offer is hard to fathom (entender, Náut.: sondear). Rotten: podrido, (tooth) cariada, -- to the core (corrompidos hasta la medulla). They rake in (se embolsan) millions of $ 2. Abusive (grosero, insultante) =/= obsceno or lujurioso or lascivo: lascivious, lecherous, lustful. Harry (hostigar + bother, pester); harried (agobiado) by new entrants =/= I'm in a hurry (prisa) =/= hastily (apresuradamente) written; hasten back to the house. Console/comfort (consolar). I'm sorry, I'm late (llego con retraso). His lowbrow (popular, poco intelectual) antics (payasadas, travesuras). Abhorrend (detestable, aborrecible) =/= detestable: (pers.) hateful, (costumbre) detestable. Act without violence & do so expeditiously (rápidamente), an expeditious (rápida) settlement (resolución) of the dispute (conflict). It sparked (desencadenó) American's consumer debt culture. Slippery (resbaladizo), slope (cuesta, pendiente) → -- -- (camino de) bankruptcy; be on -- -- (terreno resbaladizo). Be weighing (pesado) wether (si) ... Criticised for censorship (censura) & bias (inclinaciones, parcialidades). Clear-cut (dejar sin árboles). Muscle in (meterse por medio) → -- -- on (introducirse en) their market. Google unveiled (estatua/placa:

descubrir, cifras/informe: dar a conocer) a credit card. A blockbuster (éxito de taquilla, bestseller) video to be wipped out (barrido, eliminado, deficit: cancelado) by tech. shift. Defer (diferir, retrasar) consumption. Banking is late (con retraso) to the smartphone age. Be nibbling (mostrar interés por; the costs of branches are nibbling (mordisqueando) at customer basis. Mine: mina, (gold) extraer, (area/seam: filón) explotar, (Mil.) minar. Underwriters: aseguradores, de Stock exchange (SE): suscriptores. Banking is backward (retrasada), inefficient & hidebound (retrograda, rígida, aferrada a la tradición). Productivity gains are hard to come by (conseguir, hacerse con). The enthusiasm generates foolhardiness (imprudencia, insensatez). Mire/sludge (lodo) → Huawei is mired (envuelto, atascado) in political controversial. China is deliberately overloading (sobrecargando) weak states with loans. When they buckle (hebilla, abrochar, torcer, doblarse) it seizes (confisca) their assets & influence on ... Pacesetter: (Ma., busssiness) persona que marca la pauta. Compel (obligar) any Chinese firm to do whatever it wants. China is a hacker (pirata informático): purloin (hurtar sin fuerza) everything from the plans for F-35 to a database of millions American civil servants. Bill: factura, cuenta, billete; proyecto de ley; cartel/anuncio. The horse has bolted (se ha desbocado, no tuvo freno, (pers.) salir disparado). Chinese firms rely on western tech. ↔ Western rely on Chinese parts & factories to assemble. Get snippets (algunos datos sueltos) of outstanding (excepcional) talent. Snowden tried to put a back door into a cryptographic standard to give information to American spies, they get skill/flair (aptitud) to read communications. Differents status tastes sunder (rompen, henden) Europe. Self-made female billonaries (mujeres hechas billonarias gracias a sus esfuerzos). Lingering (entretenerse, persistir) fears among conservatives. Skeptic (=, incrédulo). The law has been caught up (quedado bloqueada en) ... His job was to wring costs out (escurrir, sacar) of the company's supply chain. China-Apple: the existing network would take years to unscramble (descifrar, descodificar, poner en orden) … Apple can develop a product that no self-respecting (que se precia) affluent (acomodado) Chinese could do without. Payments & other services show it is trying (duro, difícil). Insouciance: indiferencia, despreocupación + lack of concern, don't take care. China's mettle (temple: naturaleza, entereza: integridad): protectionism is making it harder to obtain vital tech. from abroad. Show one's temple (lo que vales). China must take the road of self-reliance (independence, not autarky). It angered (enojó, enfadó) China =/= annoyed (enojado/enfadado). Enriched Uranium spin (hacer girar, centrifugar). The nuclear deal is hanging on (espera, sigue, aguanta, depende de) → -- -- tight (agarrarse fuerte). Barter (trueque)-based channel. Public service utilities (empresa de servicio public). Mourn (llorar) for sb → --ful (muy triste). Mournful reports from post-industrial strongeholds (fortalezas, bastiones) to local resentful (resentimiento) of big cities. En latín *faneros* es abierto y *criptos* es cerrado → it rocked (balanceó) the cryptocurrency world. Entrust (confiar) over $ 666. Meet: (pb., pers.) encontrar, (he came out to -- me), (enemy) enfrentarse, (condiciones) satisfacer. It supplies (suministra) at a price of (por) $ 55. Compliance (conformidad) with sth, in -- with your wishes/the law. Shrine: santuario, sepulcro, hermita → ground- breaking (pionero, innovador) ceremony to enshrined (encerrados) Kami. They are the killjoys (pers. aficionadas a perturbar el negocio de otros) of Russian finances. The bankers are kin (entsiastas) to … ↔ be not kin (reluctant: reacio). Frown (ceñir el cejo) at sb: ponerle cara de pocos amigos, con ceño fruncido. Victorious, winners; triunphants. Remunerar (pay, remunerate); salary, remuneration to be agreed (a convenir). Overachiever (pers. que rinde más de lo esperado). His almost discomfiting (desconcertdo) poise (porte, elegancia, desenvoltura). Deck sth with sth (adornar, engalanar algo con algo). Brim (borde) over: (desbordar, rebosar) with enthusiasm → --ful (lleno hasta el borde). Distrust (desconfianza + suspicion) of elite institutions. A self-defeating (contraproducente) populist jesture. Ignore the booms (estruendos,V) of the incoming artillery. Jihadists are sweeping (se extienden, barren) across the Sahel's arid swathe (ringleras; envolver, vendar) of scru(bland) (monte bajo, matorral). The bearded zealot (fanático) waxed (creció, aumentó) enthusiasm about Africa. A scheme which match (emparejar, igualar, ajustarse a, enfrentar) them. Arms looted (saqueados) from the arsenal of Libya. Recipient (receptor, destinatario) =/= recipe (receta culinaria, prescripción Med.) =/= receipt (recibo, recepción (of goods, etc.). The regime corners (acorrala, acapara, monopoliza) much of India's wealth through its vast business empire. Limbs (miembros, extremidades). A raft (montón/pila, balsa) of top French private-sector companies. Create a generic template (plantilla) that an user could finetune (ajustar, poner a tono). Hurtar: purloin, steal, tienda (shoplift). The angst (angustia) surrounding its parent company/corporation (empresa matriz) is a measure of their raising global relevance (=, significación). Their links were regarded looser (más flojos, poco rígidos). Transfer of sensitive tech. are being scotched (frustrados, echados por tierra). Congress beefed up (fortaleció) the screening (revision, investigación) regime for foreign investments. A popular dating service (servicio de contactos) + dating agency (agencia matrimonial de contactos). Charge sb + inf. (encargarle + inf.). Help to switch (cambiar) jobs faster. The school does not charge (acusa, cobra) students upfront (inicial, por adelantado) to attent (asistir, esperar). Admissions are competitive. Online tuition (clases) is live (en directo) & interactive (recíproco). Cash cows: productos muy rentables, actividades que generan mucha caja. The Monarchy promote congenital defects rather than intelligence; it is designed to prevent diversity & personal merit, from creeping into (entrar sigilosamente en) its inborn (connatural, innato) & inbred (engendrado por endogamia, innato) ranks. The monarchies have gone out of brands this century. Quantum computer outperform the classical one. China throws (da, tira, proyecta) a revealing (revelador) party. Bristle (pelo, cerda; erizar) → ships bristling with (están repletos de) weaponery. Dwarfing: (hace parecer pequeño, eclipsa + =, outshine) foreign visitors. Attempts to leave the EU show up (revelan, ponen en evidencia) constitutional shortcomings (defectos, deficiencias) =/= shortage/deficit (escasez). Rollo: (tela, papel) roll, (cuerda, cable) reel. Government lays out (presenta) its policy agenda, with 45 seats short of a majority. Crime hogged (acaparó) the stage ... Crypto- derivatives are too dicey (inciertos, dudosos), risky & hazardous (arriesgados, peligrosos). Prices differ widely between crypto exchanges. A moot (discutible + atable, arguable) point; his impartiality is datable (fechable), dubious (dudosa, sospechosa). The battle lines of an American regulatory assault are being drawn (trazadas). Thank goodness (bondad, calidad) for stockmarkets. Helmet (casco), blue (de las Naciones unidas) --, safety (de seguridad) -- =/= old quartier (casco viejo) of a city. Towering (grande, alto, destacado, imponente) landmark (hito, monumento, punto de referencia). In Linxia (China's little Mecca) they have vied (competido dispudado) outdo (superar) eah other. Witting (inteligencia, ingenio, agudeza), unwitting (involuntario)ly: sin estar consciente, sin darse cuenta. Governments benefits (beneficios, prestaciones). Public profligacy (prodigalidad, despilfarto) has crowded out (desplazado) private philanthropy. The benefits of programmes targeting poor children yield (rinde, produce) returns many times higher than those targeting poor adults. Dokdo island: disputed with South Korea, Japan claims its own. Green revolution began with seeds: dwarf varieties of rice & wheat with more energy into edible bits & did not topple (over) (caerse, volcarse, perder el equilibrio) when fed with fertilisers. Mobsters (gangsters, mafias). Boot: bota, maletero + trunk (tronco, trompa, maleta). Urban fabric (tejido). Camps (campamentos). They plant saplings (árboles jóvenes) & later they are thinned (rebajados, aclarados). Talar: fell, cut down + pers.: derribar; cut down. Fibres turned into textiles. Offcuts (trozos, restos). Wastes (desperdicios) that becomes raw materials for other processes. Coax (convencer una pers. engatusando, lograr) these cells becoming nervous tissue. Overwieu (perspectiva general). Unimpeded (libre de obstáculos). Come up (problema) surgir, (pers.) subir, (sol) salir. Its beef imports grow 40-fold between … A break of more than three month. It spans (comprende) the period between the ages of 6 & 15. The mid - to-late 1990. Dubious clients were scooped up (recogidos con pala/cuchara) by rivals unaware of … Spill (derramar) the beans (judias): descubrir el pastel. Twig (ramita, darse cuenta) of the the political scandals of the whole world. Vet (investigar, examinar) to ensure he do not overstep (sobrepasa, rebasa) his role as figurehead (figura decorativa). Flanked (flanqueado) by torchbearing priests. Tender: (Com.) oferta,V → put in or make a -- (presentarse a concurso o a una licitación); tierno, sensible delicado; a child needs -- loving care + take care of him, look after him). Prices are tending upwards. Declaim (declamar, recitar en voz alta). Weave (tejer), spin (hacer girar, hilar). Obliquely (=, reply: indirectamente). Jagged (irregulares), charred (carbonizados) tree stumps (tocones) =/= scorched (quemados) woods & flog (azotar, vender) it as a charcoal (carbón vegetal). Stiff (duros) speechs. Fiscal restrain (limitación). The election was widely deemed (considerada, juzgada) to have been rigged. Text attack, assault, aggression. Espina dorsal: spinal column, spine, backbone. Pay tribute to those killed. They bridle (brida,V, frenar; se molestan, se ofenden) at his attempts to atone (expiar) for Japanese's behaviours. A third of Britons have seen her in the flesh (en carne y hueso): like Akihito, she is the soul of discretion. Spanish scandal-ridden Monarchy. She swore her coronation oath to God + he swore allegiance (lealtad) to the Constitution, to the Crown; oath (juramento) of allegiance, make/swear/ take an oath (jurar). A similar addition (suma) =/= addiction → drugs -- (drogadicción). Give smart speakers vision as well as hearing (oído). Bounce off sth (rebotar contra algo). A Lidar works as a radar: by bouncing (rebotando) a beam of electronic waves off its surrounding & measuring how quikly those waves return; build up an image of what the beam is pointing (señala). What those gestures are intended to convey (transportar, transmitir, expresar)? Satellite internet: its hability to slash (disminuir drasticamente) the cost of rocketry (cohetería) has given it a bulging (repleto) order book. Space X has lodged (interpuesto, depositado, hospedado) plans for such ground stations. The satellites must be able to hand customers off (ceder, rechazar) quickly to one another; they are designed to communicate with each other via lasers. Formula E: electrical cars are catching up (alcanzan) fast with petrol-driven ones. Receive a ballot paper in the post. Whittle (tallar) down: quitar, cesar → some Tory party's Members of the parliament (MPS) have been whittled down (cesados). Association, the membership (los socios) of the club. Any truth in these rumors? Bloody-minded (difícil, empecinado, de mala intención) Prime minister =/= cruel/blood-thirsty (sanguinario). Standing (posición, prestigio) → energy,... --. State of mind/ animosity (estado de ánimo). Years of constitutional stasis/ stagnation come to an end. Dice (dado)y: incierto, arriesgado (risky, hazardous). Winding (hacer girar, dar vueltas a, serpentear) state roads alike (parecido, del mismo modo). Cockeyed (desatinado, disparatado torcido) nature of Airbus's supply chain. Giant looms (telares + textile mill) to weave. Autopilot (piloto automático). Mutual +self-interest (interés personal) involved queasy (que marean o intranquilizan) compromises (arreglos, transigencias, soluciones intermediarias). Accountable, responsible manager =/= countable/accountant =/= account (cuenta en el banco, informe/explicación) of failures. Western will be thrown out (rechazado, tirado a la basura) before China opens up, if enough know how becomes self-reliant (independiente). Crown jewels (joyas de la corona). What is afoot (se trama, se pone en marcha)? Vow: promesa, voto,Vs, jurar → break one's -- (faltar a un comporomiso). Advocate: (of sth) defensor, (law) defense lawyear, (idea, course of action) recomendar/abogar por → the US longtime --ed for Taiwan. Be deputised: reemplazado, desempeñado las funciones de alguien. Trample (pisotear) the newspaper of your enemy. The diplomatic niceties (sutilezas). Being anti-Union soviet socialist republics (USRR) is a downside (inconveniente + =, drawback, disadvantage, objection). Trump can be riled (irritado) by advisers (asesores) telling him that China is stealing American secrets. Deal that can be branded (marcado, tildado de) a climb-down (marcha atrás). China'rightful (justa, legítima) place is the World more powerful country. Sore (úlcera; dolorido, irritado) → I'm -- everywhere. String (cuerda, cinta; fila, serie) of sensors hanging down of a buoy (boya); buoy up: (Ec.) fortalecer, (pers.) animar, (boat, pers.) mantener a flote =/= I feel a bit of a sting (aguijón, picadura, escozor) for a couple of years. The humbling of imperial China by smaller European powers. Because he is not going to let anyone push him around (darle empujones, mangonearle). Pro-China protests have ensued (seguido) in Canada. Chinese puzzlement is disingenuous (insincero + "="). Wage freeze (congelación) to fight the crissis. Beyond trade, people-to-people exchanges look like sturdy (robusto, tenaz) guardrails (barrera de protección). Americans regulatory wrestle (lucha, forcejeo) with Chinese tones. Cofucious institute → Chinese funded (financiado) outpost (puesto de avanzada) based in American universities. Plainly (claramente, sin rodeos, es obvio que) fraud to Democracy in any corner of the planet. China is tough (fuerte, exigente, estricta) on acts of piracy. Honorary chairmanship. A very vocal (que se hace oir) minority, not all senators are as -- as him. 70% of firms are profitable. View (vista; opinión, parecer) → these views are nuanced (matizados) =/= clarify a thin nº of points. Now downplay (quitar importancia a) these targets. Shut foreign rivals out (dejar fuera, no dejar entrar). Avión de carga (freight plane, cargo plane), avión de personas (airliner). The in-house (en la empresa) think-thank examined the origins of the leading speakers (oradores de la House of Commons del Reino Unido y de la House of Representatives de los Estados unidos (EEUU). Plana mayor: (Mil.) staff officers, (jefes de empresa) top brass. Pull off (quitar, conseguir) → China is on the track to -- -- this feat (proeza) to dominate 5G mobile telecommunications. Data speeds about 20 times those of 4G. It is unhelpful (poco servicial) that Trump is a techno-curmudgeon (cascarrabias). Trump signed a bipartisan bill. China has a lead in hypersonic glide (vuelo sin motor, planear) weapons (armas). All-out (total, suprema) war. We'll have to scoot (salir pitando) to get there in time (llegar a tiempo). The path (sendero) up to (hasta) the house; go up to Oxford. Greenfield (zona rural). Abroad, it means rebuilding frayed (deshilachadas, desgastadas, crispadas) alliances. Endear sb to (ganarse la voluntad de) → this did not -- him to the public, the US endear (se ganan la voluntad) to China in its back. Bitterness: amargura, crudeza, rencor; lo enconado, lo implacable → I accepted it without --, I have no -- towards you. Punzar: prick, pierce, (tiquet) punch. Shape: forma, configuración, (events) determinar, stay in shape. Perjudicar: harm, be detrimental, (salud) damage, (interés, derechos) prejudice. Defendand (demandado) ↔ plaintif (demandante, querellante). The law of supply & demand is undeniable, indisputable, irrefutable. He has brought a lawsuit (pleito, acción) against them + I sued him (lo demandé) & I brought a lawsuit against him for damages. I cannot agree to your request (petición, solicitud). He is an odd character (tipo muy raro). Plagiarize, plagiarism, piracy (piratería). Blink (pestañeo,V, petardeo)er: intermitente + flashing. Pisotear: tread down, trample → they were trampled to death (murieron pisoteados) =/= atropellar: run over/knock down. Flash point (punto de inflamación), critical (álgido) point. Helpful/obliging (servicial). Sacudida: shake, (golpeando) beat, (terreno) tremor, (explosión) blast, (tren, coche) jerk, jolt, lurch. Simpático: (pers.) nice, pleasant, likeable, (detalle) nice, lovely, (paseo, ambiente) pleasant, congenial, delightful. Chequered, sheckered: (past, period, epoch ...) accidentado + eventful, (trip/journey) con altibajos + ups & downs, (terreno) rough, rugged. I enjoyed the book/wine, ..., enjow o.s. (divertirse), he enjoys (goza) good health, ... Cojear (limp, hobble), be lame (estar cojo). Wobble: (voz) temblar, (wheel) bailar, (chair) tambalear → --y: flojo, tembloroso, tambaleante (ej.: a bridge, German-French axis). Falter: (pers.) titubear, vacilar, balbucear, (engine, heart, interest, courage, enthusiasm) fallar, (pers., Ec., business) tambalear. I can recall the day ... Don't remind me (no me hagas recordar), ... which remind me (lo que me recuerda), sift (tamizar) applications. With soldierly (marcial, militar) bravado (bravatas: fanfarronadas). Attempts at breakout (fuga, escape) =/= breakaway (ruptura, disidente) party. Brinkmanship (política arriesgada o suicida). Erdogan strong-armed (pone mano dura a) his country's electoral watchdog (guardián, organismo de control). Have sth up one's sleeve (tener algo planeado). A sinister (siniestro: izquierda; triste, daño que sufren las pers. o propiedades) plan. Istambul gave the challenger (rival, aspirante) an emphatic (=, rotunda) victory. Contender (aspirante) for the title/presidency. He wish to be awarded scholarships. The road ahead for him is strewn (esparcida, desparramada) with obstacles. On the doorstep (a la vuelta de la esquina, muy cerca). Stambul meets the contempt (desprecio) it deserves. His resolve (resolver, determinación). Grid (rejilla, red) =/= Amerian grit (polvo, arenilla, agallas + a girl with guts) & ingenuity. Mountain tops (cumbres). Put them together (montar, reunir). Switch to digital payments in droves (a manadas, a montones). A gold chain, put the chain on (the door), the prisoners are chained up. They propose to fly a kite (cometa): tantear el terreno. The tether (soga, atar) uncoils (desenrosca) spinning (haciendo rodar) a drum. Iran is poised (listo, preparado) to breach (violar) the 300 kg. cap (límite, tope). He told pollsters (encuestradores) ... Carve (tallar, esculpir, cortar, trinchar) a conglomerate into three parts. Gargantuan (gigantesco, descomual). The trend that the merger underscores (subraya, pone de relieve). Trigger-happy (disparar a la menor provocación). Genberal electric (GE) has been through (pasado por, estado sometido a) pointless (vanas, inútiles) contortions (contorsiones). Chequered (accidentadas, con altibajos) histories. Scions (descendientes, vástagos) of industrial dynasties. The bank's hard-won (ganado con esfuerso) credibility. Lay off (despedir) the workers made redundant (disminución de plantilla) by labour-saving tech. Scraps (sobras) =/= scrapes (roces, raspaduras) & dents (abolladuras, marcas) he leaves behind turn to rust (óxido, herrumbre). Toxin-generation blooms (floración,V; vello, pelusa). Money doesn't make the World go (a)round (andar, circular). Empower (conceder poderes) to people. If the project lives up (está a la altura) to the mock-ups (maquetas) it will become a doddle (pan comido). Relocations: (employees, assets) trasladar, (to cheaper market) deslocalizar. The government chipped in (intervino, contribuyó) by allowing banks to hire & fire more readily. An EU more dirigist (intervencionista) & with inflexible rulebook (reglas, normas). Venturesome: pers. atrevida, acción arriesgada. It seeks redress (corregir, reparar) the bust-ups (rupturas, peleas) originated in the region. Overmatched (derrotados, superados) policymakers. Put growth ahead of their goals. In 2014 the n^{os} spiked (incrementaron bruscamente). Gangs (bandas, grupos, pandillas) laundering (blanqueando) drug profits. Shell (proyectil) controls in America, where incorporation of public registers is at state levels, are among the World's most secretive (reservadas). Provide ion drives (transmisiones) to … Clutter (abarrotar) sth with sth, she's --ed up my home with junk (me abarrotó la casa de porquería). Cosmic rays randomely (al azar) flip (golpean) the ones & ceros that computers operate on. Risk of debris (escombros, deshechos). Brainstorm (devanarse los sesos) for new products. Untapped (sin explotar) potential of millions of brains in the third world. Armed forces will be World-class (de talla mundial) by 2050. Subdue (dominar, contener) the environment. Flay (despellejar, hacer trizas) their most successful progeny (descendencia). Ejecutar: (reo) execute, (plan) implement, carry out, execute, (imno nacional) play, perform. Texas seems more likely to push ahead of California. Steer: (ship, car: dirigir; pers., animal: conducir; timón). Be bogged down (quedar empantando) in their ideological bunkers. Flow: (Electr., fluid) fluir, (tide) subir, (blood) correr, (wound) manar, (traffic) circular. A not glat reminder: mangled (destrozado) steel & concrete remains (restos) of a jetty. Swipe card (carta magnética). Foray (incursión) into the territory, into piracy. The western clash (enfrentamiento) subsides (disminuye). Bestow sth on/upon sb (otorgar algo a alguien). I've burdened (me cargaron) with all the responsibility. Three porcentaje points more than national rate. Young man are put off (aplazados, apagados, desconcertados) by the lack of potential brides. America & India bicker (discuten) about … There are muttering (gruñen, refunfuñan) in London. Fly in-fly out (entrar y salir volando). The signs of rejection can be … Maid (sirvienta, doncella), servant (sirviente/a) → the servants. Hong kong: home of the World's fourth- largest services market. Lock onto: acoplar + fit, put together, (Electr.) connect.

Empate: tie, split, draw → break the tie, scoreless tie. Nos dejó helados, estupefactos: we were stunned/staggered. The water's freezing (helada), my feet are --/frozen; wine well chilled; drink/oom (cool). Pet (animal domestic, acariciar) → pet shop & canine hairdresser. Ecological store (tienda). Trip without laggages. Print your photos from your smartphone. Artisan bakery (pastelería). 10% discount on shipping (envíos), the canal is open to --, ship by air, rail, road, sea. Ship charge (gastos de envio). Remittance: remesa, envío, pago. Shopping in Pineda. Desengañar (disilusion) → it is best not to -- her =/= delusion: engaño, delirio, falsa illusion → -- of grandeur, she's labouring under the -- that she's going to get the job. Frenar: rein in; brake; (proceso, deterioro) slow ... down, check; (alza, inflación) curb, check, slow ... down; (progreso) hold ... back, slow ... up/down. Pure grape (de uva) juice (zumo), pure wool, thoroughbred (pura sangre). Patronage: clientela, (sponsorship) patrocinio, auspicio + tutela), ej.: -- of arts. Raid: (Mil., bank, supermarket) asaltar, incursión, bombardeo, air --, (police) redada. Raider (asaltante). Recession cause loosen fiscal policy. Dust himself down (sacudirse el polvo). The root cause of Ec. woe (aflicción + =). Overshadow (eclipsar, ensombrecer). Riot suppression & policy massing (incremento) across the border. Tank (depósito, cisterna, tanque; venirse abajo + slump, tumble) → tank Hong kong's stock - & property markets. The rot (putrefacción + "=") is deeper =/= rotten (podridos) European politics. Widespread (extendidos, generalizados) defaults in the EU. African áreas are haphazard (al azar; incoherentes, irregulares). The new minority hold the key to political change. Half of Arab families fall below. Israel's official poverty line. Plants use for their photosynthesis the blue & red wavelengths at either end of the spectrum. Green in the middle. Unload frozen mackerel. Flooded plains: tierras inundables en las crecidas de los ríos. Sea wall (malecón). Artificial islands to sell off (vender, cerrar) Jakarta Bay. Hundimiento):

(barco) sinking, (edificio, empresa, familia) collapse, ruin, fall, (terreno) cave-in, subsidence. Residents tap into (explotan, sacan provecho de) aquifers. Unreliable (poco fidedigno, informal, tiempo, …: inestable) supply of water. Sculpted (=) 1,000 Ha of reclaimed land into new waterfront (que rodea al lago, casas a sus orillas) city. He god cold feet (cogió miedo y se echó atras). They doused (light: apagada, pers./cosa: empapada) themselves with petrol. The government has incarcerated the culprits (culpables). As the planet heads up (dirige, está a la cabeza de …). Smo(u)ldering (provocativo, =, que arde lentamente, latente) → the building was -- (ardiendo); her eyes --ed with passion. Baba: (echar) drool; (niños) dribble → drool over you (le cae la baba port tí). Saudi Arabia has shaken up (agitado, sacudido, reorganizado completamente, aclarado ideas en) its oil hierarchy. Aramco's vulnerability has been laid bare (desnuda, escueta): se ha puesto al descubierto. The prices have jumped (subido, incrementado) & slid (deslizado, caido). He squeaked a victory over her (fue elegido por un mínimo). A mooted (discutible, planeado) point/trade deal, … Shield (proteger, escudo) its state- oil industry. In/out tide (marea), high/low --; raising -- (oleada) of violence; a tidal surge (fuerza, oleaje) submerged, … A surge (oleada) of people. Pre- empt (adelantarse a) → she --ed their criticism by apologizing + -- complaints. Deeds (hechos) echo (resonan) the experience of its counterparts in other states. Exaggerate, overstate. Round up (reunir, acorralar, hacer una redada a) his corrupt allies. He has pawned (empeñado) his gold jewelry (alhajas). Age of majority have to be extended. Split a laser beam in twain (2). Hint: insinuación, indirecta, consejo → -- that he contemplates (=, medita sobre, prevé) suicide; a gentle (suave, moderado) -- (consejo) for travellers. Enforcing the cap (hacer respetar el tope). Properly (correctamente, debidamente) enforced rules that prevent over-indebtedness of borrowers & insure fair treatment. Offer microloans at dearer (más caro, querido, adorable) & buy it on instalments or hire purchase (plazos). Placards nailed (clavados) to shrapnel (metralla)-ridden coconuts & palm trees. The remnants (restos) of supernova. Salir: the train leaves at ..., don't go out without a coat, the outbound (los que salen) airline passengers. Pointing hand-held (de mano) bombs at, ... The visual system they have come up with (devised: ideado, set out: planteado) are bespoke (hechos a medida). Chinks (aberturas, grietas) in an algorithm's armo(u)r (armadura, coraza) → find a -- in her armo(u)r: encontrarle el punto flaco. The ideas for subverting (minar, socavar) it. Build atop (sobre) the gold standard. Covert (encubiertas) trickeries (artimañas). Tree top (copa del árbol)-skimming missile. Capable of skirting (bordear) those defences. A central cog (piñón) of America's ind-machine. Knock- on - effect (repercusiones, impacto) → the rise in interest rates will have a -- on the housing market (mercado inmobiliario) =/= Knock-on cost (consecuencas del coste) on ... Flipside (la otra cara de la moneda) is also true. Que suerte tienes! (¡you are so lucky!). We're in luck (estamos de suerte), lucky nº, lucky man, wish me luck. Luckily, fortunately I wasn't alone, with a bit of luck I'll finish today, it brings bad luck. Cash flow (flujo de caja). Wide-bodied (armazón, fusilaje) jets. Pasillo: (house) corridor, (theatre, plane) aisle → a twin (gemelo, doble)-aisle (pasillo) plane to replace, ... Response (respuesta, reacción) to the seizure of Crimea. In Ukraine's east they set off (desencadenan) a separatist fighting. Russia pulled that off (sacó, consiguió) it with help from suporters (partidarios, Sp.: seguidores) in Ukraine. Fabrications (invenciones, mentiras) against Baltic democraties that crop up (surgen) relentlessly in online. Tallying (cuadrar, coincidir) even the seemingly (aparentemente) trivial. Russia recruits (recluta) by blackmailing (chantaje) visitors who accept the advances (anticipos, adelantos; insinuaciones + =, hints) of beautiful women. Russia is likely to step up (incrementar) efforts to stoke (up) (alimentar, avivar, agudizar) divsions & undermine trust (confianza) in Baltic states. Alibaba get into partnership (se asoció) with Mail Ru. Meekly/gently (dócilmente). Pull out: (car) arrancar, (section) separarse, (troops, partner) retirarse, (nail, plug) sacar. A loyalist (partidario del regimen) of Trump. Double-hulled (casco). Those misgivings (dudas, recelos) grew after the September 1tth attacks. A poisoned chalice (cáliz). Cortafuego: (bosque) firebreak, fireguard, fire line, (building) fire wall. Heist (golpe, atraco) in social media. Hoary (anciano, vetusto) old carbon-belchers (que eructan carbon) like Exxon Mobil. A reminder (recordatorio) of that data breaches (brechas, infracciones, violaciones) bear an unhealthy resemblance to oil spills (derrames, vertidos). Parry (rechazar, aludir) every jab (pinchazo, with elbow: codazo). Crushing (aplastante) liability (responsabilidad, taxes: pasivo, …). Score: Tanto,V, marcar, puntuar, -- over (superar) sth/sb, (a political vitory …) lograr, … Scores (montones) of people (una veintena) =/= pay off/settle old scores (saldar cuentas pendientes). Preservation (conservación) of ancient models. Pay heed (hacer caso) to, … Socially staid (serio, formal). In America & in much rest of the World conservative political parties are challenged, taken over by reactionary nationalism. They gingerly (delicadamente, cautelosamente) chose her as their leader. Storm: tempestad, (city, fortress) tomar por asalto, (house) irrumpir en → --ing on the Bastille. Undermined (debilitado, socavado) by the liberal centrist of Ciudadanos. Blast furnaces (altos hornos). Reckon: (cálculo, opinión, juicio) → the day of --ing (del juicio final), the final reckoning (la hora de la verdad), by my -- (juicio). Courtesy (=, gentileza) for the governors. He fêted/celebrated (celebró, agasajó) the re-election. Inclinado: (terreno) sloping, (plano) inclined, he left-leaning (inclinado) Congress party → corruption & fiscally helpless & landslide (irresponsable, sin objetivos) victory. Disenchanted with their erstwhile (antiguo) champion. The child looked around (alrededor) in bewilderment (desconcierto), a bewilderingly complicated (de una complejidad increible) matter. Impressive (admirables, impresionantes) reforms in Egypt. Ration cards give access to cut-rate (precios rebajados, tiendas de occasión) staples. The government subsidies to a social safety-net (red de seguridad). Gusto: taste, pleasure, he indulges (satisface) all his children's whims. He wear tasteful (de muy buen gusto) clothes. Tacto: sense of touch, a towel rough (áspera) to the --, a towel feels rough, he told it her with gread tact, she identifies coins by touch. Set-in: sentada, (en el trabajo) encierro. It had been adversised online. Local authorities usually disallowed (desestimaron, rechazaron; goal: anularon) the event. Cops (la policía) discouraged him to participate in a rally. Handed back to mainland in 1999. Like Hong kong, Macao institutions are flawed (con imperfecciones). Dole out (dar, repartir) to interest groups. Give ideas to tinker with (hacer pequeños ajustes). Hong kong's curriculum (programa, plan de estudios) caused a backlash (contragolpe, reacción violenta) that presaged (= + predicted, forestalled, heralded) the recent unrests. Wildfire (fuego arrasador) & peat (turba) fire. Soggy (empapados) wetlands (humedales). It dried out the landscape, producing tinder (yesca) for forest fires. Blank (space: en blanco, tape: virgen; vacío)et: cubrir; manta, capa; global)…, → blanketing (cubriendo) much of Siberia. Three topics dominating the election. Top up (glass: llenar, battery: cargar) of public pension. In Japan the Liberal democratic party (LDP) ruled for all but a handful (pocos, un puñado) of the past 65 years. China's muttering (refunfuñeo). A hike (excursión, subida) in tax consumption. The reindeer (renos) are backed up (pers./efford: respaldar, driver/car: dar marcha atrás) with their sleighs (trineos). Broker: (bonds, commodities) hacer corretaje. Exhibir: (m., película, colección): show, display; (arte) exhibit, (regalos, trofeos) show off. Princely: principesco, (sum) bonita, (gift) magnífico. The carrier (empresa de transportes, portaavones) yields (cedió) to the pressure & fired four staff. Patriotero: jingoistic, chauvinistic. Cram (meter, empollar, llenar a reventar) ever more transistors on chips; transistor size of dozens of atoms. Bypass faulty cores (corazones, centros, núcleos). He points at/to a solitary coca bush (mata, arbusto). A sideline (actividad complementaria) in drug trafficking. Littered (lleno, plagado) with the bodies of fallen (caidos) champions. A doughty (valiente) political dynasty. The hotheaded (exaltada), warlike, bellicose America. The EU throws its weight around/about (despilfarra). Face up (hacer frente) to a challenge (reto, desafio). His peremptory (autoritario, imperioso) removal (extracción, eliminación, traslado) from unsettled markets. A state of disarray (desorganización, confusion). It raided (atacó) its coffers (arcas). British petroleum (BP) & Chevron packed their bags (hicieron las maletas) & left. Mismanagement: (business) mala adminitración, (situation) manejo inadecuado. Petrobras took nosedive (bajó en picado). Brives to politicians in ecchange of padded (cobrar más de, inflados, acolchonados) contracts. China's market capitalisation shrivelled (se marchitó, se secó) by $ 200 bn. The sleaze (sordidez, sinvergüenza) is cleaned up. He set about (acometió, se puso a) boosting (estimular, fomentar) production. Pemex has overtaken (adelantado) petrobras. Beneath (por debajo de) the seabed. A fanciful, crazy, ridiculous (descabellado) goal. Argentina has been scared (cicatrizada, marcada) by … Tap (explotar, aprovechar) Argentina's rich shale deposits. Underdone (poco cocida) meat for the carnivorous God's creatures, … The timing (fecha escogida) by/for … Bring forward: (idea) presentar, (meeting) adelantar, (witness) hacer comparecer. A surface strewn (esparcida) with terrestrial rocks. Heavy-handed (torpe, inepta) German performance for open borders. Fraught with (con mucho) danger, a -- (tensa) region. The overlord/tyrant (cacique) doesn't accept left- leaning (inclinación). Japan & South Korea are fraying (se deshilachan, se desgastan) alarmingly. Lax: laxo, relajado, poco estricto. Run (carreras) for covers (cubiertas). Forecast: (weather) pronosticar, (result, trend) prever → insurers forecasting climate-induced losses. Merkel era draws to a close/an end. Clue (pista, idea) → they're completely clueless (negados) for practicalities (aspectos prácticos). Ageing population push up health-care costs. Digital entrepreneurs have spied (=, descubierto) an opening. Dismiss (despedir, descartar, desestimar) insurtechs as cute (guapos, listos, cucos) little things. Meltdown: fisión accidental del núcleo de un reactor, (finances) colapso + crash. Build anything sizeable (considerable, importante) → a -- sum; (bastante) → it's quite a -- house. Less strangled (ahogado) in red tape (papeleo). Scaremongering (alarmismo + "="). Good ideas are fast-tracked (llegan lejos). Big tech. is gearing up (se prepara) to enter insurance. He was adamant (firme, categórico, inflexible) to not reconsider the idea. Parents want to spare their offspring the horrors of China's gruelling (penosos, duros, agotadores) University-entrance exams. It is top of the list/class for eight out of every ten of his clients. The required investment is bigger. Profit margin/mark-up (margen de beneficios). Point-of-sale. Oddly (curiosamente, de manera extraña). Greek developer (promotor inmobiliario). She is a would-be (aspirante a) star. Keynes once fantasised (=, soñaba con) a World of permanent low interest rates. Without loose money chomage would have been higher. Long-standing (que viene de lejos) aspiration, engagement (compromiso, noviazgo). Lasers to correct eyesight (vista). Mesh (malla, engranaje, engranar) of ulta-thin electrodes to capture information of the brain. $ 50 notes (=, billetes). Steam engines. Scant (escaso) recognition (reconocimiento) of the service rendered, it's all out of recognition (irreconciliable), by your own -- (según Ud. mismo reconoce). Lauded, flattered, praised (elogiado, alavado) by his fellows. On the bring (a punto de) explosion. Basin (bol, tazón; cuenca). The farm lobby led him to withdraw his threat to leave Paris climate agreement. The tip of the iceberg; if the tipping point is transgressed (=, sobrepasado), the rest follows. Expelled (expulsado) from the party. Heaven's high canopy (bóveda, cubierta exterior). Exercises to streamline (estilizar) thighs (muslos) & hips (caderas), streamline (racionalizar) production, organization. Follow the patterns (hábitos, pautas) of consum; the familiar patterns of events (la historia de siempre); predictable --s of climate anomalies. Saplings (árboles jóvenes) have shot up (crecido; precios: disparado) among the ashes of their giants forebears. The first flickers (parpadeos) of permanent changes: the carbon dioxide declining. Covetousness (codicia) for previous minerals. The trees stood bare (desnudos). Summon up (courage: armarse de, memnory: evocar) the courage to rock the boat (hacer olas) without causing it to capsize. Sink: lavaplatos; (ship, stone) hundirse, (output, moral, level, price) decaer + decrease, drop, fall. Gentle: (moderate, not violent or harsh), (murmur: murmullo, susurro, rumor) suave, (slope) poco empinada, (exercise) moderado, (heat, breeze) suave, (dog) friendly (simpático), tame (domesticado), docile (manso). The forethought (previsión, reflexión previa) reflects the broader approach. Afirmar: state, declare, assert. An unusual amount of the chaos & upheaval (agitación, trastorno). Parliaments called in polls early (temprano, anticipadamente) + snap polls (elecciones anticipadas). Stable two-party system gave way to wobbly (tambaleante) five-party system. Increasing nº of people losing patience. A thrice (tres veces)- repeated defeat. Crash (estrellarse) out (quedarse dormido, estar hecho polvo). Republicans controlled both branches of government but failed in their main legislative goal: repeal (revocar) the affordable (asequible) Care act. Trump shut down (cerró, apagó, desconectó) the federal government twise in a year; shut down: (hotel, college) cerrar, (power) corte, (services) paralize. Reminder: recordatorio, nota para recordar. Trump flouted (desobedeció) Congress over a tax law & urged his administration to resist. Congressional request (solicitud, petición,Vs) for information. Running on fumes (gases): marcha echando chispas. The mob (populacho) rule: la ley de la calle. Governments are stalemated (en punto muerto, paralizados, en un impasse) + (chess) tablas, (negotiationes) en punto muerto. Whammy (palo, revés) of unpopularity =/= wane (menguar, declinar) interest in diplomacy. Secular: dura más de un siglo, muy viejo; seglar/laico. Voters are more fickle (veleidosos, inconstantes). Glut (superabundancia, saturación). Current-account surplus: saves more than invest at home & sells abroad more than it imports. A highly unequal distribution of wealth: in 2019 Germany is one of the most unequal of the 35 countries of the Organization for economic cooperation & development (OECD): the median household wealth of $ 68,000, slightly more than Poland. Though German's authorities tend to blame an ageing society for its high savings rate, the true culprits (culpables) appear to be the moguls (magnates) of Mittlestand (clase media). A much-vaunted (tan cacareado) Ec. model. Outstanding: (ability, beauty) extraordinario, (achievement) destacado, (debt, account) pendiente → the amount (cantidad, deuda) -- is $ 6666. These institutions, hair & teeths are fallen out. His leadership came under fire (cayó en línea de fuego). Uphold: (principle, faith) mantener, (tradition, custom) conserver, (verdict) confirmer. A country banking counting on/relying on (contando con) coal to fire. Archivar: (documentos) file, (investigaciones por un tiempo) shelve, (para siempre) close the file on. Britain impounded (retuvo, confiscó, incautó), seized, confiscated an Iranian tanker. Insurance premiums for the strait have climbed by an average of 10%. Individual defences are spotty (irregulares, desiguales; cara llena de granos). Packed (llena, repleta) court. Iran could shut this space down (desconectar, cerrar, apagar) with a few missiles. The mean (mezquino, humilde, media) annual rainfall. The spell (encanto, …) of U. v. d. Leyen as German defence minister was a debacle (disastre). Slugguish (lento) ness: aletargamiento, (mercado) atonía. A narrow majority: she said less about her authority than about the strategic feints (ademans de engaño o regate), procedural grumble (queja, refunfuñeo) & face-savings (cubrir las apariencias). Fire 300 warning shots. Make hay (heno): sacar tajada. Grunmetal (gris plomoso) skies. Amid (en medio de) dismay (consternación) of Merkel. Incite, encourage sb into sth. Map out (planificar), draw up a plan for… He declared loftily/haughty (altaneramente, con arrogancia + =). Space has since become a sinew (tendón, nervio; vigor) of terrestrial military power. Even a fleck (salpicadura) of paint can cause damage. Vet (examinar, investigar) orbits. Clearing-house (centro de intercambio de información; finanzas: cámara de compensación). Unbridled (desenfrenada) competition inside the UE. Sparsely (escasamente) populated. Lessen (atenuar, disminuir) the likelihood (probabilidad). Overfly/lew/own (sobrevolar) =/= overflow (desbordarse). Nigh/almost/nearly (casi). Heavenly (paradisíaco). Rollout (lanzamiento o presentación) of a new product. Bureaucracy in Algeria deterred foreign investments. It looks stuck (atascado) at an impasse. Luxury goods (artículos de lujo). He lives on/he still lives (perdura) in our memory. Put paid (acabar con, echar pot tierra) French-German dreams. Brainstorming (devanarse los sesos). Invoicing department (departamento de facturación). That remains a moot (discutible) point. He was thrown out (echado) for being a troublemaker. Trounced (derrotado, apalizado, aplastado) in Star Craft II: a video game in real-time, rather than turn-by-turn (por tiempos). Inscrutability (=, hermetismo). The outset (inicio) of the war. Sensor-scattering (dispersión, community: diseminada) in the jungle. A prospective (possible, eventual) president, when the lead (principal) candidate … African & South east asian infrastructure often peters out (se van apagando) at borders, the road --ed out in the dunes. European cities are build around pedestrian (peatón, pedestre: vulgar, inculto, bajo) cores rather than grids (redes) of the motor age. Many city-scapes (paisajes urbanos) in central Europa follow a medieval German layout (plan, trazado) of a castle on a hill ... Germany's interest rates: politicians hope championing (defender) savers. Squirrel away (guardar) a tenth of their disposable income for lean periods. Look into (considerar, investigar, estudiar) the practicalities (las utilidades, lo práctico). They appear some way off (a cierta distancia). The Central bank (CB) depositors rate is -0,4: rather than paying interest on the reserves kept by lenders, it charges to hold them. The boldest offering to have surfaced (emergido, aparecido). Carat: quilate (205 gr.). A month-long assault by America has pummelled (apalizado) Huawei, whose global networks it suspects of allowing China to spy on others. Poner alguien en evidencia (show sb up); poner algo en evidencia (demonstrate sth). Huawei: forced to transform it from making & sell hardware into one to also make many components of the integrated circuits that it used to buy to others. Take an ice-cream scoop (palada, cucharada) to the Earth's crust. Russian gems (=, piedra preciosa, joya, alhaja) are not bloodied by strife (lucha, conflicto). Provenance (procedencia) is our competitive advantage. Our Ec. splutters (chisporrotea). Because generic (común a muchas especies) drugs are so cheap. Apple censors (censores) app (se aplican) in China when the Communist party tells it to. A backup (de respaldo, de refuerzo) combustion engine. Uber runs an app - based taxi-hailing service. Fannie Mae & Freddie Mac: two giand government-sponsored enterprises, back (respaldan, avalan) much of America's mortage industry, were bailed out to the tune of $ 188 bn. Change rainfall (lluvia, precipitación) patterns threaten an artery of global trade. Umbilical cord =/= Panama's lifeblood (sangre vital, alma, sustento). Man-made fibers (fibras sintéticas). Panama: below 24 m. hulls would risk bumping on the bottom of the locks (esclusa) when enter & leave the lake. China approves (acuerdo, aceptación gustosa) of an institution. A brass (latón, placa de latón, mandamás) nameplate (placa). An incense-scented (perfume, aroma) haven of woodwork & grey stones. Monks were harried (hostigados, agobiados) to death. The Red guards tried to ransack (registrar) the place. Eels (anguilas). Crosses are torn off (arrancadas). Bonded (unido, en aduana) warehouse: almacén de depósito, depósito aduanero. Featureless/humdrum (monótono, anodino), monotonous. Future-proof (con garantias de futuro). Castrar: (caballo) geld, (pers., toro) castrate. Uprooting (desarraigado) capitalism. Standing: posición, prestigio; permanente, de pie, (agua) estancada + stagnant). Wrong-headed: (pers.) obstinada, (attemept) desatinado. Decolorar: (pelo) bleach, (ropa) fade. Shunt: cambio de vía, she was --ed into (lo relegaron a) other team; they --ed him off (se lo quitaron de encima) to other office. The planet is damned (condenado) to die. Wondrous (maravilloso, extraordinario, unusual) life. Its loses are frequently mourned (muy lloradas, lamentadas). Lessen (atenuar, reducir) the challenge. Put aside money for stiffer green policies. The Ec. in such a bumpy (desigual, con desniveles) patch (territorio). Build apace (a ridmo acelerado). The Victorian memorabilia (recuerdos). Dissent (discrepar) =/= dissident. Xi's work is not acknowledged (reconocido, admitido) in the EU. A rope tightened around the neck. Thereafter (a partir de entonces) =/= therefore (por consiguiente). Dollop (dosis, cucharada, porción); a portion o helping of chips (de patatas fritas), cheese portion, large chunks of or a large part of the budgt. Europe needs more than blather (parlotear, decir tonterias). Professional liability (responsibility), tax liability (carga fiscal). Tie a bow (hacer un lazo, moño) around the calf (pantorrilla). Uncoupled (desenganchado). Privacy (intimacy). Outlining (contorno, bosquejo, trazar un mapa, explicar resumidamente) her agenda. He perceived, sensed, noticed the danger. In 1781 Tupack Katari (indigenous) laid siege to/ besieged Spanish La Paz below. Airway: (Med.) vía respiratoria, (avión) ruta aérea. Window- blinds (persianas). Camera-equipped fridges. Bee hives (colmenas). Chore (tarea) → household --; lata → ironing is a --. Nudge: codear, empujar suavevemente; rondar → unemployment is --ing 30%; give them a little -- (refrescarles la memoria). Cream off (llevarse) the lowest risk/young musicians. Bendable (flexible, =). Wear out: (pers.) agotarse, (clothes, batteries) gastarse. It provokes derision (escarnio, ultraje) & mockery (mofa, burla). Be on the tenterhooks: inquieto + worried, enterprising, restless; sobresaltado, asustado + startled. Seize: (object, hand) agarrar, (opportunity) aprovechar, (forest, town, power) tomar, (assets, property) confiscate, (arms, drugs) incautar; her remarks were --ed on/upon (aprovechadas) by the opposition. Seizure: toma, confiscación, incautación. Trampa: (con lazo) snare, (ardid para animales) trap → I didn't fall into the --, they laid/set a -- for me; that's cheating. Dire: (warning, prediction) serio, grave, alarmante; (news, fate, consequences) funestas, nefastas, (need, misery) extrema; be in -- strait (situación desesperada). Ill-gotten (mal habida) wealth. Sparser/scarcer (más escasos) amounts of data. Scarcely: apenas (+ barely, hardly) → -- furnished room, -- anybody, I can -- believe it =/= scarcity: (money, food, teachers, resources) escasez. Reino: animal, mineral, vegetable kingdom; kingdom of God/of Heaven; realm of fantasy. Apenas: barely, scarcely, hardly enough to live + as soon as he found out (lo supo), she ran to tell him, barely furnished (amueblada) room. Ignot/bullion (lingote). Dim: débil, oscuro; atenuar, debilitar. Nephew/niece → my nephews (sobrinos); grandson/granddaughter) → grandchidren (nietos). Muddle (lío, follón) → get into a -- (enredarse, hacerse un lío). Stall: puesto, tenderete; pararse, ahogarse, atascarse: (negociaciones) impasse, llegar al punto muerto. Simple: =, ingenuo, naïf; sencillo + straightforward. Whip (azotar) up: provocar, incitar. Staggered: estupefacto, pasmado. The terms of the distribution, the loan (préstamo) will expire. Aloof: (pers., attitude) distante → more -- than previous emperors. The nº of cases handled (tratados) shot up (subieron mucho, se dispararon). I shall refer (remitiré) your proposal + the reader (lector en biblioteca: usuario) is --ed (remitido) to. Surreptitiously (=, a escondidas) → he was -- stuffing himself (atiborrándose) with chocolate. Debug: (system) depurar, (room) localizar y eliminar los microbios ocultos. Extravagante (raro, ridículo): eccentric, bizarre, outlandish, flamboyant, outrageous. Anti-gamble law. Congestioned roads with traffic. Sano: (persona, animal, árbol, órgano, clima) healthy. Sacudida: (agitando) shake, shaking, (de terremoto) tremor, (de explosión) blast. Admonish (amonestar, reprender) =/= (multar) fine. Upheaval (trastorno, perturbación, Pol,: agitación) → disgruntled (descontentos, contrariados) investors. Stumbling-block (escollo, impedimento (=), obstáculo (=). Statesmanship (habilidad política). Pole (poste, mástil; palo de esquí, pértiga) =/= shaft (mango, hasta, saeta, eje). Vageries (caprichos) of the wind, of the climate change. Lifeline (cuerda de salvamento) → throw a -- (tender una mano). Penpushers (chupatintas). Multi-bn. $ loan to struggling (luchar contra) coal-fired plants to keep emergency fuel on standby (alerta); standby time (tiempo de autonomía). A young man with no future/prospects (porvenir). Spring/source (manantial) =/= fountain =/= hot/termal spring or spa (balneario). Misgivings: dudas, recelos. Xi stands out (sobresale) from his predecessors. Excursion, trip, outing (si dura mucho) tour. Arrive out of puff (aliento, soplo) to the second round. In the still (tranquilidad, calma) of a wooded forest. Good/bad omen (augurio); predict, foretell (augurar); there was an ominous (que no auguraba nada bueno) silence. Hulking (muy grande, descomunal) purpose (=, determinación, intención). Stricture (crítica) → the reviewer's -- are quite valid (fundadas + =). View, perspective =/= good/poor sight, he lost his (eye)sight. Rattle (ruido, traqueteo, perder la calma, ponerse nervioso) → a -- somewhere in the car, of hailstones, the hail --ed on the plastic, (hacer sonar) he was --ing coins in a box, business are rattled; there was an ominous -- coming from thr engine; the wind -- (hace vibrar) the windous; he banged (golpeaba) on he table, --ing the cups (haciendo tintinear las tazas). Off-putting (desagradable, desalentador, molesto). Bout: (negotiations) ronda, tanda, (of illness) ataque, (of flu) gripe muy fuerte, (of activity) racha. Stockpile: almacenar, (coal, oil) reservas, (weapons) arsenal =/= warehouse: almacén, depósito,Vs). Pampered (mimados, consentidos) & pricky (espinosos, que pican; quisquillosos, irritables) sultans. Boon (ayuda, favour) to humanity. Tailored (adaptada) to bind (atar, unir) to protein. Exhaust (pipe): tubo de escape, exhausted (agotado + m.: sold out; existencias, provisiones: finished, exhausted; libro: out of stock). Tourists flock to reminisce (recordar, rememorar) old times. A disused: abandonado, (máquina) en desuso. Nail-biting (angustiosos, de mucha emoción) days of Sino-Soviet hostility. Plenty of Russian visitors to China's border towns, but they do not head (encabezan, se dirigen a) main sightseeing (de turistas) atractions. Putin flaunts (alardea) Russia's influence. Shore up (apunta, refuerza) its regime. Conflating (combinando) the brazenness (descaro (+ brazen: descarado) of Russia with … Color (raciales) prejudices. The outcome (resultado) will be pleasing (grato, agradable). The police are overworked, underpaid & understaffed. Grisly (espeluznante, horrorífico) crime. Waved (blandía) a slipper (chancleta) but didn't hit anyone. He tipped off (se chivó) to the suspicious police. Ordenanza: ordinance, decree, (Mil.) orderly + metódico, ordenado, obediente). Police shortcomings (límites) to remote places. A pistol-wielding youth shot into a crowd. Assign (destinar) officers to the back of beyond (quien sabe donde, al quinto pino). A solace (consuelo) in an injust world, solace o.s. with. Bishops tell their flock whom to vote for. A plum (ciruela, fantasía) sinecure (poco trabjo y buen sueldo). The hitch (problema, pega) is that ... Heady (embriagador, vertiginoso) price. Acces for high-rollers (jugadores empedernidos; (de vicio: inveterated; de alcohol: heavy drinker). Spool (carrete, bobina) → the allegations have spooled out to ensnare (atrapar, coger en la trampa) him. D. Trump lobbied (presionó) Abe on behalf of (en nombre de) American casino firms. Buttonhole (enganchar) → I was --ed by him (él me enganchó & no me dejaba irme); tricked (engañado) into becoming drug mules (testarrudos + stubborn). Pare (cortar), pare down (reducir) to a minimum → set about (empezar). D. Trump is hellbend/determined (empeñado) on three measures: be rid of some immigrants, illegal immigrants do not will have acces to subsidized health, bring down the cost of prescription drugs. Weighty (pesadas, importantes) tasks. Undermine (socavar, debilitar) outreach programs (para usuarios potenciales). Bait (cebo, tormento,Vs) the Supreme Court into taking a case. China's flagship (punta de lanza) foreign policy is the way to put it at the centre of the world once again. Scrabble about/around for sth (revolverlo todo buscando) → he scrabled about in the coal; hard scrabbled border town. A digital silk road undersea cables & 5G. It mesh with (engrana con) its major resource supplies worldwide. A transshipment (transbordo) hub. The spillover (derrame, exceed, Ec.: incidecia indirecta en el gasto público) effects, ej.: from finance into politics, culture & security. A win-off (donde todos ganan) cooperation. BRI is predatory (depredador) of economics; in it Pakistan is a place where it should naturally take hold of (coger, agarrar). China can fumble (meter la pata) in the politics of its prime (principal) foreign policy. Be littered with (lleno de) papers, rubbish, ... He misread (malinterpretó) Pakistan's policy. It can ill (mal puede) afford (permitirse) ... Raw sewage (aguas residuals sin tratar). Adorn (=), decorate

(=), embellish (=). Fashioned (formado, fabricado, diseñado) as tribute to the Emperor. Downplay (disminuir la importancia de) such notions. Enmesh (coger en una red) → get enmeshed (enredarse en). Draw (atraer) other states into its embrace (=, oferta: aceptar). Choke (interrumpir, asfixiar, ..., estarter) off (cortar) supply. Ethnic cleaning (limpieza). Europe faces China's wrath (ira). 5G proposals are pitched (montados, graduados...) to help drive the next phase. (Hard) cash (dinero en efectivo), pay cash (down) (al contado, en efectivo), I haven't any -- on me, -- advance (adelanto), -- desk (caja), -- in: (investment & assurance policy): cobrar. Excluded for having needlework (bordados) verses from the Koran on his wall. The project is heading for (se dirige, va en camino de) buffer (amortiguar, parachoque) ... Fix up (fijar, arreglar) their communal areas. Creeping (progresivas + =) coalitions, inflations. Yank out (sacar de un tirón) the cable & disconnect the live wires. Two-prong (flancos, puntas, dientes) affaire; -- -- fork. The companies lobby their domestic governmrnts. It prides itself (se precia, está orgulloso) on having the toughest regulations. A mental block (bloqueo) =/= the blocks into which the EU build this power are shuddering (se estremecen), I shudder to thing (sólo pensarlo me da horror). Fitness test (prueba de estado físico). Miniaturised sensors that will allow people to wear the monitoring (proceso/ley: supervisar, elecciones: observer) equipment throughout their daily lives. Work out (calcular) beforehand (antes, de antemano) who will pass advanced (avanzado, superior) military training. The initial training lasts 20 days. Their own volition (voluntad propia, de libre albedrío). Rate (considerar) their pain. Mars's exploration continues apace (a ridmo acelerado). Heavenly (celestes) bodies. The Moon's far side. Winnow (discernir) truth from lies. Flow (corriente, flujo, curso; fluir, manar) → the flow of traffic is a washout (desastre), you're a -- as a coach (como entrenador eres un desastre). Scour (fregar, registrar) deliveries & nab (cosas: agarrar; personas: pillar) them & stalk (acechar) ... Similar missile is enough to bring down (precios: rebajar; Mil.: abatir, gobierno: derrocar) the enemy & purloin (hurtar, sustraer) its freight (carga). To qualify as a pilot (titularse, conseguir la capacitación de piloto). It's as badly off (mal de dinero) as Esat Germany. The € teetered (tambaleaba). An outbreak (destello, brote) of stability by having petty (insignificantes) rows (disputas). Brussels: reassuringly (de modo tranquilizador, alentador) & dull (aburrida). Spice up (dar más sabor) to diplomacy. Cough up (apoquinó) only a wisker (pelo) more than … Tightwad (agarrado, cicatero). Rip (desgarrón,V) → -- up (romper, hacer pedazos) its treaties. Half-backed (mal concebida) migratory strategy. Mid-life (de los 40) crisis. A man in balaclavas (pasamontañas) gagged (amordazó) him. Cabecilla (ringleader). The aim of forcibly (por la fuerza) changing Russia. Social media are seething (hierven, están furiosos). Visitors are given a snifter (copa, trago). His favourite tipple is Cointreau, what's your --? (¿qué quiere tomar?). A road-roller (apisonadora) flattened the pad (hombrera, almohailla; plataforma de lanzamiento para helicópteros). Hide the virus impact. Jumpy (nerviosos, saltones, asustadizos) rural officials. China's pop-up (emergentes) hospitales awe (sobrecojen, intimidan) foreigners.

Sección segunda: frases más largas, muchas veces ya compuestas

Además de la vertiente propiamente lingüística, se captan también muchos conceptos de temas diversos:

An outspoken (franca, abierta, declarada) critic of the government; he dropped dinky (preciosas) British phrases onto her conversation & explot (se aprovecha de) the smart British names; Anglophilia litter (recoge) plenty of flotsam & jetsam (restos de naufragio); he allowed clever Brits to get away (salir, escaparse) with (llevarse) thinks. D. Trump used the Atlantic alliance as a way of beating (apalizar) the EU; Brexit, simultaneously deprived Britian of its position of bridge between Amedita & the EU; he destroyed the Britain's reputation as a well-run country capable of calm American frequent temper tantrum (berrinche); downturns (Ec: deterioro; producción/ venta: disminución) are particularly difficult when you are poor; the proportion of Americans saying that they are able to pay the rent is falling. Pretty (bonito, ...; bastante) much (más o menos) → households disponible income will increase by 4 %, pretty much in line with (conforme a, de acuerdo con) its growth before the pandemics; Europe's bail-outs have a nasty side-effects; they threaten the single market; bail-outs come with nationalistic strings (condiciones → without --). The risk of an uneven (desigual, irregular) playing field will be ease if bail-outs money is distributed evenly around the EU. All bail-outs need to be carefully policed: ensure that companies are not using public cash to run large loses or to pay for their expansion plans once the Ec. opens up. Th EU is taking a pace that would have been bloked by its former members; for instance the scheme to issue a mix of grands worth 500 € bn & 250 bn. to countries struggling against C-19; the frugal four are bound to rebates (rebajas, descuentos; devoluciones, reembolsos). It would be foolhardy (temerario) to ignore the signals; it was fucking awful (fue de puta pena) → he is a fucking weird (persona rara). Dingy basements (sótanos deslucidos) featured prominently (tuvieron un papel destacado) in ... Clash (choque, conflicto) between individual fredom & social obligations was put on hold (fue puesto en espera); there was widespread compliance (conformidad, sumisión) from the start. Warrant: justificación, autorización, (Ec., Com.) cédula, certificado; mandamiento → there is a -- out for his arrest (se ha ordenado su detención), merecer → his complaint --s further investigation, conditions did not -- calling a doctor, garantizar → he didn't do it legally, I'll -- (you). The short-term fallout has rattled (desconcertado) South Korea Ec.; fallout shelter (reugio atómico nuclear). The startups are a long way from replacing the *cheabolas* as engine of growth, there is a danger of sluggishlty o slowly economic growing. Young women are more vocal (ruidosas) than previous generations & this tendency will continue. Korean women are too well-educated to submit (presentar, someterse, rendirse) meekly (dócilmente, sumisamente) to second-class status. They have cut their hair, thrown away their make-up & sworn off (renunciado) to discriminatory relationship with men; ithching (deshacerse de) make- up (estructura) is still a fringe (marginal) position, even if it's necessary for them to tie the knock (hacer un nudo) one day. The explanations are burdensome (onerosas, costosas), what is the -- of this? There must be some --, they gave no -- for the delay. Defer to sb knowledges (deferir a los conocimientos de alguien); (Mil.) dar una prórroga → his military service was --ed (le concedieron una prórroga) =/= difer: (=, discrepar, ser distinto). She was sexually abused & treated dismissively (despectivamente) & unfairly/in a biased way (discriminatoriamente). There's no score (resultado, puntuación) yet: todavá no han inaugurado el marcador, the final -- was 4-1, --s of people (montones de gente), five games without --ing a point, -- a hit (dar en el blanco), -- 75 % in an examen, the test --s of job candidates. The police officer took my statement (declaración, exposición de hechos y problemas) & asked why I didn't play it cool (no mantuve el tipo, no actué como si nada). His theories topped charts (fueron nº 1 de la lista de éxitos o superventas) all over the world. After a lot of soul-searching (después de revolverlo muchas veces) they played a dirty trick on him (le jugaron una mala partida). A man who spends money on a date (fecha, cita, compromiso) expect sexual favours in return or he tend to break off relationship. Parental-leave (permiso parental) arrangements, parental guidance (los consejos de los padres), parental authority (patria potestad). Ask for patriarchy (patriarcado). Reclamación: (queja) complaint, (reivindicación) claim → presentar una --: make or lodge a complaint; she is claiming his share of the profits; claim damages (daños y perjuicios); they're demanding better working conditions. Men are the primary (principales, primordiales) breadwinners, they must work a lot to generate enough growth to sustain a rapidly ageing country. The feminists target us (fuimos su blanco, su objetivo) just because we are men, we didn't obey them enough. The crew (tripulación) abandoned the ship while most passengers were still on board. Kep taps on people (vigilar la gente) who spoke up (decían lo que pensaban) & sometimes blamed they friends. Promote: ascender, fomenter, promover =/= prompt: rápido, puntual; empujar, provocar, dar lugar → they --ed a drive (impulso) to reform the political system, prompting two civil guards to resign. Without any reason there was orders to stay up (mantenerse de pie) as the ferry sank. Respite (respiro, tregua) → without -- (sin descanso), we get no -- from the heat (el calor apenas nos dejó respirar). Advocate: defensor, defender; recomendar, abogar por → --ing feminism & gay rights alongside (al lado de its main platform. A third of eligible voters (electores) succeed forcing the shaking up (agitar, espavilar, reorganizar) the party system from within. A flickering (tembloroso, vacilante, tambaleante) legacy leads towards breaking the deadlock (punto muerto) between the two major parties. The deal with the looming (inminentes, que amenazan) pbs. of the north is looking shaky (tembloroso, inestable, pers.: débil; knowledge: flojo; salud/finanzas: precarios). Débil: weak feeble, (pore dad) frail, (voz, ruido) faint. Seventy years military stalemate (punto muerto, paralización) of the peninsula; reach a -- (estancarse). Paralizar: stop, (Med.) paralize, (trade) bring to a *standstill*), everything came to a complete standstill (la paralzación fue total). Surge (oleada) in/into, out: entrar, salir en tropel → refugees would -- southwards; the crowd --d into (la multitud entró en tropel en) the building. German case: much of the fiscal aid to the East ended up (terminó) on the balance sheeds of West German landloards (propietarios, dueños). West Germans were twise as rich as their cousins in the East, where they cannot rely on (depender de) the state for their livelihood. A diversion (desvío) of citizens'loyalties (lealtades, fidelidades) from the state to smoller social groupings such as family. China has build new fences & video-surveillance systems & we observe an American response to North Korea resumption (reanudación) of missile tests. The alliance must be ironclad (irrefutable, incuestionable) but cooperation has waned (disminuido). Pond (charca; artificial: estanque), pond life (fauna de las charcas/estanques), pond weed (planta acuática), … a lifeless (desolada) carp (=) floats in the pond. I hope reunification will happen but it probably won't, so we muse on/about (reflexionamos) the possibilities of it =/= (considerar) reflect, (antes de actuar) think. When I finished I didn't know what to do & my parents didn't either. Her country is lavishing (colmando) awards (premios, condecoraciones,Vs) on her, even if she don't deserve them. The government, like many others, hat failed to live up (vivir de acuerdo con) the promises of democratisation. He is heartened (animado, alentado) by willingness (voluntad, buena disposición) to help the affair have a happy ending. Accountable: responsable + =, liable; the person in charge, responsible for the department, responsible for/in charge of council policy (política municipal), the manufacturer is liable for the damage caused. The pressure to do it as everyone else is strong; a -- of 44 Kg to the square metre, high/low --, can you check the tyre --?, because of parental --, she felt the -- of her hand on his shoulder. Weather: tiempo; aguantar, soportar; rock: erosionar; skin: curtir) → it helped South Korea -- C-19 pandemic. Long-standing (antiguo) habit; old traditions, vintage car rallies, in the old-fashioned way, a medicine that has been used from time immemorial. The potential to retard (= + tren: delay/make late) the development is infuriating (desesperante), but nobody react … It looks as though (como si) the pandemic …, have a look at sth/round a house, take a -- at this! (¡mira esto!/¡Échale un vistazo a esto!), a -- (cara) of despair (desesperación). Frequently/often mothers kitting their job to care for children & other relatives display/exhibit (muestran) too much altruism. We care a lot about external validations (convalidaciones) of our choices, we are forced to it. Depending of how widespread (extendido, generaslizado) … & advancing (avanzando, fomentando, adelantando) the goals of Souh Korea feminists. They fight to hold on (aguantarse, esperarse; agarrarse) to their hard-on socal & Ec. gains. The embattled (asediado, en orden de batalla) Spanish government finds difficult answers for a definitive/final battle againt the Co-19. Community centres (centros sociales) & parish (paroquias) are full of/crammed with immigrants needing medical care & other assistances. Sanchez secured a final extension of the emergency, but only by agreeing to let the regional governments fix most of the rules; in Brussels Sanchez's presence was telling (eficaz, reveladora). Initially there will only be enough jabs (pinchazos, inyecciones) to treat the most exposed groups & there remain basic needs that are going unmet (que no están satisfechos). A network of firms with Chinese roots, united by Confucian values of dialogue & drift (movimiento, cambio, significado). Tie-up: vínculo, enlace, (entre empesas) acuerdo → a -- to carry out a project. China's state & diaspora business are mostly a result of happenstance (casualidad), not a master plan. Multinationals which thrive (prosperan) in China without cultural connections are risking a new kind of tensions & some come back to their's own country. This will tap (golpear, pulsar) various sources of data, there was a tap at or on the door, they were tapping their feet in time to the music, he was tapping a rhythm on the table. Its ranks (rangos, categorías; hileras) are set to almost double within a few years. Pull its infrastructure into sth like a workbend (mesa, banco de trabajo) is not easy at all, quite the opposite, quite the reverse. Cleaning at sea is done by teams of divers (escafandristas, buzos, submarinistas), but the results are not ever satisfactory. Tanker (buque cisterna, petrolero), a petrol tanker (un camión cisterna) =/= tankful (tanque) → get a -- of petrol (llenar el depósito de gasolina). Foul (asquear, contaminar, sucio, grosero,Vs) → antifauling tech., defoul a ship's hull. The robot is piloted remotely, he piloted the negotiations through (condujo las negociaciones a buen fin). They have leverage (influencia, palanca) & can choose how to apply it; lever sth up/out/off (levanter, sacar, quitar algo con palanca). Diplomatic risk will loom (surgir, aparecer) large (grande, extenso, importante) for China; it would be better for it to respect the western rules. Freewheeling (desenvuelto, libre, espontáneo, irresponsible) capital flows; the -- (circulación) of traffic, the river --s through the valley =/= the rain has caused the river to burst its banks or to overflow over its banks (se desbordó), water was --ing from the pipe (tubería). Profits have exceeded all our forecasts. Provisión: (funds, accommodations, jobs) provisión, (food, water) suministrar, abastecer, (service, care) prestación. Straits: apuros → be in dire -- (estar en un gran apuro); the Ec. --s we are in (en el que nos encontramos). Harrow (torturar, destrozar), harrowed (destrozado, torturado + tortured) victim), harrowing (angustioso, terrible, conmovedor) → harrowed with the world distracted (distraído, loco), China heightens (aumenta, acrecenta) military tensions. Its deepest dowturn (deterioro) & its sternest (más severo) Ec. test; a stern glance (una mirada severa), he was very stern (duro) with me. Northerners have long resisted mutualisation for fear of underwriting (asegurar, aprobar, respaldar) laxity in the south. Japanese women rebel against painful (dolorosos, penosos) dress codes in the work, always in heels, her toes bleeding. Chinese tanks hidden in a copse (bosquecillo), about as inconspicuously (sin llamar la ateción) as possible & Chinese speedboats had attacked/rushed at (embestido) one of its cutters (patrulleros, guardacostas). Condemned to death, the --ed cell (la celda de los condenados a muerte), the --ed man (el reo de muerte), such conduct is to be --ed. Dead Sea scrolls: (of parchment) rollo; scraps of parchment (pedacitos de pergamino). Apparently bought without looking too closely into their origin; apparently (por lo visto) they're getting divorce, be -- calm (tranquilo), an -- harmless question (una pregunta aparentemente inocente). Curatorial (conservador) official; curatorial expertise (conocimientos de conservación), --'s staff (equipo de conservación de museos). Fewer turists have been swinging by (se han dejado caer por casa) to see its treasures, a sudden swing (cambio) in opinion, they need a -- of 5 % (un desplazamiento de los votos de un 5 %) to win. Faiths reactions have ranged (se han alineado, extendido) from meek (dócil, sumiso) compliance (sumisión, conformidad) to truculent (agresiva, feroz) defiance. Cooperation in tracing (localizar) them, the search for traces of life on Mars, remove all --s of him from the flat (piso, apartamento), there no --s of him having been there, they found --s of an ancient settlement. Dust down/off (desempolvar), there was a thick --, raise a cloud of --, -- storm, he stood (se levantó) & --ed down his suit, -- cloth (trapo de polvo). The growing of human population outruns (sobrepasa, déja atrás) diminishing natural resources. Broadcast: (radio, TV) emisión, programa, (news, rumours) divulgación; --ing satellite (satélite de retransmisiones), the broadcasters deliver slanted (inclinadas, parciales) news & data alongside (al lado de) public- health announcements. Even the freest country is overstepping (se excede), -- the mark (pasarse de raya, excederse). Declare state of emergency (excepción) tended (tendido, desplegado) in Twitter; quick! This is an --!, prepared for any --, there is a national -- (crisis). The Ec. mainstays (pilares, sostenes principales) such as tourism & remittances; remittance advise (aviso de pago). Official tallies (cuentas, totales) → keep the -- of …, tally up (contar, hacer recuento de). Mildly (ligeramente, suavemente) affected, Putin is no doubt feeling smug (creído, engreido), even if that has sent the rouble sliding (caer) & it don't bolster (refuerza) the state. Attendance (asitencia) → is my -- necessaire?, -- figures, money, officer, record; attendant: (car park, museum) guarda, (teatro) acomodador; sirviente. Bare: (pers.) desnuda, (head) descubierta, (feet) descalzo, (landscape) pelado, … → a ghost town, its streets bare but (excepto) for some dogs & homeless people. Trump administration stop receiving apps & suspended hearings (audiencias), he never got a good hearing (nunca se le permitió explicar su punto de vista), within/out of -- (al alcance/fuera del alcance del oído). Their faint hopes of refuge have dimmed (light: bajar, hopes: hacer perder, …) further. He does not thing he would have got better on his own. Trapped (atrapado) on a tropical island after a stint (período) of volunteering for a charity (obra benéfica). Charter (alquilar) a privat jet at their own expense (cuenta) → at my expense, with all --s (gastos) paid. He was holed up (escondico) on a little island, where once fell head first out of a coconut tree. Even if you have a pothole (bache, cueva, grupa) you need to get ahead (adelantar, ir por delante) of the looming catastrophe. Remotely (en lugar apartado) → -- situated, -- related (pariente lejano); it wasn't even -- amusing (ni por asomo era divertido); say the -- (minimamente) interesting, negotiating this stage -- is an unwelcomed (desagradable, poco grata, inoportuna) complication. He wears a mask as he flattens (aplana) chiken breasts at the stall (puesto) outside (frente a) his house; outside the city (fuera de la ciudad). Thrash out: (pb., difficulty) discutir a fondo, (plan) idear, (deal) alcanzar → a deal in future relations is meant to be --ed out. Companies are piling in (se lanzan al ataque) to provide specialisation. Sweeping: (movement) amplio, (view) magnífica, (change) radical; overwhelmingly (arrolladora, aplastante) victory; place -- restrictions on the everyday life. A painful (dolorosa, penosa) conclusion; a slow & -- death, my ankle is still -- (todavía me duele el tobillo), his wrist was -- at the touch, it will be a long & -- process. The failure of reform treaties puts a burden (carga) on the European court of justice (ECJ) & rule of law. German subsidies risk undermining (minar, socavar) the single mrket; Ec. stagnation will poison the €. They show how Germany has moved from its caricature as a deficit-obsessed tightward "agarrado". A respected medical journal retracted (retiró, se retractó de) a high- profile (prominente) paper published a month previously. Language is a telling (blow: certero; argument: eficaz; remark: revelador) clue (pista, índice, indicación) to unacknowledged racial attitudes. The word thug (matón, bruto) is not politically correct; thuggery (brutalidad), thuggish (desalmado, conducta propia de un matón). Wrappers (envolturas), wrapping paper (papel de envolver), under wraps (en secreto, tapado) → keep sth -- --, -- the rug (manta) round your legs. It remains an inescapably (ineludiblemente) inefficient (method: ineficiente; pers.: incompetente; factory, mine, industry: poco productivos) subject =/= productivo: (tierra, fábrica, encuentro) productivo, (negocio) profitable, (de interés) interest-bearing. Keep an eye (vigilar, echar una mirada) on what rival powers are doing trying to defeat you (derrotarle). Chinese settlers overrunning (invadiendo, rebasando) its sparsely peopled east & no help was forthcoming for them (no obtuvieron ninguna ayuda) ↔ new government funds are forthcoming for roads, schools & hospitals. High walled (amuralladas, tapiadas) factories run with paramilitary discipline which hastily (apresuradamente) built housing blocks. The scheme has repeatedly missed his delivery targets as droughts have hit the Yangzi basin (Cuenca). There is a painfully (dolorosa, penosamente) unequal distribution of water in China, but many residents downplay (quitan importancia a) the threat. Takeover: (company) adquisición, compra, (new government) toma de posesión, (Mil.) toma del poder → takeover bid: oferta pública de adquisición (de acciones) (OPA) for a Latinoamerican banks. This bank has not been free of the faults of such institutions, such as bureaucracy & a degree of cronyism. D. Trump doesn't like gentlement agreements & his administration broke this one. For Iberoamerica the loss of its presidency is a big diplomatic defeat. London, New York & Paris not shrugged off (no han hecho caso) of a dot. com crash; he just --ed it off (se encogió de hombros y no hizo caso). One in every four of these operations is done privately (en clínicas privadas) =/= privately the government believes ... We could see the reflection of the earthquacke in the ionosphere (a layer of the atmosphere beyond 75 km. above the Earth's surface). Wring (escurrir, torcer, retorcer) → I'll wring (retorcer) your neck for that, he wrung my hand (me dio un apretón de manos), wring one's hands (retorcerse las manos), eventually we wrung the truth out of them, give the clothes a -- information can be wrung out (sacada, escurrida) of the atmosphere. The movement of high-altitude charged particles in response to passing waves can be picked up in several ways. After understand the basic Science, proceed the second stage: field trails; be on sb's-- (seguir la pista de alguien), pick up sb's -- (dar con alguien). What he said was spot-on (dio en el clavo con lo que dijo), she guessed -- - -- (lo adivinó exactamente). Crude oil: a crash in prices from 2014 to 2016 has sapped appetite for big, risky projects. Customers browsing (curiosear, echar una hojeada) shelves, bockshops. A functoning single market needs an iron will (férrea disciplina), the EU must move closer together to find responses to a wayward (rebelde) Washington. The ongoing (en curso) stokmarket rout (desbandada, derrota aplastante). The erstwhile (antiguos) title-holders =/= -- of nobility. Visa can get away with (bastarle, llevarse) charging more for services. Authorities fed up vith visa are setting up national lookalikes (dobles) & the EU wants payment rails (carriles, vías) it can control; visa will be hard to dislodge. Be quick on the uptake (ser muy listo) ↔ be slow -- -- --. Don't shout! (¡No grites!), the patient couldn't stop screaming (de chillar) =/= I controlled or restrained myself so as not to cry (llorar) ↔ irrepressible (irrefrenable, incontenible). Down the drain (desagüe): perdido → go -- -- -- (perderse, echarse a perder). Putin is hunkered down (agachado, trata de no llamar la atención) in his residence, enlivening (animando) political campaigns. Putin did one of his trademark (marca personal/de fábrica) publicity stunts for TV cameras, donned (ataviado con) a bright yellow pullover/ jumper to compensate the absence of leadership & empathy. Amnesty international, a watchdog (perro guardian, organismo protector) comments that it is staggering (asombroso, pasmoso) that… The Saudis tone down (suavizan) their austere brand of Islam. Their rash (temerario) & ruthless side has been getting more attention; a brainchild (invento, parto del ingenio) of the Prince. Hand over: (power) ceder, (property bussines) traspasar, (tool) pasar, (driving licence, passport) entregar → locked up handreds of Saudy tycoons in a luxury hotel until they handed over chunks of their fortune. Entrance card (pase), -- exam, -- fee, -- hall (vestibule), -- ramp (=). There are twice as much water on Earth as land, but with the thaw of the Poles it will be yet more water =/= deshielo del congelador (defrosting). Stealthy (sigilosos) fighter planes; get into very stealthily (entrar con mucho sigilo). Lacquered (lacado, barnizado) cardboard + varnish (barnizar), nail polishy/nail varnish. Flotadores: rubber rings, (para mediciones) floats → the floats are designed to scuttle themselves at the end of their missions. Plastics objects floating in the sea are get snared (atrapados) in their alimentary canal. Both models feature (ofrecen, están provistos de; se ocupan de; cine: figuran) solar panels. Synchronous (sincrónico) → geo--. Floating vote (voto de los indecisos) =/= plastic floating & jetsam (restos de naufragio). Russia uses larger floating reactors for its nuclear-powered icebreaker. Oil is usually stored in giant ships as the aptly (acertadamente) … Political union is the essential glue (pegamento) of any currency union. Seemingly (aparentemente) doomed (condenao a) … The picture becomes fuzzier (más velloso, más confuso) in today's settling (marco, scenario). The commitments of a shared currency are not easily shaken off (sacudidos, dado esquibazo, liberarse de). It can swiftly bring to bear (poner en marcha) powerful tools in a crisis. Plea: súplica/petición → he made a -- for money, (Jur.) alegato/defensa → a -- of insanity (demencia, locura)/of guilty, non guilty; enter a -- of innocent (declararse inocente). He stood before cameras, his face like thunder (con cara de furia, de pocos amigos). By pitting (enfrentarse con) frugal northerns we could better find a conclusive/definitive (definitiva) solution. The differences are as salient (tan notables); salient (principales) points. The non-partisan (imparcial/fair) prime minister is disappointed from some of his partisan counterparts. The left would be happy to harness (aprovechar) the blow/setback (descalabro) of the right. Euro-zone wards (pupilos) like Greece; he is her -- (él está bajo su tutela). The court rule out (descarta, excluye) C-19 but the citizens asked for new blood tests. Excess: I don't smoke in --, she was sick (harta) of his live of --, the -- of the regime, remove the -- fat from the pork, lose the -- weight. Drug-dealing (traficantes) groups, arms dealer, slave trader, drugs traffic. Farmer's livelihood (sustento) offers an alternative. You are gona (going to) have to spray the room with a paint spray (pistola de pintura), -- the roses with insecticide. It's too steep to land properly; the staff are not -- trained/dressed, I had not -- (como es debido) eaten, sit up -- (como es debido). Pull up coca bushes, -- -- one's roots (desarraigarse), the gun-toting (armado) police --ed him up (lo paró) from speeding. Baton (=, police: porra), tell sb to go to hell (mandar a la porra a alguien). Hazardous (peligroso, arriesgado), dangerous (arriesgadas) ideas. Men working in pairs uproot coca bushes with a shovel & a two-handed tug (tirón, V, remolcador). Farmers were flown in (traídos en avión), so they cannot be identified by the gangs (pandillas). Wipe out (limpiar, pers.: aniquilar, enfermead: erradicar) coca. *Cocaleros* replanted slightly (ligeramente) more, -- better (algo major), -- (levemente) injured, -- less (un poco menos), it smells -- of vanilla. Snort (resoplido, esnifar; whisky: trago) cocaine, he --ed with anger (bufó enojado), he --ed (resopló) with impacience. If erradication reduces supply, the price would rise, raising the incentive to plant more. The forest stretches to the horizon, punctuated (=, reducido) only by the smouldering (el arder lentamente) gaps (claros) where it has been slashed (cortado, sobre todo con machete) to make way for coca bushes. Some well-bounded (bien atadas) solutions, …, it's out of --s to civilians (los civiles tienen la entrada prohibida), set --s (límites) to one's ambitions. A book about facebook paints a vivid (vivo, intenso, fuerte) picture of the firm's size, not in terms of revenues or share price but in the sheer (pura, absoluta) amount of human activity through its services. Dizzying (heighs/numbers: mareantes; speed: vertiginosa) valuations (=). cooling system/tower/fa. Electricity offers big advantages over steam power in terms of both efficiency & convenience (comodidad, ventaja, provecho). Content: contento, satisfacción; contener, contenido. In retrospect (retrospección), the government should have proved the scientist's advise more deeply. Public health services (servicios de seguridad social), which were responsible for testing & tracing, failed. This shortcomings have claimed (reivindicado, reclamado) many victims. Give sth into sb's trust (confiar algo a alguien). As a privileged fantasist (fantaseador) brought up in a manor house (casa señorial). B. Johnson picked up a pair of skimpy (mezquinos) shorts (pantalones cortos) on his gab year (año sabático). Johnson has repainted the Tories as a classless, plain-speaking (lenguaje franco, llano) … Britain will restore trade ties to the Commonwealth. Trade negotiations are likely to be hard-nosed (duras) & uncomfortable (incómodas) for British farmers. Rave at sb (despotricar contra alguien), rave about sth (entusiasmarse por algo). Abandon a rally after being drowned out (ahogado) by chanting (gritones) demonstators. Deal with: ocuparse de → he -- -- all the paperwork; tratar con → you are --ing -- professionals; solucionar → have you dealt with that paperwork yet? On the security side, plans for the UN were fleshed (desarrollados). Bog (ciénaga, pantano) → --ged down (atascada) in Middle east & Aphganistan, America has grown weary (cansada) & inwardlooking (Pers.: intrometido; estado: cerrado en sí mismo). The UN's oil for food programme with Iak led to a $ 1.8 bn. scam (timo, estafa). The structures of UN built in 1945 are not just fit for 2021, let alone beyond it. Outsiders (forasteros, desconocidos) face a forbidding (severo, intimidante) confusion of agencies with acronyms (siglas). Hotting up (animándose, acalorándose) the British empire in India lives on (sigue vivo). Countries of formality are hard to slough (on) (deshacerse de, desprenderse); le's dispense with -- (prescindamos de formalidades). Hold sb in thrall (retener alguien en la esclavitud); be in -- with (ser esclavo de); China is -- of nationalism. This is a time of slumping (de caída de) global demand for China's goods & interrupted supply chains. To repair transatlantic alliances, countries should co-operate in their handling (manejo) of China. He is pitilessly (despiadadamente) clear- eyed (clarevidente) about how China has fobbed Eurpe off (engatusado) with unkept promises. Repression in Xingiang, the far-western region, that China has turned into a police state. France & other EU's countries tighten (hacen más severo) investment rules to shield Covit-battered tech. firms from being snapped up (agotadas); snap up a bargain (agarrar una ganga). Shortlived (efímero). Teem (abundar) → streets --ing with (con mucha) people. Separate the bling (joyas) from the chaff (cascarilla, pienso, paja). Purpose (propósito, objetivo; utilidad) → what is the -- of this tool? We all shared a common --? What was the -- on going?; fashion weeks have been cancelled, repurposed as posh (elegantes) catwalk weblines. Most purveyors (proveedores) of luxury (lujo, artículo the lujo) are European (America is home to some of the lesser (menores) marques. Just reopening, wondering what to do with stocks of pre-Covit-19 vintage (vendimia, cosecha; añada, antiguo). The world of personal luxury goods has been in liberation; most of Chinese buyers purchased in overseas (extranjero), frequently on jaunts (excursiones) to Europe; new ways to get Euro- chi<u>c</u> (elegante) into Chinese hands =/= chic<u>k</u> (pajarito, chavala). Go on a shopping spree (ir de compras gastando mucho dinero). These successes do not compensate for the failures. Rather, they leave America stuck between two poles (palos, postes, mástiles, ...). Mr Trump's expressed commitment to pegging back (hacer perder la ventaja) of a more assertive China was timely (oportuno). A foreshadowing (presagio) of Armaggedon (the war of --: la guerra del fin del mundo) & final political dissolution. Change the world in ways fundamentally inimical (hostiles, adversos) to their creators'interest. Post Covit-19: as Ec. adjust, there is likely to be substantial reallocation of people & resources. Unlock: abrir, (secret) descubir, (mistery) resolver, (potential) liberar → -- the productivity- boosting benefits of new tech. & business models. Keep struggling companies & jobs afloat (a flote) to meet (encontrar, satisfacer) the government deadline (fecha tope): terminar en ese plazo. Anathema (maldición; Rel.: excomunión) → he is anathema for me (no lo puedo ni ver, es inaguantable); the idea is -- to her (la idea le resulta abominable). U. von der Leyen is in charge of the Commission, but is A. Merkel who is the undisputed top dog (mandamás). German hands now grip the EU's levers (palancas) of power, just as the bloc overhauls (replantea, revisa, alcanza) itself to cope with the Covit-19; being coy (tímida, coqueta, reticente) on the European stage, as it used to work well for Germany; for many economists, the model for a Covit-19 furlough (permiso) scheme has been Germany; go under: (emterprise) quebrar, (ship) hundirse → Spanish firms are likely to -- -- due to lack of state support, while stodgy German competitors are kept alive by German taxpayers; undermine fair fight logic: German constitutional court aimed a blow (intentó un golpe) at the ECB's effords to inject more liquidty into Euro-zone Ec.; they brought into (introdujeron) a cause against Germany. During the Euro-zone crisis, the debate over bail-outs was steeped (impregnado) in the idea that diligent Germans were bailing out feckless (débiles, irresponsables) Greeks. Arguments for recovery of funds are couched (redactados) in terms of self-interest (interés propio). The EU is supposed a convergence machine, spreading prosperity rather than embedding (arraigando, incrustando, clavando) differences between rich & power countries. The world needs to work together on vaccines, on economic recovery & to support the most vulnerable countries. Ideas that were once off-limits (prohibidas) such as the long-winded (interminables) politically difficult task of ... American couples are more likely to meet each other through online-dating (de contact) services than through personal contacts. Two calamities that no one can blame him for, even before the kick-off (cominzo del) rally for Catholics. The demand for cash was relatively subdued (suave) + (luz) suave, (pers.) apagada, sumisa, deprimida. Hum (canturrear, zumbar; be busy: bullir, hervir) → the market place was --ming (el merado era un hervidro de actividad). Claw back: take up again (retomar) the ground they once surrended (entregaron, cedieron, se rindieron). In early 1970s the Middle east oil nationalism was stirring (despertaba); members of OPEC were tearing up (rompian, destrozaban) a post-war system in which western oil companies fixed the prise of crude. Electric cars could be charged wirelessly; around 50 Km. of range per hour of charging. Fish writhed (se retorcía) frantically (frenéticamente) in the shallow pool as their schoolmates stranded (se encallaban) on the exposed sandbank (banco de arena) & breathe their last (exhalaban el últmo suspiro); while the bank (orilla) of the river Mekong is so parched (abrasado, reseco) the earth has cracked. In Vietnam visitors have flocked to the desiccated river bed, to se how the measly (miserable, mezquino) flow spurred (estimulaba, espoleaba) saltwater intrusion (=, invasión) in the delta. Exacerbate: (pain, disease) exacerbar, (relations, situations) empeorar → the eleven dams of the Chinese portion -- the water shortage. Panchan Lamas identify each other's reincarnation, so China has tersely (locamente, tercamente) declared … Each of three powers (legislative, executive, judicial) must exerce control & agency (acción) over its fellow branches. Mr Trump alleged hush-money (soborno) payoff (pago, liquidación, recompensa) to an adult film star. The deal/trade war between China & the US left tariffs six times higher. As firms have foundered (fracasaron), fears have mounted that foreign state-supported companies will swoop in (descender bruscamente, hacer una redada) & snap them up (agotarlas). The Chinese giant's networking gar (equipo) lets spooks (espectro, aparición,V, espía) in Beijing eavesdrop (escuchar a escondidas) consumer' communications. Be "particular vigilant" in making sure that businesses are not sold off (liquidados). The fleet (flota) submarine activity is at its highest level since the cold war, for exemple American sallies into the Artic circle; make a sally (hacer una salida). A separate Russian naval force could also target the thicket (matorral) of undersea cables that cross the Atlantic. Buses fill to overflowing (desagüe, rebosar; en exceso), passengers dangling (colgando) out of open doors. The White house has sidelined (marginado, ejercido una actvidad secunaria) the world's premier (primera, principal) pblic-health agency. America has it in for (la tiene tomada con) Huawei, for instance its salvo (reserva, salvedad) against it. America risks "surrendering dominance" to China if it cannot blunt (despuntar, desafilar, debilitar) its 5G supremacy. The scaly (escamoso) anteater/pangolin (oso hormiguero) has the ability to roll into a small ball when threatened. Near the Russian border, the Ortodox Church regains a toehold (punto de apoyo, espacio). Put a curb on (frenar, dominar; spending: restringir) → Vietnam has curbed the virus on the cheap (en plan barato). Europan Ec. is build partly on the promise that northern governments do not unduly aid "their" firms. Never have the rules been loosened to the extend they have been today; politicians are brockering (=, negocian) aid packages. Now a breach has been opened in a set of rules that has curtailed (restringido, acortado) politicians'penchants (predilecciones, inclinaciones) for picking winners. Few countries support the principles behind state-aid rules nowadays, so the new relaxed norms may not endure behind the crisis. Merging companies is one way to create champions, but gorging (atracar) them with state aids is as effective. Smaller & poorer countries worry that their firms (less generously aided) will get globbed (up) (sean engullidas). China has never revealed even a rough, approximate figure (cifra aproximada); China's unchecked (libremente, sin restricciones) build-up (concentraciones) of such weapons. In China there are a glut (exceso) of new coal- fired power stations; nuclear plants & renewable have to elbow then off the grid. Teeter (tambalear, vacilar) on the brink of dissolution (=), for instace Nissan bred (raza, variedad; engendrar, criar) discontent. A failure (fracaso, avería, Med.: crisis, Ec.: quiebra) at some point in the system means the whole thing might grind to a halt (pararse en seco). An approach has shifted from punishment to pre-emption (anticipación, prevención). First drive wedges (abrir brechas) between America & its friends & later develop a layered (por capas) adaptation plan. The guides have braved (afrontado) sheer (absoluto, puro) rock in Everest, mountaineers cling (se agarran, se pegan) to a single (sola) safety rope. Ground crew/staff (personal de tierra); ground troops → its crews & ground staff furloughed (fueron de permiso). D. Trump needs only three points more than his approval ratings (cota de popularidad). Dismal (deprimente, sombrío) backdrop: not bristling (enérgicos) bulletproof vests & few spare (de reserva, sobras; de recambio) armament. Bucking the trend (ir en contra de la corriente) in the European integration & -- -- system (revelarse contra) the dominant states. The $ underpins (sustenta, apuntala) four-fifths of global supply & the Yuan is not yet ready to substitute it. Thousands of seasonal farmhands (obreros agrarios) for the harvest of … Bias: propensión, predisposisión, tendencia → a right-wing -- (tendencia); prejuicio; sesgo → cut sth on the --. A queasy (revuelto, intranquilo) long term rise in borrowing & the unprecedented plunge in demand will up-end (volcar) the industry; what the author skips over (pasa por alto). The frosty (helado, glacial) March embarras its technicians for shody (baja calidad) workmanship (trabajo, habilidad). Its Galaxy devices edged past (pasó con dificultades) Apple's iPhone in sales volume. South korea's third-most-valuable (valiosa) company retain a godlike (divino) status. Those steep (empinadas) descends provide the ideal setting (marco, escenario) for hydropower projects. The river slosh (echa) water away over the border; their neighbours downstream are twitchy (nerviosos). Parched (resecas, muertas de sed) crops, collapsed fisheries, salty farmlands, & as Country's leaders are mesmerised (fascinados) by big projects, bickering (discutiendo) over the flow is a source of discrimination. Even when rainfall a year is normal, siltation (sedimentación, "=") is causing saltwater to intrude (intrometerse) into the Mecong delta. The tributaries flow through China for just a tantalising (tentadores) couple of Km. Even if China's rulers cannot overcome their engineering fetish (obsessión), they could do plenty more to reassure (tranquilizar + calm down) their neighbours. Provide flood warnings to villagers downstream & allow farmers in the lower reaches (alcances) time to prepare. That would send a flood (diluvio, inundación) of gratitude flowing uphill (cuesta arriba). The nightmare scenario (peor panorama) comes from a patch of land he has rented in a nearby (cercano) village. The governments help landing out (repartiendo, distribuyendo) food or regulating prices, but there are suspicions of fraudulently inflating those. Women were trampled (pisoteadas) & police fired (disparó) tear-gas, as thousands of people jostled for a giveaway (regalo, revelación involuntaria) from wellwishers (admiradores). Many are part- time famers, topping up (llenando, dando suplemento a) their earnings with wage labour. While Nigerian polices have put up (aumentado) the brives they extort from drivers, in Uganda vendors sleep in their stalls (quiosco, puesto, caseta; establo). As farmers are lugging (arrastrando) sacks & herding (llevan en manada) goats, the traders have clubbed together (unido fuerzas) to hire them. The lessons of the truncated (=, cortado, omitido, suprimido) drill (taladradora; surco; instrucción, ejercicios) are vital for western war plans; a revived NATO strung (ensartó) 5,000 or so troops in four modest battlegroups. Shifting troops & equipments across borders was a logistical headache (quebadero de cabeza). In the attention-starving (esquivar o evadir) world of EU politics, officials & politicians like to vaunt themselves (jactarse). The court is a mere umpire (árbitro), it simply clears up any confusions left over (dejado, quedado; sobrar) in the bloc's treaties. Today its remit (=, competencias) include everything & is hellbent (resuelta a) federalising Europe. Such a mandate gives EU's judges a scope to roam (rondar, vagar; divagar). Increasingly, judges in national courts have chafed (rozado, irritado, impacientado) rulings (fallos, resoluciones) from their European peers. Indian capitalism: India Inc (incorporated)'s profits are inceasingly preserve (=, conserva; dominio) of a tiny clutch (nidada) of companies. They think that was sobering (alecionador, que da que pensar) news for budding (en ciernes) Americasn capitalists. They include state-controlled remnants (remanentes, restos) of Nehruvian socialism. A stand-up comedian (cómico), stand-buffed (comida tomada de pie). The ballot (votación) measure gained support from politcians of both parties. The snub (desaire) to dismal (sombrío, deprimente, pésima) Science makes they tend to scoff (reirse). Journals have responded to sharp rises on submissions (=, presentación, entrega; propuesta) by working overtime. Jaunty (alegre, garboso) → he replied jauntily (contestó alegremente) =/= jingle (tintineo, bells: tintinear) =/= jingoism/chauvinism (patriotería). Friends & relatives (amigos y parientes); blood relatives; blood relationship/ kindship (parentesco) may entail/involve deafness, dumbness/ muteness & blindness. Show: demostración, manifestacón; -- of hand (votación a mano alzada); Amrican impresive -- (exhibición) of power; exposición; fashion -- (desfile de modelos), (theater) espectáculo. Blasé (desagradable, apático, de mal humor) attitude of premarital sex; born out of wedlock (matrimonio), her childrenbearing years (de edad fértil). Exposed (=, descubiertos) upper arms (brazos superiores), be exposed to the view (estar a la vista de todos) =/= according to what has been stated/set about. Fall short of the targed (no alanzar el objetivo). Reinforcing bar (armadura de hormgón) =/= ironclad/battleship (acorazado); leader clad (con ropa de cuero), concrete -- (revestimiento de cemento). Yarn (hilo; cuento, historia; contar historias) → Trump yarns an history about ... =/= yawn (bostezar) =/= yearn (añorar, anhelar, ansiar) → have a --ing to do sth. Void: vacío → a -- in my life; inválido, nulo, Vs, be --ed (desprovisto) of sth + lack means (estar desprovisto de medios); make the -- (anular, invalidar algo) + they have declared the vote null & void because of irregularities; -- sth. of sb (sacar algo a alguien, ej.: I managed to -- it out from her). Fracasar: mess up, make a mess of, fail, be unsuccessful + bakfire (petardeo,V, fracasar) → his plan --ed on him (le salió por la culata). Keep (guardar)/loose (perder) the count of sth + wear one's hair loose (suelto), the button is -- (por caer), he was chased (perseguido) by a -- (suelto) dog, a dress -- round the waist, a -- confederation of sovereign republics. In compliane (conforme a) your wishes; the result is consistent (conforme) with our expectations; I did it as you told me to; there was no agreement (conformidad) on this subjet. The Ec. was a vortex (torbellino en sentido general) threatening the € zone =/= whirlwind (torbellino de viente), eddy/whirlpool (de agua), dust cloud (de polvo). He threatened to fire me (despedirme). Spirit (espíritu)ed: brioso, lleno de vida; evil (malignos) --s, good/bad -- (alta, baja moral) =/= a moral education, a morally obliged to ..., -- strength. a film with dubious morality, my moral sank (cayó por los suelos) when ... Dear (querido, caro) friends, he's a -- boy, but rather impetuous; the values & beliefs which our society holds -- (aprecia), your country is very -- to me (tengo su pais en mucha estima) + our beloved country. Relinquish (renunciar, ceder (sth to sb) → she --ed his grip on my arm (me soltó el brazo). Keep pace with her (seguirle el ridmo), at a slow -- (ridmo), the -- of city life (ridmo de vida) =/= a very good or strong sense of rhythm, clap in time to the music, Paris sets the fashion trends, fast pace of he work, heart rate, I'll do it at my own pace, flat out (a todo ritmo). Stand proxy for sb (representar a alguien), vote by --, I gave him -- (autorización, poder) to act on my behalf (nombre), (document) poder de representación =/= in this painting the vulture represents death political parties represented in parliament, the Spanish delegation in the fair, I went as a representative of the company, diplomatic representation. I envy his luck (suerte), with a bit of -- we can win, be in -- (estar de suerte), this is my lucky number, how unlucky! Good --! =/= lock (cerradura, cerrar) → put sth under -- & key (guardar algo bajo llave) =/= lack (carencia) of resources, sleep & originality, there was no -- of applications for the job, he --s self-confidence (confianza en sí mismo). Tablet/pill (pastilla) gallantly (galantemente) provided (pr<u>o</u>vista) by ... =/= they didn't have enough food with them, the TV comes with remote control included =/= the reunion planned (pr<u>e</u>vista) for the 20th, it started on time (a la hora prevista), every thing went as planned. Fairly: justamente, equitativamente; bastante → I'm -- sure; fairness (justicia, imparcialidad) → in all -- (a decir verdad), he had to admit that she had a point (que ella llevaba algo de razón). Promote sales, promote/encourage & boost industry + sales promotion, it's on offer =/= (class, year): promoción → the 1975 class, he was from my class/year. Manner (actitud, moda, estilo) → -- of paiment, in a -- of speaking (por así deirlo), I don't like this -- (forma de ser); manners: modales → forgot one's -- (perder la compostura), -- of adversaries; (costumbre) a novel of -- (cosumbrista). Bedraggled: (pers.) desaliñada, (hair, feathers, fur) enmarañados, (flowers) mustias =/= begrudge (envidiar + envy) → -- sb sth, I don't -- him his sucess, I don't -- all the money I've spent, I -- (me da rabia, me duele) his attitude. Desordenar: (hábito) make untidy, mess, (fichas, hojas) got out of order; the burglars turned the home upside down/in a terrible mess =/= (causar confusión) throw into confusion. Spare: there's a -- blanket if you're cold, keep a -- (de reserva) pair of glasses, I leave a -- key with the neighbour, -- nobody (no dejar títere con cabeza), tear sb to shreds (tiras, trozos, trizas; triturar, …): dejar a alguien como un trapo. Her daughter disappointed her, she has been --ed in love, terribly --ed when she hears the news, havig to give up the career. Deshacer: loose my belt, (nudo, lazo) untie, undo, (costura) unpick, (maleta) unpack, (paquete) undo, unwrap, (cama para cambio de sábanas) strip → what had been done couldn't be undone. Aspecto: I don't like the look of him, he looked like an executive, a healthy- looking man, look well (tener buen aspecto), outward appearance (aspecto exterior), the aspects to bear in mind (a tener en cuenta) when …, all aspects of an issue. Roughness (aspereza, rudeza) of a fabric (tela). Astucia: astuteness, cleverness, guile, schrewdness, cunning → act cunningly, crafy. Cumplir: (orden, deseo, amenaza) carry out, (condiciones, normativa) comply with, (plazo) to expire → spiry data (fecha de vencimiento), (obligación, deber) fulfill a duty; fulfilling a remarkable forecast (pronóstico). Engañar: they lied to their mother, you have been had!, this river is deceptive (It's deeper than it looks), the alliance was a sham (farsa), the victim of a swindle (timo), racketer (chantajista, timador). The influx of Greek scholars & texts after Turkish conquest of Constantinopla (1453) changed the world: for the first time world physicians had direct access to ancient Greck learning, so the Renaissance. Guardar: he keeps everything, keep the concert tickets, store it in the warehouse, keep/save me a bit of cake (tarta), keep me a place (asiento), keep my place in the queue, I have fond memories (buenos recuerdos) of that time (época), keep calm (-- la calma), keep in secret, I have no ill feeling (rencor) towards him, keep silent/quiet (silencio). Escapar: don't run away, I need you; escape → there is no -- from this prison; flee, fled, fled (huir) → -- de country, they fled to the mountains =/= fly, flew, flown (volar) → fly the nest (abandoner el nido). Less: fruit--, effort--, tire--, thank-- (ingrato), defence-- (indefenso), use--, taste-- (inodoro), odour-- (insípedo), root-- (desarraigado), pain-- (indoloro), worth-- (inútil, sin valor), match-- (inigualable) beauty, count-- (infinidad) times (de veces) =/= inefectiveness (ineficacia), nervousness & restlessness (nerviosismo) … → ineffective measures, inefficient person. Depth: (water, hole, shelf) profundidad → at a -- of 4 m., (room, building) fondo. Coser: sew, (herida) stitch ↔ unstitch, unpick =/= desencajar: (mandíbula) dislocate, the smash (choque) pushed the joint out of position =/= detach: despegar/separar algo. Neighborhood (barrio) → smart (alto) --, working- class (obrero) --; suburbio: suburb, slum area/quarter (barrio) on the outskirts (alrededores) of a town; residential district (barrio residencial); outlying (distante) area. His contract runs out/expire (expira, vence); expiration (vencimiento + espiración) ↔ inhalation =/= she got the inspiration to compose a song, the wars have provided for many nobels, Spanish inspired ballets. Popular: (cultura) popular; (música) popular, folk; (lengüaje) popular, colloquial; (de clase obrera) working-class neighbourhood, (muy conocido) a very popular actor. I'm so worried, … It's about so (más o menos así) high. Rock (mecer) → she --ed the child in her arms, his death --ed (sacudió) the fashion business, the ship --ed (se balanceaba) gently (suavemente) on the waves =/= rack (estante, rejilla, portaequiàjes, ...), racket (follón, raqueta) =/= I racked (sacudí) my brains over: me mate penando; -- with doubt, -- with pain (sufrir dolores atroces), -- with guil<u>t</u> (atormentado de culpabilidad) ↔ guil<u>d</u> (gremio).). Look after (cuidar, atender, vigilar), -- into (investigar, estudiar, considerar), -- through/over (revisar, chequear), -- on/upon (considerer), -- (around) for sth (buscar algo), I just --ed in (pasé) to say hellow (a saludarles). Tuck: meter, ej. the blanket (manta)/ sheet (sábana) under the mattress, his office is tucked away (guardada, escondida) in a nondescript (sin nada particular) building. Stalk (talllo, pedúnculo, tronco; acechar, acosar) =/= Stem: tallo, pedúnculo; (Ling.) raiz → -- from (provenir de), (flow) contener, (outbreak, decline) detener. The film was a failure/flop (fracaso), the book fell flop (dió un golpe) on the table. Mind-numbing (soporífero, inclinado al sueño) =/= mind-numbly (atontado) =/= I had a feeling of numbness (entumecimiento) in my legs. Choke: starter, ahogado por el humo/espuma =/= smother: (pers.) asfixiar, ahogar, (fear) dominar, (flames) apagar, (giggle: risita) reprimir, (opposition) acallar, (his anger) dominar. Bully: acosar (ej. el escolar)/intimidar (ej. he --ed him); matones → matonismo (thuggishness) + thug (voyau, gangster); bully (acosar) firms into saving (salvar) jobs; bullish: (market) alcista, (attitude, forecast) optimista. Breakdown: (machine) avería, (services, communications) interrupcción, (business) fracasar, (Comp.) colapso; electrical --, -- in traditional values, -- services (de servicios de asistencia en carretersa), -- truck (grúa). Rigged (amañado) system =/= rugged: áspero, escarpado, (engine: motor) resistente, (condiciones, facciones) duras, (estilo) tosco, rudo, grosero, -- countenance (semblante/rostro duros. That's just the trouble (allí está la madre del cordero), be in great -- (estar muy apurado). Lock (cerradura, cerrojo; esclusa; mechón) =/= bolt (tornillo, cerrojo; desbocar). Ancho: (river, way, bed, table) wide; (face, hands, shoulder) broad, (wall) thick, (trousers) loose, (swimming pool, measurement) width =/= enlarge: (socios, membership) aumento, (photo, picture, area, trousers) agrandar, (vein, pore, heart) dilatar, (room) ampliphy, lenghten one's stride. The novel reflects the social problems, she wore a worried expression (su expresión reflejaba inquietud), -- of the light/of public anease, good --es =/= metallic glint. Dash: (unas gotas/poco) of vinegar, chorro, a -- rash for the exit, -- in/out, 100 m -- (lisos), the waves are --ing against the rock, -- sth to the ground. Dread (terror)full: terriblemente lleno, fill sb with --, I -- (tengo pavor) going to dentist =/= dreary (gris), (trabajo, vida) monótonos (=), deprimidos (depressed). Come to terms with (asumir, asimilar + "=") the failure of its model; be in bad terms with sb (llevarse mal con alguien) =/= the major should take or assume responsibility for the accident. Come around → -- round: -- -- (pasa por casa) whenever you like, (convencerse) she'll soon -- -- to my way of thinking; he came -- after five minutes, he'll soon -- -- (se le pasará pronto, ya se calmará); -- -- (llegando) to the long-held British view that … The closest bank is in the next street downwards; the closest relative (pariente) gives sb a hug (abrazo), I hugged my knees to my chest, the ship --ged the shore (avanzaba pegado a la costa). Be glat about sth (felicitarse). Trap: trampa, atrapar, (liquid, gas, light, heat) retener + his family is what keeps him there, they held or detained the immigrants at customs, keep o retain the league title, a last-minute phone call held me up or kept me back at the office. Convey: --ed (llevaron, transmitieron) kind (clase, amables) regards (consideraciones); (goods, oil) transportar, (personas) conducir, acompañar) =/= transmitir: (radio, TV) transmit, (programa) broadcast, (bienes, recados, saludos) pass on, (enfermedad) give, pass on, (Jur.) transfer. Play down/downplay (disminuir de importancia) =/= downsides (pegas, desvetajas) =/= downsize (disminuir la plantilla, el tamaño). Take a back seat (meterse en segundo plano); whoever/whoever (quienquiera) doesn't know that can have no hope of passing (aprobar) lenghty (extenso, largo y pesado) document. Whack: intento,V → another --; parte → he want his --; golpe, porrazo,Vs → -- the contenders (competidores) with the cudgel (porra) proffered by … =/= wacky: chalado, extravagante =/= wicked (cruel, malvado). Brood: (birds) nidada, (mammals: mamíferos) camada, (pers.) prole; estar melancólicos → for those whom -- about Israel's influence in American politics. Looters (saqueadores) ransacked (registraron, saquearon, obra lit.: fusilaron) … Placard/banner (pancarta), sing/notice (letrero) → neon sign; entertainment guide (cartelera de espectáculos en el diario), publicity board (cartelera de cine y teatro), bulletin board/notice board (tablón de anuncios). Scuttle (escotilla del barco, hundir el barco) the inquiry: desperdiciar el plan, sabotear la investigación =/= risk of scuppering (hundir el barco, echar el plan por tierra) his second term. Britain at the heigh of the empire was distracted (trastornada + disrupted, disturbed, upset) by the grief (dolor, pena profunda)/by the noise, from his work. Noticeable (perceptible, evidente) → --y: we got -- (sensiblemente, perceptiblemente) colder the higher we wend (a medida que subíamos). Cumbersome/cumbrous (torpe y pesado). Stockpiles (reservas, almacenes) of rice with price support scheme (=, plan) =/= scheming (intrigante, maquinador) =/= intellect schasm (abys) =/= sham (falso, fingido). Recuperación: (Ec.,, dinero, enfermo) recovery, recuperation, ej. after a pest, a plague or blight (roya, plaga, arruinar), (edificio) restoration. Cartoons (dibujos animados) lampooning (satirizando) him =/= spoof (burla, parodia) =/= stooge (títere + puppet, lackey) =/= the histrionic (cómico, con payasadas) pageantry (pompa, boato) tinged (matizado) with regret (pesar, arrepentimiento, lamentación, Vs). Jettison (echar al mar, deshacerse de, prescindir) of scores (resultados, puntuaciones …) of flawed (erroneas, defectuosas) assumptions. Portray (retratar, describrir) as a hapless (desventurado, desafortunado) egghead (lumbrera + whiz(z): ser un as en algo) =/= bigwig (pez gordo) =/= boffin (cerebrito) =/= bigheaded (engreido, cabeza gorda) =/= hotshot (personaje celebre) =/= highbrow (intellectual) =/= ringleader (cabecilla) =/= pointy headed (intelectualoide). Rife: (corrupción) abundante, (inflación, paro) hacer estragos, -- with errors/unrest =/= rip (desgarrar) out/ off (arrancar) =/= madurar: (fruta) ripen, (plan, pers.) mature. Obstreperous (escandaloso) =/= shoking (horrible, vergonzoso, escandaloso) =/= outrageous (escandaloso, vergonzoso, atroz) =/= excruciating (atroz, horrible, insoportable) noise, pain =/= harrowing (angustiosa, terrible) experience. Let out: (visitor) acompañar a la puerta, (prisoner) poner en libertad, (del corral/aprisco) dejar salir, let me out! (¡déjenme salir!, they are -- -- of the school at four, let the aire out of the tyre, let the water out of the bath, (secret, new) contar, revelar, -- out of the contract (eximir de las obligaciones contractuales), (yell: grito, chillido,Vs) soltar, guffaw: (carcajada) soltar. Equate with sth (corresponder a, ej.: a la idea que tienes de algo) → -- sth with sth (equiparar algo a algo, comparar dos cosas). Drag (arrrastrar) → she --ed herself over the Tf., be --d to a ridiculous plan, the meeting really --ed (duró mucho), -- on: (business, speech) hacerse largo y pesado, -- away (llevarse a la fuerza). Intake: air/gas/agua intake (entrada), protein -- (consumo), an -- (toma) of 100 students, hazardous (peligroso) drinking habit of alcohol intake. Dodgy (mal funcionamiento, mala pinta, arriesgado) =/= dogged (emperrado, obstinado) + (perseguido) --ed by ill luck =/= underdog (el que tiene menos posibilidades, desamparado, desvalido). Whistleblowers (que desvelan una situación interna ilegítima). Welding (soldadura) =/= wield: (espada) blandir, (cuchillo) manejar, (influencia) ejercer ↔ un-- (difícil de manejar). Pickup: (wages, sales, prices) increase; (Ec.) mejorar, -- point (lugar de recojida), -- truck/arm ↔ he is unpicking (descosiendo, deshaciendo) a rent control law. Lash (látigo, azote, azotar), lashing (azote) of the sea, of the wind → the wind --ed the sea into a fury, the rain --ed against the window, he --ed at the donkey =/= bash (golpear) with oomph (brío) to fuse (fundir) sth + blow a fuse. Sewage (aguas residuales) → -- system (red de alcantarillado/cloaca (sewer); -- disposal (plantas de tratamiento de aguas residuals); -- works. A roaring/thunderous (estruendoso) business. Caution: cautela,V, advertencia; he ignored (hizo caso omiso) of my warnings, a warning shot, let this be a warning to you (espero que esto te sirva de advertencia). Relations marred (estropeadas) by fraught (tenso) disagreement + the relations between the two are very strained, it's a very tense situation. Torpe: clumsy, awkward, heavy =/= necio (dim, slow) → I'm very dim (débil, tenue, poco ptometedor, tarugo) or slow when it comes to (para) computers, how clumsy o stupid of me! I'm afraid I've offended her. Perseguir: (fugitive/fleeing, prey: presa) pursue, chase, (hound/harass: acosar) hunt, (ideology) persecute those who opposed; hounded by the press; he pestered me to lend him the car. Sound: sonido, (tocar) the horn, -- retreat (retirada) =/= (door bell, Tf.) ring, (claxon) blow, (instrument) play; it sounds funny (raro, gracioso), hollow, metallic, worried). Do the disches (limpiar los platos); sell sth for a mess of potage (vender algo por un plato de lentejas), it's not my cup of tea (no es mi plato favorito). Pretty: (bonito, guapo) → he thinks good looks are all he needs in life (va de guapo por la vida), who's brave enough to go in first? (¿quien es el guapo que entra primero?), (bastante) → -- goods results. Border: frontera, borde, limitar con → the -- is uneven (irregular) =/= kerb (borde de la acera), on the verge (borde) of collapse, you were very nasty (borde) to him, get stroppy/nasty (ponerse borde) with him .... Foreground (primer plano) ↔ background (al fondo), b of the strike, b (antecedents) of the story (caso), CV, ambiente. Rozar: I brushed past her (al pasar), the table scraped the wall, the ball chaffed the post, the arrow gazed the ear, the seagull skimed over the sea, (family/politics & make fire) friction. Ordinary/every day: normal, corriente, ordinario, de cada día → ordinary/common people (de la calle) ↔ out of ordinary (fuera de lo común), they have a serie of features in common. Overpower: dominar (the guards …): the guards were overpowered (dominados) by the attackers, by the sound (aturdidos), by the smell (mareados), by the head (sofocados), by a person (intimidados). Swallow (golondrina, tragar) one's feeling: tragar saliva; the tablet will be easier to swallow with a little of water; I bit my tonge (tragué saliva) out of respect for his father. Healthiness (salud, salubridad) → get better (mejorar de salud), enjoy good health, the country's moral welfare (salud moral), be prepared/take precaution (curarse en salud) before the explosion. Selfconscious (tímido, cohibido) → his -- (su sentio del ridículo)ness: timidez + shyness, timidity, coyness =/= unconscious ↔ aware, conscious. The sense of the word, he sensed (percibió) sth in the darkness, common sense, sense/lack of responsibility, (sense, feeling, sensation) of space, in a sense (en cierto sentido) =/= a whistle was the signal for them to keep quiet (se callasen), warning -- has gone, -- (hacer señas) to the helicopter, distress (de socorro, auxilio) -- =/= Road/stop/traffic signs, the sign the things are improving, sign of cross, plus/equal/minus --. They availed/took advantage (aprovecharon + made good use of …) of the darkness to escape; it's of no avail (no sirve para nada) =/= take profit: realizar beneficios. A dismal (triste, sombría, pésima) place of the World Bank ranking: strikingly (sorprendentemente extra) bold (atrevidas, audaces) promises. Glitzy (ostentoso, deslumbrante) ads (advertisements) lure (ceba, encanta, atrae,Vs) students. Lust: (dinero) codicia + greed, covetousness; (poder) ansia + yearning/lounging for freedom/love; deseo, (sexo) lujuria + lechery =/= Europe covets (codicia) Chinese investments. Greed (avaricia) blinds (deslumbra + dazzle: --ed by the light, --ed (deslumbrado) by his knowledge of the world. Far-off (lejano) → in the not distant future (en un futuro no muy lejano), in those distant or far-off times =/= a far-out (extraña, muy moderna, genial) Ec. frontier is snapped up (agarrada) by hungry investors. Screaming (llorosos) eyes, blood -- from the cut, --s of people (torrente de personas) ..., people --ed into the hall, water --es from the cracked (agrietada) pipe, light --ed (entraba) through the window, tears -- from the cheeks, go against the -- (corriente) ... Continuar: continue her studies abroad, went on/continued his life as if nothing has happened, his disciples continued/carried on/went on with the work. Draw: sorteo, lotería; Sp.: empate (courtain, bolt) descorrer, -- your chair up to the table, a car --n by a horse, the chairman (president) --s the meeting to an end/a close, (tooth/cork) sacar, (sword) desenvainar, -- water from a well, he drew a $ 100 bill from his wallet (cartera, billetera), -- blood, -- money from a bank, -- a conclusion, --n into (envuelto en) the argument, -- the attention to sb, -- the story out of him (sonsacarle lo que había pasado), dibujar/trazar un plan. Distort: (distorsionar, deformar) the plans; artists can deform limbs, the impact (=) disorted or deformed the chassis, if you keep pulling at your sweater you'll put it out of shape, the heat warped the wood. Maternity leave (permiso), he asked for permission to leave the meeting, excuse me but I must go (con permiso de Uds. me voy), excuse me, may I come in? (¿Se puede?), driving licence (permiso de conducir), gun licence, export licence, residence permit, planning permission o building permit. Swing: movimiento → with a quick -- of his axe he felled the tree; cambio → a sudden -- in opinion, oscilación → the -- of the market; ritmo → be in full -- (estar en pleno apogeo), columpio → have a swing (columpiarse); balancearse/oscilar → it --s in the wind, he was --ing his legs, the pendulum swung back & forth, the door --s on its hinges (bisagras), his mood (humor) --s wildly (descontroladamente); -- bridge (puente giratorio). Ruina: the alcohol will be his downfall (ruina, caída, perdición); he was on the wedge/fringe of (financial) ruin, the venture (empresa) ruined him, they have discovered some Roman ruins. Clutch (embrague, poder; garra + claw) → put in/depress (apretar) the clutch ↔ release the clutch; fall to sb's clutch. Unwary/careless/rash/imprudent =/= weary (cansado, cansancio; pesado, aburrido)some: fatigoso, pesado, aburrido; wearied (cansado) of the city/of sb/of the travel; do the weariest (lo más imposible) to succeed. Toll (peaje; nº de víctimas → the death -- in the roads; efectos graves → the disease takes a heavy -- each year; provocar daños) → the severe weather has taken his -- on the crops. Break up (descomponer, disolver; desguazar, separar)→ they broke up after ten years of mariage =/= breakup (fracaso de las negociacines, desintegración familiar, ruptura de matrimnio, disolver un partido político, desmembrar una empresa) =/= break out: (prisioneros) fugarse, (guerra, epidemia) estallar, (lucha, discusión) producirse. Enlist: (alistarse) in sth, (soldados, miembros) reclutar, (ayuda) conseguir + he always achieves (consigue) what he sets out to do (se propone); they won or gained (consiguieron) an absolute majority; if we keep trying we'll manage to (lo conseguiremos), I managed to pass the examen. Distrust (desconfinza) → --ful (desconfiado de, receloso) & doubtful/uncertain (dudoso); (pers.) estar dudosa: be undecided, be in two minds; use of suspect or dubious tactics. Workers council (consejo de empresa), advisory board (-- asesor), board of directors (-- de administración), court-martial (consejo de guerra), cabined meeting (consejo de ministros), editorial board (consejo de redacción), Security council (Consejo de cegdad). Cue: entrada → give sb his --, that gave me my -- (eso me sirvió de indicación), come in on -- (entrar en el momento preciso), take ones's -- from sb (seguir el ejemplo de alguien). =/= clue: pista, indicio, indicación → give sb a --; a -- about his whereabouts (paradero) ↔ clueless (sin pistas) =/= they clung (se pegaron) one another, the smell -- to the clothes. Rally: =, (Ec., Med.) recuperación; (pers.) unir, congregar; concentrarse, miting) → -- behind sb (soportar, solidarizarse con). Internet gateway (puerta, acceso)/access. Feedback (reacción, retroalimentación) of the staff (del personal); there was a negative/positive -- from customers =/= setback/mishap (revés, contratiempo) =/= upset: volcar, tirar, derramar; ofender, disgustar, (distress) afectar, (planes) desbartar; contratiempo, malestar =/= turmoil (confusión, desorden). Hasta: as far as, up to → the water came -- -- -- ..., their land stretch -- -- -- the mountains, -- -- -- the eyes can see; until eleven, to date ↔ later, from now on. Squeamish (escrupuloso, delicado, aprensivo: ve en todo peligros para la salud) =/= finicky (maniático, demasiado delicado, melindroso) =/= prudish (santurrón, mojigato, beato) =/= prudent (prudente). Facebook outshines (eclipsa) google in advertisers affectations (afectaciones: pedantería, que no existe naturalidad) =/= love/affection (=, cariño) → he showed great love or affection for his daughters, lack of affection, win sb's --, I've a great -- for him, "pero" great displays (muestras, demostraciones), she takes loving care of her plants, I've fond memories of it. Stage (escenario, etapa, organizar; poner en escena/escenificar → the dull (soso, aburrido, apagado, desanimado) leader stages a come back; set the -- for sth (crear el marco idóneo para algo), he occupies the centre of the political -- (escena), the project is still in its early --s, the war was in its last --. Tempest/storm → a sudden -- sweeping away (barriendo, arrasando; azotando) a pond; there was a poltical storm (hubo un gran revuelo político), take a town by -- (por asalto). Conceal: (object, news) ocultar, (emotion, thinking) disimular → ensconced (acomodado, instalado) → -- o.s., -- in the capital's prime (de primera) properties (=, inmuebles). Premise: (=, que va delante, cada una de las dos -- de un silogismo; local, establecimiento) → licensed premises (locales donde se permite vender bebidas alcohólicas). Flicker (destello, parpadeo) → he said it without a -- of expression (sin inmutarse), (vibrar, parpadear, vacilar) → the candel --ed & went out. Compromiso: commitment, pledge; he has undertaken/pledged to bring them up (educar, crier) in this faith; undertaking: tarea, compromiso, empresa, garantía + guarantee, warrant,Vs. → not such undertaking has been given by them. Slight chances of ... Falso: (billete) counterfeit, (cuadro, documento) forget, (joya, news) fake, false testimony, false information & false statement, (jurar en falso) perjury, (falso/a (bogus) queja, médico, policías. Pesky (latoso, molesto) =/= chirp: decir alegremente; gorjeo, chirrido, piar + tweet =/= perky/chirpy: (alegre + happy, cheerful, lively); (animado + cheerful, lively, in good spirits). Sorrow (dolor, pena, aflicción) overwhelmed (aplastó, abrumó, oprimió, agobió, venció) him. Overwhelmed with grief (dolor, pena, tristeza)/ with joy (rebosante de alegría) → grievous: (loss) dolorosa, (grief; pain: dolor físico) fuerte, (clash/blow: golpe) severo, (task, job) penoso, (crime, murder) gave; grievance (injusticia, motivo de queja). Handsome (apuesto, bello, noble) → --ly (habilmente, generosamente, espléndidamente) their audiences ("=", público, espectadores) bellow (rugen, braman) their scorn (desprecio, menosprecio). A flurry (oleada) of emotion; of wind (ráfaga), a flurry (aluvión) of proposals =/= the flags fluttered (se agitaban, en revuelo) alongside each other (juntas codo a codo) =/= flatter (halagar, favorecer) ↔ unflattering (poco alagüeño) =/= flatten (allanar) =/= glaring: (luz) deslumbrante, (injusticia) grande, (flaw: defecto) flagrante, evidente. Curl: bucle, curva..., (hair) rizo, (smoke) espiral, (chard/paper) arollar, (snake) enrollarse sobre, (leaf) abarquillarse, (waves) encresparse, -- up (acurrucarse + snuggle). He got nothing out/ derived no benefits (provechos) from the course (rumbo, curso de río, curso universitario); for his own benefit (bien, provecho) =/= make profits (ganancias); sell sth at a profit, take profits (realizar beneficios). Hark back to (recordar, volver a) → he is always --ing back to that (… con la misma canción); -- -- to the XVIII century (tener su origen en). Snap: ruido seco, brio/energia, instantanea, it's a -- (está tirado) → -- up a bargain (llevarse una ganga), our stock was --ed up (se lo llevaron) at once (enseguida). They piled into him (se avalacharon/arremetieron contra él), be piled into the car, he made a pile (montón, dineral) in the deal. Scope: (of a job) magnitud, (for action, …) libertad, oportunidad, (range of law, activity) ámbito, (capacity of persons, minds) alcance, (room for manoeuvre) campo de accion. Teeter (tambalear, titubear) =/= titter (risa tonta ahogada) =/= taut (tenso, tirante) =/= tout: (ir a la caza) for customers, (idea, producto) promocionar; vender información privilegiada; revender tickets; the theme is --ed (re)vendido, ofrecido) as a spur (estímulo) for talking =/= tatty (gastado, estropeado) =/= utter: completo, total → he's an -- fool; pronunciar, decir → he didn't say a word; I --ly (completamente) despise (desprecio) him. Peek (miradita → no --ing! = don't peek), -- over the fence, -- around (por detrás) the courtains; -- in at the kids (echarles una mirada) =/= peep: espiar, asomar, echar un vistazo → -- under the dress =/= pep (energía, dinamismo) up: animar, estimular; peppy (lleno de vida). Buff Shine/polish: lustrar. Buff (aficionado, entusiasta; lustrar) → jazz -- ↔ rebuff (desaire, rechazo,V) of unknown authorship (autoría) =/= bluff: prosaico, categórico; embaucar, farolear. Bone up (estudiar, ponerse al día sobre; empollar) =/= empollar (Zoo.): hatch =/= cram (estudiar/empollar, meter → -- money into his pokets =/= swot (empollón) up: empollar para un examen. A well-off (con dinero) neighbourhood that kick in (puerta: derribar; apoquinar/contribuir). The shaming (vergonzoso) of tax havens is fraught (tenso, difícil) with (cargado de) folly (locura)/danger); it is disgraceful that (es vergonzoso que). Flick with the tail, -- the hair out of my eyes, -- a duster (drapo) round the room (al conjunto de los muebles) =/= Click (golpe seco) → the door --ed shut; taconeo, chasquido de dedos y lengua; -- with sb (congeniar, gustarse). Fret (preocuparse) ful: inquieto + anxious, worried =/= faithful (fiel, digno de confianza); in an atmosphere (clima) of confidence (confianza), a reliable (de confianza) person, mutual trust (confianza mutual), speak to s.o. you trust, a product I have complete faith or confidence in. His political party is readying (se prepara) for bruising (penosa, violenta, dolorosa) defeat =/= dent (abollar, causar efecto, hacer mella) America's idea. Move on: (tiempo) pasar, (multitud) hacer circular; cambiar → things have moved on =/= move out: (pers., objeto) desalojar, (tropas) retirar, -- -- (muda) of a flat. Race: carrera → we --ed (nos dimos prisa), it was a -- to finish in time, the arms --, they --ed a vintage (antiguo; cosecha, vendimia, añejo; año: excelente) car (de 1919- 30); competir → the elections will be a very close --, -- against sb; raza. Spot: mancha,V → -- of blood/grease, on the -- (en el acto), pizca, dar cuenta, precio del momento; grano → she broke out or came out in --s (le salieron granos en la piel), lugar → I always have to be in the -- (de servicio), lunar → a red dress with white --s. Get into a trouble (pb, molestia, preocupación) =/= muddle/mix-up (lío, confusión) =/= fuss (alboroto, escándalo, conmoción, bulla) → such a -- to get a passport. Strewn (esparcido, desparramado) → the terminals's run-down (débiles, en decadencia, con salud que declina) moorings (amarraderos) are -- in the whole region =/= run down: (pers.) tropezar con, battery (agotarse), (decrease/drop) disminuir, (pedestrian) atropellar. Seethe: borbotear (agua en ebullición), hervir, estar furioso + fume =/= dither (estar nervioso, titubear, vacilar) =/= tether (soga,V, cadena)ed: atados, amarrados =/= sheaths (fundas, cubiertas,V) being passed off (hechas pasar) as popular brands. Outlay: (gastos, desembolsar + pay out, lay out) =/= layout: (building) plan, distribución; (city, garden) trazado, (newspaper) diseño, maqueta =/= lay out: diseñar, arreglar, desembolsar/invertir; dejar sin sentido, fuera de combate. Hover: (pájaro) planear, (pers.) rondar →

-- where soaring (planeadores) birds do → hover about/around (revolotear), -- (ronda) 40$ =/= vacuum cleaner or hoover (aspiradora), hoover (pasar la aspiradora), it hoovered up (aspiró) all the profits; -- -- unexpected surpluses. Spotter (observador) of a plane to feed him with information =/= spatter: (blood, mud) salpicar, (wine/water on the floor) sprinkle, (mud, painting) splash, the host of islands dotted about (que salpican) the ocean. Restricted (restringido, limitado) =/= restrained (cohibido/reservado; sobrio, moderado) =/= strained: tenso/crispado, (Ec.) débil → straitened circumstances (condiciones difíciles). Shredded (triturado) of lowgrade (de baja calidad) components; shredder: (papel) trituradora + (crushing, grinding) machine, (vegetales) cortador, (basura) garbage disposal unit, waste disposal unit. Wrath cólera, ira) → the -- of God =/= wreath (engalanar, adornar, ceñir, coronar) + lay --e (coronas, guirnaldas) of poppies (amapolas) at the cenotaph (=, tumba vacía). Made principals (=, escuela: directores) accountable (responsible) of the students's unwillingness or reluctance =/= the accountant (contable) is responsible for test scores (puntuaciones); made it easier to sack bad teachers. Bump (sacudida; golpe, choque)y: (surface, way) accidentados, (trip, flight) agitados =/= accidental: (no deliberado) unintentional, (fugaz) brief, transient, a temporary job. Skewed (desvió, torció) medical science, alter the course of or divert the river, change the subject (conversación), they dissuaded him from his intention, turn sb from their vocation, wean sb away from bad company. Coax (sonsacar) sth from/out of sb =/= coax sb into (convencer) of doing sth + you won't convince/persuade me otherwise (de lo contrario), they persuaded me to vote for them, we are not entirely convinced, I'm not very impressed with her latest record, his speech failed to win over (convencer) the voters. Enchufar: (Electr.) plug in, (objectos) fit in/together, (en el trabajo) set/lined up for secretary, get a cushy job, wrangle (arreglárselas para coger) o.s. a job. Canvases (lienzos, lonas) & prints (grabados) → under canvases (en tienda de campaña) =/= canvass: (Pol.) hacer campaña (to campaign), sondear, (pedidos, voto, …) solicitor, discutir, (idea) proponer. Chase off (ahuyentar + frighten off/away); drown one's sorrows in wine (ahuyentar las penas con vino). =/= stave off: (derrota, desastre) evitar → He --ed off (no volvió a) drink. Relieve: (pain) calmar/aliviar, (tension) relajar; liberar, relieve the soldiers on guard duty → rlief: alivio/auxilio, (Mil.) liberación, relevo. Civil unrest (malestar social), a general feeling of discomfort (malestar generalizado), he felt slightly unwell (sentía un lijero malestar), her behaviour disturbed her deeply. Till (caja registradora, cultivar la tierra) → a field of studies has been tilled =/= the socialist party is stuck (atascado) near the tally (cuenta, total) of 25%; keep the tally of (llevar la cuenta de) ... Bring about (ocasionar, provocar); bring forward (adelantar, presentar/exponer, hacer comparecer); bring up (T, precios) hacer subir, criar niños, vomitar. Eje: (Astron. Física, Mat.) axis =/= (Auto, Mec) axle, Talgo (1942): a system of axles (front/ rear axle) to avoid wear (desgaste por uso) & tear of wheels unlocking the bolt (cerradura). When it encounter the guides (=) it transfer the weigh, frreing up the wheels. Keep: (away) mantenerse a distancia, (off) no acercarse, (back) retener, (in) impeder salir, (out) impedir entrar, (up) continuar, (to) limitarse a. Move: movimiento, mudanza, (around) cambiar de trabajo/vivienda, (along) avanzar, (back) retroceder, (in) instalarse, (on) seguir adelante; be always on the -- (de un lado pra otra). Skeleton: armadura, estructura, → they don't want the -- into de cupboard to come out (… sacar trapos sucios) ↔ they wash their line in public; they were raking up (sacaron a relucir; conseguir, rastrillar) his past. Insight (idea, novedad, nueva percepción sobre algo) → a book full of remarquable (excelentes) --, a pers. of -- (perspicacia), do -- into sth (comprender bien). Rash: erupción, racha (of strikes), (pers.) precipitada, impetuosa → he --ly (temerariamente) returned from self-imposed exile =/= rush: prisa, apuro, ráfaga de aire, hacer deprisa → he --ed (corrió) after her; in a --/hurry (precipitadamente). Throttle: regulador, (automóvil) acelerador; ahogar, silenciar, (tax rises, …) estrangular; full -- (acelerar al máximo), at full -- (a toda máquina) ↔ throttle down/back the engine (moderar la marcha). Bluster (bravuconear, fanfarronear; viento: rugir)y: tempestuoso, borrascoso =/= blister: (in burn: en quemaduras) ampolla, (bubble) burbuja → --ing: (heat, day) abrasadores, (angry, attack) violentos, (rythm, pace) vertiginoso. Excel (superar) at: destacar en =/= excel as (destacar como) =/= extoll (alabar, elogiar + praise, eulogize). Reel (película de cine) =/= coil: (wire, rope, parchement/scroll) rollo; (hair) rizo, (snake, screw) enroscarse, (smoke) (subir en) espiral; bobinar, enrrollar (↔ unroll: desenrollar), -- sth around sth → recoil (retroceder) as if afraid/in fear/at the sight of the corpse (cadáver), from the embrace. Glare: deslumbrar, luz deslumbradora =/= flare: bengala, destello, llamarada, erupción del sol → -- up: (fuego) llamear, (pers.) enfurecerse, disturbios/violencia (riots) estallar, (epidemia) declararse =/= blaze: llamarada, hoguera; brillar. Let up: (storm) amainar, (trabajo) disminuir, without --ing up (sin parar), don't -- -- (parar) now! =/= let-up: descanso, interrupción, tregua, disminución de la demanda → there was not no -- - -- in fighting. Despite pleas (súplicas, peticiones) from the government =/= plead (alegar, defender, suplicar) sb's cause: intercede por + I --ed & --ed (supliqué mil veces); I --ed for mercy (misericordia), -- the rights of the oppressed. Manchado: smudged, dirty, stained =/= reputation tarnished + falta de brillo ↔ brillante: bright, brilliant, shiny, glossy, sparkling, glittering. Hook (gancho, percha) up: enganchar (to the grid …), conexión/ transmisión en cadena → a satellite -- - (connexion vía satellite). It's a follow up (continuación) of the meeting → the subsequent -- - (seguimiento) is a part of the program. Live up (pasarlo en grande) to (vivir conforme a) my expectations/his ideas + the upturn (mejora: (Ec.: repunte) has failed to -- -- -- (estar a la alura de) the promise. Stifle (ahogar, suprimir) growth of … =/= Str<u>a</u>fe: ametrallar machine- gun → -- of civilisations; hacer trizas → the play (obra) was --ed by the critics =/= str<u>i</u>fe (lucha, conflicto)-prone (propenso) + -- ridden (cargado de) conflicts; cease from -- (deponer las armas) =/= a horse ridden (montado) by … Drift: movimiento, cambiar de dirección, ir a la deriva → -- from the lands (éxodo rural), -- of the events, -- downstream (dejarse llevar por la corriente, sin rumbo fijo) =/= drive: -- a bus, -- (pilotar) a racing car, he drove me home, the wind drove the dust into our faces, I don't want to -- you away (echarte) but …, the Indians were --en off their lands, the smoke drove him out of the home, he drove the nail through the plank (table) + can you --? His aim is --ing me crazy, it drove her to the despair, we were droven to it by fear (miedo), -- too fast, go for a -- (dar una vuelta en coche), a four -- wehicle, -- belt (correa de transmisión), I asked be drived/ referred (me mandasen) to a specialist; refer (remitir, enviar) → data-driven referral system, spending patterns based on users. Principal: she plays (interpreta) the leading role, the main thing is the pb. has been solved, core business (actividad principal), core subject (asignatura --); principalmente: principally, chiefly, mainly. Aprieto: fix, hardship, predicament, bind → he precludes (excluye, descarta) easier fixes (arreglos, posiciones; aprietos,V); fix (grabar) in the memory, -- his eyes on her, -- arrival. Instead of building flyovers (pasos elevados) to ease (aliviar) congestions, just fix the traffic lights. A casual (fortuito, ocasional) encounter; casual clothed (ropa sport) & trainers → ca<u>sua</u>lly (de manera informal, sin darle importancia) he moved near to … =/= c<u>au</u>sally (c<u>au</u>salmente) → they are -- related (guardan relación causa/efecto). <u>C</u>linch: (elections) ganar, (deal) cerrar, (nail: clavo) remachar; debt is a --ing (decisivo) problem =/= <u>f</u>linch (estremecerse) at the pain; flinch from + inf. (resistirse a + inf.), he never -- from his duty (nunca dejó de cumplir sus obligaciones) ↔ unflinching (valiente, impávido, inmutable, resuelta) rivalry. Shuffle arrastrar los pies; (cartas) barajar; papeles, ej. papeleo administrativo (paperwork) revolver, traspapelar =/= scuffle (refriega, ej.: with the police; escaramuza) → the police -- into a riot (desorden, disturbio); -- with the protesters. Taint: the army-tainted (contaminado, manchado) policies; his writing is --ted with racism. Upthrust (empuje hacia arriba) =/= push: he pushed de door open (de un empujón), with one -- (de un --), give sb the -- (ponerle de patitas a la calle), -- (esfuerzo) for Ec. growth, when -- comes to shove (empujón, V, meter): a la hora de la verdad; they pushed & shoved their way onto the bus. Herd (manada, rebaño) =/= Fold: redil, aprisco, establo; pliegue, doblar, cruzar (one's arms); price increased five fold (se multiplicaron por 5), fold sth in half/two. Woo (galantear, buscar, cortejar), ej. disgruntled (descontentos, malhumorados) Sunnis; (investments) atraer =/= wow (exitazo, cautivar, enloquecer) → fans --ed by the speed. Contrive (idear, ingeniárselas)d (artificioso) nod (signo positivo); greet/receive with a nod, he gave a nod of agreement & we set off (salimos). Grudge (resentment/bitterness; be jealous, envy,V) → I don't envy your success/bear you a malice (guardarle rencor). Furrow (surco,V; on forehead: arruga,V). Vocational (=, profesional): -- guidance (orientación), -- training (formación). Formar: prevent milk forming curds (grumos)/the blood forming clots, a new party is to be formed, the Europe that is taking shape or that is in formation, our aim is to train (formar) tech staff. Supply (de oferta) strategy → America has 300 - year -- (reservas) of coal, oil supplies (reservas) are running down, use up (agotar) supplies (reservas) of medicines/medicaments (medicamentos), an adequate -- of food (suficientes provisiones), make supplies/provosions of sth (hacer provisions de algo). Stave off (evitar) German attempts to promote an pan-Islamic Jihad. At he first attempt, this is my first --, after several --s they gave up (se dieron por vencidos), he made no -- to help (ni siquiera intentó ayudar), make an -- on the record (tratar de batir record), -- suicide. Greeted (recibido) with amazement (asombro). Meet sb (ir a recibir a alguien) at the station, welcome sb with open arms, the king refused to receive them. At his behest (a petición suya); with reference to your request (petición) of May 25 th, by popular request, at the request of the family; Jur.: petition for divorce, appeal for a reprieve (indulto). A serene & calm people. Traer: bring, have you brought the money? Can you bring or fetch or get me a glass of water?, the lad (muchacho) who delivers or brings me newspapers, can we have the bill, please? (¿Nos trae la cuenta, por favour?). Pay (presta) close attention (mucha atención) to ..., you need to take greater care (poner más atención) over what you do, customer service (atención al cliente). A spiral stair (case): espiral de escalera, stairwell (hueco de la escalera), inflamatory --, a -- of violence, spiralbound notebook. Hélice: (barco, avión) propeller, (anatomía, Mat.) helix, (muelle) spring. Bid, bad(e), bidden: mandar → -- sb to do sth; pujar → the highest bit (la major oferta), -- (intentar) to do sth; bit farewell to sb (despedirse de alguien) for ever, ... Protracted (prolongada, excesivamente larga) Ec. war; the road goes on (se prolonga) beyond the wood, the meeting went along quite a long time (se prolongó bastante)/ went on until the early hours (hasta la madrugada). Resbalar: it had been raining & she slipped, the car skidded into a tree, tears were trickling down her cheeks, he slipped walking down the street, sllippery slope: (terreno, cuesta) resbaladizos. Hotly (con pasión, vehemencia) → he was -- pursued (seguido muy de cerca) by the policeman. Inc.: included, incorporated =/= incluso: he even hit her (ilcluso él le pegó), it isn't simple (sencillo, simple) (not) even for us; we all liked it (nos gustó a todos), even or including the most stubborn of us. Subrayar: (en cursiva) italizice, (con una línea) underline, underscore =/= (poner énfasis) underline, emphasize, stress → underscore (subrayar, recalcar) a shift in the timeline (calendario, =; de trabajo: chedule). Sideline: actividad suplementaria, línea de banda, marginar los accionistas (shareholders) → be out of -- (al margen, fuera del terreno de juego); it's easy to criticize from the --, bellow (rugir, bramar) from the --. Upper management (altos cargos administrativos), upper Nile, -- chamber/-- house, -- class, -- Egypt, -- jaw, -- lip; properties (=, inmuebles) at the upper end (sección más carca) of the market. Blatant: (injustice, lie) flagrantes: que se ejecutan ahora, ostensibles, ej. attempts (intentos), (bully, coward, thief, lier) descarado → he was quite -- about cheating in the exam; blatantly: descaradamente, obviamente → his faults are -- obvious (sus defectos saltan a la vista), it's -- obvious that (es a todas luces evidebte que). Cast (molde, escayola; reparto; lanzar, echar, mudar, arrojar …) the current (actual, vigente, corriente) lot (montón, grupo, lote; terreno) =/= cast out/expel (expulsar) =/= Russian companies are casting (buscando) elsewhere for new customers to replace … Whisk (llevar rápido) visitors up to pray at those giant feet. Whisker: bigote de animal, pelo, patillas (+ sideborn), barba (beard) → by a whisker (pelo), he was within a whisker of falling down. Ruthless: (enemy) despiadado/implacable, (persecution) implacable, (determination) firme =/= relentless: (enemy) implacable, (criticism) despiadado, (pursuit) incesante ↔ relent: (transigir) give in/away on sth, (tolerar) tolerate; (tormenta) calm. Gormless (idiota, corto) → diffident (tímido, poco seguro de sí mismo) → despondent (desanimado, abatido + downhearted, dispirited) =/= gapping: (herida, boca) abierta, (abismo, agujero) enormes. Trash: basura, tonterías; destrozar, poner verde → --/garbage bag (bolsa de basuras), -- heap (basurero + rubbish dump); papelera: wastepaper bin/basket; (calle) litter bin, trash can; (pers.) dustman, garbage collector; dustbin (cubo de basura) → throw in … Light them up (iluminarlos) =/= encender: (cigarrilo) light; he alighted (encendió, se apeó + went off) on (dio con, cayó en la cuenta de, encontró) a new tactic + set sth alight (encender algo), be sth alight (estar ardiendo); encased (encerrado) in car tyres, doused (rociado, mojado) & lighted. Zealotry (fanatismo, fervor ciego) =/= a snooty (pretencioso, altanero) resentment =/= have a snooze (echar una cabezada). Seedling (planta de semillero) =/= seedbed (semillero); nursery (guardería, vívero, semillero (ex. of young talents) =/= semillero de delincuencia: hotbed, breeding ground for crime. Front: (building) fachada, (shirt, dress) pechera, (book) portada → her dress has ripped down the front (roto por delante), you've spilled food all down your --; there's a dedication (=) at the -- of the book, there are still some seats at the --, the -- of the train, at the -- of the line or queue, be in front (ir primero, delante), front door (puerta principal), the house fronts the river (da al río) ↔ back door, back/rear wheel. Chuffed (descontento) =/= chaff (desperdicios del trigo y granos, broza) =/= chafe (rozar, irritar) =/= scoff (burlarse) at =/= scoffing (mofa, burla) =/= scuffed (se enfrentó, hizo una escaramuza) with the protesters. Yet/still (aún, todavía), (al)though (aunque) → this is his best film yet (por ahora), there's hope for me -- (todavá tengo esperanzas), he may yet succeed, -- again (una vez más), I told him several times, thoug he still hasn'done it (se lo dije varias veces, sin embargo todavía no lo a hecho. Advertencia: (1) warning → he ignored my --, (hacer una --) give a warning, let this be a warning for you (espero que esto os sirva de --); (2) give some advise; (3) caveat → with the -- (salvedad) that ..., such caveat (advertencia) rarely ... Overdo (exagerar: with garlic, ...) =/= overrate (sobrevalorar) =/= overdue (plazo vencido) =/= subdue (contener, dominar, someter)d: tenue, apagado, deprimido =/= Outdo (superar, mejorar) America's pbs. =/= undo: desabrocharse, (knot) deshacerse, (zipper) abrir; desatar (+ untie), (damage) reparar + compensate), (error) correct =/= unpick (deshacer, descoser) =/= come undone (deshacerse) =/= override (ignorar, anular, no hecer caso)ing (preponderante, primordial). Buzz: (zumbar) → my head is --ing, -- word (palabra de moda), give sb a -- (dar un telefonazo a alguien), driving fast give me a -- (me encanta), the school --ed with the news (toda la escuela comentaba la noticia). Drench: (soak) empapar, (culinario) macerar (+ ablandar, prensar) =/= dampen: humedecer, (hopes) frustar, (enthusiasm) enfriar → the news --ed the mood (humor, clima); dampen sb's spirits (desmoralizar, entristecer). Further (más, más lejos, fomenter) =/= farther (lejano + far-off, distant → further farther/farther away (más lejos, en otras partes); they are not further ahead that they were (no han progresado), further forward (más para adelante). Flub/gaffe: meter la pata, pifiarla =/= chapuza: botched job, shoddy piece of work, bungle → a --ed (fallido) attempt, a -- (mal ejecutada) operation =/= bundle: bulto, fardo, lío, haz, paquete. Oil sloshing (borrachera) through the region; get --ed (emborracharse) =/= shushing (acallando) fussy (exigentes, quisquillosos) babies =/= huffy (enfuruñado,V, susceptible, quisquilloso) =/= fuzzy (velloso, idea confusa) =/= coo (arrullar para enamorar, adormecer un niño; divulgar cosas secretas) → she enjoyed cooing press reports. Picante: (food, taste) hot, spicy, (wine) tart, sour, (comment) sharp, cutting, (joke) dirty, (film, person) naughty, (especia) chilli; this sauce is very hot or spicy. Couch (expresar, formular; sofa) =/= coach (coche, vagón; entrenar, (trainer) entrenador) → coaching (entrenamiento, preparación, help) on public hospitals. Founder: fundador; hundirse, fracasar + fail =/= flounder: debatirse (--ing in the water), perder el hilo al hablar, tropezar (the Ec. is --ing), revolcarse → the oxen --ed through the mud. Watershed: cuenca → the -- of the Duero; linea divisoria de las aguas; make a -- (marcar un hito), a -- (crucial) year for industry, she had reached a -- in her career (había llegado a un momento decisivo de su carrera professional). Flop: fracasar estrepitosamente), she flopped down (se dejó caer) into a chair =/= flap (solapa, tapa del bolsillo;

agitarse, aletazo: el batir las alas) =/= flip: tirar algo, -- one's lid: perder la cabeza; -- a coin to decide; ligereza, indiferencia, poca seriedad). Curse: (maldición) → put a -- on sb; (azote) drought is the -- of Spain; (blasfemia: =). It tarnish (deslustra, quita el brillo; mancha el honor, la reputación a) China's image rather than burnish (zapatos/muebles: dar brillo/pulir; reputacón: mejorar) it =/= bull (en alta) market, bullish (optimista, Ec. alcista) ↔ bearish. Balanceo,V: rock, swing (balanceo de un objeto colgante, las piernas en un columpio) =/= (tree, boat, train) sway + dominio, influir → his -- over the party, bring a people under one's -- (sojuzgar un pueblo), hold -- over a nation (gobernar, dominar una nación). Sham (falsa, fingida) Democracy whets (aviva, estimula) pers. to win bogus (falsas, fraudulentas) elections; the walk whetted (estimulaba) our appetites. Cluster: (casas) grupo, (plátanos) racimo, (estrellas) grupo, (plantas) macizo; apiñar, agrupar =/= clump: grupo de plantas, macizo de flores, terrón de tierra. Juggle: hacer malabarismos; (statistics, facts) añadir, manipular → -- (compaginar) a career & a family =/= jumble (revoltijo, embrollo; cosas usadas, revueltas) → -- sale charity (de beneficencia) market of second-hand (usadas) things =/= jockey: (maniobras) for position; convince sb into doing sth; (quitar, disuadir con artimañas) → he was --ed out of chairmanship. Dereliction (abandono) → the --ed (abandonado) lot (mucho, montón; terreno, solar) drags on (arrastra, debilita) the value of nearly homes. Course: (plane) rumbo, (river) curso, desviar → a boat was blown off the course; in the -- (tanscurso) of our conversation, in the normal -- (curso, recorrido) of events (en circunstancias normales); the only -- (way) open to us, in due curse (a su debido tiempo). Embedded: (grabado) in the memory; (insertado) in the US forces; idea --ed (arraigada) in public mind. Teñir: dye, ed, eing (tintura) =/= morir: die, died, dying (moribundo)=/= acostarse: lie, lay, lain, lying. Subyacer: underlies, underlay, underlain, underlying (subyacente). Ridden: a horse -- by (montado por) …, -- with (cargado de) debts, conflict ridden (muy conflictivo), guilt -- (atormentado por remordimientos) =/= riddled with bullets (acrivillado a balas), riddled with corruption (presente en todos los rincones). Thumb: pulgar, (hojear, manosear) his nose: hacer burla; under sb's -- (dominio), a well --ed (usado) book =/= thump (golpear, golpetazo)ing (aplastante) majority; Trump is tub-thumping (demagógico + =). Lively (animado) =/= lovely: belleza, (pers., naturaleza: nature) encantadores, (face, voice, figure) bonitas, preciosas; amoroso, agradable. Sluggishness (aletargamiento), drowsy (somnoliento, adormilado) =/= torpor: letargo (pérdida de las funciones vitales + letargy). Trap: (trampa/estafar: cheating) → fall into a --, keep one's -- shut (no abras la boca), cazar (+ hunt, shoot), atrapar → a driver --ed into the wreckage (escombros), he --ed me (me tendió una trampa) into admitting it. Beneficio: (finanzas) profits of his business, (ventaja, bien) benefit, a collection (colecta) for the victims, in the interest of everyone (todos), gains from migrants, natives & born in the host country). Swirl: remolino,V, girar de las bailarinas, de la falda, espiral de humo, the debate is --ing about … =/= twirl: retorcer el bigote, (bailarina, bastón) dar vueltas =/= whirl: (pers.) girar, dar vueltas, (leaves, dust) arremolinarse, (head) dar vueltas → the room was --ing (todo me daba vueltas) =/= torcer: (arm, ankle, waist, body) twist, (head, corner) turn, winced with pain, (clothes) wring, (wrist: muñeca) sprain. Bore: taladro, perforación,V, → (agua/petróleo) well; (pozo de mina) shaft; (hollow of elevator) hacer → they --ed a hole into the rock; bore for oil; pesado, pelmazo, lata → what a -- he is. Arrasar: razing buildings + Barça swept to victory; wind devastated a region. Negotiate with the French vying (compitiendo) to prevail (justice/common sense: prevalecer; enemy: imponerse) in the chaos engulfing (tragando, sumergiendo) Ukraine. Snuff (rapé, apagar) out: apagar, extinguir =/= sniff (olfatear, husmear) out: (dog) descubrir husmeando, (danger) olerse. Decay: descomponer, pudrirse, deteriorar, edificio en ruinoso estado, decadencia de valores + the decay of globalisation is compared with an steady (constante, firme) demoralisation of the transnational companies. Loath → loathe (odiar, detester); be loath to + inf.: resistirse a, ser reacio a. Loathsome: detestable (+ hateful, atrocious), repugnante (+ repugnant), despreciable (+ despicable). The hounding (acoso) is dis<u>turb</u>ing (alarmante, perturbante, inquietante); disturbance (disturbio Pol., trastorno mental, perturbación de la paz), I found the play deeply disturbing (la obra me afectó mucho), some of the scenes are disturbing (hieren la susceptibilidad) =/= dis<u>rupt</u>: (relaciones, tráfico) afectar, deteriorar; (class, plan) trastocar, perturbar); disruptive: prejudicial, perturbador. Estorbar: you just get in the way, you are just a nuisance (lo único que haces es perturbar), the vehicule blocks, obstruct the traffic, children are a hindrance (obstáculo). Provision: social -- (servicios sociales), educational -- (recursos para educación), food supplies (suministros alim.), funding -- (previsiones financieras); dispositions of a treaty, provisions for the future. Spin: (wheel) hacer giar, (ball) darle efecto, (wool, coton) hilar → spin-off: product derivado, consecuencia indirecta (ej.: from defence to industry ...); it spins out: (story, meeting) alargar, (money, salary) estirar. Hazy (confuso, ..., neblinoso) → I'm a bit -- about what happens, the -- outline (perfil) of the tower. Criar: (niño) bring up, raise, (amamantar) nurse, suckle, feed, (ganado) rear, raise, (para competición: breed + reproducirse). Boats that are honed (afilados, puestos a punto) for speed are difficult to handle when pottering about → potter about/around: entretenerse trabajando, (in the garden) pequeños trabajos, hacer un poco de esto y de aquello. Refugio: =, shelter → air-raid --, (refugio antinuclear): fallout --, tax --, (Mil.): underground --; mountain hut. Subdue: sojuzgar, (pers.) someter, dominar, (passion, anger) contener, (spirits) apagar =/= subyugate an state/the people =/= summit the agreement to his approval. Stalward: fiel, incondicional; fornido (robusto, fuerte) + burley, sturdy, robust, strong. Wham (pegar con fuerza, golpe resonante, zas!) =/= he hit me, we hit a wall (pegamos contra un muro) =/= I have to stick the photos into the album, I picked up the habit off him (él me pegó la costumbre). Rural tourism has not yet reached its peak, the peak of Internet, in the peak or height of his popularity, the rapid rise of fundamentalism, an increasingly popular fashion, feminism is increasingly successful or influential. Ponder (considerar, reflexionar), winnow (discernir) truth from lies, pander (consentir) to the pressure, to her whim. Flake: copo, escama, astilla, (painting, varnish, plaster: yeso) descascarillarse. Twinge (punzada) → feel a -- of remorse (de remordimiento de conciencia) =/= fickle (cambiante, inconstante, voluble), fickleness (inconstancia, volubilidad), =/= tickle (cosquillas,V, divertir, hacer gracia) → he enjoyed tickling the baby =/= skittish (caprichoso, delicado; nervioso, asustadizo). Convocar: (elecciones, referendun, huelga) call, (asamblea, reunión) call, convene, (manifestaciones) call for, (concurso oposición) announce → he called a press conference, they have called or convened a special conference (congreso extraordinario) for Monday, they called the journalists to a press conference. Genio: (temperamento) temper → he's got such a temper! (¡menudo genio tiene!), she's a quick-tempered (de mucho --) women, a leopard cannot change his spots (genio y figura hasta la sepultura), be good natural or even tempered (tener buen --), be in good -- ↔ be in bad --; the spirit of Andalucía (el genio andaluz). Engañoso: deceptive, deceitful, misleading =/= decepcionar: disappoint, let down =/= engañar: cheat, deceive, mislead =/= engaño: deceit, deception, ploy, trick, fake =/= swindle (estafa, timo,Vs) → it's a --! (¡Nos han timado!), swindler. Causes for disquiet (inquietud); they expressed they concern (inquietud) for their children's future (de sus hijos), the rumours have aroused concern among investors, they anxiously (con inquietud) awaited her call. Likeness (parecido) =/= they have similar surnames, the houses are all similar or alike, look like sb (tener similar aspecto a alguien), be like sb (ser similar de carácter); likewise (así mismo, de la misma manera). Fancy: (price) exorbitante, (spending) barbaridad, (casualidad) meeting (encontrar) them, they took a -- to each other (quedaron prendados uno al otro), a passing -- (capricho pasajero), I -- (me apetece) an ice cream, do you -- going to ...? (idea) extravagante, mere -- (pura fantasía). Repay: (money, loan) devolver, (debt) pagar → a click on the phone & you can draw down (bajar) $ repay funds. Revolve (girar) → his words are --ing in my brain, -- around sb/sth (ej. -- the Earth, -- around the Sun). Revolt (revuelta, sublevación)ing: repugnante, asqueroso; horrible → provide (proveer, proporcionar) revolting consumer credit. Crunch: credit crunch (crisis), if it comes to the -- (si llega el momento), -- (mascar) a biscuit (galleta), the tyres --ed on the gravel (los neumáticos hacían crujir la graba). Settle: (región, estado) colonizar, (colonists: colonos) establecer, (prices, terms) fijar, (pb.) resolver, (nonsense) acabar con, calmar, (bill, account) pagar; settling (inquietante/perturbador + worrying, disturbing) referendum ↔ unsettled (agitado, intranquilo, inestable; pendiente, sin resolver) → if this gets into the papers it will only -- people. Stop abiding (acatando) parts of the pact. The schok wave has temporarily subsidiced: (floods; swelling: Med.: hinchazón) decrecer, (storm/wind) amainar) + (laughter: carcajada/anger) calmarse, (road, land) hundirse. Five years stint (período) in the army, his second -- (parte) in office, I've done my -- for today, don't --/skimp (escatimar) on butter, he --ed herself (se privó) of food for our sake (por nosotros). Advance on (sobre) a city, with the -- (paso) of old age (años), -- in tech. -- of $ 88, tickets are $ 6 in advance, I arrived in -- of my friends, a woman in -- for her time, --ed (por adelantado) booking is essential, -- notice (preaviso) → I arrived without notice; the project is far --ed. Sharp: afilado, (bend) cerrada, (eyesight/hearing) fino, (wit, mind) agudo, (desire) intense, (TV, picture) nítidos, (rebuke, criticism) duras, (shrewd, pers.) listo, astuto. When troops rely on high-tech kit (equipo), cyber-attacks can kill, because 70 % high tech. is cyber, much of it coming from the Silicon-valley. Uncompromising/diehard (intransigente, "="). American armed forces are at grave risk from hacking & high-tech. sabotage (hacer mal el trabajo, desbaratar el taller). Scour (registrar, fregar) defence contract for Chinese companies, down to third-tier supliers (proveedores a tres niveles). Partnership (asociación) → the teachers work in -- (conjuntamente) with the parents; this societies have been in -- for years; he aspires to a -- (ser socio) with the firm; its taiwanese partner (compañero, socio, pareja) steals trade secrets. Conllevar: bring, entail → the responsibility which it --/--; a task which is fraught (llena) with serious difficulties =/= involve: (suponer) → it --s a lot of work; implicar/involucrar → -- her in the scandal, -- me in your problems. Powerhouse (central eléctrica) + intellectual -- (motor); the nerve center (centro neurálgico) & powerhouse (centro motriz) of the corporation; global -- in high-tech. fields. Lay out: (park, garden) diseñar, (town) hacer el trazado, (objeto) disponer, (argumento) planear, exponer → as laid out in China 2025. The first advantage that offers huge rewarts to state/business that take an early lead (se coloque en cabeza) & allowing to set standards that later entrants have little choice but to follow. American firms took an early lead in 4G, setting standards for new handsets (auricular; telecomunicacions: aparato) & apps that spread worldwide. Separar con un muro (wall off) =/= China & America walk off (se marchan de) their respective digital market from one another, each will look for growth in the rest of te World. Keep ahead of Chinese work on computers that harness (arreos, utilizan) the laws of quantum physics to achieve processing speeds out of a science fiction film. Mr Xi: quizzing (concurso, cuestionando, poniendo a prueba) scientists who have returned from quantum laboratories in America & Europe. Not up to the job ↔ up to (capaz de) taking over (hacerme cargo) of the enterprise; that's up to you (como quieras); sb must have put them up to it (haberles dado la idea, incitados a ello); she put him up to the idea of claiming the subsidy. When smaller neighbours complain that China is threatening them, China is convinced that America have put the tiddlers (pececitos pequeños) up to it. Nation states nuclear stand-off (punto murerto, empate; callejón sin salida) during the cold war. China schemed (mostraba intriga, proyectaba, conspiraba + =) & cheated (engañaba, hacía trampas) ... It is sobering (sobrio, grave, formal, aleccionador) that they feel like be winners. Jam: mermelada, get ino a -- (aprieto, meterse en un lío), bloquear, atascarse, (traffic --) embtellamiento, --med (atestado) with people, -- (meter) sth with sth =/= jab (codazo, golpe, inyccección → I --bed o.s. with a needdle =/= jar (tarro; choque, sacudida,Vs, enervar) =/= jagged (dentado, irregular). Slay, slew, slain: matar, hacer morir de risa =/= slew: torcer; cambio de dirección) → the car --ed to the left =/= give a clout (tortazo; peso/influencia) =/= hew (cortar, labrar; extraer; ceñirse → the unions --ed to its demand), closer to free market ideas =/= skew (torcer) → wear the hat on the -- (ladeado), -- off course (desviarse) =/= sway: (home, tree, branches) oscilación, balanceo; (by conspiracy theory, ...) influenciados, dominados, (public opinion) cambiar → hold sway: (ideas) prevalecer, preponderar, (leader) ejercer dominio, (over sb) dominar a alguien. Inverso: in reverse order, the -- side/order, the -- gear (marcha atrás), engage -- (meter marcha atrás), endorse (endosar) the check on the --, quite the --, the results are the -- of ..., the roles are --ed, -- the charges (llamar a cobro revertido), contrary to what happen, conversely (a la inversa), arrange it other way round. Sencillo: (pb., ejercicio, pers.) simple, straightforward, (vestido, estilo) simple, plain, (casa, comida, pers.) simple, modest. Invaluable ("invalorable"). A sterling (excelente, invalorable) job, a pers. of -- worth (una pers. de grandes méritos). The demonstrators have rattled (hecho ruido, pusieron nervioso) the government; this one answer with water hoses & clubs (garrotes). Readily: he -- helps (siempre está dispuesto a ayudar), I -- admid (no tengo inconveniente en aceptar), he -- agreed (accedió de buena gana), -- (fácilmente) available (possible de conseguir) =/= fairy (justamente, equitativamente, bastante). Hustle: trabajar mucho, apurar(se), meter prisa; ajetreo, bullicio, empujar → hustler (pers. muy trabajadora, dinámica); be --ed (metido a empujones) into the car =/= bustle: ajetreo, bullicio; -- about/around (ir de acá para allá), -- in/out (entrar/salir afanosamente, --ing with activity (rebosar de actividad). Come up (subir, surgir) with (idear, plantear) cool (serenos, tranquilos) new pilots; it's cool outside, keep --! (¡Tranquilo!), those shades (gafas de sol) are really -- (molan mucho), stay here in the -- (al fresco), a -- (de sangre fría) customer. Enojar (anger, upset, annoy)se: (enfadarse) lose one's temper, get angry, (irritarse) get annoyed/cross/mad. U. van der Layen: her attempt to take on (aceptar, asumir; recoger, contratar) the brass & bureaucrats by using outside experts; she hold meetings not sitting down but on foot; she belies (desdice, defrauda) her smooth (fluido, suave) public image: less twinset (juego, conjunto) & pearls than knuckleduster (nudilleras) & caffeine pills, she is wonky (poco firme, tambaleante; torcida, estropeada) & unflashy ↔ flashy: striking (imponente, llamativa), showy/ostentuous. Arruga: (piel) wrinkle, (papel) crease, wrinkle; (pliegue del pantalón) crease, he frown/knit his brow (frente), a furrowed (surcada de arrugas) brow, crumple (arrugar) a sheet of paper to a ball, his face is weather-pickered (arrugado for el tiempo). Penuria: shortage, dearth, paucity, poverty, scarcity =/= budget deficit, shortfall (menos de lo esperado) of production/harvest =/=

shortage: water --, -- of staff, housing -- (crisis de la vivienda), in times of -- (escasez). Weird/freaky (extraño, raro) =/= eerie (extraño, inquietante, misterioso). Fracasar: fail, mess up, be unsuccessful. Torcido: (línea/nariz) crooked, (palo, alambre) bent. Uso: indiscriminate use of antibiotics, a handle (mango) worn by the use, a database for the use of the scientists use only (exclusivo uso), you cannot hoot (abuchear, tocar/usar la bocina) your horn (claxon) in the vicinity (proximidades) of ..., excessive use of an expression, these matters will stand up (resistir) to a lot of wear (desgaste); the wear (desgaste) of the engine (motor). A passing fad (moda pasajera) =/= my tan soon faded (el moreno se me quitó pronto), the light was fading (estaba oscureciendo), the music/laughter (risas) faded (se fue apagando). Everyone of these must-have (que hay que tener) consumer trinkets (chucherias) is a computer in disguise (disfrazado), with innards (tripas) made from microprocesors, memory chips & circuit boards (tarjetas). Turn a blind eye, like the revellers (juerguistas, borrachos) in a night club to persuade a bouncer (gorila) to let in their mates (compañeros), even though they are weaning trainers. Streak (rasgo, parte) → there is a -- of Spanish blood in her, (mineral) veta, vena, --in/out/past (entrar, salir, pasar como un rayo) =/= it hurtled (se precipitó) along (fue a toda velocidad)/down (bajó a toda velocidad) into the Pacific. Account: explicación, informe → take sth in -- (tener algo en cuenta); on - of (debido a) his age; no satisfactory -- was given; by his own -- (según él me cuenta). Forgo, --went, --one → forego (renunciar a, privarse de); foregone conclusion (resultado inevitable); foregoing (anterior precedente). D. Trump has frequently bashed (golpeado, apalizado) China while occasionally praising Xi. America is becoming less vunerable to flag-waving (patriotismo de bandera) opportunists. Young thrusters (propulsores) can meet old fogeys (carrozas, personas chapadas a la antigua) & lobby them for jobs. Beat/bang a drum for sth (anunciar algo a bombo y platillo).

It seemed a lifetime (parecía una eternidad). B. Johnson as a child announced he would become "world king". De Gaule regarded national pride as the only cure for natiobal suicide. Johnson identifies Britain with "greatness" as natural & the general identified France with "*grandeur*". France enjoyed "*les treinte grandeurs*" (las treinta grandezas) from 1945 to 1975, when GDP grew at an average of 6 % a year. He senses (siente, percibe) that the Tories need to give more active role to the state, hence his enthusiasm for big infrastructure projects. Betrayal (traición; secret: revelación, intention, feeling: descubrimiento) → de Gaulle was a betrayal. Famous among his peers/contemporaries but obnoxious (repugnante) for his enemies. As coronavirus spreads & markets turned volatile, investors rushed to reposition their portfolios. Many governments and companies took advantage (se aprovecharon) of central-banks support & ultra-low interests rates.

TERCERA PARTE:
Sectores compuestos de varias frases en los que además del vocabulario uno se ejercita a construir aquellas, sin olvidar el aprendizaje de temas complejos

Esta presentación pedagógica conceptual lleva la atracción de tratar temas cotidianos (que luego tendrán el valor de ser históricos) y en primer lugar resaltamos su clasificación por sectores:

- (the) **Arctic**: drilling a wildfare (fauna) refuge is the hydroxycloroquine of energy policy. The Arctic National wildlife refuge in Northern Alaska is stuff of dreams. The US Department of interior released a plan to make 1.6 million acres (1 acre: 0'405 Ha) of the refuge's coastal plain available for oil gas exploration & development. The climate change is warming the Arctic twise as fast as the rest of the planet. The federal study that paved the way (preparaba el terreno) for the drilling announcement assumes that oil producton in the refuge will last for 70 years. Pollings show two-thirds of American voters oppose drilling in the Artict preserve. Investment in the region also looks increasingly dicey (dudoso) incierto, existing oil & gas infrastructure is designed for freezing (glaciales, heladas) temperature - a climate that is becoming a relic of decades past.

- **Boris Johnson's new policies:** phrases as "get Brexit done" won him the general election. It faces the socialist party led by Sir K. Stammer, from a working-class background. The junior minister (secretariado de estado) for media (medios de communicación) & data, argues that the British broadcasting (BBC) panders (consiente) Manchester's metropolitan elite. Economists find that, in the developed world, more devolved systems tend to be more equal. Measured by the percentage of total tax revenue raised centrally, regionally & locally, Britain is by some distance the most centralised country in the G7 (grupo de los 7). B. Johnson new list of peers reveals a dangerous contempt (desprecio, desdén) for governing institutions. The list of 36 new peers include the son of a Russian Security committee oif the state (KGB) agent-turned-oligarch, the prime minister's brother, sultry (various) party donors, & parasites. In the 18th & early 19th centuries the British political system was known as "old corruption": the rich treated the data as their private property, appointing their cronies to the best boroughs (municipios), ..., & buying great offices of state for themselves. The Victorians dismantled this system in the name of open competition & public duty. The sense of high seriousness that the Victorians attached to the government is being eroded before the public gaze (mirada), as insiders (emopleados de la empresa) cash in (cobran) on (sacan provecho) of their knowledge & experience. The collapse of party membership is forcing it to take desperate measures to raise money. Mr Johnson is surrounded (some would say captured) by revolutionaries who belief in tearing down (derribar) the current order. There is no sign that Britain's current master (maestro, amo, capitán) has either the firmness or purpose or philosophical conviction to wage (hacer, llevar a cabo) such a war. But he proposes a constitutional reform: weaken judicial, political & administrative limits that have been placed on the power of the executive. Brexit is only the beginning. By the time of the next election, ministers will have control over more policies, enjoy more discretion & face fewer restraints than they have faced for decades. The reforms of the past 40 years will not be overthrown, but they will be a course-correction to assert (imponer) the primacy of the politicians over the judges & officials. Lord Hailsham proposed a written constitution.

- **British relations with China**: as the relationship deteriorates, China could make Britain squirm (hacerla sufrir). (skirm: retorcerse). Britain will change its immigration rules from a low level up to 2.9 Hong kongers to gain citicenship in Britain. Several factors are behind the hardened stance: Britain says that China is in breach of (incumple) the Hong kong handover treaty; pressure to ditch (deshacerse de) Huawei from America & Australia, with which Britain hopes to seal speedly trade agreements. Britain must find homegrown alternatives to Chinese telecoms & nuclear power. Economic treaties come next. Many fret that the lost advantages are stacking up. As the reaction to Mr floyd's death showed, Midwest merits attention because it is exceptionally divided. More than elsewhere, deep racial segreggation persists. Underlying (subyacente) of this is a third reason for scrutinising (esudriñar; votos: hacer el escrutinio) America's Middle.

- **Catholic priests & politics in US**: render unto Caesar (*dar al Cesar lo que es del Cesar y a Dios lo que es de Dios*). Priestly guidance on voting is dividing the Catholic church: can Catholic vote for J. Widen & avoid damnation (perdición, maldición)? A senior Bishop doesn't think so. A priest of Wisconsin urged Catholic democrats to "repent of their support of that party ... or face the fires of the hell". American political polarisation is reflected in the leadership of the Catholic church. The nomination of a Catholic as a Democrat candidate has accelerated the progress. In so doing they echo president D. Trump's efforts to play down (disminuir importancia, minimizar) his rival faith. In 2009 socially conservative Catholic & Protestant signed an agreement saying that they would work together on gay marriage & abortion. Only the later remains a live issue. In 2016 white catolic voted Mr Trump, though by a much smaller margin than white Evangelical did.

On October 2020, polls suggest Mr Biden may be stealing some of that support. The Democrats showcased (exhibieron, mostraron) liberal Catholics … Having prayed for the unemployed, poverty-striken & desperate, he added the unborn child (feto) in the womb.

- **China's hybrid capitalism**: blooming (floreciente, radiante) for the glory of the state. Xi Jinping is blending (combina, mezcla) market mechanisms with communist party contols to remake the Chinese Ec. The time when private Chinese economies downplayed (disminuian importancia a) their links to the Communist party is gone. The communist party has greater control of all aspects of life. Mr Xi has greater control over the party. Bring to an end (terminar con algo), bring to the halt (car, thing: detener; process: interumpir) → he has had reforms that brought liberalised the Ec. to a halt & has smothered (asfixiado) market forces. Private companies have rushed to set up party committees with an increasing say over strategy. He is presiding over (conduciendo) what he hopes will be the creation of a more muscular form of state capitalism. The idea is for state-owned companies to get more market discipline & private enterprises to get more party discipline. Make state firms more efficients, & to team them up (asociarlas) with private enterprises in new industrial-policy initiatives. "To get rich is glorious", a quip (ocurrencia) of Deng Kiaoping & a mantra for his China, but so long as your pursuit of riches also benefit the state. State firms benefit from reams (montones) of subsidies & preferential rules, often opaque. Foreign companies have scant (escasa) presence in key sectors such as finance & energy. Mr Xi has been relentless in targeting anyone standing up (levantarse; ser sólido, lógico) for human rights. The case didn't standed up (la acusación no se mantuvo en el tribunal). His reassertion (reafirmación) of government control over banks, brokerages & investment firms has been brazingly (vigorosamente) hands-on (experience: práctica; knowledge:

personal). A taste for Moonshots (lanzamientos de naves espaciales a la luna): the leverage (palanca, influencia) on which the system is based also looks safer.

China is not the only controversial (=, polémica) recipient of data. America's ongoing assault on firms from China, spurred by worries about its citicens'personal data being passed to the Chinese governments. Their legal challenges against transfers of tax related data hat little success so far. But a recent ruling in Brussels could change that. War on tax evasion was officially declared in 2010, when America passed the Foreign account tax compliance act (FATCA) in response to scandals involving rich American stashing (escondites) undeclared money offshore. Europe takes privacy seriously: the EU's General data protection regulation (GDPR) is one of the basic's most treasured (preciados) legal texts. Tax authorities in Canada, Germany & elsewhere have had data stolen in cyber-attacks. In 2019 countries swapped (cambiaron) data on 84 million accounnts, covering € 10 trn (miles de billones). In the meantime, privacy is not the only worry. Security is one too.

- **Climate change** → efforts to rein in climate change will stir up (revolucionar) the geopolitics of energy: America's democratic presidential contender (=, competidor), J. Biden, wants to spend $ 2 trn decarbonising America's Ec. Today energy accounts for (representa) two-third of greenhouse- gas emissions. Renewable energy such solar & wind power could rise from 5 % of supply today to 25 % in 2035 & near 50 % by 2050. Oil & coal use will drop, although cleaner natual gas will remain central (=, fundamental). The thread of a poorly managed transition looms (surge, amenaza). Two risks stand out (sobresalen, destacan): autocratic China could temporarily gain clout (influencia, tortazo) over the global power system; because of its dominance in making key components (components clave) & developing new techs. In early 2021 Chinese firms produce 72 % of the world's solar modules, 69 % of it lithium-ion batteries & 45 % of its wind turbines.They also control much of refining of minerals of vital importance to clean energy, such as cobald & lithium. China's leverage (palanca, influencia) depends on how fast other Ecs. move. Europe is home of giant developers of wind & solar farms. America's trajectory has been affected by the rise of shale oil & gas, which has made it the largest oil producer, & by the Republican resistence to decarbonisation measures. In the world scene, the investment being contemplated (=, contado con) fall drastically short of what is need to kep temperature within 2º C of pre-industrial level, let alone the 1.5 º required to limit the environment, Ec. & political turmoil of climate change.

- **Dementia** → the perils of oblition (olvido): nowhere in the world is ready to cope with the global explosion of dementia. It may start as a "mild cognitive impairment (descapcidad, deterioro)" (MCI): forgetfulness (olvido, descuido) of senior moments. But as it progress, ataking mental aglity & eating away (desgastar, corroer) memory, it steals much of what counts as identity. When severe, people become incapable of looking after demselves: they lose the ability to read, cook & shop (ir de compras). They forget to drink & get dehydrated, or become incontinent ("="). They suffer delusions, or become frightned or angry, or they sink into (se unden, decaen en) an apathetic (=) slump (bajón, Ec.: depresión). Dementia makes it hard to understand the danger of the virus, or to remember social distanciy or higiene precautions. Of the dozens of forms o dementia identidies, Alzheimer disease is the commonest, accounting for (representando) between 60 % & 80 % of the cases. The OECD estimates that by 2030 the number of cases of dementia will increase by 50 % in the rich countries & 80 % in the poor ones. Dementia disproportiuonately affects women. The annual global cost of caring for people with dementia is of $ 1 trn. in 2018, raising to $ 2 trn by 2030, a total that could undermine socal & Ec. development globally & overwhelm health & social services. Witchcraft (bujería) is held in some African countries, where those with dementia may be shunned (rechazados) or persecuted.

- **Digital currencies**: America's Fed recognised the disruptive (perjudicial) potential of electronic money long ago. Central banking are grappling with (se confronta a) another tech. revolution: rise the mobile payments & turn away from cash. One idea gaining favour is to use a so-called central-bank digital currency (CBDC), which could exist only as electrons on a computer ship, rather than a coin or bill. The coronavirus pandemic has added to the urgency as more people shop online or pay with contactless cards or phones. The primary motivation for issuing a CBDC is likely to be definitive. The gradual demise (desaparición) of cash opens two basic risks: (1) Online payment- systems could fail, suffering outages (apagones) or hacks (cortes). To safeguard the integrity of their currencies, central banks hope to offer fail-safe (fiables) digital alternatives. (2) Private sector systems are too successful, with more people switching to payment platforms offered by big tech firms. CBDCS also give central banks more control, & it may make it easier to implement negative interest rates. After a natural disaster they could direct support to affected areas & offer consumption rebates depending on where & how the money is spent.

- **Donald Trump** will not win without Florida, which is on a knife edge (con el alma pendiente de un hilo). Just once in the past twelve presidential elections (1992) Florida voted for the loser. Organising raicous (chillones) parades of cars decked out (adornados, engalanados) in Biden flags. Polls show a tight race, much closer than the overall nationa picture. Mr Trump is overperforming with the latinos & underperforming with the elderly. Roughly one-third of Florida's Hispanics are Cuban, a group that traditionally votes Republican. It also has sizeable (considerables) Venezuelan, Colombian & Nicaraguan communities - all these groups are more favorable to Republicans than Mexican- Americans, who tend to vote more reliably for Democratic candidates.

- **Each era of Ec. confronts a new challenge**: after the 1930s the task was to prevent depresions. In the 1970s & 1980s the holy grial (santo grial) was to end the stagnation. Today the task for policimakers is to create framework that allows the business cycle to be managed & financial crisis to be fought without a policitised (politizado) takeover of Ec. The stakes are high (se apuesta fuerte, hay mucho en juego). Faiure will mean the age for free money eventually comes at a staggering (asombroso, pasmoso) price.

- **Eurpean union filling the coffers**: eutocrats have long sought to bolster the EU's budget with "own resources", i. e. revenues that accrue (se acumulan) to (confieren) it, rather than cash handed over by member countries on the basis of national income. But almost every attempt to centralise taxation has fallen foul (ha sufrido el enfrentamiento) of a national veto. Payment of € 390 will start in 2028; new own resources should contribute. Common taxes on the top of common dept would mark a decisive step towars fiscal union. There are mainly six: An EU levy on plastic waste may funnel € 7 bn. a year towards the budget from 2021; one idea is to direct revenues from the EU's carbon-trading scheme to Brussels, but that might deprive national treasures from income; another idea is a "single- market" tax on companies; a tax on financial transactions; "carbon" border-adjustment mechanism, that's to say a tariff on climate-unfriendly (poco amistosas) imports. It could raise € 5-14 bn. But it's devilish (diabólico) to design & will be challenged at the NATO; a less lucrative levy on (mainly american) tech. firms. American's opposition to a digital tax has stalled (parado) a paralel process at the OCDE.

- (the) **EU foreign policy** suffers from the same problems that once bedevilled (aquejó, plagó de problemas) the eurozone. Turkey has evolved from partner to awkward neighbour to menace. Belarus, previously a place of autocratic stability, looks wobbly (coja, insegura). Russia is regarded as an existential thread by the likes of Poland, but a potential ally by Frane. In Libya, perhaps the apogee of European foreign policy bungling (torpeza), member states managed themselves on differend sides of a civil war. Russia & Turkey carved out (esculpieron) a foothold (punto de apoyo) on the Eu's southern underbelly (parte indefensa). The EU is a victim of geography when it comes to foreign policy, but also a casually (víctima) of its own policy failures.

- **Germany** → whatever the question, the answer is Germany: that Britain should "turn to" Germany for ideas is not surprising given the long, binding ties (lazos vinculantes) between the two states. The idea of "welfare state" comes from Bismarck. Britain imported its royal family from Hanover in 1714 & Prince Albert, born in Germany, did as much as his wife to shape Victorial England. The post-war German Constitution was mostly the work of the British & Americans. Before the first world war the advocates of national eficiency insisted that Britain needed to invest in science & education to escape being crushed (aplastada) by the German chariot (carro). The university of Warwick builts one of the world's best manufacturing research centres by borrowing German methods for building tails between university & industry. The fashion for creation national champions by trying to merge companies are doomed (condenado, funesto). German's successful public-health system is built on a deep, powerful layer (capa) of local governments which does not exist Britain.

- **Finances (their future)**: capiral markets think a new era is dawning (amanece, aparece). Conventional banks now account for only 72 % of the total market value of the global banking & payments industry, down from 96 % a decade ago. Financial firms such as Ant group & Pay-pal make up 11 %: their market value has almost doubled this year to nearly $ 900 bn. Conventional non-bank payments firms such as Visa are booming (en auge), too, & make up the other 17 % of the industry. In the middle of the digital rush (torrente, ráfaga), a new business model is emerging: banks, e-commerce sites, fintechs, social networks (redes sociales), taxi apps & telecoms firms are all vying (se disputan) to become platforms: embedded finance - the integration of credit, insurance & investment into non- financial apps or websites - could in time become as valuable as payments services are today.

- Germany & Russia: the lady may toughen (up) (fortalecerse, endurecerse). Mr Putin & his officials refuse to utter (pronunciar; completo, total) the name of A. Navalny, the Kremlin's leading opponent, in public. In 2014, fed up with Mr Putin lies over Ukraine, the chanellor press-ganged (forzó) the rest of EU into imposing Ec. sanctions on Russia. Nord stream 2, an almost completed € 9.5 bn. contract of an undersea pipeline could double gas delivered from Russia's Yamal peninsula to the German coast, & from there to the rest of Europe.

- **Health care & VR**: the simulation they are watching has been modelled on the veteran's own experience in a war zone, events that have led to develop post-traumatic stress disease (PTSD). Concerning "exposure therapy", in which people are brought to face their fears in a controlled way, VR adds a way of creating detailed, carefully tuned scenarios that can elicite (suscitar, provocar) different levels of fear. Someone who is afraid of heights (alturas) will find that their heartbeat quikens & palms (=) get clammy (frias y húmedas) even if the precipitous drop (bajada, pendiente) they can see is a computer graphic in a VR headset.

- **Hybrids & evolution** → match (emparejar) & mix: despite this heavy inbreeding (endogamia) the hybrids have been sucessful. The genomes ("=") of closely related species may remain sufficiently similar to produce viable offspring (prole). But these genes frequently fit together (encajan) less well than those of parents from the same specie. As a consequence, even viable hybrids are frequently infertile (think mules) & are also at higher risk of development other types of illnes. Mixing the traits rasgos) of two parent species might actually have their hybrid offspring better off (mejor). This is called hybrid vigour or heterosis ("="). The interplay ("interacción") of two species'genes can even produce traits displayed (exhibidos, manufacturados) by neither parent. This is known as "transgresive segregation" ("="). Both the maleficient & beneficient effects of hybridisation are real. The nuclear genomes of complex organisms (animal, plants, fungi & single-celled orgasnisms such as the amoeba "=") are divided in bundles (fajos) of DNA called microsomes ("="). Such organisms are generally either aploid or diploid, meaning that each cell nucleous contains either one or two copies of every chromosome. Human being are diploid: they have 23 chromosomes pairs for a total of 46, but there are exceptions. Plant for instance are frequently polyploid, meaning that each nucleous contains copies in greater multiples than two. In the grasslands of the African Pleistocene, these ancestral groups are not alone. They were interspersed (entremezclado) with other hominids. Darwin idea of a simple, universal family tree is consigned (relegada) to oblivion (olvido). Some experts now prefer a tangled (enredada, enmarañada) bush (mata) of interconected branches. But this, too, is an imperfect comparison. A more fitting analogy is a frayed (deshilachada) rope. Species are braided (trenzadas) from individual strands (hebras). Where evolution proceeds in an ortodox Darwinian manner, braids unravel (se desenredan), strands split & new species result.

But the rope does not fray neatly: filaments of introgression criss- cross (entrecruzados,V) from braid to braid &, occasionally, two tangle (se enmarañan) to form a new traid altogether (totalmente).

- **Joe Biden presidency** might seem reassuringly (de modo traquilizadora) familiar to Latin Americans. To keep the border open to trade, Mexico's government has collaborated in shutting it to asylum seekers. Mr Trump's Latin America policy has been centred on a failed bid to overthrow the troika (dictatorship in Cuba, Venezuela, Nicaragua). His critics say its Latin America policies are based on the president's need to win Florida. Were Mr Biden win, his priorities would be the American Ec. & dealing with China. In Mr Obama second term, Vice-president Biden took responsibility for Americas. He will insist that NATO allies, two-thirds of whom fail to spend 2 % of GDP on defence, invest more in their own armed forces. He thinks there are opportunities for the US in the region, not just threats to be managed. American firms that bring supply chains back from China could benefit Mexico & Central America. A Biden presidency would revert to Mr Obama's Cuba's policy: its engagements as more likely to weaken the communist regime that Mr Trump'intensification of sanctions. It would press Mr. Bolsomoro on his failure to protect the Amazon. An immediate issue concerns the leadership of the Inter-American development bank. Biden administration would probably force the candidate of D. Trump out (lo destituiria) in favour of a less polarising figure.

- **Joe Biden & China policy**: the new president of the US has not yet to spell out his plans, but he will throw fewer wild punches. As vice-president under B. Obama, he was well remembered in Beijing for droping in at a neighbourhood early in 2011. He was also being less blunt (directo, terminante) about China's hard authoritarian turn (revolución, viraje) under Mr Xi. He seems stuck in the mindset of the B. Obama administration, which describedit co-operation with China as "unprecedented" in scope. Since the elections on November, he has called Mr Xi a thug (matón) & he has criticised Mr Trump for praising Mr Xi. Before Mr Trump presidency, there has been a long tradition of candidates berating (regañar) China on the campaign trail (sendero). He will be constrained by a Congress that has become far more hostile to China in recent years. In the Obama era, Mr Biden supported effords to TPP deal among 12 countries, including America, around the Pacific - hoping it would eventually draw in China & bind it to Western traditional norms. He will continue arms sales to Taiwan. He is likely to retain some of Mr Trump's toughest measures against China related to national security & he will persist with efforts to strangle Huawei. The new president will stress the need for America to keep ahead of China in technology. "Decoupling" in high-tech area will remain the trend. As for as the human rights, he is likely to maintain sanctions on China imposed by Mr Trump administration. But he will abandon aspects of Mr Trump's China policy that he views as harmful to openness & tolerance, for instance he may remove the visa-related impediments to study in America by people from China. Investigations will continue into suspected espionage involving Chinese researchers. He can also be expected to rejoin the WHO & try to resume the stationing in China of specialists from America's Centres for disease control. He may rejoin the Paris agreement on climate change & seek to persuade China to stop building carbon-belching projects such as coal-fired power plants in other countries, without forget his ambition to encourage a race with China to develop a green Ec. But the Senate, if it remains in Republican control, could frustrate such ambitions. Advisers suggest that he wait longer than usual to take a congratulatory call from Mr Xi, & not fall for (enamorarse de, interesarse por) any language Mr Xi may use to suggest a new framework for the relationship.

- **Mars**: consider the textures of the rocks & the distribution within them of potentially telltale (reveladores, indicadores) minerals. The jackpot (premio gordo, exitazo) of this treasure hunt (caza de tesoros) would be to find thinks like sugars, phospholipides (constituents of the membranes of cells), nucleoides (the "letters" of genetic materials) or amino acids (the building blocks of proteins) that are the characteristic of life in Earth. Satelites zip around it. Rovers trundle (ruedan) over its surface. A helicopter may soon blatter (estruendo, estrépito, V) through its skies. American newest rover is designed to stash (escondite, V, alijo) samples to be returned to Earth by a follow-up (posterior) mission by 2031. Lurid (escabrosas, desiguales) suggestions that Martian bugs may infect human beings ignore the fact that their biochemistry would almost certainly be too different from that of terrestrial organisms. Life in Mars, wether extant (existente) or extinct. Contamination risks disrupting understanding of that scientific bounty (generosidad, recompensa).

- **Natural disasters**: California has been roiled (agitada, enturbiada) by droughts, headaves & now two of the biggest fires on record. The webcam ("=") above the nest shows Inoko, a Californian codor, high in the tries of the Ventana ("=") wilderness (desierta) area, looking out as flames advance towards her. She is part of a twenty year breeding (reproducción: pers.: educación, crianza) programme to reintroduce the giant birds, which were stinct in the wil, to California's central'cost. She is alone & cnnot fly. One day the webcam shows a flash (marca) of wing feathers, then the life stream (arroyo; corriente, flujo) goes dark, as the flames presumably engulf the nest.

- (the) **New financial epoch**. It has four definingn features: (1) The jaw-dropping (alucinante) scale of today's government borrowing: rich countries toguether this year $ 4.2 trn (miles de bllones) in expending & tax cuts, (2) The whirring (zumbido) of the printing press: in America, Britain, Japan

& euro- zone, central banks have created new resources of money worth $ 3.7 trn in 2020, (3) The state's growing role as allocator (distribuidor, asignador)- in-chief, (4) The most important feature: the inflation. Yet the new era also presents grave risks: if the inflation jumps unexpectedly, the entire edifice of debt will shake, as central banks have to raise their policy rates & in turn pay out (gastar) vast sums of money on the new resources that they have created to buy bonds. And even if the inflation stays low, the new machinery is vulnerable to capture the lobbyists (cabilderos, grupos de presión), unions & cronies (amigotes).

- (a) **New generation of ambulatory machines** is striding (avanzan rápido) to the market: putting robots into factories is hardly (difícilmente) a new idea. Those few that have de mobility to manage (dirigir, gestionar, conseguir) like delivery (entregar, repartir) components, do so by scooting along (marchar) on wheels. Currently/at present (actualmente) the robots are little more tan giant arms, bolted (sujetados) firmly to the ground. They may appear cutesy (cursi) but a pair of robots that tuned up recently, are practical working machines: the new devices can walk. With laser scanners mounted on their backs, they can scamper (corretear) around the 200,000 square metter plan collecting data. This pair can climb stairs & crawl into (entrar lentamente en) hart-to-reach areas. Sone of them will have advantages in planetary exploration, negotiating (franquear; stream: cruzar) difficult terrain & entering caves, for instance. Some researches are using the new knowledge of robot locomotion to develop lightweight prostetic devices & powered exoskeletons fo those who cannot walk at all. This raises a tantalising (tentador) prospect that walking robots will one day help rid the world of wheelchairs. Walkimg robots making door-to-door deliveries might need some kind of digital material of the neighbouring (vecindad).

That might involve a big data- adquisition effort. It remains a long way off.

- (the) **Passport-free zone of Shengen** is important, but for the reasons many think: with four times more caravans per head than the European average, the Netherlands'holidaying families are the nemesis ("castigo") of other vacation-bound (que van rumbo a) drivers. In normal times, the EU's Shengen area extends across 26 countries inside & outsie the EU, without needing passport to go from … to … In pandemic times, the EU's cherished passport-free zone is under thread. The border checks are still in force in a handful (small number: puñado) of countries. E. Macron put the situation bluntly (francamente, directamente): "the risk we are facing is the death of Shengen". Only a tiny (diminut, minuscule) minority (about 2 millions of 440 millions), clostered (agrupados, apiñados) in a few places, such as Slovakia & Luxembourg, cross the border to go to work. The single market is estimated to have added 90 % to the EU's GDP since the inception (inicio). A. de Gasperi, K. Adenauer & R. Schuman, hailed from (eran naturales de) their country's borderlands (zonas fronterizas). When the C-19 hit, member states had to come up (aparecer; Jur,: comparecer) with a common list of which non- Eurpean citizens were allowed in.

- **Quantum computing is attracting commercial interest**: they could probable be much more rapid than any classical computer at researching a database. It can aid the development of drugs, catalysts & batteries. It can give boon (gran ayuda) to the transport industry (by finding efficient routes) & to finance (by maximising profits). Boston consultancy group foresees quantum computers improving the operating income of their users by between $ 450 bn. & 850 bn. a year by 2050. Unfortunately, big, stable quantum computers do not yet exist. But small, unestable ones do. They are dubbed (apodados) NISQS-Noisi, Intermediate-scale quantum computers. Some of NISQS are mere stepping stones (pasarelas) towards size & stability. If they can master (dominar) them, they will bestow (conferir) an advantage over their competitors. Microsoft is working on a topological qantum computer that relies on interactions of super-cold electrons. Psiquantum does its computing with photons that run along waveguides etched onto (gravadas sobre) ordinary silicon chips. The delicate quantum states they rely on (dependen de) break down (analiza, desglosa) in fractions of a second, so calculations must be completed in those slivers (tajadas of time). This influx of money has, though, let some researchers to worry that hype may be overtaking (adelantando) reality.

- **Reciprocity** is a buzzword (palabra de moda) **in diplomacy between China & the West**: it is not a cure all (curalotodo, panacea + "="). Relations must be guided by the principle of fairnes (justicia, imparcialidad). Trade law is a flawed (defectuosa) template (plantilla). Trade lawyers in China are of less use (sirven menos) in solving questions of high politics. Earlier in September Mr Xi called on the Communist party to strenghten its oversight (descuido, supervisión) over private companies. The ultimate (final, máximo, total) ambition of China'srulers isn't to trade with the US. It is to raid (asaltar, invadir) the US. Decoupling (escindiendo, desconectando) would make America safer than remaining open to China. Biden will reject decoupling. Breezy (alegres, despreocupados) arguments are not heard today. China is far more assertive (presumida, ostentosa, alardeante). America enjoys such a surplus of strength, that showing off (presumir, destacar) to Chinese visitors is a form of deterrence. Rather than attack the US head-on, (frontal), China has mounted trade & diplomatic boycots against American allies, that is seen as doing America's bidding (oferta, orden, mandato). China & America have spelled each other's journalists. Major American new bureaux in China have been gutted (destripados, dejados con sólo las paredes) by expulsion of their reporters. America could never win a race to the bottom on press freedom with China without betraying its liberal values the American presidents before Mr Trump, at least, have held dear (han apreciado). Alarmed & enraged to realise how it is distrusted (desconfiado) by western countries, its diplomates & state media are lashing out (arremeten contra) & threatening relations or legitimate countermesures; so warm words about fairness will not solve much. That version of reciprocity amounts to (equivale a) tell the world: "stay open to China or China will hurt you".

- **Regional Ecs. in Britain**. Many wealthy countries contain poor regions: the rural south in America, the Mexican border area, the former east Germany, the lower part of the boot in Italy, the poor south & other regions of Spain, etcetera. Britain, on a regional level, is exceptionally unbalanced. Poorest parts of it are larger than in other rich countries. The richest bit (Camden & "the City") is thirty times richer than the poorer. He uses various yardsticks (patrón, criterio, medida) to make comparisons.

Between 1949s & 1960s businesses & people where pushed out of London & other big cities. The population of the capital fell by two millions. Since the 1960s London & the regions next to it have powered ahead relentlessly. The streets of central London are quieter than elsewhere.

- **Shadow banking**: the Fed has underwritten (Ec.: suscribir; assurance: asegurar) financial markets like never before. That is because banks still pay second fiddle (desempeñan papel secundario) to capital markets in the provisions of credit. In most countries banks have dominated lending to households & firms ever since (desde entonces). America has long been different: banks have played a big role in economic developpement. But capital markets have played a mighty role too. Today that is truer than ever, which in turn helps explain the stunning (sensacional, asombroso) scope (ámbito, esfera;

alcance) of the Federal reserve's response to the latest economical crisis. From 1933 to 1999 comercial banks were legally required to be separated from investment banks (bancos de inversión). Banks have become safer, including investment banks, most of which are now part of the banking conglomerates. Last year (2019), however, banks went relatively unscathed (ilesos) as capital markets seized up (se agarrotaron). Rather than acting as a lender of last ressort (como último recurso) to banks, the Fed became marketmaker of last ressort, intervening on credit markets with a total size (magnitud, tamaño, talla) of about $ 23.5 trn. Separate the activities of the "real" banks from shadow firms is harder. Some non-banks, such as private-credit lending arms, make loans just as banks do. What we do in the shadows: untangling (desenredar) this complex interlinking is triky. But to get an idea of the financial landscape is changing America, simply look across the range of typical banks activities, from the bread-&-butter (básico) work of lending to households & firms, to advisory services & market-making. Lending to mid- sized firms is also drawing in new types of investment. This shift is mirrowed (reflejado) by trends in the private-equity (PE) industry over the past decade or so. Shadow banks are also muscling into (introduciéndose por la fuerza en) businesses that used to be the sole preserve (dominio) of the giant investment banks. Banks have a fight on their hands: they are les profitable in a world where they must hold low-yielding safe assets & carry huge safety buffers. Rather than acting as lender of last ressort to the banking system, the Fed has ben forced to act as a market-maker of last- ressort. Now the Fed has intruded (intrometido) a bewildering (desconcertante) array (serie) of financial markets. The consequences of bailing out capital markets on such a scale could linger (durar, persistir). The broad & forceful (convincentes, contundentes, enérgicos) provisions of liquidity have stemmed (detenido) market disfunctions, but it has also shored up (reforzado, sostenido) asset prices across a wider risk spectrum.

- **Simulation** (simulación) → reality bytes (=, octeto): Industrial light & magic (ILM) went on (empezó) to create special effects for dozens of films, including some of the earliest computer-generated 3D (tres dimensiones) characters, pioneering a new industry in the process. 3D product rendering has been adopted by other industries as a convenient way to produce everything from cars to industrial machinery to smartphones. The architects can use the technology to simulate rather than simply render images of the building they are working on. For self-driving cars become a reality, they need to recognise street signs, traffic lights & road marking (señales de tráfico). They need to be able to deal with dozens of hundreds of moving objects (pers., cars, bikes, animals, ...) at complex junctions. By populating proposed designs with intelligent virtual occupants, designers can identify potential problems before having to break ground. Chemists might use virtual environments to carry out billions of experiments using virtual chemicals.

- **Single market** → European's single market still need changing: the products of EU single market do not have a single price. In an integrated market, prices are supposed to come together (reunirse, juntarse, confluir) over time. Wages in Eastern Europe are not growing as rapidly as they were expected. Services make up a greater proportion of the EU Ec. Mollycoddled (mimadas, sobreprotegidas) companies still dominate some industries. Markets remain stubbornly (tercamente) national even online. Cross a state border in America & not much changes, for most business. Do it in the EU & you will face a new legal regime in a foreign language, with a different consumer culture.

- **Sino-American tusless** (luchas): a Chinese chipmaker brusches off (quita con el cepillo, con la mano; no hace caso de) Uncle sam's semiconductor "sabre-rattling". Our analyse shows how fragile consumer confidence can be. Large pagodas on the shoreline (línea de la costa), were designed to prevent blasts (wind: ráfaga; agua, ...: chorros) from doing damage to the surrounding (circundantes) wetlands (zonas húmedas, tierras pantanosas). Some rich countries are best placed to bounce back (recuperarse). No one knows for sure yet who has fared well or badly (pasado bien o mal).

American firms have over $ 700 bn. in assets in China & book about $ 500 millions a year in domestic sales. That could change if he decided to go all out (a toda marcha) & cut China off from the global payment system, which America controls thanks to the $'s status as the world reserve currency. He can slap an embargo in its financial system threatening to punish any foreign/domestic investment that uses $. China would retaliate (aplicar represalias): shut its market to western banks & firms, block them from its infrastructure projects & limit American access to resources & basic goods it control.

- **Spain's monarchy**: a tarnished (manchada, deslustrada) crown. His father's shenanigans (chanchullos, travesuras) are hurting king Felipe. King Felipe has renounced his inheritance & cancelled the salary of € 194.232 he was paying his father. King Felipe was beneficiary of two foundations linked to J. Carlos, both registered in tax havens. The emeritus King played a crucial role in quashing (sofocar, rechazar) a coup in 1981. The Monarchy is not doomed (muerta, funesta) ↔ doomed to failure (condenada al fracaso). His clubbable (sociable) manner concealed (ocultaba, disimulaba, incubría) insecurities. J. Calos's fall from grace began in 2012, when he broke his hip while elehant- hunting with Ms Larsen. Keep a level head (no perder la cabeza) → his level-headed (sensato, equilibrado) successor has largely lived up to his promise of a renovated Monarchy for a new era. Ousted three times between 1808 & 1975 the Spanish Bourbons are still on probation (provisión).

- **Vatican finances**: unravelling (desenmarañando) the Holy seat later financial embroglios (enredos, embrollos). Despite Pope Francis's avowed intention of overhawling (revisión de) its tangled (enredadas) finances. The works of religion (IOR) is ensnared (atrapada) in litigating. The IOR renegued (no cumplió la palabra) on a commitment to … It is dotted with departments jealously (celosamente) guarding substantial pots of the cash that are either undeclared or unquantified. Hundreds of millions of € … tucked away (escondidos) in accounts off the Vatican's balance-sheet. The cardinal was tried, convicted & acquitted (absuelto) on appeal (en recurso de apelación). He said that it was impossible for anyone to know accurately what was going on (que pasaba) overall (en conjunto).

- **Virtual reality (VR)** → reaching into other worlds: as the show began, the stage (escenario) exploded & Mr Scott appeared as a giant, stomping (dando fuertes pisotones) across surreal game landsape. The Scott's performance took place in a world of sorts (de verdad) - not merely in a screen. Top-of-the-range (los más altos de la gama) headsets completely replace the wearer's field of vision with a computer-generated world using tiny screens in front of the eye. Sensors in the goggles (anteojos) detected movements, & the imagery (imágenes, imaginaria) is adjustly accordingly, providing the illusion of being immerged in another world. VR & Augmented reality (AR) have the potential to add \$1.5 trn. to the world Ec. by 2030. A phone slotted into (introducido en) a cardboard viewer (espectador) with a couple of lenses can serve as a rudimentary VR headset. The most famous example of this is "Pokémon Go", a game that involves catching virtual monsters hidden around the real world. A first-perdon-shooter game called "quake (temblar)": set in a gothic 3D world, it challenged players to navigate a maze (laberinto)-like environment while fighting monsters.

Índice

Editorial LibrosEnRed

LibrosEnRed es la Editorial Digital más completa en idioma español. Desde junio de 2000 trabajamos en la edición y venta de libros digitales e impresos bajo demanda.

Nuestra misión es facilitar a todos los autores la edición de sus obras y ofrecer a los lectores acceso rápido y económico a libros de todo tipo.

Editamos novelas, cuentos, poesías, tesis, investigaciones, manuales, monografías y toda variedad de contenidos. Brindamos la posibilidad de comercializar las obras desde Internet para millones de potenciales lectores. De este modo, intentamos fortalecer la difusión de los autores que escriben en español.

Ingrese a www.librosenred.com y conozca nuestro catálogo, compuesto por cientos de títulos clásicos y de autores contemporáneos.

www.ingramcontent.com/pod-product-compliance
Lightning Source LLC
Chambersburg PA
CBHW031701230426
43668CB00006B/64
* 9 7 8 1 6 2 9 1 5 4 9 4 7 *